Applying Cultural Anthropology

An Introductory Reader

Fourth Edition

Aaron Podolefsky
University of Northern Iowa

Peter J. Brown
Emory University

Mayfield Publishing Company
Mountain View, California
London • Toronto

This edition is dedicated to the memory of Ms. Jacqueline Shapiro and to Sidney Shapiro for their love and friendship over the years, and for raising a wonderful daughter who makes my life complete.

—AP

Library of Congress Cataloging-in-Publication Data

Applying cultural anthropology : an introductory reader / [selected by] Aaron Podolefsky, Peter J. Brown. — 4th ed.
    p.   cm.
    Includes index.
    ISBN 0-7674-0466-1
    1. Applied anthropology.   2. Ethnology.   I. Podolefsky, Aaron.
II. Brown, Peter J.
GN397.5.A68   1998
301—dc21   98-20617
                                                              CIP

Manufactured in the United States of America
10 9 8 7 6 5 4 3 2 1

Mayfield Publishing Company
1280 Villa Street
Mountain View, California 94041

Sponsoring editor, Janet M. Beatty; production, Strawberry Field Publishing; manuscript editor, Jennifer Gordon; art director and cover designer, Jeanne M. Schreiber; illustrator, Alice Thiede; manufacturing manager, Randy Hurst. The text was set in 10/12 Palatino by ExecuStaff Composition Services and printed on 45# Amherst Matte by Malloy Lithographing, Inc.

Cover photograph: Japanese businessmen with Western visitor, ©MCMXCV L. D. Gordon; Tonganese with Coke cans, © Joel Simon 1998; huntsmen on horses with hounds, © Tony Stone Images/Hilarie Kavanagh

To the Student

An introductory course in any discipline is full of new terminology, concepts, and facts. Sometimes students forget that these new ideas and vocabulary are actually intellectual tools that can be put to work for analyzing and solving problems. In preparing this book, we have selected readings that will show you how anthropological concepts, discoveries, and methods can be applied in today's world.

The study of anthropology can help you view the world in a completely different way than you ever have before. You can come to appreciate the great diversity of human cultures and the interrelatedness of economic, sociopolitical, and religious systems. Anthropology can give you a broad perspective on humanity and help you understand other people's beliefs and customs. In doing so, it can help you become a better citizen in an increasingly global society. But your motivation need not be completely altruistic—there are many examples in this book of how cross-cultural awareness can improve performances in business, negotiations, and clinical medicine.

The fascinating side of anthropology seems obvious to most educated people, but there is also a lesser known practical side of the discipline. The readings we have selected demonstrate that practical, applied side. Many of the articles depict anthropological ideas and research methods in action—as they are used to understand and solve practical problems. We have included career profiles of anthropologists working outside the academic setting to show how they are applying anthropology. We believe that the fundamental lessons of anthropology can be applied to many careers and all areas of human endeavor.

To benefit from the study of anthropology, you need to study effectively. Over the years, we have found that students often read assignments without planning, and this actually makes studying less efficient. Before you read a selection, spend a few moments skimming it to get an idea of what it is about, where it is going, and what you should look for. This kind of preliminary reading is a poor idea for mystery novels but is essential for academic assignments. Without this preparation, the article may become a hodgepodge of facts and figures; details may be meaningless because you have missed the big picture. By planning your reading, you can see how the details are relevant to the central themes of an article.

To help you plan your reading, at the beginning of each article we have included questions and a list of glossary terms. By studying these questions in advance, you may gain an idea of what is to come and why the article is important. This will help make the time you spend reading more fruitful. Most of the questions highlight the central themes of the selection or draw your attention to interesting details. Some of the questions, however, do not have straightforward answers—they are food for thought and topics for discussion.

These articles have been selected with you, the student, in mind. We hope they convey our excitement about the anthropological adventure, and we expect that you will find them both enjoyable and thought-provoking.

If you are interested in reading more about applied anthropology, there are several excellent books available, such as *Applied Anthropology: A Practical Guide*, by Erve Chambers; *Applied Anthropology: An Introduction*, by John van Willigen; *Anthropological Praxis: Translating Knowledge into Action*, by Robert M. Wulff and Shirley J. Fiske; *Applied Anthropology in America*, by Elizabeth M. Eddy and William L. Partridge; and *Making Our Research Useful*, by John van Willigen, Barbara Rylko-Bauer, and Anne McElroy. If you are interested in medical matters, you may want to consult *Understanding and Applying Medical Anthropology*, by Peter J. Brown. You might also want to look at the journals *Human Organization* and *Practicing Anthropology*, both of which are published by the Society for Applied Anthropology. The National Association of Practicing Anthropologists (NAPA) has also published interesting works on specific fields such as medical anthropology.

To the Instructor

Introductory anthropology has become an established part of the college curriculum, and through this course our profession communicates with a large and diverse undergraduate audience. Members of that audience differ in experience, academic concentration, and career aspirations. For those students considering anthropology as a major, we need to provide (among other things) a vision of the future, a view of anthropological work to be done in the public domain as well as within academia. For them, we need to provide some answers to the question, What can I do with a degree in anthropology? For students majoring in other areas, such as business, engineering, or psychology, we need to address the question, How can anthropological insights or research methods help me understand and solve human problems? If we can provide such a service, we increase the likelihood that students will find creative solutions to the professional problems that await them, and we brighten the future for our anthropology majors by underscoring the usefulness of an anthropological perspective in attempts to solve the practical problems of today's world.

Over the years, we have found that most introductory texts have done little more than include a chapter on applied anthropology at the end of the book. This suggests, at least to students, that most of anthropology has no relevance to their lives. Such treatment also implies that the application of anthropological knowledge is a tangent or afterthought—at best an additional subject area, such as kinship or politics.

We disagree. We believe that the applications of anthropology cut across and infuse all the discipline's subfields. This book is a collection of articles that provide examples of both basic and applied research in cultural anthropology and linguistic anthropology.

One of our primary goals is to demonstrate some of the ways our discipline is used outside the academic arena. We want anthropology to be seen as a field that is interesting as well as relevant to the real world. Like the public at large, students seem well aware that the subject matter of anthropology is fascinating, but they seem unaware of both the fundamental questions of humanity addressed by anthropologists and the

practical applications of the field. Increased public awareness of the practical contributions of anthropology is a goal that we share with many in the profession. In fact, this is a major long-term goal of the American Anthropological Association.

Although people distinguish between basic and applied research, much of anthropology falls into a gray area, having elements of both. Many selections in this book fall into that gray zone—they are brief ethnographic accounts that contain important implications for understanding and resolving problems. We could have included a large number of articles exemplifying strictly applied research—an evaluation report of agency performance, for example. Although this sort of research is fascinating and challenging to do, it is usually not exciting for students to read. We have selected articles that we believe are fascinating for students and convey the dual nature (basic/applied) of social science research.

Any student who completes an introductory course in cultural anthropology should learn that anthropological work, in its broadest sense, may include (or at least contribute to) international business, epidemiology, program evaluation, social impact studies, conflict resolution, organizational analysis, market research, and nutrition research, even though their introductory anthropology texts make no mention of those fields. The selections in this book should help students understand why anthropology is important in today's world and also make the course more memorable and meaningful.

FEATURES OF THIS EDITION

- We chose the readings in this book to complement the typical course in introductory cultural anthropology. The sequence of articles follows the organization of standard anthropology textbooks, grouped under traditional headings such as kinship and marriage, rather than headings based on the applied areas such as medical anthropology or the anthropology of development. As in most contemporary textbooks, linguistic anthropology is included under culture and communication. Had we meant this book to be a reader on applied anthropology, our organization would have been different. Although this book could be used in courses on applied anthropology (earlier editions have been), this was not our intended audience. And, for this reason, we have not provided extensive discussion of the history or definition of applied anthropology. For students interested in this, there are a number of fine books on the subject. These include *Applied Anthropology: A Practical Guide*, by Erve Chambers; *Applied Anthropology: An Introduction*, by John van Willigen; *Anthropological Praxis: Translating Knowledge into Action*, by Robert M. Wulff and Shirley J. Fiske; *Applied Anthropology in America*, by Elizabeth M. Eddy and William L. Partridge; and *Making Our Research Useful*, by John van Willigen, Barbara Rylko-Bauer, and Anne McElroy.

- To emphasize how anthropology can be put to work in different settings, we have included a number of profiles of anthropologists whose careers involve applying anthropology outside the university setting.

- To help students better understand the subject matter, we have included a number of pedagogical aids: introductions, a list of glossary terms, and guiding questions for each article; a world map that pinpoints the locations of places and peoples discussed in the articles; and, for easy reference, an extensive glossary and index.

- To help busy instructors, we have provided an instructor's manual that includes for each article a brief summary, glossary terms, and test questions.

NEW TO THIS EDITION

Questions of race arouse significant interest both in anthropology and in society at large. For this reason we have added a new section entitled "Culture and Race." Race is a cultural category, not a biological one, so this section belongs in this cultural anthropology reader. One of the readings—the draft statement on race by the American Anthropological Association—is very short and to the point. We think all introductory anthropology students should read this. A companion piece by Jared Diamond entitled "Race Without Color" should help students realize that racial categories are culturally constructed. Also in

this new section is a reading by Peggy McIntosh concerning white privilege, which should promote interesting classroom discussions.

Related to the question of race is a new reading in the "Culture and Communication" section on the topic of Black English vernacular. Recent social events—such as the O. J. Simpson trial, attacks on affirmative action, and *The Bell Curve*—have led to a national dialogue on race. Anthropologists and students of anthropology need to be involved in that dialogue, as this responsibility is an important tradition in our discipline, dating back to Franz Boas.

Additionally, we have changed readings in other areas, such as economics and economic development. In all cases, the changes were made to offer better examples of the relevance of anthropology to solving practical problems in today's world.

ACKNOWLEDGMENTS

We want to thank the entire staff at Mayfield Publishing Company, and especially our editor, Jan Beatty, for her vision, good humor, tolerance, and friendship. Jan has consistently demonstrated a clear understanding of what we are trying to accomplish with this book; we particularly appreciate her support of the new additions on race as part of the cultural anthropological curriculum.

We are grateful to the many instructors who returned questionnaires evaluating the selections: C. Adams, Indiana University; S. Adrian, University of Arizona; N. Allison, Toccoa Falls College; L. Ammons, Assumption College; P. Barlett, Emory University; K. Barlow, University of Minnesota; E. Bigler, Rhode Island College; B. Bigony, University of Wisconsin at Menomonie; G. Bogdan, Orange Coast College; A. Bolyanatz, Wheaton College; C. Brettell, Southern Methodist University; J. Brown, Oakland University; D. Bruner, University of North Carolina at Greensboro; J. Cahoon, College of St. Scholastica; D. Chasin, Newport Beach, CA; J. Coggeshall, Clemson University; K. Costa, Fall River, MA; J. Culbert, San Diego State University; D. Darlington, Western Wyoming Community College; S. Dauria, Bloomsburg University; J. Dempsey, Phoenix, AZ; D. Duchon, Georgia State University; M. Findlay, California State University at Chico; T. Fitzgerald, University of North Carolina at Greensboro; M. Fong, Chaffey College; P. Fontane, St. Louis College of Pharmacy; M. Freedman, Syracuse University; D. Gamble, Southwest Baptist University; D. Gibson, El Camino College; D. Gordon, Fort Lewis College; T. Greaves, Bucknell University; C. Hartse, Olympic College; T. Headland, Summer Institute of Linguistics; E. Hegeman, John Jay College, City University of New York; M. Helms, University of North Carolina at Greensboro; J. Herron, Ottawa, KS; B. Howell,

University of Tennessee at Knoxville; C. Hull, Grand Valley State University; S. Jen, California State University at Fresno; B. Joans, Merritt College; C. Johnson, Indiana University Northwest; C. Kahrs, Saddleback Community College; P. Kilbride, Bryn Mawr College; S. Kus, Rhodes College; S. Lamb, Brandeis University; G. Landsman, State University of New York at Albany; J. Levi, Carleton College; P. Little, University of Kentucky; W. Lohrer, California State University at Chico; K. Lorenz, Shippensburg University; K. Maines, Pennsylvania State University; B. Mathieu, West Los Angeles College; M. Mazzarelli, Massachusetts Bay Community College; C. McCall, Hiwassee College; J. McCall, Southern Illinois University at Carbondale; C. Moyers, Cabrillo College; E. Nelson, University of Utah; C. Nowak, Chicago, IL; B. Pate, University of Tennessee; K. Platt, Babson College; K. Porter, Rochester, NY; M. Pulford, University of Wisconsin at Superior; S. Rachelle, Mt. San Jacinto College; R. Rajner, University of Toledo; S. Rasmussen, University of Houston; S. Rorbakken, University of Iowa; J. Ryan, Texas Christian University; B. Schmitz, Orange Coast College; D. Seelow, State University of New York at Old Westbury; D. Shepherd, Rubbindale, MN; V. Smith, California State University at Chico; J. Stimpfl, University of Nebraska at Lincoln; H. Swanson, Mohave Community College; M. Taylor, University of Memphis; T. M. Taylor, University of South Colorado; J. Thompson, Tennessee Wesleyan College; J. Tizon, University of Southern Maine; K. Wilcoxson, University of Sioux Falls; P. Wohlt, Ball State University; and Z. Zelazo, Montclair State University.

Peter would like to thank the following colleagues who have so willingly shared their viewpoints in compiling this volume: George Armelagos, Alan Goodman, Bruce Knauft, Peggy Barlett, Marcia Inhorn, Mel Konner, Michelle Lampl, and Cory Kratz. Special thanks go to Erin Finley, who provided valuable advice from the student's point of view. Rob Goddard did a fine job with the additions to the maps, copy editing and following up on our mistakes. Aaron would like to thank Pat Woelber and Jessica Moon. We both thank April Wells-Hayes and Melanie Field for their very professional job in the production process. Finally, we would like to thank our past and present students for their insights, practical observations, optimism, and view of the future.

Contents

CULTURE AND COMMUNICATION

Introduction:

Understanding Humans and Human Problems

To the uninitiated, the term *anthropology* conjures up images of mummies' tombs, Indiana Jones, and treks through steaming jungles or over high alpine peaks. Anthropologists agree that their chosen field is exciting, that they have been places and seen things that few experience firsthand, and that they have been deeply and emotionally involved in understanding the human condition. At the same time, however, the vision of anthropology presented by Hollywood has probably done more to obscure the true nature of the profession than it has to enlighten the public about what we really do.

Providing an accurate image of anthropology and anthropological work is both simple and complex. Essentially, anthropology is the study of people, or more properly, of humankind. But, you may say, many disciplines study people: psychology, sociology, history, biology, medicine, and so on. True, but anthropology is different in that it seeks to integrate these separate and narrow views of humanity. To understand ourselves, we need to join these disparate views into a single framework, a process that begins with our biological and evolutionary roots, explores the development of culture through the prehistoric and historical periods, probes the uniquely human ability to develop culture through communication, and examines the diversity of recent and present-day cultures that inhabit the globe.

From this conception of the *holistic* and *comparative* study of humankind emerge what are termed the four fields of anthropology: biological (or physical) anthropology, archaeology, anthropological linguistics, and cultural anthropology. Some universities offer an introductory course that covers all four subfields. Other schools cover the subfields in two or three separate introductory courses. Each approach has its advantage. The former may more fully integrate the biocultural and historical dimensions of humanity; the latter allows students to explore each subfield in greater depth. This book introduces you to the field of cultural anthropology and how it is used in today's world.

Another way to divide the discipline—in fact almost any discipline—is into *basic* and *applied* research. These categories are important in this reader because we would like students to appreciate both the basic and the applied sides of cultural anthropology. A survey of natural and social scientists and engineers conducted by the U.S. Census Bureau for the National Science Foundation used the following definitions of these fundamental concepts: *Basic research* is study directed toward gaining scientific knowledge primarily for its own sake. *Applied research* is study directed toward gaining scientific knowledge in an effort to meet a recognized need.

Anthropology is a discipline concerned primarily with basic research. It asks "big" questions concerning the origins of humankind, the roots of human nature, the development of civilization, and the functions of our major social institutions (such as marriage and religion). Nevertheless, anthropologists have put the methods and skills developed in basic research to use in solving human problems and fulfilling the needs of society. Anthropologists have, for example, worked with medical examiners in the identification of skeletal remains. They have also helped communities preserve their cultural heritage and businesses and government agencies understand the social impacts of programs or development projects.

Although the application of anthropology has a long history, it has, until recent years, remained in the shadows of pure or basic research. The last twenty years have seen a change. Anthropologists have moved beyond their traditional roles in universities and museums and now work in a broad range of settings. They are employed in many government agencies, in the private sector, and in a variety of nonresearch capacities (such as administrator, evaluator, or policy analyst).

In response to the growing opportunities for anthropologists outside academia and to the demands of students, an increasing number of master's degree and doctoral programs provide training specifically in the applications of anthropology. This is not to say that the classified ads list jobs titled "anthropologist." Rather, for those interested in anthropology, there are increasing opportunities to find careers that draw on anthropological training and skills. Profiles of people in nonacademic careers (consumer marketing, high-tech industry, and school administration) can be found in this reader. At the same time, studies have shown that there will be increasing job opportunities for anthropologists in universities and colleges during the 1990s and beyond.

These new opportunities are particularly evident in this era of multiculturalism and in the increasing public recognition that our society must be a culturally diverse social mosaic. Exploration of this reality has always been the domain of cultural anthropology; a usual pedagogical goal of teachers of cultural anthropology is to increase a student's appreciation and tolerance of cultural differences. Living in a multicultural society presents real challenges of social tensions caused by chronic persistent ethnocentrism and racism. But living in a multicultural society also brings a cultrual richness, a luxuriant wealth, to our lives.

School administrators, engineers, doctors, business leaders, lawyers, medical researchers, and government officials have become aware that the substantive knowledge, the unique perspective, and the research skills of anthropologists are applicable to practical problems—in the United States as well as other countries.

As we explore anthropology, keep in mind the interplay between and interdependence of basic cultural research and the applications of anthropological knowledge and research methods to the solution of human problems.

CULTURAL ANTHROPOLOGY

Cultural anthropology is concerned with the description and analysis of people's lives and traditions. In the past, cultural anthropologists almost always did research in far-off "exotic" societies, but today we have expanded our research interests to include our own society. Cultural anthropology can add much to both the basic and the applied scientific understanding of human behaviors and beliefs. The study and interpre-

tation of other societies—of their traditions, history, and view of the world—is inherently interesting and important because it documents the diversity of human lifestyles. The anthropological approach to understanding other societies also has practical value for addressing contemporary human problems and needs.

The concept of *culture* is central to anthropology. It refers to the patterns of economy, social organization, and belief that are learned and shared by members of a social group. Culture is traditional knowledge that is passed down from one generation to the next. Although generally stable over time, culture is flexible and fluid, changing through borrowing or invention. The influential American anthropologist Franz Boas championed the concept of culture for understanding human diversity; culture, Boas argued, is distinct from biological "race" or language. Anthropologists believe that all cultural lifestyles have intrinsic value and validity. Other societies deserve to be studied and understood without being prejudged using our own narrow (and sometimes intolerant) beliefs and values; this universal tendency to prejudge based on the supposed superiority of one's own group, called *ethnocentrism*, is something everyone should avoid.

Culture is the crowning achievement of human evolution. To understand ourselves is to appreciate cultural diversity. Dependence on culture as our primary mechanism of survival sets humans apart from other members of the animal kingdom. This dependence is responsible for the tremendous evolutionary success of our species, which has grown in population (sometimes to the point of overpopulation) and can inhabit nearly every niche on the planet.

The paradox of culture is that, as we humans learn to accept our own cultural beliefs and values, we unconsciously learn to reject those of other peoples. At birth, we are capable of absorbing any culture and language. We are predisposed to cultural learning, but we are not programmed to adopt a particular culture. As we grow, our parents, our schools, and our society teach us what is right and wrong, good and evil, acceptable and unacceptable. At the subconscious level, we learn the symbolic meanings of behavior and through them interpret the meanings of actions. Beliefs, values, and symbols must be understood within the context of a particular culture. This is the principle of *cultural relativity*. At the same time, culture supplies us with the cognitive models—software programs, if you will—that allow us to perceive or "construct" a particular version of reality. Culture permeates our thinking and our expectations; this is the principle of *cultural construction*.

In addition to the concept of culture, the anthropological approach to the study of human behavior and belief has two essential characteristics: a holistic approach and a comparative framework. The *holistic approach* means that anthropologists see a particular part of culture—for example, politics, economy, or religion—in relation to the larger social system. Individuals are viewed, not in isolation, but as part of an intricate web of social relationships. Although an anthropological study may have a particular focus, the holistic approach means that the broader cultural context is always considered important because the different parts of a cultural system are interrelated. When, for example, the economy or the technology changes, other aspects of the culture will change as well.

The *comparative framework* means that explanations or generalizations are achieved through cross-cultural research. Questions about humanity cannot be based on information from a single society or a single type of society—such as the industrial societies of the United States and Europe. Such a limited framework is simply too narrow for understanding the big picture that basic anthropological research seeks. By studying others within a comparative framework, we can better understand ourselves. If other cultures are a mirror in which we see ourselves, then anthropology is a mirror for humankind.

The broad generalizations about culture and society that we have been talking about are based on detailed knowledge of the world's cultures. To gain this knowledge, anthropologists go to the people. Often accompanied by spouses and children, we pack our bags and travel to far-off lands—to the highlands of New Guinea, the frozen arctic, the savannas of Africa, or the jungles of South America. Increasingly, anthropologists are bringing their research methods and comparative, holistic perspective into the cities and suburbs of America, the American schoolroom, and the corporate jungle. This "research adventure" has become the hallmark of cultural anthropology.

The research methods used by the cultural anthropologist are distinctive because they depend, to a large extent, on the firsthand experiences and interpretations of the field researcher. Cultural anthropologists conduct research in natural settings rather than in laboratories or over the telephone. This method for studying another society is often called *participant observation, ethnography,* or *qualitative methods.* The goal of describing, understanding, and explaining another culture is a large task. It is most often accomplished by living in the society for an extended period, by talking with people, and, as much as possible, by experiencing their lives.

One important tool that cultural anthropologists depend on in field research is *language.* They need to learn the local language not only for their own survival in the field, but, more importantly, because language is a key to understanding someone else's culture. Many anthropologists study descriptive linguistics to make it easier for them to learn an unwritten language in the field. By looking at speech and language categories, such as the

focus on the uses of silence in Apache culture (Selection 6) or the complex problems of male–female miscommunication (Selection 7), anthropologists can learn a great deal about the culture they are studying.

The fieldwork experience usually involves a kind of culture shock in which the researcher questions his or her own assumptions about the world. In this way, fieldwork is often a rewarding period of personal growth. In their work, anthropologists expect to find that other people's behavior, even when it seems bizarre when seen from the outside, makes sense when viewed from the people's own point of view. This is why anthropological research often means letting people speak for themselves. While doing research, the anthropologist often thinks of herself or himself as a child—as being ignorant or uninformed and needing to be taught by the people being studied. This approach often involves in-depth interviewing with a few key informants and then interpreting (and writing about) that other culture for the researcher's own society. The ethnographic method, pioneered and developed in anthropology, is now being used in a range of applied areas, including marketing, management research, and school evaluation. Although ethnography is an important research style, the selections in this book demonstrate that many different methods are used in anthropology today.

The applications of cultural anthropology are diverse. Internationally, anthropologists are involved in programs of technical assistance and economic aid to Third World nations. These programs address needs in such areas as agriculture and rural development; health, nutrition, and family planning; education; housing and community organizing; transportation and communication; and energy. Anthropologists do many of the same things domestically as well. They evaluate public education, study agricultural extension programs, administer projects, analyze policy (such as U.S. refugee resettlement programs), and research crime and crime prevention, for example.

In the private sector, cultural anthropologists can add a fresh perspective to market research. They analyze office and industrial organization and culture. They create language and cultural training workshops for businesspeople and others who are going overseas. These workshops reduce the likelihood of cross-cultural misunderstanding and the problems of culture shock for the employee and, often more important, for his or her family. A good example of this is the work of Richard Reeves-Ellington (Selection 22), who has demonstrated how the training of corporate managers in Japanese culture significantly improves their business productivity.

Applied anthropological work can be divided into four categories. In the first group, applied research and basic research look very much alike, except that the goal of applied research is more directly linked with a particular problem or need. For example, in Selection 33, Aaron Podolefsky studies the causes of the re-emergence of tribal warfare in New Guinea. Or, in a more general analysis, Bruce Bower (Selection 32) identifies the cross-culturally important variables in the escalation of local feuds to all-out war. Such studies provide planners and policymakers with important insights for understanding the problem. This knowledge can help in the design and implementation of programs that help bring an end to warfare in the region. Similarly, Philippe Bourgois's sensitive ethnography of the culture of crack users may help in the implementation of drug treatment programs (Selection 3).

In the second category, anthropologists may work as researchers for a government agency, corporation, or interest group on a specific task defined by the client.

In the third category, anthropologists work as consultants to business and industry or to government agencies that need in-depth cultural knowledge to solve or prevent a problem. Anthropologists often act as cultural brokers, mediating and translating between groups who are miscommunicating not because of their words but because of cultural meanings.

Finally, a few anthropologists have developed and administered programs. Gerald F. Murray's work in reforestation in Haiti (Selection 16) exemplifies the development and actual administration of a project in which cultural understanding is a fundamental component. The overwhelming success of this agroforestry project attests to the practical value of cultural understanding for solving human problems.

A great deal of anthropological work remains to be done, although this seems to be a well-kept secret. People have a far easier time focusing on the individual as the level of analysis. When divorce, drug abuse, or suicide affects small numbers of people, we may look to the individual and to psychology for answers. When divorce rates climb to 50 percent of all marriages and the suicide rate increases tenfold, however, we must look beyond the individual to forces that affect society at large. Because we are so immersed in our own culture, we have difficulty seeing it as a powerful force that guides—even controls—our behavior. We begin these readings, therefore, with three selections that convey the hidden, but powerful, nature of culture.

The readings in this book are subdivided into traditional anthropological categories, such as economy, gender, social organization, politics, and religion. In each category you will find reading selections that demonstrate not only the relevance of anthropology theory and methods in the understanding of human problems, but also the application of anthropology to the specific problems or issues.

1

Body Ritual Among the Nacirema

Horace Miner

Generations of anthropologists have traveled the globe, reaching to the far corners of the five continents to discover and describe the many ways of humankind. Anthropologists have gathered a diverse collection of exotic customs, from the mundane to the bizarre. Understanding and appreciating other societies requires us to be culturally relative. But people tend to judge others by their own cultural values in a way that is ethnocentric. This is because people take their cultural beliefs and behaviors for granted; they seem so natural that they are seldom questioned. Among the most interesting social customs on record are the rituals of the Nacirema. By viewing Nacirema behaviors as rituals, we gain insight into their culture and into the meaning of the concept of culture. We also gain insight into the problem of ethnocentrism.

Ritual is a cultural phenomenon. Ritual can be found in all societies. It can be defined as a set of acts that follow a sequence established by tradition. In Selection 38, for example, we will examine hospital operating room procedure as ritualized behavior.

Throughout the world, ritual reflects the fundamental cultural beliefs and values of a society by giving order to important activities and particular life crises like death and birth. Every day, however, mundane rituals are performed unconsciously. In fact, most Nacirema people do these things without being aware of their underlying symbolic meanings. Pay particular attention to the quotation at the end of the selection.

As you read this selection, ask yourself the following questions:

☐ How do the Nacirema feel about the human body?

☐ Do you think that the charms and magical potions used by the Nacirema really work?

☐ Can you list those aspects of social life in which magic plays an important role?

☐ What is your opinion of the importance of body ritual, and if you went to live among the Nacirema, would you tell them of your opinion?

☐ Viewed in this way, Nacirema behaviors sometimes appear bizarre. Do you think the Nacirema themselves feel this way?

The following terms discussed in this selection are included in the Glossary at the back of the book:

clan
culture
ethnocentrism
ritual

The anthropologist has become so familiar with the diversity of ways in which different peoples behave in similar situations that he is not apt to be surprised by even the most exotic customs. In fact, if all of the logically possible combinations of behavior have not been found somewhere in the world, he is apt to suspect that they must be present in some yet undescribed tribe. This point has, in fact, been expressed with respect to clan organization by Murdock (1949:71). In this light, the magical beliefs and practices of the Nacirema present such unusual aspects that it seems desirable to describe them as an example of the extremes to which human behavior can go.

Professor Linton first brought the ritual of the Nacirema to the attention of anthropologists twenty years ago (1936:326), but the culture of this people is still very poorly understood. They are a North American group living in the territory between the Canadian Cree, the Yaqui and Tarahumare of Mexico, and the Carib and Arawak of the Antilles. Little is known of their origin, although tradition states that they came from the east. According to Nacirema mythology, their nation was originated by a culture hero, Notgnihsaw, who is otherwise known for two great feats of strength—the throwing of a piece of wampum across the river Pa-To-Mac and the chopping down of a cherry tree in which the Spirit of Truth resided.

Nacirema culture is characterized by a highly developed market economy which has evolved in a rich natural habitat. While much of the people's time is devoted to economic pursuits, a large part of the fruits of these labors and a considerable portion of the day are spent in ritual activity. The focus of this activity is the human body, the appearance and health of which loom as a dominant concern in the ethos of the people. While such a concern is certainly not unusual, its ceremonial aspects and associated philosophy are unique.

The fundamental belief underlying the whole system appears to be that the human body is ugly and that its natural tendency is to debility and disease. Incarcerated in such a body, man's only hope is to avert these characteristics through the use of the powerful influences of ritual and ceremony. Every household has one or more shrines devoted to this purpose. The more powerful individuals in the society have several shrines in their houses and, in fact, the opulence of a house is often referred to in terms of the number of such ritual centers it possesses. Most houses are of wattle and daub construction, but the shrine rooms of the more wealthy are walled with stone. Poorer families imitate the rich by applying pottery plaques to their shrine walls.

While each family has at least one such shrine, the rituals associated with it are not family ceremonies but are private and secret. The rites are normally only discussed with children, and then only during the period when they are being initiated into these mysteries. I was able, however, to establish sufficient rapport with the natives to examine these shrines and to have the rituals described to me.

The focal point of the shrine is a box or chest which is built into the wall. In this chest are kept the many charms and magical potions without which no native believes he could live. These preparations are secured from a variety of specialized practitioners. The most powerful of these are the medicine men, whose assistance must be rewarded with substantial gifts. However, the medicine men do not provide the curative potions for their clients, but decide what the ingredients should be and then write them down in an ancient and secret language. This writing is understood only by the medicine men and by the herbalists who, for another gift, provide the required charm.

The charm is not disposed of after it has served its purpose, but is placed in the charm-box of the household shrine. As these magical materials are specific for certain ills, and the real or imagined maladies of the people are many, the charm-box is usually full to overflowing. The magical packets are so numerous that people forget what their purposes were and fear to use them again. While the natives are very vague on this point, we can only assume that the idea in retaining all the old magical materials is that their presence in the charm-box, before which the body rituals are conducted, will in some way protect the worshipper.

Beneath the charm-box is a small font. Each day every member of the family, in succession, enters the shrine room, bows his head before the charm-box, mingles different sorts of holy water in the font, and proceeds with a brief rite of ablution. The holy waters are secured from the Water Temple of the community, where the priests conduct elaborate ceremonies to make the liquid ritually pure.

In the hierarchy of magical practitioners, and below the medicine men in prestige, are specialists whose designation is best translated "holy-mouthmen." The Nacirema have an almost pathological horror of and fascination with the mouth, the condition of which is believed to have a supernatural influence on all social relationships. Were it not for the rituals of the mouth, they believe that their teeth would fall out, their gums bleed, their jaws shrink, their friends desert them, and their lovers reject them. They also believe that a strong relationship exists between oral and moral

---

The author of this article used the term *man* to refer to humanity in general. This term is not used by modern anthropologists because, to many people, it reflects an unconscious sexist bias in language and rhetoric. At the time that this article was written, however, the generalized *man* was a common convention in writing. In the interest of historical accuracy we have not changed the wording in this article, but students should be aware that nonsexist terms (*humans, people, Homo sapiens*, and so on) are preferred. —The Editors.

characteristics. For example, there is a ritual ablution of the mouth for children which is supposed to improve their moral fiber.

The daily body ritual performed by everyone includes a mouth-rite. Despite the fact that these people are so punctilious about care of the mouth, this rite involves a practice which strikes the uninitiated stranger as revolting. It was reported to me that the ritual consists of inserting a small bundle of hog hairs into the mouth, along with certain magical powders, and then moving the bundle in a highly formalized series of gestures.

In addition to the private mouth-rite, the people seek out a holy-mouth-man once or twice a year. These practitioners have an impressive set of paraphernalia, consisting of a variety of augers, awls, probes, and prods. The use of these objects in the exorcism of the evils of the mouth involves almost unbelievable ritual torture of the client. The holy-mouth-man opens the client's mouth, and using the above mentioned tools, enlarges any holes which decay may have created in the teeth. Magical materials are put into these holes. If there are no naturally occurring holes in the teeth, large sections of one or more teeth are gouged out so that the supernatural substance can be applied. In the client's view, the purpose of these ministrations is to arrest decay and to draw friends. The extremely sacred and traditional character of the rite is evident in the fact that the natives return to the holy-mouth-men year after year, despite the fact that their teeth continue to decay.

It is to be hoped that, when a thorough study of the Nacirema is made, there will be careful inquiry into the personality structure of these people. One has to but watch the gleam in the eye of a holy-mouth-man as he jabs an awl into an exposed nerve, to suspect that a certain amount of sadism is involved. If this can be established, a very interesting pattern emerges, for most of the population shows definite masochistic tendencies. It was to these that Professor Linton referred in discussing a distinctive part of the daily body ritual which is performed only by men. This part of the rite involves scraping and lacerating the surface of the face with a sharp instrument. Special women's rites are performed only four times during each lunar month, but what they lack in frequency is made up in barbarity. As part of this ceremony, women bake their heads in small ovens for about an hour. The theoretically interesting point is that what seems to be a preponderantly masochistic people have developed sadistic specialists.

The medicine men have an imposing temple, or latipso, in every community of any size. The more elaborate ceremonies required to treat very sick patients can only be performed at this temple. These ceremonies involve not only the thaumaturge but a permanent group of vestal maidens who move sedately about the temple chambers in distinctive costume and headdress.

The latipso ceremonies are so harsh that it is phenomenal that a fair proportion of the really sick natives who enter the temple ever recover. Small children whose indoctrination is still incomplete have been known to resist attempts to take them to the temple because "that is where you go to die." Despite this fact, sick adults are not only willing but eager to undergo the protracted ritual purification, if they can afford to do so. No matter how ill the supplicant or how grave the emergency, the guardians of many temples will not admit a client if he cannot give a rich gift to the custodian. Even after one has gained admission and survived the ceremonies, the guardians will not permit the neophyte to leave until he makes still another gift.

The supplicant entering the temple is first stripped of all his or her clothes. In every-day life the Nacirema avoids exposure of his body and its natural functions. Bathing and excretory acts are performed only in the secrecy of the household shrine, where they are ritualized as part of the body-rites. Psychological shock results from the fact that body secrecy is suddenly lost upon entry into the latipso. A man, whose own wife has never seen him in an excretory act, suddenly finds himself naked and assisted by a vestal maiden while he performs his natural functions into a sacred vessel. This sort of ceremonial treatment is necessitated by the fact that the excreta are used by a diviner to ascertain the course and nature of the client's sickness. Female clients, on the other hand, find their naked bodies are subjected to the scrutiny, manipulation and prodding of the medicine men.

Few supplicants in the temple are well enough to do anything but lie on their hard beds. The daily ceremonies, like the rites of the holy-mouth-men, involve discomfort and torture. With ritual precision, the vestals awaken their miserable charges each dawn and roll them about on their beds of pain while performing ablutions, in the formal movements of which the maidens are highly trained. At other times they insert magic wands in the supplicant's mouth or force him to eat substances which are supposed to be healing. From time to time the medicine men come to their clients and jab magically treated needles into their flesh. The fact that these temple ceremonies may not cure, and may even kill the neophyte, in no way decreases the people's faith in the medicine men.

There remains one other kind of practitioner, known as a "listener." This witch-doctor has the power to exorcise the devils that lodge in the heads of people who have been bewitched. The Nacirema believe that parents bewitch their own children. Mothers are particularly suspected of putting a curse on children while teaching them the secret body rituals. The counter-magic of the witch-doctor is unusual in its lack of ritual. The patient simply tells the "listener" all his troubles and fears, beginning with the earliest difficulties he can remember. The memory displayed by the Nacirema in these exorcism sessions is truly remarkable. It is not uncommon for the patient to bemoan the rejection he felt upon being weaned as a babe, and a few individuals even see their troubles going back to the traumatic effects of their own birth.

In conclusion, mention must be made of certain practices which have their base in native esthetics but which depend upon the pervasive aversion to the natural body and its functions. There are ritual fasts to make fat people thin and ceremonial feasts to make thin people fat. Still other rites are used to make women's breasts larger if they are small, and smaller if they are large. General dissatisfaction with breast shape is symbolized in the fact that the ideal form is virtually outside the range of human variation. A few women afflicted with almost inhuman hypermammary development are so idolized that they make a handsome living by simply going from village to village and permitting the natives to stare at them for a fee.

Reference has already been made to the fact that excretory functions are ritualized, routinized, and relegated to secrecy. Natural reproductive functions are similarly distorted. Intercourse is taboo as a topic and scheduled as an act. Efforts are made to avoid pregnancy by the use of magical materials or by limiting intercourse to certain phases of the moon. Conception is actually very infrequent. When pregnant, women dress so as to hide their condition. Parturition takes place in secret, without friends or relatives to assist, and the majority of women do not nurse their infants.

Our review of the ritual life of the Nacirema has certainly shown them to be a magic-ridden people. It is hard to understand how they have managed to exist so long under the burdens which they have imposed upon themselves. But even such exotic customs as these take on real meaning when they are viewed with the insight provided by Malinowski when he wrote (1948:70):

> Looking from far and above, from our high places of safety in the developed civilization, it is easy to see all the crudity and irrelevance of magic. But without its power and guidance early man could not have mastered his practical difficulties as he has done, nor could man have advanced to the higher stages of civilization.

REFERENCES

Linton, Ralph, 1936, *The Study of Man*. New York, D. Appleton-Century Co.

Malinowski, Bronislaw, 1948, *Magic, Science, and Religion*. Glencoe, The Free Press.

Murdock, George P., 1949, *Social Structure*. New York, The Macmillan Co.

2

Loading the Bases:

How Our Tribe Projects Its Own Image into the National Pastime

Bradd Shore

Culture is a remarkable human invention not only because it allows us to adapt and survive, but also because it requires us to make meaning of the world and our lives. People use cultural concepts and symbolic rituals to construct a view of reality.

This selection provides an insightful view of American culture by interpreting the hidden meanings of baseball. Baseball is both a game and a ritual that appeals to particular cultural notions of space, time, and social relationships. Some of the symbolic meanings in baseball hinge on the structural asymmetries of the game, especially when the lone heroic batter faces the communal efforts of the defense. Bradd Shore does not believe that baseball is just a game; he sees it as a symbolic way of expressing central cultural ideas and paradoxes. Natives might not agree with the symbolic interpretation here, but they may be too close to their own ritual to analyze it. Interestingly, when games are exported to other societies, like baseball to Japan or cricket to the Trobriand Islands, the meanings and nuances of the cultural forms are changed remarkably.

As you read this selection, ask yourself the following questions:

☐ *Why does baseball seem boring and tedious to some people? What is the meaning of contingent time?*

☐ *Why is it permissible for fans to shout derogatory things at the umpire? Why do team managers display anger when they know that the umpire will not change his or her mind?*

☐ *Do you think that the appeal of and fascination with baseball is gender linked? Why or why not?*

☐ *How do baseball fields project an open and endless image of time and space?*

☐ *What does baseball have to do with the concept of culture?*

The following terms discussed in this selection are included in the Glossary at the back of the book:

institutions   *walkabout*
ritual

Americans will recall the night of October 25, 1986, not because of any political upheaval, scientific breakthrough or natural cataclysm but because of certain events involving one William Hayward Wilson, known since childhood as Mookie. Thirty years old, five feet ten inches tall and weighing 168 pounds, Mookie Wilson was, at that time, a much cherished outfielder for the New York Mets. His playing record, comfortably better than mediocre, had been spiced with flashes of brilliance. True, he struck out a bit too often, could have drawn a few more walks and had a weak throwing arm. But he was a joy to watch for the wide sweep of his swing and the gleeful abandon with which he scampered around the bases. And he was beloved by fans and players alike for his unfailing good nature.

Thus did Mookie Wilson stand in the batter's box that autumn evening, in the bottom of the tenth inning of the sixth game of the 1986 World Series. Only minutes before, Shea Stadium had been funereal. The visiting Boston Red Sox had opened up a 5–3 lead in the top of the tenth and had retired the first two Mets on outfield flies in the bottom of the inning. With one more out, what had been a glorious season for New York would have ended ignobly, and Boston would have had its first world championship since 1918. On the field several Red Sox flashed grins, while in their clubhouse preparations were being made for the customary champagne-bath celebration. Over on the Mets' side the fiery first baseman Keith Hernandez, the inning's second out, sat sipping beer and dragging on a cigarette, sullenly awaiting the inevitable.

Then it started. In swift succession singles by Gary Carter, Kevin Mitchell and Ray Knight made it 5–4, with runners on first and third, bringing William Hayward Wilson to the plate and the crowd to its feet. Another hit would tie the score; one of Wilson's occasional home runs would win it for New York.

Wilson worked the count to two balls and two strikes against Boston's Bob Stanley, then fouled off two superlative pitches to stay alive. The next delivery followed a sinking trajectory in the direction of Wilson's ankles. Had he been struck by the pitch, he would have been sent to first, loading the bases. But the agile outfielder jumped, twisted and fell to the ground, avoiding the ball, which eluded the grasp of the catcher Rich Gedman and skipped on toward the backstop, allowing Mitchell, the barrel-chested rookie, to score the tying run and, no less important, moving Knight down to second.

Moments later Stanley pitched and Wilson took one of his enormous swings, spinning off a lazy,

squirming hopper toward the gallant Boston first baseman Bill Buckner, playing despite excruciating pain in his legs. With Wilson sprinting desperately toward first, Buckner reached down for the ball to make the kind of routine defensive play he'd executed countless times over the previous seventeen years.

He missed it. The ball squirted through his legs and rolled into right field as Knight ran home with the run that brought the Mets a 6–5 victory and forced the Series to a seventh game. Buckner meanwhile stared off toward the outfield, aware perhaps that in one split second he had tarnished indelibly a distinguished career during which he had made 2,464 base hits and earned a reputation for unsurpassed competitive spirit. In the stands and all over the New York area people danced and screamed and kissed perfect strangers as if they had just heard of the end of a major war. In New England—even though the Series was not yet over—many prepared to spend a long dour winter contemplating yet another Red Sox collapse. (Rightly so, as it turned out, for the Mets again came from behind to win game seven.) And across the nation millions of people would never forget where they were when they saw Mookie Wilson's at bat climax what may well have been the most extraordinary inning of major league baseball ever played.

Well, one could reasonably ask, as many do: So what? Why all the fuss? Baseball is, after all, just a game, a diversion from life's serious business. Maybe. But a more considered view suggests that while it is incontestably a game, our national pastime is also something more. Baseball symbolizes for many Americans a nostalgia for childhood and summer and a lost agrarian age; it engages our passions, shapes our weekends and helps lubricate our casual social relationships; it transcends the control of the clock over our harried lives; and understood as a kind of ritual drama, baseball takes us beyond the uncertainty of play in motion to the enduring forms that make it a cultural institution—confirming the oft-quoted observation by the historian Jacques Barzun, professor emeritus of Columbia University, that "whoever wants to know the heart and mind of America had better learn baseball."

Many attempts have been made to define the elusive fit between baseball and the American character. Most of them have focused on certain general aspects of the game—its leisurely pace, its concern for precision and self-control and its alleged stress on fair play. Few if any observers, however, have analyzed baseball as a pageant linked closely with the American world view, emphasizing the structural patterns that shape baseball time, baseball space and the social relationships choreographed by the rules of the game.

Like the anthropologist who studies an exotic culture, I came to baseball as a kind of outsider, never

This article is reprinted by permission of *The Sciences* and is from the May/June 1990 issue.

having been especially interested in the game. I knew its basic rules and had played a few dismal years out in left field as a Little Leaguer. But I had never really understood what made this sport so special. Frankly, I had always found watching baseball pretty dull. So my latter-day appreciation of it is inevitably that of an outside observer—a kind of convert—not that of a player or even an avid fan.

What strikes me most about baseball is that compared with other American field sports it is so consistently asymmetrical. Almost everywhere in the game one finds an endearing oddness instead of the efficient balance of basketball, football or hockey. There is barely an even number associated with baseball: nine players, nine innings, three strikes, three outs and a seventh-inning stretch. A full count is five—three balls and two strikes. Even the apparent symmetry of the diamond is broken by its division into three square bases and the lopsided pentagon that serves as home plate. Charmingly skewed, the game gives us no quarters and no halftimes. Baseball play may be fair, but it is not even.

This asymmetry shapes the odd sense of time in baseball. As many writers have noted, baseball is unique among American field sports in its utter disregard for the clock. Baseball time is controlled by innings and the contingencies of events. A game is over only when the losing team has had at least nine at bats and when a difference between the teams has been generated. The rare exceptions are when umpires call a game, say for darkness or bad weather. Otherwise, the fearful symmetry of a tie score is not allowed. The open-endedness of baseball is guaranteed by the theoretically endless moments of the game. The batter might foul off an infinite number of pitches and thus remain at the plate to dig in and take his cuts for eternity. The team at bat could mount an interminable hitting streak and prolong indefinitely its half of the inning. Or the score might be inextricably deadlocked, sending the contest sprawling into an infinity of extra innings.

Detractors of the game are fond of pointing to its leisurely pace as its most glaring defect. Aficionados rarely deny the charge and instead locate much of the genius of baseball in its alternation of long periods of languor with sudden bursts of action. For the fan the drawling rhythm of the game allows a continuous shift of attention from the public spectacle at hand to more private pursuits: staring at the field, the scoreboard, the sky or the cityscape; discussing the game and arguing over what's to come; eating, drinking and making small talk. For the uninitiated these long breaks account for the tedium of baseball; but for true believers the resolute pokiness of the game allows for a kind of imaginative engagement impossible to achieve while watching a safety blitz, a fast break or a power play. This kind of intellectual involvement differs from the

kinesthetic rush we feel when, as spectators, we sprint along with Carl Lewis in the 100-yard dash or add our own body English to Ray Leonard's feints, jabs and uppercuts. It is, rather, what Roger Angell, one of the more elegant baseball scribes, has called the "inner game—baseball in the mind": the cerebral interplay of strategy, anecdote and realignment of the all important statistics.

The romance of baseball with time, its genius for defying the clock, is equally apparent in its capacity to subdue the flow of history. For many Americans baseball encapsulates their own biographies through a seamless chain of teams that propels youth into age and projects age back to reclaim its lost vitality. From Little League to Babe Ruth League, high school, college, the Minors and the Majors, baseball is an idiom by which the dream of the endless summer is tied up with an individual life history. This may be why it is with a swing of the bat that most old-timers seem to think they can recapture youth. As the San Francisco columnist Herb Caen mused: "Whereas we cannot imagine ourselves executing a two-handed slam-dunk or a 50-yard field goal, we are still certain we have one base hit left in us."

If baseball time is open-ended, it nonetheless maintains its fundamental asymmetry by insistently fixing its beginnings. If the conclusion of a game is contingent on subsequent events, the start is always ritually precise: the national anthem and the umpire's cry "Play ball!" The baseball season may end with a contingent world series, but it begins with a single, sacred act: the presidential toss on opening day, a tradition that dates to 1910 and the beaming, corpulent William Howard Taft. In fact, the opening of the season is itself a re-enactment of the birth of professional baseball. Game one of each new National League campaign is always played in Cincinnati, in memory of the Cincinnati Red Stockings, which in 1869 became the first salaried team.

The same need to demarcate its beginnings may well have inspired the invention of the mythical birth of baseball. In 1903 Henry Chadwick, the premier baseball authority in his day, testified in the *Baseball Guide* that the American game was without doubt a natural offspring of the British game rounders. Such heresy riled Albert Goodwill Spalding, a great pitcher of the 1870s who had by then become the nation's leading sporting goods magnate. The influential Spalding called for the formation of a fact-finding committee to determine the true pedigree of baseball. And in 1907 this august body certified that, Chadwick's compelling evidence notwithstanding, baseball was a deliberate and authentic American creation.

The baseball nativity story can be traced to the colorful reminiscences of one Abner Graves, a friend of a

Civil War major general named Abner Doubleday. Graves claimed to recall how in 1839 Doubleday—who conveniently enough happened also to be acquainted with Abraham G. Mills, the fact-finding committee's chairman—had cleaned up an anarchic game called town ball played by boys in Cooperstown, New York. By mapping out a precise and orderly diamond on a pasture and by codifying the loose rules of the game, this latter-day Justinian was said to have single-handedly given America its national pastime. Like our nation itself, baseball could now lay claim to a fixed domestic origin, a certifiable beginning in an act of deliberate reason—the rationalization of a cow pasture on a summer's day in 1839.

Thus, baseball time juxtaposes the fixed beginning and the open end, the determinate and the contingent, in a characteristic asymmetrical relation. This pattern is paralleled closely by the game's orchestration of space. Baseball is the only American field sport that does not use a symmetrical field, defined by sides and ends. The baseball park defines a tension between an ever narrowing inner point, called home, and an ever widening outer field. The diamond, which includes the home area, is marked out with exacting precision and is the same in every park. The modern baseball diamond consists of a focal plate, located at home, and of three bases (or bags) situated at ninety-foot intervals around the diamond. Exactly sixty feet six inches from home plate is the pitcher's mound, raised no more than fifteen inches above the level of the bases.

Whereas this diamond area is precisely and uniformly measured, there are no rules governing the size or the outer boundaries of the outfield. It is the indeterminacy of the outfield that has given the classic ballparks—Wrigley Field in Chicago, Ebbets Field in Brooklyn, Yankee Stadium in the Bronx, Fenway Park in Boston—their distinctive souls. Moreover, outfields are subject to historical revision: only in baseball can the field be reshaped to accommodate new configurations of talent on the home team. There have been more than a few examples of outfield fences' being raised or lowered or moved closer to or farther from home plate. The most notorious instance of such boundary manipulation was the adjustable-height fence concocted by Bill Veeck, Jr., owner of the hapless Saint Louis Browns during the early 1950s. An inveterate showman, Veeck was renowned for the outlandish marketing gimmicks with which he enticed fans into watching his abysmal team. To enhance the Browns' home-field advantage, he installed an outfield fence that could be raised or lowered depending on who was at bat. The innovation lasted one game, after which a rule forbidding the practice was passed.

Whereas other field sports present focal goals for the object in play at each end of the field, the baseball park extends into the community. In a sense, the batter's goal lies beyond the park itself, on the city streets; in fact, according to ballplayers' slang, to hit a home run is to "go downtown." Through the home run, baseball celebrates the possibility of a heroic action's momentarily overcoming the limits of the contest. The home run is an authentic sacred event—not so much the everyday homer that merely drops into the stands, but the electric smash, announced by the loud crack of a bat, that sails clear of the park, beyond the fielder's futile leap, beyond the reach of the riotous fans, beyond the bounds of the game itself. That is why the royalty of baseball—the likes of Babe Ruth, Hank Aaron, Willie Mays and Mickey Mantle—are nearly always home-run kings.

The spatial open-endedness of baseball differs sharply from the "bowls" associated with football, arenas that surround the players totally, cutting the game space off completely and symmetrically from the surrounding community. The recent introduction of hybrid stadiums suitable for both baseball and football is for baseball purists an unfortunate development. If, traditionally, baseball parks were engagingly idiosyncratic, the modern era surely has encouraged a standardization alien to the game's authentic locale.

The most powerful of the asymmetries of baseball is social: it is the only American field sport that never directly confronts one team with another. Instead, the game pits a team—nine players on the field—against a lone batter and no more than three base runners at one time. Moreover, the team at bat remains out of sight, with members in a dugout awaiting their trips to the plate. Each player has two personas—a reactive defensive identity in which he plays a part in a highly coordinated communal enterprise on the field, and an aggressive offensive persona, in which he faces the opposing team as an individual batter and base runner. Although he functions as part of the communal fielding unit, the pitcher is the only player whose primary roles are aggressive on offense and defense alike.

The social asymmetry is reflected in baseball talk. Take for instance the difference between "playing" and "being." Those in the field merely "play" positions; but the batter "is" at bat, and the pitcher "pitches." Consider the awkwardness of such phrases as "Jose Canseco is playing the batter for the Oakland A's" or "Whitey Ford played pitcher for the Yankees." The more active a role is in baseball, the more the players *are* what they do, whereas "playing" is relegated to more passive, defensive roles. The language of being rather than of playing is also associated with proximity to "home." These speech conventions reflect a world view in which being is linked to an individual activity in a domestic, or home, environment. In contrast, social role playing is linked to an "outer" field.

In other field sports one team tries to move an object from one end of the field, through a hostile set of defenders, to a goal at the opposite end. The object, not the players, makes the score. In baseball it is the runner alone who scores. The ball is controlled largely by the fielders, whose ability to move it around the field works against the runner's interest. The batter, meanwhile, opposes the ball, hoping to knock it free of the fielders' control—out of the park, if possible. When he fails—if the ball is caught in the air or is returned to confront him or one of the base runners—he has made an "out." This essentially hostile relationship between offensive players and the ball is a distinctive characteristic of the game.

The action of baseball, then, can be conceived of as a series of travels by individuals who attempt to leave home and make a circuit through a social field marked with obstacles. It is not getting through the field itself that scores, however, but returning safely home. Baseball is our version of what Australian aborigines call a walkabout—a circular journey into alien territory, with the aim of returning home after making contact with sacred landmarks and braving hazards along the way.

Thus baseball dramatizes a recurrent cultural problem: how to reconcile communal values with a tradition of heroic individualism and privatism. But the power of baseball as a ritual comes from more than a simple opposition between the social and the individual. It derives from the dramatization of the tension between the two and from an attempt to reconcile them symbolically. So baseball can be viewed as several kinds of contest going on simultaneously, each representing a different aspect of the relation between self and society.

On the first and broadest level, baseball is a contest between two teams, a clash that involves some profound social loyalties. The spatial opposition between home and outfield around which the game is organized is mimicked by the opposition between home team and visitors, or outsiders, a contest that provokes powerful community allegiances among fans. The second level of competition in baseball is the contest between the batsman at home plate and his opponents arrayed on the field. It is here that the game most vividly reflects the American dilemma: reconciling ideas of community and fair play with those of privacy and heroic individualism.

At the third level the teams disappear altogether, and baseball becomes a showdown between pitcher and batter, who face off in a mythic shoot-out scenario, each struggling to control the ball and unnerve the other. This dimension of the game has been greatly amplified by the advent of television, which in more ways than one has brought baseball home. By zooming in on the batter and the pitcher, televised baseball blocks out the fielding game for all but a few action-packed moments and is almost exclusively confined to the intimate battle taking place between the mound and the plate.

Finally there is a fourth level, where not only the teams fade from view but also the game, the season and the decade. At this level, through statistics, each player enters into a kind of ongoing universal supergame, beyond time and space, in which each is pitted against every other player who has ever worn a uniform. The lure of the "stats" has been perhaps the most commonly noted distinctive aspect of baseball. As Angell has written, a host of statistics "swarm and hover above the head of every pitcher, every fielder, every batter, every team, recording every play with an accompanying silent shift of digits." Thus Ty Cobb's .367 career batting average (the all-time standard) has merged with his name, his dates of birth and death and the memory of his irascible disposition.

An obsession with batting average, RBI, ERA and such is characteristic of a society at once democratic and individualistic, egalitarian and fiercely competitive, a nation preoccupied with enforcing a vision of community upon a vastly heterogeneous population. What statistics do for baseball, polls and elections do for society at large. As Rousseau noted long ago, in *A Discourse Upon the Origin and Foundation of the Inequality Among Mankind*, in a democracy the general will of the people can never really be general. It can only be manifest through the assertion of numerical superiority—the will of the majority.

Thus it is altogether fitting that stats are an important way in which the spectator can participate in a professional's game. If gradations in players' skills can be translated through statistics into a quantitative hierarchy of value, so too can differences in skill and devotion among fans be ranked through a contest that engages their knowledge of the numbers. This is metabaseball; one can be bored with the actual events of a game—yet relish the ongoing Pythagorean drama of numbers piling up against numbers in the mind's own ballpark.

Children enter early into this cosmic contest through baseball cards. In their incarnations as cards, players can be lifted out of their local team context and placed into the wider marketplace of baseball, their stats compared, their value calculated. When my seven-year-old son, his box of baseball cards tucked under his arm, sets off to close a deal with a boy down the block, he joins the ranks of baseball owners. Through a combination of shrewd business savvy and raw hero worship he connects with the most atomistic dimension of baseball.

The central Christian rite of Communion involves confronting and momentarily overcoming basic theological contradictions: life and death, body and spirit, god and human being. Whether religious or secular, ritual thrives on such paradoxes, crystallizing for the participants a fleeting reconciliation of opposites. As a civic ritual baseball enacts tensions between domestic, private and individual concerns, on the one hand, and social, public and communal concerns, on the other. Americans often use the language of the game metaphorically to represent other activities that involve the problematic nexus of self-interest and social responsibility, and no activity is more frequently so described than sexual behavior. Consider these expressions: "I can't get to first base"; "making a hit with him"; "he struck out with her"; "going all the way"; "I scored last night." Along the same lines American schoolboys commonly liken a sexual interlude to an epic dash around the base paths, in which they achieve more daring levels of physical intimacy with every base—and, with any luck, go all the way.

At first glance one might assume that baseball terminology is applied to all realms of sexual endeavor. Yet "My wife and I went all the way last night" and "I couldn't get to first base with the prostitute" seem jarringly inappropriate. Evidently, the baseball metaphor doesn't apply to sex when sex either is fully domesticated and private or is a fully public and commercial transaction. Baseball lingo is linked to sexual adventurism in dating behavior, in which a male must negotiate a perilous field of play with at least the possibility of coming home to score.

Like all games, baseball has rules to govern the competitive relationships between players. But possibly because it is a game that calls into question issues of individual freedom and social regulation, the attitude toward rules in baseball is notoriously ambivalent. Behind home plate, at the very apex of the infield, stands the embodiment of the rule book: the umpire, whose judgments represent the final authority in the game. But while umpires hold absolute power, managers, coaches and some players regularly treat their decisions as if they are open to protracted, sometimes violent negotiation. Such legendary figures as John McGraw, Leo Durocher and Billy Martin earned folkloric niches as much for their profane, dirt-kicking, tobacco-spewing debates with arbiters as for their managerial skills. This venerable ritual of challenging authority endures even though umpires rarely change decisions—certainly not in response to abuse by a player or a coach.

This leitmotiv of rebellion extends from the field to the grandstand: In no other American sport is there any counterpart of the traditional cry to kill the ump, a recurring ritual rebellion aimed not only at a particular call but also at the dominion of the rule book itself. In the nineteenth century club owners encouraged their patrons to humiliate the umpires. As Albert Spalding suggested, fans who harassed umpires were merely expressing a democratic right to protest tyranny. In fact, nineteenth-century fans were called cranks, an appropriate sobriquet, given their predilection for razzing and, on occasion, rioting.

The same reckless spirit can be found within the game itself. Spitters and brushback pitches, phantom double plays and the hidden-ball trick: these moments of petty villainy have a revered place in the sport. A reputation for insouciance has followed baseball almost from the start: as Harvey Frommer notes in *Baseball: The First Quarter-Century of the National Pastime*, Cincinnati's Red Stockings—models of Victorian propriety in their daguerreotypes—were loved in the 1860s not just for their on-field adventures but for their rowdy off-field antics.

For the most part the challenge of baseball to social order has always had an endearing tameness about it: it is the schoolboy playing hooky or swiping penny candy from a glass jar at the sweet shop, not the darker sins of elders. The authentic hero of American baseball is not the rapacious Hun but the errant knight—not the man but the Babe. Thus, as Paul Gardner points out in his 1975 book, *Nice Guys Finish Last: Sport and American Life*, George Herman Ruth was the perfect embodiment of the game's ambiguous relation with the idea of order:

> He had come up the hard way. He had reached the top without special training, without a college education; he was a graduate of "the school of hard knocks." He was a big man, with big appetites. He was irreverent and scornful of authority. He liked kids. And he made a lot of money. . . . He drank and he ate enough for two men, ignored the training rules and curfews, yet he played baseball better than anyone else around. . . . Ruth, it seemed, could get away with anything, while Americans chuckled and muttered in envious admiration, "That Babe. . . ."

For its millions of devotees baseball, though obviously a game to be played, is also a ritual to be observed; and ritual, by most definitions, is religion in motion, constituted by activities directed toward the sacred. In his book *The Savage Mind*, the French anthropologist Claude Lévi-Strauss reflects on the relation between games and rituals:

> Games thus appear to have a *disjunctive* effect: they end in the establishment of a difference between individual players or teams. . . . At the end of the game they are distinguished into winners and losers. Ritual, on the other hand, is the exact inverse; it *conjoins*, for it brings about a union . . . between two initially separate groups.

For Lévi-Strauss the crucial difference between games and rituals hinges on the relation between the fixed rules, or structural forms, and the unpredictable events to which they give rise. In games the structure of play is taken for granted and recedes into the background like the bass line in a piece of music: a barely perceptible but deeply resonant grounding on which the melody dances with illusory freedom. Games use the rules to create disequilibrium between players and teams that ostensibly started out as equals. Rituals, on the other hand, bring the shared framework of forms* and rules forward into consciousness. A ritual can serve as a kind of public social memory, an enacted recollection of shared experience. It brings us together.

An oft-noted characteristic of games is that they are not for real: they are "just play." All games take place within an agreed-upon "play frame" that suspends to some extent the seriousness of ordinary activity. The play frame is defined by both time and space, so that the suspension of workaday reality is understood to be in effect only within the confines of the park, or game space, and only for as long as the game is in play.

Ritual shares with games this framing of reality. Often, however, a ritual is assumed to be more important than everyday behavior. Whereas games seem to operate on a level just below ordinary business, rituals rise transcendently above it, largely because ritual— particularly religious ritual—is frequently believed to be the repetition of sacred primal events. To devout worshipers, the rites of their faith may fairly be characterized as more real than reality or, at least, part of a higher reality. At the same time, ritual draws much of its power from the interplay of its immutable forms and the possibility that a real event may chance upon the scene. At the edge of performance, ritual flirts with reality: Rites of passage can come unnervingly close to bodily experience, whether for novices in New Guinea or fraternity pledges on college campuses. Real pain, authentic danger and, not infrequently, body mutilation figure prominently in such rites, throwing into doubt their status as performance.

Baseball, it seems, is neither game nor ritual alone but both at once. Our experience of the sport as player or spectator exemplifies what might be called—to use a musical metaphor—the polyphonic mind. That is, a thick, complex texture of conscious experience is made possible by the simultaneous interaction of several layers of knowledge. From our box at the ballpark our immediate attention may be riveted on the flow of the events of the game. But the total experience of baseball includes the embodied awareness of the recurrent forms and traditions of the game, which have a resonance all their own.

The interplay of game, ritual and reality in baseball was brought into sharp relief last fall, when a major earthquake struck before the third game of the World Series between the San Francisco Giants and the Oakland Athletics. There is no more sacred event in American sport than the Series, in which two major league titlists duel for what is a bit jingoistically called the World Championship. Feats accomplished during this festival are transcendent, and those who achieve them are enshrined in myth. When the earthquake struck the Bay Area, game, ritual and reality collided violently. We were jolted, confused by the sight of uniformed players huddling with their wives and children in Candlestick Park, reacting to an all too real intrusion from beyond game space. In the aftermath the reality of leveled buildings and of cars crushed on a freeway bridge seemed at first to render baseball absurdly insignificant. Even at World Series time, it *was* only a game. Or was it? As bodies were being pulled from wreckage, questions of when, where and whether or not the Series should resume were being hotly debated. And when, after what was deemed a respectable interlude, the Giants and the Athletics took to the field, the restoration of baseball, game and ritual, was for many like awakening from a nightmare to look again on the real world.

3

Crack in Spanish Harlem

Philippe Bourgois

Urban America vibrates with the intensity of a taut drum. The cadence of street life is a constant reminder that things are different here. Suburban folks who meander into some of these inner-city neighborhoods immediately notice the contrasts between these streets and their hometowns. Beset by what has been called the "signs of incivility," outsiders are uneasy and often afraid. Outsiders seldom understand the subculture of the inner city, and most don't want to.

Yet, it is in the inner city that many of our most serious social problems are found, including unemployment, homelessness, broken families, poor medical care, and crime. Survival in this milieu, particularly in the drug scene, requires a deep understanding of the subculture. In the same way, effective public policy is more likely to result if policymakers understand the cultural meaning of people's behavior. But how can they achieve such an understanding?

This riveting account reveals how anthropological work can lend an important dimension to our comprehension of a way of life almost as foreign to most of us as is the life of an Amazon warrior, a !Kung bushman, or a rain forest pygmy.

As you read this selection, ask yourself the following questions:

☐ *What is meant by the culture of resistance, and what effects does this culture have on a community and society?*

☐ *In what ways is the underground economy like a business?*

☐ *How is a job in the underground economy different from a legal job in terms of respect and an individual's feeling of self-worth?*

☐ *What is meant by the culture of terror, and what is the role of violence in maintaining social status?*

☐ *What can be learned through ethnographic fieldwork as opposed to questionnaires and surveys?*

The following terms discussed in this selection are included in the Glossary at the back of the book:

cultural reproduction
ethnography
ghetto

A MUGGING IN SPANISH HARLEM

The heavy-set, white undercover policeman pushed me across the ice-cream counter, spreading my legs and poking me around the groin. As he came dangerously close to the bulge in my right pocket I hissed in his ear "It's a tape recorder." He snapped backwards,

"Crack in Spanish Harlem: Culture and Economy in the Inner City" by Philippe Bourgois, from *Anthropology Today*, vol. 5, no. 4, 1989. Royal Anthropological Institute of Great Britian and Ireland. Reprinted with permission.

releasing his left hand's grip on my neck and whispering a barely audible "Sorry." Apparently, he thought he had clumsily intercepted an undercover from another department because before I could get a close look at his face he had left the *bodega* grocery-store cum numbers-joint. Meanwhile, the marijuana sellers stationed in front of the *bodega* that Gato and I had just entered to buy 16-ounce cans of Private Stock (beer), observing that the undercover had been rough with me when he searched through my pants, suddenly felt safe and relieved—finally confident that I was a white drug addict rather than an undercover.

As we hurried to leave this embarrassing scene we were blocked by Bennie, an emaciated teenager high on angel dust who was barging through the door along with two friends to mug us. I ran to the back of the *bodega* but Gato had to stand firmly because this was the corner he worked, and those were his former partners. They dragged him onto the sidewalk surrounding him on all sides, shouting about the money he still owed, and began kicking and hitting him with a baseball bat. I found out later that Gato owed them for his share of the supply of marijuana confiscated in a drug bust last week . . . After we finished telling the story at the crack/*botanica*[1] house where I had been spending most of my evening hours this summer, Chino, who was on duty selling that night with Julio (pronounced Jew-Lee-oh), jumped up excitedly calling out 'what street was that on? Come on, let's go, we can still catch them—How many were they?' I quickly stopped this mobilization for a revenge posse, explaining that it was not worth my time, and that we should just forget about it. Chino looked at me disgustedly sitting back down on the milk crate in front of the *botanica*'s door and turned his face away from me, shrugging his shoulders. Julio, whom I knew better and had become quite close to for a number of weeks last year, jumped up in front of me raising his voice to berate me for being "pussy." He also sat back down shortly afterwards feigning exasperated incredulity with the comment "Man you still think like a *blanquito*." A half dozen spectators—some of them empty-pocketed ("thirsty!") crack addicts, but most of them sharply dressed teenage drug-free girls competing for Chino's and Julio's attentions—giggled and snickered at me.

CULTURE AND MATERIAL REALITY

The above extract from sanitized fieldwork notes is merely a personalized glimpse of the day-to-day struggle for survival *and for meaning* by the people who stand behind the extraordinary statistics on inner city violent crime in the United States.[2] These are the same Puerto Rican residents of Spanish Harlem, New York City, that Oscar Lewis in *La Vida* declared to be victims of a "culture of poverty" enmired in a "self-perpetuating cycle of poverty" (Lewis 1966: 5). The culture of poverty concept has been severely criticized for its internal inconsistencies, its inadequate understanding of "culture" and ethnicity, its ethnocentric/middle class bias, its blindness to structural forces, and its blame-the-victim implications (cf. Leacock ed. 1971, Valentine 1968, Waxman 1977, Stack 1974). Despite the negative scholarly consensus on Lewis's theory, the alternative discussions either tend towards economic reductionism (Ryan 1971, Steinberg 1981, Wilson 1978) or else ultimately minimize the reality of profound

marginalization and destruction—some of it internalized—that envelop a disproportionate share of the inner city poor (cf. Stack 1974, Valentine 1978; see critiques by Maxwell 1988, Wilson 1988). More importantly, the media, public policy-makers and a large proportion of inner city residents themselves continue to subscribe to a popularized blame-the-victim/culture of poverty concept that has not been adequately rebutted by scholars.

The inner city residents described in the ethnographic vignette above are the pariahs of urban industrial US society. They seek their income and subsequently their identity and the meaning in their life through what they perceive to be high-powered careers "on the street." They partake of ideologies and values and share symbols which form the basis of an "inner city street culture" completely excluded from the mainstream economy and society but ultimately derived from it. Most of them have a few direct contacts with non–inner city residents, and when they do it is usually with people who are in a position of domination: teachers in school, bosses, police officers, and later parole or probation officers.

How can one understand the complicated ideological dynamic accompanying inner city poverty without falling into a hopelessly idealistic culture of poverty and blame-the-victim interpretation? Structural, political economy reinterpretations of the inner city dynamic emphasize historical processes of labour migration in the context of institutionalized ethnic discrimination. They dissect the structural transformations in the international economy which are destroying the manufacturing sector in the United States and are swelling the low wage, low prestige service sector (cf. Davis 1987; Sassen-Koob 1986; Steinberg 1981; Tabb and Sawers, eds., 1984; Wilson 1978, 1987). These analyses address the structural confines of the inner city dynamic but fall prey to a passive interpretation of human action and subscribe to a weakly dialectic interpretation of the relationship between ideological processes and material reality, or between culture and class.

Although ultimately traceable directly to being products of international labour migrations in a transnational world economy, street-level inner city residents are more than merely passive victims of historical economic transformations or of the institutionalized discrimination of a perverse political and economic system. They do not passively accept their fourth-class citizen fate. They are struggling determinedly—just as ruthlessly as the railroad and oil robber-barons of the previous century and the investment-banker "yuppies" of today—to earn money, demand dignity and lead meaningful lives. Tragically, it is that very process of struggle against—yet within—the system which exacerbates the trauma of their community and which destroys hundreds of thousands of lives on the individual level.

In the day-to-day experience of the street-bound inner city resident, unemployment and personal anxiety over the inability to provide one's family with a minimal standard of living translates itself into intra-community crime, intra-community drug abuse, intra-community violence. The objective, structural desperation of a population without a viable economy, and facing systematic barriers of ethnic discrimination and ideological marginalization, becomes charged at the community level into self-destructive channels.

Most importantly, the "personal failure" of those who survive on the street is articulated in the idiom of race. The racism imposed by the larger society becomes internalized on a personal level. Once again, although the individuals in the ethnographic fragment at the beginning of this paper are the victims of long-term historical and structural transformations, they do not analyse their difficult situation from a political economy perspective. In their struggle to survive and even to be successful, they enforce on a day-to-day level the details of the trauma and cruelty of their lives on the excluded margins of US urban society.

CULTURAL REPRODUCTION THEORY

Theorists of education have developed a literature on processes of social and cultural reproduction which focus on the ideological domination of the poor and the working class in the school setting (cf. Giroux 1983). Although some of the social reproduction approaches tend towards an economic reductionism or a simple, mechanical functionalism (cf. Bowles and Gintis 1977), the more recent variants emphasize the complexity and contradictory nature of the dynamic of ideological domination (Willis 1983). There are several ethnographies which document how the very process whereby students resist school, channels them into marginal roles in the economy for the rest of their lives (cf. Willis 1977; Macleod 1987). Other ethnographically-based interpretations emphasize how success for inner city African-American students requires a rejection of their ethnic identity and cultural dignity (Fordham 1988).

There is no reason why these theories of cultural resistance and ideological domination have to be limited to the institutional school setting. Cultural reproduction theory has great potential for shedding light on the interaction between structurally induced cultural resistance and self-reinforced marginalization at the street-level in the inner city experience. The violence, crime and substance abuse plaguing the inner city can be understood as the manifestations of a "culture of resistance" to mainstream, white racist, and

economically exclusive society. This "culture of resistance," however, results in greater oppression and self-destruction. More concretely, refusing to accept the outside society's racist role playing and refusing to accept low wage, entry-level jobs, translates into high crime rates, high addiction rates and high intra-community violence.

Most of the individuals in the above ethnographic description are proud that they are not being exploited by "the White Man," but they feel "like fucking assholes" for being poor. All of them have previously held numerous jobs in the legal economy in their lives. Most of them hit the street in their early teens working odd jobs as delivery boys and baggers in supermarkets and *bodegas*. Most of them have held the jobs that are recognized as among the least desirable in US society. Virtually all of these street participants have had deeply negative personal experiences in the minimum-wage labour market, owing to abusive, exploitative and often racist bosses or supervisors. They see the illegal, underground economy as not only offering superior wages, but also a more dignified work place. For example, Gato had formerly worked for the ASPCA, cleaning out the gas chambers where stray dogs and cats are killed. Bennie had been fired six months earlier from a night shift job as security guard on the violent ward for the criminally insane on Wards Island; Chino had been fired a year ago from a job installing high altitude storm windows on skyscrapers following an accident which temporarily blinded him in the right eye. Upon being disabled he discovered that his contractor had hired him illegally through an arrangement with a corrupt union official who had paid him half the union wage, pocketing the rest, and who had not taken health insurance for him. Chino also claimed that his foreman from Pennsylvania was a "Ku Klux Klanner" and had been especially abusive to him as he was a black Puerto Rican. In the process of recovering from the accident, Chino had become addicted to crack and ended up in the hospital as a gunshot victim before landing a job at Papito's crack house. Julio's last legal job before selling crack was as an off-the-books messenger for a magazine catering to New York yuppies. He had become addicted to crack, began selling possessions from out of his home and finally was thrown out by his wife who had just given birth to his son, who carried his name as Julio the IIIrd, on public assistance. Julio had quit his messenger job in favour of stealing car radios for a couple of hours at night in the very same neighbourhood where he had been delivering messages for ten hour days at just above minimum wage. Nevertheless, after a close encounter with the police. Julio begged his cousin for a job selling in his crack house. Significantly, the sense of responsibility, success and prestige that selling crack gave him enabled him to kick his crack habit and replace it by a less expensive and destructive powder cocaine and alcohol habit.

The underground economy, consequently, is the ultimate "equal opportunity employer" for inner city youth (cf. Kornblum and Williams 1985). As Davis (1987: 75) has noted for Los Angeles, the structural economic incentive to participate in the drug economy is overwhelming:

> With 78,000 unemployed youth in the Watts-Willowbrook area, it is not surprising that there are now 145 branches of the rival Crips and Bloods gangs in South L.A., or that the jobless resort to the opportunities of the burgeoning 'Crack' economy.

The individuals "successfully" pursuing careers in the "crack economy" or any other facet of the underground economy are no longer "exploitable" by legal society. They speak with anger at their former low wages and bad treatment. They make fun of friends and acquaintances—many of whom come to buy drugs from them—who are still employed in factories, in service jobs, or in what they (and most other people) would call "shitwork." Of course, many others are less self-conscious about the reasons for their rejection of entry-level, mainstream employment. Instead, they think of themselves as lazy and irresponsible. They claim they quit their jobs in order to have a good time on the street. Many still pay lip service to the value of a steady, legal job. Still others cycle in and out of legal employment supplementing their bouts at entry-level jobs through part-time crack sales in an almost perverse parody of the economic subsidy of the wage labour sector by semi-subsistence peasants who cyclically engage in migratory wage labour in third world economies (cf. Meillassoux 1981; Wallerstein 1977).

THE CULTURE OF TERROR IN THE UNDERGROUND ECONOMY

The culture of resistance that has emerged in the underground street-level economy in opposition to demeaning, underpaid employment in the mainstream economy engenders violence. In the South American context of extreme political repression and racism against Amerindians and Jews, anthropologist Michael Taussig has argued that "cultures of terror" emerge to become ". . . a high-powered tool for domination and a principal medium for political practice" (1984:492). Unlike Taussig's examples of the 1910s Putumayo massacres and the 1970s Argentine torture chambers, domination in the case of the inner city's culture of terror is self-administered even if the root cause is generated or even imposed externally. With the exception of occasional brutality by policemen or

the bureaucratized repression of the social welfare and criminal justice institutions (cf. Davis 1988), the physical violence and terror of the inner city are largely carried out by inner city residents themselves.

Regular displays of violence are necessary for success in the underground economy—especially at the street-level drug dealing world. Violence is essential for maintaining credibility and for preventing rip-off by colleagues, customers and hold-up artists. Indeed, upward mobility in the underground economy requires a systematic and effective use of violence against one's colleagues, one's neighbours and, to a certain extent, against oneself. Behaviour that appears irrationally violent and self-destructive to the middle class (or the working class) outside observer, can be reinterpreted according to the logic of the underground economy, as a judicious case of public relations, advertising, rapport building and long-term investment in one's "human capital development."

The importance of one's reputation is well illustrated in the fieldwork fragment at the beginning of this paper. Gato and I were mugged because Gato had a reputation for being "soft" or "pussy" and because I was publicly unmasked as *not being* an undercover cop: hence safe to attack. Gato tried to minimize the damage to his future ability to sell on that corner by not turning and running. He had pranced sideways down the street, though being beaten with a baseball bat and kicked to the ground twice. Significantly, I found out later that it was the second time this had happened to Gato this year. Gato was not going to be upwardly mobile in the underground economy because of his "pussy" reputation and he was further cementing his fate with an increasingly out of control addiction to crack.

Employers or new entrepreneurs in the underground economy are looking for people who can demonstrate their capacity for effective violence and terror. For example, in the eyes of Papito, the owner of the string of crack franchises I am currently researching, the ability of his employees to hold up under gunpoint is crucial as stick-ups of dealing dens are not infrequent. In fact, since my fieldwork began in 1986, the *botanica* has been held up twice. Julio happened to be on duty both times. He admitted to me that he had been very nervous when they held the gun to his temple and had asked for money and crack. Nevertheless, not only did he withhold some of the money and crack that was hidden behind the bogus *botanica* merchandise, but he also later exaggerated to Papito the amount that had been stolen in order to pocket the difference.

On several occasions in the midst of long conversations with active criminals (i.e., once with a dealing-den stick-up artist, several times with crack dealers, and once with a former bank robber) I asked them to explain how they were able to trust their partners in crime sufficiently to ensure the longevity and effectiveness of their enterprise. To my surprise I was not given any righteous diatribes about blood-brotherhood trustworthiness or any adulations of boyhood loyalty. Instead, in each case, in slightly different language I was told somewhat aggressively: "What do you mean how do I trust him? You should ask 'How does he trust me?'" Their ruthlessness is their security: "My support network is me, myself and I." They made these assertions with such vehemence as to appear threatened by the concept that their security and success might depend upon the trustworthiness of their partner or their employer. They were claiming—in one case angrily—that they were not dependent upon trust: because they were tough enough to command respect and enforce all contracts they entered into. The "How can they trust me?" was said with smug pride, perhaps not unlike the way a stockbroker might brag about his access to inside information on an upcoming hostile takeover deal.

At the end of the summer Chino demonstrated clearly the how-can-I-be-trusted dynamic. His cocaine snorting habit had been degenerating into a crack addiction by the end of the summer, and finally one night he was forced to flee out of state to a cousin's when he was unable to turn in the night's receipts to his boss Papito following a binge. Chino also owed Papito close to a thousand dollars for bail that Papito had posted when he was arrested for selling crack at the *botanica* a few months ago. Almost a year later when Papito heard that Chino had been arrested for jumping bail he arranged through another associate incarcerated in the same prison (Rikers Island) to have Chino beaten up before his trial date.

My failure to display a propensity for violence in several instances cost me the respect of the members of the crack scene that I frequented. This was very evident when I turned down Julio and Chino's offer to search for Bennie after he mugged Gato and me. Julio had despairingly exclaimed that I "still [thought] like a *blanquito*," genuinely disappointed that I was not someone with common sense and self-respect.

These concrete examples of the cultivation of violent public behaviour are the extreme cases of individuals relying on the underground economy for their income and dependent upon cultivating terror in order to survive. Individuals involved in street activity cultivate the culture of terror in order to intimidate competitors, maintain credibility, develop new contacts, cement partnerships, and ultimately to have a good time. For the most part they are not conscious of this process. The culture of terror becomes a myth and a role model with rules and satisfactions all its own which ultimately has a traumatic impact on the majority of Spanish Harlem residents—who are drug free and who work honestly at poorly remunerated legal jobs, 9 to 5 plus overtime.

PURSUING THE AMERICAN DREAM

It is important to understand that the underground economy and the violence emerging out of it are not propelled by an irrational cultural logic distinct from that of mainstream USA. On the contrary, street participants are frantically pursuing the "American dream." The assertions of the culture of poverty theorists that the poor have been badly socialized and do not share mainstream values is wrong. On the contrary, ambitious, energetic, inner city youths are attracted into the underground economy in order to try frantically to get their piece of the pie as fast as possible. They often even follow the traditional US model for upward mobility to the letter by becoming aggressive private entrepreneurs. They are the ultimate rugged individualists braving an unpredictable frontier where fortune, fame and destruction are all just around the corner. Hence Indio, a particularly enterprising and ambitious young crack dealer who was aggressively carving out a new sales point, shot his brother in the spine and paralysed him for life while he was high on angel dust in a battle over sales rights. His brother now works for him selling on crutches. Meanwhile, the shooting has cemented Indio's reputation and his workers are awesomely disciplined: "If he shot his brother he'll shoot anyone." Indio reaffirms this symbolically by periodically walking his turf with an oversized gold chain and name plate worth several thousand dollars hanging around his neck.

The underground economy and the culture of terror are experienced as the most realistic routes to upward mobility. Entry-level jobs are not seen as viable channels to upward mobility by high school dropouts. Drug selling or other illegal activity appear as the most effective and realistic options for getting rich within one's lifetime. Many of the street dealers claim to be strictly utilitarian in their involvement with crack and they snob their clients despite the fact that they usually have considerable alcohol and powder cocaine habits themselves. Chino used to chant at his regular customers "Come on, keep on killing yourself; bring me that money; smoke yourself to death; make me rich."

Even though street sellers are employed by the owner of a sales point for whom they have to maintain regular hours, meet sales quotas and be subject to being fired, they have a great deal of autonomy and power in their daily (or nightly) routine. The boss only comes once or twice a shift to drop off drugs and pick up money. Frequently, it is a young messenger who is sent instead. Sellers are often surrounded by a bevy of "thirsty" friends and hanger-oners—frequently young teenage women in the case of male sellers—willing to run errands, pay attention to conversations, lend support in arguments and fights and provide sexual favours for them on demand because of the relatively large amounts of money and drugs passing through their hands. In fact, even youths who do not use drugs will hang out and attempt to befriend respectfully the dealer just to be privy to the excitement of people coming and going, copping and hanging; money flowing, arguments, detectives, and stick-up artists—all around danger and excitement. Other non-users will hang out to be treated to an occasional round of beer, Bacardi or, on an off night, Thunderbird.

The channel into the underground economy is by no means strictly economic. Besides wanting to earn "crazy money," people choose "hoodlum" status in order to assert their dignity at refusing to "sling a mop for the white man" (cf. Anderson 1976:68). Employment or better yet self-employment—in the underground economy—accords a sense of autonomy, self-dignity and an opportunity for extraordinary rapid short-term upward mobility that is only too obviously unavailable in entry-level jobs. Opulent survival without a "visible means of support" is the ultimate expression of success and it is a viable option. There is plenty of visible proof of this to everyone on the street as they watch teenage crack dealers drive by in convertible Suzuki Samurai jeeps with the stereo blaring, "beem" by in impeccable BMWs, or—in the case of the middle-aged dealers—speed around in well waxed Lincoln Continentals. Anyone can aspire to be promoted to the level of a seller perched on a 20-speed mountain bike with a beeper by their side. In fact, many youths not particularly active in the drug trade run around with beepers on their belts just pretending to be big-time. The impact of the sense of dignity and worth that can accompany selling crack is illustrated by Julio's ability to overcome his destructive addiction to crack only after getting a job selling it: "I couldn't be messin' up the money. I couldn't be fucking up no more! Besides, I had to get respect."

In New York City the insult of working for entry-level wages amidst extraordinary opulence is especially painfully perceived by Spanish Harlem youths who have grown in abject poverty only a few blocks from all-white neighbourhoods commanding some of the highest real estate values in the world. As messengers, security guards or xerox machine operators in the corporate headquarters of the Fortune 500 companies, they are brusquely ordered about by young white executives who sometimes make monthly salaries superior to their yearly wages and who do not even have the time to notice that they are being rude.

It could be argued that Manhattan sports a *de facto* apartheid labour hierarchy whereby differences in job category and prestige correlate with ethnicity and are often justified—consciously or unconsciously—through a racist logic. This humiliating confrontation with New York's ethnic/occupational hierarchy drives the street-bound cohort of inner city youths deeper into the confines of their segregated neighbourhood and the underground economy. They prefer to seek out meaning and upward mobility in a context that does not constantly oblige them to come into contact with people of a different, hostile ethnicity wielding arbitrary power over them. In the underground economy, especially in the world of substance abuse, they never have to experience the silent subtle humiliations that the entry-level labour market—or even merely a daily subway ride downtown—invariably subjects them to.

In this context the crack high and the rituals and struggles around purchasing and using the drug are comparable to the millenarian religions that sweep colonized peoples attempting to resist oppression in the context of accelerated social trauma—whether it be the Ghost dance of the Great Plains Amerindians, the "cargo cults" of Melanesia, the Mamachi movement of the Guaymi Amerindians in Panama, or even religions such as Farrakhan's Nation of Islam and the Jehovah's Witnesses in the heart of the inner city (cf. Bourgois 1986, 1989). Substance abuse in general, and crack in particular, offer the equivalent of a millenarian metamorphosis. Instantaneously users are transformed from being unemployed, depressed high school dropouts, despised by the world—and secretly convinced that their failure is due to their own inherent stupidity, "racial laziness" and disorganization—into being a mass of heart-palpitating pleasure, followed only minutes later by a jaw-gnashing crash and wideawake alertness that provides their life with concrete purpose: get more crack—fast!

One of the most dramatic illustrations within the dynamic of the crack economy of how a cultural dynamic of resistance to exploitation can lead contradictorily to greater oppression and ideological domination is the conspicuous presence of women in the growing cohort of crack addicts. In a series of ten random surveys undertaken at Papito's crack franchises, women and girls represented just under 50% of the customers. This contrasts dramatically to the estimates of female participation in heroin addiction in the late 1970s.

The painful spectacle of young, emaciated women milling in agitated angst around crack copping corners and selling their bodies for five dollars, or even merely for a puff on a crack stem, reflects the growing emancipation of women in all aspects of inner city life, culture and economy. Women—especially the emerging generation which is most at risk for crack addiction—are no longer as obliged to stay at home and maintain the family. They no longer so readily sacrifice public life or forgo independent opportunities to generate personally disposable income. This is documented by the frequent visits to the crack houses by pregnant women and by mothers accompanied by toddlers.

A more neutral illustration of the changed position of women in street culture outside the arena of substance abuse is the growing presence of young women on inner city basketball courts. Similarly, on the national level, there are conclusive statistics documenting increased female participation in the legal labour market—especially in the working class Puerto Rican community. By the same token, more women are also resisting exploitation in the entry-level job market and are pursuing careers in the underground economy and seeking self-definition and meaning through intensive participation in street culture.

Although women are using the drug and participating intensively in street culture, traditional gender relations still largely govern income-generating strategies in the underground economy. Most notably, women are forced disproportionately to rely on prostitution to finance their habits. The relegation of women to the traditional street role of prostitution has led to a flooding of the market for sex, leading to a drop in the price of women's bodies and to an epidemic rise in venereal disease among women and newborn babies.

Contradictorily, therefore, the underlying process of emancipation which has enabled women to demand equal participation in street culture and to carve out an expanded niche for themselves in the underground economy has led to a greater depreciation of women as ridiculed sex objects. Addicted women will tolerate a tremendous amount of verbal and physical abuse in their pursuit of a vial of crack, allowing lecherous men to humiliate and ridicule them in public. Chino, who is married and is the father of nine children, refers to the women who regularly service him with oral sex as "my moufs" [mouths]. He enjoys calling out to these addicted women from across the street, "Yo, there goes my mouf! Come on over here." Such a public degradation of a cohort of women who are conspicuously present on the street cannot be neutral. It ultimately reinforces the ideological domination of women in general.

DE-LEGITIMIZING DOMINATION

How can one discuss and analyse the phenomenon of street-level inner city culture and violence without reproducing and confirming the very ideological relationships that are its basis? In his discussion of the culture of terror, Taussig notes that it is precisely the narratives about the torture and violence of the repressive societies which ". . . are in themselves evidence of the process whereby a culture of terror was created and sustained" (1984:279). The superhuman power that

the media has accorded to crack serves a similar mythical function. The *New York Times* has run articles and interviews with scientists that portray crack as if it were a miraculous substance beyond the power of human beings to control (cf. 25 June, 1988: 1). They "prove" this by documenting how quickly rats will ecstatically kill themselves when provided with cocaine upon demand. Catheterized rats push the cocaine lever to the exclusion of the nutrient lever until they collapse exhausted to die of thirst.

The alleged omnipotence of crack coupled with even the driest recounting of the overpowering statistics on violence ultimately allows US society to absolve itself of any real responsibility for the inner city phenomena. The mythical dimensions of the culture of terror push economics and politics out of the picture and enable the US to maintain in some of its larger cities a level of ethnic segregation and economic marginalization that are unacceptable to any of the other wealthy, industrialized nations of the world, with the obvious exception of South Africa. Worse yet, on the level of theory, because of the continued domination—even in their negation—of the North America-centred culture of poverty theories, this discussion of the ideological implications of the underground economy may take readers full circle back to a blame-the-victim interpretation of inner city oppression.

NOTES

1. A *botanica* is a herbal pharmacy and *santeria* utility store.
2. This research was funded by the United States Bureau of the Census, the Wenner-Gren Foundation for Anthropological Research, two Washington University Junior Faculty Summer Research grants, and Lottery Funds and an Affirmative Action Grant from San Francisco State University. An expanded version of this article will be appearing in a special issue of *Contemporary Drug Problems* devoted to crack in the United States.

Pseudonyms have been used in order to disguise identities of persons referred to.

REFERENCES

Anderson, Elijah. 1976. *A Place on the Corner*. Chicago: U. of Chicago.

Bourgois, Philippe. 1986. The Miskitu of Nicaragua: Politicized Ethnicity. *A.T.* 2(2): 4–9.

———. 1989. *Ethnicity at Work: Divided Labour on a Central American Banana Plantation*. Baltimore: Johns Hopkins U.P.

Bowles, Samuel, and Herbert Gintis. 1977. *Schooling in Capitalist America*. New York: Basic Books.

Davis, Mike. 1987. *Chinatown*, Part Two? The "Internationalization" of Downtown Los Angeles. *New Left Review* 164: 65–86.

Davis, Mike, with Sue Ruddick. 1988. Los Angeles: Civil Liberties Between the Hammer and the Rock. *New Left Review* 1970: 37–60.

Fordham, Signithia. 1988. Racelessness as a Factor in Black Students' School Success: Pragmatic Strategy or Pyrrhic Victory? *Harvard Educational Review* 58(1): 54–84.

Giroux, Henry. 1983. Theories of Reproduction and Resistance in the New Sociology of Education: A Critical Analysis. *Harvard Educational Review* 53(3): 257–293.

Kornblum, William, and Terry Williams. 1985. *Growing Up Poor*. Lexington, MA.: Lexington Books.

Leacock, Eleanor Burke, ed. 1971. *The Culture of Poverty: A Critique*. New York: Simon and Schuster.

Lewis, Oscar. 1966. The Culture of Poverty. In *Anthropological Essays*, pp. 67–80. New York: Random House.

Macleod, Jay. 1987. *Ain't No Makin' It*. Boulder, Colorado: Westview P.

Maxwell, Andrew. 1988. The Anthropology of Poverty in Black Communities: A Critique and Systems Alternative. *Urban Anthropology* 17(2&3): 171–191.

Meillassoux, Claude. 1981. *Maidens, Meal and Money*. Cambridge: Cambridge U.P.

Ryan, William. 1986[1971]. Blaming the Victim. In *Taking Sides: Clashing Views on Controversial Social Issues*, pp. 45–52, ed. Kurt Finsterbusch and George McKenna. Guilford, CT: Dushkin Publishing Group.

Sassen-Koob, Saskia. 1986. New York City: Economic Restructuring and Immigration. *Development and Change* 17(1): 87–119.

Stack, Carol. 1974. *All Our Kin: Strategies for Survival in a Black Community*. New York: Harper & Row.

Steinberg, Stephen. 1981. *The Ethnic Myth: Race, Ethnicity and Class in America*. New York: Atheneum.

Tabb, William and Larry Sawers, eds. 1984. *Marxism and the Metropolis: New Perspectives in Urban Political Economy*. New York: Oxford U.P.

Taussig, Michael. 1984. Culture of Terror—Space of Death, Roger Casement's Putumayo Report and the Explanation of Torture. *Comparative Studies in Society and History* 26(3): 467–497.

Valentine, Charles. 1968. *Culture and Poverty*. Chicago: U. of Chicago P.

Valentine, Bettylou. 1978. *Hustling and Other Hard Work*. NY: Free Press.

Wallerstein, Emanuel. 1977. Rural Economy in Modern World Society. *Studies in Comparative International Development* 12(1): 29–40.

Waxman, Chaim. 1977. *The Stigma of Poverty: A Critique of Poverty Theories and Policies*. NY: Pergamon.

Willis, Paul. 1983. Cultural Production and Theories of Reproduction. In *Race, Class and Education*, pp. 107–138, ed. Len Barton and Stephen Walker. London: Croom-Helm.

———. 1977. *Learning to Labor: How Working Class Kids Get Working Class Jobs*. Aldershot, England: Gower.

Wilson, William Julius. 1978. *The Declining Significance of Race: Blacks and Changing American Institutions*. Chicago: U. of Chicago P.

———. 1987. *The Truly Disadvantaged: The Inner City, the Underclass and Public Policy*. Chicago: U. of Chicago.

4

PROFILE OF AN ANTHROPOLOGIST

Corporate Anthropologists

Jennifer J. Laabs

Most anthropological work is still done in other cultures. Today, however, an increasing number of anthropologists are bringing their expertise to the corporate world. The concept of culture and the ethnographic methods of anthropology that originally developed on the African savannas, the Australian outback, the arctic tundra, and the bush country of the New Guinea highlands are now being applied to understand and advance corporate cultures as well as to enhance the social organization of shops and offices. From Xerox to General Motors to Nissan, corporate executives find that anthropologists can help them to see through different eyes.

Recent business anthropology aims to improve working conditions within offices, develop an understanding of the importance of corporate culture, provide market research insights through participant observation rather than survey research, develop products through observation of people in natural settings, and provide insights into other cultures to facilitate a corporation's expansion into the global economy.

Although anthropologists have been working with businesses since the 1930s, the 1980s witnessed exceptional growth in this field because of the globalization of business activity and the increased awareness of the importance of culture for business.

As you read this selection, ask yourself the following questions:

☐ *What are the four fields of anthropology, and what are some of the areas of applied anthropological work?*

☐ *What are the similarities and differences between business anthropology and other forms of cultural anthropology?*

☐ *What is meant by the culture of a business?*

☐ *How can anthropologists help corporations perform better in a global environment?*

☐ *How can a corporate origin myth stimulate creative thinking?*

The following terms discussed in this selection are included in the Glossary at the back of the book:

archaeology
biological anthropology
corporate culture
cultural anthropology
linguistic anthropology
origin myth

Chances are, an anthropologist wouldn't be the first business expert you'd call if you wanted to build a better mousetrap—or a better HR program. Anthropologists aren't exactly listed as consultants in the phone book between *accountant* and *attorney*. But maybe they should be.

Although calling an anthropologist might seem like an unusual answer to a business dilemma, many companies have found that anthropologists' expertise as cultural scientists is quite useful in gaining insight about human behavior within their corporate digs.

Anthropology, by definition, is "the science of human beings," and studies people in relation to their "distribution, origin, classification, relationship of races, physical character, environmental and social relations and culture" (according to *Webster's Ninth New Collegiate Dictionary*).

Although there are many types of anthropologists (see "They Dig up Rocks, Don't They?"), most people have only heard of the archaeology (stones and bones) variety. But there's much more to them than that.

Anthropologists study many different areas of business, but essentially they're all people-watchers of one sort or another. Business anthropologists have been studying the corporate world for years (since the early 1900s), on such varied topics as how to encourage more creativity or how best to integrate multicultural learning techniques into an organization's training program.

There are only a dozen business anthropologists who actually use the title of *anthropologist*, but there are about 200 currently working in and for corporate America.

Lorna M. McDougall, a staff anthropologist at Arthur Andersen's Center for Professional Education in St. Charles, Illinois, for example, currently is studying why people from some cultures learn best from lectures, although others learn best through interactive learning.

Her background includes linguistics study at Trinity College in Dublin, Ireland, and social anthropological study at Oxford. She also has a specialty in medical anthropology, and has worked in a variety of organizations and universities.

McDougall has been a key player in shaping the firm's Business English Language Immersion Training (ELIT) program, directed by the company's management development group, to which McDougall reports.

The ELIT program builds both a common language skill for communication between people who speak English as a second language (there are approximately 800 million in the world), and an awareness of each culture's unique approach to business encounters. The results of her work have helped instructors, who train Andersen consultants working in 66 countries, be better teachers. They've also helped students become better learners.

The center is almost a mini-United Nations, and has many of the same kinds of intercultural opportunities and challenges, but also is a melting pot of sorts in which she studies many types of cultural issues. "We're in a unique position to be able to use people's information and exchange it," says McDougall.

Arthur Andersen's product essentially is its people, and keeping them trained and in top shape to consult alongside other Andersen employees in many different countries is a cultural and business challenge that many global firms are facing these days. Although the company has been global for many years, delivering clear, effective training for consultants continues to be an issue.

McDougall is part of Andersen's corporate strategy, says Pete Pesce, managing director for Arthur Andersen's human resources worldwide. "An anthropologist brings a lot of value to an organization," says Pesce. Although McDougall is the company's first onsite anthropologist and has been with Arthur Andersen only one year, she's going to be even more valuable in the future because of the increasing worldwide scope of the company's operations, says Pesce.

Because the organization has more than 56,000 employees and has spent, for example, 7.4% of its annual revenue in 1990 ($309 million) on training and education, the company is committed to enhancing its education programs using expertise that such disciplines as anthropology can offer.

What is that expertise? "Business anthropology, like all anthropology, is based on observing and analyzing group values and behavior in a cultural context. We focus on *what* people in a cultural group do, *how many* of them do it and *how what they do* affects the individuals in the group," she says.

"Business anthropologists seek to identify the connections between national culture and organizational culture," explains McDougall. Just as other cultural scientists, she helps identify some of the major cultural variables within and between organizations and the various ways that these differences impact:

- Structure
- Strategy
- Operations
- Communications
- Behavior.

From a cross-cultural standpoint, McDougall's job was to analyze what Arthur Andersen instructors (usually partners) and students do in the classroom and how they interpret those events.

THEY DIG UP ROCKS, DON'T THEY?

When most people think of anthropologists, they think of the most popular kind—those who dig up ancient artifacts and try to make sense of past life forms and cultures. These "stones and bones" scientists are only a fraction of the forms that anthropology takes: *Academic anthropology* dates back to the late 19th century. It was formalized by the establishment of the American Anthropological Association (AAA) in 1902, which currently has 11,000 members. In contrast with anthropology in Europe and Latin America, American academic anthropology is distinguished by its "four-field approach" including:

• Cultural anthropology
• Archaeology
• Biological anthropology
• Linguistic anthropology.

There are many other subgroups within these four areas.

Applied anthropology dates back to World War II when anthropologists worked for the federal government. The Society for Applied Anthropology (SFAA), founded in 1941, has 3,000 members. The National Association for the Practice of Anthropology (NAPA) was formed in 1983 and overlaps membership of the SFAA. Many of these *applied* and *practicing* anthropologists work for government agencies and non-profit groups. Their work includes:

• Agricultural development
• Education
• Family planning
• Legal system development
• Natural resources management
• Public health and nutrition
• Social impact assessment.

Business anthropology traces its origins to the 1930s, but only since the early 1980s have anthropologists been working for such major corporations as General Motors, Xerox, Nissan and McDonnell Douglas.   —*J.L.*

"When I came in to study this program, I used an anthropological methodology to take a look at what was happening," she says. She listened in on classroom sessions and conducted many face-to-face interviews. "I then analyzed that data from an anthropological perspective," says McDougall. She noticed, for example, that people from certain cultures are used to two-way communication in the classroom, although others just sit quietly while the "professor lectures." To do otherwise, in their minds, would be disrespectful.

"It isn't necessarily an inherent feature of the human mind that people learn in one way or another," says McDougall. It's more a question of how people have *learned to learn,* and how the company's training can incorporate all types of learning styles for the best possible retention of the material by everyone. "What we're really doing is facilitating," she says.

Changes were made in the objectives of the training program. For example, another component was added—a cultural orientation module, which helps the company's staff and managers become more aware of multicultural diversity issues and how those behaviors are affecting their business interactions.

As a result of the changes, the "students" have been more cooperative and better learners inside the classroom, explains McDougall. Noticeably more intercultural socializing has taken place outside the classroom as well—something management hadn't anticipated. "It's important to realize that when you're looking at the effectiveness of cross-cultural training, you want to look at the outcome in improved relations between the people involved," she explains.

Pesce, from a human resources perspective, has found that the organizational values are the same throughout the firm's many offices globally because of the company's emphasis on homogeneous training and orientation. "I've travelled around the world and talked to employees," he says. "What I see clearly is that the values of the firm are very, very consistent. When our people talk about our organization, they talk about it in the same light in terms of quality, values, delivering client service and developing our people."

McDougall also teaches some of the management development classes, and is involved in the company's "train the trainers" program. In addition, she presents special classes to the company's human resources managers on cultural sensitivity issues.

"Recently, I was in London meeting with our directors of human resources for our Europe, the Middle East, India and Africa divisions," says Pesce. "Their

AN ANTHROPOLOGIST'S TOOL KIT

By Lorna M. McDougall

Anthropologists rely on a large historical and current geographical data bank for new ideas and new applications of old ideas. For example, when we look at the history of work, we can trace it from the survival activities common to higher primates—getting food and shelter—through the stages of human evolution and history.

What we see is that, as work becomes further removed from the direct provision of needs, the issue of motivation arises. We know that many of the great states: Greek, Roman, Mayan, Egyptian, African, Indian, Chinese, to mention only a few, approached work and productivity using a variety of rewards, incentives and disciplinary measures. They also had to deal with what we would recognize as business issues: strategic planning, accounting, finance and inventory management.

A wide-ranging cultural approach shows us that the issues any society faces today aren't necessarily new—nor are the issues new for management. On the contrary, approaching things from a comparative perspective, we can see that in our time we have made progress in finding creative alternatives for productivity in the context of today's values and culturally diverse work force.

The value of this knowledge is that it can readily stimulate creative thinking. It helps us to realize that nothing is written in stone, and that we are dealing with situations that always have been challenging. We aren't deficient just because these situations continue.

On the contrary, we need to realize that our current proactive approach to such situations, which involves actually studying how to improve them, rather than just wrestling with them, is a significant advancement. Management problems have been around a long time, but management development is our creative response to dealing with them.

interest in dealing with working standards is very keen. The challenge is to understand the differences in cultures, and in work and family values—the differences between Spain and Germany, for example. Lorna will be very helpful to us in that whole process."

Other areas she is studying involve such topics as:

- Leadership
- Creativity
- Productivity
- Delegation.

Areas for McDougall's anthropological study have been identified in a variety of ways. Sometimes members of the management development team propose ideas; other times, McDougall identifies them. Some recent topics have included teaching associates the cultural meaning of gestures and selecting colors for computer screens used in training.

"Colors have symbolic connections that are culture-specific," explains McDougall. "For example, in some cultures, white is associated with marriage, but in others it's associated with death. Others associate blue with death. In some cultures pink is considered feminine and in others yellow is."

Another project that McDougall is helping develop is an Experienced Hire Orientation program to help new hires assimilate more rapidly into the company's corporate culture. "We would apply what anthropologists call *oral transmission* of beliefs, practices and values by having established personnel pass on the firm's history and traditions by word of mouth, rather than in writing," explains McDougall.

For now, her work has been centered at the St. Charles facility, but in the future she might travel to the company's other worldwide locations for other research projects.

ANTHROPOLOGY BOOSTS CREATIVITY

"What good are zero defects, if you aren't even making the right product?" asks Roger P. McConochie, a St. Charles, Illinois-based anthropologist who consults with businesses on a variety of topics.

McConochie asks a thought-provoking question. Some companies are looking to people like him to help answer it, because it opens up the corporate agenda to the bigger picture: What really is a company's business all about?

One business person, who has benefited from the anthropological approach, came to this conclusion:

"What is our product? It isn't hardware, and it isn't even customer satisfaction, excellence, quality, TQM, or those other buzzwords from the '80s," says Mark T. Grace, operations development manager for Houston-based Generon Systems (a division of Dow Chemical and British Oxygen Corp.). Although the company manufactures nitrogen-separation equipment, Grace says: "We have only one product: innovation."

"Today we're the best in the world at what we do," says Grace, "but if we keep doing things the same way for another two or three years, we'll be out of business. That's how quickly this industry is changing and that's how tough our competition is. Our challenge on a daily basis is to redesign our equipment so that it's more efficient: space-efficient, weight-efficient, cost-efficient."

In his business, creativity is everything, he continues. "The problem is putting people into a group and having them freely share their ideas. Each person wants individual credit for his or her ideas, yet the best ideas emerge from interaction." Although the company even has "idea rooms" in which people can draw their ideas and put them up on the wall, Grace explains, "We were stuck. So at one meeting, I said, 'We've tried everything else, why not bring in an anthropologist?'"

He called McConochie, president of Corporate Research International, for suggestions on how to incorporate culturally correct ways of getting staff to contribute. Since then, McConochie, and his associate, Harvard-educated Anthony Giannini, president of The Corporate DaVinci, Ltd., have been an anthropological sounding board for Grace.

Generon's problem is fairly typical in business. But it isn't the company's fault, say these anthropologists, because today's business people are products of the competitive jungle in which they live and work. Although competition may be good among rivals, it often doesn't work within a single organizational culture, as evidenced by the fact that creativity gets stifled. People have a hard time leaving their cultural imprints at the front door.

To understand present society, anthropologists look to the past. From their perspective, McConochie and Giannini liken successful business strategy to the Renaissance period in Europe (between the 14th and 16th centuries), when such individuals as Leonardo da Vinci were guided by many values, including the aesthetics of beauty and the spiritual and emotional sides of humanity.

"During the Renaissance, new institutions were being formed and reformed and the individual was rediscovered," says Giannini. Da Vinci's *The Last Supper*, for example, was the first painting that got away from depicting human figures in a flat and monochromatic way. "You had, for the very first time, real people," he notes.

At that time, there was a blending of many human interests and cultures into almost every facet of life, including work. But that approach, for the most part, was abandoned somewhere along the way.

What was lost? "A concern with the human side of things, a concern with the non-quantifiable," says McConochie. He and Giannini say they think business would benefit from getting back to that holistic approach to thinking. "We believe in numbers; and we believe in measurements, but we also believe that there are elements to life and elements to corporate practice that can't be put into numbers."

Today, compartmentalization of human thinking is rampant, but the challenge of globalization requires businesses to rethink that strategy. Such techniques as "bridging" or "scaffolding" allow workers to use the many facets of their collective conscious to come up with solutions to current problems. It also can help them better understand colleagues from other cultures. Anything less, they say, falls short.

Giannini and McConochie created *The Corporate DaVinci*—a program for corporate Renaissance, in which they help organizations rethink their corporate history and recreate their corporate myths. "In anthropological terms, we would call it an *origin myth*. Every tribe in the jungle has a story of how it came to be," says McConochie. And so do companies. They don't usually think about it, but it often helps people remember how they came to be, and how they fit into history.

For example, when Giannini took the program to Ford Motor Co., he began the first session with a brief history of the wheel: From its invention to modern-day transportation. "In just 15 minutes, they had a fresh way of looking at the work they were doing day by day," says McConochie. "It was no longer just going out and pushing cars off the assembly line and selling them to get their sales figures up for the year. They were participating in the human drama."

Why is this so important? Because companies need a clear "ego sense": a continual sense of organizational self over time, says McConochie. Most anthropologists talk in terms of thousands, or even millions, of years. People begin to see that their lives, in the grander scheme of things, last only an instant. They also see, however, that what they do has an impact on the historical continuum and gives workers a feeling of oneness.

"What defines us as human beings is that, despite the differences across cultures, we're all trying to create meaning in our lives," says McConochie. "From my experience in corporations, the people on the shop floor have as much need for meaning in their lives as the people in the boardroom," he explains. "Everybody wants fewer defects at a lower cost. That's fine," says McConochie. "I'm not sure that's enough."

TEN DIMENSIONS OF CORPORATE BEAUTY

1. Purpose. Is there a clear and unifying purpose to the product or service you're auditing?
2. Integrity. Does the product or service do what it was originally designed to do?
3. Simplicity. Is the product or service as simple as possible in structure, content, operation, and so on? Do corporate standards exist for simplicity in design?
4. Symmetry/Asymmetry. Is it physically symmetrical? *Pleasing to the eye?* Is it logically symmetrical? *Pleasing to the mind?* Is there operational harmony between the various parts? *Pleasing to the ear?* Does it feel symmetrical? *Pleasing to the touch? Smell? Taste?* Is it pleasing to your sense of proportional order in all respects? *Pleasing to the emotions?*
5. Balance. Does the product or service justify its existence? Are its gains worth its costs? Does it fit in with the rest of your product or service family?
6. Brilliancy. Compared to other competitive products and services, does this product or service sparkle on its own? Where does it lack sparkle?
7. Suggestiveness. Does the use of this product or service strongly evoke images of client or customer success in multiple domains, such as how designer clothes may suggest a boost in social status?
8. Clarity. Is the product or service easily understood? Is it easily used?
9. Adaptability. How adaptable to sudden change in the marketplace is the product or service? Are there any breakthroughs looming on the technology horizon that will change the picture?
10. Perenniality. Is the product or service an annual or perennial entity? Will it last at least two years? More than five, 10 or 15 years?

Corporations have been trapped by the concept that all that people on the shop floor need is to sleep, eat and get paid at the end of the week—and if you give them those basics, it's enough to motivate them. This isn't so, explains McConochie, who has consulted with many types of businesses, including aviation companies. Even chief executive officers won't work any harder if you double their salaries. "What you need to do is give them an opportunity to be creative, and an opportunity for challenge and growth," he explains. Creativity also must be supported in corporate culture—in word and deed.

"Right at the top of their corporate mission statement, organizations ought to have a special credo that reads 'Beauty in our products and services, and in the creative means of their production, is a corporate goal of the highest order,'" says Giannini.

Everyone can be creative—they just need some tools to help broaden their thinking. Giannini and McConochie's Corporate DaVinci program includes a segment called *The Aesthetic Audit* (see "Ten Dimensions of Corporate Beauty"), which gives people a guide to use as a springboard into the creative process.

For example, if you went to the hardware store, and picked up a simple screw or nut, you could examine it and ask, "Does it suit its purpose?" Then you'd move on to the other points. Does it demonstrate integrity? If it's corroded, has sharp edges that might cut the person using it, or lacks brilliancy and symmetry, for example, you might round the edges and paint it.

"Typically, I find that executives give low ratings to 60 to 70% of their products and services in at least half of these dimensions," says Giannini. Looking at their own products with *focused eyes*, companies then go on to make better products, and also create new ones. It gives colleagues a set of questions from which to start, so they can work together creatively.

Employees also can benefit from cognitive and cultural training, so they understand where ideas come from and how those ideas vary across societal boundaries. For example, these anthropologists include such topics in their program as:

• Organization of Thought Across Cultures

• The Multicultural Technician

- Cognitive Emotions Across Cultures

- Multicultural Business Thinking in Action

Can corporations actually blend science with poetry? Production with art? Business with aesthetics?

Anthropologists who reach from one culture to another—bringing the best cognitive and cultural artifacts from the past into the present—say it *is* possible, and may be just the bridge that sparks innovation of the future.

5

Shakespeare in the Bush

Laura Bohannan

Communication is an essential characteristic of human social life. Through language we socialize our children and pass down cultural values from generation to generation. Communication forms and defines relations among individuals as well as among groups. Because communication is so natural, we seldom ask a critical question: When we speak, does the listener understand?

At a minimum, communication involves a sender, a receiver, and a shared code for exchanging information. When an individual or a group sends a message, the sender anticipates that those who receive the message will interpret and understand the message in the way the sender intended. Miscommunication is, of course, an unfortunately common phenomenon that can lead to fist fights, divorces, and wars.

What most of us do not appreciate is the degree to which culture affects our interpretation of messages. As Laura Bohannan tells the tale of Hamlet, we gradually discover how particular behaviors or events can have very different meanings in different places. What is interesting is that the miscommunication of interpretational differences is not a result of poor language or translation abilities. Miscommunication is not a result of speaking too quickly or not loudly enough. It reflects cultural differences.

As you read this selection, ask yourself the following questions:

- ☐ *What were the author's original beliefs about the universality of the classics—such as* Hamlet?

- ☐ *How did the Tiv elders react to the marriage of Hamlet's mother to his uncle? How was this different from Hamlet's own emotional reaction?*

- ☐ *Why do the Tiv believe that a chief should have more than one wife?*

- ☐ *As the author tells the story, consider how the elders interpret various actions to fit Tiv culture and in so doing redefine the central meaning of the play.*

The following terms discussed in this selection are included in the Glossary at the back of the book:

age grade
agnatic
chiefdom
cultural relativism
levirate
polygyny
socialization

Just before I left Oxford for the Tiv in West Africa, conversation turned to the season at Stratford. "You Americans," said a friend, "often have difficulty with Shakespeare. He was, after all, a very English poet, and one can easily misinterpret the universal by misunderstanding the particular."

From *Natural History*, 1966. Reprinted by permission of the author.

I protested that human nature is pretty much the same the whole world over; at least the general plot and motivation of the greater tragedies would always be clear—everywhere—although some details of custom might have to be explained and difficulties of translation might produce other slight changes. To end an argument we could not conclude, my friend gave me a copy of *Hamlet* to study in the African bush: it would, he hoped, lift my mind above its primitive surroundings, and possibly I might, by prolonged meditation, achieve the grace of correct interpretation.

It was my second field trip to that African tribe, and I thought myself ready to live in one of its remote sections—an area difficult to cross even on foot. I eventually settled on the hillock of a very knowledgeable old man, the head of a homestead of some hundred and forty people, all of whom were either his close relatives or their wives and children. Like the other elders of the vicinity, the old man spent most of his time performing ceremonies seldom seen these days in the more accessible parts of the tribe. I was delighted. Soon there would be three months of enforced isolation and leisure, between the harvest that takes place just before the rising of the swamps and the clearing of new farms when the water goes down. Then, I thought, they would have even more time to perform ceremonies and explain them to me.

I was quite mistaken. Most of the ceremonies demanded the presence of elders from several homesteads. As the swamps rose, the old men found it too difficult to walk from one homestead to the next, and the ceremonies gradually ceased. As the swamps rose even higher, all activities but one came to an end. The women brewed beer from maize and millet. Men, women, and children sat on their hillocks and drank it.

People began to drink at dawn. By midmorning the whole homestead was singing, dancing, and drumming. When it rained, people had to sit inside their huts: there they drank and sang or they drank and told stories. In any case, by noon or before, I either had to join the party or retire to my own hut and my books. "One does not discuss serious matters when there is beer. Come, drink with us." Since I lacked their capacity for the thick native beer, I spent more and more time with *Hamlet*. Before the end of the second month, grace descended on me. I was quite sure that *Hamlet* had only one possible interpretation, and that one universally obvious.

Early every morning in the hope of having some serious talk before the beer party, I used to call on the old man at his reception hut—a circle of posts supporting a thatched roof above a low mud wall to keep out wind and rain. One day I crawled through the low doorway and found most of the men of the homestead sitting huddled in their ragged clothes on stools, low plank beds, and reclining chairs, warming themselves against the chill of the rain around a smoky fire. In the center were three pots of beer. The party had started.

The old man greeted me cordially. "Sit down and drink." I accepted a large calabash full of beer, poured some into a small drinking gourd, and tossed it down. Then I poured some more into the same gourd for the man second in seniority to my host before I handed my calabash over to a young man for further distribution. Important people shouldn't ladle beer themselves.

"It is better like this," the old man said, looking at me approvingly and plucking at the thatch that had caught in my hair. "You should sit and drink with us more often. Your servants tell me that when you are not with us, you sit inside your hut looking at a paper."

The old man was acquainted with four kinds of "papers": tax receipts, bride price receipts, court fee receipts, and letters. The messenger who brought him letters from the chief used them mainly as a badge of office, for he always knew what was in them and told the old man. Personal letters for the few who had relatives in the government or mission stations were kept until someone went to a large market where there was a letter writer and reader. Since my arrival, letters were brought to me to be read. A few men also brought me bride price receipts, privately, with requests to change the figures to a higher sum. I found moral arguments were of no avail, since in-laws are fair game, and the technical hazards of forgery difficult to explain to an illiterate people. I did not wish them to think me silly enough to look at any such papers for days on end, and I hastily explained that my "paper" was one of the "things of long ago" of my country.

"Ah," said the old man. "Tell us."

I protested that I was not a storyteller. Storytelling is a skilled art among them; their standards are high and the audiences critical—and vocal in their criticism. I protested in vain. This morning they wanted to hear a story while they drank. They threatened to tell me no more stories until I told them one of mine. Finally, the old man promised that no one would criticize my style "for we know you are struggling with our language." "But," put in one of the elders, "you must explain what we do not understand, as we do when we tell you our stories." Realizing that here was my chance to prove *Hamlet* universally intelligible, I agreed.

The old man handed me some more beer to help me on with my storytelling. Men filled their long wooden pipes and knocked coals from the fire to place in the pipe bowls; then, puffing contentedly, they sat back to listen. I began in the proper style, "Not yesterday, not yesterday, but long ago, a thing occurred. One night three men were keeping watch outside the homestead of the great chief, when suddenly they saw the former chief approach them."

"Why was he no longer their chief?"

"He was dead," I explained. "That is why they were troubled and afraid when they saw him."

"Impossible," began one of the elders, handing his pipe on to his neighbor, who interrupted, "Of course it wasn't the dead chief. It was an omen sent by a witch. Go on."

Slightly shaken, I continued. "One of these three was a man who knew things"—the closest translation for scholar, but unfortunately it also meant witch. The second elder looked triumphantly at the first. "So he spoke to the dead chief saying, 'Tell us what we must do so you may rest in your grave,' but the dead chief did not answer. He vanished, and they could see him no more. Then the man who knew things—his name was Horatio—said this event was the affair of the dead chief's son, Hamlet."

There was a general shaking of heads round the circle. "Had the dead chief no living brothers? Or was this son the chief?"

"No," I replied. "That is, he had one living brother who became the chief when the elder brother died."

The old men muttered: such omens were matters for chiefs and elders, not for youngsters; no good could come of going behind a chief's back; clearly Horatio was not a man who knew things.

"Yes, he was," I insisted, shooing a chicken away from my beer. "In our country the son is next to the father. The dead chief's younger brother had become the great chief. He had also married his elder brother's widow only about a month after the funeral."

"He did well," the old man beamed and announced to the others, "I told you that if we knew more about Europeans, we would find they really were very like us. In our country also," he added to me, "the younger brother marries the elder brother's widow and becomes the father of his children. Now, if your uncle, who married your widowed mother, is your father's full brother, then he will be a real father to you. Did Hamlet's father and uncle have one mother?"

His question barely penetrated my mind; I was too upset and thrown off balance by having one of the most important elements of *Hamlet* knocked straight out of the picture. Rather uncertainly I said that I thought they had the same mother, but I wasn't sure—the story didn't say. The old man told me severely that these genealogical details made all the difference and that when I got home I must ask the elders about it. He shouted out the door to one of his younger wives to bring his goatskin bag.

Determined to save what I could of the mother motif, I took a deep breath and began again. "The son Hamlet was very sad because his mother had married again so quickly. There was no need for her to do so, and it is our custom for a widow not to go to her next husband until she has mourned for two years."

"Two years is too long," objected the wife, who had appeared with the old man's battered goatskin bag. "Who will hoe your farms for you while you have no husband?"

"Hamlet," I retorted without thinking, "was old enough to hoe his mother's farms himself. There was no need for her to remarry." No one looked convinced. I gave up. "His mother and the great chief told Hamlet not to be sad, for the great chief himself would be a father to Hamlet. Furthermore, Hamlet would be the next chief: therefore he must stay to learn the things of a chief. Hamlet agreed to remain, and all the rest went off to drink beer."

While I paused, perplexed at how to render Hamlet's disgusted soliloquy to an audience convinced that Claudius and Gertrude had behaved in the best possible manner, one of the younger men asked me who had married the other wives of the dead chief.

"He had no other wives," I told him.

"But a chief must have many wives! How else can he brew beer and prepare food for all his guests?"

I said firmly that in our country even chiefs had only one wife, that they had servants to do their work, and that they paid them from tax money.

It was better, they returned, for a chief to have many wives and sons who would help him hoe his farms and feed his people; then everyone loved the chief who gave much and took nothing—taxes were a bad thing.

I agreed with the last comment, but for the rest fell back on their favorite way of fobbing off my questions: "That is the way it is done, so that is how we do it."

I decided to skip the soliloquy. Even if Claudius was here thought quite right to marry his brother's widow, there remained the poison motif, and I knew they would disapprove of fratricide. More hopefully I resumed, "That night Hamlet kept watch with the three who had seen his dead father. The dead chief again appeared, and although the others were afraid, Hamlet followed his dead father off to one side. When they were alone, Hamlet's dead father spoke."

"Omens can't talk!" The old man was emphatic.

"Hamlet's dead father wasn't an omen. Seeing him might have been an omen, but he was not." My audience looked as confused as I sounded. "It *was* Hamlet's dead father. It was a thing we call a 'ghost.'" I had to use the English word, for unlike many of the neighboring tribes, these people didn't believe in the survival after death of any individuating part of the personality.

"What is a 'ghost'? An omen?"

"No, a 'ghost' is someone who is dead but who walks around and can talk, and people can hear him and see him but not touch him."

They objected. "One can touch zombis."

"No, no! It was not a dead body the witches had animated to sacrifice and eat. No one else made Hamlet's dead father walk. He did it himself."

"Dead men can't walk," protested my audience as one man.

I was quite willing to compromise. "A 'ghost' is the dead man's shadow."

But again they objected. "Dead men cast no shadows."

"They do in my country," I snapped.

The old man quelled the babble of disbelief that arose immediately and told me with that insincere, but courteous, agreement one extends to the fancies of the young, ignorant, and superstitious, "No doubt in your country the dead can also walk without being zombis." From the depths of his bag he produced a withered fragment of kola nut, bit off one end to show it wasn't poisoned, and handed me the rest as a peace offering.

"Anyhow," I resumed, "Hamlet's dead father said that his own brother, the one who became chief, had poisoned him. He wanted Hamlet to avenge him. Hamlet believed this in his heart, for he did not like his father's brother." I took another swallow of beer. "In the country of the great chief, living in the same homestead, for it was a very large one, was an important elder who was often with the chief to advise and help him. His name was Polonius. Hamlet was courting his daughter, but her father and her brother . . . (I cast hastily about for some tribal analogy) warned her not to let Hamlet visit her when she was alone on her farm, for he would be a great chief and so could not marry her."

"Why not?" asked the wife, who had settled down on the edge of the old man's chair. He frowned at her for asking stupid questions and growled, "They lived in the same homestead."

"That was not the reason," I informed them. "Polonius was a stranger who lived in the homestead because he helped the chief, not because he was a relative."

"Then why couldn't Hamlet marry her?"

"He could have," I explained, "but Polonius didn't think he would. After all, Hamlet was a man of great importance who ought to marry a chief's daughter, for in his country a man could have only one wife. Polonius was afraid that if Hamlet made love to his daughter, then no one else would give a high price for her."

"That might be true," remarked one of the shrewder elders, "but a chief's son would give his mistress's father enough presents and patronage to more than make up the difference. Polonius sounds like a fool to me."

"Many people think he was," I agreed. "Meanwhile Polonius sent his son Laertes off to Paris to learn the things of that country, for it was the homestead of a very great chief indeed. Because he was afraid that Laertes might waste a lot of money on beer and women and gambling, or get into trouble by fighting, he sent one of his servants to Paris secretly, to spy out what Laertes was doing. One day Hamlet came upon Polonius's daughter Ophelia. He behaved so oddly he frightened her. Indeed"—I was fumbling for words to express the dubious quality of Hamlet's madness—"the chief and many others had also noticed that when

Hamlet talked one could understand the words but not what they meant. Many people thought that he had become mad." My audience suddenly became more attentive. "The great chief wanted to know what was wrong with Hamlet, so he sent for two of Hamlet's age mates (school friends would have taken long explanation) to talk to Hamlet and find out what troubled his heart. Hamlet, seeing that they had been bribed by the chief to betray him, told them nothing. Polonius, however, insisted that Hamlet was mad because he had been forbidden to see Ophelia, whom he loved."

"Why," inquired a bewildered voice, "should anyone bewitch Hamlet on that account?"

"Bewitch him?"

"Yes, only witchcraft can make anyone mad, unless, of course, one sees the beings that lurk in the forest."

I stopped being a storyteller, took out my notebook and demanded to be told more about these two causes of madness. Even while they spoke and I jotted notes, I tried to calculate the effect of this new factor on the plot. Hamlet had not been exposed to the beings that lurk in the forest. Only his relatives in the male line could bewitch him. Barring relatives not mentioned by Shakespeare, it had to be Claudius who was attempting to harm him. And, of course, it was.

For the moment I staved off questions by saying that the great chief also refused to believe that Hamlet was mad for the love of Ophelia and nothing else. "He was sure that something much more important was troubling Hamlet's heart."

"Now Hamlet's age mates," I continued, "had brought with them a famous storyteller. Hamlet decided to have this man tell the chief and all his homestead a story about a man who had poisoned his brother because he desired his brother's wife and wished to be chief himself. Hamlet was sure the great chief could not hear the story without making a sign if he was indeed guilty, and then he would discover whether his dead father had told him the truth."

The old man interrupted, with deep cunning, "Why should a father lie to his son?" he asked.

I hedged: "Hamlet wasn't sure that it really was his dead father." It was impossible to say anything, in that language, about devil-inspired visions.

"You mean," he said, "it actually was an omen, and he knew witches sometimes send false ones. Hamlet was a fool not to go to one skilled in reading omens and divining the truth in the first place. A man-who-sees-the-truth could have told him how his father died, if he really had been poisoned, and if there was witchcraft in it; then Hamlet could have called the elders to settle the matter."

The shrewd elder ventured to disagree. "Because his father's brother was a great chief, one-who-sees-the-truth might therefore have been afraid to tell it. I think it was for that reason that a friend of Hamlet's father—a witch and an elder—sent an omen so his friend's son would know. Was the omen true?"

"Yes," I said, abandoning ghosts and the devil; a witch-sent omen it would have to be. "It was true, for when the storyteller was telling his tale before all the homestead, the great chief rose in fear. Afraid that Hamlet knew his secret, he planned to have him killed."

The stage set of the next bit presented some difficulties of translation. I began cautiously. "The great chief told Hamlet's mother to find out from her son what he knew. But because a woman's children are always first in her heart, he had the important elder Polonius hide behind a cloth that hung against the wall of Hamlet's mother's sleeping hut. Hamlet started to scold his mother for what she had done."

There was a shocked murmur from everyone. A man should never scold his mother.

"She called out in fear, and Polonius moved behind the cloth. Shouting, 'A rat!' Hamlet took his machete and slashed through the cloth." I paused for dramatic effect. "He had killed Polonius!"

The old men looked at each other in supreme disgust. "That Polonius truly was a fool and a man who knew nothing! What child would not know enough to shout, 'It's me!'" With a pang, I remembered that these people are ardent hunters, always armed with bow, arrow, and machete; at the first rustle in the grass an arrow is aimed and ready, and the hunter shouts "Game!" If no human voice answers immediately, the arrow speeds on its way. Like a good hunter Hamlet had shouted, "A rat!"

I rushed in to save Polonius's reputation. "Polonius did speak. Hamlet heard him. But he thought it was the chief and wished to kill him to avenge his father. He had meant to kill him earlier that evening. . . ." I broke down, unable to describe to these pagans, who had no belief in individual afterlife, the difference between dying at one's prayers and dying "unhousell'd, disappointed, unaneled."

This time I had shocked my audience seriously. "For a man to raise his hand against his father's brother and the one who has become his father—that is a terrible thing. The elders ought to let such a man be bewitched."

I nibbled at my kola nut in some perplexity, then pointed out that after all the man had killed Hamlet's father.

"No," pronounced the old man, speaking less to me than to the young men sitting behind the elders. "If your father's brother has killed your father, you must appeal to your father's age mates; they may avenge him. No man may use violence against his senior relatives." Another thought struck him. "But if his father's brother had indeed been wicked enough to bewitch Hamlet and make him mad that would be a good story indeed, for it would be his fault that Hamlet, being mad, no longer had any sense and thus was ready to kill his father's brother."

There was a murmur of applause. *Hamlet* was again a good story to them, but it no longer seemed quite the same story to me. As I thought over the coming complications of plot and motive, I lost courage and decided to skim over dangerous ground quickly.

"The great chief," I went on, "was not sorry that Hamlet had killed Polonius. It gave him a reason to send Hamlet away, with his two treacherous age mates, with letters to a chief of a far country, saying that Hamlet should be killed. But Hamlet changed the writing on their papers, so that the chief killed his age mates instead." I encountered a reproachful glare from one of the men whom I had told undetectable forgery was not merely immoral but beyond human skill. I looked the other way.

"Before Hamlet could return, Laertes came back for his father's funeral. The great chief told him Hamlet had killed Polonius. Laertes swore to kill Hamlet because of this, and because his sister Ophelia, hearing her father had been killed by the man she loved, went mad and drowned in the river."

"Have you already forgotten what we told you?" The old man was reproachful. "One cannot take vengeance on a madman; Hamlet killed Polonius in his madness. As for the girl, she not only went mad, she was drowned. Only witches can make people drown. Water itself can't hurt anything. It is merely something one drinks and bathes in."

I began to get cross. "If you don't like the story, I'll stop."

The old man made soothing noises and himself poured me some more beer. "You tell the story well, and we are listening. But it is clear the elders of your country have never told you what the story really means. No, don't interrupt! We believe you when you say your marriage customs are different, or your clothes and weapons. But people are the same everywhere; therefore, there are always witches and it is we, the elders, who know how witches work. We told you it was the great chief who wished to kill Hamlet, and now your own words have proved us right. Who were Ophelia's male relatives?"

"There were only her father and her brother." Hamlet was clearly out of my hands.

"There must have been many more; this also you must ask of your elders when you get back to your country. From what you tell us, since Polonius was dead, it must have been Laertes who killed Ophelia, although I do not see the reason for it."

We had emptied one pot of beer, and the old men argued the point with slightly tipsy interest. Finally one of them demanded of me, "What did the servant of Polonius say on his return?"

With difficulty I recollected Reynaldo and his mission. "I don't think he did return before Polonius was killed."

"Listen," said the elder, "and I will tell you how it was and how your story will go, then you may tell me if I am right. Polonius knew his son would get into trouble, and so he did. He had many fines to pay for fighting, and debts from gambling. But he had only two ways of getting money quickly. One was to marry off his sister at once, but it is difficult to find a man who will marry a woman desired by the son of a chief. For if the chief's heir commits adultery with your wife, what can you do? Only a fool calls a case against a man who will someday be his judge. Therefore Laertes had to take the second way: he killed his sister by witchcraft, drowning her so he could secretly sell her body to the witches."

I raised an objection. "They found her body and buried it. Indeed Laertes jumped into the grave to see his sister once more—so, you see, the body was truly there. Hamlet, who had just come back, jumped in after him."

"What did I tell you?" The elder appealed to the others. "Laertes was up to no good with his sister's body. Hamlet prevented him, because the chief's heir, like a chief, does not wish any other man to grow rich and powerful. Laertes would be angry, because he

would have killed his sister without benefit to himself. In our country he would try to kill Hamlet for that reason. Is this not what happened?"

"More or less," I admitted. "When the great chief found Hamlet was still alive, he encouraged Laertes to try to kill Hamlet and arranged a fight with machetes between them. In the fight both the young men were wounded to death. Hamlet's mother drank the poisoned beer that the chief meant for Hamlet in case he won the fight. When he saw his mother die of poison, Hamlet, dying, managed to kill his father's brother with his machete."

"You see, I was right!" exclaimed the elder.

"That was a very good story," added the old man, "and you told it with very few mistakes. There was just one more error, at the very end. The poison Hamlet's mother drank was obviously meant for the survivor of the fight, whichever it was. If Laertes had won, the great chief would have poisoned him, for no one would know that he arranged Hamlet's death. Then, too, he need not fear Laertes' witchcraft; it takes a strong heart to kill one's only sister by witchcraft.

"Sometime," concluded the old man, gathering his ragged toga about him, "you must tell us some more stories of your country. We, who are elders, will instruct you in their true meaning, so that when you return to your own land your elders will see that you have not been sitting in the bush, but among those who know things and who have taught you wisdom."

6

"To Give up on Words":
Silence in Western Apache Culture[1]

Keith H. Basso

Can you imagine working on a four-person cattle crew for several days without being introduced to or speaking with one of the other members, whom you did not know? For the Apache, this is a normal occurrence; they do not feel obligated to introduce strangers to one another. Instead, the Apache believe that when the time is right, the strangers will begin speaking to one another.

Would you find it uncomfortable to go on a date and sit in silence for an hour because you had only recently met your companion? What would you think if after returning home from several months' absence your parents and relatives didn't speak to you for several days? Although these situations seem unusual to us, they are considered appropriate among the Apache. Although it seems natural to us that when people first meet introductions are in order and that when friends and relatives reunite greetings and catching up will immediately follow, this is not the case for all cultures.

Those familiar with the television show "Northern Exposure" may consider how the reticence of Native American character Marilyn Whirlwind contrasts with the behavior of the other characters. This example demonstrates how communicating across cultural boundaries can be fraught with uncertainty and misunderstanding. In this selection Keith Basso shows how, among the Apache, certain situations call for silence rather than communication and how silence makes sense within its cultural context.

As you read this selection, ask yourself the following questions:

☐ *What are some of the ways silence is used in European American communication, and how are they different from those in Apache culture?*

☐ *How are the meaning and function of silence affected by the social and cultural context?*

☐ *What is the critical factor in an Apache's decision to speak or keep silent?*

☐ *How do Apaches interact upon meeting a stranger, courting, welcoming children home, "getting cussed out," and being with people who are sad?*

☐ *Despite the variety of situations in which Apaches are silent, what is the underlying determinant?*

The following terms discussed in this selection are included in the Glossary at the back of the book:

hypothesis
informant
kinship
socialization
sociolinguistics
status

From *Southwestern Journal of Anthropology*, vol. 26, no. 3, Autumn 1970, pp. 213–230. Reprinted with permission.

It is not the case that a man who is silent says nothing.

—Anonymous

I

Anyone who has read about American Indians has probably encountered statements which impute to them a strong predilection for keeping silent or, as one writer has put it, "a fierce reluctance to speak except when absolutely necessary." In the popular literature, where this characterization is particularly widespread, it is commonly portrayed as the outgrowth of such dubious causes as "instinctive dignity," "an impoverished language," or, perhaps worst of all, the Indians' "lack of personal warmth." Although statements of this sort are plainly erroneous and dangerously misleading, it is noteworthy that professional anthropologists have made few attempts to correct them. Traditionally, ethnographers and linguists have paid little attention to cultural interpretations given to silence or, equally important, to the types of social contexts in which it regularly occurs.

This study investigates certain aspects of silence in the culture of the Western Apache of east-central Arizona. After considering some of the theoretical issues involved, I will briefly describe a number of situations—recurrent in Western Apache society—in which one or more of the participants typically refrain from speech for lengthy periods of time.[2] This is accompanied by a discussion of how such acts of silence are interpreted and why they are encouraged and deemed appropriate. I conclude by advancing an hypothesis that accounts for the reasons that the Western Apache refrain from speaking when they do, and I suggest that, with proper testing, this hypothesis may be shown to have relevance to silence behavior in other cultures.

II

A basic finding of sociolinguistics is that, although both language and language usage are structured, it is the latter which responds most sensitively to extra-linguistic influences (Hymes 1962, 1964; Ervin-Tripp 1964, 1967; Gumperz 1964; Slobin 1967). Accordingly, a number of recent studies have addressed themselves to the problem of how factors in the social environment of speech events delimit the range and condition the selection of message forms (cf. Brown and Gilman 1960; Conklin 1959; Ervin-Tripp 1964, 1967; Frake 1964; Friedrich 1966; Gumperz 1961, 1964; Martin 1964). These studies may be viewed as taking the now familiar position that verbal communication is fundamen-

tally a decision-making process in which, initially, a speaker, having elected to speak, selects from among a repertoire of available codes that which is most appropriately suited to the situation at hand. Once a code has been selected, the speaker picks a suitable channel of transmission and then, finally, makes a choice from a set of referentially equivalent expressions within the code. The intelligibility of the expression he chooses will, of course, be subject to grammatical constraints. But its acceptability will not. Rules for the selection of linguistic alternates operate on features of the social environment and are commensurate with rules governing the conduct of face-to-face interaction. As such, they are properly conceptualized as lying outside the structure of language itself.

It follows from this that for a stranger to communicate appropriately with the members of an unfamiliar society it is not enough that he learn to formulate messages intelligibly. Something else is needed: a knowledge of what kinds of codes, channels, and expressions to use in what kinds of situations and to what kinds of people—as Hymes (1964) has termed it, an "ethnography of communication."

There is considerable evidence to suggest that extra-linguistic factors influence not only the use of speech but its actual occurrence as well. In our own culture, for example, remarks such as "Don't you know when to keep quiet?" "Don't talk until you're introduced," and "Remember now, no talking in church" all point to the fact that an individual's decision to speak may be directly contingent upon the character of his surroundings. Few of us would maintain that "silence is golden" for all people at all times. But we feel that silence is a virtue for some people some of the time, and we encourage children on the road to cultural competence to act accordingly.

Although the form of silence is always the same, the function of a specific act of silence—that is, its interpretation by and effect upon other people—will vary according to the social context in which it occurs. For example, if I choose to keep silent in the chambers of a Justice of the Supreme Court, my action is likely to be interpreted as a sign of politeness or respect. On the other hand, if I refrain from speaking to an established friend or colleague, I am apt to be accused of rudeness or harboring a grudge. In one instance, my behavior is judged by others to be "correct" or "fitting"; in the other, it is criticized as being "out of line."

The point, I think, is fairly obvious. For a stranger entering an alien society, a knowledge of when *not* to speak may be as basic to the production of culturally acceptable behavior as a knowledge of what to say. It stands to reason, then, that an adequate ethnography of communication should not confine itself exclusively to the analysis of choice within verbal repertoires. It should also, as Hymes (1962, 1964) has suggested, specify those conditions under which the members of the society regularly decide to refrain from verbal behavior altogether.

III

The research on which this paper is based was conducted over a period of sixteen months (1964–1969) in the Western Apache settlement of Cibecue, which is located near the center of the Fort Apache Indian Reservation in east-central Arizona. Cibecue's 800 residents participate in an unstable economy that combines subsistence agriculture, cattle-raising, sporadic wage-earning, and Government subsidies in the form of welfare checks and social security benefits. Unemployment is a serious problem, and substandard living conditions are widespread.

Although Reservation life has precipitated far-reaching changes in the composition and geographical distribution of Western Apache social groups, consanguineal kinship—real and imputed—remains the single most powerful force in the establishment and regulation of interpersonal relationships (Kaut 1957; Basso 1970). The focus of domestic activity is the individual "camp," or *gowáá*. This term labels both the occupants and the location of a single dwelling or, as is more apt to be the case, several dwellings built within a few feet of each other. The majority of *gowáá* in Cibecue are occupied by nuclear families. The next largest residential unit is the *gotáá* (camp cluster), which is a group of spatially localized *gowáá*, each having at least one adult member who is related by ties of matrilineal kinship to persons living in all the others. An intricate system of exogamous clans serves to extend kinship relationships beyond the *gowáá* and *gotáá* and facilitates concerted action in projects, most notably the presentation of ceremonials, requiring large amounts of manpower. Despite the presence in Cibecue of a variety of Anglo missionaries and a dwindling number of medicine men, diagnostic and curing rituals, as well as the girls' puberty ceremonial, continue to be performed with regularity (Basso 1966, 1970). Witchcraft persists in undiluted form (Basso 1969).

IV

Of the many broad categories of events, or scenes, that comprise the daily round of Western Apache life, I shall deal here only with those that are coterminous with what Goffman (1961, 1964) has termed "focused gatherings" or "encounters." The concept *situation*, in keeping with established usage, will refer inclusively to the location of such a gathering, its physical setting, its point in time, the standing behavior patterns that accompany it, and the social attributes of the persons involved (Hymes 1962, 1964; Ervin-Tripp 1964, 1967).

In what follows, however, I will be mainly concerned with the roles and statuses of participants. The reason for this is that the critical factor in the Apache's decision to speak or keep silent seems always to be the nature of his relationships to other people. To be sure, other features of the situation are significant, but apparently only to the extent that they influence the perception of status and role.[3] What this implies, of course, is that roles and statuses are not fixed attributes. Although they may be depicted as such in a static model (and often with good reason), they are appraised and acted upon in particular social contexts and, as a result, subject to redefinition and variation.[4] With this in mind, let us now turn our attention to the Western Apache and the types of situations in which, as one of my informants put it, "it is right to give up on words."

V

1. "Meeting strangers" (*nda dòhwáá'iłtsééda*). The term, *nda*, labels categories at two levels of contrast. At the most general level, it designates any person—Apache or non-Apache—who, prior to an initial meeting, has never been seen and therefore cannot be identified. In addition, the term is used to refer to Apaches who, though previously seen and known by some external criteria such as clan affiliation or personal name, have never been engaged in face-to-face interaction. The latter category, which is more restricted than the first, typically includes individuals who live on the adjacent San Carlos Reservation, in Fort Apache settlements geographically removed from Cibecue, and those who fall into the category *kii dòhandáágo* (non-kinsmen). In all cases, "strangers" are separated by social distance. And in all cases it is considered appropriate, when encountering them for the first time, to refrain from speaking.

The type of situation described as "meeting strangers" (*nda dòhwáá'iłtsééda*) can take place in any number of different physical settings. However, it occurs most frequently in the context of events such as fairs and rodeos, which, owing to the large number of people in attendance, offer unusual opportunities for chance encounters. In large gatherings, the lack of verbal communication between strangers is apt to go unnoticed, but in smaller groups it becomes quite conspicuous. The following incident, involving two strangers who found themselves part of a four-man round-up crew, serves as a good example. My informant, who was also a member of the crew, recalled the following episode:

One time, I was with A, B, and X down at Gleason Flat, working cattle. That man, X, was from East Fork [a community nearly 40 miles from Cibecue] where B's wife was from. But he didn't know A, never knew him before, I guess. First day, I worked with X. At night, when we camped, we talked with B, but X and A didn't say anything to each other. Same way, second day. Same way, third. Then, at night on fourth day, we were sitting by the fire. Still, X and A didn't talk. Then A said, "Well, I know there is a stranger to me here, but I've been watching him and I know he is all right." After that, X and A talked a lot. . . . Those two men didn't know each other, so they took it easy at first.

As this incident suggests, the Western Apache do not feel compelled to "introduce" persons who are unknown to each other. Eventually, it is assumed, strangers will begin to speak. However, this is a decision that is properly left to the individuals involved, and no attempt is made to hasten it. Outside help in the form of introductions or other verbal routines is viewed as presumptuous and unnecessary.

Strangers who are quick to launch into conversation are frequently eyed with undisguised suspicion. A typical reaction to such individuals is that they "want something," that is, their willingness to violate convention is attributed to some urgent need which is likely to result in requests for money, labor, or transportation. Another common reaction to talkative strangers is that they are drunk.

If the stranger is an Anglo, it is usually assumed that he "wants to teach us something" (i.e., give orders or instructions) or that he "wants to make friends in a hurry." The latter response is especially revealing, since Western Apaches are extremely reluctant to be hurried into friendships—with Anglos or each other. Their verbal reticence with strangers is directly related to the conviction that the establishment of social relationships is a serious matter that calls for caution, careful judgment, and plenty of time.

2. "Courting" (*líígoláá*). During the initial stages of courtship, young men and women go without speaking for conspicuous lengths of time. Courting may occur in a wide variety of settings—practically anywhere, in fact—and at virtually any time of the day or night, but it is most readily observable at large public gatherings such as ceremonials, wakes, and rodeos. At these events, "sweethearts" (*zééde*) may stand or sit (sometimes holding hands) for as long as an hour without exchanging a word. I am told by adult informants that the young people's reluctance to speak may become even more pronounced in situations where they find themselves alone.

Apaches who have just begun to court attribute their silence to "intense shyness" (*'isté'*) and a feeling of acute "self-consciousness" (*dàyééxi'*) which, they claim, stems from their lack of familiarity with one another. More specifically, they complain of "not knowing what to do" in each other's presence and of the fear that whatever they say, no matter how well thought out in advance, will sound "dumb" or "stupid."[5]

One informant, a youth 17 years old, commented as follows:

It's hard to talk with your sweetheart at first. She doesn't know you and won't know what to say. It's the same way towards her. You don't know how to talk yet . . . so you get very bashful. That makes it sometimes so you don't say anything. So you just go around together and don't talk. At first, it's better that way. Then, after a while, when you know each other, you aren't shy anymore and can talk good.

The Western Apache draw an equation between the ease and frequency with which a young couple talks and how well they know each other. Thus, it is expected that after several months of steady companionship sweethearts will start to have lengthy conversations. Earlier in their relationship, however, protracted discussions may be openly discouraged. This is especially true for girls, who are informed by their mothers and older sisters that silence in courtship is a sign of modesty and that an eagerness to speak betrays previous experience with men. In extreme cases, they add, it may be interpreted as a willingness to engage in sexual relations. Said one woman, aged 32:

This way I have talked to my daughter. "Take it easy when boys come around this camp and want you to go somewhere with them. When they talk to you, just listen at first. Maybe you won't know what to say. So don't talk about just anything. If you talk with those boys right away, then they will know you know all about them. They will think you've been with many boys before, and they will start talking about that."

3. "Children, coming home" (*čogoše nakáii*). The Western Apache lexeme *iltá'ìnatsáá* (reunion) is used to describe encounters between an individual who has returned home after a long absence and his relatives and friends. The most common type of reunion, *čogoše nakáii* (children, coming home), involves boarding school students and their parents. It occurs in late May or early in June, and its setting is usually a trading post or school, where parents congregate to await the arrival of buses bringing the children home. As the latter disembark and locate their parents in the crowd, one anticipates a flurry of verbal greetings. Typically, however, there are few or none at all. Indeed, it is not unusual for parents and child to go without speaking for as long as 15 minutes.

When the silence is broken, it is almost always the child who breaks it. His parents listen attentively to everything he says but speak hardly at all themselves.

This pattern persists even after the family has reached the privacy of its camp, and two or three days may pass before the child's parents seek to engage him in sustained conversation.

According to my informants, the silence of Western Apache parents at (and after) reunions with their children is ultimately predicated on the possibility that the latter have been adversely affected by their experiences away from home. Uppermost is the fear that, as a result of protracted exposure to Anglo attitudes and values, the children have come to view their parents as ignorant, old-fashioned, and no longer deserving of respect. One of my most thoughtful and articulate informants commented on the problem as follows:

> You just can't tell about those children after they've been with White men for a long time. They get their minds turned around sometimes . . . they forget where they come from and get ashamed when they come home because their parents and relatives are poor. They forget how to act with these Apaches and get mad easy. They walk around all night and get into fights. They don't stay at home.
>
> At school, some of them learn to want to be White men, so they come back and try to act that way. But we are still Apaches! So we don't know them anymore, and it is like we never knew them. It is hard to talk to them when they are like that.

Apache parents openly admit that, initially, children who have been away to school seem distant and unfamiliar. They have grown older, of course, and their physical appearance may have changed. But more fundamental is the concern that they have acquired new ideas and expectations which will alter their behavior in unpredictable ways. No matter how pressing this concern may be, however, it is considered inappropriate to directly interrogate a child after his arrival home. Instead, parents anticipate that within a short time he will begin to divulge information about himself that will enable them to determine in what ways, if any, his views and attitudes have changed. This, the Apache say, is why children do practically all the talking in the hours following a reunion, and their parents remain unusually silent.

Said one man, the father of two children who had recently returned from boarding school in Utah:

> Yes, it's right that we didn't talk much to them when they came back, my wife and me. They were away for a long time, and we didn't know how they would like it, being home. So we waited. Right away, they started to tell stories about what they did. Pretty soon we could tell they liked it, being back. That made us feel good. So it was easy to talk to them again. It was like they were before they went away.

4. "Getting cussed out" (*šiłditéé*). This lexeme is used to describe any situation in which one individual, angered and enraged, shouts insults and criticisms at another. Although the object of such invective is in most cases the person or persons who provoked it, this is not always the case, because an Apache who is truly beside himself with rage is likely to vent his feelings on anyone whom he sees or who happens to be within range of his voice. Consequently, "getting cussed out" may involve large numbers of people who are totally innocent of the charges being hurled against them. But whether they are innocent or not, their response to the situation is the same. They refrain from speech.

Like the types of situations we have discussed thus far, "getting cussed out" can occur in a wide variety of physical settings: at ceremonial dancegrounds and trading posts, inside and outside wickiups and houses, on food-gathering expeditions and shopping trips—in short, wherever and whenever individuals lose control of their tempers and lash out verbally at persons nearby.

Although "getting cussed out" is basically free of setting-imposed restrictions, the Western Apache fear it most at gatherings where alcohol is being consumed. My informants observed that especially at "drinking parties" (*dá'idlą́ą́*), where there is much rough joking and ostensibly mock criticism, it is easy for well-intentioned remarks to be misconstrued as insults. Provoked in this way, persons who are intoxicated may become hostile and launch into explosive tirades, often with no warning at all.

The silence of Apaches who are "getting cussed out" is consistently explained in reference to the belief that individuals who are "enraged" (*haškéé*) are also irrational or "crazy" (*bìné'idį́í*). In this condition, it is said, they "forget who they are" and become oblivious to what they say or do. Concomitantly, they lose all concern for the consequences of their actions on other people. In a word, they are dangerous. Said one informant:

> When people get mad they get crazy. Then they start yelling and saying bad things. Some say they are going to kill somebody for what he has done. Some keep it up that way for a long time, maybe walk from camp to camp, real angry, yelling, crazy like that. They keep it up for a long time, some do.
>
> People like that don't know what they are saying, so you can't tell about them. When you see someone like that, just walk away. If he yells at you, let him say whatever he wants to. Let him say anything. Maybe he doesn't mean it. But he doesn't know that. He will be crazy, and he could try to kill you.

Another Apache said:

> When someone gets mad at you and starts yelling, then just don't do anything to make him get worse. Don't try to quiet him down because he won't know why you're doing it. If you try to do that, he may just get worse and try to hurt you.

As the last of these statements implies, the Western Apache operate on the assumption that enraged persons—because they are temporarily "crazy"—are difficult to reason with. Indeed, there is a widely held belief that attempts at mollification will serve to intensify anger, thus increasing the chances of physical violence. The appropriate strategy when "getting cussed out" is to do nothing, to avoid any action that will attract attention to oneself. Since speaking accomplishes just the opposite, the use of silence is strongly advised.

5. "Being with people who are sad" (*nde dò- biłgòzóóda bigą́ą́*). Although the Western Apache phrase that labels this situation has no precise equivalent in English, it refers quite specifically to gatherings in which an individual finds himself in the company of someone whose spouse or kinsman has recently died. Distinct from wakes and burials, which follow immediately after a death, "being with people who are sad" is most likely to occur several weeks later. At this time, close relatives of the deceased emerge from a period of intense mourning (during which they rarely venture beyond the limits of their camps) and start to resume their normal activities within the community. To persons anxious to convey their sympathies, this is interpreted as a sign that visitors will be welcomed and, if possible, provided with food and drink. To those less solicitous, it means that unplanned encounters with the bereaved must be anticipated and prepared for.

"Being with people who are sad" can occur on a foot-path, in a camp, at church, or in a trading post; but whatever the setting—and regardless of whether it is the result of a planned visit or an accidental meeting—the situation is marked by a minimum of speech. Queried about this, my informants volunteered three types of explanations. The first is that persons "who are sad" are so burdened with "intense grief" (*dółgozóóda*) that speaking requires of them an unusual amount of physical effort. It is courteous and considerate, therefore, not to attempt to engage them in conversation.

A second native explanation is that in situations of this sort verbal communication is basically unnecessary. Everyone is familiar with what has happened, and talking about it, even for the purpose of conveying solace and sympathy, would only reinforce and augment the sadness felt by those who were close to the deceased. Again, for reasons of courtesy, this is something to be avoided.

The third explanation is rooted in the belief that "intense grief," like intense rage, produces changes in the personality of the individual who experiences it. As evidence for this, the Western Apache cite numerous instances in which the emotional strain of dealing with death, coupled with an overwhelming sense of irrevocable personal loss, has caused persons who were formerly mild and even-tempered to become abusive, hostile, and physically violent.

That old woman, X, who lives across Cibecue Creek, one time her first husband died. After that she cried all the time, for a long time. Then, I guess she got mean because everyone said she drank a lot and got into fights. Even with her close relatives, she did like that for a long time. She was too sad for her husband. That's what made her like that; it made her lose her mind.

My father was like that when his wife died. He just stayed home all the time and wouldn't go anywhere. He didn't talk to any of his relatives or children. He just said, "I'm hungry. Cook for me." That's all. He stayed that way for a long time. His mind was not with us. He was still with his wife.

My uncle died in 1911. His wife sure went crazy right away after that. Two days after they buried the body, we went over there and stayed with those people who had been left alone. My aunt got mad at us. She said, "Why do you come over here? You can't bring my husband back. I can take care of myself and those others in my camp, so why don't you go home." She sure was mad that time, too sad for someone who died. She didn't know what she was saying because in about one week she came to our camp and said, "My relatives, I'm all right now. When you came to help me, I had too much sadness and my mind was no good. I said bad words to you. But now I am all right and I know what I am doing."

As these statements indicate, the Western Apache assume that a person suffering from "intense grief" is likely to be disturbed and unstable. Even though he may appear outwardly composed, they say, there is always the possibility that he is emotionally upset and therefore unusually prone to volatile outbursts. Apaches acknowledge that such an individual might welcome conversation in the context of "being with people who are sad," but, on the other hand, they fear it might prove incendiary. Under these conditions, which resemble those in Situation No. 4, it is considered both expedient and appropriate to keep silent.

6. "Being with someone for whom they sing" (*nde bìdádìstááha bigą́ą́*). The last type of situation to be described is restricted to a small number of physical locations and is more directly influenced by temporal factors than any of the situations we have discussed so far. "Being with someone for whom they sing" takes place only in the context of "curing ceremonials" (*gòjitáł; èdotáł*). These events begin early at night and come to a close shortly before dawn the following day. In the late fall and throughout the winter, curing ceremonials are held inside the patient's wickiup or house. In the spring and summer, they are located outside, at some open place near the patient's camp or at specially designated dance grounds where group rituals of all kinds are regularly performed.

Prior to the start of a curing ceremonial, all persons in attendance may feel free to talk with the patient;

indeed, because he is so much a focus of concern, it is expected that friends and relatives will seek him out to offer encouragement and support. Conversation breaks off, however, when the patient is informed that the ceremonial is about to begin, and it ceases entirely when the presiding medicine man commences to chant. From this point on, until the completion of the final chant next morning, it is inappropriate for anyone except the medicine man (and, if he has them, his aides) to speak to the patient.[6]

In order to appreciate the explanation Apaches give for this prescription, we must briefly discuss the concept of "supernatural power" (*diyi'*) and describe some of the effects it is believed to have on persons at whom it is directed. Elsewhere (Basso 1969:30) I have defined "power" as follows:

> The term *diyi'* refers to one or all of a set of abstract and invisible forces which are said to derive from certain classes of animals, plants, minerals, meteorological phenomena, and mythological figures within the Western Apache universe. Any of the various powers may be acquired by man and, if properly handled, used for a variety of purposes.

A power that has been antagonized by disrespectful behavior towards its source may retaliate by causing the offender to become sick. "Power-caused illnesses" (*kásití diyi' bił*) are properly treated with curing ceremonials in which one or more medicine men, using chants and various items of ritual paraphernalia, attempt to neutralize the sickness-causing power with powers of their own.

Roughly two-thirds of my informants assert that a medicine man's power actually enters the body of the patient; others maintain that it simply closes in and envelops him. In any case, all agree that the patient is brought into intimate contact with a potent supernatural force which elevates him to a condition labeled *gòdiyó'* (sacred, holy).

The term *gòdiyó'* may also be translated as "potentially harmful" and, in this sense, is regularly used to describe classes of objects (including all sources of power) that are surrounded with taboos. In keeping with the semantics of *gòdiyó'*, the Western Apache explain that, besides making patients holy, power makes them potentially harmful. And it is this transformation, they explain, that is basically responsible for the cessation of verbal communication during curing ceremonials. Said one informant:

> When they start singing for someone like that, he sort of goes away with what the medicine man is working with (i.e., power). Sometimes people they sing for don't know you, even after it (the curing ceremonial) is over. They get holy, and you shouldn't try to talk to them when they are like that . . . it's best to leave them alone.

Another informant made similar comments:

> When they sing for someone, what happens is like this: that man they sing for doesn't know why he is sick or which way to go. So the medicine man has to show him and work on him. That is when he gets holy, and that makes him go off somewhere in his mind, so you should stay away from him.

Because Apaches undergoing ceremonial treatment are perceived as having been changed by power into something different from their normal selves, they are regarded with caution and apprehension. Their newly acquired status places them in close proximity to the supernatural and, as such, carries with it a very real element of danger and uncertainty. These conditions combine to make "being with someone for whom they sing" a situation in which speech is considered disrespectful and, if not exactly harmful, at least potentially hazardous.

VI

Although the types of situations described above differ from one another in obvious ways, I will argue in what follows that the underlying determinants of silence are in each case basically the same. Specifically, I will attempt to defend the hypothesis that keeping silent in Western Apache culture is associated with social situations in which participants perceive their relationships *vis-à-vis* one another to be ambiguous and/or unpredictable.

Let us begin with the observation that, in all the situations we have described, *silence is defined as appropriate with respect to a specific individual or individuals*. In other words, the use of speech is not directly curtailed by the setting of a situation nor by the physical activities that accompany it but, rather, by the perceived social and psychological attributes of at least one focal participant.

It may also be observed that, in each type of situation, *the status of the focal participant is marked by ambiguity*—either because he is unfamiliar to other participants in the situation or because, owing to some recent event, a status he formerly held has been changed or is in a process of transition.

Thus, in Situation No. 1, persons who earlier considered themselves "strangers" move towards some other relationship, perhaps "friend" (*šìdikéê*), perhaps "enemy" (*šìkédndíí*). In Situation No. 2, young people who have had relatively limited exposure to one another attempt to adjust to the new and intimate status of "sweetheart." These two situations are similar in that the focal participants have little or no prior knowledge of each other. Their social identities are not as yet clearly defined, and their expectations, lacking the foundation of previous experience, are poorly developed.

Situation No. 3 is somewhat different. Although the participants—parents and their children—are well known to each other, their relationship has been seriously interrupted by the latter's prolonged absence from home. This, combined with the possibility that recent experiences at school have altered the children's attitudes, introduces a definite element of unfamiliarity and doubt. Situation No. 3 is not characterized by the absence of role expectations but by the participants' perception that those already in existence may be outmoded and in need of revision.

Status ambiguity is present in Situation No. 4 because a focal participant is enraged and, as a result, considered "crazy." Until he returns to a more rational condition, others in the situation have no way of predicting how he will behave. Situation No. 5 is similar in that the personality of a focal participant is seen to have undergone a marked shift which makes his actions more difficult to anticipate. In both situations, the status of focal participants is uncertain because of real or imagined changes in their psychological makeup.

In Situation No. 6, a focal participant is ritually transformed from an essentially neutral state to one which is contextually defined as "potentially harmful." Ambiguity and apprehension accompany this transition, and, as in Situations No. 4 and 5, established patterns of interaction must be waived until the focal participant reverts to a less threatening condition.

This discussion points up a third feature characteristic of all situations: *the ambiguous status of focal participants is accompanied either by the absence or suspension of established role expectations.* In every instance, non-focal participants (i.e., those who refrain from speech) are either uncertain of how the focal participant will behave towards them or, conversely, how they should behave towards him. Stated in the simplest way possible, their roles become blurred with the result that established expectations—if they exist—lose their relevance as guidelines for social action and must be temporarily discarded or abruptly modified.

We are now in a position to expand upon our initial hypothesis and make it more explicit.

1. In Western Apache culture, the absence of verbal communication is associated with social situations in which the status of local participants is ambiguous.

2. Under these conditions, fixed role expectations lose their applicability and the illusion of predictability in social interaction is lost.

3. To sum up and reiterate: keeping silent among the Western Apache is a response to uncertainty and unpredictability in social relations.

VII

The question remains to what extent the foregoing hypothesis helps to account for silence behavior in other cultures. Unfortunately, it is impossible at the present time to provide anything approaching a conclusive answer. Standard ethnographies contain very little information about the circumstances under which verbal communication is discouraged, and it is only within the past few years that problems of this sort have engaged the attention of sociolinguists. The result is that adequate cross-cultural data are almost completely lacking.

As a first step towards the elimination of this deficiency, an attempt is now being made to investigate the occurrence and interpretation of silence in other Indian societies of the American Southwest. Our findings at this early stage, though neither fully representative nor sufficiently comprehensive, are extremely suggestive. By way of illustration, I quote below from portions of a preliminary report prepared by Priscilla Mowrer (1970), herself a Navajo, who inquired into the situational features of Navajo silence behavior in the vicinity of Tuba City on the Navajo Reservation in east-central Arizona.

I. *Silence and Courting:* Navajo youngsters of opposite sexes just getting to know one another say nothing, except to sit close together and maybe hold hands.... In public, they may try not to let on that they are interested in each other, but in private it is another matter. If the girl is at a gathering where the boy is also present, she may go off by herself. Falling in step, the boy will generally follow. They may just walk around or find some place to sit down. But, at first, they will not say anything to each other.

II. *Silence and Long Absent Relatives:* When a male or female relative returns home after being gone for six months or more, he (or she) is first greeted with a handshake. If the returnee is male, the female greeter may embrace him and cry—the male, meanwhile, will remain dry-eyed and silent.

III. *Silence and Anger:* The Navajo tend to remain silent when being shouted at by a drunk or angered individual because that particular individual is considered temporarily insane. To speak to such an individual, the Navajo believe, just tends to make the situation worse.... People remain silent because they believe that the individual is not himself, that he may have been witched, and is not responsible for the change in his behavior.

IV. *Silent Mourning:* Navajos speak very little when mourning the death of a relative.... The Navajo mourn and cry together in pairs. Men will embrace one another and cry together. Women, however, will hold one another's hands and cry together.

V. *Silence and the Ceremonial Patient:* The Navajo consider it wrong to talk to a person being sung over. The only people who talk to the patient are the medicine man and a female relative (or male relative if the patient is male) who is in charge of food preparation. The only time the patient speaks openly is when the medicine man asks her (or him) to pray along with him.

These observations suggest that striking similarities may exist between the types of social contexts in which Navajos and Western Apaches refrain from speech. If this impression is confirmed by further research, it will lend obvious cross-cultural support to the hypothesis advanced above. But regardless of the final outcome, the situational determinants of silence seem eminently deserving of further study. For as we become better informed about the types of contextual variables that mitigate against the use of verbal codes, we should also learn more about those variables that encourage and promote them.

NOTES

1. At different times during the period extending from 1964–1969 the research on which this paper is based was supported by U. S. P. H. S. Grant MH-12691-01, a grant from the American Philosophical Society, and funds from the Doris Duke Oral History Project at the Arizona State Museum. I am pleased to acknowledge this support. I would also like to express my gratitude to the following scholars for commenting upon an earlier draft: Y. R. Chao, Harold C. Conklin, Roy G. D'Andrade, Charles O. Frake, Paul Friedrich, John Gumperz, Kenneth Hale, Harry Hoijer, Dell Hymes, Stanley Newman, David M. Schneider, Joel Sherzer, and Paul Turner. Although the final version gained much from their criticisms and suggestions, responsibility for its present form and content rests solely with the author. A preliminary version of this paper was presented to the Annual Meeting of the American Anthropological Association in New Orleans, Louisiana, November 1969. A modified version of this paper is scheduled to appear in *Studies in Apachean Culture and Ethnology* (ed. by Keith H. Basso and Morris Opler), Tucson: University of Arizona Press, 1970.

2. The situations described in this paper are not the only ones in which the Western Apache refrain from speech. There is a second set—not considered here because my data are incomplete—in which silence appears to occur as a gesture of respect, usually to persons in positions of authority. A third set, very poorly understood, involves ritual specialists who claim they must keep silent at certain points during the preparation of ceremonial paraphernalia.

3. Recent work in the sociology of interaction, most notably by Goffman (1963) and Garfinkel (1967), has led to the suggestion that social relationships are everywhere the major determinants of verbal behavior. In this case, as Gumperz (1967) makes clear, it becomes methodologically unsound to treat the various components of communicative events as independent variables. Gumperz (1967) has presented a hierarchical model, sensitive to de-

pendency, in which components are seen as stages in the communication process. Each stage serves as the input for the next. The basic stage, i.e., the initial input, is "social identities or statuses." For further details see Slobin 1967:131–134.

4. I would like to stress that the emphasis placed on social relations is fully in keeping with the Western Apache interpretation of their own behavior. When my informants were asked to explain why they or someone else was silent on a particular occasion, they invariably did so in terms of *who* was present at the time.

5. Among the Western Apache, rules of exogamy discourage courtships between members of the same clan (*kii àłhánigo*) and so-called "related" clans (*kii*), with the result that sweethearts are almost always "non-matrilineal kinsmen" (*dòhwàkíída*). Compared to "matrilineal kinsmen" (*kii*), such individuals have fewer opportunities during childhood to establish close personal relationships and thus, when courtship begins, have relatively little knowledge of each other. It is not surprising, therefore, that their behavior is similar to that accorded strangers.

6. I have witnessed over 75 curing ceremonials since 1961 and have seen this rule violated only 6 times. On 4 occasions, drunks were at fault. In the other 2 cases, the patient fell asleep and had to be awakened.

REFERENCES

Basso, Keith H. 1966. *The Gift of Changing Woman.* Bureau of American Ethnology, bulletin 196.

———. 1969. *Western Apache Witchcraft.* Anthropological Papers of the University of Arizona, no. 15.

———. 1970. *The Cibecue Apache.* New York: Holt, Rinehart and Winston, Inc.

Brown, R. W., and Albert Gilman. 1960. "The Pronouns of Power and Solidarity," in *Style in Language* (ed. by T. Sebeok), pp. 253–276. Cambridge: The Technology Press of Massachusetts Institute of Technology.

Conklin, Harold C. 1959. Linguistic Play in Its Cultural Context. *Language* 35:631–636.

Ervin-Tripp, Susan. 1964. "An Analysis of the Interaction of Language, Topic and Listener," in *The Ethnography of Communication* (ed. by J. J. Gumperz and D. Hymes), pp. 86–102. *American Anthropologist*, Special Publication, vol. 66, no. 6, part 2.

———. 1967. *Sociolinguistics.* Language-Behavior Research Laboratory, Working Paper no. 3. Berkeley: University of California.

Frake, Charles O. 1964. "How to Ask for a Drink in Subanun," in *The Ethnography of Communication* (ed. by J. J. Gumperz and D. Hymes), pp. 127–132. *American Anthropologist*, Special Publication, vol. 66, no. 6, part 2.

Friedrich, P. 1966. "Structural Implications of Russian Pronomial Usage," in *Sociolinguistics*, (ed. by W. Bright), pp. 214–253. The Hague: Mouton.

Garfinkel, H. 1967. *Studies in Ethnomethodology.* Englewood Cliffs, N. J.: Prentice-Hall, Inc.

Goffman, E. 1961. *Encounters: Two Studies in the Sociology of Interaction.* Indianapolis: The Bobbs-Merrill Co., Inc.

———. 1963. *Behavior in Public Places.* Glencoe, Ill.: Free Press.

————. 1964. "The Neglected Situation," in *The Ethnography of Communication* (ed. by J. J. Gumperz and D. Hymes), pp. 133–136. *American Anthropologist*, Special Publication, vol. 66, no. 6, part 2.

Gumperz, John J. 1961. Speech Variation and the Study of Indian Civilization. *American Anthropologist* 63: 976–988.

————. 1964. "Linguistic and Social Interaction in Two Communities," in *The Ethnography of Communication* (ed. by J. J. Gumperz and D. Hymes), pp. 137–153. *American Anthropologist*, Special Publication, vol. 66, no. 6, part 2.

————. 1967. "The Social Setting of Linguistic Behavior," in *A Field Manual for Cross-Cultural Study of the Acquisition of Communicative Competence (Second Draft)* (ed. by D. I. Slobin), pp. 129–134. Berkeley: University of California.

Hymes, Dell. 1962. "The Ethnography of Speaking," in *Anthropology and Human Behavior* (ed. by T. Gladwin and W. C. Sturtevant), pp. 13–53. Washington, D. C.: The Anthropological Society of Washington.

————. 1964. "Introduction: Toward Ethnographies of Communication," in *The Ethnography of Communication* (ed. by J. J. Gumperz and D. Hymes), pp. 1–34. *American Anthropologist*, Special Publication, vol. 66, no. 6, part 2.

Kaut, Charles R. 1957. *The Western Apache Clan System: Its Origins and Development*. University of New Mexico Publications in Anthropology, no. 9.

Martin, Samuel. 1964. "Speech Levels in Japan and Korea," in *Language in Culture and Society* (ed. by D. Hymes), pp. 407–415. New York: Harper & Row.

Mowrer, Priscilla. 1970. Notes on Navajo Silence Behavior. MS, University of Arizona.

Slobin, Dan I. (ed.). 1967. *A Field Manual for Cross-Cultural Study of the Acquisition of Communicative Competence (Second Draft)*. Berkeley: University of California.

7

A Cultural Approach to Male–Female Miscommunication

Daniel N. Maltz and Ruth A. Borker

Of the 60,000 or so words in the English language, the typical educated adult uses about 2,000. Five hundred of these words alone can convey over 14,000 meanings. But even with all these alternatives, this is not the central problem of miscommunication in North America. Rather, interethnic and cross-sex conversations are the central problem, because the participants possess different subcultural rules for speaking.

Conversation is a negotiated activity. Within a given culture, conversations rely on unspoken understandings about tone of voice, visual cues, silence, minimal responses (such as "mm hmm"), and a variety of other subtle conventions. A cultural approach to male–female conversation highlights unconscious meanings that can lead members of one group to misinterpret the intent of others. Evidence suggests, for example, that women use the response "mm hmm" to indicate they are listening, whereas men use the same response to indicate they are agreeing. Thus, a man who does not provide such cues may indicate to a female conversation partner that he is not listening, whereas a woman may appear to keep changing her mind when giving the same cue. This and similar insights are found throughout this selection and indicate the need for paying attention to communication across cultural and subcultural boundaries.

As you read this selection, ask yourself the following questions:

☐ *What are some of the differences in the ways men and women talk to each other that have been noted in earlier research?*

☐ *How do differences between men and women in conversational style reflect differences in power in the larger society?*

☐ *If men and women exist in different linguistic subcultures, how and when were these subcultures learned? How does the world of girls differ from the world of boys?*

☐ *What kinds of miscommunications occur in cross-sex conversation?*

☐ *Can you think of situations that have occurred in your own life that can be better understood after reading this cultural analysis of cross-sex conversation?*

The following terms discussed in this selection are included in the Glossary at the back of the book:

gender	*social networks*
metalinguistics	*sociolinguistics*
sex roles	*subculture*

From John L. Gumperz (ed.), *Language and Social Identity*, 1982.
Reprinted with the permission of Cambridge University Press.

INTRODUCTION

This chapter presents what we believe to be a useful new framework for examining differences in the speaking patterns of American men and women. It is based not on new data, but on a reexamination of a wide variety of material already available in the scholarly literature. Our starting problem is the nature of the different roles of male and female speakers in informal cross-sex conversations in American English. Our attempts to think about this problem have taken us to preliminary examination of a wide variety of fields often on or beyond the margins of our present competencies: children's speech, children's play, styles and patterns of friendship, conversational turn-taking, discourse analysis, and interethnic communication. The research which most influenced the development of our present model includes John Gumperz's work on problems in interethnic communication (1982) and Marjorie Goodwin's study of the linguistic aspects of play among black children in Philadelphia (1978, 1980a, 1980b).

Our major argument is that the general approach recently developed for the study of difficulties in cross-ethnic communication can be applied to cross-sex communication as well. We prefer to think of the difficulties in both cross-sex and cross-ethnic communication as two examples of the same larger phenomenon: cultural difference and miscommunication.

THE PROBLEM OF CROSS-SEX CONVERSATION

Study after study has shown that when men and women attempt to interact as equals in friendly cross-sex conversations they do not play the same role in interaction, even when there is no apparent element of flirting. We hope to explore some of these differences, examine the explanations that have been offered, and provide an alternative explanation for them.

The primary data on cross-sex conversations come from two general sources: social psychology studies from the 1950s such as Soskin and John's (1963) research on two young married couples and Strodbeck and Mann's (1956) research on jury deliberations, and more recent sociolinguistic studies from the University of California at Santa Barbara and the University of Pennsylvania by Candace West (Zimmerman and West 1975; West and Zimmerman 1977; West 1979), Pamela Fishman (1978), and Lynette Hirschman (1973).

WOMEN'S FEATURES

Several striking differences in male and female contributions to cross-sex conversation have been noticed in these studies.

First, women display a greater tendency to ask questions. Fishman (1978:400) comments that "at times I felt that all women did was ask questions," and Hirschman (1973:10) notes that "several of the female–male conversations fell into a question–answer pattern with the females asking the males questions."

Fishman (1978:408) sees this question-asking tendency as an example of a second, more general characteristic of women's speech, doing more of the routine "shitwork" involved in maintaining routine social interaction, doing more to facilitate the flow of conversation (Hirschman 1973:3). Women are more likely than men to make utterances that demand or encourage responses from their fellow speakers and are therefore, in Fishman's words, "more actively engaged in insuring interaction than the men" (1978:404). In the earlier social psychology studies, these features have been coded under the general category of "positive reactions" including solidarity, tension release, and agreeing (Strodbeck and Mann 1956).

Third, women show a greater tendency to make use of positive minimal responses, especially "mm hmm" (Hirschman 1973:8), and are more likely to insert "such comments throughout streams of talk rather than [simply] at the end" (Fishman 1978:402).

Fourth, women are more likely to adopt a strategy of "silent protest" after they have been interrupted or have received a delayed minimal response (Zimmerman and West 1975; West and Zimmerman 1977:524).

Fifth, women show a greater tendency to use the pronouns "you" and "we," which explicitly acknowledge the existence of the other speaker (Hirschman 1973:6).

MEN'S FEATURES

Contrasting contributions to cross-sex conversations have been observed and described for men.

First, men are more likely to interrupt the speech of their conversational partners, that is, to interrupt the speech of women (Zimmerman and West 1975; West and Zimmerman 1977; West 1979).

Second, they are more likely to challenge or dispute their partners' utterances (Hirschman 1973:11).

Third, they are more likely to ignore the comments of the other speaker, that is, to offer no response or acknowledgment at all (Hirschman 1973:11), to respond slowly in what has been described as a "delayed minimal response" (Zimmerman and West 1975:118), or to respond unenthusiastically (Fishman 1978).

Fourth, men use more mechanisms for controlling the topic of conversation, including both topic development and the introduction of new topics, than do women (Zimmerman and West 1975).

Finally, men make more direct declarations of fact or opinion than do women (Fishman 1978:402), including suggestions, opinions, and "statements of orientation" as Strodbeck and Mann (1956) describe them, or "statements of focus and directives" as they are described by Soskin and John (1963).

EXPLANATIONS OFFERED

Most explanations for these features have focused on differences in the social power or in the personalities of men and women. One variant of the social power argument, presented by West (Zimmerman and West 1975; West and Zimmerman 1977), is that men's dominance in conversation parallels their dominance in society. Men enjoy power in society and also in conversation. The two levels are seen as part of a single social-political system. West sees interruptions and topic control as male displays of power—a power based in the larger social order but reinforced and expressed in face-to-face interaction with women. A second variant of this argument, stated by Fishman (1978), is that while the differential power of men and women is crucial, the specific mechanism through which it enters conversation is sex-role definition. Sex roles serve to obscure the issue of power for participants, but the fact is, Fishman argues, that norms of appropriate behavior for women and men serve to give power and interactional control to men while keeping it from women. To be socially acceptable as women, women cannot exert control and must actually support men in their control. In this casting of the social power argument, men are not necessarily seen to be consciously flaunting power, but simply reaping the rewards given them by the social system. In both variants, the link between macro and micro levels of social life is seen as direct and unproblematic, and the focus of explanation is the general social order.

Sex roles have also been central in psychological explanations. The primary advocate of the psychological position has been Robin Lakoff (1975). Basically, Lakoff asserts that, having been taught to speak and act like 'ladies,' women become as unassertive and insecure as they have been made to sound. The impossible task of trying to be both women and adults, which Lakoff sees as culturally incompatible, saps women of confidence and strength. As a result, they come to produce the speech they do, not just because it is how women are supposed to speak, but because it fits with the personalities they develop as a consequence of sex-role requirements.

The problem with these explanations is that they do not provide a means of explaining why these specific features appear as opposed to any number of others, nor do they allow us to differentiate between various types of male–female interaction. They do not

really tell us why and how these specific interactional phenomena are linked to the general fact that men dominate within our social system.

AN ALTERNATIVE EXPLANATION: SOCIOLINGUISTIC SUBCULTURES

Our approach to cross-sex communication patterns is somewhat different from those that have been previously proposed. We place the stress not on psychological differences or power differentials, although these may make some contribution, but rather on a notion of cultural differences between men and women in their conceptions of friendly conversation, their rules for engaging in it, and, probably most important, their rules for interpreting it. We argue that American men and women come from different sociolinguistic subcultures, having learned to do different things with words in a conversation, so that when they attempt to carry on conversations with one another, even if both parties are attempting to treat one another as equals, cultural miscommunication results.

The idea of distinct male and female subcultures is not a new one for anthropology. It has been persuasively argued again and again for those parts of the world such as the Middle East and southern Europe in which men and women spend most of their lives spatially and interactionally segregated. The strongest case for sociolinguistic subcultures has been made by Susan Harding from her research in rural Spain (1975).

The major premise on which Harding builds her argument is that speech is a means for dealing with social and psychological situations. When men and women have different experiences and operate in different social contexts, they tend to develop different genres of speech and different skills for doing things with words. In the Spanish village in which she worked, the sexual division of labor was strong, with men involved in agricultural tasks and public politics while women were involved in a series of networks of personal relations with their children, their husbands, and their female neighbors. While men developed their verbal skills in economic negotiations and public political argument, women became more verbally adept at a quite different mode of interactional manipulation with words: gossip, social analysis, subtle information gathering through a carefully developed technique of verbal prying, and a kind of second-guessing the thoughts of others (commonly known as 'women's intuition') through a skillful monitoring of the speech of others. The different social needs of men and women, she argues, have led them to sexually differentiated communicative cultures, with each sex learning a different set of skills for manipulating words effectively.

The question that Harding does not ask, however, is, if men and women possess different subcultural rules for speaking, what happens if and when they try to interact with each other? It is here that we turn to the research on interethnic miscommunication.

INTERETHNIC COMMUNICATION

Recent research (Gumperz 1977, 1978a, 1978b, 1979; Gumperz and Tannen 1978) has shown that systematic problems develop in communication when speakers of different speech cultures interact and that these problems are the result of differences in systems of conversational inference and the cues for signalling speech acts and speaker's intent. Conversation is a negotiated activity. It progresses in large part because of shared assumptions about what is going on.

Examining interactions between English-English and Indian-English speakers in Britain (Gumperz 1977, 1978a, 1979; Gumperz et al. 1977), Gumperz found that differences in cues resulted in systematic miscommunication over whether a question was being asked, whether an argument was being made, whether a person was being rude or polite, whether a speaker was relinquishing the floor or interrupting, whether and what a speaker was emphasizing, whether interactants were angry, concerned, or indifferent. Rather than being seen as problems in communication, the frustrating encounters that resulted were usually chalked up as personality clashes or interpreted in the light of racial stereotypes which tended to exacerbate already bad relations.

To take a simple case, Gumperz (1977) reports that Indian women working at a cafeteria, when offering food, used a falling intonation, e.g., "gravy," which to them indicated a question, something like "do you want gravy?" Both Indian and English workers saw a question as an appropriate polite form, but to English-English speakers a falling intonation signalled not a question, which for them is signalled by a rising intonation such as "gravy," but a declarative statement, which was both inappropriate and extremely rude.

A major advantage of Gumperz's framework is that it does not assume that problems are the result of bad faith, but rather sees them as the result of individuals wrongly interpreting cues according to their own rules.

THE INTERPRETATION OF MINIMAL RESPONSES

How might Gumperz's approach to the study of conflicting rules for interpreting conversation be applied to the communication between men and women? A simple example will illustrate our basic approach: the case of positive minimal responses. Minimal responses such as nods and comments like "yes" and "mm hmm" are common features of conversational interaction. Our claim, based on our attempts to understand personal experience, is that these minimal responses have significantly different meanings for men and women, leading to occasionally serious miscommunication.

We hypothesize that for women a minimal response of this type means simply something like "I'm listening to you; please continue," and that for men it has a somewhat stronger meaning such as "I agree with you" or at least "I follow your argument so far." The fact that women use these responses more often than men is in part simply that women are listening more often than men are agreeing.

But our hypothesis explains more than simple differential frequency of usage. Different rules can lead to repeated misunderstandings. Imagine a male speaker who is receiving repeated nods or "mm hmm"s from the woman he is speaking to. She is merely indicating that she is listening, but he thinks she is agreeing with everything he says. Now imagine a female speaker who is receiving only occasional nods and "mm hmm"s from the man she is speaking to. He is indicating that he doesn't always agree; she thinks he isn't always listening.

What is appealing about this short example is that it seems to explain two of the most common complaints in male–female interaction: (1) men who think that women are always agreeing with them and then conclude that it's impossible to tell what a woman really thinks, and (2) women who get upset with men who never seem to be listening. What we think we have here are two separate rules for conversational maintenance which come into conflict and cause massive miscommunication.

SOURCES OF DIFFERENT CULTURES

A probable objection that many people will have to our discussion so far is that American men and women interact with one another far too often to possess different subcultures. What we need to explain is how it is that men and women can come to possess different cultural assumptions about friendly conversation.

Our explanation is really quite simple. It is based on the idea that by the time we have become adults we possess a wide variety of rules for interacting in different situations. Different sets of these rules were learned at different times and in different contexts. We have rules for dealing with people in dominant or subordinate social positions, rules which we first learned as young children interacting with our parents and teachers. We have rules for flirting and other sexual encounters which we probably started learning at or near adolescence. We have rules for dealing with service personnel and bureaucrats, rules we began learning when we first ventured into the public domain. Finally, we have rules for friendly interaction, for carrying on friendly conversation. What is striking about these last rules is that they were learned not from adults but from peers, and that they were learned during precisely that time period, approximately age 5 to 15, when boys and girls interact socially primarily with members of their own sex.

The idea that girls and boys in contemporary America learn different ways of speaking by the age of five or earlier has been postulated by Robin Lakoff (1975), demonstrated by Andrea Meditch (1975), and more fully explored by Adelaide Haas (1979). Haas's research on school-age children shows the early appearance of important male–female differences in patterns of language use, including a male tendency toward direct requests and information giving and a female tendency toward compliance (1979:107).

But the process of acquiring gender-specific speech and behavior patterns by school-age children is more complex than the simple copying of adult "genderlects" by preschoolers. Psychologists Brooks-Gunn and Matthews (1979) have labelled this process the "consolidation of sex roles"; we call it learning of gender-specific 'cultures.'

Among school-age children, patterns of friendly social interaction are learned not so much from adults as from members of one's peer group, and a major feature of most middle-childhood peer groups is homogeneity; "they are either all-boy or all-girl" (Brooks-Gunn and Matthews 1979). Members of each sex are learning self-consciously to differentiate their behavior from that of the other sex and to exaggerate these differences. The process can be profitably compared to accent divergence in which members of two groups that wish to become clearly distinguished from one another socially acquire increasingly divergent ways of speaking.[1]

Because they learn these gender-specific cultures from their age-mates, children tend to develop stereotypes and extreme versions of adult behavior patterns. For a boy learning to behave in a masculine way, for example, Ruth Hartley (1959, quoted in Brooks-Gunn and Matthews 1979:203) argues that:

both the information and the practice he gets are distorted. Since his peers have no better sources of information than he has, all they can do is pool the impressions and anxieties they derived from their early training. Thus, the picture they draw is oversimplified and overemphasized. It is a picture drawn in black and white, with little or no modulation and it is incomplete, including a few of the many elements that go to make up the role of the mature male.

What we hope to argue is that boys and girls learn to use language in different ways because of the very different social contexts in which they learn how to carry on friendly conversation. Almost anyone who remembers being a child, has worked with school-age children, or has had an opportunity to observe school-age children can vouch for the fact that groups of girls and groups of boys interact and play in different ways. Systematic observations of children's play have tended to confirm these well-known differences in the ways girls and boys learn to interact with their friends.

In a major study of sex differences in the play of school-age children, for example, sociologist Janet Lever (1976) observed the following six differences between the play of boys and that of girls: (1) girls more often play indoors; (2) boys tend to play in larger groups; (3) boys' play groups tend to include a wider age range of participants; (4) girls play in predominantly male games more often than vice versa; (5) boys more often play competitive games, and (6) girls' games tend to last a shorter period of time than boys' games.

It is by examining these differences in the social organization of play and the accompanying differences in the patterns of social interaction they entail, we argue, that we can learn about the sources of male–female differences in patterns of language use. And it is these same patterns, learned in childhood and carried over into adulthood as the bases for patterns of single-sex friendship relations, we contend, that are potential sources of miscommunication in cross-sex interaction.

THE WORLD OF GIRLS

Our own experience and studies such as Goodwin's (1980b) of black children and Lever's (1976, 1978) of white children suggest a complex of features of girls' play and the speech within it. Girls play in small groups, most often in pairs (Lever 1976; Eder and Hallinan 1978; Brooks-Gunn and Matthews 1979), and their play groups tend to be remarkably homogeneous in terms of age. Their play is often in private or semi-private settings that require participants be invited in. Play is cooperative and activities are usually organized in noncompetitive ways (Lever 1976; Goodwin 1980b). Differentiation between girls is not made in terms of power, but relative closeness. Friendship is seen by girls as involving intimacy, equality, mutual commitment, and loyalty. The idea of 'best friend' is central for girls. Relationships between girls are to some extent in opposition to one another, and new relationships are often formed at the expense of old ones. As Brooks-Gunn and Matthews (1979:280) observe, "friendships tend to be exclusive, with a few girls being exceptionally close to one another. Because of this breakups tend to be highly emotional," and Goodwin (1980a:172) notes that "the non-hierarchical framework of the girls provides a fertile ground for rather intricate processes of alliance formation between equals against some other party."

There is a basic contradiction in the structure of girls' social relationships. Friends are supposed to be equal and everyone is supposed to get along, but in fact they don't always. Conflict must be resolved, but a girl cannot assert social power or superiority as an individual to resolve it. Lever (1976), studying fifth-graders, found that girls simply could not deal with quarrels and that when conflict arose they made no attempt to settle it; the group just broke up. What girls learn to do with speech is cope with the contradiction created by an ideology of equality and cooperation and a social reality that includes differences and conflict. As they grow up they learn increasingly subtle ways of balancing the conflicting pressures created by a female social world and a female friendship ideology.

Basically girls learn to do three things with words: (1) to create and maintain relationships of closeness and equality, (2) to criticize others in acceptable ways, and (3) to interpret accurately the speech of other girls.

To a large extent friendships among girls are formed through talk. Girls need to learn to give support, to recognize the speech rights of others, to let others speak, and to acknowledge what they say in order to establish and maintain relationships of equality and closeness. In activities they need to learn to create cooperation through speech. Goodwin (1980a) found that inclusive forms such as "let's," "we gonna," "we could," and "we gotta" predominated in task-oriented activities. Furthermore, she found that most girls in the group she studied made suggestions and that the other girls usually agreed to them. But girls also learn to exchange information and confidences to create and maintain relationships of closeness. The exchange of personal thoughts not only expresses closeness but mutual commitment as well. Brooks-Gunn and Matthews (1979:280) note of adolescent girls:

> much time is spent talking, reflecting, and sharing intimate thought. Loyalty is of central concern to the 12- to 14-year old girl, presumably because, if innermost secrets are shared, the friend may have 'dangerous knowledge' at her disposal.

Friendships are not only formed through particular types of talk, but are ended through talk as well. As Lever (1976:4) says of 'best friends,' "sharing secrets binds the union together, and 'telling' the secrets to outsiders is symbolic of the 'break-up.'"

Secondly, girls learn to criticize and argue with other girls without seeming overly aggressive, without being perceived as either 'bossy' or 'mean,' terms girls use to evaluate one another's speech and actions. Bossiness, ordering others around, is not legitimate because it denies equality. Goodwin (1980a) points out that girls talked very negatively about the use of commands to equals, seeing it as appropriate only in role play or in unequal relationships such as those with younger siblings. Girls learn to direct things without seeming bossy, or they learn not to direct. While disputes are common, girls learn to phrase their arguments in terms of group needs and situational requirements rather than personal power or desire (Goodwin 1980a). Meanness is used by girls to describe nonlegitimate acts of exclusion, turning on someone, or withholding friendship. Excluding is a frequent occurrence (Eder and Hallinan 1978), but girls learn over time to discourage or even drive away other girls in ways that don't seem to be just personal whim. Cutting someone is justified in terms of the target's failure to meet group norms and a girl often rejects another using speech that is seemingly supportive on the surface. Conflict and criticism are risky in the world of girls because they can both rebound against the critic and can threaten social relationships. Girls learn to hide the source of criticism; they present it as coming from someone else or make it indirectly through a third party (Goodwin 1980a, 1980b).

Finally, girls must learn to decipher the degree of closeness being offered by other girls, to recognize what is being withheld, and to recognize criticism. Girls who don't actually read these cues run the risk of public censure or ridicule (Goodwin 1980). Since the currency of closeness is the exchange of secrets which can be used against a girl, she must learn to read the intent and loyalty of others and to do so continuously, given the system of shifting alliances and indirect expressions of conflict. Girls must become increasingly sophisticated in reading the motives of others, in determining when closeness is real, when conventional, and when false, and to respond appropriately. They must learn who to confide in, what to confide, and who not to approach. Given the indirect expression of conflict, girls must learn to read relationships and situations sensitively. Learning to get things right is a fundamental skill for social success, if not just social survival.

THE WORLD OF BOYS

Boys play in larger, more hierarchically organized groups than do girls. Relative status in this everfluctuating hierarchy is the main thing that boys learn to manipulate in their interactions with their peers. Nondominant boys are rarely excluded from play but are made to feel the inferiority of their status positions in no uncertain terms. And since hierarchies fluctuate over time and over situation, every boy gets his chance to be victimized and must learn to take it. The social world of boys is one of posturing and counterposturing. In this world, speech is used in three major ways: (1) to assert one's position of dominance, (2) to attract and maintain an audience, and (3) to assert oneself when other speakers have the floor.

The use of speech for the expression of dominance is the most straightforward and probably the best-documented sociolinguistic pattern in boys' peer groups. Even ethological studies of human dominance patterns have made extensive use of various speech behaviors as indices of dominance. Richard Savin-Williams (1976), for example, in his study of dominance patterns among boys in a summer camp uses the following speech interactions as measures of dominance: (1) giving of verbal commands or orders, such as "Get up," "Give it to me," or "You go over there"; (2) name calling and other forms of verbal ridicule, such as "You're a dolt"; (3) verbal threats or boasts of authority, such as "If you don't shut up, I'm gonna come over and bust your teeth in"; (4) refusals to obey orders; and (5) winning a verbal argument as in the sequence: "I was here first" / "Tough," or in more elaborate forms of verbal duelling such as the 'dozens.'[2]

The same patterns of verbally asserting one's dominance and challenging the dominance claims of others form the central element in Goodwin's (1980a) observations of boys' play in Philadelphia. What is easy to forget in thinking about this use of words as weapons, however, is that the most successful boy in such interaction is not the one who is most aggressive and uses the most power-wielding forms of speech, but the boy who uses these forms most successfully. The simple use of assertiveness and aggression in boys' play is the sign not of a leader but of a bully. The skillful speaker in a boys' group is considerably more likeable and better liked by his peers than is a simple bully. Social success among boys is based on knowing both how and when to use words to express power as well as knowing when not to use them. A successful leader will use speech to put challengers in their place and to remind followers periodically of their nondominant position, but will not browbeat unnecessarily and will therefore gain the respect rather than the fear of less dominant boys.

A second sociolinguistic aspect of friendly interaction between boys is using words to gain and maintain an audience. Storytelling, joke telling, and other narrative performance events are common features of the social interaction of boys. But actual transcripts of such storytelling events collected by Harvey Sacks (Sacks 1974; Jefferson 1978) and Goodwin (1980a), as opposed to stories told directly to interviewers, reveal a suggestive feature of storytelling activities among boys: audience behavior is not overtly supportive. The storyteller is frequently faced with mockery, challenges and side comments on his story. A major sociolinguistic skill which a boy must apparently learn in interacting with his peers is to ride out this series of challenges, maintain his audience, and successfully get to the end of his story. In Sacks's account (1974) of some teenage boys involved in the telling of a dirty joke, for example, the narrator is challenged for his taste in jokes (an implication that he doesn't know a dirty joke from a nondirty one) and for the potential ambiguity of his opening line "Three brothers married three sisters," not, as Sacks seems to imply, because audience members are really confused, but just to hassle the speaker. Through catches,[3] put-downs, the building of suspense, or other interest-grabbing devices, the speaker learns to control his audience. He also learns to continue when he gets no encouragement whatever, pausing slightly at various points for possible audience response but going on if there is nothing but silence.

A final sociolinguistic skill which boys must learn from interacting with other boys is how to act as audience members in the types of storytelling situations just discussed. As audience member as well as storyteller, a boy must learn to assert himself and his opinions. Boys seem to respond to the storytelling of other boys not so much with questions on deeper implications or with minimal-response encouragement as with side comments and challenges. These are not meant primarily to interrupt, to change topic, or to change the direction of the narrative itself, but to assert the identity of the individual audience member.

WOMEN'S SPEECH

The structures and strategies in women's conversation show a marked continuity with the talk of girls. The key logic suggested by Kalčik's (1975) study of women's rap groups, Hirschman's (1973) study of students and Abrahams's (1975) work on black women is that women's conversation is interactional. In friendly talk, women are negotiating and expressing a relationship, one that should be in the form of support and closeness, but which may also involve criticism and distance. Women orient themselves to the person they are talking to and expect such orientation in return. As interaction, conversation requires participation from those involved and back-and-forth movement between participants. Getting the floor is not seen as particularly problematic; that should come about automatically. What is problematic is getting people engaged and keeping them engaged—maintaining the conversation and the interaction.

This conception of conversation leads to a number of characteristic speech strategies and gives a particular dynamic to women's talk. First, women tend to use personal and inclusive pronouns, such as 'you' and 'we' (Hirschman 1973). Second, women give off and look for signs of engagement such as nods and minimal response (Kalčik 1975; Hirschman 1973). Third, women give more extended signs of interest and attention, such as interjecting comments or questions during a speaker's discourse. These sometimes take the form of interruptions. In fact, both Hirschman (1973) and Kalčik (1975) found that interruptions were extremely common, despite women's concern with politeness and decorum (Kalčik 1975). Kalčik (1975) comments that women often asked permission to speak but were concerned that each speaker be allowed to finish and that all present got a chance to speak. These interruptions were clearly not seen as attempts to grab the floor but as calls for elaboration and development, and were taken as signs of support and interest. Fourth, women at the beginning of their utterances explicitly acknowledge and respond to what has been said by others. Fifth, women attempt to link their utterance to the one preceding it by building on the previous utterance or talking about something parallel or related to it. Kalčik (1975) talks about strategies of tying together, filling in, and serializing as signs of women's desire to create continuity in conversation, and Hirschman (1973) describes elaboration as a key dynamic of women's talk.

While the idiom of much of women's friendly talk is that of support, the elements of criticism, competition, and conflict do occur in it. But as with girls, these tend to take forms that fit the friendship idiom. Abrahams (1975) points out that while 'talking smart' is clearly one way women talk to women as well as to men, between women it tends to take a more playful form, to be more indirect and metaphoric in its phrasing and less prolonged than similar talk between men. Smartness, as he points out, puts distance in a relationship (Abrahams 1975). The target of criticism, whether present or not, is made out to be the one violating group norms and values (Abrahams 1975). Overt competitiveness is also disguised. As Kalčik (1975) points out, some stories that build on preceding ones are attempts to cap the original speaker, but they tend to have a form similar to supportive ones. It is the intent more than the form that differs. Intent is a central element in the concept of 'bitchiness,' one of women's terms for evaluating their talk, and it relates to this contradiction between form and intent, whether putting negative messages in overtly positive forms or acting supportive face to face while not being so elsewhere.

These strategies and the interactional orientation of women's talk give their conversation a particular dynamic. While there is often an unfinished quality to particular utterances (Kalčik 1975), there is a progressive development to the overall conversation. The conversation grows out of the interaction of its partici-

pants, rather than being directed by a single individual or series of individuals. In her very stimulating discussion, Kalčik (1975) argues that this is true as well for many of the narratives women tell in conversation. She shows how narrative "kernels" serve as conversational resources for individual women and the group as a whole. How and if a "kernel story" is developed by the narrator and/or audience on a particular occasion is a function of the conversational context from which it emerges (Kalčik 1975:8), and it takes very different forms at different tellings. Not only is the dynamic of women's conversation one of elaboration and continuity, but the idiom of support can give it a distinctive tone as well. Hannerz (1969:96), for example, contrasts the "tone of relaxed sweetness, sometimes bordering on the saccharine," that characterizes approving talk between women, to the heated argument found among men. Kalčik (1975:6) even goes so far as to suggest that there is an "underlying esthetic or organizing principle" of "harmony" being expressed in women's friendly talk.

MEN'S SPEECH

The speaking patterns of men, and of women for that matter, vary greatly from one North American subculture to another. As Gerry Philipsen (1975:13) summarizes it, "talk is not everywhere valued equally; nor is it anywhere valued equally in all social contexts." There are striking cultural variations between subcultures in whether men consider certain modes of speech appropriate for dealing with women, children, authority figures, or strangers; there are differences in performance rules for storytelling and joke telling; there are differences in the context of men's speech; and there are differences in the rules for distinguishing aggressive joking from true aggression.

But more surprising than these differences are the apparent similarities across subcultures in the patterns of friendly interaction between men and the resemblances between these patterns and those observed for boys. Research reports on the speaking patterns of men among urban blacks (Abrahams 1976; Hannerz 1969), rural Newfoundlanders (Faris 1966; Bauman 1972), and urban blue-collar whites (Philipsen 1975; LeMasters 1975) point again and again to the same three features: storytelling, arguing and verbal posturing.

Narratives such as jokes and stories are highly valued, especially when they are well performed for an audience. In Newfoundland, for example, Faris (1966:242) comments that "the reason 'news' is rarely passed between two men meeting in the road—it is simply not to one's advantage to relay information to such a small audience." Loud and aggressive argument is a second common feature of male–male speech. Such arguments, which may include shouting, wagering, name-calling, and verbal threats (Faris 1966:245), are often, as Hannerz (1969:86) describes them, "debates over minor questions of little direct import to anyone," enjoyed for their own sake and not taken as signs of real conflict. Practical jokes, challenges, put-downs, insults, and other forms of verbal aggression are a third feature of men's speech, accepted as normal among friends. LeMasters (1975:140), for example, describes life in a working-class tavern in the Midwest as follows:

> It seems clear that status at the Oasis is related to the ability to "dish it out" in the rapid-fire exchange called "joshing": you have to have a quick retort, and preferably one that puts you "one up" on your opponent. People who can't compete in the game lose status.

Thus challenges rather than statements of support are a typical way for men to respond to the speech of other men.

WHAT IS HAPPENING IN CROSS-SEX CONVERSATION

What we are suggesting is that women and men have different cultural rules for friendly conversation and that these rules come into conflict when women and men attempt to talk to each other as friends and equals in casual conversation. We can think of at least five areas, in addition to that of minimal responses already discussed, in which men and women probably possess different conversational rules, so that miscommunication is likely to occur in cross-sex interaction.

1. There are two interpretations of the meaning of questions. Women seem to see questions as a part of conversational maintenance, while men seem to view them primarily as requests for information.

2. There are two conventions for beginning an utterance and linking it to the preceding utterance. Women's rules seem to call for an explicit acknowledgment of what has been said and making a connection to it. Men seem to have no such rule and in fact some male strategies call for ignoring the preceding comments.

3. There are different interpretations of displays of verbal aggressiveness. Women seem to interpret overt aggressiveness as personally directed, negative, and disruptive. Men seem to view it as one conventional organizing structure for conversational flow.

4. There are two understandings of topic flow and topic shift. The literature on storytelling in particular seems to indicate that men operate with a system in which topic is fairly narrowly defined and adhered to until finished and in which shifts between topics are abrupt, while women have a system in which topic is developed progressively and shifts gradually. These two systems imply very different rules for and interpretations of side comments, with major potential for miscommunication.

5. There appear to be two different attitudes towards problem sharing and advice giving. Women tend to discuss problems with one another, sharing experiences and offering reassurances. Men, in contrast, tend to hear women, and other men, who present them with problems as making explicit requests for solutions. They respond by giving advice, by acting as experts, lecturing to their audiences.[4]

CONCLUSIONS

Our purpose in this paper has been to present a framework for thinking about and tying together a number of strands in the analysis of differences between male and female conversational styles. We hope to prove the intellectual value of this framework by demonstrating its ability to do two things: to serve as a model both of and for sociolinguistic research.

As a model *of* past research findings, the power of our approach lies in its ability to suggest new explanations of previous findings on cross-sex communication while linking these findings to a wide range of other fields, including the study of language acquisition, of play, of friendship, of storytelling, of cross-cultural miscommunication, and of discourse analysis. Differences in the social interaction patterns of boys and girls appear to be widely known but rarely utilized in examinations of sociolinguistic acquisition or in explanations of observed gender differences in patterns of adult speech. Our proposed framework should serve to link together these and other known facts in new ways.

As a model *for* future research, we hope our framework will be even more promising. It suggests to us a number of potential research problems which remain to be investigated. Sociolinguistic studies of school-age children, especially studies of the use of speech in informal peer interaction, appear to be much rarer than studies of young children, although such studies may be of greater relevance for the understanding of adult patterns, particularly those related to gender. Our framework also suggests the need for many more studies of single-sex conversations among adults, trying to make more explicit some of the differences in conversational rules suggested by present research. Finally, the argument we have been making suggests a number of specific problems that appear to be highly promising lines for future research:

1. A study of the sociolinguistic socialization of 'tomboys' to see how they combine male and female patterns of speech and interaction;

2. An examination of the conversational patterns of lesbians and gay men to see how these relate to the sex-related patterns of the dominant culture;

3. An examination of the conversational patterns of the elderly to see to what extent speech differences persist after power differences have become insignificant;

4. A study of children's cultural concepts for talking about speech and the ways these shape the acquisition of speech styles (for example, how does the concept of 'bossiness' define a form of behavior which little girls must learn to recognize, then censure, and finally avoid?);

5. An examination of 'assertiveness training' programs for women to see whether they are really teaching women the speaking skills that politically skillful men learn in boyhood or are merely teaching women how to act like bossy little girls or bullying little boys and not feel guilty about it.

We conclude this paper by reemphasizing three of the major ways in which we feel that an anthropological perspective on culture and social organization can prove useful for further research on differences between men's and women's speech.

First, an anthropological approach to culture and cultural rules forces us to reexamine the way we interpret what is going on in conversations. The rules for interpreting conversations are, after all, culturally determined. There may be more than one way of understanding what is happening in a particular conversation and we must be careful about the rules we use for interpreting cross-sex conversations, in which the two participants may not fully share their rules of conversational inference.

Second, a concern with the relation between cultural rules and their social contexts leads us to think seriously about differences in different kinds of talk, ways of categorizing interactional situations, and ways in which conversational patterns may function as strategies for dealing with specific aspects of one's social world. Different types of interaction lead to different ways of speaking. The rules for friendly conversation between equals are different from those for service encounters, for flirting, for teaching, or for polite formal interaction. And even within the apparently uniform domain of friendly interaction, we argue that there are systematic differences between men and women in the way friendship is defined and thus in the conversational strategies that result.

Third and finally, our analysis suggests a different way of thinking about the connection between the gender-related behavior of children and that of adults. Most discussions of sex-role socialization have been based on the premise that gender differences are greatest for adults and that these adult differences are learned gradually throughout childhood. Our analysis, on the other hand, would suggest that at leastsome aspects of behavior are most strongly gender-differentiated during childhood and that adult patterns of friendly interaction, for example, involve learning to overcome at least partially some of the gender-specific cultural patterns typical of childhood.

NOTES

1. The analogy between the sociolinguistic processes of dialect divergence and genderlect divergence was pointed out to us by Ron Macaulay.

2. In the strict sense of the term, 'dozens' refers to a culturally specific form of stylized argument through the exchange of insults that has been extensively documented by a variety of students of American black culture and is most frequently practiced by boys in their teens and preteens. Recently folklorist Simon Bronner (1978) has made a convincing case for the existence of a highly similar but independently derived form of insult exchange known as 'ranking,' 'mocks,' or 'cutting' among white American adolescents. What we find striking and worthy of note is the tendency for both black and white versions of the dozens to be practiced primarily by boys.

3. 'Catches' are a form of verbal play in which the main speaker ends up tricking a member of his or her audience into a vulnerable or ridiculous position. In an article on the folklore of black children in South Philadelphia, Roger Abrahams (1963) distinguishes between catches which are purely verbal and tricks in which the second player is forced into a position of being not only verbally but also physically abused as in the following example of a catch which is also a trick:

   A: Adam and Eve and Pinch-Me-Tight
      Went up the hill to spend the night.
      Adam and Eve came down the hill.
      Who was left?
   B: Pinch-Me-Tight
   [A pinches B]

   What is significant about both catches and tricks is that they allow for the expression of playful aggression and that they produce a temporary hierarchical relation between a winner and loser, but invite the loser to attempt to get revenge by responding with a counter-trick.

4. We thank Kitty Julien for first pointing out to us the tendency of male friends to give advice to women who are not necessarily seeking it and Niyi Akinnaso for pointing out that the sex difference among Yoruba speakers in Nigeria in the way people respond verbally to the problems of others is similar to that among English speakers in the U.S.

REFERENCES

Abrahams, R. D. 1975. Negotiating respect: patterns of presentation among black women. In *Women in Folklore*, C. R. Farrat, ed. Austin: University of Texas Press.

Abrahams, R. D. 1976. *Talking Black.* Rowley, Mass.: Newbury House.

Bauman, R. 1972. The La Have Island General Store: Sociability and verbal art in a Nova Scotia community. *Journal of American Folklore* 85:330–43.

Brooks-Gunn, J. and Matthews, W. S. 1979. *He and She: How Children Develop Their Sex-Role Identity.* Englewood Cliffs, NJ: Prentice Hall.

Eder, D. and Hallinan, M. T. 1978. Sex differences in children's friendships. *American Sociological Review* 43:237–50.

Faris, J. C. 1966. The dynamics of verbal exchange: A Newfoundland example. *Anthropologica* (Ottawa) 8(2):235–48.

Fishman, P. M. 1978. Interaction: The work women do. *Social Problems* 25(4):397–406.

Goodwin, M. 1978. Conversational practices in a peer group of urban black children. Doctoral dissertation. University of Pennsylvania, Philadelphia.

Goodwin, M. 1980a. Directive-response speech sequences in girls' and boys' task activities, In *Women and Language in Literature and Society.* S. McConnell-Ginet, R. Borker, and N. Furman, eds. New York: Praeger.

Goodwin, M. 1980b. He-said-she-said: Formal cultural procedures for the construction of a gossip dispute activity. *American Ethnologist* 7(4):674–95.

Gumperz, J. J. 1977. Sociocultural knowledge in conversational inference. In *Linguistics and Anthropology.* M. Saville-Troike, ed. Washington DC: Georgetown University Press (Georgetown University Round Table on Languages and Linguistics, 1977).

Gumperz, J. J. 1978a. The conversational analysis of interethnic communication. In *Interethnic Communication.* E. Lamar Ross, ed. Athens, Ga.: University of Georgia Press.

Gumperz, J. J. 1978b. Dialect and conversational inference in urban communication. *Language in Society* 7(3):393–409.

Gumperz, J. J. 1979. The sociolinguistic basis of speech act theory. In *Speech Act Ten Years After.* J. Boyd and S. Fertara, eds. Milan: Versus.

Gumperz, J. J. 1982. *Discourse Strategies.* Cambridge: Cambridge University Press.

Gumperz, J. J., Agrawal, A., and Aulakh, G. 1977. Prosody, paralinguistics and contextualization in Indian English. Language Behavior Research Laboratory, typescript. University of California, Berkeley.

Gumperz, J. J. and Tannen, D. 1979. Individual and social differences in language use. In *Individual Differences in*

Language Ability and Language Behavior. W. Wang and C. Fillmore, eds. New York: Academic Press.

Hass, A. 1979. The acquisition of genederlect. In Language, Sex and Gender: Does La Différence Make a Difference? J. Orasnu, M. Slater, and L. Adler, eds. *Annals of the New York Academy of Sciences* 327:101–13.

Hannerz, U. 1969. *Soulside,* New York: Columbia University Press.

Harding, S. 1975. Women and words in a Spanish village. In *Towards an Anthropology of Women.* R. Reiter, ed. New York: Monthly Review Press.

Hirshman, L. 1973. Female–male differences in conversational interaction. Paper presented at Linguistic Society of America, San Diego.

Jefferson, G. 1978. Sequential aspects of storytelling in conversation. In *Studies in the Organization of Conversation Interaction.* J. Schenker, ed. New York: Academic Press.

Kalčik, S. 1975. ". . . Like Anne's gynecologist or the time I was almost raped": Personal narratives in women's rap groups. In *Women and Folklore.* C. R. Farrar, ed. Austin: University of Texas Press.

Lakoff, R. 1975. *Language and Women's Place.* New York: Harper and Row.

LeMasters, E. E. 1975. *Blue Collar Aristocrats: Life-Styles at a Working-Class Tavern.* Madison: University of Wisconsin Press.

Lever, J. 1976. Sex differences in the games children play. *Social Problems* 23:478–83.

Lever, J. 1978. Sex differences in the complexity of children's play and games. *American Sociological Review* 43:471–83.

Meditch, A. 1975. The development of sex-specific speech patterns in young children. *Athropological Linguistics* 17:421–33.

Philipsen, G. 1975. Speaking "like a man" in Teamsterville" Cultural patterns of role enactment in an urban neighborhood. *Quarterly Journal of Speech* 61:13–22.

Sacks, H. 1974. An analysis of the course of a joke's telling in conversation. In *Explorations in the Ethnography of Speaking.* R. Bauman and J. Scherzer, eds. Combridge: Cambridge University Press.

Savin-Williams, R. C. 1976. The ethological study of dominance formation and maintenance in a group of human adolescents. *Child Development* 47:972–9.

Soskin, W. F. and John, V. P. 1963. The study of spontaneous talk. In *The Stream of Behavior.* R. G. Barker, ed. New York: Appleton-Century-Croft.

Stodbeck, F. L. and Mann, R. D. 1956. Sex role differentiation in jury deliberations. *Sociometry* 19:3–11.

West, C. 1979. Against our will: male interruptions of females in cross-sex conversation. In Language, Sex and Gender: Does La Différences Make a Difference? J. Oranzanu, M. Slater and L. Adler, eds. *Annals of the New York Academy of Sciences* 327:81–100.

West, C. and Zimmerman, D. H. 1977. Women's place in everyday talk: reflectivos on parent–child interaction. *Social Problems* 24(5):521–9.

Zimmerman, D. H. and West, C. 1975. Sex roles, interruptions, and silences in conversation. In *Language and Sex: Differences and Dominance.* B. Thorne and N. Henley, eds. Rowley, Mass.: Newbury House.

8

Suite for Ebony and Phonics

John R. Rickford

The musical **My Fair Lady** *is the story of a lower-class flower girl, Eliza Doolittle, who is transformed by a linguistics professor, Henry Higgins. The transformation is based on teaching Eliza "proper" patterns of speech, grammar, and presentation of self. Motivated by a simple wager, this human experiment in social and linguistic transformation is a success, at least in the sense that Eliza is able to pass as a lady at a society ball. The experiment also exposes the professor's class-based arrogance and dehumanized attitudes about the poor. The relationship between speech patterns and social class is real and observable, but what is the significance of that connection?*

Linguistic anthropologists often make a distinction between language and speech. Language is a rule-based and patterned system; speech refers to the actual performance— how people talk. The study of sociolinguistics focuses on how speech patterns reflect social realities like social class. Sociolinguists document regional differences in dialects, specialized vocabularies of particular groups, and "code switching" to exclude or include people in a conversation.

This selection concerns linguistic relativity in a multicultural society. In 1996 the Oakland City School District passed a resolution recognizing Ebonics, or black English vernacular (BEV), as the primary language of African American students in this poor urban area. As such, schools officials reasoned, the differences between Standard English and Ebonics needed to be explicitly recognized in the classroom. As you will see in this selection, there was a national uproar in the media against this idea. Ebonics was ridiculed, in part because nonstandard dialects of English are stigmatized in our society. This selection argues that the debate over Ebonics missed the point, which was, just like in **My Fair Lady,** *the significance of the social construction of class differences and the politics of economic opportunity. The connection between this argument and the idea of the social construction of race (Selections 10, 30, 31, and 32) in U.S. society should be clear.*

As you read this selection, ask yourself the following questions:

☐ *What are the five present tenses of black English vernacular?*

☐ *How are differences between Ebonics and Standard English both phonological and grammatical?*

☐ *Do you think it would be easier to learn Standard English for children who regularly speak a dialect at home if the differences between Standard English and the vernacular are made explicit?*

☐ *Who speaks Ebonics? What role might speech play in marking and maintaining ethnic identity or social class?*

☐ *Why did the Oakland schools' decision about Ebonics prompt such a negative public outcry?*

☐ *In a multicultural and multiethnic society, what are the goals of bilingual education programs? What are the best ways to provide educational opportunities to all?*

The following terms discussed in this selection are included in the Glossary at the back of the book:

Afrocentric
creole
dialect
Ebonics
language
linguistic relativity
slang

John R. Rickford /© 1997 Discover Magazine.

To James Baldwin, writing in 1979, it was "this passion, this skill . . . this incredible music." Toni Morrison, two years later, was impressed by its "five present tenses" and felt that "the worst of all possible things that could happen would be to lose that language." What these novelists were talking about was Ebonics, the informal speech of many African Americans, which rocketed to public attention a year ago this month after the Oakland School Board approved a resolution recognizing it as the primary language of African American students.

The reaction of most people across the country—in the media, at holiday gatherings, and on electronic bulletin boards—was overwhelmingly negative. In the flash flood of e-mail on America Online, Ebonics was described as "lazy English," "bastardized English," "poor grammar," and "fractured slang." Oakland's decision to recognize Ebonics and use it to facilitate mastery of Standard English also elicited superlatives of negativity: "ridiculous, ludicrous," "VERY, VERY STUPID," "a terrible mistake."

However, linguists—who study the sounds, words, and grammars of languages and dialects—though less rhapsodic about Ebonics than the novelists, were much more positive than the general public. Last January, at the annual meeting of the Linguistic Society of America, my colleagues and I unanimously approved a resolution describing Ebonics as "systematic and rule-governed like all natural speech varieties." Moreover, we agreed that the Oakland resolution was "linguistically and pedagogically sound."

Why do we linguists see the issue so differently from most other people? A founding principle of our science is that we describe *how* people talk; we don't judge how language should or should not be used. A second principle is that all languages, if they have enough speakers, have dialects—regional or social varieties that develop when people are separated by geographic or social barriers. And a third principle, vital for understanding linguists' reactions to the Ebonics controversy, is that all languages and dialects are systematic and rule-governed. Every human language and dialect that we have studied to date—and we have studied thousands—obeys distinct rules of grammar and pronunciation.

What this means, first of all, is that Ebonics is not slang. Slang refers just to a small set of new and usually short-lived words in the vocabulary of a dialect or language. Although Ebonics certainly has slang words—such as *chillin* ("relaxing") or *homey* ("close friend"), to pick two that have found wide dissemination by the media—its linguistic identity is described by distinctive patterns of pronunciation and grammar.

But is Ebonics a different language from English or a different dialect of English? Linguists tend to sidestep such questions, noting that the answers can depend on historical and political considerations. For instance, spoken Cantonese and Mandarin are mutually unintelligible, but they are usually regarded as "dialects" of Chinese because their speakers use the same writing system and see themselves as part of a common Chinese tradition. By contrast, although Norwegian and Swedish are so similar that their speakers can generally understand each other, they are usually regarded as different languages because their speakers are citizens of different countries. As for Ebonics, most linguists agree that Ebonics is more of a dialect of English than a separate language, because it shares many words and other features with other informal varieties of American English. And its speakers can easily communicate with speakers of other American English dialects.

Yet Ebonics is one of the most distinctive varieties of American English, differing from Standard English—the educated standard—in several ways. Consider, for instance, its verb tenses and aspects. ("Tense" refers to *when* an event occurs, "aspect" to *how* it occurs, whether habitual or ongoing.) When Toni Morrison referred to the "five present tenses" of Ebonics, she probably had usages like these—each one different from Standard English—in mind:

1. He runnin. ("He is running.")

2. He be runnin. ("He is usually running.")

3. He be steady runnin. ("He is usually running in an intensive, sustained manner.")

4. He bin runnin. ("He has been running.")

5. He BIN runnin. ("He has been running for a long time and still is.")

In Standard English, the distinction between habitual or nonhabitual events can be expressed only with adverbs like "usually." Of course, there are also simple present tense forms, such as "he runs," for habitual events, but they do not carry the meaning of an ongoing action, because they lack the "-ing" suffix. Note too that "bin" in example 4 is unstressed while "BIN" in example 5 is stressed. The former can usually be understood by non-Ebonics speakers as equivalent to "has been" with the "has" deleted, but the stressed BIN form can be badly misunderstood. Years ago, I presented the Ebonics sentence "She BIN married" to 25 whites and 25 African Americans from various parts of the United States and asked them if they understood the speaker to be still married or not. While 23 of the African Americans said yes, only 8 of the whites gave the correct answer. (In real life a misunderstanding like this could be disastrous!)

Word pronunciation is another distinctive aspect of dialects, and the regularity of these differences can be very subtle. Most of the "rules" we follow when speaking Standard English are obeyed unconsciously.

Take for instance English plurals. Although grammar books tell us that we add "s" to a word to form a regular English plural, as in "cats" and "dogs," that's true only for writing. In speech, what we actually add in the case of "cat" is an s sound; in the case of "dog" we add z. The difference is that s is voiceless, with the vocal cords spread apart, while z is voiced, with the vocal cords held closely together and noisily vibrating.

Now, how do you know whether to add s or z to form a plural when you're speaking? Easy. If the word ends in a voiceless consonant, like "t," add voiceless s. If the word ends in a voiced consonant, like "g," add voiced z. Since all vowels are voiced, if the word ends in a vowel, like "tree," add z. Because we spell both plural endings with "s," we're not aware that English speakers make this systematic difference every day, and I'll bet your English teacher never told you about voiced and voiceless plurals. But you follow the "rules" for using them anyway, and anyone who doesn't—for instance, someone who says "bookz"—strikes an English speaker as sounding funny.

One reason people might regard Ebonics as "lazy English" is its tendency to omit consonants at the ends of words—especially if they come after another consonant, as in "tes(t)" and "han(d)." But if one were just being lazy or cussed or both, why not also leave out the final consonant in a word like "pant"? This is not permitted in Ebonics; the "rules" of the dialect do not allow the deletion of the second consonant at the end of a word unless both consonants are either voiceless as with "st," or voiced, as with "nd." In the case of "pant," the final "t" is voiceless, but the preceding "n" is voiced, so the consonants are both spoken. In short, the manner in which Ebonics differs from Standard English is highly ordered; it is no more lazy English than Italian is lazy Latin. Only by carefully analyzing each dialect can we appreciate the complex rules that native speakers follow effortlessly and unconsciously in their daily lives.

Who speaks Ebonics? If we made a list of all the ways in which the pronunciation and grammar of Ebonics differ from Standard English, we probably couldn't find anyone who always uses all of them. While its features are found most commonly among African Americans (*Ebonics* is itself derived from "ebony" and "phonics," meaning "black sounds"), not all African Americans speak it. The features of Ebonics, especially the distinctive tenses, are more common among working-class than among middle-class speakers, among adolescents than among the middle-aged, and in informal contexts (a conversation on the street) rather than formal ones (a sermon at church) or writing.

The genesis of Ebonics lies in the distinctive cultural background and relative isolation of African Americans, which originated in the slaveholding South. But contemporary social networks, too, influence who uses Ebonics. For example lawyers and doctors and their families are more likely to have more contact with Standard English speakers—in schools, work, and neighborhoods—than do bluecollar workers and the unemployed. Language can also be used to reinforce a sense of community. Working-class speakers, and adolescents in particular often embrace Ebonics features as markers of African American identity, while middle-class speakers (in public at least) tend to eschew them.

Some Ebonics features are shared with other vernacular varieties of English, especially Southern white dialects, many of which have been influenced by the heavy concentration of African Americans in the South. And a lot of African American slang has "crossed over" to white and other ethnic groups. Expressions like "givin five" ("slapping palms in agreement or congratulation") and "Whassup?" are so widespread in American culture that many people don't realize they originated in the African American community. Older, nonslang words have also originated in imported African words. *Tote,* for example, comes from the Kikongo word for "carry," *tota,* and *hip* comes from the Wolof word *hipi,* to "be aware." However, some of the distinctive verb forms in Ebonics—he run, he be runnin, he BIN runnin—are rarer or nonexistent in white vernaculars.

How did Ebonics arise? The Oakland School Board's proposal alluded to the Niger-Congo roots of Ebonics, but the extent of that contribution is not at all clear. What we do know is that the ancestors of most African Americans came to this country as slaves. They first arrived in Jamestown in 1619, and a steady stream continued to arrive until at least 1808, when the slave trade ended, at least officially. Like the forebears of many other Americans, these waves of African "immigrants" spoke languages other than English. Their languages were from the Niger-Congo language family, especially the West Atlantic, Mande, and Kwa subgroups spoken from Senegal and Gambia to the Cameroons, and the Bantu subgroup spoken farther south. Arriving in an American milieu in which English was dominant, the slaves learned English. But how quickly and completely they did so and with how much influence from their African languages are matters of dispute among linguists.

The Afrocentric view is that most of the distinctive features of Ebonics represent imports from Africa. As West African slaves acquired English, they restructured it according to the patterns of Niger-Congo languages. In this view, Ebonics simplifies consonant clusters at the ends of words and doesn't use linking verbs like "is" and "are"—as in, for example, "he happy"—because these features are generally absent from Niger-Congo languages. Verbal forms like habitual "be" and BIN referring to a remote past, it is argued, crop up in Ebonics because these kinds of tenses occur in Niger-Congo languages.

Most Afrocentrists, however, don't cite a particular West African language source. Languages in the Niger-Congo family vary enormously, and some historically significant Niger-Congo languages don't show these forms. For instance, while Yoruba, a major language for many West Africans sold into slavery, does indeed lack a linking verb like "is" for some adjectival constructions, it has another linking verb for other adjectives. And it has *six* other linking verbs for nonadjectival constructions, where English would use "is" or "are." Moreover, features like dropping final consonants can be found in some vernaculars in England that had little or no West African influence. Although many linguists acknowledge continuing African influences in some Ebonics and American English words, they want more proof of its influence on Ebonics pronunciation and grammar.

A second view, the Eurocentric—or dialectologist—view, is that African slaves learned English from white settlers, and that they did so relatively quickly and successfully, retaining little trace of their African linguistic heritage. Vernacular, or non-Standard features of Ebonics, including omitting final consonants and habitual "be," are seen as imports from dialects spoken by colonial English, Irish, or Scotch-Irish settlers, many of whom were indentured servants. Or they may be features that emerged in the twentieth century, after African Americans became more isolated in urban ghettos. (Use of habitual "be," for example, is more common in urban than in rural areas.) However, as with Afrocentric arguments, we still don't have enough historical details to settle the question. Crucial Ebonics features, such as the absence of linking "is," appear to be rare or nonexistent in these early settler dialects, so they're unlikely to have been the source. Furthermore, although the scenario posited by this view is possible, it seems unlikely. Yes, African American slaves and whites sometimes worked alongside each other in households and fields. And yes the number of African slaves was so low, especially in the early colonial period, that distinctive African American dialects may not have formed. But the assumption that slaves rapidly and successfully acquired the dialects of the whites around them requires a rosier view of their relationship than the historical record and contemporary evidence suggest.

A third view, the creolist view, is that many African slaves, in acquiring English, developed a pidgin language—a simplified fusion of English and African languages—from which Ebonics evolved. Native to none of its speakers, a pidgin is a mixed language, incorporating elements of its users' native languages but with less complex grammar and fewer words than either parent language. A pidgin language emerges to facilitate communication between speakers who do not share a language; it becomes a creole language when it takes root and becomes the primary tongue among its users. This often occurs among the children of pidgin speakers—the vocabulary of the language expands, and the simple grammar is fleshed out. But the creole still remains simpler in some aspects than the original languages. Most creoles, for instance, don't use suffixes to mark tense ("he walk*ed*"), plurals ("boy*s*"), or possession ("John*'s* house").

Creole languages are particularly common on the islands of the Caribbean and the Pacific, where large plantations brought together huge groups of slaves or indentured laborers. The native languages of these workers were radically different from the native tongues of the small groups of European colonizers and settlers, and under such conditions, with minimal access to European speakers, new, restructured varieties like Haitian Creole French and Jamaican Creole English arose. These languages do show African influence, as the Afrocentric theory would predict, but their speakers may have simplified existing patterns in African languages by eliminating more complex alternatives; like the seven linking verbs of Yoruba I mentioned earlier.

Within the United States African Americans speak one well-established English creole, Gullah. It is spoken on the Sea Islands off the coast of South Carolina and Georgia, where African Americans at one time constituted 80 to 90 percent of the local population in places. When I researched one of the South Carolina Sea Islands some years ago, I recorded the following creole sentences. They sound much like Caribbean Creole English today:

1. E. M. run an gone to Suzie house. ("E. M. went running to Suzie's house.")

2. But I does go to see people when they sick. ("But I usually go to see people when they are sick.")

3. De mill bin to Bluffton dem time. ("The mill was in Bluffton in those days.") Note the creole traits: the first sentence lacks the past tense and the possessive form; the second sentence lacks the linking verb "are" and includes the habitual "does"; the last sentence uses unstressed "bin" for past tense and "dem time" to refer to a plural without using an *s*.

What about creole origins for Ebonics? Creole speech might have been introduced to the American colonies through the large numbers of slaves imported from the colonies of Jamaica and Barbados, where creoles were common. In these regions the percentage of

Africans ran from 65 to 90 percent. And some slaves who came directly from Africa may have brought with them pidgins or creoles that developed around West African trading forts. It's also possible that some creole varieties—apart from well-known cases like Gullah—might have developed on American soil.

This would have been less likely in the northern colonies, where blacks were a very small percentage of the population. But blacks were much more concentrated in the South, making up 61 percent of the population in South Carolina and 40 percent overall in the South. Observations by travelers and commentators in the eighteenth and nineteenth centuries record creole-like features in African American speech. Even today, certain features of Ebonics, like the absence of the linking verbs "is" and "are," are widespread in Gullah and Caribbean English creoles but rare or nonexistent in British dialects.

My own view is that the creolist hypothesis incorporates the strengths of the other hypotheses and avoids their weaknesses. But we linguists may never be able to settle that particular issue one way or another. What we can settle on is the unique identity of Ebonics as an English dialect.

So what does all this scholarship have to do with the Oakland School Board's proposal? Some readers might be fuming that it's one thing to identify Ebonics as a dialect and quite another to promote its usage. Don't linguists realize that nonstandard dialects are stigmatized in the larger society, and that Ebonics speakers who cannot shift to Standard English are less likely to do well in school and on the job front? Well, yes. The resolution we put forward last January in fact stated that "there are benefits in acquiring Standard English." But there is experimental evidence both from the United States and Europe that mastering the standard language might be easier if the differences in the student vernacular and Standard English were made explicit rather than entirely ignored.

To give only one example: At Aurora University, outside Chicago, inner-city African American students were taught by an approach that contrasted Standard English and Ebonics features through explicit instruction and drills. After eleven weeks, this group showed a 59 percent reduction in their use of Ebonics features in their Standard English writing. But a control group taught by conventional methods showed an 8.5 percent increase in such features.

This is the technique the Oakland School Board was promoting in its resolution last December. The approach is not new; it is part of the 16-year-old Standard English Proficiency Program, which is being used in some 300 California schools. Since the media uproar over its original proposal, the Oakland School Board has clarified its intent: the point is not to teach Ebonics as a distinct language but to use it as a tool to increase mastery of Standard English among Ebonics speakers. The support of linguists for this approach may strike nonlinguists as unorthodox, but that is where our principles—and the evidence—lead us.

9

Ancient Genes and Modern Health

S. Boyd Eaton and Melvin Konner

The best available evidence about prehistory is that early humans were scavengers and gatherers of wild plants, not mighty hunters. This idea might at first seem far removed from the daily worries of people in complex societies like the United States. What do the food-getting methods of prehistoric people have to do with us and our world?

Two points are relevant here. First, anthropologists believe that food-getting and food-producing systems have been important factors in historical change, as we will see in Selection 14, "The Worst Mistake in the History of the Human Race." Second, a major problem confronting Western society has been the rise in particular chronic illnesses—sometimes called the diseases of civilization—that ultimately kill most Americans. In this article, Boyd Eaton and Melvin Konner demonstrate how information from paleoanthropology and the study of contemporary hunters and gatherers can shed new light on the origins of some present-day health problems.

As you read this selection, ask yourself the following questions:

☐ What is the difference between biological and cultural evolution?

☐ Do biological and cultural evolution advance at the same rate? If not, what sorts of things might happen as cultural changes occur faster than biological changes?

☐ What was the diet of our Paleolithic ancestors?

☐ What sort of nutritional changes accompanied the development of agriculture?

☐ What sort of illnesses are found in the West but not among hunters and gatherers?

☐ In addition to diet, what other lifestyle differences are related to chronic illness in the Western world?

The following terms discussed in this selection are included in the Glossary at the back of the book:

agricultural development
Cro-Magnon
cultural evolution
dental anthropology
epidemiology
foraging
hunter-gatherers
Paleolithic
paleontology
prehistoric

For the past ten years we have been investigating the proposition that the major chronic illnesses which afflict humans living in affluent industrialized Western nations are promoted by a mismatch between our genetic constitution and a variety of lifestyle factors which have bioenvironmental relevance. The diseases include atherosclerosis with its sequels of heart attacks, strokes and peripheral vascular disease; adult-onset diabetes; many important forms of cancer; hypertension (high blood pressure); emphysema; and obesity. The main lifestyle variables are diet, exercise patterns and exposure to abusive substances—chiefly alcohol and tobacco. We have taken the basic position that the genetic constitution of humanity, which controls our physiology, biochemistry and metabolism, has not been altered in any fundamental way since *Homo sapiens sapiens* first became widespread. In contrast, cultural evolution during the relatively brief period since the appearance of agriculture has been breathtakingly rapid, so that genes selected over the preceding geologic eras must now function in a foreign and, in many ways, hostile Atomic Age milieu.

In order to better understand our current lifestyle/genetic discord and to appreciate what steps might be taken to eliminate its harmful etiologic consequences, we needed to determine, as best we could, the actual constituents of our ancestral lifestyle. For most people speculation about our Stone Age ancestors exerts a strong fascination: How did they live, what did they look like, how did they differ from us and how were they similar? For us, the effort to characterize their nutritional practices and the exercise patterns necessitated by their daily activities has been exciting as well as scientifically rewarding. The bulk of our understanding has come from the fields of paleontology, anthropology, epidemiology and nutritional science.

Paleontology is the study of fossil remains. For example, the stature of Paleolithic humans can be estimated from the length of femora (thigh bones) according to a formula which relates total height to femoral length; it is not necessary to have all the bony components of a skeleton to make this determination. Such studies have shown that humans living in the eastern Mediterranean area 30,000 years ago were probably tall; males averaged 177.1 cm (5'9¾") and females 166.5 cm (5'5½"), whereas in 1960 Americans averaged 174.2 cm (5'8½") and 163.4 cm (5'4½") respectively.

Skeletal height and pelvic depth both probably reflect nutritional factors, especially protein intake. With the advent of agriculture, animal protein intake decreased markedly so that average stature for both men and women ultimately declined by over 10 centime-

ters. The same phenomenon, a decrease in the animal protein content of the diet around the time that agriculture first appeared, is also documented by analysis of strontium/calcium ratios in bony remains. Strontium reaches the skeletons of living animals mainly through ingestion of plant foods so that herbivores have higher strontium levels in their bones than do carnivores. Studies of strontium/calcium ratios in the bones of humans who lived just before and during the changeover to agriculture confirm that the consumption of meat declined relative to that of vegetable foods around this period.

Skeletons also indicate muscularity; the prominence of muscular insertion sites and the area of articular surfaces both vary directly with the forces exerted by the muscles acting on them. Analyses of these features show that average preagricultural humans were apparently generally stronger than those who lived thereafter, including us today. Because of their hardness, teeth are very well represented in paleontological material. It is a telling comment about our current consumption of sugar (which approaches 125 lbs per person per year in the United States) that only about two percent of teeth from the Late Paleolithic period exhibit dental caries whereas some recent European populations have had more than 70 percent of their teeth so affected.

Anthropology is a broad discipline which includes the study of recent hunter-gatherers whose lives can be considered to mirror those of our remote ancestors in many ways. Of course, there are important differences: Such people have been increasingly forced from the most environmentally desirable areas into desert, arctic or jungle habitats where the food quest must be far more difficult than it was for Paleolithic hunter-gatherers who exploited the most abundant and fruitful regions then available without competition from encroaching civilization. On the other hand, the technology of recent foragers is more advanced than that available to those living 25,000 years ago; an excellent example is the bow and arrow, perhaps developed no earlier than 10 to 15 thousand years ago. Nevertheless, study of recent hunter-gatherers does provide a kind of window into the Stone Age world; the nutrition, physical attributes and health of individuals who have such parallel lives must be reasonably similar despite the millennia which separate them in time.

Anthropologists have studied over 50 hunter-gatherer societies sufficiently well to justify nutritional generalizations about them. When data from these groups are analyzed statistically, the average values all center around a subsistence pattern of 35 percent meat and 65 percent vegetable foods (by weight). There is, of course, considerable variation; arctic peoples may eat up to 90 percent animal products, whereas arid desert dwellers may obtain only 15 percent of their diet from

"Diet: Paleolithic Genes and Twentieth Century Health," S. Boyd Eaton and Melvin Konner, *Anthroquest* 1985. Reprinted by permission of the L.S.B. Leakey Foundation.

such sources. Nevertheless, these data allow us to reasonably conclude that Paleolithic humans had a roughly similar range of subsistence patterns.

Epidemiology is the study of disease patterns. When a pathologic condition, such as lung cancer, is common in a specified population, for example, cigarette smokers, and uncommon in another specified group, such as nonsmokers, differences between the two groups may bear on the etiology of the disease condition under scrutiny. Information derived from various epidemiologic investigations can be used to help estimate what sorts of diseases might have afflicted Paleolithic humans and which ones must have been uncommon. For example, in today's world, people who consume a minimal amount of saturated fat tend to have little coronary heart disease and a relatively low incidence of cancer involving the breast, uterus, prostate and colon. If we could be confident that the Stone Age diet contained little saturated fat we could rationally assume that individuals living then had a lower incidence of heart disease and cancers related to fat intake than do persons living in affluent, industrialized Western nations today. Similar arguments might be made concerning hypertension (as related to dietary sodium, potassium and calcium) and, of course, lung cancer and emphysema (cigarettes). A tempting assumption is that, since illnesses of this sort tend to become manifest in older persons, Paleolithic humans (whose life expectancy was less than ours) would not have had the opportunity to develop them, no matter what their lifestyle. However, epidemiologists and pathologists have shown that young people in the Western world commonly have developing, asymptomatic forms of these illnesses, but hunter-gatherer youths do not. Furthermore, those members of technologically primitive cultures who survive to the age of 60 or more remain relatively free from these disorders, unlike their "civilized" counterparts.

Nutritional science furthers evaluation of Paleolithic life by providing analyses of the foods such people were likely to have eaten. An understanding of their overall nutrition is impossible without knowing that, although they ate more red meat than we do now, they nevertheless consumed much less saturated fat since wild game has less than a fifth the fat found in the domesticated animals currently bred and raised for meat production. Similarly, nutrition analyses of the wild, uncultivated fruits, vegetables and nuts eaten by recent hunter-gatherers allow us to estimate the average nutritional values of the plant foods our ancestors ate. To this end we have been able to accumulate nutritional data characterizing 43 different wild animals ranging from kangaroos to wart hogs and 153 different wild vegetable foods—mainly roots, beans, nuts, tubers and fruit but including items as diverse as truffles and seed pods. The search for this information has

been challenging but entertaining; how else would one learn that bison meat contains only 40 mg of cholesterol per 100 grams of tissue or that the Australian green plum has the world's highest known vitamin C content (3150 mg per 100 grams)!

When information from these disparate scientific disciplines is correlated and coordinated, what is the picture that emerges? What was the diet of our ancestors; what are other important ways in which their lifestyle differs from ours; and do these differences have any relationship to the chronic illnesses from which we suffer, but from which recent hunter-gatherers seem immune?

To address the most straightforward, but certainly not unimportant, issues first, it is clear that our Stone Age ancestors were rarely if ever exposed to tobacco and alcohol. The manufacture of barley beer can be dated as early as 7000 years ago, but there is no convincing evidence for consumption of alcohol before this time, and recent technologically primitive groups have not been found to manufacture alcoholic beverages. Similarly, there is no indication that tobacco was available in Eurasia prior to the voyages of discovery only 500 years ago. But Late Paleolithic peoples were probably not altogether free from abusive substances; several recent hunter-gatherer groups have used some form of consciousness-altering drugs for ceremonial purposes and it seems likely that similar agents may have been available in the Late Stone Age although their use could hardly have been as prevalent as is currently the case.

The physical demands of life in the Late Paleolithic period insured that our ancestors, both men and women, were strong, fit, lean, and muscular. Their bones prove that they were robust—they resemble those of today's superior athletes. Furthermore, hunter-gatherers studied in the last 150 years have been trim and athletic in their appearance.

Modern nutritionists generally feel that items from four basic food groups—meat and fish, vegetables, nuts and fruits, milk and milk products, and breads and cereals—are necessary for a balanced diet. But during the Paleolithic period older children and adults derived all their nutrients from the first two groups: wild game and vegetables, fruits and nuts. Except for very young children, who were weaned much later than they are today, no one had any dairy foods at all and they apparently made comparatively little use of grain. Their only "refined" carbohydrate was honey, available only seasonally and obtained painfully. They seem to have eaten little seafood until fairly late in prehistory, though this assumption is questionable since the ancient sea level was much lower (because of water locked up in the extensive glaciers of that period), and the sites of Paleolithic seacoast dwellers are now under water.

After weaning, Paleolithic humans drank water, but the beverages we now consume generally deliver an appreciable caloric load as they quench our thirst. Mundane as it is, this example illustrates a pervasive pattern—caloric concentration. Since our meat is fattier, it contains more calories per unit weight (typically two to three times as many) than does wild game. Furthermore, the plant foods we eat are commonly refined and adulterated so that their basic caloric load is multiplied: french fries have more than twice and potato chips over five times the calories present in an equal weight of baked potato. Pumpkin pie has ten times the calories found in the same weight of pumpkin served alone.

The salt added to our foods as a seasoning and as a preservative insures that we now consume an average of six times the daily sodium intake of Paleolithic humans. In a similar vein, the process of refining carbohydrate foods provides us with quantities of sugar and white flour far in excess of what was available to our ancestors while reducing our complex carbohydrate (starch) and dietary fiber intake much below the levels they consumed. Not only do we eat twice the fat eaten by Stone Agers, its nature is different. Structural fat is a necessary constituent of cellular membranous structures; this type of fat is predominantly polyunsaturated in nature and was the major fat consumed by our remote ancestors. Conversely, depot or storage fat is the main type found in the adipose tissue stores of domesticated animals; this variety of fat is largely saturated and is very prominent in today's diets. Like game available now, the wild animals eaten 25,000 years ago had minimal depot fat; accordingly humans then ate considerably more polyunsaturated than saturated fat—but the reverse obtains in 20th century affluent Western nations.

To summarize, these observations indicate that the Cro-Magnons and similar Late Paleolithic peoples consumed nearly three times the amount of protein we do, about a sixth of the sodium, more potassium, more calcium (which is very interesting in view of the prevalence of osteoporosis in today's society), and considerably more vitamin C (though not the amounts megavitamin enthusiasts would recommend). They ate about the same amount of carbohydrate that we do; however, it was predominantly in the form of starch and other complex carbohydrates, providing a good deal more dietary fiber than we have in our diet. For them refined carbohydrate and simple sugar, from honey and fruit, were available only seasonally and in limited amounts. They ate only half the fat we consume in 20th century America and their fat was more polyunsaturated than saturated in nature.

Certain aspects of our ancestors' physical fitness bear further emphasis: Their "exercise program" was lifelong, it developed both endurance and strength, it applied to men and women alike, and the activities which comprised their "workouts" varied predictably with seasonal changes. Today's fitness enthusiasts might well ponder these Paleolithic training guidelines. Preagricultural humans were more like decathlon athletes than either marathoners or power lifters; our genes appear to have been programmed for the synergism which results when endurance and strength occur together. A lifelong program was unavoidable for them; for us it requires strategic planning. Really long-term training in just one exercise mode is almost impossible to maintain; overtraining, boredom and burn-out tend to overcome even the most intense dedication. Paleolithic men and women were spared these phenomena because the activities of each season differed from those of the next. The Russians have perhaps unconsciously recreated these circumstances in a training approach they call "periodization." This system employs planned daily, weekly and quarterly variation in the mode, volume and intensity of exercise so that training remains fresh and invigorating, not dull and endlessly repetitive. Perhaps this recapitulation of our ancestral pattern partially explains the success their athletes have experienced in international competition.

What about the proposition we advanced at the beginning of this article: Do the diseases of civilization result from the mismatch between our genes and our current lifestyle? The evidence is strong that such a connection exists. In important respects the lifestyle of Paleolithic humans, that for which our genes have been selected, parallels recommendations made by the American Cancer Society, the American Heart Association, the American Diabetes Association and the Senate Select Committee on Nutrition. Furthermore, recent hunter-gatherers have been essentially free from the chronic illnesses which kill most Americans.

Anthropology, paleontology, medicine, epidemiology and nutrition can be likened to the facets of a prism, each providing a different view of the same subject. Our subject is the health and disease of persons living in affluent, industrialized Western society and when views provided by diverse scientific disciplines converge, the resulting implications acquire profound significance. There is nothing especially distinctive about human hunter-gatherers in biochemical and physiological terms. What they ate and how they lived fall well within the broad mammalian spectrum. During the past 10,000 years, however, humans have exceeded the bounds. Many of the lifestyle factors we now take for granted (particularly sedentary living, alcohol, tobacco and our high salt, high saturated fat, high refined carbohydrate diet) are unique in free-living vertebrate experience. They constitute a deviation so extreme that our bodies have responded by developing forms of illness not otherwise seen in nature. These are the diseases of civilization.

10

Ancient Bodies, Modern Customs, and Our Health

Elizabeth D. Whitaker

Culture determines the way we have children and how we raise children. The American way of childbirth—with the woman in a hospital, lying on her back with her legs up in stirrups, connected to a fetal monitor and numbed with an epidural anesthetic—is a cultural creation that has developed in recent history. Rarely do we question our cultural traditions, especially when there are experts and expert opinions. People in all cultures take comfort in the fact that they are doing things the "right way," that is, the way things are supposed to be as dictated by tradition. The comfort derived from our traditions is most evident in rituals, like weddings or funerals. But cultural traditions (and dependence on cultural experts) also play a major role in how people go about being parents. In the United States, mothers and fathers try to do the best they can for their children, often unaware how the larger cultural context shapes or limits the possibilities. Children, in turn, get not just their genes but also their ideas, beliefs, and values from their parents, thus perpetuating the culture. But people also have minds of their own, and there are more rational ways to choose one's child-rearing practices than to simply accept the opinions of "experts" and authorities. After all, it is also part of our culture to question authority!

Biological anthropologists believe that evolution has shaped our bodies and therefore strongly influences our health. In this selection, Elizabeth Whitaker reviews evidence from evolutionary medicine about the health implications of infant feeding and sleeping patterns. She demonstrates that American cultural ideas emphasizing the individual have detracted from the fact that mothers and their infants form a biological interacting pair during pregnancy and continuing in infancy. Patterns of breast-feeding in other cultures are undoubtedly linked to health issues such as birth spacing, allergies, and infant diarrhea and dehydration. It is less obvious, however, that the disappearance of evolutionary patterns of breast-feeding are also linked to the increasing incidence of breast cancer in countries like the United States. Finally, there is solid evidence that the cultural pattern of babies sleeping in their own cribs—by themselves, in a separate room, and often placed on their stomachs—is linked to the risk of sudden infant death syndrome.

As you read this selection, ask yourself the following questions:

☐ *What benefits does breast-feeding have for the mother? What benefits does it have for the child?*

☐ *Why do people get fevers? Why do people take medicine to stop fevers?*

☐ *Does the U.S. socioeconomic system shape our patterns of breast-feeding and weaning?*

☐ *Is evolutionary medicine against progress?*

The following terms discussed in this selection are included in the Glossary at the back of the book:

diseases of civilization   *ovulation*
evolutionary medicine   *SIDS*
food foragers

Mothers and infants are physiologically interconnected from conception to the termination of breast-feeding. While this mutual biological relationship is obvious during pregnancy, to many people it is less clear in the period following birth. In Western society, individuals are expected to be autonomous and independent, and this ideal extends to mothers and their babies. Individual autonomy is a core value in our economy, society, and family life: even to our understanding of health and disease. However, it is not a widely shared notion, as more *sociocentric* conceptions of personhood are very common in other cultures and have prevailed in other time periods. Until the Industrial Revolution, Western society also recognized the dependence relationships among individuals and families, and this matched an agrarian social structure involving mutual responsibilities and obligations. Mothers and infants were considered interdependent and there was relatively little cultural intervention in or manipulation of gestation or lactation.

Until a century ago, medical experts followed Aristotle, Hippocrates, and Galen in saying that *not* to breast-feed was to have half a birth, because mother's milk came from the same blood which nourished the fetus. Today, in many cultures around the world, infants are not expected to be independent of their mothers for as long as they breast-feed—that is, for at least the first few years of life. These beliefs reflect an appreciation of the fact that breast-feeding represents a physiological process for both mothers and infants and is more than a simple question of nutrition.

Cultural interventions in the mother–infant relationship are bound to bring significant biological outcomes. Common infant feeding practices in Western societies, such as timed, widely spaced meals, early weaning, pacifier use, and isolated infant sleep with few or no nighttime feedings, are very new and rare in human history, and do not reflect "natural" needs or optimal behaviors, as is commonly presumed. They result in partial or short-term breast-feeding that is very different from the "traditional" or ancient pattern humans have known over evolutionary time. This pattern involves frequent, exclusive, and prolonged breast-feeding, and brings the greatest benefits to mothers and infants. These benefits include reduced risk of breast cancer and the Sudden Infant Death Syndrome (SIDS), diseases which share a common thread in their history: the decline in breast-feeding in the Western industrial societies. By examining them together, we will try to overcome the assumption of individual autonomy, which is so entrenched in Western culture that studies on breast-feeding commonly focus on either the mother or child, but not both.

OLD GENES, NEW LIFESTYLES

Beyond the level of personal experience, breast-feeding concerns both biological processes and cultural interpretation and manipulation. Biocultural anthropology examines such a topic by bringing together cross-cultural comparison and evolutionary considerations. This can mean, for example, comparing human physiology and behavior to those of other primates, such as chimpanzees and gorillas, with whom we share common ancestors and diverge genetically by less than 2%. It also involves looking at different strategies for making a living among human populations. In particular, anthropologists are interested in comparing hunter-gatherers, or foragers, to agricultural or industrial societies. We study modern-day foragers such as the !Kung San of Botswana or the Gainj of Papua New Guinea because their diet, exercise, and health patterns roughly represent those of humans for the vast majority of evolutionary history.

With a few exceptions, our genetic endowment has not changed since the first foraging groups began to practice settled agriculture and animal husbandry between 13,000 and 9,000 years ago (the *Neolithic Revolution*). From the start, the lifestyle change produced notable health consequences. Early agriculturists had shorter stature, greater nutritional stress, and higher infant mortality, especially at the age of weaning. Whereas foragers suffered annual seasonal food shortages, these were less severe than the famines that resulted when crops or livestock were lost. Although famines are rare now, especially in the wealthier countries, constant over-nutrition produces new health problems. At the same time, the diet in many impoverished countries remains scanter and less varied than the foraging diet.

In contrast to what we think of as proper nutrition, foragers subsist on a low-calorie diet made up exclusively of wild plant parts (roots, seeds, stalks. leaves, nuts, fruits) and game or fish. There are no dairy products (except mother's milk) or processed grains in their diet. Most of the food comes from plants, while meat is a less reliable but highly valued supply of concentrated protein, fat (though only one-seventh the amount in the meat of domesticated animals), and vitamins and minerals.

Foragers collect these foods over distances of 10 or more kilometers per day, often carried out in a pattern of one or two days of work for six to eight hours and one or two days of other activities. This averages out to more than 6½ kilometers per day. Women routinely carry up to 15 kilograms (almost 35 pounds) of food, a bundle which can reach half their body weight. They also carry children up to three or four years of age, adding up to another 15 kilograms. In addition to this physical activity, foragers move camp several times each year. Because they work outdoors and do not have climate control indoors, they are constantly exposed to the elements.

Unlike people in affluent societies, foragers do not experience any "natural" rise in blood pressure with age. They do not undergo hearing loss or overweight as inevitable consequences of aging, nor does their body mass increase. They are not free of disorders including accidents and injuries, degenerative bone disease, complications of childbirth, and infectious disease, but the major health problems of the Western societies are very rare. These "diseases of civilization" or "chronic diseases" include heart disease, hypertension, strokes, and cancer, as well as emphysema, cirrhosis, diabetes, and obesity and overweight.

While we all share a genetic propensity for the chronic diseases, it is our lifestyle and environment which cause their wide expression today. Our biological characteristics are those of Stone Age humans practicing a hardy foraging lifestyle, making our bodies adept at storing fat against the likelihood of periodic food shortage. This helps to explain why overweight and obesity are so common wherever physical activity and exposure to the elements are minimal while food supplies are plentiful and steady.

Similarly, the perspective of evolutionary medicine helps us to understand cancer as the cost of the beneficial biological adaptation of tissue repair and regeneration through cell division. In all living things, the body's various ways of regulating and suppressing cell division become less effective in older age. However, over the past centuries, cancer rates have risen way beyond those which would result simply from the increase in the proportion of individuals living into old age. Beyond exposure to carcinogenic and viral agents, this can be explained in terms of changes in diet and lifestyle away from the foraging pattern. Our diet is scarce in protective micro-nutrients such as beta-carotene and selenium, but abundant in macro-nutrients such as fat, protein, and calories which, in themselves and in relation to body composition and size, promote cancer.

Compared to the chronic diseases, we have been adapting to infectious organisms for ages, and vice versa. In many cases, fever is an adaptive defense against infection. It raises the body's temperature and speeds up its metabolic processes, helping to eliminate viruses and bacteria. When ectothermic ("cold-blooded") animals are injected with virus, they seek out a hotter place, and are more likely to die from the infection if prevented from doing so. Recent studies have found that people who take antipyretics (drugs such as aspirin or acetaminophen which suppress fever) are infectious longer and take longer to recover from colds, flu, and chicken pox.

Fever also promotes the sequestration of iron which takes place as a defense against many kinds of infection. The iron is bound more tightly to protein and hidden in the liver, reducing the amount that circulates in the blood. The resulting anemia is typically treated with iron supplements, but iron is a necessary mineral to many bacteria and their need for it is increased by fever. This pair of evolved defensive systems—increased heat and decreased iron—is therefore blocked by human interventions such as iron supplements and antipyretics. On the other hand, some pathogens actually reproduce better or become more toxic in the presence of fever and reduced iron, which would be expected since their rapid reproductive rates and short lives give them an evolutionary advantage. What this suggests is that an evolutionary perspective is needed to better target and treat symptoms appropriately, just as it contributes to our analysis of lactation and the health outcomes of variations in its practice.

MOTHERS AND INFANTS

When breast-feeding patterns are compared across mammals (from *mamma,* Latin for "breast"), non-human primates, and humans, "on-demand" or baby-fed feeding emerges as the evolutionary norm for our species. Many aspects of the ancestral pattern are shared by non-Western societies today and were common in Western populations until a few generations ago. A relationship of interdependence and mutuality is expressed in parent–infant co-sleeping and exclusive, unrestricted breast-feeding well beyond the first year.

The ancestral pattern involves frequent feedings (from several times an hour to once every hour or two) all day and night with no limit on their duration; no supplementary foods before six months and low to moderate use of pre-chewed foods or very ripe fruits thereafter; and complete weaning at 2½ to 4 years, when the child is able to walk long distances on its own. Mother's milk remains the principal food until 15 to 18 months, after which it continues to be a significant source of nutrition. When these conditions prevail, infants are more likely to survive, pregnancy is prevented for 2 to 3 years or more, and births are spaced 3 to 5 years apart. In all but one family of primates, lactation implies *anovulation* (lack of ovulation). In our closest relatives, births are spaced as far as 5 (in chimpanzees) to 8 (in orangutans) years apart.

In foraging societies such as the !Kung, the mother carries her child in a sling against her body, providing constant physical contact and access to the breast. Infants hardly ever cry, and are not expected to cry. Their signs of distress bring an immediate response from their mother or another relative, but never with any kind of pacifier other than the breast. Infants are constantly cuddled and kissed all over the body, including the genitals. Parents are bewildered to hear that Western infants cry and are left alone in a crib, swaddled perhaps, to do so for long periods without being held or allowed to suckle. They do not share the idea that infants and children need to be denied what they want or they will grow up spoiled or dependent. Indeed, the opposition between independence and dependence has relatively little meaning in these societies.

Milk production and release are regulated by pituitary hormones secreted in response to nipple stimulation, the emptying of the breast, and psychological factors. Prolactin is released in response to suckling, stimulating the synthesis of milk in the lacteal cells within a couple of hours. Oxytocin is also released in response to nipple stimulation, and immediately causes the cells around the milk-producing bulbs and ducts to contract and secrete milk. This pathway can be affected by psychological factors in positive and negative ways. A thought, emotion, or sound or sight of an infant can cause the release of oxytocin. Contrariwise, fear and other stressful emotions lead to the secretion of epinephrine, which impedes the circulation of oxytocin to breast tissue by constricting the blood vessels around it.

After the surge following nipple stimulation, prolactin levels drop off quickly, reaching baseline levels within two hours. Consequently, to maintain continuous milk production it is necessary to breast-feed at short intervals and keep prolactin levels high. Especially in the early months, more frequent feedings result in greater milk production. Milk that is not secreted but left in the breast has an independent dampening effect on production through both a substance in the milk and the mechanical pressure it exerts on the surrounding cells. This kind of control over milk production seems to apply in a preponderant way after the first two or three months, against a diminishing but still important background of hormonal regulation. Moreover, more frequent feedings and complete removal of milk lead to higher average fat and calorie content. Infants fed without restrictions are able to vary feed frequencies and the degree of breast-emptying and thereby regulate their nutrition very closely. They tend to be satiated and satisfied after feedings.

High prolactin levels inhibit ovulation, so that infrequent feedings and reduced time at the breast lead to less effective suppression of fertility. In addition, other hormones involved in the menstrual cycle are affected by frequent breast-feeding, interfering with normal follicle growth, ovulation (should a egg mature), development of the endometrium, and implantation of a fertilized ovum. As women space feedings at wider intervals, introduce supplementary foods, and reduce nighttime feeding, the contraceptive effect of breast-feeding weakens and ovulation and menstruation resume.

The composition of human milk also indicates that it is made to be given frequently. Unlike other mammals such as rabbits or tree shrews, who keep their young in nests and leave them all day or even longer, primates carry their babies and thereby provide them with transportation and temperature regulation, for which their milk is less fatty. Primate infants are born less mature and grow more slowly, explaining why protein is relatively scarce in the milk. Continuous breast-feeding and physical contact also protect the infant from predators, as well as illness. Contact with others is reduced, while exposure to the same diseases leads to the production of immunological substances which are then transmitted in the mother's milk.

In recent years, there has been wide publication of the wonderful properties of breast-milk, from nutritional components to immunological factors, sedative substances to anti-allergenic properties. These benefits make breast-fed infants better able to resist and overcome infections, including those of the gastrointestinal and respiratory tract (which includes the middle ear). Breast-feeding promotes optimal growth and development of the body's systems, such as the cardiovascular, immune, nervous, and gastrointestinal systems. It also protects breast-fed infants from protein malnutrition, even in areas of the world in which it is common. This is because the quality of milk is remarkably constant across mothers, regardless of their diet or nutritional status.

The uniform quality of mother's milk, even in conditions of stress, brings up two points. It implies that we should focus upon infant demand and suckling behavior when there are problems in breast-feeding, but the tendency is instead to search for maternal causes. Secondly, by focusing on the benefits of breast-feeding in terms of the useful properties of the milk, we may fail to acknowledge the impacts of breast-feeding on the mother. Mothers who are overworked and poorly nourished may become depleted, their lives shortened by repeated cycles of gestation and lactation.

On the other hand, assuming good conditions breast-feeding has many positive effects on mothers. It helps the uterus to return to its normal size and shape after childbirth, hastens weight loss and moderates digestion, metabolism, blood circulation, and sensations of well-being. It favors bone consolidation, preventing osteoporosis and hip and other fractures in later life, and reduces the risk of women's reproductive cancers. In order to appreciate these benefits, we must go beyond looking at breast-milk as a mere product manufactured for the advantage of the child.

Whereas in foraging and agricultural societies mothers and their fetuses or infants are considered inseparable, even when physically divided after childbirth, in Western society they are considered independent even during gestation. In evolutionary biology, this is an appropriate concept since the interests of the child and the mother may conflict: for example, the fetus of humans and all placental animals taps into the mother's blood circulation, injecting fetal hormones into it and drawing nutrients from the mother's organs if they are not available through her diet. Yet, the biological concept of individuality simultaneously presumes physiological interdependence. The cultural concept of the autonomous individual denies it. After childbirth, the separation between mother and child is complete, and the physiological interrelationship in breast-feeding is obscured by a focus on the infant's nutritional and psychological independence. This has notable health outcomes for both mothers and infants, some of which we will now examine in light of an evolutionary perspective.

BREAST CANCER

Until the 19th century, European medical philosophers observed that well-off women who lived in cities were much more susceptible to breast cancer than women who lived in the countryside. They attributed this difference to the abandonment of breast-feeding, which, they noted, caused numerous other maladies and grave health effects. Even today, not only is breast cancer more common in affluent societies, but within them it is more frequent among the wealthier classes.

The decline in breast-feeding has been part of a broad change in reproductive and child-rearing patterns since the Industrial Revolution. Urban women were the first to undergo the *secular trend* of earlier maturation and greater achieved stature. They experienced earlier puberty, delayed marriage and first birth, fewer pregnancies, and reduced or forsaken breast-feeding. Over time, these patterns diffused through the entire population.

Many of the things we consider "natural" are therefore more like aberrations or deviations from what evolution has produced. To illustrate, a typical woman of a foraging or pre-industrial society reaches puberty and her first menstrual period (*menarche*) at the age of 16 to 18. She becomes pregnant within three or four years, breast-feeds for three or four years, and has a subsequent child four or five years after the first. This sequence repeats itself between four and six times before she reaches menopause at around the age of 45. As a result, she has about 150 ovulations in her lifetime, taking account of non-ovulatory cycles at the near and far end of her reproductive years. Periodic nutritional and exercise stress reduce the number of ovulations even more. Because only half of her children survive long enough to reproduce, population grows very slowly, as was the case until historical times. Lactation has represented humankind's main method of birth control for most of our existence.

In contrast, Western women enjoy a stable food supply, including foods concentrated in fat, protein, and calories, and experience very little stress from exercise and exposure. Over the past centuries, this has caused them, and men, to reach higher stature and lower age at puberty. Girls arrive at menarche at the age of 12 or 13, while menopause is delayed to 50 or 55 years. Significantly, the first birth is postponed for 13 or 14 years, to the age of 25 or 26, and the average number of births is reduced to two or three. The average Western woman breast-feeds for a few months, if at all. Because she spaces feedings at long intervals and supplements with other foods, breast-feeding does not inhibit ovulation for long. As a result, population growth was very rapid in Europe for several centuries (and in many developing countries today) not only because mortality rates were falling but also because women did not have a long interval of infertility associated with lactation.

If she does not take oral contraceptives, the average woman will ovulate around 450 times over her lifetime. Ovulation will rarely be suppressed due to physiological constraints associated with nutritional or exercise stress. This amounts to three or four times as many ovulations over the life-span, and some scholars have suggested that the proportion may be as high as nine times.

The differences in reproductive patterns between women in foraging as opposed to affluent societies match some of the currently known risk factors for women's reproductive cancers (breast, endometrium, ovary), including age at menarche and menopause, *parity* (number of births), and breast-feeding. Differences in diet and physical activity, as well as body composition, also agree with identified non-reproductive risk factors such as fat intake and percent body fat. Together with other factors, they give Western women, especially below the age of 60, at least 20 times the risk of reproductive cancer. The risk for breast cancer may be more than 100 times higher. In nonhuman primates, these cancers are extremely rare.

For all three cancers, earlier age at menarche and later age at menopause increase risk, while greater parity reduces risk. Like these factors, breast-feeding is protective against ovarian cancer because it inhibits ovulation. This reduces the monthly mechanical injury to the ovarian epithelium and the release of hormones by the follicle, which are considered the main elements in the etiology of ovarian cancer. For breast cancer, lactation and earlier first birth are also protective factors.

The breast's susceptibility to carcinogenesis is directly related to the rate of epithelial cell proliferation. Consequently, the lengthening of the period between menarche and first birth widens the window of time in which undifferentiated structures destined to become secretory glands are vulnerable to carcinogenic agents and therefore the initiation of tumors. In breast tissue, cell proliferation is promoted by exposure to estrogen, apparently in concert with progesterone, and cell division rates are highest during the first five years after menarche. With pregnancy and lactation, these structures differentiate and develop, devoting themselves less ardently to cell proliferation. Their cell cycle is longer, and they are more resistant to chemical carcinogens. Subsequent pregnancies may also be protective because they increase the proportion of fully differentiated secretory lobules, until in advanced age pregnancy increases risk by favoring the expansion of initiated tumors.

While the age at first pregnancy seems to be of primary importance and may even modulate the protective effect of breast-feeding and later pregnancies, breast-feeding in itself provides protection against breast cancer in step with the number of children breast-fed and the cumulative duration of breast-feeding. The reason some studies have found no effect or a weak one is that they were based upon the experiences of Western women, who do not generally conform to the ancient pattern of breast-feeding at close intervals for at least a year. Short periods of breast-feeding may in fact provide very little protection.

At the level of the breast fluid, there are lower levels of a potential carcinogen, cholesterol-epoxide, as well as cholesterol, in breast-feeding women, a reduction that persists for two years after childbirth or lactation. Estrogen levels are also lower, protecting the breast tissue directly as opposed to systemically through variations in blood estrogen levels. Breast-feeding also affects the turnover rate of substances in the breast fluid, so that prolonged breast-feeding reduces exposure of the breast epithelial tissue to potential exogenous carcinogens.

Exercise, high consumption of dietary fiber, and low fat consumption and percent body fat are all protective against breast and other cancers. High dietary levels of fat and protein (especially from animal sources) and total calories are associated with higher levels of breast cancer across populations and within subpopulations of single countries. Animal studies have shown that dietary protein promotes tumor development while restriction of protein intake inhibits tumor growth. The enzymes in adipose tissue convert precursor adrenal hormones into active estrogens. Dietary fat raises serum estrogen levels and promotes tumor development and may also play a role in originating tumors. In contrast to Western women, women in foraging societies have low serum estrogen levels.

Western women's skinfold thickness (a measure of the proportion of body fat) is almost twice that of pre-agricultural women. Compared to college athletes, women who are not athletic in college (and less active in adolescence and somewhat less active after college) have two to five times the rates of breast, uterine, and ovarian cancer. Women in affluent societies consume 40% or more of their calories in the form of fat, against 20 to 25% among pre-agricultural women, but only 20 as opposed to 100 grams of fiber per day. Dietary fiber is protective because it reduces free estrogen levels in the blood. It helps to prevent bowel dysfunction, which has been associated with breast cancer, and the severe constipation which can lead to the migration of mutagenic substances from the gastrointestinal tract to the breast fluid.

The protective effect of breast-feeding goes beyond the current generation to the next one, for early nutritional influences seem to have an important effect on later susceptibility to cancer. Breast-feeding contributes to the development and regulation of the immune system, which plays a central role in suppressing the initiation and growth of tumors. It prevents over-consumption of fat, protein, and calories. This influences body size and composition, the baseline against which nutrition works throughout life. That is, breast-feeding prevents the accelerated growth of muscles and fat stores associated with breast cancer risk factors: faster growth rates, earlier menarche, and greater achieved stature and size. Women who have been breast-fed themselves are less likely to develop breast cancer.

We have seen that breast-feeding benefits both the mother and child with respect to prevention of breast cancer. In the mother, breast-feeding according to the ancient pattern influences systemic hormone levels and the micro-environment of the breast tissue, reducing exposure to exogenous and endogenous carcinogens. In the child, breast-milk provides an appropriate balance of nutrients that prevents over-nutrition, rapid growth, and early maturation. This circular interaction of factors expresses and can be predicted by the concept of the mother–infant dyad as a biological interacting pair.

SUDDEN INFANT DEATH SYNDROME

From a global perspective, Western society's expectation that infants should sleep alone for long hours away from their parents stands out as anomalous, even if it fits well in its cultural context. One unfortunate consequence is that the diffusion of lone infant sleep over the past several generations may be related to the rise in the frequency of infant death from the Sudden Infant Death Syndrome (SIDS).

The meaning of reproduction and child-rearing changed with the emergence of industrial society and its predominance of small, simple families (couples plus children). In this kind of society, the crib symbolizes the child's place and is usually placed in a separate room. By contrast, in rural pre-industrial Europe and in a survey of over 90 contemporary non-Western societies, infants invariably slept in the same bed or room as their parents. SIDS does not appear to exist in these societies, nor is it found among non-human primates or other mammals. In many Western societies, SIDS is the major cause of infant death, though rates are very low among sub-populations in which there is co-sleeping and nocturnal breast-feeding. Peak mortality is between the ages of two and four months, with 90% of all deaths occurring before the age of six months.

While there seem to be many intrinsic and secondary factors that affect infants in different ways to bring about SIDS events, one common factor is that SIDS usually happens during sleep. While breast-feeding in itself reduces risk, it is the frequent, intensive, prolonged breast-feeding implying mother–infant co-sleeping that may provide the best environment for avoiding the disease.

Co-sleeping infants lay on their backs or sides with their heads turned toward the breast and feed through the night, often without waking their mothers. Even newborns and very young infants are able to attach to the breast on their own, provided it is within reach. In non-industrialized societies, it is rare for infants younger than one year to sleep long hours with only a few arousals or feedings. They do not increase the length of their longest sleep episode within the first few months, nor do they stop feeding at night, as parents in Western societies expect.

These same patterns are observed in sleep laboratories, where mothers report waking up and feeding their child many times fewer than the number recorded on the monitors. They and their infants move through the various stages of sleep in synchrony, shifting between them more frequently and spending less time in the deep sleep which makes arousal more difficult. If in the laboratory the breast-feeding mother spends the night in a separate room from her child, on average she breast-feeds less than half as often. She also tends to put the child on its stomach when leaving it to sleep alone. Notably, breast-feeding mothers who routinely sleep in a separate room from their infants actually sleep for a shorter amount of time during the night, even though they feed their infants less often and for a shorter overall time period than mothers who co-sleep.

One factor common to a majority of cases is that the infant had been placed on its stomach to sleep: the opposite of the position used by infants who sleep with their mothers and breast-feed throughout the night. This may be due to suffocation because the child is unable to move out of pockets of its own carbon dioxide in puffy mattresses or bean bag cushions. It also may be the result of developmental changes related to a shift in the position of the larynx (windpipe) which takes place at four to six months.

At birth, the larynx is in contact with the back of the palate, allowing air inhaled by the nostrils to go by its own route to the lungs. It then begins to descend in the throat to a position below the back of the tongue, so that the two openings leading to the lungs and stomach lie side by side (which is why food sometimes "goes down the wrong tube"). During this shift, problems can occur if breathing through the nose (which infants greatly prefer) is impeded by a cold or other factor. Breathing through the mouth can be blocked by the uvula (the fleshy structure hanging over the back of the tongue) if it enters the descending larynx, especially if the child is lying at the wrong angle. Huge reductions in SIDS rates have taken place over the past decade in many European countries and the United Kingdom since the initiation of campaigns against the face-down position, and the U.S. is also beginning to show rapid improvement in SIDS rates.

There is more to the story than sleep position which itself inculpates the crib since co-sleeping is associated with the safer position. More directly, the crib implies isolated, prolonged, deep sleep. Like adults, infants are able to fall into deep sleep, but they are less equipped to arouse themselves out of it. All people have temporary lapses in breathing during the night, but their brains generally respond to them appropriately. Infants are different, for they are born at a much earlier stage of neurological development than other primates, even our closest relatives.

During sleep, infants may need frequent arousals to allow them to emerge from episodes of apnea or cardiorespiratory crisis. External stimuli and parental monitoring from co-sleeping and breast-feeding give them practice at doing so, and keep them from spending long periods of time in deep stages of sleep. SIDS deaths peak at the same age at which the amount of deep sleep relative to REM sleep increases dramatically, at two to three months. Moreover, at this time infants begin to exercise more voluntary control of breathing, as parents notice in their more expressive cries. This is a step toward the speech breathing they will use later, but may complicate breathing in the short term.

The rhythm of sound and silence in the mother's breathing gives the infant auditory stimulation, while contact with her body provides tactile stimulation. The carbon dioxide which her breathing releases into the air they share induces the infant to breathe. Frequent waking for breast-feeding is a behavior common to primates and prevents hypoglycemia, which has been implicated in some SIDS deaths. Human milk also provides immunological protection against several infectious organisms (and preparations of them given as immunizations) considered responsible for some deaths. This protection is especially needed after two months, when inherited maternal antibodies become scarce but the infant's own immune system is not yet developed. Breast-feeding and constant physical contact prevent overheating and the exhausting crying spells which seem to be factors in the disease. In addition, the infant is sensitive to other aspects of its micro-environment, including temperature, humidity, and odors.

While many experts and parents advise against or avoid co-sleeping because they fear suffocating the infant, in fact this risk is very low, especially where people sleep on hard bedding or the floor. Modern bedding is dangerous because of the conformation of bed frames and the use of soft mattresses and heavy coverings. Yet, these factors are at least as relevant to cribs as parents' beds. On the other hand, some parents should not sleep with their infants, such as those who go to bed affected by drugs or alcohol. Cigarette smoke in the sleeping room could cancel the benefit of co-sleeping.

While isolated infant sleep may be consistent with parents' desires and the primacy of the conjugal bond and other Western values, it is a new behavioral norm in human history and does not represent a "natural" need. It is neither in the infant's best interest nor in conformity with behavioral patterns and biological conditions established long before our time. By contrast, parent–infant co-sleeping matches evolutionary considerations such as the need for temperature regulation, frequent nutrition, and protection from predators and disease. There may be some wisdom to the popular term, "crib death," or "cot death," for it points to the crib and the Western concept of infant independence as major factors in the disease.

SOCIAL AND CULTURAL INTERVENTION

We have seen that mothers and infants are physiologically bound together from conception to weaning, not just conception to birth. The Western ideal of the autonomous individual, even the neonate, is not shared by other societies today or by those of the past. The biocultural model shows that evolution has favored frequent, exclusive, and prolonged breast-feeding in humans. This entails constant physical contact, parent–infant co-sleeping, and nighttime breast-feeding. It leads to postpartum infertility and protects against SIDS and breast and other reproductive system cancers. Breast-feeding therefore has significant health outcomes, beyond the usual benefits of breast-milk which have been popularized in recent years.

Unfortunately, the health benefits of breast-feeding, especially for mothers, are generally overshadowed by assertions regarding the supposed convenience of bottle feeding and the nutritional adequacy of artificial milk. Even the promotion of breast-feeding on the basis of the milk's value to infants does not always induce women to breast-feed, since there is little if any mention of a benefit to them. To the contrary, there are many disincentives to breast-feeding, such as beliefs that it causes the breasts to sag and makes it difficult to lose weight, or that it makes the husband feel jealous and left out. The lack of familiarity with breast-feeding which has resulted from a couple of generations of preference for the bottle also discourages it. Many people have never seen a woman breast-feed, and would prefer not to.

The degree to which our culture has come to favor intervention in the fundamental relationship between nurslings and mothers is evident in the nearly-universal use of pacifiers. This has been promoted by the notion, sanctioned by professional medicine, that infants need to suckle, and better a scientifically designed object than the thumb or finger (the nipple is not even among the choices). However, in evolutionary perspective, a pacifier is completely unnecessary since infants who are breast-fed according to the ancient pattern are allowed to suckle to their heart's content. Not surprisingly, pacifier use has been found to reduce the duration of breast-feeding.

The birthing process is focused upon the infant, while the mother is considered and often treated as an impediment to the physician's efforts to extract the child. Afterward, the medical care of the two is split between obstetricians and pediatricians, reflecting the conceptual splitting of the mother–infant relationship at birth. There is little or no breast-feeding (in the United States, only one half of all infants begin life feeding at the breast). Weaning takes place within a few months and almost always within the first year, and the mother resumes her menstrual cycle within a few months. Mothers are strongly encouraged to put their children on feeding schedules and eliminate nighttime feeding as quickly as possible, and to teach them to get to sleep and stay asleep on their own, in their own bed and room. Instead of being carried and cuddled throughout the day and night, infants are left in cribs, strollers, and playpens and are touched relatively rarely. They are expected to cry and left to do so, sometimes for hours. Often, the door to their room is closed at nap time and during the night.

On a social-structural level, cultural interference in breast-feeding seems to be more common in societies which are based upon vertical inheritance and the simple family structure, than societies in which families are wide and inheritance is lateral. In the former, the institution of marriage is emphasized over kin relationships. Women's sexual and conjugal duties take precedence over their role as kinswomen and mothers, while children are considered heirs rather than links in a kinship network. These conditions can make breast-feeding seem to interfere with sexuality, and pit the husband against the child in competition over the woman's sexualized breast.

Notably, our culture describes breasts as "secondary *sexual* characteristics," highlighting a tendency to regard them as objects of display rather than functional organs. In medieval to modern Europe, the postpartum taboo against sex during lactation was circumvented among the elite classes by wet-nursing, so that women could be available to their husbands instead of breast-feeding. This was subsequently replaced by formula feeding and practiced by a much wider segment of the population.

The rise of the modern nation-state over the past two centuries meanwhile has brought an expansion of the authority of medical experts. Beginning with early industrialization, the state and its emerging medical system sought to shape public morality and oppose traditional authority by reaching into the private, intimate world of the family. As a result, reproduction and child-rearing became medicalized well before professional medicine had much legitimate knowledge or expertise in these areas. As multiple families broke up due to socioeconomic changes, families became more dependent upon outside experts in areas which had previously been handled by older relatives or other authorities such as midwives and clerics.

By now, it is rare for anyone to question the authority of the medical community in questions such as birth control or infant feeding. This phenomenon has emerged hand-in-hand with the notion of the autonomous individual. By considering fetuses and infants as beings independent of their mothers, Western society has allowed and welcomed experts into the life of the dyad and granted them predominant authority in decisions regarding the care and upbringing of the young. Mothers are not encouraged to think of themselves as competent or knowledgeable enough to breast-feed without expert intervention and surveillance. This is reinforced by the regimen of ever-more numerous obstetric and pediatric examinations before and after childbirth, and the literature directed at mothers by the medical and pharmaceutical communities.

In contrast to agricultural and foraging societies, in ours breast-feeding does not easily fit into women's work or social lives. Few professions allow women much flexibility in time scheduling, and there is a deep, underlying expectation that the new mother will immediately be independent from her child. Many working women are forced to pump their milk in bathrooms, often in secrecy. Women who do not work outside the home are targeted by formula manufacturers, who capitalize on cultural values such as work and efficiency by suggesting that formula feeding with an increasingly complex array of products demonstrates a woman's capability in scientific mothering.

Firms that sell formula, pacifiers, and other infant care products distribute samples and coupons through hospitals and physicians' offices, lending their products a medical stamp of approval that appeals to many parents. Often, they are able to "hook" babies even before they leave the hospital because the staff supplements the mother's milk with formula or sugar water, and the infant comes to prefer the easier flow of the bottle.

Thus, even when breast-feeding is promoted and women feel committed to it, social and cultural obstacles can make it difficult. A biocultural understanding of breast-feeding as an evolved, two-way process could help to make conditions more favorable. It would highlight the fact that women are normally able to breast-feed without medical approval, surveillance, and intervention and reduce the public's receptiveness to industrially produced formula and baby foods. Most importantly, the biocultural perspective would foster an appreciation of the intricate mechanisms linking mothers and infants together in a dynamic system of nutrition that benefits them both.

SUGGESTED READING

Cohen, Mark Nathan. 1989. *Health and the Rise of Civilization.* New Haven: Yale University Press.

Daly, S. E. J., and P. E. Hartmann. 1995. Infant Demand and Milk Supply. *Journal of Human Lactation* 11(1):21–37.

Dettwyler, Katherine. 1995. A Time to Wean. In Patricia Stuart-Macadam and Katherine Dettwyler (eds.) *Breast-feeding. Biocultural Perspectives.* New York: Aldine de Gruyter.

Eaton, S. Boyd, Melvin Konner, and Marjorie Shostak. 1988. *The Paleolithic Prescription.* New York: Harper and Row.

Eaton, S. Boyd, et al. 1994. Women's Reproductive Cancers in Evolutionary Perspective. *The Quarterly Review of Biology* 69(3):353–367.

Ellison, Peter. 1995. Breast-feeding, Fertility, and Maternal Condition. In Patricia Stuart-Macadam and Katherine Dettwyler (eds.) *Breast-feeding. Biocultural Perspectives.* New York: Aldine de Gruyter.

Ewald, Paul W. 1994. *Evolution of Infectious Disease.* New York: Oxford University Press.

Konner, Melvin, and Marjorie Shostak. 1987. Timing and Management of Birth among the !Kung. *Cultural Anthropology* 2(1):11–28.

Konner, Melvin, and Carol Worthman. 1980. Nursing Frequency, Gonadal Function, and Birth Spacing among !Kung Hunter-Gatherers. *Science* 207:788–791.

Maher, Vanessa (ed.). 1992. *The Anthropology of Breast-feeding.* Oxford: Berg.

McKenna, James. 1986. An Anthropological Perspective on the Sudden Infant Death Syndrome (SIDS): The Role of Parental Breathing Cues and Speech Breathing Adaptations. *Medical Anthropology* 10(1):9–53.

McKenna, James, and Sarah Mosko. 1990. Evolution and the Sudden Infant Death Syndrome (SIDS). Part 3: Infant Arousal and Parent–Infant Co-Sleeping. *Human Nature* 1(3):291–330.

Micozzi, Marc. 1995. Breast Cancer, Reproductive Biology, and Breast-feeding. In Patricia Stuart-Macadam and Katherine Dettwyler (eds.) *Breast-feeding. Biocultural Perspectives.* New York: Aldine de Gruyter.

Nesse, Randolph M., and George C. Williams. 1994. *Why We Get Sick: The New Science of Darwinian Medicine.* New York: Random House.

Riordan, Jan, and Kathleen Auerbach. 1993. *Breast-feeding and Human Lactation.* Boston: Jones and Bartlett.

Scheper-Hughes, Nancy, and Margaret Lock. 1987. The Mindful Body: A Prolegomenon to Future Work in Medical Anthropology. *Medical Anthropology Quarterly* 1(1):6–41.

Stuart-Macadam, Patricia. 1995. Breast-feeding in Prehistory. In Patricia Stuart-Macadam and Katherine Dettwyler (eds.) *Breast-feeding. Biocultural Perspectives.* New York: Aldine de Gruyter.

Williams, George C., and Randolph M. Nesse. 1991. The Dawn of Darwinian Medicine. *The Quarterly Review of Biology* 66(1):1–22.

Wood, James W. et al. 1985. Lactation and Birth Spacing in Highland New Guinea. *Journal of Biosocial Sciences, Supplement* 9:159–173.

Woolridge, Michael W. 1995. Baby-Controlled Breast-feeding. In Patricia Stuart-Macadam and Katherine Dettwyler (eds.) *Breast-feeding. Biocultural Perspectives.* New York: Aldine de Gruyter.

11

You Are What You Eat:
Religious Aspects of the Health Food Movement

Jill Dubisch

Food is a basic biological need, a fundamental ingredient for the survival of a group. The environment often determines what sorts of foods are available and also influences which foods are culturally preferred and which are prohibited. Culture, however, is the final arbiter of what is acceptable to eat. We eat cows but not horses. We eat pheasant but not the bald eagle, because the latter is a sacred symbol. We eat lettuce but avoid dandelion in our salads. We may find eating raw fish disgusting but don't mind cooking the unborn young of a dumb and helpless bird that doesn't know enough to hide its eggs.

Culture defines what is appropriate to eat, and at the same time, what you eat may define your membership in a culture or subculture. What a family eats for breakfast or lunch often reflects its ethnic background or geographic location—bagels and lox, grits, or refried beans. Some people are conspicuous in their pronouncements of what they do or do not eat because this projects their self-image. In that very real sense, you are what you eat.

As you read this selection, ask yourself the following questions:

☐ *The author indicates that she is looking at food as a system of symbols expressing a world view. What does that mean?*

☐ *In what ways does the health food movement seem to you like a religion?*

☐ *The author notes a number of symbolic oppositions, like nature–culture and pure–impure. What are some of the other oppositions she mentions and what is their significance?*

☐ *How does what you eat (for example, wheat germ and honey) communicate membership in the movement?*

☐ *How might understanding the dynamics of health food beliefs be helpful in improving public health by reducing tobacco, alcohol, and crack consumption?*

The following terms discussed in this selection are included in the Glossary at the back of the book:

mana
taboo
world view

Dr. Robbins was thinking how it might be interesting to make a film from Adelle Davis' perennial best seller, *Let's Eat Right to Keep Fit*. Representing a classic confrontation between good and evil—in this case nutrition versus unhealthy diet—the story had definite box office appeal. The role of the hero, Protein, probably should be filled by Jim Brown, although Burt Reynolds undoubtedly would pull strings to get the part. Sunny Doris Day would be a clear choice to play the heroine, Vitamin C, and Orson Welles, oozing saturated fatty acids from the pits of his flesh, could win an Oscar for his interpretation of the villainous Cholesterol. The film might begin on a stormy night in the central nervous system. . . .

—Tom Robbins, *Even Cowgirls Get the Blues*

From *The American Dimension*, 1981. Reprinted by permission of the author.

I intend to examine a certain way of eating; that which is characteristic of the health food movement, and try to determine what people are communicating when they choose to eat in ways which run counter to the dominant patterns of food consumption in our society. This requires looking at health foods as a system of symbols and the adherence to a health food way of life as being, in part, the expression of belief in a particular world view. Analysis of these symbols and the underlaying world view reveals that, as a system of beliefs and practices, the health food movement has some of the characteristics of a religion.

Such an interpretation might at first seem strange since we usually think of religion in terms of a belief in a deity or other supernatural beings. These notions, for the most part, are lacking in the health food movement. However, anthropologists do not always consider such beliefs to be a necessary part of a religion. Clifford Geertz, for example, suggests the following broad definition:

> A religion is (1) a system of symbols which acts to (2) establish powerful, pervasive, and long-lasting moods and motivations in men by (3) formulating conceptions of a general-order of existence and (4) clothing these conceptions with such an aura of factuality that (5) the moods and motivations seem uniquely realistic. (Geertz 1965:4)

Let us examine the health food movement in the light of Geertz's definition.

HISTORY OF THE HEALTH FOOD MOVEMENT

The concept of "health foods" can be traced back to the 1830s and the Popular Health movement, which combined a reaction against professional medicine and an emphasis on lay knowledge and health care with broader social concerns such as feminism and the class struggle (see Ehrenreich and English 1979). The Popular Health movement emphasized self-healing and the dissemination of knowledge about the body and health to laymen. One of the early founders of the movement, Sylvester Graham (who gave us the graham cracker), preached that good health was to be found in temperate living. This included abstinence from alcohol, a vegetarian diet, consumption of whole wheat products, and regular exercise. The writings and preachings of these early "hygienists" (as they called themselves) often had moral overtones, depicting physiological and spiritual reform as going hand in hand (Shryock 1966).

The idea that proper diet can contribute to good health has continued into the twentieth century. The discovery of vitamins provided for many health food people a further "natural" means of healing which could be utilized instead of drugs. Vitamins were promoted as health-giving substances by various writers, including nutritionist Adelle Davis, who has been perhaps the most important "guru" of health foods in this century. Davis preached good diet as well as the use of vitamins to restore and maintain health, and her books have become the best sellers of the movement. (The titles of her books, *Let's Cook It Right, Let's Get Well, Let's Have Healthy Children*, give some sense of her approach.) The health food movement took on its present form, however, during the late 1960s, when it became part of the "counterculture."

Health foods were "in," and their consumption became part of the general protest against the "establishment" and the "straight" life-style. They were associated with other movements centering around social concerns, such as ecology and consumerism (Kandel and Pelto 1980:328). In contrast to the Popular Health movement, health food advocates of the sixties saw the establishment as not only the medical profession but also the food industry and the society it represented. Food had become highly processed and laden with colorings, preservatives, and other additives so that purity of food became a new issue. Chemicals had also become part of the food-growing process, and in reaction terms such as "organic" and "natural" became watchwords of the movement. Health food consumption received a further impetus from revelations about the high sugar content of many popular breakfast cereals which Americans had been taught since childhood to think of as a nutritious way to start the day. (Kellogg, an early advocate of the Popular Health movement, would have been mortified, since his cereals were originally designed to be part of a hygienic regimen.)

Although some health food users are members of formal groups (such as the Natural Hygiene Society, which claims direct descent from Sylvester Graham), the movement exists primarily as a set of principles and practices rather than as an organization. For those not part of organized groups, these principles and practices are disseminated, and contact is made with other members of the movement, through several means. The most important of these are health food stores, restaurants, and publications. The two most prominent journals in the movement are *Prevention* and *Let's Live*, begun in 1920 and 1932 respectively (Hongladarom 1976).

These journals tell people what foods to eat and how to prepare them. They offer advice about the use of vitamins, the importance of exercise, and the danger of pollutants. They also present testimonials from faithful practitioners. Such testimonials take the form of articles that recount how the author overcame a physical problem through a health food approach, or letters from readers who tell how they have cured their ailments by following methods advocated by the journal or suggested by friends in the movement. In this manner, such magazines not only educate, they also articulate a world view and provide evidence and support for it. They have become the "sacred writings" of the movement. They are a way of "reciting the code"—the cosmology and moral injunctions—which anthropologist Anthony F. C. Wallace describes as one of the important categories of religious behavior (1966:57).

IDEOLOGICAL CONTENT OF THE HEALTH FOOD MOVEMENT

What exactly is the health food system? First, and most obviously, it centers around certain beliefs regarding the relationship of diet to health. Health foods are seen as an "alternative" healing system, one which people turn to out of their dissatisfaction with conventional medicine (see, for example, Hongladarom 1976). The emphasis is on "wellness" and prevention rather than on illness and curing. Judging from letters and articles found in health food publications, many individuals' initial adherence to the movement is a type of conversion. A specific medical problem, or a general dissatisfaction with the state of their health, leads these converts to an eventual realization of the "truth" as represented by the health food approach, and to a subsequent change in life-style to reflect the principles of that approach. "Why This Psychiatrist 'Switched,'" published in *Prevention* (September 1976), carries the following heading: "Dr. H. L. Newbold is a great advocate of better nutrition and a livelier life style. But it took a personal illness to make him see the light." For those who have experienced such conversion, and for others who become convinced by reading about such experiences, health food publications serve an important function by reinforcing the conversion and encouraging a change of life-style. For example, an article entitled "How to Convert Your Kitchen for the New Age of Nutrition" (*Prevention*, February 1975) tells the housewife how to make her kitchen a source of health for her family. The article suggests ways of reorganizing kitchen supplies and reforming cooking by substituting health foods for substances detrimental to health, and also offers ideas on the preparation of nutritious and delicious meals which will convert the family to this new way of eating without "alienating" them. The pamphlet *The Junk Food Withdrawal Manual* (Kline 1978), details how an individual can, step by step, quit eating junk foods and adopt more healthful eating habits. Publications also urge the readers to convert others by letting them know how much better health foods are than junk foods. Proselytizing may take the form of giving a "natural" birthday party for one's children and their friends, encouraging schools

to substitute fruit and nuts for junk food snacks, and even selling one's own baking.

Undergoing the conversion process means learning and accepting the general features of the health food world view. To begin with, there is great concern, as there is in many religions, with purity, in this case, the purity of food, of water, of air. In fact, there are some striking similarities between keeping a "health food kitchen" and the Jewish practice of keeping kosher. Both make distinctions between proper and improper foods, and both involve excluding certain impure foods (whether unhealthful or non-kosher) from the kitchen and table. In addition, a person concerned with maintaining a high degree of purity in food may engage in similar behavior in either case—reading labels carefully to check for impermissible ingredients and even purchasing food from special establishments to guarantee ritual purity.

In the health food movement, the basis of purity is healthfulness and "naturalness." Some foods are considered to be natural and therefore healthier; this concept applies not only to foods but to other aspects of life as well. It is part of the large idea that people should work in harmony with nature and not against it. In this respect, the health food cosmology sets up an opposition of nature (beneficial) versus culture (destructive), or, in particular, the health food movement against our highly technological society. As products of our industrialized way of life, certain foods are unnatural; they produce illness by working against the body. Consistent with this view is the idea that healing, like eating, should proceed in harmony with nature. The assumption is that the body, if allowed to function naturally, will tend to heal itself. Orthodox medicine, on the other hand, with its drugs and surgery and its non-holistic approach to health, works against the body. Physicians are frequently criticized in the literature of the movement for their narrow approach to medical problems, reliance on drugs and surgery, lack of knowledge of nutrition, and unwillingness to accept the validity of the patient's own experience in healing himself. It is believed that doctors may actually cause further health problems rather than effecting a cure. A short item in *Prevention*, "The Delivery Is Normal—But the Baby Isn't," recounts an incident in which drug-induced labor in childbirth resulted in a mentally retarded baby. The conclusion is "nature does a good job—and we should not, without compelling reasons, try to take over" (*Prevention*, May 1979:38).

The healing process is hastened by natural substances, such as healthful food, and by other "natural" therapeutic measures such as exercise. Vitamins are also very important to many health food people, both for maintaining health and for healing. They are seen as components of food which work with the body and are believed to offer a more natural mode of healing than drugs. Vitamins, often one of the most prominent products offered in many health food stores, provide the greatest source of profit (Hongladarom 1976).

A basic assumption of the movement is that certain foods are good for you while others are not. The practitioner of a health food way of life must learn to distinguish between two kinds of food: those which promote well-being ("health foods") and those which are believed to be detrimental to health ("junk foods"). The former are the only kind of food a person should consume, while the latter are the antithesis of all that food should be and must be avoided. The qualities of these foods may be described by two anthropological concepts, *mana* and *taboo*. Mana is a type of beneficial or valuable power which can pass to individuals from sacred objects through touch (or, in the case of health foods, by ingestion). Taboo, on the other hand, refers to power that is dangerous; objects which are taboo can injure those who touch them (Wallace 1966:60–61). Not all foods fall clearly into one category or the other. However, those foods which are seen as having health-giving qualities, which contain *mana*, symbolize life, while *taboo* foods symbolize death. ("Junk food is . . . dead. . . . Dead food produces death," proclaims one health food manual [Kline 1978:2–4].) Much of the space in health food publications is devoted to telling the reader why to consume certain foods and avoid others ("Frozen, Creamed Spinach: Nutritional Disaster," *Prevention*, May 1979; "Let's Sprout Some Seeds," *Better Nutrition*, September 1979).

Those foods in the health food category which are deemed to possess an especially high level of *mana* have come to symbolize the movement as a whole. Foods such as honey, wheat germ, yogurt, and sprouts are seen as representative of the general way of life which health food adherents advocate, and Kandel and Pelto found that certain health food followers attribute mystical powers to the foods they consume. Raw food eaters speak of the "life energy" in uncooked foods. Sprout eaters speak of their food's "growth force" (1980:336).

Qualities such as color and texture are also important in determining health foods and may acquire symbolic value. "Wholeness" and "whole grain" have come to stand for healthfulness and have entered the jargon of the advertising industry. Raw, coarse, dark, crunchy, and cloudy foods are preferred over those which are cooked, refined, white, soft, and clear. (See chart on the next page.)

Thus dark bread is preferred over white, raw milk over pasteurized, brown rice over white. The convert must learn to eat foods which at first seem strange and even exotic and to reject many foods which are components of the Standard American diet. A McDonald's

hamburger, for example, which is an important symbol of America itself (Kottak 1978), falls into the category of "junk food" and must be rejected.

Just as the magazines and books which articulate the principles of the health food movement and serve as a guide to the convert can be said to comprise the sacred writings of the movement, so the health food store or health food restaurant is the temple where the purity of the movement is guarded and maintained. There individuals find for sale the types of food and other substances advocated by the movement. One does not expect to find items of questionable purity, that is, substances which are not natural or which may be detrimental to health. Within the precincts of the temple adherents can feel safe from the contaminating forces of the larger society, can meet fellow devotees, and can be instructed by the guardians of the sacred area (see, for example, Hongladarom 1976). Health food stores may vary in their degree of purity. Some sell items such as coffee, raw sugar, or "natural" ice cream which are considered questionable by others of the faith. (One health food store I visited had a sign explaining that it did not sell vitamin supplements, which it considered to be "unnatural," i.e., impure.)

People in other places are often viewed as living more "naturally" and healthfully than contemporary Americans. Observation of such peoples may be used to confirm practices of the movement and to acquire ideas about food. Healthy and long-lived people like the Hunza of the Himalayas are studied to determine the secrets of their strength and longevity. Cultures as yet untainted by the food systems of industrialized nations are seen as examples of what better diet can do. In addition, certain foods from other cultures—foods such as humus, falafel, and tofu—have been adopted into the health food repertoire because of their presumed healthful qualities.

Peoples of other times can also serve as models for a more healthful way of life. There is in the health food movement a concept of a "golden age," a past which provides an authority for a better way of living. This past may be scrutinized for clues about how to improve contemporary American society. An archaeologist, writing for *Prevention* magazine, recounts how "I Put Myself on a Caveman Diet—Permanently" (*Prevention*, September 1979). His article explains how he improved his health by utilizing the regular exercise and simpler foods which he had concluded from his research were probably characteristic of our prehistoric ancestors. A general nostalgia about the past seems to exist in the health food movement, along with the feeling that we have departed from a more natural pattern of eating practiced by earlier generations of Americans (see, for example, Hongladarom 1976). (Sylvester Graham, however, presumably did not find

HEALTH FOOD WORLD VIEW

	Health Foods	Junk Foods	
cosmic *oppositions*	LIFE, NATURE	DEATH, CULTURE	
basic values and desirable attributes	holistic, organic harmony with body and nature natural and real harmony, self-sufficiency, independence homemade, small scale layman competence and understanding	fragmented, mechanistic working against body and nature manufactured and artificial disharmony, dependence mass-produced professional esoteric knowledge and jargon	undesirable attributes
beneficial qualities of food	whole coarse dark crunchy raw cloudy	processed refined white soft cooked clear	harmful qualities
specific foods with mana	yogurt* honey* carob soybeans* sprouts* fruit juices herb teas foods from other cultures: humus, falafel, kefir, tofu, stir-fried vegetables, pita bread	ice cream, candy sugar* chocolate beef overcooked vegetables soft drinks* coffee*, tea "all-American" foods: hot dogs, McDonald's hamburgers*, potato chips Coke	specific taboo foods
	return to early American values, "real" American way of life	corruption of this original and better way of life and values	

*Denotes foods with especially potent mana or taboo.

the eating habits of his contemporaries to be very admirable.)

The health food movement is concerned with more than the achievement of bodily health. Nutritional problems are often seen as being at the root of emotional, spiritual, and even social problems. An article entitled "Sugar Neurosis" states "Hypoglycemia (low blood sugar) is a medical reality that can trigger wife-beating, divorce, even suicide" (*Prevention*, April 1979: 110). Articles and books claim to show the reader how to overcome depression through vitamins and nutrition and the movement promises happiness and psychological well-being as well as physical health. Social problems, too, may respond to the health food approach. For example, a probation officer recounts how she tried changing offenders' diets in order to change their behavior. Testimonials from two of the individuals helped tell "what it was like to find that good nutrition was their bridge from the wrong side of the law and a frustrated, unhappy life to a vibrant and useful one" (*Prevention*, May 1978:56). Thus, through more

healthful eating and a more natural life-style, the health food movement offers its followers what many religions offer: salvation—in this case salvation for the body, for the psyche, and for society.

Individual effort is the keystone of the health food movement. An individual can take responsibility for his or her own health and does not need to rely on professional medical practitioners. The corollary of this is that it is a person's own behavior which may be the cause of ill health. By sinning, by not listening to our bodies, and by not following a natural way of life, we bring our ailments upon ourselves.

The health food movement also affirms the validity of each individual's experience. No two individuals are alike: needs for different vitamins vary widely; some people are more sensitive to food additives than others; each person has his or her best method of achieving happiness. Therefore, the generalized expertise of professionals and the scientifically verifiable findings of the experts may not be adequate guides for you, the individual, in the search of health. Each person's experience has meaning; if something works for you, then it works. If it works for others also, so much the better, but if it does not, that does not invalidate your own experience. While the movement does not by any means disdain all scientific findings (and indeed they are used extensively when they bolster health food positions), such findings are not seen as the only source of confirmation for the way of life which the health food movement advocates, and the scientific establishment itself tends to be suspect.

In line with its emphasis on individual responsibility for health, the movement seeks to deprofessionalize knowledge and place in every individual's hands the information and means to heal. Drugs used by doctors are usually available only through prescription, but foods and vitamins can be obtained by anyone. Books, magazines, and health food store personnel seek to educate their clientele in ways of healing themselves and maintaining their own health. Articles explain bodily processes, the effects of various substances on health, and the properties of foods and vitamins.

The focus on individual responsibility is frequently tied to a wider concern for self-sufficiency and self-reliance. Growing your own organic garden, grinding your own flour, or even, as one pamphlet suggests, raising your own cow are not simply ways that one can be assured of obtaining healthful food; they are also expressions of independence and self-reliance. Furthermore, such practices are seen as characteristic of an earlier "golden age" when people lived natural lives. For example, an advertisement for vitamins appearing in a digest distributed in health food stores shows a mother and daughter kneading bread together. The heading reads "America's discovering basics." The copy goes on, "Baking bread at home has been a basic family practice throughout history. The past several decades, however, have seen a shift in the American diet to factory-produced breads. . . . Fortunately, today there are signs that more and more Americans are discovering the advantage of baking bread themselves." Homemade bread, home-canned produce, sprouts growing on the window sill symbolize what are felt to be basic American values, values supposedly predominant in earlier times when people not only lived on self-sufficient farms and produced their own fresh and more natural food, but also stood firmly on their own two feet and took charge of their own lives. A reader writing to *Prevention* praises an article about a man who found "new life at ninety without lawyers or doctors," saying "If that isn't the optimum in the American way of living, I can't imagine what is!" (*Prevention*, May 1978:16). Thus although it criticizes the contemporary American way of life (and although some vegetarians turn to Eastern religions for guid-

ance—see Kandel and Pelto 1980), the health food movement in general claims to be the true faith, the proponent of basic American-ness, a faith from which the society as a whole has strayed.

SOCIAL SIGNIFICANCE OF THE HEALTH FOOD MOVEMENT FOR AMERICAN ACTORS

Being a "health food person" involves more than simply changing one's diet or utilizing an alternative medical system. Kandel and Pelto suggest that the health food movement derives much of its popularity from the fact that "food may be used simultaneously to cure or prevent illness, as a religious symbol and to forge social bonds. Frequently health food users are trying to improve their health, their lives, and sometimes the world as well" (1980:332). Use of health foods becomes an affirmation of certain values and a commitment to a certain world view. A person who becomes involved in the health food movement might be said to experience what anthropologist Anthony F. C. Wallace has called "mazeway resynthesis." The "mazeway" is the mental "map" or image of the world which each individual holds. It includes values, the environment and the objects in it, the image of the self and of others, the techniques one uses to manipulate the environment to achieve desired end states (Wallace 1966:237). Resynthesis of this mazeway—that is, the creation of new "maps," values, and techniques—commonly occurs in times of religious revitalization, when new religious movements are begun and converts to them are made. As individuals, these converts learn to view the world in a new manner and to act accordingly. In the case of the health food movement, those involved learn to see their health problems and other dissatisfactions with their lives as stemming from improper diet and living in disharmony with nature. They are provided with new values, new ways of viewing their environment, and new techniques for achieving their goals. For such individuals, health food use can come to imply "a major redefinition of self-image, role, and one's relationship to others" (Kandel and Pelto 1980:359). The world comes to "make sense" in the light of this new world view. Achievement of the desired end states of better health and an improved outlook on life through following the precepts of the movement gives further validation.

It is this process which gives the health food movement some of the overtones of a religion. As does any new faith, the movement criticizes the prevailing social values and institutions, in this case the health-threatening features of modern industrial society. While an individual's initial dissatisfaction with prevailing beliefs and practices may stem from experiences with the conventional medical system (for example, failure to find a solution to a health problem through visits to a physician), this dissatisfaction often comes to encompass other facets of the American way of life. This further differentiates the "health food person" from mainstream American society (even when the difference is justified as a return to "real" American values).

In everyday life the consumption of such substances as honey, yogurt, and wheat germ, which have come to symbolize the health food movement, does more than contribute to health. It also serves to represent commitment to the health food world view. Likewise, avoiding those substances, such as sugar and white bread, which are considered "evil" is also a mark of a health food person. Ridding the kitchen of such items—a move often advocated by articles advising readers on how to "convert" successfully to health foods—is an act of ritual as well as practical significance. The symbolic nature of such foods is confirmed by the reactions of outsiders to those who are perceived as being inside the movement. An individual who is perceived as being a health food person is often automatically assumed to use honey instead of sugar, for example. Conversely, if one is noticed using or not using certain foods (e.g., adding wheat germ to food, not eating white sugar), this can lead to questions from the observer as to whether or not that individual is a health food person (or a health food "nut," depending upon the questioner's own orientation).

The symbolic nature of such foods is especially important for the health food neophyte. The adoption of a certain way of eating and the renunciation of mainstream cultural food habits can constitute "bridge-burning acts of commitment" (Kandel and Pelto 1980:395), which function to cut the individual off from previous patterns of behavior. However, the symbolic activity which indicates this cutting off need not be as radical as a total change of eating habits. In an interview in *Prevention*, a man who runs a health-oriented television program recounted an incident in which a viewer called up after a show and announced excitedly that he had changed his whole life-style—he had started using honey in his coffee! (*Prevention*, February 1979:89). While recognizing the absurdity of the action on a practical level, the program's host acknowledged the symbolic importance of this action to the person involved. He also saw it as a step in the right direction since one change can lead to another. Those who sprinkle wheat germ on cereal, toss alfalfa sprouts with a salad, or pass up an ice cream cone for yogurt are not only demonstrating a concern for health but also affirming their commitment to a particular life-style and symbolizing adherence to a set of values and a world view.

CONCLUSION

As this analysis has shown, health foods are more than simply a way of eating and more than an alternative healing system. If we return to Clifford Geertz's definition of religion as a "system of symbols" which produces "powerful, pervasive, and long-lasting moods and motivations" by "formulating conceptions of a general-order of existence" and making them appear "uniquely realistic," we see that the health food movement definitely has a religious dimension. There is, first, a system of symbols, in this case based on certain kinds and qualities of food. While the foods are believed to have health-giving properties in themselves, they also symbolize a world view which is concerned with the right way to live one's life and the right way to construct a society. This "right way" is based on an approach to life which stresses harmony with nature and the holistic nature of the body. Consumption of those substances designated as "health foods," as well as participation in other activities associated with the movement which also symbolize its world view (such as exercising or growing an organic garden) can serve to establish the "moods and motivations" of which Geertz speaks. The committed health food follower may come to experience a sense of spiritual as well as physical well-being when he or she adheres to the health food way of life. Followers are thus motivated to persist in this way of life, and they come to see the world view of this movement as correct and "realistic."

In addition to its possession of sacred symbols and its "convincing" world view, the health food movement also has other elements which we usually associate with a religion. Concepts of mana and taboo guide the choice of foods. There is a distinction between the pure and impure and a concern for the maintenance of purity. There are "temples" (health food stores and other such establishments) which are expected to maintain purity within their confines. There are "rabbis," or experts in the "theology" of the movement and its application to everyday life. There are sacred and instructional writings which set out the principles of the movement and teach followers how to utilize them. In addition, like many religious movements, the health food movement harkens back to a "golden age" which it seeks to recreate and assumes that many of the ills of the contemporary world are caused by society's departure from this ideal state.

Individuals entering the movement, like individuals entering any religious movement, may undergo a process of conversion. This can be dramatic, resulting from the cure of an illness or the reversal of a previous state of poor health, or it can be gradual, a step-by-step changing of eating and other habits through exposure to health food doctrine. Individuals who have undergone conversion and mazeway resynthesis, as well as those who have tested and confirmed various aspects of the movement's prescriptions for better health and a better life, may give testimonials to the faith. For those who have adopted, in full or in part, the health food world view, it provides, as do all religions, explanations for existing conditions, answers to specific problems, and a means of gaining control over one's existence. Followers of the movement are also promised "salvation," not in the form of afterlife, but in terms of enhanced physical well being, greater energy, longer life-span, freedom from illness, and increased peace of mind. However, although the focus is this-worldly, there is a spiritual dimension to the health food movement. And although it does not center its world view around belief in supernatural beings, it does posit a higher authority—the wisdom of nature—as the source of ultimate legitimacy for its views.

Health food people are often dismissed as "nuts" or "food faddists" by those outside the movement. Such a designation fails to recognize the systematic nature of the health food world view, the symbolic significance of health foods, and the important functions which the movement performs for its followers. Health foods offer an alternative or supplement to conventional medical treatment, and a meaningful and effective way for individuals to bring about changes in lives which are perceived as unsatisfactory because of poor physical and emotional health. It can also provide for its followers a framework of meaning which transcends individual problems. In opposing itself to the predominant American life-style, the health food movement sets up a symbolic system which opposes harmony to disharmony, purity to pollution, nature to culture, and ultimately, as in many religions, life to death. Thus while foods are the beginning point and the most important symbols of the health food movement, food is not the ultimate focus but rather a means to an end: the organization of a meaningful world view and the construction of a satisfying life.

REFERENCES

Ehrenreich, Barbara, and Deidre English. 1979. *For Her Own Good: 150 Years of the Experts' Advice to Women*. Garden City, N.Y.: Anchor Press/Doubleday.

Geertz, Clifford. 1965. "Religion as a Cultural System." In Michael Banton, ed., *Anthropological Approaches to the Study of Religion*. A.S.A. Monograph No. 3. London: Tavistock Publications Ltd.

Hongladarom, Gail Chapman. 1976. "Health Seeking Within the Health Food Movement." Ph.D. Dissertation: University of Washington.

Kandel, Randy F., and Gretel H. Pelto. 1980. "The Health Food Movement: Social Revitalization or Alternative Health Maintenance System." In Norge W. Jerome, Randy F. Kandel, and Gretel H. Pelto, eds., *Nutritional Anthropology*. Pleasantville, N.Y.: Redgrave Publishing Co.

Kline, Monte. 1978. *The Junk Food Withdrawal Manual*. Total Life, Inc.

Kottak, Conrad. 1978. "McDonald's as Myth, Symbol, and Ritual." In *Anthropology: The Study of Human Diversity*. New York: Random House.

Shryock, Richard Harrison. 1966. *Medicine in America: Historical Essays*. Baltimore: Johns Hopkins University Press.

Wallace, Anthony F. C. 1966. *Religion: An Anthropological View*. New York: Random House.

12

Chinese Table Manners:
You Are *How* You Eat

Eugene Cooper

I had been looking forward to this dinner with an important client for over a week. We were going to close the biggest deal of my career. He arrived on time, and I ordered a bit of wine. It was a fancy restaurant and I was trying to behave appropriately; I tucked my napkin neatly on my lap and lifted my wine glass carefully with my little finger extended in the way I had always seen it done. But what began well, began to go awry. I looked on in horror as my client ladled a number of different dishes together into a soup bowl, lifted it to his mouth and began to shovel it in. I was so embarrassed by this display of bad manners that I hoped no one I knew would happen by. My face must have betrayed my thoughts, but my client did not let on. He simply asked if I was not enjoying my food because I had left the dishes flat on the table. This took me by surprise, because I realized for the first time that he was looking at me and finding my behavior odd. Our smiles became realizations and turned to laughter. Luckily, we had a good sense of humor about our ethnocentrism. Somebody should have warned us; this could have been a real disaster.

Consider yourself warned. Table manners, like a great many everyday events, are heavily laden with cultural meaning. Understanding culturally prescribed behaviors is of practical importance, not merely interesting. More anthropologists need to be involved in cross-cultural training for situations where there is likely to be interaction between people from different cultures or ethnic groups.

As you read this selection, ask yourself the following questions:

- [ ] *How does one determine which culture's table manners are better? Why do we judge people by their manners?*

- [ ] *What are the important distinctions in Chinese food?*

- [ ] *Which food is the most basic and a necessary part of every Chinese meal? What about your own culture?*

- [ ] *What does it mean in China if you leave your rice bowl on the table while eating from it?*

- [ ] *What is the overriding rule of Chinese table customs?*

- [ ] *How do the Chinese feel about eating alone? Why?*

The following terms discussed in this selection are included in the Glossary at the back of the book:

cultural values
ethnology
symbol

Reproduced by permission of Society for Applied Anthropology from *Human Organization* 45(2):179–184, 1986.

"Etiquette of this kind (not putting half eaten meat back in the bowl, [not] wiping one's nose on one's sleeve) is not superficial, a matter for the surface rather than the depths; refined ways of acting are so internalized as to make alternative behavior truly 'disgusting,' 'revolting,' 'nauseous,' turning them into some of the most highly charged and deeply felt of intra-social differences, so that 'rustic' behavior is not merely quaint but barbarous" (Goody 1982:140).

"Probably no common practice is more diversified than the familiar one of eating in company, for what Europeans consider as correct and decent may by other races be looked upon as wrong or indelicate. Similarly, few social observances provide more opportunities for offending the stranger than the etiquette of the table" (Hammerton 1936:23).

Our shrinking world makes encounters with people of other cultures increasingly common in our life experiences. Whether in the conduct of business, in interactions with our "ethnic" neighbors, or as visitors to other countries, we are frequently called on to communicate with others whose assumptions about what constitutes appropriate behavior are widely different from our own.

In such contexts, it is often difficult to know whether habits and customs one takes for granted in one's own home may be creating unfavorable impressions in one's host's home. No less an authority than Confucius, writing more than two thousand years ago, was aware of the potential difficulties involved in intercultural communication, and provided the following advice: "When entering a country inquire of its customs. When crossing a border, inquire of the prohibitions" (Li Chi 1971:17).

Among such customs and prohibitions, those associated with behavior at the table can make an enormous difference in the way one is perceived by a foreign host.

As regards the Chinese in particular, the way one handles oneself at the table gives off signals of the clearest type as to what kind of a person one is, and it is all too easy to offend, as I hope to show. At the same time, however, it is easy enough to equip oneself with a few simple points to bear in mind that will not only pleasantly surprise one's Chinese host, but also convince him or her that one is a sensitive, cultivated, courteous, respectful, and considerate individual.

Surprisingly, for a civilization which has generated so many handbooks of its various cuisines, China has not produced any popular guidebooks for table manners of the Emily Post variety. The field, of course, has for the most part been preempted by the *Li Chi*—records of etiquette and ceremonial—most of which is said to date from the early Han. Indeed, many of the themes which characterize contemporary Chinese table manners are present in the minute descriptions of behaviors appropriate to people of various stations in all the gradations of Han social structure, such as the prescription to yield or defer. However, one is hard pressed to find a general rough and ready guide to contemporary Chinese table manners of anything more than the most superficial kind, usually present in popular Chinese cookbooks for Western audiences.

The absence of attention to table manners may be the result of the fact that table manners are among those habits most taken for granted—rules no grown-up needs instruction in. A Chinese culinary enthusiast of my acquaintance assures me that table manners are not important in Chinese history, being far outweighed by the scarcity of food generally as the major issue. Nevertheless, an examination of Chinese table manners provides sufficient contrast with Western table habits in terms of structure and performance, as to make significant features of Chinese etiquette emerge in comparison—features taken for granted by the native.

Those few who have written on the subject (Chang 1977; Hsü and Hsü 1977) generally qualify as bicultural individuals with sufficient experience of both Chinese and Western rules to tease out the areas of contrastive significance. My five years of field research (and eating) in Hong Kong, and eight years of marriage to a Chinese woman who taught me Chinese table manners as to a child, also qualify me for the assignment, although my former European colleagues at the University of Hong Kong might question my credentials as an expert on Western etiquette, to be sure.

BASIC STRUCTURES AND PARAPHERNALIA

To begin with, it is useful to consider K. C. Chang's (1977) broad outline of the important distinctions in Chinese food between food (*shih*) and drink (*yin*), and then within the category food, between *fan* (grain/rice) and *ts'ai* (dishes). Chang establishes a hierarchy with grain as the base, vegetables and fruit as next least expendable, and meat as most expendable in the preparation of a meal. Fish would probably fall between vegetables and meat at least as far as contemporary Hong Kong is concerned, particularly if one includes the enormous variety of preserved fish available.

In any event, it is fair to say that a Chinese meal is not a meal without *fan*. The morning food event, at which rice is not normally taken, or if so is taken as gruel, is not thought of as a meal. When Chinese speak of a full day's eating fare, it is two square meals per day rather than three. Thus rice (or grain) defines a meal, and its treatment and consumption are circumscribed in a number of ways.

It will be helpful, however, to lay out the general paraphernalia with which the diner is equipped, and the structure in which it is deployed before returning to the rules governing rice. On this subject, Hsü and Hsü (1977:304) have written:

> The typical Chinese dining table is round or square, the *ts'ai* dishes are laid in the center, and each participant in the meal is equipped with a bowl for *fan*, a pair of chopsticks, a saucer, and a spoon. All at the table take from the *ts'ai* dishes as they proceed with the meal.

The *ts'ai* dishes are typically shared by all, and must be treated much as common property, whereas one's bowl is a private place which comes directly in touch with the mouth. The chopsticks are of both the mouth and the table, and mediate between. They are thin, and when employed appropriately only touch the one piece or small quantity a person touches first. Many Westerners find the habit of sharing from a common plate potentially unhygienic, and one might be tempted to dismiss this as a bit of ethnocentricity. However, the point has recently been made by no less an authority than Communist party secretary Hu Yaobang, who called attention to the unsanitary character of traditional Chinese eating habits and urged change.

One employs the chopsticks to take from the common plate and place food in one's bowl, then one raises the bowl to the mouth and pushes food into the mouth with the chopsticks. Hsü and Hsü state, "The diner who lets his *fan* bowl stay on the table and eats by picking up lumps of *fan* from the bowl is expressing disinterest in or dissatisfaction with the food. If he or she is a guest in someone's house, that is seen as an open insult to the host" (1977:304). Since one's bowl is a private place, "good manners do not preclude resting a piece of meat (or other items) in one's bowl between bites" (1977:304). However, one never puts a partially chewed piece of anything back into one of the common plates (I would not have thought this necessary to mention; however, an otherwise culturally sensitive person I know had the audacity to do so recently so it may bear mentioning.) Also, it is extremely poor manners to suck or bite your chopsticks.

In some cases the bowl may be substituted for by a spoon, as, for example, when one goes out to lunch with one's workmates, and each diner is supplied with a flat plate piled high with rice topped with roast pork, chicken, duck and/or *lap cheong* (Chinese sausage), or with a helping of a single *ts'ai* dish (the latter known as *hui fan*).

Eating rice off a flat plate with chopsticks alone is not an easy task. Westerners exasperated with the use of chopsticks often feel their most intense frustration when trying to accomplish this task, and are often reduced to picking up small bits of rice with the ends of their chopsticks and placing them in the mouth. Seeming to pick at one's food in this way is not good manners and marks one as an incompetent foreign devil, confirming in most Chinese minds all of their previous prejudices about *guailos*.

No self-respecting Chinese would attempt to eat rice directly from a flat plate without first piling the rice onto, or scooping the rice into, a spoon. One eats the *ts'ai* or meat with one's chopsticks, but rice is most often carried to the mouth in a spoon. The spoon stands in for the bowl in the mini-context of an individual serving, and one can also think of the bowl itself as serving in the capacity of an enlarged spoon in the context of regular dining as well.

Rice is usually doled out from a common pot by the host or hostess. When someone has filled your rice bowl for you, it is accepted with two hands. To accept rice with one hand suggests disinterest, disrespect, and carelessness. One places the full bowl in front of oneself and waits until everyone has been served. It is very impolite to begin eating before everyone at the table has had his bowl filled with rice. When one has finished the rice in one's bowl, one does not continue to eat of the common *ts'ai* dishes. To eat *ts'ai* without rice in one's bowl is to appear a glutton interested only in *ts'ai*, of which one must consume a great deal to get full without rice. Depending on the degree of intimacy of a relationship, one may, when eating at the home of a friend or acquaintance, rise from the table to refill one's bowl with rice from the rice pot in the kitchen. However, at formal occasions one's host will usually be alert enough to notice when one's rice bowl is empty and move to fill it before one might be forced to request more rice. When one rises to get more rice, the host will usually insist on taking one's bowl and filling it. One may decline such assistance if the host is a close friend by simply saying "I'll serve myself."

At banquets one is expected to fill up on *ts'ai*, and consumption of too much rice may be a sign of disrespect to the quality of the *ts'ai* dishes. No rice should ever be left over in one's bowl at the end of the meal.

> As children we were always taught to leave not a single grain of *fan* in our bowl when we finished. Our elders strongly impressed on us that each single grain of rice or corn was obtained through the drops of sweat of the tillers of the soil (Hsü and Hsü 1977:308).

A corollary of this rule is never to take so much rice, or anything else for that matter, in your bowl as to be unable to finish it. It is also extremely disrespectful of the meal and of one's host to leave bits of rice on the table around one's bowl, and Chinese children are often told that each of these grains will materialize as a pockmark on the face of their future spouse.

As regards the *ts'ai*, it is important to note again that it is arrayed for all to share. Generally speaking, especially on formal occasions, one does not serve oneself without first offering to others, at least those seated immediately to either side. This applies also to the taking of tea, and one generally fills a neighbor's cup before taking tea for oneself. When tea is poured for you, it is customary to tap the table with your fingers to convey your thanks.

The overriding rule of Chinese table customs is deference. Defer to others in everything. Be conscious of the need to share what is placed in common. This means don't eat only from those dishes that you like.

> One very common point of instruction from parents to children is that the best mannered person does not allow co-diners to be aware of what his or her favorite dishes are by his or her eating pattern (Hsü and Hsü 1977:304).

When taking from the common dishes one should also only take in such proportions that everyone else will be left with a roughly equivalent amount. It is polite to take the remains of a common *ts'ai* dish after a new dish has been brought out. The desirability of the remains is diminished by the introduction of a new dish, and the remains of the old become fair game. However, it is rather poor manners to incline a common plate toward oneself and scrape the remains into one's bowl. This "looking in the mirror" evokes the idea of narcissistic concern with oneself.

In general, young should defer to old in order of eating, and on formal occasions when guests are present children may even be excluded from the dining table until the adults are finished, or seated at a table separate from the adults. In the household of the boss of the factory where I did my fieldwork, apprentices commonly sat with the boss at the family table, but were relegated to the children's table at the New Year's feast.

A host will usually signal that it is appropriate to begin eating, after each person at the table has taken rice, by picking up his chopsticks and saying "*sik fan*." When a guest has eaten his fill, he indicates that he is finished by putting down his chopsticks and encouraging others still eating to take their time. They in turn will inquire if the guest is full, and if he is he should say so. Upon finishing one may either remain at the table or leave. A guest of honor is expected to remain until all are finished.

In addition, one should be careful not to take large mouthfuls, to refrain from making noise while chewing, and to try to maintain the same pace of eating as others at the table. In contrast to Western etiquette in which "toothpicks are never used outside the privacy of one's room" (McLean 1941:63), toothpicks are provided at most Chinese tables and it is not impolite to give one's teeth a thorough picking at the table, provided one covers one's mouth with the opposite hand.

Spitting is not good manners at a Chinese table, although this is a rule often honored more in the breach. Spittoons are often provided in Chinese restaurants, both as a repository for waste water and tea used to sterilize one's utensils, and for expectorations of various sorts. Often the contents of the spittoons threaten to get up and walk away, so vile are the contents. The floor is fair game in many restaurants for just about anything remaining in one's mouth not swallowable, such as small bits of bone or gristle. Hong Kong has improved considerably in this regard in the recent years, but in working-class restaurants and *daipaidongs*, spitting is still quite common.

INFLECTIONS OF GENERAL PRINCIPLES

Having laid out these basic ground rules, it remains to explore how these rules are inflected in the various contexts in which food events occur in contemporary Hong Kong. These contexts are many and varied, ranging from informal and intimate occasions when the family is together at home for a meal, to the more formal occasions involving elaborate feasts usually held in restaurants. Somewhat intermediate between these are the meals eaten out, but in somewhat less formal contexts—from breakfast taken at *dim saam* houses, lunches taken at foodstalls with workmates, to evening meals prepared in restaurants for individual diners (*hak fan*), and midnight snacks. Expectations as to appropriate comportment at the table will also vary with region of origin, age, and class position.

For example, for Cantonese a full meal usually includes soup, and many Cantonese feel uncomfortable leaving the table without having partaken of soup. The minimal structure of the Cantonese meal includes not just *fan* (grain) and *ts'ai* (dishes), but also soup. This minimal structure is served up in what is known as *hak fan*, a specialty of some restaurants (usually Shanghainese) in which one may choose from a daily set menu of *hak* dishes, served with an extra large bowl of rice and the soup of the day. *Hak fan* is designed for people who must eat alone for some reason, not considered the most desirable circumstances. Two Chinese who knew each other would not sit down at the same table and order two individual dishes of *hak fan*. They would surely grasp the opportunity of sharing the greater variety available to each through social eating.

Jack Goody has likened eating alone to defecating in public (1982:306) because of the absence of the social in meeting essentially biological needs. *Hak fan* assures that even taken alone, the minimum structural entity of a Cantonese meal is available to be consumed. This basic structure is also revealed in a variety of thermos containers used for carrying lunch to work which are equipped with compartments for rice, *ts'ai* and soup. Since the contexts in which food events occur in Hong Kong are so varied, soup is not always the focus of attention. Proceeding through the ordinary day's food events from morning to evening will give us occasion to note context-linked inflections of our general principles.

As mentioned previously, the morning food event does not pass muster as a meal, largely due to the absence of rice. Still, there are a variety of contexts in which this event may take place. At home, the morning food event usually involves rice from the evening before boiled down to congee with a variety of pickles and condiments tossed in or served on the side. This is usually grabbed quickly in the kitchen on the way out to work, if it is eaten at all, and seldom involves the entire family seated at a single table.

Eaten out, the morning food event may take several forms. Consistent with the quick and superficial character of the event at home is the food event taken at a food stall of *daipaidong*, of which several different types serve suitable breakfast fare—congee (most commonly with preserved egg and pork), *yautiu* (unsweetened fried dough strips), hot *dao-jeung* (soy bean milk), *jucheung fen* (rolled rice noodles), all served with tea, usually in a glass.

Eating at a *daipaidong*, and even in some restaurants, one assumes the probability that the chopsticks, stuffed together in a can and set at the center of the table for individual diners to take, as well as one's cup, bowl, and spoon, will not have been properly washed. A brief ritualized washing usually precedes the meal in which one pours a glass of boiling hot tea into one's glass, stirring the ends of the chopsticks in the water to sterilize them, pouring the still hot water into one's bowl where one's cup and spoon are immersed and sterilized. The wash water is then thrown out, usually on the street in the case of a *daipaidong*, or in a spittoon at a restaurant, and one is prepared to commence eating. Occasionally, one is even provided with a separate bowl for washing one's eating implements, filled by one's waiter with boiling water from a huge kettle.

At a *daipaidong* for breakfast, one usually shares a table with a stranger, or perhaps a neighbor or workmate, depending on whether one eats near home or near work. In any case, one's portion is usually one's own, and the rules of formal dining apply only in the most general terms. Food is usually taken with dispatch, as one is usually rushing to work or to school, and the idea is just to put something in one's stomach to suppress hunger till the first meal of the day—*ng fan* (lunch).

The slightly more formal morning food event is *dim saam*, referred to most often as *yam ch'a* (drink tea). "Drinking tea" again refers to something less than a "meal," although on weekends, taken with one's family at a large table, *dim saam* often involves the consumption of large quantities of buns, dumplings, rice noodles in various shapes, a variety of innards, and the

like. One sits down, is approached by one's waiter, or in fancier restaurants by a host or hostess, who will inquire what kind of tea one will be drinking—*sao mei, bo lei, soy sin*, and that old perceived favorite of *guailos*—*heung pien* (jasmine). When the tea arrives the host will fill everyone's cup and the meal may begin.

One acquires food from carts pushed around by young children and/or aged women, and less frequently by older men. One may find oneself sharing a table with strangers, or with regular customers who eat at the same restaurant at the same time every morning. Going to *yam ch'a* on a regular schedule assures one of continuous contact with the usual crowd, and it is common to find oneself seated at the same table with many of the same people each morning. While polite conversation is the general rule, more juicy gossip is not inappropriate as the relationship between morning diners becomes more familiar.

Generally, each diner is aware of what he has consumed, and the position of the plates may be adjusted where they have been ambiguously placed so the waiter can figure the tab. One eats from one's own plates under such circumstances, and pays for one's own plates; however, it is polite to fill the tea cup of one's neighbor from one's own pot if one is acquainted with him or her. There are still some restaurants in Hong Kong which serve tea in a covered bowl, quite literally stuffed with tea, and poured into a cup to be drunk, extremely dark, but the standard tea pot has replaced the bowl as a tea vessel in most restaurants.

A table shared with strangers or neighbors is usually an informal arrangement in which one eats one's own food. However, taking *dim saam* may also be a more formal occasion, especially on weekends, or when one has been *cheng*-ed (asked out). In such circumstances many of the rules of formal dining apply, i.e., the food on the table is common and should only be taken in such proportions that enough is left for others. One may order dishes one likes from the passing wagons, but one should always offer to others before taking from the dish for oneself. The dishes accumulate somewhat at random due to the vagaries of the itinerary of the carts, so there is no formal order to the dishes' arrival, although sweeter dishes are usually taken last.

Dim saam often trails off into lunch on formal or informal occasions, and by noon after the diners have warmed up with a few *dim saam* dishes, it is polite to inquire of one's fellow diners whether a plate of noodles or rice (a real meal) is in order, and if so, to order such dishes from the kitchen from one's waiter. Varieties of *dim saam* are also available from *daipaidong* as well, sometimes served up in individual portions to go.

The midday food event in Hong Kong includes rice or a reasonable substitute (rice noodles, bean noodles, wheat noodles), and is most often taken during a lunch hour break from factory or office labor. A variety of choices confront the Hong Kong worker eating out for lunch. Food stalls serve a variety of dishes, usually in individual portions on flat plates heaped high with rice, and covered with a single *ts'ai* dish. A glass of tea is usually served, and doubles again as a vessel for sterilizing one's chopsticks and spoon. Blue collar workers I knew in Hong Kong would often consume a full-to-the-brim tea tumbler of high octane spirits with such meals, and trundle back to work with the warm glow and slightly glazed look of a two-martini-lunch executive.

A plate of noodles may also be ordered from stalls specializing in such things. These may be served in individual portions, but given the easy divisibility of noodle dishes it is common for workmates to order a variety of noodle dishes and share them in common. A portion is lifted from the plate to one's bowl; with chopsticks initially, when the noodles are easily grasped in quantity; with help from the spoon as the plate gets progressively emptied. The setting of shared common dishes makes the general rules of the table outlined above once again applicable.

Co-workers will often go out to lunch at large *dim saam* restaurants, catch the tail end of the morning *dim saam* and order a variety of more substantial noodle or rice dishes. Where eating has taken place in common, and occasionally even where individual portions have been served, it is unusual for the check to be divided. Someone usually pays the whole tab. Among workmates, or those who often eat together, there is an implicit assumption that in the long run reciprocity will be achieved. It is not impolite among status equals to grab the check and pay for one's fellow diner, but this is not polite if the status difference is too great. Fights over the check occasionally occur in a way which evokes the potlatches of Northwest Coast Indians in which a status hierarchy is confirmed. Paying the check validates one's status superiority over one's fellow diners. Of course, the wider social setting must also be taken into account. One may be desirous of seeking a favor of an important person, in which case paying the check may serve as a mild form of pressure in which the obligation of reciprocity is finessed, enjoining one's fellow diner to comply with one's request. Food events are first and foremost social events.

The evening meal taken at home usually includes some warmed over *ts'ai* from the previous day's meal plus an increment of newly prepared dishes. It is not good manners to ignore the leftovers, despite the fact that they may not be quite as attractive as when served the day before. The general rules of the table apply, although the intimate setting of the family at home makes their application somewhat less formal. Still

and all, parents will most commonly instruct children as to the appropriate forms of behavior at the table in this setting, and the children must show that they understand and are learning. In many working-class homes in Hong Kong it is still common for the men to eat first, with the women joining later and/or hovering over the meal without ever formally sitting down.

At more formal dinners or at banquets or feasts associated with weddings, New Year's, funerals or festivals, the primacy of the *fan* and the secondary character of the *ts'ai* dishes is reversed, with attention devoted to the quality of the *ts'ai* dishes (Hsü and Hsü 1977:307), and rice not served till last. Thus at a banquet one may eat *ts'ai* without rice in one's bowl, and one is expected to fill up on *ts'ai* such that when the rice is finally served, one can only take a token portion, which is to say, this has been a real feast.

> During festivals and especially when acting as hosts all Chinese seem to ignore their sense of frugality and indulge in extravagance. *Ts'ai* dishes are served in abundance. The host or hostess will heap the guests' saucers with piece after piece of meat, fish, chicken and so on, in spite of repeated excuses or even protests on the guests' part. When *fan* is finally served, most around the table are full and can at best nibble a few grains (Hsü and Hsü 1977:307).

By the time the rice has been served at a banquet the diner has already had a share of cold appetizer, several stir fry dishes, or whole chickens, ducks, fish, soup, and a sweet/salty dessert. The emphasis on whole items (with head and tail attached) symbolizes completeness and fullness, and evokes these meanings at the table. One tries to serve fish, *yü*, a homophone for surplus, *yü*, to sympathetically bring about that condition in one's guests.

It is not polite to turn over a fish at the table. Rather, when the side facing up has been finished, the skeleton is lifted off to leave the meat underneath exposed. Apparently, turning over the fish is taboo among boat people, since the fish symbolizes the boat which will capsize sympathetically if a fish is turned over. Waiters in Hong Kong are never sure which of their customers are boat folk and might take offense, so they generally refrain from turning over any fish and apparently the practice has now become general.

A variety of prestige foods, such as shark's fin soup and the various eight precious dishes, are served at banquets more for the social recognition they confer than for the pleasure derived from their consumption (see de Garine 1976:150).

Conceptually, whiskey belongs with grain from which it is distilled and may be taken with food as a rice substitute. On formal occasions in Hong Kong scotch or VSOP Cognac is the rule, served straight in water tumblers, and often diluted with Seven-Up.

Another food event of note in Hong Kong is *siu yeh*—loosely translated as snacks. Usually taken late in the evening, they may include anything from congee, noodles and won ton, to roast pork, duck or chicken, to *hung dao sa* (sweet red bean soup—hot or iced) and *dao-fufa* (sweet bean curd usually flavored with almond). *Siu yeh* is usually served in individual portions. If you go out for won ton mein, everyone gets his own bowl. If you order duck's neck soup with rice, you are served an individual helping of soup, and an individual bowl of rice. Depending on the class of restaurant you take your *siu yeh* in, you may or may not find it advisable to wash your utensils with tea.

Itinerant street vendors with wheeled carts dispense a variety of prepared *siu yeh* in some residential neighborhoods, calling housewives and amahs to the street clutching their large porcelain bowls, or doling out cuttlefish parts to schoolchildren on street corners.

In all these contexts the general pattern that emerges is one that centers on deference, in thinking first of the other, in suppressing one's inclination to satiate oneself before the other has had a chance to begin, in humility. One yields to the other before satisfying one's own urges. At the macro level of China's great tradition, one finds such behavior characteristic of the *chün-tzu*, the individual skilled in the *li* (etiquette, rites, and ceremonies). He is one also skilled in the art of *jang*—of yielding, of accomplishing without activity, of boundless generosity, of cleaving to the *li*. There is even something of a Taoist resonance in all this, getting at things indirectly, without obvious instrumental effort.

Generally, it can be stated that the degree to which a Chinese practices the rules of etiquette marks his class position with respect to his fellow Chinese; although the degree to which the behavior of lower-class people at the table is informed by these rules should not be underestimated. Disregard of the rules on the part of a Chinese is regarded with as much distaste by their fellows as the faux pas normally committed by Westerners, except that the latter can be excused by their hopeless, if expected, ignorance.

It does not take much study for a Westerner to perform well enough at the table to impress most Chinese, since their expectations are exceedingly low. Keeping in mind a few simple things without slavishly parading one's knowledge, one can usually avoid provoking disgust and revulsion, and convince one's fellow diners that one is sensitive to others on their own terms, as well as to the world at large. Among the most basic of cultural patterns, learned early in life, the degree to which one observes these patterns has a lot to do with the way one is perceived as a person in Chinese terms.

Simple knowledge of the structural contexts, behavioral expectations, and symbolic associations of food events can provide access across social boundaries that would otherwise be less easily breached, and make it possible to more easily achieve one's goals. Table manners are part of an inventory of symbolic behaviors that may be manipulated, finessed, and encoded to communicate messages about oneself. For the Chinese, as for almost everyone else, you are *how* you eat.

REFERENCES

Chang, K. C. (ed.), 1977, Introduction. In *Food in Chinese Culture*. New Haven: Yale University Press.

de Garine, I., 1976, Food, Tradition and Prestige. In *Food, Man and Society*. D. Walcher, N. Kretchmer, and H. L. Barnett, eds. New York: Plenum Press.

Goody, J., 1982, *Cooking, Cuisine and Class*. Cambridge: Cambridge University Press.

Hammerton, J. A., 1936, *Manners and Customs of Mankind*, Vol. I. New York: W. M. A. Wise.

Hsü, F. L. K., and V. Y. N. Hsü, 1977, Modern China: North. In *Food in Chinese Culture*. K. C. Chang, ed. New Haven: Yale University Press.

Li Chi, 1971, *Chü Li, Part I*. Taipei: World Publishing.

McLean, N. B., 1941, *The Table Graces: Setting, Service and Manners for the American House without Servants*. Peoria, IL: Manual Arts Press.

13

Culture and the Evolution of Obesity

Peter J. Brown

As a people, Americans rank as one of the fattest societies in history. This epidemiological fact remains despite the tremendous amount of money, effort, and worry that Americans put into diet, exercise, and the quest for the perfect body. For some people, particularly young women, the quest to be thin can become such an obsession that they develop life-threatening eating disorders, like anorexia nervosa. But in other cultures, young women may go to great lengths to try to gain weight to look attractive. There are no universal standards of physical beauty; in fact, there is considerable cross-cultural variation. Culture defines normality.

How do conditions like obesity come to be expressed? Biologists usually say that it is a combination of genes and environment. There is good evidence that genes predispose people toward conditions, but there is seldom evidence that the chain of causation is entirely genetic. A complete explanation must be both biological and cultural. In other words, if a condition like obesity is caused by an interaction of genetic and cultural/behavioral predispositions, then both the genes and culture must be the product of evolutionary processes.

In this selection, Peter Brown provides a cross-cultural and evolutionary analysis of how both biological and cultural factors in obesity evolved. This analysis explains the sociological distribution of obesity today. It also emphasizes that peripheral body fat (characteristic of women) is a small health hazard compared to abdominal fat (characteristic of men).

Dietary patterns are obviously shaped by culture. But human tendencies to value meat, fatty foods, and sweets must be understood in the context of our evolutionary past.

As you read this selection, ask yourself the following questions:

☐ Have you ever noticed that there are gender differences in the locality of fat storage in the body? Why would this be the case?

☐ Why are fat people ridiculed and discriminated against in the United States? Are these social reactions worse for men or for women?

☐ What does the author mean when he says that in a rich society, slenderness can be an individual symbol of conspicuous consumption?

☐ Given the difference in health risk between peripheral body fat and central body fat, why might weight not be the best way to measure one's risk?

☐ Why do humans like foods that are "bad" for them?

The following terms discussed in this selection are included in the Glossary at the back of the book:

adipose tissue

cultural ideals

culture

epidemiology

food scarcity

gender dimorphism

ideal body images

obesity

sexual dimorphism

The etiology or cause of obesity can be understood in the context of human cultural and genetic evolution. The cause of human obesity and overweight involves the interaction of genetic traits with culturally patterned behaviors and beliefs. Both these genes and culture traits, remarkably common in human societies, are evolutionary products of similar processes of selection related to past food scarcities. This idea is not new: The notion of "thrifty phenotypes rendered detrimental by progress" was introduced more than a quarter-century ago. In recent years, the evidence for the existence of genes that enable individuals to use food energy efficiently and store energy reserves in the form of fat has been increasingly impressive; those individuals with "fat phenotypes" are likely to develop adult obesity (Stunkard et al. 1986, 1990).

It is important to recognize that these "thrifty" genes are, at least in the human context, necessary but not sufficient factors in the causation of obesity. In actuality, the new discoveries in the genetics of obesity highlight our ignorance about the role of nongenetic or cultural factors, which are usually subsumed in the term *environment* in the medical literature. The purpose of this paper is to examine why and how cultures have evolved behaviors and beliefs that appear to predispose individuals to develop obesity. I believe that an anthropological model of culture has significant advantages over the commonly used undifferentiated concept of "environment" for generating hypotheses about behavioral causes of obesity. This cultural approach is particularly useful for improving our understanding of the social epidemiological distribution of obesity.

It is valuable to raise an obvious question at the outset: Why do people find it very difficult to reduce their intake of dietary fat and sugar even when the medical benefits of this behavioral change are well known to them? The answer is not obvious, since neither the physiological nor the cultural attraction of these foods is well understood. The proximate mechanisms for this attraction are linked to brain physiology and biochemistry (Wurtman and Wurtman 1987). The ultimate answers are linked to our *evolutionary heritage.* Human predispositions to obesity are found in both genetic and cultural traits that may have been adaptive in the context of past food scarcities but are maladaptive today in the context of affluence and constant food surpluses.

THE PROBLEMS OF OBESITY AND OVERWEIGHT

Throughout most of human history, obesity was neither a common health problem nor even a realistic possibility for most people. Today, particularly in affluent societies like the United States, obesity is very common, affecting about 12 percent of adult men and women; overweight is even more common, affecting an additional 20 to 50

percent of adult Americans depending on the definitions used (Bray 1987). Not only are overweight and obesity relatively common conditions in our society, they are also extremely complex and intractable. Obesity is a serious public health problem because of its causal connection to major causes of morbidity and mortality from chronic diseases, including cardiovascular disease, type 2 diabetes mellitus (NIDDM), and hypertension. On the individual level, obesity and overweight bring with them an enormous amount of personal psychological pain. The fact that the obese are subjected to significant social and economic discrimination is well documented.

Fat is extraordinarily difficult to shed because the body guards its fat stores. The evidence concerning the effectiveness over a 5-year period of diet therapies indicates that nearly all of the weight that is lost through diets is eventually regained. The remarkable failure of diet therapies has made some researchers rethink their commonsensical theory of obesity as being caused by overeating; the clinical evidence of the past 40 years simply does not support this simplistic notion.

Even in the absence of scientific data about the effectiveness of diet therapy, the diet and weight-loss industry in the United States is remarkably successful in its ability to capture the hope and money of people who perceive themselves to be overweight. This industry thrives because of a complex of cultural beliefs about the ideal body and sexual attractiveness rather than medical advice and the prevention of chronic diseases per se. The American cultural concern about weight loss and the positive valuation of slenderness for women of the middle and upper classes are difficult to overemphasize. Chernin (1981) has referred to this cultural theme as an "obsession" and the "tyranny of slenderness." In this light, it is impossible to claim that obesity is purely a medical issue.

OBESITY AND HUNGER

It is important to remember that for most citizens of the world today, as it has been in the past, the possibility of obesity is remote whereas the possibility of hunger is close to home. There is a palpable irony in the fact of an epidemic of obesity in a world characterized by hunger. For example, in the United States an estimated 20 million people are hungry because they are on a "serious diet"; generally these people are of the middle and upper classes, and most are women. At the same time in the same rich nation, another estimated 20 million Americans are hungry and poorly nourished largely because they lack sufficient money; generally these people are elderly, homeless, or rural inhabitants. This sad symmetry in the estimates of voluntary and involuntary hunger in the United States is a valuable starting point for a discussion of the etiology of obesity. From an evolutionary standpoint, past food shortages have acted as powerful agents of natural selection, shaping both human genetics and behavior.

A theory of the etiology of obesity must not only account for the influences of genes and learned behaviors but also explain its social distribution. Before the problem of causation is addressed, it is worthwhile to examine the nature of human obesity.

CHANGING DEFINITIONS OF OBESITY

The most basic scientific issues regarding obesity are, in fact, controversial. The definitions of obesity and overweight have been the subject of substantial medical debate, in part because they must be based on inferred definitions of normality or "ideal" body proportions. Although obesity refers to excessive adiposity (fat deposits), the most common measurement is not of fat tissue at all but an indirect inference based on measures of stature and total body weight (Bray 1987).

The social history of height and weight standards in the United States is interesting. Until recently, the task of defining both obesity and ideal weights has been the domain of the life-insurance industry. The most well-known table of desirable weights was developed by the Metropolitan Life Insurance Company using correlation statistics between height/weight and mortality among insurance applicants. Ideal weights were based on data from 25-year-old insurance applicants, despite the nonrepresentative nature of the "sample" pool and the fact that in most human populations, individuals increase in weight until around age 50. Obesity was defined as 120 percent of the Ideal Body Weight (IBW), and overweight was defined as 110 percent IBW. Individual life-insurance applicants outside the recommended weight range were required to pay a surcharge on insurance premiums. In 1959, the concept of "frame size" was introduced, although the resulting categories were never given operational definitions using anthropometric measures.

Definitions of obesity have changed throughout history. From 1943 to 1980, definitions of "ideal weights" for women of a particular height were consistently lowered, while those for men remained approximately the same. In 1983, a major debate on the definition of obesity began when Metropolitan Life revised its tables upward, based on new actuarial studies of mortality. Many organizations and experts in the diet industry, including experts in medical fields, rejected these new standards.

In the current medical literature, weight and height tables have been replaced by the Body Mass Index (BMI), defined as body weight (in kilograms) divided by the square of body height (in meters). BMI (W/H^2) is strongly correlated with total body fat, and a value greater than 30 is generally considered obese. Current recommendations include slight increases in BMI with age (Bray 1987). Nevertheless, there continues to be little agreement on precise definitions of either overweight or obesity.

An important added dimension to the questions of definition of obesity involves the distribution of fat around the body trunk or on the limbs. Central or trunk body fat distribution is closely correlated with serious chronic diseases, such as cardiovascular disease, whereas peripheral body fat in the hips and limbs does not carry similar medical risks. Because of this clinically important distinction, measures of fat distribution like waist to hips ratio (WHR), wherein lower WHR values indicate lower risk of chronic disease consequences, will be a valuable addition to future definitions of obesity.

FOUR FACTS ABOUT THE SOCIAL DISTRIBUTION OF OBESITY

Humans are among the fattest of all mammals, and the primary function of our fat is to serve as an energy reserve. The nonrandom social distribution of adiposity within and between human populations may provide a key to understanding obesity. Four facts about this social distribution are particularly cogent for an evolutionary reconstruction: (1) the gender difference in the total percent and site distribution of body fat, as well as the prevalence of obesity; (2) the concentration of obesity in certain ethnic groups; (3) the increase in obesity associated with economic modernization; and (4) the powerful and complex relationship between social class and obesity. Any useful theory concerning the etiology of obesity must account for these social epidemiological patterns.

Sexual Dimorphism

Humans show only mild sexual dimorphism in variables like stature. Males are only 5 to 9 percent taller than females. The sample of adults from Tecumseh, Michigan seen in Figure 1 are typical. Men are larger than women in height and total body mass, but women have more subcutaneous fat as measured by skinfold thicknesses in 16 of 17 sites (the exception is the suprailiac region—so-called "love handles"). The greatest degree of sexual dimorphism is found in the site of distribution of fat tissue; women have much more peripheral fat in the legs and hips (Kissebah et al. 1989). This difference is epidemiologically important because the greater proportion of peripheral fat in females may be associated with reduced morbidity compared to males with identical BMI values.

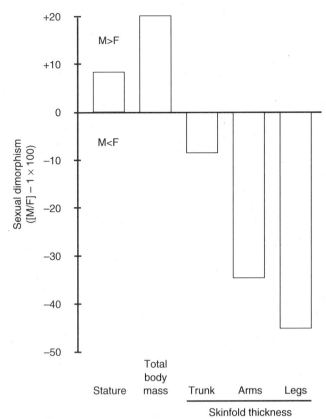

Figure 1
Sexual dimorphism in stature, body mass, and fat measures among white Americans aged 20 to 70 in Techumseh, Michigan. Sexual dimorphism is calculated by comparing male and female means; positive figures refer to greater male measures. Skinfold thicknesses are means of four sites on the trunk or five sites on the arms and legs; the mean dimorphism for all 17 fat measures is –19 percent. (From Brown, P. J., and M. Konner, An Anthropological Perspective on Obesity. In *Human Obesity*, R. J. Wurtman and J. J. Wurtman, eds. *Annals of New York Academy of Sciences* 499:29–46. Copyright © 1987. Reprinted with permission.)

Sex differences are also seen in the prevalence of obesity. Despite methodological differences in the categorization of obesity, data from the 14 population surveys shown in Figure 2 indicate that in *all* of the studies, females have a higher prevalence of obesity than males. A greater risk of obesity for females appears to be a basic fact of human biology.

Economic Modernization

The social distribution of obesity varies among societies, depending on their degree of economic modernization. Studies of traditional hunting and gathering populations report *no obesity*. In contrast, numerous studies of traditional societies undergoing the process of economic modernization demonstrate rapid increases

in the prevalence of obesity. Trowell and Burkitt's (1981) 15 case studies of epidemiological change in modernizing societies conclude that obesity is the first of the "diseases of civilization" to appear. The rapidity with which obesity becomes a common health problem in the context of modernization underscores the critical role of cultural behaviors in the causation of obesity, since there has been insufficient time for changes in gene frequencies.

Figure 2 also suggests that variations in the male-female ratio of obesity prevalence are related to economic modernization. In less industrially developed societies female obesity is much more common than male obesity, but in more affluent societies the ratio is nearly equivalent. Recent World Health Organization data on global obesity also support this observation (Gurney and Gorstein 1988).

Cultural changes with modernization include the seemingly invariable pattern of diet in industrial countries—decreased fiber intake and increased consumption of fat and sugar. Modernization is also associated with decreased energy expenditures related to work,

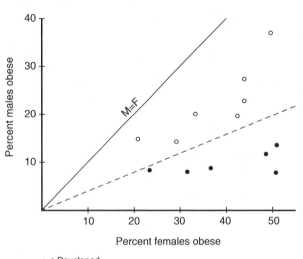

Figure 2
Gender differences in prevalences of obesity in 14 populations by general industrial development. Operational definitions of obesity differ between studies. See Brown and Konner (1987) for references. The unbroken line demarcates equal male-female obesity prevalences. The broken line indicates an apparent distinction in gender proportions of obesity in developed and underdeveloped countries. (From Brown, P. J., and M. Konner, An Anthropological Perspective on Obesity. In *Human Obesity*, R. J. Wurtman and J. J. Wurtman, eds. *Annals of New York Academy of Sciences* 499:29–46. Copyright © 1987. Reprinted with permission.)

recreation, or daily activities. From the perspective of the populations undergoing economic modernization, increasing average weight might be seen as a good thing rather than a health problem.

Ethnicity

The idea that particular populations have high rates of a genotype that predisposes individuals to obesity and related diseases is not new but is now supported by a convincing body of adoption and twin data (Stunkard et al. 1986, 1990) and by studies of particular obesity-prone populations like the Pima Indians (Ravussin et al. 1988). In the United States, ethnic groups with elevated rates of obesity include African Americans (particularly in the rural South), Mexican Americans, Puerto Ricans, Gypsies, and Pacific Islanders (Centers for Disease Control 1989).

The fact that certain ethnic groups have high rates of obesity is not easy to interpret because of the entanglement of the effects of genetic heredity, social class, and cultural beliefs. The association of obesity with ethnicity is not evidence for the exclusive role of genetic transmission, since social factors like endogamy (marriage within the group) or group isolation are critical for defining the population structure—that is, the social system through which genes are passed from generation to generation.

Social Class

Social class (socioeconomic status) can be a powerful predictor of the prevalence of obesity in both modernizing and affluent societies, although the direction of the association varies with the type of society. In developing countries, there is a strong and consistent *positive association* between social class and obesity for men, women, and children; correspondingly, there is an inverse correlation between social class and protein-calorie malnutrition. In heterogeneous and affluent societies, like the United States, there is a strong *inverse correlation* of social class and obesity for females. The association between obesity and social class among women in affluent societies is not constant through the life cycle. Economically advantaged girls are initially fatter than their low-income counterparts, but the pattern is reversed beginning at puberty. For females, social class remains the strongest social epidemiological predictor of obesity.

OBESITY AND HUMAN EVOLUTION

Human biology and behavior can be understood in the context of two distinct processes of evolution. Biological evolution involves changes through time in the fre-

quency of particular genes, primarily because of the action of natural selection on individuals. Cultural evolution involves historical changes in the configurations of cultural systems, that is, the learned patterns of behavior and belief characteristics of social groups. Cultural evolution includes the striking and rapid transformation of human lifestyles from small food-foraging societies to large and economically complex states in a span of less than 5,000 years.

The Context of Food Scarcities

Food shortages have been very common in human prehistory and history; in fact, they could be considered a virtually inevitable fact of life for most people. As such, they have been a powerful evolutionary force.

A cross-cultural ethnographic survey of 118 nonindustrial societies (with hunting and gathering, pastoral, horticultural, and agricultural economies) found some form of food shortages for *all* of the societies in the sample (Whiting 1958). Shortages occur annually or even more frequently in roughly half of the societies, and every 2 to 3 years in an additional 24 percent. The shortages are "severe" (i.e., including starvation deaths) in 29 percent of the societies sampled. Seasonal availability of food results in a seasonal cycle of weight loss and weight gain in both hunting and gathering and agricultural societies, although the fluctuation is substantially greater among agriculturalists.

Scarcity and Cultural Evolution

A hunting and gathering economy was characteristic of all human societies for more than 95 percent of our history, yet it is represented by only a handful of societies today. In general, food foragers enjoy high-quality diets, maintain high levels of physical fitness, suffer the risk of periodic food shortages, and are generally healthier than many contemporary populations that rely on agriculture. Without romanticizing these societies, the evidence is persuasive enough to suggest a "paleolithic prescription" of diet and exercise for the prevention of chronic diseases (Eaton et al. 1988). This recommendation refers to the quality of preindustrial diets and not to their dependability or quantity.

Approximately 12,000 years ago, some human groups shifted from a food-foraging economy to one of food production. This economic transformation allowed the evolution of urban civilizations. Many archaeologists believe that people were "forced" to adopt the new agricultural economy because of ecological pressures from population growth and food scarcities or because of military coercion. The archaeological record clearly shows that agriculture was associated with nutritional stress, poor health, and diminished stature (Cohen and Armelagos 1984). The beginning of agriculture is also linked to the emergence of social stratification, a system of inequality that improved the Darwinian fitness of the ruling class relative to that of the lower classes. Social inequality, particularly differential access to strategic resources, plays a critical role in the distribution of obesity in most societies.

Certain ecological zones appear to be prone to severe food shortages. For example, archaeological analysis of tree rings from the southwestern United States shows that the prehistoric past was characterized by frequent and severe droughts. The impressive agricultural societies of the prehistoric Southwest had expanded during an extended period of uncharacteristically good weather and could not be maintained when the lower and more characteristic rainfall patterns resumed. Ecological conditions leading to severe scarcity may have acted as strong forces of selection for "thrifty" genotypes.

Scarcity and Genetic Evolution

Since food shortages were ubiquitous for humans under natural conditions, selection favored individuals who could effectively store calories in times of surplus. For most societies, these fat stores would be called on at least every 2 or 3 years. Malnutrition increases infectious disease mortality, as well as decreasing birth weights and rates of child growth. The evolutionary scenario is this: Females with greater energy reserves in fat would have a selective advantage over their lean counterparts in terms of withstanding the stress of food shortages, not only for themselves but also for their fetuses or nursing children. Humans have evolved the ability to "save up" food energy for inevitable food shortages through the synthesis and storage of fat.

Selection has favored the production of peripheral body fat in females, whose reproductive fitness is influenced by the nutritional demands of pregnancy and lactation. This peripheral fat is usually mobilized after being primed with estrogen during the late stages of pregnancy and during lactation. In addition, a minimal level of fatness increases female reproductive success because of its association with regular cycling and early menarche (Frisch 1987).

In this evolutionary context the usual range of human metabolic variation must have produced many individuals with a predisposition to become obese; yet they would, in all likelihood, never have had the opportunity to do so. Furthermore, in this context there could be little or no natural selection against this tendency. Selection could not provide for the eventuality of continuous surplus simply because it had never existed before.

CULTURE AND ADAPTATIONS TO FOOD SCARCITY

Food scarcities have shaped not only our genes but also, and perhaps more important, human cultures. Because the concept of culture is rarely considered in medical research on obesity, and because I am suggesting that this concept has advantages over the more common and undifferentiated term *environment,* it is necessary to review some basic aspects of this anthropological term. *Culture* refers to the learned patterns of behavior and belief characteristic of a social group. As such, culture encompasses *Homo sapiens'* primary mechanism of evolutionary adaptation, which has distinct advantages of greater speed and flexibility than genetic evolution.

Cultural behaviors and beliefs are usually learned in childhood and they are often deeply held and seldom questioned by adults, who pass this "obvious" knowledge and habits to their offspring. In this regard, cultural beliefs and values are largely unconscious factors in the motivation of individual behaviors. Cultural beliefs define "what is normal" and therefore constrain the choices of behaviors available to an individual.

One useful way of thinking about culture in relation to obesity is a cultural materialist model as seen in Figure 3. This model divides culture into three layers. The material foundation of a cultural system is the economic mode of production, which includes the technology and the population size that the productive economy allows and requires. Population size is maintained by the social system, sometimes called the mode of reproduction. Contingent on the first layer is the system of social organization, which includes kinship patterns, marriage and family practices, politics, and status differentiation. Contingent on the social structure is the ideology or belief system, including ideas, beliefs, and values, both secular and sacred. Most anthropologists believe that the ideology is an extremely important part of culture, in part because it rationalizes and reinforces the economy and social structure. Ideology enables people to make sense of their world and to share their common world view through symbols. As such, ideology includes sacred concepts from

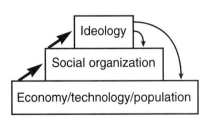

Figure 3
A materialist model of culture.

religion as well as secular concepts (with symbolic components) like health or sexual attractiveness.

A culture is an integrated system: A change in one part causes changes in the other layers. The materialist model indicates that the direction of causal change is from the bottom layer upward (the solid arrows in Figure 3). An economic change, like the invention of agriculture or the Industrial Revolution, has drastic implications for population size, social organization, and associated beliefs. On the other hand, most people *within* a society tend to explain things from the top down. Of course, people can hold contradictory beliefs and values that are not necessarily linked to their actual behavior.

CULTURAL PREDISPOSITIONS TO OBESITY

Obesity is related to culture in all three levels of the materialist model.

Productive Economy and Food Scarcity

Humans have evolved a wide variety of cultural mechanisms to avoid or minimize the effects of food scarcities. The most important adaptation to scarcity is the evolution of systems of food production and storage. As noted previously, the primary weakness of preindustrial systems of food production is a vulnerability to food shortages. The universality of food shortages discussed above is largely because of the technological limitations in food production and storage.

On the other hand, the energy-intensive (and energy-inefficient) system of agriculture in industrialized societies produces large surpluses of food. These agricultural surpluses are seldom used to eliminate hunger; rather they are used to transform and process foods in particular ways—often to add calories, fat, or salt. For example, we feed "extra" grain to beef cattle to increase the proportion of fat in their meat; consumers say that this overfeeding makes the meat "juicy." Similarly, potatoes are transformed into french fries and potato chips. From a nutritional standpoint the original vegetable is actually reduced to a vehicle for fat and salt. Endemic hunger exists even in the most affluent societies, where it is caused not by poor production but by inequitable distribution.

Technological changes associated with cultural evolution almost exclusively reduce the energy requirements of human labor. In general, cultural evolution has meant the harnessing of greater amounts of energy through technology (one aspect of the mode of production). To prevent obesity, people in developed societies must burn energy through daily workouts rather than daily work.

Reproduction and Energy Expenditure

The concept of the *mode of reproduction* is also related to predispositions to obesity. Pregnancy and lactation represent serious and continuing energy demands on women in societies that have not undergone the demographic transition. Industrial and nonindustrial societies differ in terms of the historical changes from high to low fertility and the reduction of mortality attributable to infectious disease. Higher numbers of pregnancies and longer periods of breast-feeding place high energy demands on women, especially if they cannot supplement their diet during these critical periods. As a result, women suffer greater risk of protein-energy malnutrition. Conversely, with fewer pregnancies and the reduction of breast-feeding, women in industrial societies have less opportunity to mobilize peripheral fat stores and suffer greater risk of obesity. In contemporary societies like the United States, mothers in lower social classes tend to have more children and to feed their infants with bottled formula rather than breast milk. Use of infant formulas allows women to retain their fat stores. These different social patterns in reproduction may play a role in the inverse association of obesity and social class for females.

Social Structure and Obesity

Characteristics of social organization may function as predispositions to obesity. In highly stratified and culturally heterogeneous societies, the distribution of obesity is associated with ethnicity and social class. Marriage patterns typically illustrate ethnic or social class endogamy, that is, marriage within the group. In the United States, members of ethnic minorities choose marriage partners from the same group at extremely high rates. This social practice may concentrate the genetic predispositions to conditions like obesity in particular subpopulations. Similarly, data suggest a pattern of "assortative mating" by social class as well as body type (particularly stature), which may be related to the genetic etiology of obesity. Genetic admixture with Native American groups of the Southwest has been suggested as a cause of elevated rates of type 2 diabetes mellitus and obesity among Mexican Americans (Gardner et al. 1984).

The pervasive and complex relationship between obesity and social class, or socioeconomic status (SES), is important. SES is related to particular behavior patterns that cause obesity. This statement underemphasizes the fact that these learned behaviors are *characteristic* of particular social groups or classes. In other words, the cultural patterns of social class groups are primary, not the individual behaviors themselves.

From a cross-cultural perspective, the general association between obesity and social position is positive: The groups with greater access to economic resources have higher rates of obesity. This pattern is logical and expected because socially dominant groups with better access to strategic resources should have better nutrition, better health, and consequently greater reproductive success.

As discussed earlier, the remarkable and important exception is women in industrial societies, who exhibit a strong *inverse* correlation between obesity and social class. The challenge for researchers is to explain why and how upper-class women in industrial societies remain thin. For many women the ideal of thinness requires considerable effort, restrained eating, and often resources invested in exercise. The social origins of the ideal of thinness in American women are associated with historical changes in women's economic roles, marriage patterns, and family size.

Low-income people in industrial societies might be considered well off by worldwide standards, and this access to resources is reflected in obesity prevalences. Yet in the context of perceived relative deprivation and economic stability, many people in societies like the United States live in stressful conditions—just one paycheck away from hunger. In terms of life priorities, economic security may be a higher and more immediate objective than more elusive goals like an "ideal body" or even long-term health. Amid the daily stresses of poverty, food may be the most common avenue of pleasure and psychological relief. Ethnographic studies of low-income urban black communities in the United States show a social emphasis on food sharing as a tool for marking family ties and demonstrating community cohesiveness.

Cultural Beliefs as Predispositions to Obesity

The third and possibly most important level of the model of culture shown in Figure 3 encompasses cultural symbols, beliefs, and values. Aspects of ideology relevant to the etiology of obesity include the symbolic meaning of fatness, ideal body types, and perceived risks of food shortages.

Fatness is symbolically linked to psychological dimensions, such as self-worth and sexuality, in many societies of the world, but the nature of that symbolic association is not constant. In mainstream U.S. culture, obesity is socially stigmatized, but for most cultures of the world, fatness is viewed as a welcome sign of health and prosperity. Given the rarity of obesity in preindustrial societies, it is not surprising that they lack ethnomedical terms for obesity. Much more attention is placed on "thinness" as a symptom of starvation, like among the !Kung San (Lee 1979), or in contemporary Africa as a sign of AIDS (sometimes called "the slim disease"). In the context of the AIDS epidemic, plumpness is indeed a marker of health.

Perhaps it is large body size, rather than obesity per se, that is admired as a symbol of health, prestige, prosperity, or maternity in agricultural societies. The Tiv of Nigeria, for example, distinguish between a very positive category, "too big" (*kehe*), and an unpleasant condition "to grow fat" (*ahon*) (Bohannan and Bohannan 1969). The first is a compliment because it is a sign of prosperity; the second is a rare and undesirable condition.

For women, fatness may also be a symbol of maternity and nurturance. In traditional societies in which women attain status only through motherhood, this symbolic association increases the cultural acceptability of fatness. A fat woman, symbolically, is well taken care of, and in turn she takes good care of her children. Fellahin Arabs in Egypt describe the proper women as fat because she has more room to bear the child, lactates abundantly, and gives warmth to her children. The cultural ideal of thinness in industrial societies, in contrast, is found where motherhood is not the sole or even primary means of status attainment for woman. The idea that fat babies and children are healthy children is very widespread. Food can be treated as a symbol of love and nurturance; in some cultures it may be impolite for a guest to refuse food that has been offered, but it is taboo to refuse food from one's mother.

In the industrialized United States, ethnic variation in culturally accepted definitions of obesity is significant. Some Mexican Americans have coined a new term, *gordura mala* (bad fatness), because the original term *gordura* continues to have positive cultural connotations (Ritenbaugh 1982). For this group cultural identity has a stronger and independent effect on risk of obesity than socioeconomic status. An ethnographic study of the cultural meanings of weight in a Puerto Rican community in Philadelphia (Massara 1989) documents the positive associations and lack of social stigma of obesity. Additional quantitative evidence suggests significant differences in ideal body preferences between this ethnic community and mainstream American culture. Positive evaluations of fatness may also occur among lower-class African Americans and Mexican Americans. These ethnic groups are heterogeneous, however, and upwardly mobile ethnics tend to resemble mainstream American culture in their attitudes about obesity and ideal body shape.

In a low-income housing project in Atlanta, Georgia, a sociological interviewer was asked by a group of obese black women, "Don't you know how hard it is to keep this weight *on*?" Their views of the advantages of a large body included being given respect and reduced chances of being bothered by young "toughs" in the neighborhood. For these women, fatness was part of their positive self-identity, and if a friend lost weight she was thought to look sickly. Among lower-income groups, the perceived risk of a food shortage—not for the society as a whole but for the immediate family—may be very important, especially if lack of food was personally experienced in the past. The perception of the risk of future "bad times" and insufficient food is the reality upon which people act.

FATNESS AND CROSS-CULTURAL STANDARDS OF BEAUTY IN WOMEN

Culturally defined standards of beauty vary between societies. In a classic example, Malcom (1925) describes the custom of "fattening huts" for elite Efik pubescent girls in traditional Nigeria. A girl spent up to 2 years in seclusion and at the end of this rite of passage possessed symbols of womanhood and marriageability—a three-tiered hairstyle, clitoridectomy, and fatness. Fatness was a primary criterion of beauty as it was defined by the elites, who alone had the economic resources to participate in this custom. Similarly, fatter brides demand significantly higher bridewealth payments among the Kipsigis of Kenya (Borgerhoff Mulder 1988).

Among the Havasupai of the American Southwest, if a girl is thin at puberty, a fat woman "stands" (places her foot) on the girl's back so she will become attractively plump. In this society, fat legs and, to a lesser extent, arms are considered essential to beauty. The Tarahumara of northern Mexico consider fat legs a fundamental aspect of the ideal feminine body; an attractive woman is called a "beautiful thigh." Among the Amhara of Ethiopia in northern East Africa, thin hips are called "dog hips" in a typical insult (Messing 1957).

It is difficult to know how widespread among the world's cultures is the association of plumpness and beauty. A preliminary indication can be found through a cross-cultural survey based on data from the Human Relations Area Files (a cross-indexed compilation of ethnographic information on more than 300 of the most thoroughly studied societies). The results of this survey are summarized in Table 1. Although conclusions made from these data are weak because of the small number and possibly nonrepresentative nature of the cases, as well as the fact that most ethnographies are difficult to code on this variable, some preliminary generalizations are possible. Cultural standards of beauty do not refer to physical extremes. No society on record has an ideal of extreme obesity. On the other hand, the desirability of "plumpness" or being "filled out" is found in 81 percent of the societies for which this variable can be coded. This standard, which probably includes the clinical categories of overweight and mild obesity, apparently refers to the desirability of fat deposits, particularly on the hips and legs.

Although cross-cultural variation is evident in standards of beauty, this variation falls within a certain range. American ideals of thinness occur in a setting in which it is easy to become fat, and preference for plumpness occurs in settings in which it is easy to remain lean. In context, both standards require the investment of individual effort and economic resources; furthermore, each in its context involves a display of wealth. Cultural beliefs about attractive body shape in mainstream American culture place pressure on females to lose weight and are involved in the etiology of anorexia and bulimia.

IDEAL BODY-TYPE, SIZE, AND SYMBOLIC POWER IN MEN

The ethnographic record concerning body preferences for males is extremely weak, yet preliminary research suggests a universal preference for a muscular physique and for tall or moderately tall stature. In general, members of all human societies appear to admire large body size as an attribute of attractiveness in men, because it symbolizes health, economic success, political power, and social status. "Big men," political leaders in tribal New Guinea, are described by their constituents in terms of their size and physical well-being: He is a man "whose skin swells with 'grease' [fat] underneath" (Strahern 1971). The spiritual power (*mana*) and noble breeding of a Polynesian chief is expected to be seen in his large size. In American society vestiges of a similar idea remain; for example, a "fat cat" is a wealthy and powerful man who can "throw his weight around." The political metaphor of weight and power in American society has been explored by social historians.

Table 1 CROSS-CULTURAL STANDARDS OF FEMALE BEAUTY

	Number of societies	Percent of societies
Overall body		
Extreme obesity	0	0
Plump/moderately fat	31	81
Thin/abhorrence of fat	7	19
Breasts		
Large or long	9	50
Small/abhorrence of large	9	50
Hips and Legs		
Large or fat	9	90
Slender	1	10
Stature		
Tall	3	30
Moderate	6	60
Small	1	10

Source: Brown and Konner 1987.

Most male college students in the U.S., in contrast with women, want to gain weight because it is equivalent to gaining muscle mass and physical power in a process called "bulking up."

CONCLUSIONS

Two sets of conclusions can be drawn from this discussion of culture and its relationship to obesity—one practical and one theoretical. First, recognition of cultural variation in beliefs and behaviors related to obesity needs to be incorporated into health programs aimed at reducing the prevalence of obesity. The second conclusion regards the need for more research on the role of culture, as it interacts with genes, on the etiology of obesity.

The Importance of Culture in Health Interventions

Existing cultural beliefs must be taken into account in the design and implementation of health promotion projects. In an obesity prevention campaign in a Zulu community outside of Durban, one health education poster depicted an obese woman and an overloaded truck with a flat tire, with a caption "Both carry too much weight." Another poster showed a slender woman easily sweeping under a table next to an obese woman who was using the table for support; it had the caption "Who do you prefer to look like?" The intended message of these posters was misinterpreted by the community because of a cultural connection between obesity and social status. The woman in the first poster was perceived to be rich and happy, since she was not only fat but had a truck overflowing with her possessions. The second poster was perceived as a scene of an affluent mistress directing her underfed servant.

Health interventions must be culturally acceptable, and we cannot assume that people place the highest priority on their health. The idea of reducing *risk factors* for chronic diseases that may develop later may not be an effective strategy for populations who do not feel empowered or who live in a fundamentally risky world.

Implications for the Etiology of Obesity

The frequency of past food shortages, the social distribution of obesity, and the cultural meanings of fatness, when taken together, suggest a biocultural hypothesis of the evolution of obesity. Both genetic and cultural predispositions to obesity may be products of the same evolutionary pressures, involving two related processes: first, genetic traits that cause fatness were selected because they improved chances of survival in the face of food scarcities, particularly for pregnant and nursing women; second, in the context of unequal access to food, fatness may have been socially selected because it is a cultural symbol of social prestige and an index of general health. Under Western conditions of abundance, our biological tendency to regulate body weight at levels above our ideal cannot be easily controlled even with a reversal of the widespread cultural ideal of plumpness.

This evolutionary model is obviously congruent with the current etiological theory about obesity, which combines genetic predispositions with "environmental" causes. Recent research both in epidemiology and human laboratory research demonstrates without a doubt the central role of genetic heredity in the etiology of obesity. Similar genetic evidence exists for variables like the distribution of fat on the body and basal metabolic rates. To an anthropologist, these important studies are welcome and expected.

The recent advances in understanding the genetic bases of obesity remind us, however, of our ignorance about the precise role of the "environment." One problem is that "environment" has been poorly defined and treated as if it were idiosyncratic for every individual or family. Another problem is that "environment" is essentially treated as a residual category—one that cannot be explained by genetic heredity. This paper has attempted to show how the anthropological concept of culture may be useful in conceptualization of the different components of the "environment" and the generation of hypotheses for future research in behavioral medicine.

The most convincing demonstrations of a strong genetic component for obesity have been in populations with relatively high levels of cultural homogeneity. In social contexts like Denmark, Iowa, or among Pima Indians, the influence of culture—including learned behaviors and beliefs—is minimized by the sample selected for study in order to emphasize the importance of genotypical variation. Essentially, cultural variation has been treated as if it were "noise." An essential goal in future research must be the identification of specific cultural factors—whether economic, social, or ideological—that predispose people to obesity.

From the standpoint of the prevention of obesity, it is critical to stress that genetic predisposition is not destiny. Genetic predispositions to obesity have apparently been maintained in populations throughout most of our species' history, yet it has rarely been expressed phenotypically. Culture is adaptive because it can be changed. Habitual patterns of behavior—of an individual or an entire society—can be changed to reduce morbidity and mortality linked to obesity and overweight. These changes must include social and political efforts to reduce the risk of hunger and food scarcity, even in affluent societies.

REFERENCES

Bohannan, P., and L. Bohannan. 1969. *A Source Notebook on Tiv Religion.* New Haven, CT: Human Relations Area Files.

Borgerhoff Mulder, M. 1988. Kipsigis Bridewealth Payments. In *Human Reproductive Behavior*, L. Betzig, M. Borgerhoff Mulder, and P. Turke, eds. Pp. 65–82. Cambridge: Cambridge University Press.

Bray, G. A. 1987. Overweight Is Risking Fate: Definition, Classification, Prevalence and Risks. In *Human Obesity*, R. J. Wurtman and J. J. Wurtman, eds. *Annals of the New York Academy of Sciences* 499:14–28.

Brown, P. J., and M. Konner. 1987. An Anthropological Perspective on Obesity. In *Human Obesity*, R. J. Wurtman and J. J. Wurtman, eds. *Annals of the New York Academy of Sciences* 499:29–46.

Centers for Disease Control. 1989. Prevalence of Overweight— Behavioral Risk Factor Surveillance System, 1987. *Morbidity and Mortality Weekly Report* 38:421–423.

Chernin, K. 1981. *The Obsession: Reflections on the Tyranny of Slenderness.* New York: Harper & Row.

Cohen, M. N., and G. J. Armelagos, eds. 1984. *Paleopathology at the Origins of Agriculture.* New York: Academic Press.

Eaton, S. B., M. Shostak, and M. Konner. 1988. *The Paleolithic Prescription.* New York: Harper & Row.

Frisch, R. E. 1987. Body Fat, Menarche, Fitness and Fertility. *Human Reproduction* 2:521–533.

Gardner, L. I., M. P. Stern, S. M. Haffner, S. P. Gaskill, H. Hazuda, and J. H. Relethford. 1984. Prevalence of Diabetes in Mexican Americans. *Diabetes* 33:86–92.

Gurney, M., and J. Gorstein. 1988. The Global Prevalence of Obesity—An Initial Overview of Available Data. *World Health Statistics Quarterly* 41:251–254.

Kissebah, A. H., D. S. Freedman, and A. N. Peiris. 1989. Health Risks of Obesity. *Medical Clinics of North America* 73:11–138.

Lee, R. B. 1979. *The !Kung Sun: Men, Women, and Work in a Foraging Society.* Cambridge, MA: Harvard University Press.

Malcom, L. W. G. 1925. Note on the Seclusion of Girls Among the Efik at Old Calabar. *Man* 25:113–114.

Massara, E. B. 1989. *Que Gordita! A Study of Weight Among Women in a Puerto Rican Community.* New York: AMS Press.

Messing, S. D. 1957. *The Highland Plateau Amhara of Ethiopia.* Ph.D. dissertation, Department of Anthropology, University of Pennsylvania, Philadelphia.

Ravussin, E., S. Lillioja, and W. C. Knowler, et al. 1988. Reduced Rate of Energy Expenditure as a Risk Factor for Body-Weight Gain. *New England Journal of Medicine* 318:467–472.

Ritenbaugh, C. 1982. Obesity as a Culture-Bound Syndrome. *Culture, Medicine and Psychiatry* 6:347–361.

Strahern, A. 1971. *The Rope of Moka.* New York: Cambridge University Press.

Stunkard, A. J., T. I. A. Sorenson, C. Hanis, T. W. Teasdale, R. Chakaborty, W. J. Schull, and F. Schulsinger. 1986. An Adoption Study of Obesity. *New England Journal of Medicine* 314:193–198.

Stunkard, A. J., J. R. Harris, N. L. Pedersen, and G. McClearn. 1990. The Body-Mass Index of Twins Who Have Been Reared Apart. *New England Journal of Medicine* 322:1483–1487.

Trowell, H. C., and D. P. Burkitt. 1981. *Western Diseases: Their Emergence and Prevention.* Cambridge, MA: Harvard University Press.

Whiting, M. G. 1958. *A Cross-Cultural Nutrition Survey.* Doctoral Dissertation, Harvard School of Public Health, Cambridge.

Wurtman, R. J., and J. J. Wurtman, eds. 1987. *Human Obesity.* Annals of the New York Academy of Sciences 499.

14

The Worst Mistake in the History of the Human Race

Jared Diamond

What we eat and how we eat are important both nutritionally and culturally. This selection suggests that how we get what we eat—through gathering and hunting versus agriculture, for example—has dramatic consequences. This seems pretty obvious. We all imagine what a struggle it must have been before the development of agriculture. We think of our ancestors spending their days searching for roots and berries to eat, or out at the crack of dawn, hunting wild animals. We now know, as discussed by Boyd Eaton and Melvin Konner in Selection 9 ("Ancient Genes and Modern Health"), that this was not quite the case. Nevertheless, isn't it really *better to simply go to the refrigerator, open the door, and reach for a container of milk to pour into a bowl of flaked grain for your regular morning meal? What could be simpler and more nutritious?*

There are many things that we seldom question; the truth seems so evident and the answers obvious. One such sacred cow is the tremendous prosperity brought about by the agricultural revolution. This selection is a thought-provoking introduction to the connection between culture and agriculture. The transition from food foraging to farming (what archaeologists call the Neolithic revolution) may have been the worst mistake in human history or its most important event. You be the judge. But for better or worse, this cultural evolution has occurred, and the world will never be the same again.

As you read this selection, ask yourself the following questions:

☐ *What is the fundamental difference between the progressivist view and the revisionist interpretation?*

☐ *How did the development of agriculture affect people's health?*

☐ *What three reasons explain the changes brought about by the development of agriculture?*

☐ *How did the development of agriculture affect social equality, including gender equality?*

The following terms discussed in this selection are included in the Glossary at the back of the book:

agricultural development
civilization
domestication of plants and animals
hunter-gatherers
Neolithic
paleontology
paleopathology
social stratification

Jared Diamond / © 1987 Discover Magazine.

To science we owe dramatic changes in our smug self-image. Astronomy taught us that our earth isn't the center of the universe but merely one of billions of heavenly bodies. From biology we learned that we weren't specially created by God but evolved along with millions of other species. Now archaeology is demolishing another sacred belief: that human history over the past million years has been a long tale of progress. In particular, recent discoveries suggest that the adoption of agriculture, supposedly our most decisive step toward a better life, was in many ways a catastrophe from which we have never recovered. With agriculture came the gross social and sexual inequality, the disease and despotism, that curse our existence.

At first, the evidence against this revisionist interpretation will strike twentieth century Americans as irrefutable. We're better off in almost every respect than the people of the Middle Ages, who in turn had it easier than cavemen, who in turn were better off than apes. Just count our advantages. We enjoy the most abundant and varied foods, the best tools and material goods, some of the longest and healthiest lives, in history. Most of us are safe from starvation and predators. We get our energy from oil and machines, not from our sweat. What neo-Luddite among us would trade his life for that of a medieval peasant, a caveman, or an ape?

For most of our history we supported ourselves by hunting and gathering: we hunted wild animals and foraged for wild plants. It's a life that philosophers have traditionally regarded as nasty, brutish, and short. Since no food is grown and little is stored, there is (in this view) no respite from the struggle that starts anew each day to find wild foods and avoid starving. Our escape from this misery was facilitated only 10,000 years ago, when in different parts of the world people began to domesticate plants and animals. The agricultural revolution gradually spread until today it's nearly universal, and few tribes of hunter-gatherers survive.

From the progressivist perspective on which I was brought up, to ask "Why did almost all our hunter-gatherer ancestors adopt agriculture?" is silly. Of course they adopted it because agriculture is an efficient way to get more food for less work. Planted crops yield far more tons per acre than roots and berries. Just imagine a band of savages, exhausted from searching for nuts or chasing wild animals, suddenly gazing for the first time at a fruit-laden orchard or a pasture full of sheep. How many milliseconds do you think it would take them to appreciate the advantages of agriculture?

The progressivist party line sometimes even goes so far as to credit agriculture with the remarkable flowering of art that has taken place over the past few thousand years. Since crops can be stored, and since it takes less time to pick food from a garden than to find it in the wild, agriculture gave us free time that hunter-gatherers never had. Thus it was agriculture that enabled us to build the Parthenon and compose the B-minor Mass.

While the case for the progressivist view seems overwhelming, it's hard to prove. How do you show that the lives of people 10,000 years ago got better when they abandoned hunting and gathering for farming? Until recently, archaeologists had to resort to indirect tests, whose results (surprisingly) failed to support the progressivist view. Here's one example of an indirect test: Are twentieth century hunter-gatherers really worse off than farmers? Scattered throughout the world, several dozen groups of so-called primitive people, like the Kalahari Bushmen, continue to support themselves that way. It turns out that these people have plenty of leisure time, sleep a good deal, and work less hard than their farming neighbors. For instance, the average time devoted each week to obtaining food is only 12 to 19 hours for one group of Bushmen, 14 hours or less for the Hadza nomads of Tanzania. One Bushman, when asked why he hadn't emulated neighboring tribes by adopting agriculture, replied, "Why should we, when there are so many mongongo nuts in the world?"

While farmers concentrate on high-carbohydrate crops like rice and potatoes, the mix of wild plants and animals in the diets of surviving hunter-gatherers provides more protein and a better balance of other nutrients. In one study, the Bushmen's average daily food intake (during a month when food was plentiful) was 2,140 calories and 93 grams of protein, considerably greater than the recommended daily allowance for people of their size. It's almost inconceivable that Bushmen, who eat 75 or so wild plants, could die of starvation the way hundreds of thousands of Irish farmers and their families did during the potato famine of the 1840s.

So the lives of at least the surviving hunter-gatherers aren't nasty and brutish, even though farmers have pushed them into some of the world's worst real estate. But modern hunter-gatherer societies that have rubbed shoulders with farming societies for thousands of years don't tell us about conditions before the agricultural revolution. The progressivist view is really making a claim about the distant past: that the lives of primitive people improved when they switched from gathering to farming. Archaeologists can date that switch by distinguishing remains of wild plants and animals from those of domesticated ones in prehistoric garbage dumps.

How can one deduce the health of the prehistoric garbage makers, and thereby directly test the progressivist view? That question has become answerable only in recent years, in part through the newly emerging techniques of paleopathology, the study of signs of disease in the remains of ancient peoples.

In some lucky situations, the paleopathologist has almost as much material to study as a pathologist today. For example, archaeologists in the Chilean deserts found well preserved mummies whose medical conditions at time of death could be determined by autopsy. And feces of long-dead Indians who lived in dry caves in Nevada remain sufficiently well preserved to be examined for hookworm and other parasites.

Usually the only human remains available for study are skeletons, but they permit a surprising number of deductions. To begin with, a skeleton reveals its owner's sex, weight, and approximate age. In the few cases where there are many skeletons, one can construct mortality tables like the ones life insurance companies use to calculate expected life span and risk of death at any given age. Paleopathologists can also calculate growth rates by measuring bones of people of different ages, examining teeth for enamel defects (signs of childhood malnutrition), and recognizing scars left on bones by anemia, tuberculosis, leprosy, and other diseases.

One straightforward example of what paleopathologists have learned from skeletons concerns historical changes in height. Skeletons from Greece and Turkey show that the average height of hunter-gatherers toward the end of the ice ages was a generous 5'9" for men, 5'5" for women. With the adoption of agriculture, height crashed, and by 3000 B.C. had reached a low of only 5'3" for men, 5' for women. By classical times heights were very slowly on the rise again, but modern Greeks and Turks have still not regained the average height of their distant ancestors.

Another example of paleopathology at work is the study of Indian skeletons from burial mounds in the Illinois and Ohio river valleys. At Dickson Mounds, located near the confluence of the Spoon and Illinois rivers, archaeologists have excavated some 800 skeletons that paint a picture of the health changes that occurred when a hunter-gatherer culture gave way to intensive maize farming around A.D. 1150. Studies by George Armelagos and his colleagues then at the University of Massachusetts show these early farmers paid a price for their new-found livelihood. Compared to the hunter-gatherers who preceded them, the farmers had a nearly 50 percent increase in enamel defects indicative of malnutrition, a fourfold increase in iron-deficiency anemia (evidenced by a bone condition called porotic hyperostosis), a threefold rise in bone lesions reflecting infectious disease in general, and an increase in degenerative conditions of the spine, probably reflecting a lot of hard physical labor. "Life expectancy at birth in the pre-agricultural community was about twenty-six years," says Armelagos, "but in the post-agricultural community it was nineteen years. So these episodes of nutritional stress and infectious disease were seriously affecting their ability to survive."

The evidence suggests that the Indians at Dickson Mounds, like many other primitive peoples, took up farming not by choice but from necessity in order to feed their constantly growing numbers. "I don't think most hunter-gatherers farmed until they had to, and when they switched to farming they traded quality for quantity," says Mark Cohen of the State University of New York at Plattsburgh, co-editor, with Armelagos, of one of the seminal books in the field, *Paleopathology at the Origins of Agriculture.* "When I first started making that argument ten years ago, not many people agreed with me. Now it's become a respectable, albeit controversial, side of the debate."

There are at least three sets of reasons to explain the findings that agriculture was bad for health. First, hunter-gatherers enjoyed a varied diet, while early farmers obtained most of their food from one or a few starchy crops. The farmers gained cheap calories at the cost of poor nutrition. (Today just three high-carbohydrate plants—wheat, rice, and corn—provide the bulk of the calories consumed by the human species, yet each one is deficient in certain vitamins or amino acids essential to life.) Second, because of dependence on a limited number of crops, farmers ran the risk of starvation if one crop failed. Finally, the mere fact that agriculture encouraged people to clump together in crowded societies, many of which then carried on trade with other crowded societies, led to the spread of parasites and infectious disease. (Some archaeologists think it was crowding, rather than agriculture, that promoted disease, but this is a chicken-and-egg argument, because crowding encourages agriculture and vice versa.) Epidemics couldn't take hold when populations were scattered in small bands that constantly shifted camp. Tuberculosis and diarrheal disease had to await the rise of farming, measles and bubonic plague the appearance of large cities.

Besides malnutrition, starvation, and epidemic diseases, farming helped bring another curse upon humanity: deep class divisions. Hunter-gatherers have little or no stored food, and no concentrated food sources, like an orchard or a herd of cows: they live off the wild plants and animals they obtain each day. Therefore, there can be no kings, no class of social parasites who grow fat on food seized from others. Only in farming populations could a healthy, non-producing elite set itself above the disease-ridden masses. Skeletons from Greek tombs at Mycenae c. 1500 B.C. suggest that royals enjoyed a better diet than commoners, since the royal skeletons were two or three inches taller and had better teeth (on the average, one instead of six cavities or missing teeth). Among Chilean mummies from c. A.D. 1000, the élite were distinguished not only by ornaments and gold hair clips but also by a fourfold lower rate of bone lesions caused by disease.

Similar contrasts in nutrition and health persist on a global scale today. To people in rich countries like the U.S., it sounds ridiculous to extol the virtues of hunting and gathering. But Americans are an élite, dependent on oil and minerals that must often be imported from countries with poorer health and nutrition. If one could choose between being a peasant farmer in Ethiopia or a Bushman gatherer in the Kalahari, which do you think would be the better choice?

Farming may have encouraged inequality between the sexes, as well. Freed from the need to transport their babies during a nomadic existence, and under pressure to produce more hands to till the fields, farming women tended to have more frequent pregnancies than their hunter-gatherer counterparts— with consequent drains on their health. Among the Chilean mummies, for example, more women than men had bone lesions from infectious disease.

Women in agricultural societies were sometimes made beasts of burden. In New Guinea farming communities today I often see women staggering under loads of vegetables and firewood while the men walk empty-handed. Once while on a field trip there studying birds, I offered to pay some villagers to carry supplies from an airstrip to my mountain camp. The heaviest item was a 110-pound bag of rice, which I lashed to a pole and assigned to a team of four men to shoulder together. When I eventually caught up with the villagers, the men were carrying light loads, while one small woman weighing less than the bag of rice was bent under it, supporting its weight by a cord across her temples.

As for the claim that agriculture encouraged the flowering of art by providing us with leisure time, modern hunter-gatherers have at least as much free time as do farmers. The whole emphasis on leisure time as a critical factor seems to me misguided. Gorillas have had ample free time to build their own Parthenon, had they wanted to. While post-agricultural technological advances did make new art forms possible and preservation of art easier, great paintings and sculptures were already being produced by hunter-gatherers 15,000 years ago, and were still being produced as recently as the last century by such hunter-gatherers as some Eskimos and the Indians of the Pacific Northwest.

Thus with the advent of agriculture an élite became better off, but most people became worse off. Instead of swallowing the progressivist party line that we chose agriculture because it was good for us, we must ask how we got trapped by it despite its pitfalls.

One answer boils down to the adage "Might makes right." Farming could support many more people than hunting, albeit with a poorer quality of life. (Population densities of hunter-gatherers are rarely over one person per ten square miles, while farmers average 100 times that.) Partly, this is because a field planted entirely in edible crops lets one feed far more mouths than a forest with scattered edible plants. Partly, too, it's because nomadic hunter-gatherers have to keep their children spaced at four-year intervals by infanticide and other means, since a mother must carry her toddler until it's old enough to keep up with the adults. Because farm women don't have that burden, they can and often do bear a child every two years.

As population densities of hunter-gatherers slowly rose at the end of the ice ages, bands had to choose between feeding more mouths by taking the first steps toward agriculture, or else finding ways to limit growth. Some bands chose the former solution, unable to anticipate the evils of farming, and seduced by the transient abundance they enjoyed until population growth caught up with increased food production. Such bands outbred and then drove off or killed the bands that chose to remain hunter-gatherers, because a hundred malnourished farmers can still outfight one healthy hunter. It's not that hunter-gatherers abandoned their life style, but that those sensible enough not to abandon it were forced out of all areas except the ones farmers didn't want.

At this point it's instructive to recall the common complaint that archaeology is a luxury, concerned with the remote past, and offering no lessons for the present. Archaeologists studying the rise of farming have reconstructed a crucial stage at which we made the worst mistake in human history. Forced to choose between limiting population or trying to increase food production, we chose the latter and ended up with starvation, warfare, and tyranny.

Hunter-gatherers practiced the most successful and longest-lasting life style in human history. In contrast, we're still struggling with the mess into which agriculture has tumbled us, and it's unclear whether we can solve it. Suppose that an archaeologist who had visited us from outer space were trying to explain human history to his fellow spacelings. He might illustrate the results of his digs by a 24-hour clock on which one hour represents 100,000 years of real past time. If the history of the human race began at midnight, then we would now be almost at the end of our first day. We lived as hunter-gatherers for nearly the whole of that day, from midnight through dawn, noon, and sunset. Finally, at 11:54 p.m., we adopted agriculture. As our second midnight approaches, will the plight of famine-stricken peasants gradually spread to engulf us all? Or will we somehow achieve those seductive blessings that we imagine behind agriculture's glittering façade, and that have so far eluded us?

15

Agricultural Development and the Quality of Life

Peggy F. Barlett and Peter J. Brown

U.S. culture values progress. We seem to believe that new is better, and, as a nation, we seem to think that "progress is our most important product." We expect most change to be improvement, which means, most of the time, increased production, profits, and material possessions. As a society we are rich, but in what ways are we better off? Is our diet really better? Do we have greater equality and justice? Are our families stronger? These questions lead many people to wonder about their own values and expectations for life: Are these determined by you or by your culture?

In this article, Peggy Barlett and Peter Brown discuss the ambiguous but important concept of quality of life. In rural areas throughout the world, increased agricultural production spurred on by the expansion of a world market has significantly changed people's lives. For most farmers, this progress has been possible only with some real costs—trade-offs—in traditional values and life satisfaction. From an anthropological view, economic development can bring increases in perceived needs that can never be satisfied. As cultures change through increased agricultural production, people may have more material possessions but be less satisfied.

As you read this selection, ask yourself the following questions:

☐ *What is meant by trade-offs in the process of agricultural development?*

☐ *What are some of the difficulties in defining the quality of life in a cross-culturally valid way?*

☐ *Why has the U.S. economy followed the capital-intensive pathway of agricultural development?*

☐ *What causes people to change their perceptions about the necessities of life? What is the role of culture contact in this process?*

The following terms discussed in this selection are included in the Glossary at the back of the book:

agricultural development
cultural evolution
fallow
population pressure
slash-and-burn techniques

One of the paradoxes of modern life is the persistence of suffering and deep dissatisfaction among people who enjoy an unparalleled abundance of material goods. The paradox is at least as old as our modern age. Ever since the benefits and costs of industrial technology became apparent, opinion has been divided over whether we are progressing or declining (Johnson 1982:200).

Agricultural development is usually considered synonymous with "progress" in the Western world, but does agricultural development always improve the "quality of life" for farmers and their communities?

From *Agriculture and Human Values*, 1985. Reprinted by permission.

What are the human dimensions of the transformation of agriculture? Anthropological research shows that the relationship between agricultural development and the quality of life is much more complex than simple "progress." As Johnson indicates above, there are both costs and benefits associated with major economic changes, and these costs and benefits are difficult to interpret because they vary from culture to culture. We feel that agricultural development both harms and enhances life quality. We reject the simplistic notion that "new is better" and that increased agricultural production will automatically improve peoples' lives. However, it is wrong to ignore this important question simply because it is value laden or hard to measure.

In this paper we explore the relationship between agricultural development and the quality of life using concepts and examples from cultural anthropology. We explore the question by emphasizing the systematic patterns of trade-offs inherent in economic and social transformations. The concept "quality of life" must be seen as involving both an objective, measurable reality and a subjective, unquantifiable reality, which includes a person's ability to achieve culturally prescribed goals. Agricultural development can change the objective conditions of life, but it can also alter perceptions and goals, and these changes can sometimes move in opposite directions, both to increase and decrease "quality of life."

THE ANTHROPOLOGICAL PERSPECTIVE: CULTURAL EVOLUTION AND LIFE QUALITY

Respect for the values and lifeways of other societies is essential for an accurate understanding of changing quality of life. The knowledge, technology, values and beliefs of a society form a complex interconnected whole which is passed down from generation to generation; this is the central anthropological concept of culture. Cultural systems are highly adaptable, and as such form the core of human survival, allowing our species to inhabit and prosper in all environments of the world. The interconnected aspect of culture means that if one part changes, others will be affected; if, for instance, an economy changes, then we can and should expect that people's family life, politics, and religion will also be affected. In the past anthropology was limited to the study of primitive peoples, but today it includes the study of contemporary cultures in developing as well as developed nations. In this way, anthropologists bring a cross-cultural perspective to understandings about patterns of socio-economic change.

Quality of life is seen by anthropologists not only in terms of contemporary cultural diversity but also in the dimension of time. Using a long-term evolutionary view, there are basic stages in cultural evolution from "hunting and gathering" societies, through tribal and chiefdom phases, to agricultural and industrial states. In the historical evolution of complex societies like the one in which we live, there are some clear, unmistakable trends: population sizes get larger; economic systems become more complex and specialized; more energy is harnessed and consumed; social systems become unequal; and belief systems generally become more elaborate, reinforcing the economic and political trends.

From this perspective, the domestication of plants and animals emerges as one of the most important events in human history. Current archeological evidence indicates that the emergence of farming was not a sudden revolutionary event, but a slow, gradual process which occurred independently in Mesopotamia, the Indus valley, southern China, ancient Mexico and ancient Peru (Service 1975). The economic shift towards agriculture provided the foundation of ancient civilizations that followed the economic transformation in those five locations. The production of surplus food through farming allowed the economic specialization of the first cities and the elaboration of knowledge and art which are sometimes synonymous with civilization. It is logical that Western historians have interpreted this general cultural change as "progress."

The cultural changes following the domestication of plants and animals also involved some rather hefty costs. With the first agriculturally based state societies there also appeared the first kings, armies, jails, taxes, and war. For the bulk of the population, agriculture and civilization meant more work and a less nutritious diet than had been the case with more "primitive" cultures based on hunting and gathering. When we consider early slave-based states, for example, it is obvious that civilization improved life quality only for certain social segments. Because of these types of trade-offs involved in historical processes, the anthropological perspective does not allow a simple label like "progress" to be applied to complex cultural evolution. As cultures change, things get different, not necessarily better.

An important finding of recent anthropology was that the life among hunting and gathering societies like that of the !Kung San of Botswana is not "nasty, brutish, and short," as Westerners have traditionally believed. On the contrary, the San have more leisure time than most other societies, and adults average two to three days of subsistence work per week with six to eight hours of work in each of those days (Lee 1979:256–278). The San also enjoy an abundant and nutritious diet, compared to most agricultural societies, and have a flexible and intimate social system characterized by sharing, independence, cooperation and humor. Recent research on other band societies seems to support these findings that hunting and gathering peoples live lives with few material possessions, but what might be considered a high quality of life. The !Kung themselves describe a decline in their life quality brought by government control as well as the loss of territory to herding and agricultural people.

> Before the white people came, we did what our hearts wanted. We lived in different places, far apart, and when our hearts wanted to travel, we traveled. *We were not poor.* We had everything we could carry. No one told us what to do. Now the white people tell us to stay in this place. There are too many people. There's no food to gather. Game is far away and people are dying of tuberculosis. But when I was a little girl, we left sickness behind us when we moved (Volkman 1982:20; emphasis added).

DEFINING THE QUALITY OF LIFE

In general, there are two social scientific strategies for attempting to measure the quality of life. Most common is the definition of social indicators, that is, objective material measures such as per capita income, life expectancy, employment figures, morbidity/mortality rates, and the availability of certain consumer goods. Social indicators attempt to measure objectively peoples' life conditions, both wealth and health. A second, and less widespread strategy is subjective, attempting to measure life quality in terms of individuals' assessments of their life circumstances and life satisfaction. This subjective approach emphasizes the role of perception both in terms of life expectations and current life circumstances.

The methodological rigor associated with social indicators is impressive, but there is clearly no consensus on which statistical measures best comprise a standard quality of life scale. There is always the nagging question of the cross-cultural validity of "objective" social indicators since they ignore variations in beliefs and value concerning what is important in life. Because values, life expectations, and perceptions of the "good life" vary between cultural groups, it may be as difficult to define a universal scale of life quality as it would be to define a universal scale of beauty. This is not to imply, however, that minimal requirements in terms of basic human needs for food, shelter, and clothing cannot be identified. Such material conditions for the continuation of life may be considered *necessary but not sufficient* conditions for a high quality of life.

While objective quality of life indicators may be useful scientific tools for legislators and policy makers who wish to measure the efficacy of social and economic development programs, they often obscure important variations in the quality of life. For instance, infant mortality statistics are nearly identical for two cantons in Costa Rica that have sharply distinct situations (OFIPLAN 1979). One canton includes a large urban population, some light industry, and good medical facilities. Its high infant mortality rate can be attributed to the density of population, lack of adequate urban employment for many families, very concentrated landholdings in its rural areas, and lack of alternate income sources for these landless rural families. Infant mortality would seem to be strongly correlated with social class and inadequate nourishment. The contrasting canton is a sparsely populated frontier area with less concentrated landholdings and little unemployment. Its high infant mortality rate can be attributed more to difficult transportation and poor medical facilities rather than to malnourishment and underemployment of the population. Quality of life indicators obscure the great variation of wealth in the first canton, and the much lower and less skewed income levels in the second canton.

In addition to these problems in reducing complex issues to quantitative measures, quality of life measures can in some cases be inherently ethnocentric. For example, in using a measure of formal education, access to Western medicine, or income, the researcher assumes a more Western culture is better, and movement toward Western standards of living implies "progress." People judge their life circumstances through comparisons with others; this is the basis of the social scientific concept, "relative deprivation." There may be changing standards of comparison because of new perceptions of the necessities of life, or because of new comparison groups. As the case of the !Kung San shows, lack of material possessions does not always imply poverty. A subjective perspective of quality of life, based on the people's own perceptions, needs to be added to social indicators, to achieve a less biased view.

In applying the quality of life concept, a neglected question has been the extent to which the needs, values, aspirations, and life expectations as defined by a particular group of people can be met in their current life circumstances. These needs, values, and aspirations are by necessity defined differently by diverse ethnic or class groups, and also at various points in a process of historical cultural change. Material possessions, for instance, will be important to some groups as in modern Western culture, but irrelevant in others. The ability to maintain close ties with large family groups is essential for some cultures, while such contact would be burdensome to others. This diversity is important when analyzing how the "trade-offs" of agricultural development influence the quality of life. A culturally relativistic approach would therefore first examine a people's perceived needs and desires and then compare it to the objective reality of life circumstances. Quality of life might be conceived of as a ratio of objective social indicators to culturally defined perceptions of needs and life expectations. As we show below, both parts of this equation can change simultaneously in a process of agricultural development.

This approach allows for different strategies for achieving a high quality of life: to increase the capability to meet needs, or to reduce perceived needs and life expectations. Schumacher (1973) has argued that the former is an approach to life satisfaction typical of industrial capitalism while the latter represents a "Buddhist" approach. This second strategy is not generally recognized in discussions of quality of life among developmental practitioners or government agencies, but is revealed by a less ethnocentric approach to the issue.

WHAT IS AGRICULTURAL DEVELOPMENT?

Agricultural development is one label that can be given to a complex process of change in food production systems. As human populations have grown over the centuries, early methods of shifting agriculture have been replaced by permanent plow agriculture, characterized by draft animals and a short fallow period. Research on the evolution of cultural methods shows a transition from long fallow systems in which crop land is used only one year out of 25, to medium and short fallow systems where the land is cultivated every year (Netting 1977; Boserup 1965; Brookfield and Hart 1971). Slash-and-burn techniques that are necessary to remove a forest cover are replaced by plowing techniques to remove weeds and cultivate the soil. In this process, human labor in agriculture is supplemented by draft animals or by machines. When compared with the earliest agricultural technology, plow agriculture requires not only more intensive use of land but also more human labor per unit of output (Boserup 1965).

The causes of agricultural intensification are complex, but the single most important determinant in most of the world areas is population pressure (Gleave and White 1969; Boserup 1965; Spooner 1972; Brown and Podolefsky 1976). As the numbers of people increase for a given area of territory, agricultural methods become more sophisticated. In some cases contact with other groups creates the desire for consumer goods, especially through trade, and this culture contact can also result in agricultural intensification (Rawski 1972; Barlett 1982). Increased taxation or colonial expropriation of resources can have the same effect (Geertz 1963; White 1973).

With the advent of the industrial revolution, the process of agricultural evolution split into two distinct paths. Western European nations have generally followed one path in which industrial goods are emphasized in the production process and farm labor is generally replaced with capital. The other path is best exemplified by wet rice cultivation in Asia: it involves extraordinarily high investments of human labor in very small plots. This labor-intensive path usually includes sophisticated irrigation systems and public investments in canals and terraces. A result of this type of agriculture intensification is often a complete restructuring of the ecosystem to maximize food production. Although the productivity of agricultural labor declines on this path, the productive output per acre increases.

In the capital-intensive path of agricultural development, the production process becomes increasingly more diversified. Some parts of the production process, although not commonly conceived of as agriculture, are turned over to industries separate from the farm (such as the substitution of commercial fertilizer for farm manure). These industries produce chemicals, tractors, and silos for the use of farmers, thereby adding much more capital and labor investment to the overall process of food production. Importantly, such increased specialization also removes the farmer from direct control over important aspects of agricultural production, although he or she may orchestrate the process. Industrial agriculture also modifies the ecosystem more than traditional plow methods, not only through massive clearings of plots but also with the introduction of herbicides and pesticides into the environment.

Considering either the labor-intensive path or the capital-intensive path of agricultural development, there are major changes in four areas: the amount of work required to grow food increases; the amount of energy invested in food production increases; the sophistication of necessary tools increases; and the ecosystem is dramatically altered. These are all aspects of a general process of cultural change which can be called agricultural *intensification*.

AGRICULTURAL "PROGRESS" AND THE QUALITY OF LIFE

Although agricultural development actually has two alternative paths, only the capital intensive path is considered "development" or "progress" by Western experts and policy makers. Most agricultural development programs, modeled after the Western capital-intensive path, seek to replace on-farm labor with machinery and chemicals as well as to increase the productivity of the land with commercial fertilizers and improved crop varieties. The success of increasing productivity by U.S. and Western European farmers is clear. However, important trade-offs are often not recognized in agricultural development planning. For example, we noted above the farmer's loss of control over critical aspects of the production system. Another trade-off in capital-intensive agriculture is that it sometimes results in a lower quality food product. The quality of hybrid tomatoes sold in most grocery stores is one example; the lower protein content of hybrid corn is another. The introduction of these hybrid corn varieties into the U.S. increases profits for corn producers, but forces livestock producers to find a new protein source to replace the lost food value in corn. Peruvian fishmeal was once imported for this purpose, but today soybeans are commonly used. The cost of these substitutes is often not included in the estimates of the success of hybrid corn varieties.

Has the development of agriculture in the U.S. led to an improvement in the quality of life? Most policy makers have equated "improved quality of life" with "increased consumption of purchased goods" and farmers are certainly consuming more goods now than in previous generations. But as farmers in the U.S. have become more and more linked to a complex industrial and market system, their self-sufficiency has declined. Farmers' purchases of food at the grocery store are now similar to non-farmers, and consumer goods that were once rare are now purchased regularly. There is little doubt that capital-intensive farming provides more cash with which to buy more goods now, as the result of the development process.

Farmers' increased consumption of purchased goods is achieved at the cost of certain other aspects of the quality of life. The quality of work time, for example, has clearly diminished for those people who used to be independent farmers but who today are workers in fertilizer or machine factories. These workers may not do the arduous tasks that face farmers at certain points of the year, but they lose the variety of farm work and also lose control over their daily schedule of activities. Farmers consistently place a high value on "being one's own boss" and making one's own independent decisions. Trade-offs such as this are hard to include when trying to create a total judgment of a change in the quality of life.

Quality of life, the ability to meet perceived needs, is not automatically improved by agricultural development. Despite the ability of U.S. farmers to purchase more goods, like everyone else in capitalist society, they are likely to be caught in the consumer trap. The "consumer trap" means that the more one is able to consume, the more one desires to consume. Because "needs" escalate, development does not necessarily increase the ability to meet those needs. As U.S. farmers have become more a part of the wider consumer society, they experience constant pressure for more consumer goods, for the farm as well as for the family. This increasing desire to consume leads to pressures for greater intensification in farm production, which can push the farm into yet another spiral of more work, more energy, and more capital. Just as industry finds itself on a growth treadmill, so is agriculture told: "Grow or die."

A CROSS-CULTURAL MODEL

The relationship of agricultural development to the issue of quality of life may be seen as a circular process of intensification of production and consumption. Figure 1 diagrams some aspects of that process. Agricultural intensification leads in most situations to an increase in the labor expended in food production. This labor intensification may involve a lower quality of work experience for many workers and sometimes even a lower quality product. Environmental and technological changes usually accompany the process, which results in more sales of products and more money for the consumption of goods. An increase in perceived needs accompanies this process, however, and thus increased consumption does not automatically lead to an improved subjective assessment of life quality.

The desire for further consumption may stimulate another cycle of increased intensification in order to increase production. As explained above, this spiral begins as the result of a long evolutionary history of population pressure, conquest, and trade. In contemporary developing societies, however, it is maintained by the market pressures on consumers. From this perspective, then, as long as the developmental process pushes farmers to be more and more involved in the market, the market will exert pressure to expand their perceived "needs." Since the perceived ability to meet those needs is an essential component of the quality of life, agricultural development is inherently incapable of increasing the level of satisfaction and the quality of life among farmers.

COSTA RICA

These same issues of intensification, trade-offs, and the consumer trap can be seen in a mountainous area of rural Costa Rica, where the process of agricultural intensification has occurred rapidly in one generation (Barlett 1982). Having abandoned their traditional fallow system, the majority of farmers are now using each plot of land to produce several crops each year. The adoption of tobacco as a cash crop allows many households to harvest corn, beans, and tobacco in one annual sequence on each plot. To achieve this level of production, farmers must now work much harder, both in

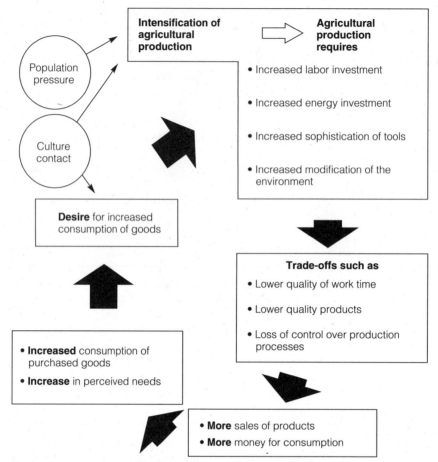

Figure 1
A model of the vicious cycle of agricultural intensification and increases in perceived needs.

terms of longer hours of work and in terms of harder work digging tobacco terraces by hand each year. Farmers in this area of Costa Rica invest over four times the work for this triple cropping sequence than for the traditional corn and beans sequence. Tobacco also requires considerably more capital (for fertilizer, chemicals, and equipment), increasing per acre costs over 700% for these "more modern" farmers.

Ecological adaptations and the security of rural life are also affected. The intensity of cultivation without the traditional fallow periods, together with the heavy use of chemicals, has increased problems with plant diseases and insect infestations in the area. Some farmers report feeling nauseated or having headaches after using the chemicals required by their tobacco contract. Another trade-off is the necessity to finance tobacco on credit, jeopardizing future income should one year's harvest be damaged. Many farmers see farming as much more stressful and risky now than it used to be.

Tobacco is, however, a profitable crop and gives farmers three times more cash per acre than any other land use option. With more money to consume, to-bacco producers are proud of their increased consumption. They are able to build nicer houses, buy televisions and refrigerators, invest in more land and livestock, and eat a more varied diet. On the other hand, development has also brought changes in cultural perceptions of the necessities of life in rural Costa Rica. Television exposes them to an urban middle-class lifestyle, and peasant farmers who were barefoot a generation ago now want stereos and cars as well as shoes and new fashions. Even for those without television, the increased contact with the city, government officials, tobacco company personnel, and bank officials all affect their perceived needs. It would be impossible for the scientific observer to say that agricultural development has clearly led to an improved ability to meet their perceived needs.

SARDINIA

Another case of trade-offs associated with agricultural intensification is the history of industrial cheese production in Sardinia, Italy (Brown 1979; Berger 1981).

Traditionally, shepherds from all zones of the island maintained flocks of sheep on non-arable land and produced *pecorino* cheese out in the countryside at the sheepfold enclosures. While most of this production was for local consumption, some cheese was sold to itinerant merchants who imported it to mainland Italy. In the local economy, cheese, meat, and lambs were bartered by shepherd families for food, services, rent payments, and necessities; the remainder of cheese sold to merchants was a source of cash for what little there was to purchase.

Around 1910, cheese production became industrialized with the advent of centralized cheese factories (*casefici*) financed by investors from Romagna in mainland Italy. Gradually, most herders in coastal and foothill zones, with the notable exception of the Barbagia highlands, were transformed into simple milk producers, selling milk daily to the factories. This economic transformation was possible not simply because local brokers for the factories offered cash for milk and hence reduced some economic risk. Industrial cheese production occurred simultaneously with an increased demand for cash and the availability of consumer goods.

The intensified production system has had a number of important consequences. On the negative side, shepherds' work lives are more monotonous, their profit margins much narrower, and their hours longer because flocks have been expanded up to four times the traditional size (Sabattini and Moro 1973). Similarly, the cheese produced by the industrial process is considered to be of inferior quality (Counihan 1981). On the positive side, the shift has allowed shepherds to live permanently in town and to purchase consumer goods like Fiats and motor scooters which make commutes to flocks easier. Most shepherds, however, must use donkeys for some part of their commute and now face the additional burden of transporting milk to roads for transfer to the cheese factory trucks. From the shepherds' view, the greatest advantage of the *caseficio* system is their ability to live a more "civilized" life in town, but the demands for cash in this modern consumer-oriented society are boundless.

Interestingly, *caseficio*-contracted shepherds envy their counterparts, primarily from the Barbagia highlands, who produce their own cheese and have remained independent of the factories. These traditional shepherds have also increased production, and they achieve much higher incomes by selling their own cheese. The original produce is considered tastier and brings a higher price in the market. Traditional producers tend to be more self-sufficient in food production, but their families still participate fully in the cash-based consumer society. In terms of material indicators, industrial and traditional shepherds may not be very different, but in terms of the strong cultural value placed on independence, the cost of industrialization has been heavy.

RURAL UNITED STATES

Agricultural development in the U.S. shows several of the trade-offs noted above. The "cost-price squeeze" currently facing U.S. farmers is a natural result of the increased diversification of capital-intensive agriculture (Schertz 1979). Today, U.S. farmers sell their products for low prices in a world market glutted with food. They operate an intensified farming system that requires capital that must be borrowed at high interest rates, fertilizers and chemicals whose prices rise sharply each year, and machinery whose costs also reflect the rising costs of living in the U.S. (Tweeten 1981). Rising energy prices provide an additional burden to the farmer (Buttel et al., 1980). The "squeeze" on farmers' profits is severe and is forcing many families out of farming. The number of farmers is declining rapidly all over the country, and farms are becoming bigger as the result. On those farms that are left, the capital and energy invested per unit of output has increased, showing the familiar intensification and the use of resources to produce food (Pimentel 1973; U.S.D.A. 1979, 1981).

Families forced off the farm usually end up in factory work or similar wage labor. Most see these jobs as much less desirable than farming and lament the monotony of the work, the loss of control over their lives, and the necessity to be "indoors" and away from growing things. For these people, agricultural development is usually a decline in the quality of work life.

In Georgia, farmers have suffered an unusually severe period of drought, together with the national cost-price squeeze (Barlett 1984). Facing profits that have fallen to zero year after year, one older farmer was asked if he thought we could go back to an era of lower consumption standards. He replied, "Most of those younger farmers would rather jump in the river." The perceived needs for cars, new homes, luxury vacations, or even an air-conditioned tractor make this period of financial hardship doubly difficult. The increased sophistication of farming has led again to an increase in perceived needs and no perceived improvement in the quality of life.

CONCLUSION

The three ethnographic examples above help illustrate the complex interaction of agricultural development and the quality of life. In this paper we have examined both the concepts of agricultural development and quality of life in the framework of cultural relativism and cultural evolution. It is important to recognize that in the process of intensified or industrialized production, both the material measures of life quality and a people's value and attitudes about "necessities" can change. In capital-intensive economic systems, perceptions of need can fuel the market demand for increased production. When this is the case, it will be impossible to assume that increased agricultural production will necessarily improve a society's quality of life.

REFERENCES

Barlett, Peggy F. 1982. *Agricultural Choice and Change: Decision Making in a Costa Rican Community.* New Brunswick, N.J.: Rutgers Press.

————. 1984. "Microdynamics of Debt, Drought & Default in South Georgia." *American Journal of Agricultural Economics* 66(5): 836–843.

Berger, Allen. 1981. "The Effects of Capitalism on the Social Structure of Pastoral Villages in Highland Sardinia." *Michigan Discussions in Anthropology,* Vol. 3.

Boserup, Ester. 1965. *The Conditions of Agricultural Growth.* Chicago: Aldine.

Brookfield, H. C. and D. Hart. 1971. *Melanesia: A Geographical Interpretation of an Island World.* London: Methuen.

Brown, Paula and Aaron Podolefsky. 1976. "Population Density, Agricultural Intensity, Land Tenure, and Group Size in the New Guinea Highlands." *Ethnology* 15:211–238.

Brown, Peter J. 1979. *Cultural Adaptations to Endemic Malaria and the Socioeconomic Effects of Malaria Eradication in Sardinia.* Ph.D. Dissertation, Department of Anthropology, S.U.N.Y. Stony Brook.

Buttel, Frederick H. et al. 1980. "Energy and Small Farms: A Review of Existing Research." Paper II of the National Rural Center, Small Farms Project. Washington, D.C.

Counihan, Carole M. 1981. *Food, Culture, and Political Economy: An Investigation of Changing Lifestyles in the Sardinian Town of Bosa.* Ph.D. Dissertation, Department of Anthropology, University of Massachusetts.

Geertz, Clifford. 1963. *Agricultural Involution.* Berkeley: University of California Press.

Gleave, M. B. and H. P. White. 1969. "Population Density and Agricultural Systems in West Africa." In *Environment and Land Use in Africa.* M. F. Thomas and G. W. Whittington, eds. (pps. 273–300). London: Methuen.

Johnson, Allen. 1982. "In Search of the Affluent Society." In *Anthropology: Contemporary Perspectives* (3d ed.). D. Hunter and P. Whitten, eds. (pp. 200–225). Boston: Little, Brown.

Lee, Richard Borshay. 1979. *The !Kung San: Men, Women and Work in a Foraging Society.* NY: Cambridge University Press.

Netting, Robert McC. 1977. *Cultural Ecology.* Menlo Park: Cummings.

OFIPLAN. 1979. *Mapa de Pobreza de Costa Rica.* San Jose: Oficina de Planificacion Nacional y Politica Economica.

Pimental, David, et al. 1973. "Food Production and the Energy Crisis." *Science* 182:443–449.

Rawsky, Evelyn Sakakida. 1972. *Agricultural Change and the Peasant Economy of South China.* Cambridge, Mass.: Harvard University Press.

Sabattini, Gianfranco and Beniamino Moro. 1973. *Il Sistema Economica della Sardegna.* Cagliari: Editrice Sarda.

Schertz, Lyle P. et al. 1979. *Another Revolution in U.S. Farming?* USDA Agricultural Economic Report #441. Washington: U.S. Government Printing Office.

Schumacher, E. F. 1973. *Small Is Beautiful.* NY: Harper and Row.

Service, Elman R. 1975. *Origins of the State and Civilization.* NY: Norton.

Spooner, Brian. 1972. *Population Growth.* Cambridge, Mass.: MIT Press.

Tweeten, Luther. 1981. "Agriculture at a Crucial Evolutionary Crossroads." *Research in Domestic and International Agribusiness Management* 2:1–15.

U.S.D.A. 1979. *Structure Issues of American Agriculture.* Economics, Statistics and Cooperatives Service: Agricultural Economic Report 438. Washington, D.C.: U.S. Government Printing Office.

————. 1981. *A Time to Choose: Summary Report on the Structure of Agriculture.* Washington, D.C.: U.S. Government Printing Office.

Volkman, Toby Alice. 1982. *The San in Transition.* Cultural Survival and D.E.R. Occasional Paper 9. Cambridge, Mass.: Cultural Survival.

White, Benjamin. 1973. "Demand for Labor and Population Growth in Colonial Java." *Human Ecology* 1(3): 217–244.

16

The Domestication of Wood in Haiti:
A Case Study in Applied Evolution

Gerald F. Murray

In its annual report on the state of the planet, the World-watch Institute describes the growing shortage of wood for fuel and construction throughout the Third World. The problem is most acute in densely populated areas with a long history of agriculture. In these areas, peasant farmers or members of their families can spend several hours each day finding firewood. Because forests take such a long time to grow and such a short time to cut down, reforestation is a worldwide ecological challenge.

As described in this selection, Haiti has a severe deforestation problem that is closely related to wider issues of poverty and overpopulation. In this context, traditional reforestation projects, with ponderous educational components on the value of trees, had failed miserably. Anthropologist Gerald Murray, who had done research on land tenure among rural Haitian peasants, had the rare opportunity to design and implement an alternative project in forestry and agricultural development. His anthropological understanding of the economic system and culture of the Haitian people clearly paid off. The project represents applying cultural anthropology at its best.

As you read this selection, ask yourself the following questions:

☐ Why does Haiti have a deforestation problem?

☐ How was Gerald Murray's anthropological alternative project different from traditional reforestation programs?

☐ Why was using particular kinds of trees important for the project?

☐ What accounted for the Haitian peasants' enthusiasm for the idea of trees as a cash crop?

☐ What is meant by the title of this piece?

The following terms discussed in this selection are included in the Glossary at the back of the book:

arable land
cadastral
domestication of plants and animals
horticulture
population pressure
reforestation
swidden cultivation
usufruct rights

PROBLEM AND CLIENT

Expatriate tree lovers, whether tourists or developmental planners, often leave Haiti with an upset stomach. Though during precolonial times the island Arawaks had reached a compromise with the forest, their market-oriented colonial successors saw trees as something to be removed. The Spaniards specialized in exporting wood from the eastern side of the island, whereas the French on the western third found it more profitable to clear the wood and produce sugar cane, coffee, and indigo for European markets. During the nineteenth century, long after Haiti had become an independent republic, foreign lumber companies cut and exported most of the nation's precious hardwoods, leaving little for today's peasants.

The geometric increase in population since colonial times—from an earlier population of fewer than half a million former slaves to a contemporary population of more than six million—and the resulting shrinkage of average family holding size have led to the evolution of a land use system devoid of systematic fallow periods. A vicious cycle has set in—one that seems to have targeted the tree for ultimate destruction. Not only has land pressure eliminated a regenerative fallow phase in the local agricultural cycle; in addition the catastrophic declines in per hectare food yields have forced peasants into alternative income-generating strategies. Increasing numbers crowd into the capital city, Port-au-Prince, creating a market for construction wood and charcoal. Poorer sectors of the peasantry in the rural areas respond to this market by racing each other with axes and machetes to cut down the few natural tree stands remaining in remoter regions of the republic. The proverbial snowball in Hades is at less risk than a tree in Haiti.

Unable to halt the flows either of wood into the cities or of soil into the oceans, international development organizations finance studies to measure the volume of these flows (50 million trees cut per year is one of the round figures being bandied about) and to predict when the last tree will be cut from Haiti. Reforestation projects have generally been entrusted by their well-meaning but short-sighted funders to Duvalier's Ministry of Agriculture, a kiss-of-death resource channeling strategy by which the Port-au-Prince jobs created frequently outnumber the seedlings produced. And even the few seedlings produced often died in the nurseries because the peasants were understandably reluctant to cover their scarce holdings with state-owned trees. Project managers had been forced to resort to "food for work" strategies to move seedlings out of nurseries onto hillsides. And peasants have endeavored where possible to plant the trees on somebody else's hillsides and to enlist their livestock as allies in the subsequent removal of this dangerous vegetation.

This generalized hostility to tree projects placed the U.S. Agency for International Development (AID)/Haiti mission in a bind. After several years of absence from Haiti in the wake of expulsion by François Duvalier, AID had reestablished its presence under the government of his son Jean Claude. But an ambitious Integrated Agricultural Development Project funded through the Ministry of Agriculture had already given clear signs of being a multimillion-dollar farce. And an influential congressman chairing the U.S. House Ways and Means Committee—consequently exercising strong control over AID funds worldwide—had taken a passionate interest in Haiti. In his worldwide travels this individual had become adept at detecting and exposing developmental charades. And he had been blunt in communicating his conviction that much of what he had seen in AID/Haiti's program was precisely that. He had been touched by the plight of Haiti and communicated to the highest AID authorities his conviction about the salvific power of contraceptives and trees and his determination to have AID grace Haiti with an abundant flow of both. And he would personally visit Haiti (a convenient plane ride from Washington, D.C.) to inspect for himself, threatening a worldwide funding freeze if no results were forthcoming. A chain reaction of nervous "yes sirs" speedily worked its way down from AID headquarters in Washington to a beleaguered Port-au-Prince mission.

The pills and condoms were less of a problem. Even the most cantankerous congressman was unlikely to insist on observing them in use and would probably settle for household distribution figures. Not so with the trees. He could (and did) pooh-pooh nursery production figures and asked to be taken to see the new AID forests, a most embarrassing request in a country where peasants creatively converted daytime reforestation projects into nocturnal goat forage projects. AID's reaction was twofold—first, to commission an immediate study to explain to the congressman and others why peasants refused to plant trees (for this they called down an AID economist); and second, to devise some program strategy that would achieve the apparently unachievable: to instill in cash-needy, defiant, pleasant charcoalmakers a love, honor, and respect for newly planted trees. For this attitudinal transformation, a task usually entrusted to the local armed forces, AID/Haiti invited an anthropologist to propose an alternative approach.

PROCESS AND PLAYERS

During these dynamics, I completed a doctoral dissertation on the manner in which Haitian peasant land tenure had evolved in response to internal population growth. The AID economist referred to above exhaustively reviewed the available literature, also focusing on the issue of Haitian peasant land tenure, and produced for the mission a well-argued monograph (Zuvekas 1978) documenting a lower rate of landlessness in Haiti than in many other Latin American settings but documenting as well the informal, extralegal character of the relationship between many peasant families and their landholdings. This latter observation was interpreted by some in the mission to mean that the principal determinant of the failure of tree planting projects was the absence among peasants of legally secure deeds over their plots. Peasants could not be expected to invest money on land improvements when at mildest the benefits could accrue to another and at worst the very improvements themselves could lead to expropriation from their land. In short, no massive tree planting could be expected, according to this model, until a nationwide cadastral reform granted plot-by-plot deeds to peasant families.

This hypothesis was reputable but programmatically paralyzing because nobody dreamed that the Duvalier regime was about to undertake a major cadastral reform for the benefit of peasants. Several AID officers in Haiti had read my dissertation on land tenure (Murray 1977), and I received an invitation to advise the mission. Was Haitian peasant land tenure compatible with tree planting? Zuvekas' study had captured the internally complex nature of Haitian peasant land tenure. But the subsequent extrapolations as to paralyzing insecurity simply did not seem to fit with ethnographic evidence. In two reports (Murray 1978a, 1978b) I indicated that peasants in general feel secure about their ownership rights over their land. Failure to secure plot-by-plot surveyed deeds is generally a cost-saving measure. Interclass evictions did occur, but they were statistically rare; instead most land disputes were intrafamilial. A series of extralegal tenure practices had evolved—preinheritance land grants to young adult dependents, informal inheritance subdivisions witnessed by community members, fictitious sales to favored children, complex community-internal share-cropping arrangements. And though these practices produced an internally heterogeneous system with its complexities, there was strong internal order. Any chaos and insecurity tended to be more in the mind of observers external to the system than in the behavior of the peasants themselves. There was a danger that the complexities of Haitian peasant land tenure would generate an unintended smokescreen obscuring the genuine causes of failure in tree planting projects.

What then were these genuine causes? The mission, intent on devising programming strategies in this domain, invited me to explore further, under a contract aimed at identifying the "determinants of success and failure" in reforestation and soil conservation projects. My major conclusion was that the preexisting land tenure, cropping, and livestock systems in peasant Haiti were perfectly adequate for the undertaking of significant tree planting activities. Most projects had failed not because of land tenure or attitudinal barriers among peasants but because of fatal flaws in one or more key project components. Though my contract called principally for analysis of previous or existing projects, I used the recommendation section of the report to speculate on how a Haiti-wise anthropologist would program and manage reforestation activities if he or she had the authority. In verbal debriefings I jokingly challenged certain young program officers in the mission to give me a jeep and carte blanche access to a $50,000 checking account, and I would prove my anthropological assertions about peasant economic behavior and produce more trees in the ground than their current multimillion-dollar Ministry of Agriculture charade. We had a good laugh and shook hands, and I departed confident that the report would be as dutifully perused and as honorably filed and forgotten as similar reports I had done elsewhere.

To my great disbelief, as I was correcting Anthro 101 exams some two years later, one of the program officers still in Haiti called to say that an Agroforestry Outreach Project (AOP) had been approved chapter and verse as I had recommended it; and that if I was interested in placing my life where my mouth had been and would leave the ivory tower to direct the project, my project bank account would have not $50,000, but $4 million. After several weeks of hemming and hawing and vigorous negotiating for leave from my department, I accepted the offer and entered a new (to me) role of project director in a strange upside-down world in which the project anthropologist was not a powerless cranky voice from the bleachers but the chief of party with substantial authority over general project policy and the allocation of project resources. My elation at commanding resources to implement anthropological ideas was dampened by the nervousness of knowing exactly who would be targeted for flak and ridicule if these ideas bombed out, as most tended to do in the Haiti of Duvalier.

The basic structural design of AOP followed a tripartite conceptual framework that I proposed for analyzing projects. Within this framework a project is composed of three essential systemic elements: a technical base, a benefit flow strategy, and an institutional delivery strategy. Planning had to focus equally on all three; I argued that defects in one would sabotage the entire project.

Technical Strategy

The basic technical strategy was to make available to peasants fast-growing wood trees (*Leucaena leuco-cephala, Cassia siamea, Azadirachta indica, Casuarina equi-setifolia, Eucalyptus camaldulensis*) that were not only drought resistant but also rapid growing, producing possible four-year harvest rotations in humid lowland areas (and slower rotations and lower survival rates in arid areas) and that were good for charcoal and basic construction needs. Most of the species mentioned also restore nutrients to the soil, and some of them coppice from a carefully harvested stump, producing several rotations before the need for replanting.

Of equally critical technical importance was the use of a nursery system that produced light-weight micro-seedlings. A project pickup truck could transport over 15,000 of these microseedlings (as opposed to 250 traditional bag seedlings), and the average peasant could easily carry over 500 transportable seedlings at one time, planting them with a fraction of the ground preparation time and labor required for bulkier bagged seedlings. The anthropological implications of this nursery system were critical. It constituted a technical breakthrough that reduced to a fraction the fossil-fuel and human energy expenditure required to transport and plant trees.

But the technical component of the project incorporated yet another element: the physical juxtaposition of trees and crops. In traditional reforestation models, the trees are planted in large unbroken monocropped stands. Such forests or woodlots presuppose local land tenure and economic arrangements not found in Haiti. For the tree to make its way as a cultivate into the economy of Haitian peasants and most other tropical cultivators, reforestation models would have to be replaced by agroforestry models that entail spatial or temporal juxtaposition of crops and trees. Guided by prior ethnographic knowledge of Haitian cropping patterns, AOP worked out with peasants various border planting and intercropping strategies to make tree planting feasible even for small holding cultivators.

Benefit Flow Strategies

With respect to the second systemic component, the programming of benefit flows to participants, earlier projects had often committed the fatal flaw of defining project trees planted as *pyebwa leta* (the state's trees). Authoritarian assertions by project staff concerning sanctions for cutting newly planted trees created fears among peasants that even trees planted on their own land would be government property. And several peasants were frank in reporting fears that the trees might eventually be used as a pretext by the government or the "Company" (the most common local lexeme used to refer to projects) for eventually expropriating the land on which peasants had planted project trees.

Such ambiguities and fears surrounding benefit flows paralyze even the technically soundest project. A major anthropological feature of AOP was a radical frontal attack on the issue of property and usufruct rights over project trees. Whereas other projects had criticized tree cutting, AOP promulgated the heretical message that trees were meant to be cut, processed, and sold. The only problem with the present system, according to project messages, was that peasants were cutting nature's trees. But once the landowner "mete fos li deyo" (expends his resources) and plants and cares for his or her own wood trees on his or her own land, the landowner has the same right to harvest and sell wood as corn or beans.

I was inevitably impressed at the impact that this blunt message had when I delivered it to groups of prospective peasant tree planters. Haitian peasants are inveterate and aggressive cash-croppers; many of the crops and livestock that they produce are destined for immediate consignment to local markets. For the first time in their lives, they were hearing a concrete proposal to make the wood tree itself one more marketable crop in their inventory.

But the message would ring true only if three barriers were smashed.

1. The first concerned the feared delay in benefits. Most wood trees with which the peasants were familiar took an impractically long time to mature. There fortunately existed in Haiti four-year-old stands of leucaena, cassia, eucalyptus, and other project trees to which we could take peasant groups to demonstrate the growth speed of these trees.

2. But could they be planted on their scanty holdings without interfering with crops? Border and row planting techniques were demonstrated, as well as intercropping. The average peasant holding was about a hectare and a half. If a cultivator planted a field in the usual crops and then planted 500 seedlings in the same field at 2 meters by 2 meters, the seedlings would occupy only a fifth of a hectare. And they would be far enough apart to permit continued cropping for two or three cycles before shade competition became too fierce. That is, trees would be planted on only a fraction of the peasant's holdings and

planted in such a way that they would be compatible with continued food growing even on the plots where they stood. We would then calculate with peasants the potential income to be derived from these 500 trees through sale as charcoal, polewood, or boards. In a best-case scenario, the gross take from the charcoal of these trees (the least lucrative use of the wood) might equal the current annual income of an average rural family. The income potential of these wood trees clearly would far offset any potential loss from decreased food production. Though it had taken AID two years to decide on the project, it took about twenty minutes with any group of skeptical but economically rational peasants to generate a list of enthusiastic potential tree planters.

3. But there was yet a third barrier. All this speculation about income generation presupposed that the peasants themselves, and not the government or the project, would be the sole owners of the trees and that the peasants would have unlimited rights to the harvest of the wood whenever they wished. To deal with this issue, I presented the matter as an agreement between cultivator and the project: We would furnish the free seedlings and technical assistance; the cultivators would agree to plant 500 of these seedlings on their own land and permit project personnel to carry out periodic survival counts. We would, of course, pay no wages or "Food for Work" for this planting. But we would guarantee to the planters complete and exclusive ownership of the trees. They did not need to ask for permission from the project to harvest the trees whenever their needs might dictate, nor would there be any penalties associated with early cutting or low survival. If peasants changed their minds, they could rip out their seedlings six months after planting. They would never get any more free seedlings from us, but they would not be subject to any penalties. There are preexisting local forestry laws, rarely enforced, concerning permissions and minor taxes for tree cutting. Peasants would have to deal with these as they had skillfully done in the past. But from our project's point of view, we relinquish all tree ownership rights to the peasants who accept and plant the trees on their property.

Cash-flow dialogues and ownership assurances such as these were a far cry from the finger-wagging ecological sermons to which many peasant groups had been subjected on the topic of trees. Our project technicians developed their own messages; but central to all was the principle of peasant ownership and usufruct of AOP trees. The goal was to capitalize on the preexisting fuel and lumber markets, to make the wood tree one more crop in the income-generating repertoire of the Haitian peasant.

Institutional Strategy

The major potential fly in the ointment was the third component, the institutional component. To whom would AID entrust its funds to carry out this project? My own research had indicated clearly that Haitian governmental involvement condemned a project to certain paralysis and possible death, and my report phrased that conclusion as diplomatically as possible. The diplomacy was required to head off possible rage, less from Haitian officials than from certain senior officers in the AID mission who were politically and philosophically wedded to an institution-building strategy. Having equated the term "institution" with "government bureaucracy," and having defined their own career success in terms, not of village-level resource flows, but of voluminous and timely bureaucracy-to-bureaucracy cash transfers, such officials were in effect marshaling U.S. resources into the service of extractive ministries with unparalleled track records of squandering and/or pilfering expatriate donor funds.

To the regime's paradoxical credit, however, the blatant openness and arrogance of Duvalierist predation had engendered an angry willingness in much of Haiti's development community to explore other resource flow channels. Though the nongovernmental character of the proposal provoked violent reaction, the reactionaries in the Haiti mission were overridden by their superiors in Washington, and a completely nongovernmental implementing mode was adopted for this project.

The system, based on private voluntary organizations (PVOs), worked as follows.

1. AID made a macrogrant to a Washington-based PVO (the Pan American Development Foundation, PADF) to run a tree-planting project based on the principles that had emerged in my research. At the Haiti mission's urging, PADF invited me to be chief of party for the project and located an experienced accountant in Haiti to be financial administrator. PADF in addition recruited three American agroforesters who, in addition to MA-level professional training, had several years of overseas village field experience under their belts. Early in the project they were supplemented by two other expatriates, a Belgian and a French Canadian. We opened a central office in Port-au-Prince and assigned a major region of Haiti to each of the agroforesters, who lived in their field regions.

2. These agroforesters were responsible for contacting the many village-based PVOs working in their regions to explain the project, to emphasize its microeconomic focus and its difference from traditional reforestation models, to discuss the conditions of entry therein, and to make technical suggestions as to the trees that would be appropriate for the region.

3. If the PVO was interested, we drafted an agreement in which our mutual contributions and spheres of responsibility were specified. The agreements were not drafted in French (Haiti's official language) but in Creole, the only language spoken by most peasants.

4. The local PVO selected *animateurs* (village organizers) who themselves were peasants who lived and worked in the village where trees would be planted. After receiving training from us, they contacted their neighbors and kin, generated lists of peasants interested in planting a specified number of trees, and informed us when the local rains began to fall. At the proper moment we packed the seedlings in boxes customized to the particular region and shipped them on our trucks to the farmers, who would be waiting at specified drop-off points at a specified time. The trees were to be planted within twenty-four hours of delivery.

5. The animateurs were provided with Creole language data forms by which to gather ecological, land use, and land tenure data on each plot where trees would be planted and certain bits of information on each peasant participant. These forms were used to follow up, at periodic intervals, the survival of trees, the incidence of any problems (such as livestock depredation, burning, disease), and—above all—the manner in which the farmer integrated the trees into cropping and livestock patterns, to detect and head off any unintended substitution of food for wood.

RESULTS AND EVALUATION

The project was funded for four years from October 1981 through November 1985. During the writing of the project paper we were asked by an AID economist to estimate how many trees would be planted. Not knowing if the peasants would in fact plant any trees, we nervously proposed to reach two thousand peasant families with a million trees as a project goal. Fiddling with his programmed calculator, the economist informed us that that output would produce a negative internal rate of return. We would need at least two million trees to make the project worth AID's institutional while. We shrugged and told him cavalierly to up the figure and to promise three million trees on the land of six thousand peasants. (At that time I thought someone else would be directing the project.)

Numbers of Trees and Beneficiaries

Though I doubted that we could reach this higher goal, the response of the Haitian peasants to this new approach to tree planting left everyone, including myself, open mouthed. Within the first year of the project, one million trees had been planted by some 2,500 peasant households all over Haiti. My fears of peasant indifference were now transformed into nervousness that we could not supply seedlings fast enough to meet the demand triggered by our wood-as-a-cash-crop strategy. Apologetic village animateurs informed us that some cultivators who had not signed up on the first lists were actually stealing newly planted seedlings from their neighbors' fields at night. They promised to catch the scoundrels. If they did, I told them, give the scoundrels a hug. Their pilfering was dramatic proof of the bull's-eye nature of the anthropological predictions that underlie the project.

By the end of the second year (when I left the project), we had reached the four-year goal of three million seedlings and the project had geared up and decentralized its nursery capacity to produce several million seedlings per season (each year having two planting seasons). Under the new director, a fellow anthropologist, the geometric increase continued. By the end of the fourth year, the project had planted, not its originally agreed-upon three million trees, but twenty million trees. Stated more accurately, some 75,000 Haitian peasants had enthusiastically planted trees on their own land. In terms of its quantitative outreach, AOP had more than quintupled its original goals.

Wood Harvesting and Wood Banking

By the end of its fourth year the project had already received an unusual amount of professional research attention by anthropologists, economists, and foresters. In addition to AID evaluations, six studies had been released on one or another aspect of the project (Ashley 1986; Balzano 1986; Buffum and King 1985; Conway 1986; Grosenick 1985; McGowan 1986). As predicted, many peasants were harvesting trees by the end of the fourth year. The most lucrative sale of the wood was as polewood in local markets, though much charcoal was also being made from project trees.

Interestingly, however, the harvesting was proceeding much more slowly than I had predicted. Peasants were "clinging" to their trees and not engaging in the clear cutting that I hoped would occur, as a prelude to the emergence of a rotational system in which peasants would alternate crops with tree cover that they themselves had planted. This technique would have been a revival, under a "domesticated" mode, of the ancient swidden sequence that had long since disappeared from Haiti. Though such a revival would have warmed anthropological hearts, the peasants had a different agenda. Though they had long ago removed nature's tree cover, they were extremely cautious about removing the tree cover that they had planted. Their economic logic was unassailable. Crop failure is so frequent throughout most of Haiti, and the market for wood and charcoal so secure, that peasants prefer to leave the tree as a "bank" against future emergencies. This arboreal bank makes particular sense in the context of the recent disappearance from Haiti of the peasant's traditional bank, the pig. A governmentally mandated (and U.S. financed) slaughter of all pigs because of fears of African swine fever created a peasant banking gap that AOP trees have now started to fill.

THE ANTHROPOLOGICAL DIFFERENCE

Anthropological findings, methods, and theories clearly have heavily influenced this project at all stages. We are dealing, not with an ongoing project affected by anthropological input, but with a project whose very existence was rooted in anthropological research and whose very character was determined by ongoing anthropological direction and anthropologically informed managerial prodding.

My own involvement with the project spanned several phases and tasks:

1. Proposal of a theoretical and conceptual base of AOP, and concept of "wood as a cash crop."

2. Preliminary contacting of local PVOs to assess preproject interest.

3. Identification of specific program measures during project design.

4. Preparation of social soundness analysis for the AID project paper.

5. Participation as an outside expert at the meetings in AID Washington at which the fate of the project was decided.

6. Participation in the selection and in-country linguistic and cultural training of the agroforesters who worked for the project.

7. Direction and supervision of field operations.

8. Formative evaluation of preliminary results and the identification of needed midcourse corrections.

9. Generation of several hundred thousand dollars of supplemental funding from Canadian and Swiss sources and internationalization of the project team.

10. Preparation of publications about the project (Murray 1984, 1986).

In addition to my own participation in the AOP, four other anthropologists have been involved in longterm commitments to the project. Fred Conway did a preliminary study of firewood use in Haiti (Conway 1979). He subsequently served for two years as overall project coordinator within AID/Haiti. More recently he has carried out revealing case study research on the harvesting of project trees (Conway 1986). Glenn Smucker likewise did an early feasibility study in the northwest (Smucker 1981) and eventually joined the project as my successor in the directorship. Under his leadership, many of the crucial midcourse corrections were introduced. Ira Lowenthall took over the AID coordination of the project at a critical transitional period and has been instrumental in forging plans for its institutional future. And Anthony Balzano has carried out several years of case study fieldwork on the possible impact of the tree-planting activities on the land tenure in participating villages. All these individuals have PhDs, or are PhD candidates, in anthropology. And another anthropologist in the Haiti mission, John Lewis, succeeded in adapting the privatized umbrella agency outreach model for use in a swine repopulation project. With the possible exception of Vicos, it would be hard to imagine a project that has been as heavily influenced by anthropologists.

But how specifically has anthropology influenced the content of the project? There are at least three major levels at which anthropology has impinged on the content of AOP.

1. *The Application of Substantive Findings.* The very choice of "wood as a marketable crop" as the fundamental theme of the project stemmed from ethnographic knowledge of the cash-oriented foundations of Haitian peasant horticulture and knowledge of current conditions in the internal marketing system. Because of ethnographic knowledge I was able to avoid succumbing to the common-sense inclination to emphasize fruit trees (whose perishability and tendency to glut markets make them commercially vulnerable) and to choose instead a fast-growing wood tree. There is a feverishly escalating market for charcoal and construction wood that cannot be dampened even by the most successful project. And there are no spoilage problems with wood. The peasants can harvest it when they want. Furthermore, ethnographic

knowledge of Haitian peasant land tenure—which is highly individualistic—guided me away from the community forest schemes that so many development philosophers seem to delight in but that are completely inappropriate to the social reality of Caribbean peasantries.

2. *Anthropological Methods.* The basic research that led up to the project employed participant observation along with intensive interviewing with small groups of informants to compare current cost/benefit ratios of traditional farming with projected cash yields from plots in which trees are intercropped with food on four-year rotation cycles. A critical part of the project design stage was to establish the likelihood of increased revenues from altered land use behaviors. During project design I also applied ethnographic techniques to the behavior of institutional personnel. The application of anthropological notetaking on 3-by-5 slips, not only with peasants but also with technicians, managers, and officials, exposed the institutional roots of earlier project failures and stimulated the proposal of alternative institutional routes. Furthermore, ethno-scientific elicitation of folk taxonomies led to the realization that whereas fruit trees are classified as a crop by Haitian peasants, wood trees are not so classified. This discovery exposed the need for the creation of explicit messages saying that wood can be a crop, just as coffee, manioc, and corn can. Finally, prior experience in Creole-language instrument design and computer analysis permitted me to design a baseline data gathering system.

3. *Anthropological Theory.* My own thinking about tree planting was heavily guided by cultural-evolutionary insights into the origins of agriculture. The global tree problem is often erroneously conceptualized in a conservationist or ecological framework. Such a perspective is very short-sighted for anthropologists. We are aware of an ancient food crisis, when humans still hunted and gathered, that was solved, not by the adoption of conservationist practices, but rather by the shift into a domesticated mode of production. From hunting and gathering we turned to cropping and harvesting. I found the analogy with the present tree crisis conceptually overpowering. Trees will reemerge when and only when human beings start planting them aggressively as a harvestable crop, not when human consciousness is raised regarding their ecological importance. This anthropological insight (or bias), nourished by the aggressive creativity of the Haitian peasants among

whom I had lived, swayed me toward the adoption of a dynamic "domestication" paradigm in proposing a solution to the tree problem in Haiti. This evolutionary perspective also permitted me to see that the cash-cropping of wood was in reality a small evolutionary step, not a quantum leap. The Haitian peasants already cut and sell natural stands of wood. They already plant and sell traditional food crops. It is but a small evolutionary step to join these two unconnected streams of Haitian peasant behavior, and this linkage is the core purpose of the Agroforestry Outreach Project.

Broader anthropological theory also motivated and justified a nongovernmental implementing mode for AOP. Not only AID but also most international development agencies tend to operate on a service model of the state. This idealized model views the basic character of the state as that of a provider of services to its population. Adherence to this theoretically naive service model has led to the squandering of untold millions of dollars in the support of extractive public bureaucracies. This waste is justified under the rubric of institution building—assisting public entities to provide the services that they are supposed to be providing.

But my anthropological insights into the origins of the state as a mechanism of extraction and control led me to pose the somewhat heretical position that the predatory behavior of Duvalier's regime was in fact not misbehavior. Duvalier was merely doing openly and blatantly what other state leaders camouflage under rhetoric. AID's search of nongovernmental implementing channels for AOP, then, was not seen as a simple emergency measure to be employed under a misbehaving regime but rather as an avenue of activity that might be valid as an option under many or most regimes. There is little justification in either ethnology or anthropological theory for viewing the state as the proper recipient of developmental funds. This theoretical insight permitted us to argue for a radically nongovernmental mode of tree-planting support in AOP. In short, sensitivity to issues in anthropological theory played a profound role in the shaping of the project.

Would AOP have taken the form it did without these varied types of anthropological input? Almost certainly not. Had there been no anthropological input, a radically different scenario would almost certainly have unfolded with the following elements.

1. AID would probably have undertaken a reforestation project—congressional pressure alone would have ensured that. But the project would have been based, not on the theme of "wood as a peasant cash-crop," but on the more traditional approach to trees as a vehicle of soil conservation. Ponderous educational programs would have been launched to teach the peasants

about the value of trees. Emphasis would have been placed on educating the ignorant and on trying to induce peasants to plant commercially marginal (and nutritionally tangential) fruit trees instead of cash-generating wood trees.

2. The project would have been managed by technicians. The emphasis would probably have been on carrying out lengthy technical research concerning optimal planting strategies and the combination of trees with optimally effective bench terraces and other soil conservation devices. The outreach problem would have been given second priority. Throughout Haiti hundreds of thousands of dollars have been spent on numerous demonstration projects to create terraced, forested hillsides, but only a handful of cooperative local peasants have been induced to undertake the same activities on their own land.

3. The project would almost certainly have been run through the Haitian government. When after several hundred thousand dollars of expenditures few trees were visible, frustrated young AID program officers would have gotten finger-wagging lectures about the sovereign right of local officials to use donor money as they see fit. And the few trees planted would have been defined as *pyebwa leta* (the government's trees), and peasants would have been sternly warned against ever cutting these trees, even the ones planted on their own land. And the peasants would soon turn the problem over to their most effective ally in such matters, the free-ranging omnivorous goat, who would soon remove this alien vegetation from the peasants' land.

Because of anthropology, the Agroforestry Outreach Project has unfolded to a different scenario. It was a moving experience for me to return to the village where I had done my original fieldwork (and which I of course tried to involve in the tree-planting activities) to find several houses built using the wood from leucaena trees planted during the project's earliest phases. Poles were beginning to be sold, although the prices had not yet stabilized for these still unknown wood types. Charcoal made from project trees was being sold in local markets. For the first time in the history of this village, people were "growing" part of their house structures and their cooking fuel. I felt as though I were observing (and had been a participant in) a replay of an ancient anthropological drama, the shift from an extractive to a domesticated mode of resource procurement. Though their sources of food energy had been domesticated millennia ago, my former village neighbors had now begun replicating this transition in the domain of wood and wood-based energy. I felt a satisfaction at having chosen a discipline that could give me the privilege of participating, even marginally, in this very ancient cultural-evolutionary transition.

REFERENCES

Ashley, Marshall D. 1986. *A Study of Traditional Agroforestry Systems in Haiti and Implications for the USAID/Haiti Agroforestry Outreach Project.* Port-au-Prince: University of Maine Agroforestry Outreach Research Project.

Balzano, Anthony. 1986. *Socioeconomic Aspects of Agroforestry in Rural Haiti.* Port-au-Prince: University of Maine Agroforestry Outreach Research Project.

Buffum, William, and Wendy King. 1985. *Small Farmer Decision Making and Tree Planting: Agroforestry Extension Recommendations.* Port-au-Prince: Haiti Agroforestry Outreach Project.

Conway, Frederick. 1979. *A Study of the Fuelwood Situation in Haiti.* Port-au-Prince: USAID.

———. 1986. *The Decision Making Framework for Tree Planting Within the Agroforestry Outreach Project.* Port-au-Prince: University of Maine Agroforestry Outreach Research Project.

Grosenick, Gerald. 1985. *Economic Evaluation of the Agroforestry Outreach Project.* Port-au-Prince: University of Maine Agroforestry Outreach Research Project.

McGowan, Lisa A. 1986. *Potential Marketability of Charcoal, Poles, and Planks Produced by Participants in the Agroforestry Outreach Project.* Port-au-Prince: University of Maine Agroforestry Outreach Research Project.

Murray, Gerald F. 1977. *The Evolution of Haitian Peasant Land Tenure: A Case Study in Agrarian Adaptation to Population Growth.* Ph.D. dissertation, Columbia University, New York.

———. 1978a. *Hillside Units, Wage Labor, and Haitian Peasant Land Tenure: A Strategy for the Organization of Erosion Control.* Port-au-Prince: USAID.

———. 1978b. *Informal Subdivisions and Land Insecurity: An Analysis of Haitian Peasant Land Tenure.* Port-au-Prince: USAID.

———. 1979. *Terraces, Trees, and the Haitian Peasant: An Assessment of 25 Years of Erosion Control in Rural Haiti.* Port-au-Prince: USAID.

———. 1984. "The Wood Tree as a Peasant Cash-Crop: An Anthropological Strategy for the Domestication of Energy." In A. Valdman and R. Foster, eds., *Haiti—Today and Tomorrow: An Interdisciplinary Study.* New York: University Press of America.

———. 1986. "Seeing the Forest While Planting the Trees: An Anthropological Approach to Agroforestry in Rural Haiti." In D. W. Brinkerhoff and J. C. Garcia-Zamor, eds., *Politics, Projects, and Peasants: Institutional Development in Haiti.* New York: Praeger, pp. 193–226.

Smucker, Glenn R. 1981. *Trees and Charcoal in Haitian Peasant Economy: A Feasibility Study.* Port-au-Prince: USAID.

Zuvekas, Clarence. 1978. *Agricultural Development in Haiti: An Assessment of Sector Problems, Policies, and Prospects under Conditions of Severe Soil Erosion.* Washington, D.C.: USAID.

17

Race Without Color

Jared Diamond

Looking at the title of this selection, you should ask yourself two questions. First, what is a reading about race doing in a cultural anthropology book? After all, it would seem that race is obviously a biological question. Second, what could the author could possibly mean by "race without color?" Doesn't that sound like an oxymoron?

An important aspect of anthropological thinking is examining ideas, beliefs, and values within their own cultural context. Our own cultural ideas and concepts, including scientific ones, are grist for the anthropological mill because they are best understood within a larger cultural framework. Sometimes cultural anthropologists focus on a single cultural concept and take it apart, demonstrating its historical roots and its relation to other social beliefs. In postmodern parlance, this kind of intensive analysis can be called "deconstructing" a concept.

In this selection, a well-known natural scientist "deconstructs" the biological concept of race. Although the term of race seems to have some use in the description of population variation in birds and in creating a taxonomy, the concept doesn't work very well for understanding human variation. In fact, from a biological standpoint, the concept of race based on skin color is scientifically useless. As the reading demonstrates, there are a lot of different ways to categorize human biological diversity, but these variations are independent from one another so that there is more variation within racial categories than between them. By deconstructing race, we see that it is a cultural category, not a biological one.

On the other hand, race is indeed an important historical and political concept—as a cultural construction that functions as a folk-biological rationalization for enforcing social inequalities. We decided to include this reading within this cultural anthropology book to emphasize the fact that race is a cultural invention. Race is not useful for understanding human biological diversity; it is essentially meaningless, like an oxymoron.

As you read this selection, ask yourself the following questions:

☐ Why does skin color seem to be such an obvious and commonsensical way to make distinctions among people?

☐ How might it be acceptable to use the concept of race for talking about birds, but not humans?

☐ What does it mean that taxonomists are "lumpers" and "splitters"?

☐ How is our understanding of most biological variations—like resistance to malaria or adults' ability to digest milk—not aided by the concept of race?

☐ If racial classifications are cultural constructions, what does the author think is the purpose of these arbitrary classifications?

The following terms discussed in this selection are included in the Glossary at the back of the book:

lactose intolerance
race
sickle-cell anemia
species

Jared Diamond/© 1994 Discover Magazine.

Basing race on body chemistry makes no more sense than basing race on appearance—but at least you get to move the membership around.

Science often violates simple common sense. Our eyes tell us that the Earth is flat, that the sun revolves around the Earth, and that we humans are not animals. But we now ignore that evidence of our senses. We have learned that our planet is in fact round and revolves around the sun, and that humans are slightly modified chimpanzees. The reality of human races is another commonsense "truth" destined to follow the flat Earth into oblivion. The commonsense view of races goes somewhat as follows. All native Swedes differ from all native Nigerians in appearance: there is no Swede whom you would mistake for a Nigerian, and vice versa. Swedes have lighter skin than Nigerians do. They also generally have blond or light brown hair, while Nigerians have very dark hair. Nigerians usually have more tightly coiled hair than Swedes do, dark eyes as opposed to eyes that are blue or gray, and fuller lips and broader noses.

In addition, other Europeans look much more like Swedes than like Nigerians, while other peoples of sub-Saharan Africa—except perhaps the Khoisan peoples of southern Africa—look much more like Nigerians than like Swedes. Yes, skin color does get darker in Europe toward the Mediterranean, but it is still lighter than the skin of sub-Saharan Africans. In Europe, very dark or curly hair becomes more common outside Scandinavia, but European hair is still not as tightly coiled as in Africa. Since it's easy then to distinguish almost any native European from any native sub-Saharan African, we recognize Europeans and sub-Saharan Africans as distinct races, which we name for their skin colors: whites and blacks, respectively.

What could be more objective?

As it turns out, this seemingly unassailable reasoning is not objective. There are many different, equally valid procedures for defining races, and those different procedures yield very different classifications. One such procedure would group Italians and Greeks with most African blacks. It would classify Xhosas—the South African "black" group to which President Nelson Mandela belongs—with Swedes rather than Nigerians. Another equally valid procedure would place Swedes with Fulani (a Nigerian "black" group) and not with Italians who would again be grouped with most other African blacks. Still another procedure would keep Swedes and Italians separate from all African blacks but would throw the Swedes and Italians into the same race as New Guineans and American Indians. Faced with such differing classifications, many anthropologists today conclude that one cannot recognize any human races at all.

If we were just arguing about races of nonhuman animals, essentially the same uncertainties of classification would arise. But the debates would remain polite and would never attract attention outside the halls of academia. Classification of humans is different "only" in that it shapes our views of other peoples, fosters our subconscious differentiation between "us" and "them," and is invoked to justify political and socioeconomic discrimination. On this basis, many anthropologists therefore argue that even if one *could* classify humans into races, one should not.

To understand how such uncertainties in classification arise let's steer clear of humans for a moment and instead focus on warblers and lions, about which we can easily remain dispassionate. Biologists begin by classifying living creatures into species. A species is a group of populations whose individual members would, if given the opportunity, interbreed with individuals of other populations of that group. But they would not interbreed with individuals of other species that are similarly defined. Thus all human populations, no matter how different they look belong to the same species because they do interbreed and have interbred whenever they have encountered each other. Gorillas and humans, however, belong to two different species because—to the best of our knowledge—they have never interbred despite their coexisting in close proximity for millions of years.

We know that different populations classified together in the human species are visibly different. The same proves true for most other animal and plant species as well, whenever biologists look carefully. For example, consider one of the most familiar species of bird in North America, the yellow-rumped warbler. Breeding males of eastern and western North America can be distinguished at a glance by their throat color. white in the east, yellow in the west. Hence they are classified into two different races, or subspecies (alternative words with identical meanings), termed the myrtle and Audubon races, respectively. The white-throated eastern birds differ from the yellow-throated western birds in other characteristics as well, such as in voice and habitat preference. But where the two races meet, in western Canada, white-throated birds do indeed interbreed with yellow-throated birds. That's why we consider myrtle warblers and Audubon warblers as races of the same species rather than different species.

Racial classification of these birds is easy. Throat color, voice and habitat preference all vary geographically in yellow-rumped warblers, but the variation of those three traits is "concordant"—that is, voice differences or habitat differences lead to the same racial classification as differences in throat color because the same populations that differ in throat color also differ in voice and habitat.

Racial classification of many other species, though, presents problems of concordance. For instance, a

Pacific island bird species called the golden whistler varies from one island to the next. Some populations consist of big birds, some of small birds; some have black-winged males, others green-winged males; some have yellow-breasted females, others gray-breasted females; many other characteristics vary as well. But, unfortunately for humans like me who study these birds, those characteristics don't vary concordantly. Islands with green-winged males can have either yellow-breasted or gray-breasted females, and green-winged males are big on some islands but small on other islands. As a result if you classified golden whistlers into races based on single traits, you would set entirely different classifications depending on which trait you chose.

Classification of these birds also presents problems of "hierarchy." Some of the golden whistler races recognized by ornithologists are wildly different from all the other races, but some are very similar to one another. They can therefore be grouped into a hierarchy of distinctness. You start by establishing the most distinct population as a race separate from all other populations. You then separate the most distinct of the remaining populations. You continue by grouping similar populations, and separating distinct populations or groups of populations as races or groups of races. The problem is that the extent to which you continue the racial classification is arbitrary, and it's a decision about which taxonomists disagree passionately. Some taxonomists, the "splitters," like to recognize many different races, partly for the egotistical motive of getting credit for having named a race. Other taxonomists, the "lumpers," prefer to recognize few races. Which type of taxonomist you are is a matter of personal preference.

How does that variability of traits by which we classify races come about in the first place? Some traits vary because of natural selection: that is, one form of the trait is advantageous for survival in one area, another form in a different area. For example, northern hares and weasels develop white fur in the winter, but southern ones retain brown fur year-round. The white winter fur is selected in the north for camouflage against the snow, while any animal unfortunate enough to turn white in the snowless southern states would stand out from afar against the brown ground and would be picked off by predators.

Other traits vary geographically because of *sexual* selection, meaning that those traits serve as arbitrary signals by which individuals of one sex attract mates of the opposite sex while intimidating rivals. Adult male lions, for instance, have a mane, but lionesses and young males don't. The adult male's mane signals to lionesses that he is sexually mature, and signals to young male rivals that he is a dangerous and experienced adversary. The length and color of a lion's mane vary among populations, being shorter and blacker in Indian lions than in African lions. Indian lions and lionesses evidently find short black manes sexy or intimidating; African lions don't.

Finally, some geographically variable traits have *no* known effect on survival and are invisible to rivals and to prospective sex partners. They merely reflect mutations that happened to arise and spread in one area. They could equally well have arisen and spread elsewhere—they just didn't.

RACE BY RESISTANCE

Traditionally we divide ourselves into races by the twin criteria of geographic location and visible physical characteristics. But we could make an equally reasonable and arbitrary division by the presence or absence of a gene, such as the sickle-cell gene, that confers resistance to malaria. By this reckoning, we'd place Yemenites, Greeks, New Guineans, Thai, and Dinkas in one "race," Norwegians and several black African peoples in another.

Nothing that I've said about geographic variation in animals is likely to get me branded a racist. We don't attribute higher IQ or social status to black-winged whistlers than to green-winged whistlers. But now let's consider geographic variation in humans. We'll start with invisible traits, about which it's easy to remain dispassionate.

Many geographically variable human traits evolved by natural selection to adapt humans to particular climates or environments—just as the winter color of a hare or weasel did. Good examples are the mutations that people in tropical parts of the Old World evolved to help them survive malaria, the leading infectious disease of the old-world tropics. One such mutation is the sickle-cell gene, so-called because the red blood cells of people with that mutation tend to assume a sickle shape. People bearing the gene are more resistant to malaria than people without it. Not surprisingly, the gene is absent from northern Europe, where malaria is nonexistent, but it's common in tropical Africa, where malaria is widespread. Up to 40 percent of Africans in such areas carry the sickle-cell gene. It's also common in the malaria-ridden Arabian Peninsula and southern India, and rare or absent in the southern most parts of South Africa, among the Xhosas who live mostly beyond the tropical geographic range of malaria.

The geographic range of human malaria is much wider than the range of the sickle-cell gene. As it happens, other antimalarial genes take over the protective function of the sickle-cell gene in malarial Southeast

Asia and New Guinea and in Italy, Greece, and other warm parts of the Mediterranean basin. Thus human races, if defined by antimalarial genes, would be very different from human races as traditionally defined by traits such as skin color. As classified by antimalarial genes (or their absence), Swedes are grouped with Xhosas but not with Italians or Greeks. Most other peoples usually viewed as African blacks are grouped with Arabia's "whites" and are kept separate from the "black" Xhosas.

RACE BY DIGESTION

We could define a race by any geographicaly variable trait—for example, the retention in adulthood of the enzyme lactase, which allows us to digest milk, Using this as our divisive criterion, we can place northern and central Europeans with Arabians and such West African peoples as the Fulani; in a "lactase-negative race," we can group most other African blacks with east Asians, American Indians, southern Europeans, and Australian aborigines.

Antimalarial genes exemplify the many features of our body chemistry that vary geographically under the influence of natural selection. Another such feature is the enzyme lactase, which enables us to digest the milk sugar lactose. Infant humans, like infants of almost all other mammal species, possess lactase and drink milk. Until about 6,000 years ago most humans, like all other mammal species, lost the lactase enzyme on reaching the age of weaning. The obvious reason is that it was unnecessary—no human or other mammal drank milk as an adult, Beginning around 4000 B.C., however, fresh milk obtained from domestic mammals became a major food for adults of a few human populations. Natural selection caused individuals in these populations to retain lactase into adulthood. Among such peoples are northern and central Europeans, Arabians, north Indians, and several milk-drinking black African peoples, such as the Fulani of West Africa. Adult lactase is much less common in southern European populations and in most other African black populations, as well as in all populations of east Asians, aboriginal Australians, and American Indians.

Once again races defined by body chemistry don't match races defined by skin color. Swedes belong with Fulani in the "lactase-positive race," while most African "blacks," Japanese, and American Indians belong in the "lactase-negative race."

Not all the effects of natural selection are as invisible as lactase and sickle cells. Environmental pressures have also produced more noticeable differences among peoples, particularly in body shapes. Among the tallest and most long-limbed peoples in the world are the Nilotic peoples, such as the Dinkas, who live in the hot, dry areas of East Africa. At the opposite extreme in body shape are the Inuit, or Eskimo, who have compact bodies and relatively short arms and legs. The reasons have to do with heat loss. The greater the surface area of a warm body, the more body heat that's lost, since heat loss is directly proportional to surface area. For people of a given weight, a long-limbed, tall shape maximizes surface area, while a compact, short-limbed shape minimizes it. Dinkas and Inuit have opposite problems of heat balance: the former usually need desperately to get rid of body heat, while the latter need desperately to conserve it. Thus natural selection molded their body shapes oppositely, based on their contrasting climates.

(In modern times, such considerations of body shape have become important to athletic performance as well as to heat loss. Tall basketball players, for example, have an obvious advantage over short ones, and slender, long-limbed tall players have an advantage over stout, short-limbed tall players. In the United States, it's a familiar observation that African Americans are disproportionately represented among professional basketball players. Of course, a contributing reason has to do with their lack of socioeconomic opportunities. But part of the reason probably has to do with the prevalent body shapes of some black African groups as well. However, this example also illustrates the dangers in facile racial stereotyping. One can't make the sweeping generalization that "whites can't jump," or that "blacks' anatomy makes them better basketball players." Only certain African peoples are notably tall and long-limbed; even those exceptional peoples are tall and long-limbed only on the average and vary individually.)

Other visible traits that vary geographically among humans evolved by means of sexual selection. We all know that we find some individuals of the opposite sex more attractive than other individuals. We also know that in sizing up sex appeal, we pay more attention to certain parts of a prospective sex partner's body than to other parts. Men tend to be inordinately interested in women's breasts and much less concerned with women's toenails. Women, in turn, tend to be turned on by the shape of a man's buttocks or the details of a man's beard and body hair, if any, but not by the size of his feet.

But all those determinants of sex appeal vary geographically. Khoisan and Andaman Island women tend to have much larger buttocks than most other women. Nipple color and breast shape and size also vary geographically among women. European men are rather hairy by world standards, while Southeast Asian men tend to have very sparse beards and body hair.

What's the function of these traits that differ so markedly between men and women? They certainly don't aid survival: it's not the case that orange nipples help Khoisan women escape lions, while darker nipples help European women survive cold winters. Instead, these varying traits play a crucial role in sexual selection. Women with very large buttocks are a turn-on, or at least acceptable, to Khoisan and Andaman men but look freakish to many men from other parts of the world. Bearded and hairy men readily find mates in Europe but fare worse in Southeast Asia. The geographic variation of these traits, however, is as arbitrary as the geographic variation in the color of a lion's mane.

RACE BY FINGERPRINTS

Probably the most trivial division of humans we could manage would be based on fingerprint patterns. As it turns out, the prevalance of certain basic features varies predictably among peoples: in the "Loops" race we could group together most Europeans, black Africans, and east Asians. Among the "Whorls" we could place Mongolians and Australian aborigines. Finally, in an "Arches" race, we could group Khoisans and some central Europeans.

There is a third possible explanation for the function of geographically variable human traits, besides survival or sexual selection—namely, no function at all. A good example is provided by fingerprints, whose complex pattern of arches, loops, and whorls is determined genetically. Fingerprints also vary geographically: for example, Europeans' fingerprints tend to have many loops, while aboriginal Australians' fingerprints tend to have many whorls.

If we classify human populations by their fingerprints, most Europeans and black Africans would sort out together in one race, Jews and some Indonesians in another, and aboriginal Australians in still another. But those geographic variations in fingerprint patterns possess no known function whatsoever. They play no role in survival: whorls aren't especially suitable for grabbing kangaroos, nor do loops help bar mitzvah candidates hold on to the pointer for the Torah. They also play no role in sexual selection: while you've undoubtedly noticed whether your mate is bearded or has brown nipples, you surely haven't the faintest idea whether his or her fingerprints have more loops than whorls. Instead it's purely a matter of chance that whorls became common in aboriginal Australians, and loops among Jews. Our rhesus factor blood groups and numerous other human traits fall into the same category of genetic characteristics whose geographic variation serves no function.

RACE BY GENES

One method that seems to offer a way out of arbitrariness is to classify peoples degree of genetic distinctness. By this standard the Khoisans of southern Africa would be in a race by themselves. African blacks would form several other distinct races. All the rest of the world's peoples—Norwegians, Navajo, Greeks, Japanese, Australian aborigines, and so on—would, despite their greatly differing external appearance, belong to a single race.

You've probably been wondering when I was going to get back to skin color, eye color, and hair color and form. After all, those are the traits by which all of us members of the lay public, as well as traditional anthropologists, classify races. Does geographic variation in those traits function in survival, in sexual selection, or in nothing?

The usual view is that skin color varies geographically to enhance survival. Supposedly, people in sunny, tropical climates around the world have generally dark skin, which is supposedly analogous to the temporary skin darkening of European whites in the summer. The

Arches

Loops

Whorls

supposed function of dark skin in sunny climates is for protection against skin cancer. Variations in eye color and hair form and color are also supposed to enhance survival under particular conditions, though no one has ever proposed a plausible hypothesis for how those variations might actually enhance survival.

Alas, the evidence for natural selection of skin color dissolves under scrutiny. Among tropical peoples, anthropologists love to stress the dark skins of African blacks, people of the southern Indian peninsula, and New Guineans and love to forget the pale skins of Amazonian Indians and Southeast Asians living at the same latitudes. To wriggle out of those paradoxes, anthropologists then plead the excuse that Amazonian Indians and Southeast Asians may not have been living in their present locations long enough to evolve dark skins. However, the ancestors of fair-skinned Swedes arrived even more recently in Scandinavia, and aboriginal Tasmanians were black-skinned despite their ancestors' having lived for at least the last 10,000 years at the latitude of Vladivostok.

Besides, when one takes into account cloud cover, peoples of equatorial West Africa and the New Guinea mountains actually receive no more ultraviolet radiation or hours of sunshine each year than do the Swiss. Compared with infectious diseases and other selective agents, skin cancer has been utterly trivial as a cause of death in human history, even for modern white settlers in the tropics. This objection is so obvious to believers in natural selection of skin color that they have proposed at least seven other supposed survival functions of skin color, without reaching agreement. Those other supposed functions include protection against rickets, frostbite, folic acid deficiency, beryillium poisoning, overheating, and overcooling. The diversity of these contradictory theories makes clear how far we are from understanding the survival value (if any) of skin color.

It wouldn't surprise me if dark skins do eventually prove to offer some advantage in tropical climates, but I expect the advantage to turn out to be a slight one that is easily overridden. But there's an overwhelming importance to skin, eye, and hair color that is obvious to all of us—sexual selection. Before we can reach a condition of intimacy permitting us to assess the beauty of a prospective sex partner's hidden physical attractions, we first have to pass muster for skin, eyes, and hair

We all know how those highly visible "beauty traits" guide our choice of sex partners. Even the briefest personal ad in a newspaper mentions the advertiser's skin color, and the color of skin that he or she seeks in a partner. Skin color, of course, is also of overwhelming importance in our social prejudices. If you're a black African American trying to raise your children in white U.S. society, rickets and overheating are the least of the problems that might be solved by your skin color. Eye color and hair form and color,

while not so overwhelmingly important as skin color, also play an obvious role in our sexual and social preferences. Just ask yourself why hair dyes, hair curlers, and hair straighteners enjoy such wide sales. You can bet that it's not to improve our chances of surviving grizzly bear attacks and other risks endemic to the North American continent.

Nearly 125 years ago Charles Darwin himself, the discoverer of natural selection, dismissed its role as an explanation of geographic variation in human beauty traits. Everything that we have learned since then only reinforces Darwin's view.

We can now return to our original questions: Are human racial classifications that are based on different traits concordant with one another? What is the hierarchical relation among recognized races? What is the function of racially variable traits? What, really, are the traditional human races?

Regarding concordance, we *could* have classified races based on any number of geographically variable traits. The resulting classifications would not be at all concordant. Depending on whether we classified ourselves by antimalarial genes, lactase, fingerprints, or skin color, we could place Swedes in the same race as either Xhosas, Fulani, the Ainu of Japan, or Italians.

Regarding hierarchy, traditional classifications that emphasize skin color face unresolvable ambiguities. Anthropology textbooks often recognize five major races: "whites," "African blacks," "Mongoloids," "aboriginal Australians," and "Khoisans," each in turn divided into various numbers of sub-races. But there is no agreement on the number and delineation of the sub-races, or even of the major races. Are all five of the major races equally distinctive? Are Nigerians really less different from Xhosas than aboriginal Australians are from both? Should we recognize 3 or 15 sub-races of Mongoloids? These questions have remained unresolved because skin color and other traditional racial criteria are difficult to formulate mathematically.

A method that could in principle overcome these problems is to base racial classification on a combination of as many geographically variable genes as possible. Within the past decade, some biologists have shown renewed interest in developing a hierarchical classification of human populations—hierarchical not in the sense that it identifies superior and inferior races but in the sense of grouping and separating populations based on mathematical measures of genetic distinctness. While the biologists still haven't reached agreement, some of their studies suggest that human genetic diversity may be greatest in Africa. If so, the primary races of humanity may consist of several African races, plus one race to encompass all peoples of all other continents. Swedes, New Guineans, Japanese, and Navajo would then belong to the same primary race; the Khoisans of southern Africa would constitute another primary race by themselves; and African "blacks" and Pygmies would be divided among several other primary races.

As regards the function of all those traits that are useful for classifying human races, some serve to enhance survival, some to enhance sexual selection, while some serve no function at all. The traits we traditionally use are ones subject to sexual selection, which is not really surprising. These traits are not only visible at a distance but also highly variable; that's why they became the ones used throughout recorded history to make quick judgments about people. Racial classification didn't come from science but from the body's signals for differentiating attractive from unattractive sex partners, and for differentiating friend from foe.

Such snap judgments didn't threaten our existence back when people were armed only with spears and surrounded by others who looked mostly like themselves. In the modern world, though, we are armed with guns and plutonium, and we live our lives surrounded by people who are much more varied in appearance. The last thing we need now is to continue codifying all those different appearances into an arbitrary system of racial classification.

18

Draft Official Statement on "Race"

American Anthropological Association

Race is an incredibly important social and political issue in the United States. News items of national interest—from the Los Angeles riots after the Rodney King verdict to the trial of O. J. Simpson—centered around sensitive cultural issues. Questions about the inclusion of mixed race and ethnicity categories for the U.S. Census for the year 2000 have been hotly debated. The publication of Herrnstein and Murray's The Bell Curve: Intelligence and Class Structure in American Life *raised a remarkable public debate; despite terrible reviews and scientific criticism, the book sold very well. President Clinton identified the need for a national dialogue about race; such a dialogue may well be an uncomfortable conversation.*

As we learned in the last selection, race is an out-of-date and useless concept from the viewpoint of understanding and explaining human biological diversity. Although many biological anthropologists privately came to such a conclusion, the public holds on to the belief that race refers to real biological categories. At the same time, discrimination based on skin color—at times overt and at other times subtle and invidious—continues to exist in the United States.

The American Anthropological Association (AAA) is the oldest and largest professional association for all four

fields of anthropology as well as applied anthropology. As a professional association, the AAA has drafted a clear statement about the biology and politics of race. The statement is clear and informational. At the time of the publication of the current edition of this book, the statement has not been approved by the AAA membership at large.

As you read this selection, ask yourself the following questions:

☐ *Why would a professional academic association think that they need to have an official statement about race?*

☐ *Why is the history of a concept like race relevant to understanding its current scientific usefulness?*

☐ *What is the relationship between racial categorizations and the distribution of privilege, power, and wealth?*

☐ *Why does race distort and prejudge our ideas about human differences and group behavior?*

The following terms discussed in this selection are included in the Glossary at the back of the book:
biophysical diversity
culture
race

Reprinted by permission of the American Anthropological Association from *Anthropology Newsletter* 38:6, September 1997.

Since the mid-20th century there has been a major transformation in thinking about "race" in the academic world, especially in the fields of anthropology and biology. For several hundred years before this time, both scholars and the public had been conditioned to viewing purported "races" as natural, distinct and exclusive divisions among human populations based on visible physical differences. However, with the vast expansion of scientific knowledge in this century, it is clear that human populations are not unambiguous, clearly demarcated, biologically distinct groups. As a result, we conclude that the concept of "race" has no validity as a biological category in the human species. Because it homogenizes widely varying individuals into limited categories, it impedes research and understanding of the true nature of human biological variations.

The following statement summarizes the findings and conclusions of experts on human biophysical variation. For a more full and extensive exploration of this topic, see the statement published by the American Association of Physical Anthropologists in 1996 (*AJPA* 101:569–570).

The human species is highly diverse, with individuals and populations varying in observable traits such as body size and shape, skin color, hair texture, facial features and certain characteristics of the skeletal structure. Populations also differ in their percentage frequencies of the blood types (A, B, AB and O) and other known genetic traits. This variation is a product of evolutionary forces operating on human groups as they have adapted to different environments over thousands of years. Some biogenetic variation results from migration and changes within isolated groups. Yet all human groups are capable of interbreeding with others and producing viable and fertile offspring. Throughout history, whenever different groups have come into contact, they have interbred. As a result, all populations share many features with other, neighboring groups.

Variations in any given trait tend to occur gradually rather than abruptly over geographic areas. And because physical traits vary independently of one another, knowing the frequencies of one trait does not predict the presence or frequencies of others. These facts render any attempt to establish lines of division among biological populations both arbitrary and subjective. Genetically there are greater differences among individuals within large geographic populations than the average differences between them. Because of our complex genetic structure, no human groups can be seen as homogeneous or "pure."

Biophysical diversity has no inherent social meaning except what we humans confer upon it. The concept of "race" is in reality a product of that process. "Race" is a set of culturally created attitudes toward, and beliefs about, human differences developed following widespread exploration and colonization by Western European powers since the 16th century. In the North American colonies, European settlers conquered an indigenous population and brought in as slaves alien peoples from Africa. By the end of the 18th century a rising antislavery movement, produced by liberal and humanistic forces mostly in Europe, compelled slave owners to find new defenses for preserving slavery. "Race" was invented as a social mechanism to justify the retention of slavery. "Race" ideology magnified differences among these populations, established a rigid hierarchy of socially exclusive categories, underscored and bolstered unequal rank and status differences and provided the rationalization that such differences were natural or God-given. The different physical traits became markers or symbols of status differences.

As they were constructing this society, white Americans fabricated the cultural/behavioral characteristics associated with each "race," linking superior traits to Europeans and negative and inferior ones to blacks and Indians. Thus arbitrary beliefs about the different peoples were institutionalized and deeply embedded in American thought. Ultimately "race" as an ideology about human differences was reified and subsequently spread to other areas of the world. It became a mechanism for dividing and ranking people, used by colonial powers everywhere. But it was not limited to the colonial situation; it was employed by Europeans to rank each other and, during World War II, became the motive for the unspeakable brutalities of the Holocaust.

"Race" evolved as a worldview, a body of prejudgments that distorts our ideas about human differences and group behavior. Such beliefs constitute myths about the diversity in the human species and about the abilities and behavior of people homogenized into "racial" categories. The myths fused behavior and physical features together in the public mind, impeding our comprehension of both biology and culture and implying that both are genetically determined. Racial myths bear no relationship to the reality of human capabilities or behavior. Scientists have found that reliance on such folk beliefs about human differences in research has led to countless errors.

At the end of the 20th century, we now understand that human behavior is learned, conditioned into infants beginning at birth and always subject to modification and change. No human is born with built-in culture traits or language. Our temperaments, dispositions and personalities, regardless of genetic propensities, are developed within sets of meanings and values that we call "culture." Studies of infant and early childhood learning and behavior attest to the reality of our cultures in forming who we are.

It is a basic tenet of anthropological knowledge that all normal human beings have the capacity to learn any cultural behavior. In the modern world we humans are constantly experiencing new cultural meanings and are, thus, capable of transforming ourselves. The American experience with immigrants from hundreds of different language and cultural backgrounds who have acquired some variation of American culture traits and behavior is the clearest evidence of this fact. We are all becoming more multicultural as we have access to both material culture and ideas that disseminate around the world.

How people have been accepted and treated within the context of their society and culture has a direct impact on how they perform within that society. The "racial" worldview was invented to assign some groups to perpetual low status while others were permitted access to privilege, power and wealth. The tragedy is that it succeeded all too well in constructing unequal populations. Given what we know about the capacity of normal humans to achieve and function within any culture, we conclude that present-day inequalities between human groups are not consequences of their biological inheritance; rather, these inequalities are products of historical and contemporary social, economic, educational and political circumstances.

19

White Privilege:
Unpacking the Invisible Knapsack

Peggy McIntosh

Although many major events of the civil rights movement happened before present-day college students were born, most students have probably seen pictures, films, or videos of police blocking African Americans from entering white schools and signs prohibiting African Americans from sitting at lunch counters or drinking from the same water fountains as whites. Though the signs indicating "for whites only" are fading from the American memory, the legacy of racism certainly remains with us today. In the absence of Cross burnings and other obvious signs of racism, however, there is a tendency for whites to assume that racism is a thing of the past, that inequality no longer plagues our nation.

The frustration in the dialogue about racism in the United States has many of the characteristics of cross-cultural miscommunication. People use the same words but with different meanings. They examine the same social situations and come away with quite different interpretations. The analogy in linguistics is that individuals from one language group may not even hear the phonemes used in a different language. In other words, individuals from one group simply cannot see the world through the eyes of the other. Throughout this book you will be reading about other cultures and trying to understand their lifeways— to see the world as they do. It is often more difficult to set aside our commonsense interpretation of the familiar world that surrounds us each day than to freshly examine a novel situation. We must strive to suspend our judg-ment and read through this selection with an anthropological imagination.

As you read this selection, ask yourself the following questions:

- [ ] *What does the author mean by "an invisible package of unearned assets?" How might this relate to the concept of ascribed status?*

- [ ] *Does the author's use of the term* oppressor *imply intentionality, or is this oppression a result of a culture and social organization that is seldom consciously recognized?*

- [ ] *Can you add to the author's list of twenty-six situations that confer privilege?*

- [ ] *Is white privilege a serious threat to equality, or is it merely an inconvenience? What should be done to achieve the U.S. ideal of social equality? Who's responsibility is it to change the culture if it is harmful?*

The following terms discussed in this selection are included in the Glossary at the back of the book:
hierarchy
meritocracy
privilege

Through work to bring materials from Women's Studies into the rest of the curriculum, I have often noticed men's unwillingness to grant that they are over-privileged even though they may grant that women are disadvantaged. They may say they will work to improve women's status, in the society, the university, or the curriculum, but they can't or won't support the idea of lessening men's. Denials which amount to taboos surround the subject of advantages which men gain from women's disadvantages. These denials protect male privilege from being fully acknowledged, lessened or ended.

Thinking through unacknowledged male privilege as a phenomenon, I realized that since hierarchies in our society are interlocking, there was most likely a phenomenon of white privilege which was similarly denied and protected. As a white person, I realized I had been taught about racism as something which puts others at a disadvantage, but had been taught not to see one of its corollary aspects, white privilege, which puts me at an advantage.

I think whites are carefully taught not to recognize white privilege, as males are taught not to recognize male privilege. So I have begun in an untutored way to ask what it is like to have white privilege. I have come to see white privilege as an invisible package of un-earned assets which I can count on cashing in each day, but about which I was "meant" to remain oblivious. White privilege is like an invisible weightless knapsack of special provisions, maps, passports, codebooks, visas, clothes, tools and blank checks.

Describing white privilege makes one newly accountable. As we in Women's Studies work to reveal male privilege and ask men to give up some of their power, so one who writes about having white privilege must ask, "Having described it, what will I do to lessen or end it?"

After I realized the extent to which men work from a base of unacknowledged privilege, I understood that much of their oppressiveness was unconscious. Then I remembered the frequent charges from women of color that white women whom they encounter are oppressive. I began to understand why we are justly seen as oppressive, even when we don't see ourselves that way. I began to count the ways in which I enjoy un-earned skin privilege and have been conditioned into oblivion about its existence.

My schooling gave me no training in seeing myself as an oppressor, as an unfairly advantaged person, or as a participant in a damaged culture. I was taught to see myself as an individual whose moral state depended on her individual moral will. My schooling followed the pattern my colleague Elizabeth Minnich has pointed out: whites are taught to think of their lives as morally neutral, normative, and average, and also ideal, so that when we work to benefit others, this is seen as work which will allow "them" to be more like "us."

I decided to try to work on myself at least by identifying some of the daily effects of white privilege in my life. I have chosen those conditions which I think in my case *attach somewhat more to skin-color privilege* than to class, religion, ethnic status, or geographical location, though of course all these other factors are intricately intertwined. As far as I can see, my African American co-workers, friends and acquaintances with whom I come into daily or frequent contact in this particular time, place, and line of work cannot count on most of these conditions.

1. I can if I wish arrange to be in the company of people of my race most of the time.

2. If I should need to move, I can be pretty sure of renting or purchasing housing in an area which I can afford and in which I would want to live.

3. I can be pretty sure that my neighbors in such a location will be neutral or pleasant to me.

4. I can go shopping alone most of the time, pretty well assured that I will not be followed or harassed.

5. I can turn on the television or open to the front page of the paper and see people of my race widely represented.

6. When I am told about our national heritage or about "civilization," I am shown that people of my color made it what it is.

7. I can be sure that my children will be given curricular materials that testify to the existence of their race.

8. If I want to, I can be pretty sure of finding a publisher for this piece on white privilege.

9. I can go into a music shop and count on finding the music of my race represented, into a supermarket and find the staple foods which fit with my cultural traditions, into a hairdresser's shop and find someone who can cut my hair.

10. Whether I use checks, credit cards, or cash, I can count on my skin color not to work against the appearance of financial reliability.

11. I can arrange to protect my children most of the time from people who might not like them.

12. I can swear, or dress in second hand clothes. Or not answer letters, without having people attribute these choices to the bad morals, the poverty, or the illiteracy of my race.

13. I can speak in public to a powerful male group without putting my race on trial.

14. I can do well in a challenging situation without being called a credit to my race.

15. I am never asked to speak for all the people of my racial group.

16. I can remain oblivious of the language and customs of persons of color who constitute the world's majority without feeling in my culture any penalty for such oblivion.

17 I can criticize our government and talk about how much I fear its policies and behavior without being seen as a cultural outsider.

18. I can be pretty sure that if I ask to talk to "the person in charge," I will be facing a person of my race.

19. If a traffic cop pulls me over or if the IRS audits my tax return, I can be sure I haven't been singled out because of my race.

20. I can easily buy posters, postcards, picture books, greeting cards, dolls, toys, and children's magazines featuring people of my race.

21. I can go home from most meetings of organizations I belong to feeling somewhat tied in, rather than isolated, out-of-place, outnumbered, unheard, held at a distance, or feared.

22. I can take a job with an affirmative action employer without having co-workers on the job suspect that I got it because of race.

23. I can choose public accommodation without fearing that people of my race cannot get in or will be mistreated in the places I have chosen.

24. I can be sure that if I need legal or medical help, my race will not work against me.

25. If my day, week, or year is going badly, I need not ask of each negative episode or situation whether it has racial overtones.

26. I can choose blemish cover or bandages in "flesh" color and have them more or less match my skin.

I repeatedly forgot each of the realizations on this list until I wrote it down. For me white privilege has turned out to be an elusive and fugitive subject. The pressure to avoid it is great, for in facing it I must give up the myth of meritocracy. If these things are true, this is not such a free country, one's life is not what one makes it; many doors open for certain people through no virtues of their own.

In unpacking this invisible knapsack of white privilege, I have listed conditions of daily experience which I once took for granted. Nor did I think of any of these perquisites as bad for the holder. I now think that we need a more finely differentiated taxonomy of privilege, for some of these varieties are only what one would want for everyone in a just society, and others give license to be ignorant, oblivious, arrogant and destructive.

I see a pattern running through the matrix of white privilege, a pattern of assumptions which were passed on to me as a white person. There was one main piece of cultural turf; it was my own turf, and I was among those who could control the turf. *My skin color was an asset for any move I was educated to want to make.* I could think of myself as belonging in major ways, and of making social systems work for me. I could freely disparage, fear, neglect, or be oblivious to anything outside of the dominant cultural forms. Being of the main culture, I could also criticize it fairly freely.

In proportion as my racial group was being made confident, comfortable, and oblivious, other groups were likely being made inconfident, uncomfortable, and alienated. Whiteness protected me from many kinds of hostility, distress, and violence, which I was being subtly trained to visit in turn upon people of color.

For this reason, the word "privilege" now seems to me misleading. We usually think of privilege as being a favored state, whether earned or conferred by birth or luck. Yet some of the conditions I have described here work to systematically overempower certain groups. Such privilege simply *confers dominance* because of one's race or sex.

I want, then, to distinguish between earned strength and unearned power conferred systematically. Power from unearned privilege can look like strength when it is in fact permission to escape or to dominate. But not all of the privileges on my list are inevitably damaging. Some, like the expectation that neighbors will be decent to you, or that your race will not count against you in court, should be the norm in a just society. Others, like the privilege to ignore less powerful people, distort the humanity of the holders as well as the ignored groups.

We might at least start by distinguishing between positive advantages which we can work to spread, and negative types of advantages which unless rejected will always reinforce our present hierarchies. For example, the feeling that one belongs within the human circle, as Native Americans say, should not be seen as privilege for a few. Ideally it is an *unearned entitlement.* At present, since only a few have it, it is an *unearned advantage* for them. This paper results from a process of coming to see that some of the power which I originally saw as attendant on being a human being in the U.S. consisted [of] *unearned advantage* and *conferred dominance.*

I have met very few men who are truly distressed about systemic, unearned male advantage and conferred dominance. And so one question for me and others like me is whether we will be like them, or whether we will get truly distressed, even outraged, about unearned race advantage and conferred dominance and if so, what we will do to lessen them. In any case, we need to do more work in identifying how they actually affect our daily lives. Many, perhaps most, of our white students in the U.S. think that racism doesn't affect them because they are not people of color; they do not see "whiteness" as a racial identity. In addition, since race and sex are not the only advantaging systems at work, we need similarly to examine the daily experience of having age advantage, or ethnic advantage, or physical ability, or advantage related to nationality, religions or sexual orientation.

Difficulties and dangers surrounding the task of finding parallels are many. Since racism, sexisms and heterosexism are not the same, the advantaging associated with them should not be seen as the same. In addition, it is hard to disentangle aspects of unearned advantage which rest more on social class, economic class, race, religion, sex and ethnic identity than on other factors. Still, all of the oppressions are interlocking, as the Combahee River Collective[1] Statement of 1977 continues to remind us eloquently.

One factor seems clear about all of the interlocking oppressions. They take both active forms which we can see and embedded forms which as a member of the dominant group one is taught not to see. In my class and place, I did not see myself as a racist because I was taught to recognize racism only in individual acts of meanness by members of my group, never in invisible systems conferring unsought racial dominance on my group from birth.

Disapproving of the systems won't be enough to change them. I was taught to think that racism could end if white individuals changed their attitudes. [But] a "white" skin in the United States opens many doors

for whites whether or not we approve of the way dominance has been conferred on us. Individual acts can palliate, but cannot end, these problems.

To redesign social systems we need first to acknowledge their colossal unseen dimensions. The silences and denials surrounding privilege are the key political tool here. They keep the thinking about equality or equity incomplete, protecting unearned advantage and conferred dominance by making these taboo subjects. Most talk by whites about equal opportunity seems to me now to be about equal opportunity to try to get into a position of dominance while denying that *systems* of dominance exist.

It seems to me that obliviousness about white advantage like obliviousness about male advantage, is kept strongly inculturated in the United States so as to maintain the myth of meritocracy, the myth that democratic choice is equally available to all. Keeping most people unaware that freedom of confident action is there for just a small number of people props up those in power and serves to keep power in the hands of the same groups that have most of it already.

Though systemic change takes many decades, there are pressing questions for me and I imagine for some others like me if we raise our daily consciousness on the perquisites of being lightskinned. What will we do with such knowledge? As we know from watching men, it is an open question whether we will choose to use unearned advantage to weaken hidden systems of advantage, and whether we will use any of our arbitrarily awarded power to try to reconstruct power systems on a broader base.

NOTE

1. Combahee River Collective: A group of black feminist women in Boston from 1974 to 1980.

20

Eating Christmas in the Kalahari

Richard Borshay Lee

An economy *is a social system for the production, exchange, and consumption of goods and services. Using this definition, anthropologists believe that all human societies have economies and that economic systems can work without money and markets.*

People in food-foraging societies, like the !Kung San described in this selection, have received much attention by anthropologists. To a large degree, this is because they represent (at least by analogy) the original lifestyle of our ancestors. A major discovery of research on food foragers is that their life is not "nasty, brutish, and short." In fact, in Selection 9 ("Ancient Genes and Modern Health") Eaton and Konner argue that food foragers' diet might be an ideal one for people living in industrialized societies.

In the hunter-gatherer economy, anthropologists have discovered that the exchange of goods is based on rules of gift giving or reciprocity. In this selection, Richard Lee tells of his surprise at the !Kung San's lack of appreciation of a Christmas gift. As we have already seen, a group's customs and rules about appropriate social behavior can reflect important cultural values. When people act in unexpected ways, anthropologists see this as an opportunity to better understand their culture and world view. That is the case in this selection.

All people give gifts to each other, but there are rules and obligations about those gifts. In our own society, there are rules about the polite way to receive a present. We are supposed to act appreciative (even if we hate the gift) be-

cause the gift is less important than the social relationship at stake. The !Kung break those rules, but in the process, Richard Lee discovers that there are important cultural messages behind their "impoliteness."

As you read this selection, ask yourself the following questions:

☐ *Why did Richard Lee feel obligated to give a valuable gift to the !Kung at Christmas? Why did they think he was a miser?*

☐ *Why did the !Kung people's insults about the impending gift bother the anthropologist so much? Were the people treating him in a special way?*

☐ *What does Lee mean by saying, "There are no totally generous acts"? Do you agree?*

☐ *What are some cultural rules about gift giving in our own society?*

The following terms discussed in this selection are included in the Glossary at the back of the book:

cultural values
economy
egalitarian society
hunter-gatherers
reciprocal gift

With permission from *Natural History*, vol. 78, no. 10. Copyright © 1969 The American Museum of Natural History.

The !Kung Bushmen's knowledge of Christmas is thirdhand. The London Missionary Society brought the holiday to the southern Tswana tribes in the early nineteenth century. Later, native catechists spread the idea far and wide among the Bantu-speaking pastoralists, even in the remotest corners of the Kalahari Desert. The Bushmen's idea of the Christmas story, stripped to its essentials, is "praise the birth of white man's god-chief": what keeps their interest in the holiday high is the Tswana-Herero custom of slaughtering an ox for his Bushmen neighbors as an annual goodwill gesture. Since the 1930s, part of the Bushmen's annual round of activities has included a December congregation at the cattle posts for trading, marriage brokering, and several days of trance dance feasting at which the local Tswana headman is host.

As a social anthropologist working with !Kung Bushmen, I found that the Christmas ox custom suited my purposes. I had come to the Kalahari to study the hunting and gathering subsistence economy of the !Kung, and to accomplish this it was essential not to provide them with food, share my own food, or interfere in any way with their food-gathering activities. While liberal handouts of tobacco and medical supplies were appreciated, they were scarcely adequate to erase the glaring disparity in wealth between the anthropologist, who maintained a two-month inventory of canned goods, and the Bushmen, who rarely had a day's supply of food on hand. My approach, while paying off in terms of data, left me open to frequent accusations of stinginess and hardheartedness. By their lights, I was a miser.

The Christmas ox was to be my way of saying thank you for the cooperation of the past year; and since it was to be our last Christmas in the field, I determined to slaughter the largest, meatiest ox that money could buy, insuring that the feast and trance dance would be a success.

Through December I kept my eyes open at the wells as the cattle were brought down for watering. Several animals were offered, but none had quite the grossness that I had in mind. Then, ten days before the holiday, a Herero friend led an ox of astonishing size and mass up to our camp. It was solid black, stood five feet high at the shoulder, had a five-foot span of horns, and must have weighed 1,200 pounds on the hoof. Food consumption calculations are my specialty, and I quickly figured that bones and viscera aside, there was enough meat—at least four pounds—for every man, woman, and child of the 150 Bushmen in the vicinity of /ai/ai who were expected at the feast.

Having found the right animal at last, I paid the Herero £20 ($56) and asked him to keep the beast with his herd until Christmas day. The next morning word spread among the people that the big solid black one was the ox chosen by /ontah (my Bushman name; it

means, roughly, "whitey") for the Christmas feast. That afternoon I received the first delegation. Ben!a, an outspoken sixty-year-old mother of five, came to the point slowly.

"Where were you planning to eat Christmas?"

"Right here at /ai/ai," I replied.

"Alone or with others?"

"I expect to invite all the people to eat Christmas with me."

"Eat what?"

"I have purchased Yehave's black ox, and I am going to slaughter and cook it."

"That's what we were told at the well but refused to believe it until we heard it from yourself."

"Well, it's the black one," I replied expansively, although wondering what she was driving at.

"Oh, no!" Ben!a groaned, turning to her group. "They were right." Turning back to me she asked, "Do you expect us to eat that bag of bones?"

"Bag of bones! It's the biggest ox at /ai/ai."

"Big, yes, but old. And thin. Everybody knows there's no meat on that old ox. What did you expect to eat off of it, the horns?"

Everybody chuckled at Ben!a's one-liner as they walked away, but all I could manage was a weak grin.

That evening it was the turn of the young men. They came to sit at our evening fire. /gaugo, about my age, spoke to me man-to-man.

"/ontah, you have always been square with us," he lied. "What has happened to change your heart? That sack of guts and bones of Yehave's will hardly feed one camp, let alone all the Bushmen around /ai/ai." And he proceeded to enumerate the seven camps in the /ai/ai vicinity, family by family. "Perhaps you have forgotten that we are not few, but many. Or are you too blind to tell the difference between a proper cow and an old wreck? That ox is thin to the point of death."

"Look, you guys," I retorted, "that is a beautiful animal, and I'm sure you will eat it with pleasure at Christmas."

"Of course we will eat it: it's food. But it won't fill us up to the point where we will have enough strength to dance. We will eat and go home to bed with stomachs rumbling."

That night as we turned in, I asked my wife, Nancy, "What did you think of the black ox?"

"It looked enormous to me. Why?"

"Well, about eight different people have told me I got gypped; that the ox is nothing but bones."

"What's the angle?" Nancy asked. "Did they have a better one to sell?"

"No, they just said that it was going to be a grim Christmas because there won't be enough meat to go around. Maybe I'll get an independent judge to look at the beast in the morning."

Bright and early, Halingisi, a Tswana cattle owner, appeared at our camp. But before I could ask him to give me his opinion on Yehave's black ox, he gave me the eye signal that indicated a confidential chat. We left the camp and sat down.

"/ontah, I'm surprised at you; you've lived here for three years and still haven't learned anything about cattle."

"But what else can a person do but choose the biggest, strongest animal one can find?" I retorted.

"Look, just because an animal is big doesn't mean that it has plenty of meat on it. The black one was a beauty when it was younger, but now it is thin to the point of death."

"Well I've already bought it. What can I do at this stage?"

"Bought it already? I thought you were just considering it. Well, you'll have to kill it and serve it, I suppose. But don't expect much of a dance to follow."

My spirits dropped rapidly. I could believe that Ben!a and /gaugo just might be putting me on about the black ox, but Halingisi seemed to be an impartial critic. I went around that day feeling as though I had bought a lemon of a used car.

In the afternoon it was Tomazo's turn. Tomazo is a fine hunter, a top trance performer . . . and one of my most reliable informants. He approached the subject of the Christmas cow as part of my continuing Bushman education.

"My friend, the way it is with us Bushmen," he began, "is that we love meat. And even more than that, we love fat. When we hunt we always search for the fat ones, the ones dripping with layers of white fat: fat that turns into a clear, thick oil in the cooking pot, fat that slides down your gullet, fills your stomach and gives you a roaring diarrhea," he rhapsodized.

"So, feeling as we do," he continued, "it gives us pain to be served such a scrawny thing as Yehave's black ox. It is big, yes, and no doubt its giant bones are good for soup, but fat is what we really crave and so we will eat Christmas this year with a heavy heart."

The prospect of a gloomy Christmas now had me worried, so I asked Tomazo what I could do about it.

"Look for a fat one, a young one . . . smaller, but fat. Fat enough to make us //gom (evacuate the bowels), then we will be happy."

My suspicions were aroused when Tomazo said that he happened to know a young, fat, barren cow that the owner was willing to part with. Was Tomazo working on commission, I wondered? But I dispelled this unworthy thought when we approached the Herero owner of the cow in question and found that he had decided not to sell.

The scrawny wreck of a Christmas ox now became the talk of the /ai/ai water hole and was the first news told to the outlying groups as they began to come in from the bush for the feast. What finally convinced me that real trouble might be brewing was the visit from u!au, an old conservative with a reputation for fierceness. His nickname meant spear and referred to an incident thirty years ago in which he had speared a man to death. He had an intense manner; fixing me with his eyes, he said in clipped tones:

"I have only just heard about the black ox today, or else I would have come earlier. /ontah, do you honestly think you can serve meat like that to people and avoid a fight?" He paused, letting the implications sink in. "I don't mean fight you, /ontah; you are a white man. I mean a fight between Bushmen. There are many fierce ones here, and with such a small quantity of meat to distribute, how can you give everybody a fair share? Someone is sure to accuse another of taking too much or hogging all the choice pieces. Then you will see what happens when some go hungry while others eat."

The possibility of at least a serious argument struck me as all too real. I had witnessed the tension that surrounds the distribution of meat from a kudu or gemsbok kill, and had documented many arguments that sprang up from a real or imagined slight in meat distribution. The owners of a kill may spend up to two hours arranging and rearranging the piles of meat under the gaze of a circle of recipients before handing them out. And I knew that the Christmas feast at /ai/ai would be bringing together groups that had feuded in the past.

Convinced now of the gravity of the situation, I went in earnest to search for a second cow; but all my inquiries failed to turn one up.

The Christmas feast was evidently going to be a disaster, and the incessant complaints about the meagerness of the ox had already taken the fun out of it for me. Moreover, I was getting bored with the wisecracks, and after losing my temper a few times, I resolved to serve the beast anyway. If the meat fell short, the hell with it. In the Bushmen idiom, I announced to all who would listen:

"I am a poor man and blind. If I have chosen one that is too old and too thin, we will eat it anyway and see if there is enough meat there to quiet the rumbling of our stomachs."

On hearing this speech, Ben!a offered me a rare word of comfort. "It's thin," she said philosophically, "but the bones will make a good soup."

At dawn Christmas morning, instinct told me to turn over the butchering and cooking to a friend and take off with Nancy to spend Christmas alone in the bush. But curiosity kept me from retreating. I wanted to see what such a scrawny ox looked like on butchering, and if there *was* going to be a fight, I wanted to catch every word of it. Anthropologists are incurable that way.

The great beast was driven up to our dancing ground, and a shot in the forehead dropped it in its tracks. Then, freshly cut branches were heaped around the fallen carcass to receive the meat. Ten men volunteered to help with the cutting. I asked /gaugo to make the breast bone cut. This cut, which begins the butchering process for most large game, offers easy access for removal of the viscera. But it allows the hunter to spot-check the amount of fat on an animal. A fat game animal carries a white layer up to an inch thick on the chest, while in a thin one, the knife will quickly cut to the bone. All eyes fixed on his hand as /gaugo, dwarfed by the great carcass, knelt to the breast. The first cut opened a pool of solid white in the black skin. The second and third cut widened and deepened the creamy white. Still no bone. It was pure fat; it must have been two inches thick.

"Hey /gau," I burst out, "that ox is loaded with fat. What's this about the ox being too thin to bother eating? Are you out of your mind?"

"Fat?" /gau shot back. "You call that fat? This wreck is thin, sick, dead!" And he broke out laughing. So did everyone else. They rolled on the ground, paralyzed with laughter. Everybody laughed except me; I was thinking.

I ran back to the tent and burst in just as Nancy was getting up. "Hey, the black ox. It's fat as hell! They were kidding about it being too thin to eat. It was a joke or something. A put-on. Everyone is really delighted with it."

"Some joke," my wife replied. "It was so funny that you were ready to pack up and leave /ai/ai."

If it had indeed been a joke, it had been an extraordinarily convincing one, and tinged, I thought, with more than a touch of malice as many jokes are. Nevertheless, that it was a joke lifted my spirits considerably, and I returned to the butchering site where the shape of the ox was rapidly disappearing under the axes and knives of the butchers. The atmosphere had become festive. Grinning broadly, their arms covered with blood well past the elbow, men packed chunks of meat into the big cast-iron cooking pots, fifty pounds to the load, and muttered and chuckled all the while about the thinness and worthlessness of the animal and /ontah's poor judgment.

We danced and ate that ox two days and two nights; we cooked and distributed fourteen potfuls of meat and no one went home hungry and no fights broke out.

But the "joke" stayed in my mind. I had a growing feeling that something important had happened in my relationship with the Bushmen and that the clue lay in the meaning of the joke. Several days later, when most of the people had dispersed back to the bush camps, I raised the question with Hakekgose, a Tswana man who had grown up among the !Kung, married a !Kung girl, and who probably knows the culture better than any other non-Bushman.

"With us whites," I began, "Christmas is supposed to be the day of friendship and brotherly love. What I can't figure out is why the Bushmen went to such lengths to criticize and belittle the ox I had bought for the feast. The animal was perfectly good and their jokes and wisecracks practically ruined the holiday for me."

"So it really did bother you," said Hakekgose. "Well, that's the way they always talk. When I take my rifle and go hunting with them, if I miss, they laugh at me for the rest of the day. But even if I hit and bring one down, it's no better. To them, the kill is always too small or too old or too thin; and as we sit down on the kill site to cook and eat the liver, they keep grumbling, even with their mouths full of meat. They say things like, 'Oh, this is awful! What a worthless animal! Whatever made me think that this Tswana rascal could hunt!'"

"Is this the way outsiders are treated?" I asked.

"No, it is their custom; they talk that way to each other too. Go and ask them."

/gaugo had been one of the most enthusiastic in making me feel bad about the merit of the Christmas ox. I sought him out first.

"Why did you tell me the black ox was worthless, when you could see that it was loaded with fat and meat?"

"It is our way," he said smiling. "We always like to fool people about that. Say there is a Bushman who has been hunting. He must not come home and announce like a braggart, 'I have killed a big one in the bush!' He must first sit down in silence until I or someone else comes up to his fire and asks, 'What did you see today?' He replies quietly, 'Ah, I'm no good for hunting. I saw nothing at all (pause) just a little tiny one.' Then I smile to myself," /gaugo continued, "because I know he has killed something big.

"In the morning we make up a party of four or five people to cut up and carry the meat back to the camp. When we arrive at the kill we examine it and cry out, 'You mean to say you have dragged us all the way out here in order to make us cart home your pile of bones? Oh, if I had known it was this thin I wouldn't have come.' Another one pipes up, 'People, to think I gave up a nice day in the shade for this. At home we may be hungry but at least we have nice cool water to drink.' If the horns are big, someone says, 'Did you think that somehow you were going to boil down the horns for soup?'

"To all this you must respond in kind. 'I agree,' you say, 'this one is not worth the effort; let's just cook the liver for strength and leave the rest for the hyenas. It is not too late to hunt today and even a duiker or steenbok would be better than this mess.'

"Then you set to work nevertheless; butcher the animal, carry the meat back to the camp and everyone eats," /gaugo concluded.

Things were beginning to make sense. Next, I went to Tomazo. He corroborated /gaugo's story of the obligatory insults over a kill and added a few details of his own.

"But," I asked, "why insult a man after he has gone to all that trouble to track and kill an animal and when he is going to share the meat with you so that your children will have something to eat?"

"Arrogance," was his cryptic answer.

"Arrogance?"

"Yes, when a young man kills much meat he comes to think of himself as a chief or a big man, and he thinks of the rest of us as his servants or inferiors. We can't accept this. We refuse one who boasts, for someday his pride will make him kill somebody. So we always speak of his meat as worthless. This way we cool his heart and make him gentle."

"But why didn't you tell me this before?" I asked Tomazo with some heat.

"Because you never asked me," said Tomazo, echoing the refrain that has come to haunt every field ethnographer.

The pieces now fell into place. I had known for a long time that in situations of social conflict with Bushmen I held all the cards. I was the only source of tobacco in a thousand square miles, and I was not incapable of cutting an individual off for noncooperation. Though my boycott never lasted longer than a few days, it was an indication of my strength. People resented my presence at the water hole, yet simultaneously dreaded my leaving. In short I was a perfect target for the charge of arrogance and for the Bushman tactic of enforcing humility.

I had been taught an object lesson by the Bushmen; it had come from an unexpected corner and had hurt me in a vulnerable area. For the big black ox was to be the one totally generous, unstinting act of my year at /ai/ai and I was quite unprepared for the reaction I received.

As I read it, their message was this: There are no totally generous acts. All "acts" have an element of calculation. One black ox slaughtered at Christmas does not wipe out a year of careful manipulation of gifts given to serve your own ends. After all, to kill an animal and share the meat with people is really no more than the Bushmen do for each other every day and with far less fanfare.

In the end, I had to admire how the Bushmen had played out the farce—collectively straight-faced to the end. Curiously, the episode reminded me of the *Good Soldier Schweik* and his marvelous encounters with authority. Like Schweik, the Bushmen had retained a thoroughgoing skepticism of good intentions. Was it this independence of spirit, I wondered, that had kept them culturally viable in the face of generations of contact with more powerful societies, both black and white? The thought that the Bushmen were alive and well in the Kalahari was strangely comforting. Perhaps, armed with that independence and with their superb knowledge of their environment, they might yet survive the future.

21

Strings Attached

Lee Cronk

Anthropologists have traditionally studied how social ties among people are created through a system of kinship and marriage; this is a universal aspect of human social systems. Marriages link families who were previously strangers into kin (affines). Such new social relations are cemented by the exchange of goods—expected gifts—at the time of the marriage; this appears to be a universal aspect of marriage systems.

People give each other gifts all the time, and in all cultures of the world. According to the French anthropologist Marcel Mauss, who first wrote about this phenomenon in 1924, gift giving is a universal way of creating and maintaining social relations among people. This is because gift giving creates social obligations. Gifts "cement" social relationships, and members of a society understand what the implicit rules of gift giving are.

In the beginning of this selection, Lee Cronk discusses possible cultural misunderstandings that were involved in the creation of the unfortunate (and racist) term **Indian giver**. These misunderstandings were offensive to both Native Americans and whites. Europeans thought that gifts should be freely given and that the gift is less valued when there are strings attached. On a worldwide survey of different cultures, however, it is far more common for the strings themselves to be the main consideration of value. Because of this, when anthropologists study economic exchanges they are more interested in the social relationship between the gift giver and the receiver than in the actual gift.

As we saw in the case of Richard Lee and the gift of the Christmas ox among the !Kung San, the cultural rules behind gift giving often involve the principle of reciprocity. There are also cases when gifts can be used to embarrass ri-vals or to foster feelings of indebtedness. These cases usually involve social groups or nations rather than individuals. It is valuable to re-examine international political relations and economic aid in light of the cross-cultural context of gift giving.

As you read this selection, ask yourself the following questions:

☐ Is it really true that "there is no such thing as a free gift"?

☐ How can gift giving be a question of social power and prestige, as in the case of one chief "burying" another with gifts?

☐ Why was Russian acceptance of humanitarian aid from the United States after the 1988 Armenian earthquake considered to be a breakthrough? How can concessions in arms reductions negotiations be considered as gifts?

☐ Do Americans devalue a gift that has strings attached? Why?

The following terms discussed in this selection are included in the Glossary at the back of the book:

dependency
exchange
kula
potlatch
reciprocity

Reprinted with permission from *The Sciences* May–June 1989, (3):2–4.

During a trek through the Rockies in the 1830s, Captain Benjamin Louis E. de Bonneville received a gift of a fine young horse from a Nez Percé chief. According to Washington Irving's account of the incident, the American explorer was aware that "a parting pledge was necessary on his own part, to prove that this friendship was reciprocated." Accordingly, he "placed a handsome rifle in the hands of the venerable chief; whose benevolent heart was evidently touched and gratified by this outward and visible sign of amity."

Even the earliest white settlers in New England understood that presents from natives required reciprocity, and by 1764, "Indian gift" was so common a phrase that the Massachusetts colonial historian Thomas Hutchinson identified it as "a proverbial expression, signifying a present for which an equivalent return is expected." Then, over time, the custom's meaning was lost. Indeed, the phrase now is used derisively, to refer to one who demands the return of a gift. How this cross-cultural misunderstanding occurred is unclear, but the poet Lewis Hyde, in his book *The Gift*, has imagined a scenario that probably approaches the truth.

Say that an Englishman newly arrived in America is welcomed to an Indian lodge with the present of a pipe. Thinking the pipe a wonderful artifact, he takes it home and sets it on his mantelpiece. When he later learns that the Indians expect to have the pipe back, as a gesture of goodwill, he is shocked by what he views as their short-lived generosity. The newcomer did not realize that, to the natives, the point of the gift was not to provide an interesting trinket but to inaugurate a friendly relationship that would be maintained through a series of mutual exchanges. Thus, his failure to reciprocate appeared not only rude and thoughtless but downright hostile. "White man keeping" was as offensive to native Americans as "Indian giving" was to settlers.

In fact, the Indians' tradition of gift giving is much more common than our own. Like our European ancestors, we think that presents ought to be offered freely, without strings attached. But through most of the world, the strings themselves are the main consideration. In some societies, gift giving is a tie between friends, a way of maintaining good relationships, whereas in others it has developed into an elaborate, expensive, and antagonistic ritual designed to humiliate rivals by showering them with wealth and obligating them to give more in return.

In truth, the dichotomy between the two traditions of gift giving is less behavioral than rhetorical: our generosity is not as unconditional as we would like to believe. Like European colonists, most modern Westerners are blind to the purpose of reciprocal gift giving, not only in non-Western societies but also, to some extent, in our own. Public declarations to the contrary, we, too, use gifts to nurture long-term relationships of mutual obligation, as well as to embarrass our rivals and to foster feelings of indebtedness. And this ethic touches all aspects of contemporary life, from the behavior of scientists in research networks to superpower diplomacy. Failing to acknowledge this fact, especially as we give money, machines, and technical advice to peoples around the world, we run the risk of being misinterpreted and, worse, of causing harm.

Much of what we know about the ethics of gift giving comes from the attempts of anthropologists to give things to the people they are studying. Richard Lee, of the University of Toronto, learned a difficult lesson from the !Kung hunter-gatherers, of the Kalahari desert, when, as a token of goodwill, he gave them an ox to slaughter at Christmas. Expecting gratitude, he was shocked when the !Kung complained about having to make do with such a scrawny "bag of bones." Only later did Lee learn, with relief, that the !Kung belittle all gifts. In their eyes, no act is completely generous, or free of calculation; ridiculing gifts is their way of diminishing the expected return and of enforcing humility on those who would use gifts to raise their own status within the group.

Rada Dyson-Hudson, of Cornell University, had a similar experience among the Turkana, a pastoral people of northwestern Kenya. To compensate her informants for their help, Dyson-Hudson gave away pots, maize meal, tobacco, and other items. The Turkana reaction was less than heartwarming. A typical response to a gift of a pot, for example, might be, "Where is the maize meal to go in this pot?" or, "Don't you have a bigger one to give me?" To the Turkana, these are legitimate and expected questions.

The Mukogodo, another group of Kenyan natives, responded in a similar way to gifts Beth Leech and I presented to them during our fieldwork in 1986. Clothing was never nice enough, containers never big enough, tobacco and candies never plentiful enough. Every gift horse was examined carefully, in the mouth and elsewhere. Like the !Kung, the Mukogodo believe that all gifts have an element of calculation, and they were right to think that ours were no exception. We needed their help, and their efforts to diminish our expectations and lessen their obligations to repay were as fair as our attempts to get on their good side.

The idea that gifts carry obligations is instilled early in life. When we gave Mukogodo children candies after visiting their villages, their mothers reminded them of the tie: "Remember these white people? They are the ones who gave you candy." They also reinforced the notion that gifts are meant to circulate, by asking their children to part with their precious candies, already in their mouths. Most of the youngsters reluctantly surrendered their sweets, only to have them immediately returned. A mother might take, at most, a symbolic nibble from her child's candy, just to drive home the lesson.

The way food, utensils, and other goods are received in many societies is only the first stage of the behavior surrounding gift giving. Although repayment is expected, it is crucial that it be deferred. To reciprocate at once indicates a desire to end the relationship, to cut the strings; delayed repayment makes the strings longer and stronger. This is especially clear on the Truk Islands, of Micronesia, where a special word—*niffag*—is used to designate objects moving through the island's exchange network. From the Trukese viewpoint, to return niffag on the same day it is received alters its nature from that of a gift to that of a sale, in which all that matters is material gain.

After deciding the proper time for response, a recipient must consider how to make repayment, and that is dictated largely by the motive behind the gift. Some exchange customs are designed solely to preserve a relationship. The !Kung have a system, called *hxaro*, in which little attention is paid to whether the items exchanged are equivalent. Richard Lee's informant !Xoma explained to him that "Hxaro is when I take a thing of value and give it to you. Later, much later, when you find some good thing, you give it back to me. When I find something good I will give it to you, and so we will pass the years together." When Lee tried to determine the exact exchange values of various items (Is a spear worth three strings of beads, two strings, or one?), !Xoma explained that any return would be all right: "You see, we don't trade with things, we trade with people!"

One of the most elaborate systems of reciprocal gift giving, known as *kula*, exists in a ring of islands off New Guinea. Kula gifts are limited largely to shell necklaces, called *soulava*, and armbands, called *mwali*. A necklace given at one time is answered months or years later with an armband, the necklaces usually circulating clockwise, and the armbands counterclockwise, through the archipelago. Kula shells vary in quality and value, and men gain fame and prestige by having their names associated with noteworthy necklaces or armbands. The shells also gain value from their association with famous and successful kula partners.

Although the act of giving gifts seems intrinsically benevolent, a gift's power to embarrass the recipient and to force repayment has, in some societies, made it attractive as a weapon. Such antagonistic generosity reached its most elaborate expression, during the late nineteenth century, among the Kwakiutl, of British Columbia.

The Kwakiutl were acutely conscious of status, and every tribal division, clan, and individual had a specific rank. Disputes about status were resolved by means of enormous ceremonies (which outsiders usually refer to by the Chinook Indian term *potlatch*), at which rivals competed for the honor and prestige of giving away the greatest amount of property. Although nearly everything of value was fair game—blankets, canoes, food, pots, and, until the mid-nineteenth century, even slaves—the most highly prized items were decorated sheets of beaten copper, shaped like shields and etched with designs in the distinctive style of the Northwest Coast Indians.

As with the kula necklaces and armbands, the value of a copper sheet was determined by its history—by where it had been and who had owned it—and a single sheet could be worth thousands of blankets, a fact often reflected in its name. One was called "Drawing All Property from the House," and another, "About Whose Possession All Are Quarreling." After the Kwakiutl began to acquire trade goods from the Hudson's Bay Company's Fort Rupert post, in 1849, the potlatches underwent a period of extreme inflation, and by the 1920s, when items of exchange included sewing machines and pool tables, tens of thousands of Hudson's Bay blankets might be given away during a single ceremony.

In the 1880s, after the Canadian government began to suppress warfare between tribes, potlatching also became a substitute for battle. As a Kwakiutl man once said to the anthropologist Franz Boas, "The time of fighting is past. . . . We do not fight now with weapons: we fight with property." The usual Kwakiutl word for potlatch was *p!Esa*, meaning to flatten (as when one flattens a rival under a pile of blankets), and the prospect of being given a large gift engendered real fear. Still, the Kwakiutl seemed to prefer the new "war of wealth" to the old "war of blood."

Gift giving has served as a substitute for war in other societies, as well. Among the Siuai, of the Solomon Islands, guests at feasts are referred to as attackers, while hosts are defenders, and invitations to feasts are given on short notice in the manner of "surprise attacks." And like the Kwakiutl of British Columbia, the Mount Hagen tribes of New Guinea use a system of gift giving called *moka* as a way of gaining prestige and shaming rivals. The goal is to become a tribal leader, a "big-man." One moka gift in the 1970s consisted of several hundred pigs, thousands of dollars in cash, some cows and wild birds, a truck, and a motorbike. The donor, quite pleased with himself, said to the recipient, "I have won. I have knocked you down by giving so much."

Although we tend not to recognize it as such, the ethic of reciprocal gift giving manifests itself throughout our own society, as well. We, too, often expect something, even if only gratitude and a sense of indebtedness, in exchange for gifts, and we use gifts to establish friendships and to manipulate our positions in society. As in non-Western societies gift giving in America sometimes takes a benevolent and helpful form; at other times, the power of gifts to create obligations is used in a hostile way.

The Duke University anthropologist Carol Stack found a robust tradition of benevolent exchange in an Illinois ghetto known as the Flats, where poor blacks engage in a practice called swapping. Among residents of the Flats, wealth comes in spurts; hard times are frequent and unpredictable. Swapping, of clothes, food, furniture, and the like, is a way of guaranteeing security, of making sure that someone will be there to help out when one is in need and that one will get a share of any windfalls that come along.

Such networks of exchange are not limited to the poor, nor do they always involve objects. Just as the exchange of clothes creates a gift community in the Flats, so the swapping of knowledge may create one among scientists. Warren Hagstrom, a sociologist at the University of Wisconsin, in Madison, has pointed out that papers submitted to scientific journals often are called contributions, and, because no payment is received for them, they truly are gifts. In contrast, articles written for profit—such as this one—often are held in low esteem: scientific status can be achieved only through giving gifts of knowledge.

Recognition also can be traded upon, with scientists building up their gift-giving networks by paying careful attention to citations and acknowledgments. Like participants in kula exchange, they try to associate themselves with renowned and prestigious articles, books, and institutions. A desire for recognition, however, cannot be openly acknowledged as a motivation for research, and it is a rare scientist who is able to discuss such desires candidly. Hagstrom was able to find just one mathematician (whom he described as "something of a social isolate") to confirm that "junior mathematicians want recognition from big shots and, consequently, work in areas prized by them."

Hagstrom also points out that the inability of scientists to acknowledge a desire for recognition does not mean that such recognition is not expected by those who offer gifts of knowledge, any more than a kula trader believes it is all right if his trading partner does not answer his gift of a necklace with an armband. While failure to reciprocate in New Guinean society might once have meant warfare, among scientists it may cause factionalism and the creation of rivalries.

Whether in the Flats of Illinois or in the halls of academia, swapping is, for the most part, benign. But manipulative gift giving exists in modern societies, too—particularly in paternalistic government practices. The technique is to offer a present that cannot be repaid, coupled with a claim of beneficence and omni-

science. The Johns Hopkins University anthropologist Grace Goodell documented one example in Iran's Khūzestān Province, which, because it contains most of the country's oil fields and is next door to Iraq, is a strategically sensitive area. Goodall focused on the World Bank–funded Dez irrigation project, a showpiece of the shah's ambitious "white revolution" development plan. The scheme involved the irrigation of tens of thousands of acres and the forced relocation of people from their villages to new, model towns. According to Goodell, the purpose behind dismantling local institutions was to enhance central government control of the region. Before development, each Khūzestāni village had been a miniature city-state, managing its own internal affairs and determining its own relations with outsiders. In the new settlements, decisions were made by government bureaucrats, not townsmen, whose autonomy was crushed under the weight of a large and strategically placed gift.

On a global scale, both the benevolent and aggressive dimensions of gift giving are at work in superpower diplomacy. Just as the Kwakiutl were left only with blankets with which to fight after warfare was banned, the United States and the Soviet Union now find, with war out of the question, that they are left only with gifts—called concessions—with which to do battle. Offers of military cutbacks are easy ways to score points in the public arena of international opinion and to shame rivals, and failure either to accept such offers or to respond with even more extreme proposals may be seen as cowardice or as bellicosity. Mikhail Gorbachev is a virtuoso, a master potlatcher, in this new kind of competition, and, predictably, Americans often see his offers of disarmament and openness as gifts with long strings attached. One reason U.S. officials were buoyed last December, when, for the first time since the Second World War, the Soviet Union accepted American assistance, in the aftermath of the Armenian earthquake, is that it seemed to signal a wish for reciprocity rather than dominance—an unspoken understanding of the power of gifts to bind people together.

Japan, faced with a similar desire to expand its influence, also has begun to exploit gift giving in its international relations. In 1989, it will spend more than ten billion dollars on foreign aid, putting it ahead of the United States for the second consecutive year as the world's greatest donor nation. Although this move was publicly welcomed in the United States as the sharing of a burden, fears, too, were expressed that the resultant blow to American prestige might cause a further slip in our international status. Third World leaders also have complained that too much Japanese aid is targeted at countries in which Japan has an economic stake and that too much is restricted to the purchase of

Japanese goods—that Japan's generosity has less to do with addressing the problems of underdeveloped countries than with exploiting those problems to its own advantage.

The danger in all of this is that wealthy nations may be competing for the prestige that comes from giving gifts at the expense of Third World Nations. With assistance sometimes being given with more regard to the donors' status than to the recipients' welfare, it is no surprise that, in recent years, development aid often has been more effective in creating relationships of dependency, as in the case of Iran's Khūzestān irrigation scheme, than in producing real development. Nor that, given the fine line between donation and domination, offers of help are sometimes met with resistance, apprehension and, in extreme cases, such as the Iranian revolution, even violence.

The Indians understood a gift's ambivalent power to unify, antagonize, or subjugate. We, too, would do well to remember that a present can be a surprisingly potent thing, as dangerous in the hands of the ignorant as it is useful in the hands of the wise.

22

Using Cultural Skills for Cooperative Advantage in Japan

Richard H. Reeves-Ellington

Cultural awareness and sensitivity have significant payoffs, helping people avoid major mistakes resulting from cultural ignorance or cultural misunderstanding. In addition, businesspeople who are more culturally aware are also more successful. In this selection, Reeves-Ellington describes a cross-cultural training program that he designed and implemented for an American company doing business in Japan. About fifty employees participated in the on-site cross-cultural training. The long-term results of their training are impressive. Project managers who took the cultural training program were able to cut project completion time nearly in half and increase the financial returns from the projects threefold (see Table 7). After the training program, managers felt much more comfortable and confident about conducting business in Japan on their own.

What might account for this dramatic success? Do the trained managers make no cultural mistakes, and are there no communication misunderstandings? Obviously, some cultural "horror stories" are instructive, like the case of the nervous American who publicly folded and then tore up a Japanese counterpart's business card during a meeting. But there is also evidence that the American efforts to learn Japanese customs and cultural rules of politeness engendered much goodwill and increased trust between employees involved in multinational business cooperation.

Reeves-Ellington teaches businesspeople to use the basic methods developed by cultural anthropologists to describe and analyze cultural settings. In this selection, he describes the cultural values and behavioral rituals implicit in day-to-day business interactions. In many ways, it is more important to recognize the different ways to observe and interpret cultural patterns than to remember the particular details of the cultural rules of business described here. There are practical advantages to being a participant observer rather than a nonobserving participant.

As you read this selection, ask yourself the following questions:

☐ *What Japanese cultural values are illustrated in the stories about business cards and identity?*

☐ *Given the cultural expectations for business entertainment described, do you think there may be special challenges facing American women doing business in Japan?*

☐ *What are aspects of American culture that Japanese people might find particularly perplexing?*

☐ *In what ways do the rules of a business meeting seem to be ritualized?*

☐ *How would you convince an American company of the value of intercultural training?*

The following terms discussed in this selection are included in the Glossary at the back of the book:

artifact   *ritual*
intercultural communication   *values*
participant observation

Reproduced by permission of Society for Applied Anthropology
from Human Organization 52(2), 1993.

Through trial and error, American managers who do business in Japan have learned to gain insight into the Japanese culture. Nonetheless, most American managers remain uneasy dealing with their Japanese counterparts, and "home office" continues to be suspicious of Japanese business practices. This situation produces ineffective business relationships and poor business results. The paradigm of discomfort and suspicion must be replaced by one of confidence and trust if American business is to succeed in Japan.

Pharmco, a pharmaceutical subsidiary of a major United States multinational, was saddled with this "home office" attitude of suspicion. Having done business in Japan for more than 20 years, it was dissatisfied with the relationships and financial arrangements with its Japanese licensees. The advent of innovative pharmaceutical technologies provided an opportunity to develop a new strategic alliance with a major Japanese company, Diversity KK. Pharmco anticipated that the alliance would facilitate rapid introduction of its technology in Japan, yield tenfold greater financial returns, and furnish the framework for learning to operate more successfully in Japan. Senior managers in the company understood that they and their staff needed to work effectively at many levels with Japanese managers and scientists in both the Japanese and American cultural environments. They had, however, no plan for learning about Japanese culture; the initial meetings between employees of the two companies resulted in more "damage control" than was desirable. The Pharmco senior manager responsible for Japanese operations, a trained anthropologist, proposed a program offering United States-based managers and scientists assistance in learning about Japanese culture. As a result of the program, American-Japanese relations at Pharmco improved considerably and business operations are running smoothly.

This paper . . . demonstrates how individuals used a cultural understanding process, ethnographic data, and participant observation (PO) to get through a business day in Japan, build their own data base, and eventually, predict Japanese social behavior in different settings. Empirical evidence is provided to demonstrate the value the program had for one company.

UNDERPINNINGS OF THE PROGRAM

Employee Needs

The purpose of education in the business setting is to resolve problems. . . . Within the Pharmco context, the people who needed cultural information were based in the United States, worked in a variety of functions, and had to operate in several different cultures, not only Japan. Two common learning methods were thereby excluded, i.e., general reading and the use of culture-specific training courses. The manager-anthropologist had to devise another method.

To determine the educational needs, he set up small-group and one-on-one meetings with managers and scientists who would be required to work on the Japanese strategic alliance. He discovered that two questions deterred employees from wanting to work with Japanese in particular and all non-Americans in general: "What do I do during a business day?" and "How can I learn to respond to the various situations I might find myself in while travelling in foreign cultures?" The initial training objective, therefore, was to offer assistance in getting through a Japanese business day while at the same time providing the tools and processes to enable employees to gain cultural understanding and apply their learning to other cultural contexts.

Involvement of an Insider Anthropologist

The manager-anthropologist responsible for Japan operations provided all training that took place over a five-year period and involved ten sets of employees. Training content included "horror" stories of what goes wrong in U.S.-Japanese relationships, examples of successful activities and processes for increasing the chances of success, and practice in using all the material discussed and presented. Material selection depended on the previous experience of members of the group in multicultural settings. Initial sessions were timed approximately two weeks before contacts with Japanese counterparts. This timing coincided with the peak interest employees had in learning the information. All training was done at the employees' work site, allowing them a greater comfort level. The manager-anthropologist was present at all initial meetings between U.S. employees and their Japanese contacts, and he continued to be present until the Americans expressed confidence that he was not needed at future meetings. . . .

The goal of training was that, through better understanding of Japan, employees would change their normal behavior patterns when working with Japanese counterparts. All improved their ability to work cross-culturally, but not all applied the material learned equally. Managers, in particular, had less patience to learn "how to do things," but rather just wanted to know "what to do." Scientists, on the other hand, tended to apply the models and processes in a much more diligent manner. . . .

Application of the "Understanding and Predicting Culture Process" in Japan

Pharmco employees started gaining understanding of Japanese culture by gathering and understanding cultural generalities. . . . Employees became more involved in the learning process by working on the tools to be used as well as applying them in a Japanese context.

Employees gathered information through visits, while in Japan, to museums, theaters, shrines, baseball games, and business meetings. . . . The initial work session was led by the manager-anthropologist but the trainees at the session participated in data entry. . . . After the introduction of the model, the anthropologist made no effort to suggest data classification according to anthropological criteria. Rather, Pharmco employees using the model defined classifications acceptable to and understood by them. For example, in the case of "insider-outsider," discussed under "artifacts" below, the visual artifact was the way people sat at business and dinner tables, with the concept rightly belonging in the cultural logic. Employees, however, skipped the visual and placed the cultural logic in the artifacts section. The point is that they understood what they meant.

The following analysis of Japanese culture used by Pharmco as baseline data is:

Artifacts. *How are things classified or what are the artifacts of an agreed classification system?* In Japan there are two basic classification systems commonly used: (1) insider-outsider and (2) front-rear. The insider is determined in the first instance by what Nakane (1970) refers to as a "frame." By frame, she means criteria that classify and identify individuals as part of a group. In business, the most obvious is the identification by company. When introducing oneself, one says, for example, "I am Pharmco's Reeves-Ellington." Japanese frames can also be determined by locality, such as the city in which one is born or family or household affiliations. In all cases frame indicates a criterion that sets a boundary and gives a common basis to a group of individuals who are located or involved in it. Outsiders are all those who are excluded from the frame. Hence, the use of the word "foreigner" (*gaijin*) is frequent in Japan. If one is not part of the frame, i.e., Japanese (insider), then one is a foreigner (outsider) (Nakane 1970).

Front and rear in the Japanese concept are not linear, as in the western world, but circular. The front, which embodies the concept of *tatamae,* is what is seen or what is commonly known, or frontstage, whereas the rear is what is hidden or backstage. This rear embodies the concept of *honne,* commonly referred to as what is "true." In the western world, these two concepts are the flip sides of a coin existing in a dichotomous relationship, but in Japan, the two concepts are a circular continuum. One folds into the next as do the rooms of a house as one walks through it. Outsiders are always kept to the front, whereas insiders are introduced to the rear (Matsumoto 1988).

The artifacts of the classifications are always determined by the situation in which people come together (Hall and Hall 1987). For example, in the inside-outside relationship, obvious manifestations are the family, localities, schools, companies, and associations. Tour groups are formed to make a group of people insiders. Outsiders are those not in a particular group, e.g., family members are outsiders to the company inside group. On the other hand, fellow employees are typically outsiders to a colleague's family group. In another context, such as going on a trip together, the family and business colleagues could both be insiders, as members of the XYZ tour group. The artifacts of the front and rear classifications can be exemplified by business meetings. Humans typically belong to a complex of groups that can be concentrically layered and are variably mutually inclusive and exclusive. The front artifacts are expressed in how people are arranged at a table and the courtesy that is extended to guests. The rear artifacts are expressed in terms of who is attending and the body language that occurs.

Social knowledge (values). *What are proper principles for behavior? What are the values that drive the categories and artifacts described above?* In Japan, adoption of the classification systems discussed above keeps as many people on the outside as possible. One keeps one's social obligations to a level that encourages self gain but eliminates all that offer less gain than one is required to give. One sees this principle in action in the Tokyo subway system. The proverbial Japanese politeness is totally absent, replaced with a "survival of the fittest" behavior pattern, which is accomplished, in part, by avoiding eye contact, thereby assuring that everyone around stays on the outside.

Keeping people on the outside embodies another principle: Minimize obligations to others. The personal value that drives this principle is the desire and need for personal relationships of a meaningful nature. If too many people are insiders, personal relationships would be weakened and a fundamental value diluted.

There is a third human principle at work: Everyone needs to be an insider somewhere. All Japanese are striving to be an insider in situations that will provide personal gain. In companies, they have a strong sense of being inside: On tour groups, they all do things together as insiders in a travel experience. The driving value that leads Japanese to strive for insider status is the value of acknowledging and accepting mutual interdependencies with others (*amae*) (Doi 1990).

Cultural logic. Social knowledge or values are based on underlying cultural logic around relationships to the environment, the nature of reality, truth, human nature, human activities, human relationships, and use of time. Within a culture, these are all taken for granted, rarely understood, and almost never expressible by those living in the culture, but they are of utmost importance to foreigners wishing to live and work in that culture. An explanation of Japanese cultural logic is contained in Table 1. . . .

Table 1 CULTURAL LOGIC

Environmental relationships

Japanese, as well as other Asians, view the physical environment and human environment as intertwined and not in opposition as do most Christians (Campbell 1960, 1989; Pelzel 1974). As exemplified in Japanese gardens, humans control and shape the environment in ways that suit the artistic feeling of people. The garden denotes the desire for environmental harmony and orderliness.

Nature of truth and reality

Truth and reality are determined by situations and social contexts in which people find themselves (Hall and Hall 1987; Lebra 1976). In a social group, only the insiders determine what is true and real. The accuracy of this determination is based on the degree of harmony and orderliness obtained within the insider group.

Nature of human nature

Humans are driven by emotion and not by logic (Doi 1990b). Mutuality of love and obligation (within the context of the concept of obligation) ties closely with that of hate (Ishida 1974). This mutuality in human relations forces the concept of consensus into human society organization. Since human nature is not believed to be inherently "bad," it is assumed this behavior is caused by ignorance and not evil intent.

Nature of human relationships

Using the concept of relational value orientation (Kluckhohn and Strodbeck 1961), collaterality in human relationships is highly valued. Within this concept is the perception that uncertainty is to be avoided and much effort is put into avoiding it. Within the basic collateral value, there exists a strong power distance within organizations and generational structures (Hofstede 1980).

Nature of human activities

Activity is focused on working toward ideals of harmonious relationships and involves an orientation toward human interdependency (Doi 1990; Lebra 1976; Hayashi 1988). Activity is necessarily done in groups and by groups.

Use of time

Time is polychronic (Hall and Hall 1988). The time system is characterized by the simultaneous occurrence of many things and by a deep involvement with people. There is more emphasis on completing transactions than holding to a schedule. A person confronted with too many subjects to be covered in too short a time chooses to expand the time available to complete the tasks rather than reduce the number of tasks.

THEORY INTO PRACTICE

To get theory into practice, Pharmco decided to learn how to do introductions, meetings, leavings, dinner, and drinking in Japan.

This analysis brings to life Pharmco's learning by relating incidents about just how badly things can go wrong when there is no basis for successful behaviors leading to appropriate judgements in the course of cross-cultural activities. In spite of the mistakes made, Diversity employees were gracious and appreciative of the efforts made to behave properly. They understand that Pharmco, being foreign, will never get it exactly right in Japan—just as the Japanese will never get it exactly right in the United States. Pharmco employees constantly remind themselves that they are involved in a continuous process they may never get entirely "right." There are always new and more subtle nuances to learn.

The Business Card (*meishi*)

During the initial meeting with the Japanese, the first item of business is introductions. (See Table 2.) Proper introductions require proper business cards (*meishi*). The word *meishi* is used by all people in Japan, including foreigners because the two words, business card and *meishi*, refer to the same card but the meaning behind the card is substantially different. For this reason, *meishi* should be prepared in Japan and be ready upon arrival to do business. At the time of presenting the *meishi*, the Japanese expect the viewer of the *meishi* to examine it carefully and to remember both name and title.

Mistreatment of a Japanese businessman's *meishi* will ruin a relationship, whether new or established. Since the *meishi* is an extension of self, damage to the card is damage to the individual. Explaining this to Pharmco staff was not sufficient. They did not understand the implications of the *meishi* until two stories were told to help their understanding.

The importance of this point is demonstrated in the following story. A major U.S. company was having problems with one of its distributors, and the parties seemed unable to resolve their differences. The president of the U.S. company decided to visit Japan, meet with his counterpart in the wholesaler organization, and attempt to resolve their differences. The two had not met previously and, upon meeting, each followed proper *meishi* ritual. The American, however, did not put the Japanese counterpart's *meishi* on the table; instead he held on to it. As the conversation became heated, the American rolled up the *meishi* in his hand. Horror was recorded on the face of the Japanese businessman. The American then tore the *meishi* into bits. This was more than the Japanese could stand; he excused himself from the meeting. Shortly afterward the two companies stopped doing business with each other.

Table 2 INTRODUCTIONS AT BUSINESS MEETINGS

Artifacts	Social knowledge	Cultural logic
Technology • Business cards • *Meishi* Visual behavior • Presentation of *meishi* by presenting card, facing recipient. • Senior people present *meishi* first. • Guest presents first, giving name, company affiliation and bowing. • Host presents *meishi* in same sequence. • Upon sitting at conference table, all *meishi* are placed front of recipient to assure name use.	• Once given a card is kept—not discarded. • *Meishi* are not exchanged a second time unless there is a position change. • Before the next meeting between parties, the *meishi* are reviewed for familiarization with the people attending the meeting. • The *meishi* provides status for the owner.	Human relations • *Meishi* provide understanding of appropriate relations between parties. • *Meishi* take uncertainty out of relationships. Environment • *Meishi* establish insider/outsider environment. • *Meishi* help establish possible obligations to environment. Human activity • *Meishi* help to establish human activities.

How Japanese use the *meishi* also helped Pharmco staff understand its importance. Japanese companies value a high degree of consistency in those with whom they work and in the handling of personnel within a company. Failure to demonstrate consistency toward internal employees indicates a probable inconsistency in relationships outside the company. The *meishi* can provide the Japanese executive with some indication of a company's attitude toward its employees. The Pharmco employees learned this lesson with a particularly painful outcome at a meeting with a senior Japanese executive. After the Pharmco team explained the purpose of the visit, this executive took a number of *meishi* from his desk. As he turned each of them up, he asked, "I see that I met with Mr. Hansen of your company ten years ago. Where is he now?" Then came the next card. "I see I met with Mr. Harman of your company eight years ago. Where is he now?" The questioning went through eight separate *meishi*. The Pharmco team leader responded each time that the particular person was no longer with the company. At the end, the Japanese executive said, "People are not treated well in your company. In our company, people do not leave until retirement." The meeting was not successful.

With this background, Pharmco staff visiting Japan have a good understanding of the *meishi* and treat it and its presentation with the respect Japanese expect.

The Conference Table

As soon as introductions are complete both sides take a seat at the conference table. In Japan, there are no round tables at business meetings. The expression "head of the table" is meaningless in a Japanese context. Understanding conference table arrangements (Table 3) leads to a successful meeting.

Seating is highly ritualistic and stylized. The power position is flanked by advisors; next come suppliers of data and information, should they be requested; and finally interested parties are seated at the extremities of the conference table (Figure 1). The person in the power seat performs all ritualistic duties for the side represented. That person directs all comments or questions to particular members of his team who are best qualified to answer them and also functions as the go-between for his team and the other side.

Contrary to usual western practice, the person in the power seat is not necessarily the most senior person present. Rather, the person designated as the official contact for his company or the person most knowledgeable about the subject matter to be discussed takes the seat. The Japanese want the powerful person to be the one who can accomplish the business at hand.

Not understanding this point led to Pharmco embarrassment. Pharmco managers believed at first that the senior person present always occupied the power seat. This assumption was based on meetings between senior managers of the companies who were addressing subject matter only they could decide. When Pharmco's R&D senior manager led Pharmco's initial discussions with Diversity regarding research philosophy and programs, he correctly took the power seat. At a subsequent meeting, called to address program execution, the senior R&D manager again took the power seat. The Japanese body language indicated he should not be there. A new lesson was learned that day: expertise and subject matter, not status, determine the occupant of the power seat. In the case of program execution, the Pharmco power seat occupant should have been the senior scientist for toxicology, not the head of R&D. By taking the power seat, the R&D manager offended the Japanese scientist because he had less status and therefore felt ineffectual. The meeting was inconclusive.

Table 3   CONFERENCE SEATING ARRANGEMENTS

Artifacts	Social knowledge	Cultural logic

Technology
  • Rectangular table
Visual behavior
  • Hosts on one side of the table and guests on the other.
  • Guests are framed by most attractive background.
  • The power seat is in the middle of the table.
  • Junior people are closest to the door.
	• Set seating allows all parties social/business understanding.
	• Person responsible for success has the authority.
	• Guests are treated as customers.
		Human relations
		  • Seating arrangements allow established order to be known, allowing a proper order and power structure to function between people.
		Reality and truth
		  • Responsibility and authority are combined for success.
		  • The inside and outside are maintained at the conference table.
		Environment
		  • Used to honor customers and guests.
		  • Used to maintain inside-outside definitions.

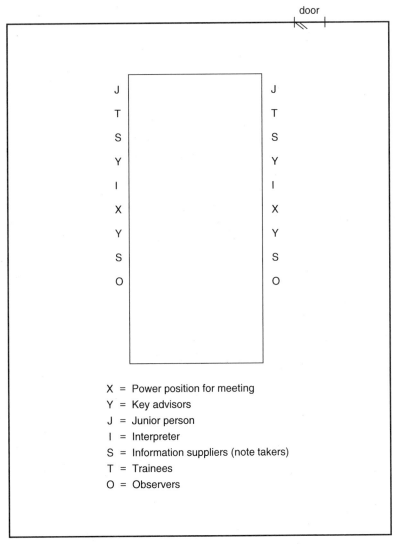

Figure 1
Meeting room

Knowing who is in the power seat offers insights to the other side's agenda. At a negotiating meeting between Diversity KK and Pharmco, the Pharmco team expected the meeting to be a confirmation of work done. When the meeting started, however, the Diversity power seat was occupied by an attorney, not the familiar businessman known by Pharmco. Pharmco immediately excused themselves for a few minutes. In private caucus, the team discussed the change of people and decided that major changes in the contract under negotiation were about to be introduced. This proved to be a correct interpretation. Even this short notice helped the Pharmco team stay in control of unfolding events. At the conclusion of the meeting, leaving is as ritualistic as arriving. Table 4 provides a grasp of the ritual.

At the conclusion of a business meeting, both sides stand up to leave; the host leads the guests out of the conference room; the host's team escorts the guests to the elevator; the entire team, excluding the host, leaves the guests as the elevator doors close, both sides bowing profusely; the host joins his guests in the elevator. The remaining host and his guests then go to the front door of the office, where, if a car has been arranged, the host will get into the car if there is room and accompany his guests back to their hotel. If no car is arranged, the host will stay with the guests until a taxi is found and the guests are safely in it and driving off. The host will remain at the curb, bowing, until the taxi is well into the traffic. The guests keep eye contact, heads nodding and arms waving until the car leaves the curb.

The respect ritualistically shown is based on the status of the individual's company, not on that of the individual. By showing this level of courtesy, the hosts expect the guests to recognize that they have an obligation to reciprocate in the future, when he is on their turf.

Once Pharmco staff understood the social importance of what the Japanese were doing in seeing them off, they immediately instituted the same policy of courtesy for the Japanese when they visited the Pharmco facilities.

Going out to Dinner

When foreigners are invited to dinner, they must be prepared to express a preference for the nationality of food to be eaten; in Japan, a preference for Japanese is obligatory because it demonstrates a willingness to engage in things "Japanese." The Japanese restaurant is likely to be more comfortable and offer more privacy than others, thus creating a better relationship. A Japanese menu includes raw fish. The Japanese host will inevitably ask "Do you like raw fish?" The answer is "yes." Accepting what is offered is a necessity for relationship building in Japan, but it does not include the necessity of eating everything. Being a guest is a simple task as all that is necessary is responding to what the Japanese host suggests or discusses. The intricacies of the organization are the responsibility of the hosts.

Hosting a dinner is much more difficult than being a guest. The host is responsible for assuring a successful relationship-building event. Hosting requires an understanding of Japanese social knowledge if the event is to be successful. Three principles of social knowledge are at work in dinner meetings: (1) have an environment that permits individual members of the companies to start to become acquainted and either start building a relationship or support and maintain one; (2) provide a setting and a meal befitting the guests' social position and thereby show that the host respects this position; and (3) send indirect signals of the status of the relationship in terms of the locale and quality of food. The meal can offer a form of celebration, a basis of apology[1] or just a feeling of comfort. The atmosphere created at dinner should be relaxed and enjoyable. The host is responsible for the comfort of the guests and, should that comfort be threatened for any reason, the host must make certain that conviviality is restored.

Table 4   LEAVING THE CONFERENCE

Artifacts	Social knowledge	Cultural logic
Visual behavior • Ritualistic thank yous end the meeting while all are seated. • Conclusion of exchange means guests initiate standing. All arise. • Power person stays with guests until they are off company premises. • Bows start upon arising and continue each time one of either side leaves.	• Politeness demands guests be treated as though they were visiting the Japanese at home.	Environment • Guests are under control while in the insider environment. They are left only when they achieve the outside environment. Truth and reality • All exchanges assure a smooth transition from one status to another. Human relations • All structured interactions require a host and a guest role.

Execution of these social values requires one to know when to host, how to select the right guests, how to select a proper restaurant, how to assure that the meal is a proper one, how to keep the conversation in an acceptable mood and assure that the event starts and ends within a culturally acceptable time frame.

Determination of who hosts must be settled well in advance of the date of the dinner. The decision should not be left open until the close of a formal business meeting. If one side has an apology to make or if they have a difficult request, then they should certainly offer to host. For dinners following routine meetings, Pharmco works on the basis that if the meetings are in Japan, then the Japanese host, and if they are in the United States, Pharmco hosts. This works well. If, however, the Japanese are insistent upon acting as host, it is best to follow their lead.

The attendees of any particular dinner must correlate to reciprocal status of individuals from both companies. Therefore the attendees must be agreed upon well in advance of the dinner. Any changes of attendee by one side must be announced well in advance of the dinner. For one side to change the status level of attendance at the last minute causes problems for the other. If the side making changes lowers the level of attendance, the other side has two problems to sort out. First, is a *honne* message being sent and why? For example, Japanese companies have been known to use this type of last-minute change as a way to tell the other company that they want to downgrade the existing relationship between the two companies. Second, how can a Japanese manager explain such changes to his superior? If, on the other hand, the level of attendance is increased at the last minute, the other might not be able to reciprocate, leading to embarrassment and a weakening of friendly relations. Attendance, once set, should not change.

The class of the restaurant must be in keeping with the status of the senior member of the party being invited, for Japanese executives have a clear understanding of where their status allows them to dine. Selection of a restaurant considered below a Japanese guest's status results in the guest losing face with his colleagues. Anticipation of this problem makes the Japanese uncomfortable during the meal, precluding the building of good social relationships. An example demonstrates the point.

Pharmco headquarters decided that the cost of entertaining in Tokyo was too high and dictated that cheaper places be found. The dictum was followed and, on the occasion of the next business meeting with a middle manager of Diversity, disaster resulted. When the guest arrived, his first comment was that one of his subordinates often brought suppliers to the restaurant. Pharmco had clearly insulted him in the choice of eating establishment, causing Pharmco managers to spend the rest of the night apologizing. Trying to rectify the situation, the next time they hosted the manager, Pharmco managers went to a very exclusive place. The first comment received was, "the president of our company likes this restaurant but I have never been here." This time, Pharmco embarrassed the Diversity manager by taking him to a location beyond his status, causing him to explain to his colleagues the next day why he was there.

Avoiding these problems requires only that foreigners ask a Japanese for a restaurant preference. The answer will be "no," followed by a comment indicating a restaurant in which he has never eaten but would like to do so. If this approach fails, a visit to the social director of the hotel in which the foreigner is staying will yield dividends. By showing the director the card of the individual to be entertained, she will make appropriate selections, based on the *meishi* information of the name of the company and the title of the person. She never errs in judgment.

Selection of the restaurant leads to the selection of a suitable menu, which is done by the host in advance and must reflect the status of the guests and the nature of the occasion. For example, if it is a dinner just to end the day, a simple meal is in order. If the relationship is particularly strong, a stop in a noodle shop can be totally appropriate. If the dinner is one of celebration or a form of apology, however, a more elaborate meal is required. As with the choice of a restaurant, use Japanese expertise. A visit to the restaurant with the guest's business card and a discussion of the room and the meal with the majordomo of the restaurant (a discussion that should also cover who will attend and the purpose of the meal) assures a proper menu and setting.

When Pharmco management decided to enter a strategic alliance with Diversity KK, they had to inform Nippon Pharmaceutical, a potential partner, that they had decided not to work with them. The business aspects of the decision were discussed with Nippon Pharma at their offices, but then at dinner the relationship aspects of the decision were covered. The choice of location and meal was more elaborate than would normally be the case, given the state of the relationship. At the end of the meal, the Nippon Pharma representatives complimented Pharmco on their ability to be a good Japanese host.

Conversation at dinners does not include heavy business negotiations under any but the most unusual circumstances. Talk focuses on recreational activities, current politics, travel, or other "cocktail party" chat. The point of conversation, as well as of the food, is to put everyone at ease. Failure to follow this principle can cause discomfort.

At a dinner hosted by Diversity management, a Pharmco manager discussed matters relating to fundamental changes in the Japanese health care system.

He did not notice that the Japanese were becoming upset until one of them exploded that "these matters were not the business of foreigners and they should not express opinions. Rather they should wait to be taught the right way to do business by the Japanese." While the foreigner thought himself at fault by not avoiding the delicate subject matter, he received an extensive apology by a colleague of the Japanese who expressed such a forceful opinion. He said "As host, I should not permit such things to happen!"

In Japan, dinners are arranged for the end of the business day which is around 6:30 p.m. The foreign host should plan to invite his guests for a 7 p.m. dinner, as doing so will give them a half an hour to get to the restaurant. Always offer an exact time. The American habit of "let's make it around 6:30 to 7" is not acceptable. The host always should arrive a few minutes early and be there to greet his guests. At the close of the meal, the host walks the guest to the front of the restaurant, where he has had the restaurant arrange transportation. The host stands at the curb and stays there, preferably bowing or waving, until the guests have been driven off. Table 5 summarizes the critical cultural factors concerning dinner engagements.

Drinking in Bars

Going out to drink after dinner is the first opportunity for colleagues of different companies to have the chance to behave as a set of "insiders." It also provides a setting in which anyone of the group can express a *honne* sentiment. Drinking provides the foreigner a sense of how relationship-building is progressing between his company, himself and his Japanese counterparts. Therefore, ethnographic understanding of ritual drinking is imperative (Table 6).

"Know how to sing," was the key learned by Pharmco management before going out drinking after dinner. Drinking in Karaoke bars is the ultimate socializing and relationship-building mechanism with and among Japanese. Power and social distance are almost completely broken down at the bars. The president as well as the most junior person present will sing, tell jokes, and generally relax. Although there is still not a round table, all the people together act as though they are at one. The environment has also changed substantially from that of the office. The bar is smaller than the office, and women are an important addition as they are to provide conversation and pour the drinks.[2] The tables are laid out so that there is little structure in physical environment. A basic assumption is that this is the one place in the entire social milieu where uncertainty is acceptable. The assumption is that, with drink, it is totally acceptable to say what is on your mind to whomever you want. A further assumption is that whatever is said cannot be held against a person after leaving the bar.

Being there makes one an insider for the time spent together in the bar. "Insidership" is created only if the proper bar is chosen—one befitting the status of the group. Unlike choosing a restaurant, however, the foreigner must ask his Japanese associates for advice as to where to go, for they know that the foreigner lacks the knowledge to make a proper selection. A Pharmco executive experienced near-disaster the one time he selected a bar without consulting a Japanese businessman. He had found the hotel social relations director helpful with restaurants so [he] thought that person would be a good source of information for bars. He was not. As soon as he walked in the bar recommended by the director, he knew there was a problem: Except for one or two Japanese, only foreigners were present; the bar was almost empty; and the hostesses ranged in age from 40 to 50—far too old for the tastes of the Japanese guests. Fortunately, relationships between the Pharmco executive and his Japanese guests [were] strong enough for everyone to get a good laugh from the situation. He is still periodically reminded of the incident.

Business is usually not done at the bar, where drinking offers the Japanese an opportunity to express *honne* opinions about his relationships with colleagues, both foreign and Japanese. These opinions are tolerable as they are expressed when the person expressing them is acceptably drunk. Within the drinking context,

Table 5   GOING TO DINNER

Artifacts	Social knowledge	Cultural logic
Physical • Guests • Restaurant • Meals • Transportation Visual behavior • Hosting • Guesting • Timing to eat	• Relationship building is purpose of eating. • Status is honored by correct dinners. • Dinner group has some "insider" attributes.	Use of time • Time at dinners is effective use of time for relations. Relationships • Identifies how two companies view peoples' position in hierarchy. • Confirms status matching through acceptance or nonacceptance of invitations.

Table 6   GOING OUT DRINKING

Artifacts	Social knowledge	Cultural logic

Physical
  • Karaoke bars
  • Tabs
  • Female social managers
Visual behavior
  • Singing
  • Joking
  • Honest opinion
	• Freedom of speech acceptable.
	• Drunken behavior acceptable.
	• Place to get things "off the chest."
	• Everyone can be an "insider."
		Human relations
		  • Provides a time for *honne* talk.
		  • Fills the need for business associates
		    to be a set of "insiders."
		Environment
		  • Setting is outside a traditional
		    "insider" setting, allowing a new
		    set of "insiders" to be formed on
		    "neutral" ground.
		Reality and truth
		  • Feelings (reality) must be expressed
		    and understood (truth) by an
		    insider group.

everyone is in the same social circle. For this reason, one must constantly be alert for signals that might indicate something is on a colleague's mind. At one drinking session, a Pharmco manager felt that something was bothering his Japanese counterpart but, as the evening wore on, nothing was said. Just before it ended, the Japanese manager put his face down on the table and muttered that he had something important to say. The American leaned forward and asked what it was. All the Japanese said was "Your Johns-san is an asshole." Nothing more was said and the subject was never raised again. The American assumed that just stating the opinion was enough to relieve the tension the Japanese had. The opinion was not reported to Johns. The next business day discussions with the Japanese gentlemen were more relaxed than had been previously experienced.

PHARMCO BUSINESS IMPROVEMENTS

Three critical factors were deemed necessary for the program to be judged a success: (1) effective working relationships with Japanese executives; (2) shortened project times; and (3) improved financial returns. The project is successful based on these factors (Table 7) and is in the process of being applied to other countries.

Before learning the methodologies and skills outlined in this paper, Pharmco executives avoided travel to Japan and working with Japanese whenever possible. Fifty Pharmco executives have been through the training program. Before the program, they were asked to evaluate their comfort level of working with Japanese and their enjoyment of business trips to Japan. The rating scale was 1 to 10 with 1 expressing no comfort and no enjoyment to 10 expressing total comfort and enjoyment. The average score was 3 with a range of 1 to 5. After exposure to the concepts, tools, and material, the average score increased to 6, with a range of 5 to 9. The final measurement was based on 15

executives who used the concepts and tools in their next series of meetings. The average score of this group was 8, with a low score of 5 and a high score of 10. Before the program, most employees wanted to be accompanied to Japan by a person experienced in Japan. After the exposure, almost all are comfortable making these trips on their own. This willingness to work in and with Japan has improved the personal effectiveness of all these employees working on Japanese projects.

Late delivery of projects was costly to Pharmco and discouraged Diversity managers from working with their Pharmco counterparts. In one case the delays were estimated to cost Pharmco $90 million over a ten-year period. The delays were of a nature that a competitor entered the market with a similar product, thereby denying innovator status to Pharmco. The improved delivery times are helping both Diversity and

Table 7   CRITICAL FACTORS OUTCOME

Effective working relationships
1. Pharmco employees are more self-assured when meeting Japanese in Japan.
2. Their Japanese counterparts state they prefer working with Pharmco over other foreign companies.

Shortened project times
1. Prior to introducing the cultural material, projects between Pharmco and Diversity averaged 15 months to completion.
2. Projects run by executives applying cultural methodologies shortened project completion times to an average of 8 months, while all others remain at 15 months.

Improved financial returns
1. Financial returns based on contracts negotiated by personnel not exposed to the cultural material average gross income of 6% of sales.
2. Financial returns of contracts negotiated by personnel applying the anthropological techniques provide gross income equal to 18% of sales.

Pharmco in gaining valuable marketing time over their key competitors.

SUMMARY

The ability to work with and within a foreign culture requires an organization to adopt and implement an interpretive strategy that permits its practitioners to set out to work proactively within the perceived meaning of the foreign environment. This strategy requires managers to become transformational in order to operate successfully in other social and institutional environments. Successful implementation of such a strategy demands the use of both business and anthropological tools and skills. By creating a base of these skills and providing a training environment in which employees individually could learn and implement such a strategy, Pharmco achieved dramatic improvements in its Japanese business relationships and business results. This success has led to adapting the training to other countries.

NOTES

1. In Japan, the concept of apology involves a great shame for not having behaved correctly or done something in the right way. To apologize is traumatic for a Japanese.
2. Apologies are necessary to my female colleagues for this chauvinistic viewpoint. It is how things are in Japan, however. I would like to point out that should a female colleague be part of the group visiting the bar, she would be treated as a colleague by her peers and be well received by the employees in the bar.

REFERENCES

Brislin, Richard W., Kenneth Cushner, Craig Cherrie, and Mehalahi Yong. 1986. *Intercultural Interactions: A Practical Guide.* Beverly Hills, CA: Sage.

Campbell, Joseph. 1960. *The Masks of God: Primitive Mythology.* New York: Viking Press.

———. 1989. *The Hero with a Thousand Faces.* New York: Viking Press.

David, Kenneth. 1985. *Participant Observation in Pharmaceutical Field Selling.* Norwich, CT: Norwich Eaton Pharmaceutical Co., Inc.

Doi, Takeo. 1990a. *The Anatomy of Dependence.* Tokyo: Kodansha International.

———. 1990b. *The Anatomy of Self.* Tokyo: Kodansha International.

Hall, Edward T., and Mildred R. Hall. 1987. *Hidden Differences.* New York: Anchor Press.

Hamada, Tomoko. 1991. *American Enterprise in Japan.* Albany: SUNY Press.

Hayashi, Shuji. 1988. *Culture and Management in Japan.* Tokyo: University of Tokyo Press.

Hofstede, Geert. 1980. *Culture's Consequences: International Differences in Work-Related Values.* Beverly Hills, CA: Sage.

Ishida, Eiichiro. 1974. A Culture of Love and Hate. In *Japanese Culture and Behavior,* Takie Sugiyama Lebra and William P. Lebra, eds. Pp. 27–36. Honolulu: University Press of Hawaii.

Kluckhohn, F. R., and F. L. Strodtbeck. 1961. *Variations in Value Orientations.* Westport, CT: Greenwood Press.

Lebra, Takie Sugiyama. 1976. *Japanese Patterns of Behavior.* Honolulu: University Press of Hawaii.

Matsumoto, Michihiro. 1988. *The Unspoken Way.* Tokyo: Kodansha International.

Nakane, Chie. 1970. *Japanese Society.* Tokyo: Charles E. Tuttle Co.

Pelzel, John C. 1974. Human Nature in the Japanese Myths. In *Japanese Culture and Behavior,* Takie Sugiyama Lebra and William P. Lebra, eds. Pp. 3–26. Honolulu: University Press of Hawaii.

Reeves-Ellington, Richard H. 1988. Relationships Between Multinationals and Peasants. Paper presented at the annual meeting of the American Anthropological Association, Chicago.

Reeves-Ellington, Richard H., and Paul Steidlmeier. 1991. *Total Quality, Institutionalism and the Retooling of American Business.* Binghamton, NY: SUNY-Binghamton, School of Management.

23

Society and Sex Roles

Ernestine Friedl

Americans pride themselves on their concern about social justice. We believe, or at least say we believe, in equal rights and equal access to education, jobs, and other opportunities. As such, understanding the social and historical origins of inequality should be important to us for both intellectual and policy reasons. One of the many inequalities that remain in our society and in societies throughout the world is the asymmetrical relations between men and women. Indeed, the dominant position of men is so pervasive that people often assume that this is the "natural" (read biological) relationship between the sexes. Anthropology, as we have seen, is a discipline that challenges us to question such fundamental assumptions.

In this selection, Ernestine Friedl examines contemporary hunter-gatherer societies and in so doing suggests that male dominance stems from economic control over resources. Differences in cultural perception about gender are closely related not only to economic patterns but also to the organization of families and the institution of marriage.

As you read this selection, ask yourself the following questions:

☐ *Looking at the historical and anthropological records, how frequently do we find gender equality?*

☐ *What is the source of male power in hunter-gatherer societies?*

☐ *Why don't women hunt?*

☐ *Based on this reading, how will the changing position of women in the American labor force affect gender roles?*

☐ *What is the value of cross-cultural studies for understanding problems such as sexism in our own society?*

The following terms discussed in this selection are included in the Glossary at the back of the book:

egalitarian society
gender
human universal
hunter-gatherers
nomadic band
reciprocal gift
sex roles
shaman

"Women must respond quickly to the demands of their husbands," says anthropologist Napoleon Chagnon describing the horticultural Yanomamo Indi-

ans of Venezuela. When a man returns from a hunting trip, "the woman, no matter what she is doing, hurries home and quietly but rapidly prepares a meal for her husband. Should the wife be slow in doing this, the husband is within his rights to beat her. Most reprimands . . . take the form of blows with the hand or with a piece of firewood. . . . Some of them chop their wives with the sharp edge of a machete or axe, or shoot them with a barbed arrow in some nonvital area, such as the buttocks or leg."

Among the Semai agriculturalists of central Malaya, when one person refuses the request of another, the offended party suffers *punan*, a mixture of emotional pain and frustration. "Enduring *punan* is commonest when a girl has refused the victim her sexual favors," reports Robert Dentan. "The jilted man's 'heart becomes sad.' He loses his energy and his appetite. Much of the time he sleeps, dreaming of this lost love. In this state he is in fact very likely to injure himself 'accidentally.'" The Semai are afraid of violence; a man would never strike a woman.

The social relationship between men and women has emerged as one of the principal disputes occupying the attention of scholars and the public in recent years. Although the discord is sharpest in the United States, the controversy has spread throughout the world. Numerous national and international conferences, including one in Mexico sponsored by the United Nations, have drawn together delegates from all walks of life to discuss such questions as the social and political rights of each sex, and even the basic nature of males and females.

Whatever their position, partisans often invoke examples from other cultures to support their ideas about the proper role of each sex. Because women are clearly subservient to men in many societies, like the Yanomamo, some experts conclude that the natural pattern is for men to dominate. But among the Semai no one has the right to command others, and in West Africa women are often chiefs. The place of women in these societies supports the argument of those who believe that sex roles are not fixed, that if there is a natural order, it allows for many different arrangements.

The argument will never be settled as long as the opposing sides toss examples from the world's cultures at each other like intellectual stones. But the effect of biological differences on male and female behavior can be clarified by looking at known examples of the earliest forms of human society and examining the relationship between the technology, social organization, environment, and sex roles. The problem is to determine the conditions in which different degrees of male dominance are found, to try to discover the social and cultural arrangements that give rise to equality or inequality between the sexes, and to attempt to apply this knowledge to our understanding of the changes taking place in modern industrial society.

As Western history and the anthropological record have told us, equality between the sexes is rare; in most known societies females are subordinate. Male dominance is so widespread that it is virtually a human universal; societies in which women are consistently dominant do not exist and have never existed.

Evidence of a society in which women control all strategic resources like food and water, and in which women's activities are the most prestigious has never been found. The Iroquois of North America and the Lovedu of Africa came closest. Among the Iroquois, women raised food, controlled its distribution, and helped to choose male political leaders. Lovedu women ruled as queens, exchanged valuable cattle, led ceremonies, and controlled their own sex lives. But among both the Iroquois and the Lovedu, men owned the land and held other positions of power and prestige. Women were equal to men; they did not have ultimate authority over them. Neither culture was a true matriarchy.

Patriarchies are prevalent, and they appear to be strongest in societies in which men control significant goods that are exchanged with people outside the family. Regardless of who produces food, the person who gives it to others creates the obligations and alliances that are at the center of all political relations. The greater the male monopoly on the distribution of scarce items, the stronger their control of women seems to be. This is most obvious in relatively simple hunter-gatherer societies.

Hunter-gatherers, or foragers, subsist on wild plants, small land animals, and small river or sea creatures gathered by hand; large land animals and sea mammals hunted with spears, bows and arrows, and blow guns; and fish caught with hooks and nets. The 300,000 hunter-gatherers alive in the world today include the Eskimos, the Australian aborigines, and the Pygmies of Central Africa.

Foraging has endured for two million years and was replaced by farming and animal husbandry only 10,000 years ago; it covers more than 99 percent of human history. Our foraging ancestry is not far behind us and provides a clue to our understanding of the human condition.

Hunter-gatherers are people whose ways of life are technologically simple and socially and politically egalitarian. They live in small groups of 50 to 200 and have neither kings, nor priests, nor social classes. These conditions permit anthropologists to observe the essential bases for inequalities between the sexes without the distortions induced by the complexities of contemporary industrial society.

The source of male power among hunter-gatherers lies in their control of a scarce, hard to acquire, but necessary nutrient—animal protein. When men in a hunter-gatherer society return to camp with game, they divide the meat in some customary way. Among the !Kung San of South Africa, certain parts of the animal are given to the owner of the arrow that killed the beast, to the first hunter to sight the game, to the one who threw the first spear, and to all men in the hunting party. After the meat has been divided, each hunter distributes his share to his blood relatives and his in-laws, who in turn share it with others. If an animal is large enough, every member of the band will receive some meat.

Vegetable foods, in contrast, are not distributed beyond the immediate household. Women give food to their children, to their husbands, to other members of the household, and rarely, to the occasional visitor. No one outside the family regularly eats any of the wild fruits and vegetables that are gathered by the women.

The meat distributed by the men is a public gift. Its source is widely known, and the donor expects a reciprocal gift when other men return from a successful hunt. He gains honor as a supplier of a scarce item and simultaneously obligates others to him.

These obligations constitute a form of power or control over others, both men and women. The opinions of hunters play an important part in decisions to move the village; good hunters attract the most desirable women; people in other groups join camps with good hunters; and hunters, because they already participate in an internal system of exchange, control exchange with other groups for flint, salt, and steel axes. The male monopoly on hunting unites men in a system of exchange and gives them power; gathering vegetable food does not give women equal power even among foragers who live in the tropics, where the food collected by women provides more than half the hunter-gatherer diet.

If dominance arises from a monopoly on big-game hunting, why has the male monopoly remained unchallenged? Some women are strong enough to participate in the hunt and their endurance is certainly equal to that of men. Dobe San women of the Kalahari Desert in Africa walk an average of 10 miles a day carrying from 15 to 33 pounds of food plus a baby.

Women do not hunt, I believe, because of four interrelated factors: variability in the supply of game; the different skills required for hunting and gathering; the incompatibility between carrying burdens and hunting; and the small size of seminomadic foraging populations.

Because the meat supply is unstable, foragers must make frequent expeditions to provide the band with gathered food. Environmental factors such as seasonal and annual variation in rainfall often affect the size of the wildlife population. Hunters cannot always find game, and when they do encounter animals, they are not always successful in killing their prey. In northern latitudes, where meat is the primary food, periods of starvation are known in every generation. The irregularity of the game supply leads hunter-gatherers in areas where plant foods are available to depend on these predictable foods a good part of the time. Some-

one must gather the fruits, nuts, and roots and carry them back to camp to feed unsuccessful hunters, children, the elderly, and anyone who might not have gone foraging that day.

Foraging falls to the women because hunting and gathering cannot be combined on the same expedition. Although gatherers sometimes notice signs of game as they work, the skills required to track game are not the same as those required to find edible roots or plants. Hunters scan the horizon and the land for traces of large game; gatherers keep their eyes to the ground, studying the distribution of plants and the texture of the soil for hidden roots and animal holes. Even if a woman who was collecting plants came across the track of an antelope, she could not follow it; it is impossible to carry a load and hunt at the same time. Running with a heavy load is difficult, and should the animal be sighted, the hunter would be off balance and could neither shoot an arrow nor throw a spear accurately.

Pregnancy and child care would also present difficulties for a hunter. An unborn child affects a woman's body balance, as does a child in her arms, on her back, or slung at her side. Until they are two years old, many hunter-gatherer children are carried at all times, and until they are four, they are carried some of the time.

An observer might wonder why young women do not hunt until they become pregnant, or why mature women and men do not hunt and gather on alternate days, with some women staying in camp to act as wet nurse for the young. Apart from the effects hunting might have on a mother's milk production, there are two reasons. First, young girls begin to bear children as soon as they are physically mature and strong enough to hunt, and second, hunter-gatherer bands are so small that there are unlikely to be enough lactating women to serve as wet nurses. No hunter-gatherer group could afford to maintain a specialized female hunting force.

Because game is not always available, because hunting and gathering are specialized skills, because women carrying heavy loads cannot hunt, and because women in hunter-gatherer societies are usually either pregnant or caring for young children, for most of the last two million years of human history men have hunted and women have gathered.

If male dominance depends on controlling the supply of meat, then the degree of male dominance in a society should vary with the amount of meat available and the amount supplied by the men. Some regions, like the East African grasslands and the North American woodlands, abounded with species of large mammals; other zones, like tropical forests and semideserts, are thinly populated with prey. Many elements affect the supply of game, but theoretically, the less meat provided exclusively by the men, the more egalitarian the society.

All known hunter-gatherer societies fit into four basic types: those in which men and women work together in communal hunts and as teams gathering edible plants, as did the Washo Indians of North America; those in which men and women each collect their own plant foods although the men supply some meat to the group, as do the Hadza of Tanzania; those in which male hunters and female gatherers work apart but return to camp each evening to share their acquisitions, as do the Tiwi of North Australia; and those in which the men provide all the food by hunting large game, as do the Eskimo. In each case the extent of male dominance increases directly with the proportion of meat supplied by individual men and small hunting parties.

Among the most egalitarian of hunter-gatherer societies are the Washo Indians, who inhabited the valleys of the Sierra Nevada in what is now southern California and Nevada. In the spring they moved north to Lake Tahoe for the large fish runs of sucker and native trout. Everyone—men, women, and children—participated in the fishing. Women spent the summer gathering edible berries and seeds while the men continued to fish. In the fall some men hunted deer but the most important source of animal protein was the jack rabbit, which was captured in communal hunts. Men and women together drove the rabbits into nets tied end to end. To provide food for the winter, husbands and wives worked as teams in the late fall to collect pine nuts.

Since everyone participated in most food-gathering activities, there were no individual distributors of food and relatively little difference in male and female rights. Men and women were not segregated from each other in daily activities; both were free to take lovers after marriage; both had the right to separate whenever they chose; menstruating women were not isolated from the rest of the group; and one of the two major Washo rituals celebrated hunting while the other celebrated gathering. Men were accorded more prestige if they had killed a deer, and men directed decisions about the seasonal movement of the group. But if no male leader stepped forward, women were permitted to lead. The distinctive feature of groups such as the Washo is the relative equality of the sexes.

The sexes are also relatively equal among the Hadza of Tanzania but this near-equality arises because men and women tend to work alone to feed themselves. They exchange little food. The Hadza lead a leisurely life in the seemingly barren environment of the East African Rift Gorge that is, in fact, rich in edible berries, roots, and small game. As a result of this abundance, from the time they are 10 years old, Hadza men and women gather much of their own food.

Women take their young children with them into the bush, eating as they forage, and collect only enough food for a light family meal in the evening. The men eat berries and roots as they hunt for small game, and should they bring down a rabbit or a hyrax, they eat the meat on the spot. Meat is carried back to the camp and shared with the rest of the group only on those rare occasions when a poisoned arrow brings down a large animal—an impala, a zebra, an eland, or a giraffe.

Because Hadza men distribute little meat, their status is only slightly higher than that of the women. People flock to the camp of a good hunter and the camp might take on his name because of his popularity, but he is in no sense a leader of the group. A Hadza man and a woman have an equal right to divorce and each can repudiate a marriage simply by living apart for a few weeks. Couples tend to live in the same camp as the wife's mother but they sometimes make long visits to the camp of the husband's mother. Although a man may take more than one wife, most Hadza males cannot afford to indulge in this luxury. In order to maintain a marriage, a man must support both his wife and his mother-in-law with some meat and trade goods, such as beads and cloth, and the Hadza economy gives few men the wealth to provide for more than one wife and mother-in-law. Washo equality is based on cooperation; Hadza equality is based on independence.

In contrast to both these groups, among the Tiwi of Melville and Bathurst Islands off the northern coast of Australia, male hunters dominate female gatherers. The Tiwi are representative of the most common form of foraging society, in which the men supply large quantities of meat, although less than half the food consumed by the group. Each morning Tiwi women, most with babies on their backs, scatter in different directions in search of vegetables, grubs, worms, and small game such as bandicoots, lizards, and opossums. To track the game, they use hunting dogs. On most days women return to camp with some meat and with baskets full of *korka*, the nut of the native palm, which is soaked and mashed to make a porridge-like dish. The Tiwi men do not hunt small game and do not hunt every day, but when they do they often return with kangaroo, large lizards, fish, and game birds.

The porridge is cooked separately by each household and rarely shared outside the family, but the meat is prepared by a volunteer cook, who can be male or female. After the cook takes one of the parts of the animal traditionally reserved for him or her, the animal's "boss," the one who caught it, distributes the rest to all near kin and then to all others residing with the band. Although the small game supplied by the women is distributed in the same way as the big game supplied by the men, Tiwi men are dominant because the game they kill provides most of the meat.

The power of Tiwi men is clearest in their betrothal practices. Among the Tiwi, a woman must always be married. To ensure this, female infants are betrothed at birth and widows are remarried at the gravesides of their late husbands. Men form alliances by exchanging daughters, sisters, and mothers in marriage and some collect as many as 25 wives. Tiwi men value the quantity and quality of food many wives can collect and the many children they can produce.

The dominance of the men is offset somewhat by the influence of adult women in selecting their next husbands. Many women are active strategists in the political careers of their male relatives, but to the exasperation of some sons attempting to promote their own futures, widowed mothers sometimes insist on selecting their own partners. Women also influence the marriages of their daughters and granddaughters, especially when the selected husband dies before the bestowed child moves to his camp.

Among the Eskimo, representative of the rarest type of forager society, inequality between the sexes is matched by inequality in supplying the group with food. Inland Eskimo men hunt caribou throughout the year to provision the entire society, and maritime Eskimo men depend on whaling, fishing, and some hunting to feed their extended families. The women process the carcasses, cut and sew skins to make clothing, cook, and care for the young; but they collect no food of their own and depend on the men to supply all the raw material for their work. Since men provide all the meat, they also control the trade in hides, whale oil, seal oil, and other items that move between the maritime and inland Eskimos.

Eskimo women are treated almost exclusively as objects to be used, abused, and traded by men. After puberty all Eskimo girls are fair game for any interested male. A man shows his intentions by grabbing the belt of a woman and if she protests, he cuts off her trousers and forces himself upon her. These encounters are considered unimportant by the rest of the group. Men offer their wives' sexual services to establish alliances with trading partners and members of hunting and whaling parties.

Despite the consistent pattern of some degree of male dominance among foragers, most of these societies are egalitarian compared with agricultural and industrial societies. No forager has any significant opportunity for political leadership. Foragers, as a rule, do not like to give or take orders, and assume leadership only with reluctance. Shamans (those who are thought to be possessed by spirits) may be either male or female. Public rituals conducted by women in order to celebrate the first menstruation of girls are common, and the symbolism in these rituals is similar to that in the ceremonies that follow a boy's first kill.

In any society, status goes to those who control the distribution of valued goods and services outside the family. Equality arises when both sexes work side by side in food production, as do the Washo, and the products are simply distributed among the workers. In such circumstances, no person or sex has greater access to valued items than do others. But when women make no contribution to the food supply, as in the case of the Eskimo, they are completely subordinate.

When we attempt to apply these generalizations to contemporary industrial society, we can predict that as long as women spend their discretionary income from jobs on domestic needs, they will gain little social recognition and power. To be an effective source of power, money must be exchanged in ways that require returns and create obligations. In other words, it must be invested.

Jobs that do not give women control over valued resources will do little to advance their general status. Only as managers, executives, and professionals are women in a position to trade goods and services, to do others favors, and therefore to obligate others to them. Only as controllers of valued resources can women achieve prestige, power, and equality.

Within the household, women who bring in income from jobs are able to function on a more nearly equal basis with their husbands. Women who contribute services to their husbands and children without pay, as do some middle-class Western housewives, are especially vulnerable to dominance. Like Eskimo women, as long as their services are limited to domestic distribution they have little power relative to their husbands and none with respect to the outside world.

As for the limits imposed on women by their procreative functions in hunter-gatherer societies, childbearing and child care is organized around work as much as work is organized around reproduction. Some foraging groups space their children three to four years apart and have an average of only four to six children, far fewer than many women in other cultures. Hunter-gatherers nurse their infants for extended periods, sometimes for as long as four years. This custom suppresses ovulation and limits the size of their families. Sometimes, although rarely, they practice infanticide. By limiting reproduction, a woman who is gathering food has only one child to carry.

Different societies can and do adjust the frequency of birth and the care of children to accommodate whatever productive activities women customarily engage in. In horticultural societies, where women work long hours in gardens that may be far from home, infants get food to supplement their mothers' milk, older children take care of younger children, and pregnancies are widely spaced. Throughout the world, if a society requires a woman's labor, it finds ways to care for her children.

In the United States, as in some other industrial societies, the accelerated entry of women with preschool children into the labor force has resulted in the development of a variety of child-care arrangements. Individual women have called on friends, relatives, and neighbors. Public and private child-care centers are growing. We should realize that the declining birth rate, the increasing acceptance of childless or single-child families, and a de-emphasis on motherhood are adaptations to a sexual division of labor reminiscent of the system of production found in hunter-gatherer societies.

In many countries where women no longer devote most of their productive years to childbearing, they are beginning to demand a change in the social relationship of the sexes. As women gain access to positions that control the exchange of resources, male dominance may be archaic, and industrial societies may one day become as egalitarian as the Washo.

24

Family Planning Outreach and Credit Programs in Rural Bangladesh

Sidney Ruth Schuler and Syed M. Hashemi

In many parts of the world, high fertility rates threaten women's health and lead to a variety of negative consequences associated with exploding populations. Many applied anthropologists argue that stabilizing population growth is critical for increased quality of life in developing nations. Yet the paradoxical coexistence of high birthrates in tandem with starvation and poverty is all too common. Governments and nongovernmental agencies spend millions and millions of dollars each year trying to reduce birthrates. Certainly there has been much success, but there is a long way to go.

As we have seen repeatedly, anthropology teaches us of the interrelationships between the various segments of our social order. If we wish to reduce the birthrate, for example, there may be ways that are less intrusive than family planning and that have additional benefits for women and their communities.

Women's participation in the economic sphere is linked to their status in society. Low status, isolation, dependence, and lack of mobility to even visit with other women limit women's opportunities and ability to act in their own interests. Empowering women by enhancing their economic role in society can have many consequences, one of which is an increased use of contraceptives.

This intriguing selection examines the case of a Grameen Bank program that provides loans for poor women in rural Bangladesh.

As you read this selection, ask yourself the following questions:

☐ *Who should make judgments about whether the fertility rate in Bangladesh is too high? And who has the right to implement programs that change the social order?*

☐ *How does purdah limit women's access to family planning services?*

☐ *What is Grameen Bank's strategy for reducing women's isolation?*

☐ *How are economic conditions linked to the use of contraceptives?*

☐ *Should family planning workers assist women in using contraceptive methods secretly?*

☐ *What do women mean when they say that through Grameen Bank they have "learned to talk"?*

The following terms discussed in this selection are included in the Glossary at the back of the book:

dependent variable　　　　*qualitative methods*
hypothesis　　　　　　　　*random sample*
purdah　　　　　　　　　　*TFR (total fertility rate)*

Reprinted with permission of Society for Applied Anthropology from *Human Organization* 54(4): 455–61, 1995.

In rural Bangladesh, women's ability to seek out family planning services is limited by their isolation and their economic and social dependence on men. Large numbers of female outreach workers—about 28,000—are being employed by the government and nongovernmental programs to bring family planning services to women in their homes. Program evaluations and research studies have documented the effectiveness of this strategy, particularly in increasing use of the oral pill and other temporary contraceptive methods. Recent studies show substantial increases in contraceptive use and a decline in estimated fertility rates—from TFR[1] of about 7 in the late 1960s and early 1970s to about 5 in 1989—and attribute this change in large part to the expansion in access to family planning services in recent years, mainly through female community-based workers (Cleland *et al.* 1994; Larson and Mitra 1992; World Bank 1992).

While the intensive door-to-door delivery strategy has been effective in raising levels of contraceptive use from low to moderate levels (e.g., from 19% in 1983 to 40% in 1991), it is obvious that intensification of service delivery can only go so far, and that other strategies will be needed if levels of contraceptive use are to be increased to a level that would stabilize population growth. Improvements in the quality of services are needed, both for achievement of higher levels of contraceptive use, and from the perspective of women's rights to better health and reproductive autonomy. Another strategy would be interventions that increase women's ability to take an active role in getting access to services—for example, programs that strengthen women's economic roles and increase their mobility. This article examines the effects of the Grameen Bank program that provides small loans for women's self-employment activities in rural Bangladesh. Survey and ethnographic research findings are used to analyze the effects of the Grameen Bank, community-based family planning outreach, and women's relative levels of physical mobility on their practice of contraception. The effects of exposure to the Grameen Bank and home visits by family planning workers are compared for members and nonmembers living in Grameen Bank villages.

BACKGROUND

Among the poor in rural Bangladesh, women's lives are severely restricted by their social and economic dependence on men. Because of *purdah* (a system based on an ideology concerned with secluding and protecting women to uphold social standards of modesty and morality) women's contacts with the world outside of the family are extremely limited. Many cannot avail themselves of family planning, health and other services that may be available unless these services are brought to their homes. Bringing services to women in or near their homes is the principal strategy of the Bangladesh Government's family planning program and of many of the nongovernmental organizations providing family planning services in rural areas. As noted above, this strategy has been very effective in increasing contraceptive use.

Grameen Bank is a quasi-governmental organization involved in lending to the poor in nearly half of all villages in rural Bangladesh. Its two million female members (and about two hundred thousand male members) come from landless rural poor families, most of whom have very few assets of any kind. The program attempts to draw women out of isolation by providing them with credit, to enable them to earn a cash income through various types of self-employment activities. In addition to supporting economic activities that require interactions in the public sphere, it increases women's mobility and access to information by requiring that they attend regular meetings. The rituals of membership help women to create a sense of identity outside of the family. Grameen Bank does not provide family planning services. We have argued, based on a previous analysis, that the program influences contraceptive use by strengthening women's economic roles and contributing to their empowerment, increasing their ability to overcome obstacles to use of contraception. The same analysis suggested that BRAC (Bangladesh Rural Advancement Committee), whose program focus is similar but somewhat broader, does not have the same effect on contraceptive use because it is less effective in strengthening women's economic roles and in helping them to establish identities outside of the family (Schuler and Hashemi 1994).

A number of studies (e.g., Koenig *et al.* 1992) have assessed the effects of family planning outreach on use of contraception in Bangladesh. Two recent studies (Simmons *et al.* 1988, 1992) argue that the role of the female family planning worker in Bangladesh goes beyond the conventional concept of "supply" of family planning methods and services, so that they function as change agents in the communities where they work. In this article we focus on the effects of credit rather than family planning programs in transforming reproductive norms, and we attempt to highlight the interactive effects of the two types interventions.

METHODOLOGY

Data Sources

The analysis is based on a survey conducted in late 1992 to measure the impact of participation in credit programs on contraceptive use. It included four separately selected samples. The first two were random samples of Grameen Bank and BRAC members.[2] . . . With a Few exceptions, the women in these two samples had been members of the programs for a minimum of 18 months. The third was a comparison group consisting of nonmembers from Grameen Bank villages who would be eligible to join BLAC or Grameen Bank (i.e., poor and functionally landless). The fourth was a second comparison group consisting of women living in villages not served by either program, who would be eligible to join the programs. One adult woman was selected from each household. The interviewers were Bangladeshi women who had previous experience in conducting demographic surveys. They received more training during the process of pretesting the questionnaires. In addition to questions related to contraceptive use, the survey included questions related to women's status within the family and community, their physical mobility and their economic roles. A total of 1305 married women younger than 50 were interviewed.[3]

The data from concurrent ethnographic research in six villages describes the credit programs in operation, from the perspectives of the field research team as well as participants in the programs. The team consisted of six women and six men, all Bangladeshi, most of whom had Masters degrees. The team received intensive training in qualitative research methods at the beginning of the project, and the principal investigators provided continuing informal training throughout the study. The male-female team in each village conducted in-depth interviews to document change processes, both in women's roles and status and in norms related to reproduction and use of contraception. This article is based primarily on the survey data, but data from the ethnographic study is taken into account in interpreting the survey results.

Hypotheses

The following analysis is intended to test several specific hypotheses. Underlying all of them is the more general hypothesis that women's isolation, dependence, and lack of mobility inhibit use of contraception, and that a variety of programmatic strategies can be used to lessen these effects. The specific hypotheses are:

1. Home visits by family planning fieldworkers are positively related to contraceptive use.

2. Membership in credit programs and residence in villages where such programs are present increase the likelihood that a woman will use contraception.

3. Women's relative physical mobility is positively related to use of contraception.

4. The higher level of physical mobility of credit program participants does not fully explain their greater propensity to use contraception.

Variables

Dependent Variable. The dependent variable indicates whether or not the respondent is currently using any method of contraception.

Exposure to Credit Programs. These variables indicate whether the respondent was a Grameen Bank member, a nonparticipant living in a Grameen Bank village, or a resident of a comparison village, where no credit program existed.

Control Variables. In order to distinguish between effects of credit program participation per se and effects of other variables that are believed to affect contraceptive use in Bangladesh, several control variables are included. These are respondent's age, whether she ever attended school, number of surviving children, existence of at least one surviving son, existence of at least one surviving daughter, and an indicator of the relative economic level of the respondent's household. The latter is a composite measure based on the number of items owned from the following list: bed, blanket/quilt, shawl/sweater/coat, radio/TV, cow/buffalo.

Indicators of Access to Family Planning Services. We include two indicators of access to family planning services. The first of these is whether the respondent was ever visited by a family planning worker and the second is whether she was visited in the three months prior to the survey. Because of the strong emphasis on community-based services in the Bangladesh family planning program, these are generally thought to be the best indicators of access to family planning services in rural Bangladesh.

Indicators of Women's Physical Mobility. For this analysis we consolidated the variables related to women's mobility to create a single score. In the survey interview the respondent was presented with a list of places (the market, a medical facility, the movies, outside the village) and asked if she had ever gone there. She was given one point for each place she had visited and an additional point if she had ever gone there alone. A dichotomous variable was then created, in which a respondent with a score of 3 or better was classified as "more mobile."

Frequency distributions and means, as applicable, for the dependent and independent variables are presented in Table 1.

Table 1   CHARACTERISTICS OF STUDY SAMPLES

	GB	GB Non-members	Comparison
% using contraception	59.0	48.0	43.0
Mean age (in years)	31.0	26.0	29.0
Mean no. surviving children	3.5	2.6	3.3
Mean no. surviving sons	1.8	1.3	1.7
Mean no. surviving daughters	1.7	1.3	1.6
% attended school	29.0	18.0	18.0
Mean wealth score	2.5	1.7	1.6
% ever visited by FP worker	83.0	67.0	78.0
% visited in past 3 months	36.0	38.0	35.0
Mean mobility score	2.3	2.1	1.9
Mean duration of membership (in months)	50.0	—	—
N of cases	312	315	424

STATISTICAL RESULTS

The first section of the analysis compares women living in villages where Grameen Bank is present with women living in villages without a credit program. As Table 1 indicates, there is a dramatic difference in levels of contraceptive use between Grameen Bank members and women living in comparison villages—a difference of 16 percentage points. . . . The presence of the Grameen Bank program in a village has a significant effect on use of contraception, both among members and nonmembers, which is not explained by the effects of outreach. Visits by family planning workers (both recent and "ever") also appear to have strong independent effects, as do age, relative wealth, and presence of a surviving son.

. . . [Further,] women who are "more mobile" are considerably more likely to use contraception. Sixty percent of the "more mobile" group were using a contraceptive method, compared with 46% of the "less mobile" group. The relatively higher level of mobility of women in Grameen Bank villages explains, at least in part, the higher level of contraceptive use.

COMBINED EFFECTS OF GRAMEEN BANK AND FAMILY PLANNING OUTREACH

Previous studies in Bangladesh have found contact with female family planning workers to be one of the most important determinants of contraceptive use. . . . In general the findings indicate that family planning outreach has a highly significant effect on contraceptive use and that the presence of Grameen Bank in a village has an added effect. However, another dimen-

sion is added when contraceptive use rates among women who have/have not been visited by family planning workers are examined separately for each of the three groups (Figure 1).

For the comparison group and for nonmembers in Grameen Bank villages, rates of contraceptive use among women who have been visited by a family planning worker are 21 and 30 points higher, respectively, than for women who have never been visited. However, for members of Grameen Bank, the rate of contraceptive use is consistently high (59%), regardless of whether the women have ever been visited by a family planning worker. This suggests that the potential of Grameen Bank to influence contraceptive use is particularly important for women whose access to family planning services is relatively limited. For nonparticipating women in Grameen Bank villages who have been visited by a family planning fieldworker, the rate of contraceptive use is almost as high as among Grameen Bank members in the same communities—58%, compared with 48% for women in the comparison group. For the nonparticipants, the combined effect of the presence of Grameen Bank in a village and family planning outreach is even more evident when one looks at visits by family planning workers within the past three months (Figure 2). Among women who were not visited within the three months preceding the survey, the rates of contraceptive use are about the same as for the comparison group, and about 20 points lower than among Grameen Bank members. The rates

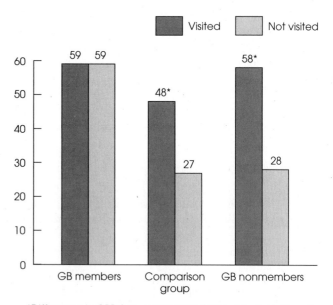

*Difference in CPR for women visited/not visited significant at p<.001 in chi square test.

Figure 1
Current contraceptive use—all methods, whether ever visited by FP worker

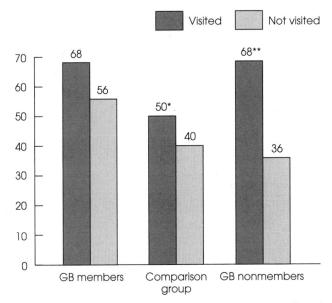

* Difference in CPR for women visited/not visited significant at p<.05 in chi square test.

**Difference in CPR for women visited/not visited significant at p<.001 in chi square test. (For GB members difference not significant at p<.05 level.)

Figure 2
Current contraceptive use—all methods, whether ever visited by FP worker past three months

of contraceptive use among women who were visited by a family planning worker within the past three months are 9 points higher for Grameen Bank members, 11 points higher for the comparison group, and 32 points higher for Grameen Bank nonmembers (65%, 50%, and 68% respectively).

. . . Family planning outreach is an important factor explaining the relatively high level of contraceptive use among nonparticipants in Grameen Bank villages, but that the even higher level of contraceptive use among participants is due to other factors.

DISCUSSION AND CONCLUSION

The strong effect of visits by community-based family planning fieldworkers on use of contraception supports the findings of previous research in Bangladesh. Because of their social and economic dependence on men, and their limited physical mobility, most women in rural Bangladesh cannot get access to family planning methods and services without assistance. As one of the respondents put it,

I am not allowed to go out and work even though we are so poor that we are sometimes desperate. Neither my husband nor his parents will let me go out to work . . . I had wanted to use family planning before my two daughters were born. I asked my husband several times

to bring me a family planning method but he wouldn't listen . . . I am a woman—I could not get it for myself.

The ethnographic study data indicate that men often fail to provide this assistance because they are generally apathetic about fertility control, or because they fear that side effects will lead to economic losses—either by interfering with work or by incurring monetary costs for treatment. Since most women are prevented from working outside of the home, and perceived as economically nonproductive, their husbands and in-laws often feel that it is wrong for them to incur expenses (Schuler *et al.* 1995).

In this context the presence of a community-based fieldworker, whether employed by the government or a nongovernmental organization, can make a great difference. By providing information and services in the home, they preempt the need for most women to go to clinics or other sources for family planning methods. They provide free pills and suggest things that women can say to persuade their husbands to allow them to use contraception. In cases where persuasion seems unlikely to be effective, they often assist women in using contraceptive methods secretly.

The survey findings suggest that, in addition to "supply-side" strategies, it is possible to influence fertility through programs that decrease women's isolation and their economic dependence on men. Such programs can help women to overcome obstacles to contraceptive use such as lack of mobility, lack of cash, lack of information about contraceptive methods and services, and opposition or lack of cooperation from their husbands and other family members. Grameen Bank strengthens women's economic roles through

Table 2   COMPARISON OF METHOD MIX IN GRAMEEN BANK VILLAGES VERSUS COMPARISON VILLAGES (N=1051)

	Grameen Bank Villages	Comparison Villages
Modern Methods		
Pills	22%	15%
Condom	1%	—
Injectables	5%	1%
IUDs	1%	1%
Female Sterilization	18%	18%
Male Sterilization	2%	3%
Traditional Methods		
Rhythm Method	4%	4%
Withdrawal	1%	—
Abstinence	1%	—
Other	1%	1%
No Method	46%*	56%*

• Totals not equal to 100% because of rounding.

credit, enabling them to contribute more substantially to their families' support. Even in cases where the woman hands her loan money over to her husband, there is usually some acknowledgment from the family that she is a source of income. Involvement in the program also gives women a socially legitimate purpose to participate in a group outside of the family. The opportunity for involvement in a nonfamily group can be important as a source of identity, new experiences, and ideas.

The ethnographic and the survey findings from this study generally support Grameen Bank's own contention that strengthening women's economic roles gives them more autonomy and more control over important decisions affecting themselves and their families, as well as contributing to their self-confidence and propensity to plan for the future. It promotes women's relative freedom to move about in public and to travel outside of the village. Where more women are employed outside of the home, and are required to walk along roads or use buses or other forms of transport, it is less difficult for them to travel within and outside of their villages to get services.

Participation in the Grameen Bank program also makes members more experienced in interacting with men outside of the family and with authority figures. Although the interactions that take place in weekly meetings with bank staff clearly cast the women in a subservient role, this nevertheless seems to give them a certain self-confidence. In all interactions with government officials and even representatives of nongovernmental organizations, the poor are in a subservient role, and at least in this case it is the woman rather than her husband who is doing the interacting. Several of the women in our study told our field investigators that through Grameen Bank they had "learned to talk," and now they were not afraid to talk to outsiders. This probably increases their ability to avail themselves of family planning and health services.

Through a combination of intimidation and confidence-building, Grameen helps women to stand up to their husbands. Normally, any savings or asset that a women might have could be legitimately (at least from her husband's point of view) appropriated by him. Having recognized that this would be a central problem in a loan program for women, Grameen Bank tells women what to say when their husbands try to take their loan money. Case studies suggest that women who have developed the self-confidence to try to protect their assets and earnings from their husbands are more likely to take initiative in other areas such as practicing family planning.

The Grameen Bank program can produce high rates of contraceptive use among members, even if they are not exposed to family planning outreach. The very high rates of contraceptive use among nonmem-

bers in Grameen Bank villages who are visited by a family planning fieldworker suggest that the presence of Grameen Bank's program in a village in combination with family planning outreach can increase use of contraception dramatically, even among women who do not join Grameen Bank. The probable explanation is that reproductive norms are changing in Grameen Bank villages, but that diffusion of innovations takes time. Nonmembers, whose level of dependence on men has not been reduced because they have not participated in the program, typically require the support of family planning workers to follow the reproductive norms that are emerging.

In considering the implications of these findings, it is important to avoid overestimating the magnitude of the changes occurring gender relations. The vast majority of women—including those who participate in the Grameen Bank program—are able to make only small cash or kind contributions to the family's support, and many have little or no control over the income. Only a quarter of the Grameen Bank members in our survey said that their contribution represented half or more of the family's income, and only 7% of the nonmembers in Grameen Bank villages and 4% in comparison villages said this. Socially, and psychologically as well, the typical Grameen Bank member, like other women, is extremely dependent on her husband, and simply has to accept inequities, extreme limitations on her autonomy, and in some cases physical abuse. Watching the realities of poverty and gender-based subordination being played out in social life in the six ethnographic study villages, most of the members of our research team did not expect to find that the small changes occurring in women's lives as a result of Grameen Bank were having a measurable impact on contraceptive use.

Our ethnographic study provided some insight into the processes through which women are asserting themselves in making reproductive decisions, but it also revealed continuing obstacles to increased and more effective fertility control. The most significant of these seems to be fear—related to method side effects, health problems that may be perceived as side effects, and the widespread belief that contraceptive methods cause physical weakness and other problems. In some cases lingering ideas that contraceptive use may be sinful are reinforced when contraceptive users suffer from side effects or experience other types of misfortunes. In addition to physical suffering and even death, contraceptive users and their families fear inability to work, and the possibility that the problems resulting from contraceptive use will require costly medical treatments. Because most women do not have an independent income or control over money, they know that if something happens to them they will be dependent on others—in most cases their husbands—

to arrange and pay for medical treatment. Generally the fieldworkers who come to their doors have limited training and are only minimally equipped to treat health problems. Women's restricted physical mobility and their economic dependence on men, as well as their general condition of poverty, limit their ability to seek treatment. In our view, a continuous and increased focus on providing economic opportunities for women and, simultaneously, on improving poor women's access to health services and improving the quality of contraceptive services is needed.

NOTES

1. TFR or Total Fertility Rate, is the average number of children born to a woman during her lifetime.
2. Since the previous analysis suggested that BRAC does not affect the level of contraceptive use among its members it was excluded from the present analysis.
3. See Schuler and Hashemi 1994 for a more detailed description of the survey methodology.

REFERENCES

Cleland, John, James E. Phillips, Sajeda Amin and G. M. Kasmal. 1994. The Determinants of Reproductive Change in Bangladesh: Success in a Challenging Environment. World Bank Regional and Sectoral Studies. Washington DC: The World Bank.

Koenig, Michael A., Ubaidur Rob, Mehrab Jali Khan, J. Chakraborty, and Vincent Fauveau. 1992. Contraceptive Use in Matlab, Bangladesh in 1990: Levels, Trends, and Explanations. Studies in Family Planning. 23(6): 352–364.

Larson, Ann and S. N. Mitra. 1992. Family Planning in Bangladesh: An Unlikely Success Story. International Family Planning Perspectives. 18(4):123–129.

Mauldin, W. Parker and John A. Ross. 1991. Family Planning Programs: Efforts and Results, 1982–89. Studies in Family Planning. 22(6):350–367.

Mitra, S. N., Ann Larson, Gillian Foo, and Shahidul Islam. 1992. Bangladesh Contraceptive Prevalence Survey. July 1991: Key Findings. Dhaka: Mitra and Associates.

Schuler, Sidney Ruth and Syed M. Hashemi. 1994. Credit Programs, Women's Empowerment and Contraceptive Use in Rural Bangladesh. Studies in Family Planning. 25(2):65–76.

Schuler, Sidney Ruth, Syed M. Hashemi and Ann Hendrix. 1995. Bangladesh's Family Planning Success Story: A Gender Perspective. International Family Planning Perspectives. 27:6.

Simmons, Ruth, Laila Baqee, Michael A. Koenig, and James E. Phillips. 1988. Beyond Supply: The Importance of Female Family Planning Workers in Rural Bangladesh. Studies in Family Planning. 19(1):29–38.

Simmons, Ruth, Rezina Mita, and Michael A. Koenig. 1992. Employment in Family Planning and Women's Status in Bangladesh. Studies in Family Planning. 23(2):97–109.

The World Bank. 1992. Population and the World Bank: Implications from Eight Case Studies. Operations Evaluations Department. The World Bank. Washington, DC.

25

Child Care in China

Bruce Dollar

In the previous two selections, we saw that gender roles are related to conditions of economic control and the exchange of resources. Such comparisons lead anthropologists to study the causes and effects of increasing numbers of women entering business, industry, and the service economy. This social and economic change affects the family and children, primarily those of preschool age.

Postrevolutionary China is a country where a large proportion of women work outside the home. China, then, provides an example of a society in which public, preschool child-care facilities are used on a large scale. Indeed, the widespread availability of child care for working parents provides a stark contrast to our own society. A second difference between China and our own culture is the values that adults attempt to instill in their children.

The schoolroom is a place where children learn models of social interaction. Much of what is learned in school is not part of the curriculum but rather has to do with cultural values and explanations of how our social systems work. Most American parents would feel comfortable with the values learned in the Chinese kindergarten. Yet these fundamental orientations and values are quite different from those actually taught in our schools. In their early encounters with public education, as we shall see in the next selection, American children learn the importance of competition and the desire to outperform their classmates.

Studies in postrevolutionary China provide a vivid cross-cultural contrast with our own society.

As you read this selection, ask yourself the following questions:

☐ *What major values do caregivers attempt to instill in Chinese children?*

☐ *What form of child care is provided for the infants of working mothers?*

☐ *What sorts of punishment are used in kindergarten?*

☐ *Why did Mao consider women working outside the home so important?*

☐ *Has the large population of women in the labor force in China contributed to the decline of the family or to social or psychological problems for youth?*

The following terms discussed in this selection are included in the Glossary at the back of the book:

cultural values
egalitarian society
institutions
sex roles

The old art of China watching is giving way to China witnessing, and one quality of the new China that seems inevitably to impress all recent visitors is the extraordinary vibrancy of Chinese children, from the very youngest to the adolescents, who already tower so noticeably over their grandparents. During my own recent trip within China, my companions and I saw for ourselves the exuberant self-confidence that seems to infuse all Chinese kids, whether they are performing for strangers, participating in a classroom exercise, or playing by themselves.

"Ours is a socialist society; everything is done according to plan." This pronouncement, with which our

With permission from *Saturday Review of Education*, May 1973.

various Chinese hosts so frequently prefaced their answers to our questions, provides a starting point for understanding how this spirit of exuberance has been achieved. Although Chinese society is largely decentralized to encourage local self-sufficiency and diversification, the whole is knit together by an administrative structure that is more or less uniform from city to city and, somewhat less, from commune (or network of villages) to commune. It is a framework that provides an efficient system of communication and has helped produce a remarkable social cohesion based on commonly held goals and values—which themselves are informed by the teachings of Mao Tse-tung.

The consensus is particularly apparent with respect to the care and training of the young. This is hardly surprising when one considers the enormous stock the Chinese place in producing what they call "revolutionary successors," an apt phrase in a country where revolutionary consciousness has been maintained largely through vivid comparisons with the "bitter past," and where the problem of continuing the revolution into succeeding generations is paramount.

Thus, throughout our visit we constantly encountered—with amazing consistency at various points along a 2,500-mile itinerary—several major ideas about child rearing in the numerous conversations we had with people in child-related institutions: families, nurseries, kindergartens, and schools. These themes—especially the subordination of personal to social needs, respect for productive labor, altruism, cooperation, and the integration of physical with intellectual labor—together describe the kind of citizen China hopes to produce. The techniques employed to achieve these values are in practice virtually from infancy.

During the years before primary schools, which begin at the age of seven, a series of public child care facilities is available to parents who wish to use them. In the cities, where patterns are more uniform, a mother's maternity leave (paid) usually terminates 56 days after birth. Since breast-feeding is the rule in China, the mother may then place her child in the nursing room at her place of work. Most work institutions—factories, hospitals, and government offices, for example—provide this facility for their employees. In a typical arrangement the mother has two half-hour breaks, plus lunch, to visit and nurse her baby during the work day. After work the baby returns home with the mother.

Nursing rooms provide care for infants up to one and a half years old; then they may be sent to one of the various kinds of nurseries. Some of these are attached to the work place or located in the home neighborhood; they may be open only during the work day, or they may be "live-in" nurseries, where children stay overnight and go home on weekends. Kindergartens, usually located in the residential areas, generally care for children from three and a half to seven years old and may also be either part-time or full-time.

In a country in which over 90 percent of all women of working age do work, it might be expected that a similar percentage of children would therefore receive some kind of institutional care. But there are options. The most common is to leave the child in the care of grandparents, who frequently live with the family. Another alternative is to make arrangements with a friend or neighbor. Estimates vary from place to place, but in most cities no more than half the children of nursery school age are in attendance. For kindergarten the figures are higher, especially in the cities, where attendance is over 80 percent.

Since child care is decentralized, different localities often make their own arrangements, which may not conform to the usual patterns. This is particularly true of rural areas, where a lack of resources and the persistence of custom probably account for a lower incidence of public child care facilities. One small village we visited, the Sha Shih Yu Brigade in northeast China, had no permanent facility; only during harvest time, when all hands were needed in the fields, was there organized care for small children. A child care center located in a coal mining area near Tangshan, on the other hand, served 314 children divided into at least five separate age groups, from 56 days to six years old.

How do these institutions work to socialize the children under their care? And what are they like for the kids? In spite of the diversity in organizational structure, the remarkable similarity from place to place, both in the values espoused and the methods used to inculcate them, seems to support a number of generalizations.

One quality that is sure to strike an American observer is the preponderance and the style of group activities. A common example is the "cultural performance," usually presented for visitors. Whether they are songs from a revolutionary opera, dances to celebrate a harvest, or a program of folk melodies played on traditional Chinese instruments, these performances are always presented by groups, and it is impossible to pick out a "star."

Although there were exceptions, many early child care facilities we visited seemed rather poorly supplied with the variety of toys and materials that the conventional wisdom in the United States says should be on hand to enrich and enliven a child's environment. Although this may have been due to a simple inability to pay for more equipment, the teachers we spoke to did not seem to consider it a shortcoming. Perhaps this is because Chinese children are generally expected to rely on each other for stimulation—at any rate, this seems to be the effect. The situation provides an interesting contrast to that in the United States, where the highly desired "rich environment" often means that kids interact with inanimate materials more than they do with other people.

The small children we saw were not without playthings, however. There was always at least one toy for each child—typically a rubber or plastic doll of a worker, a peasant, or a soldier. Rocking horses were also common, as were military toys and playground equipment that could accommodate many children. But in general the emphasis was on group play. One recent American visitor to a Chinese nursery school reports noticing that the blocks seemed awfully heavy for small children. "Exactly!" beamed the teachers. "That fosters mutual help."

Chinese teachers actively encourage such group behavior as cooperation, sharing, and altruism. "We praise a child when he shows concern for others' interests," said one kindergarten teacher. "For example, at meal time teachers give out bowls and chop sticks. If a youngster gets a nicer bowl and gives it to someone else, we praise him for it. Or when the children are asked to select a toy and a child gives the best one to a classmate, we praise that, too."

Even in a competitive situation, this teacher said, helping another is more important than winning. "When the children run in a relay race, sometimes one will fall down, especially if he's small. If another child stops to help him get up or to see if he's all right, even though his own team might fall behind, we encourage this." The approach contrasts markedly with methods used in the Soviet Union, another country that stresses the collective in its child-rearing practices. There, competition is discouraged between individuals but promoted between groups. Each child is made aware of his importance within his group—say, a row in his classroom—and then competes fiercely for the rewards of a group victory. The Chinese seem genuinely to eschew even this form of competition in favor of straightforward mutual help and cooperation.

But how do teachers deal with improper behavior and matters of discipline? Here is how the question was answered in a conversation with three staff members of a full-time kindergarten in Peking:

Q: What kinds of behavior do you discourage in the children?

A: We criticize those who take toys or other things from others. Or if children beat each other—we criticize that.

Q: Exactly how do you handle such a situation—say, two kids fighting?

A: First, the teacher must understand the reason for the fight. For instance, one might have taken a toy from the other, and the second child hit him. In that case, the teacher will criticize both. This criticism is carried out alone, unless it took place in the class; in that case it will be done in front of the class so that all the children will understand what was wrong. Criticism is to make children understand what was wrong and why.

Q: What kind of punishment do you use?

A: There is no punishment.

Q: Well, what if a child were really intractable? Would you use some mild sanction, such as depriving him of some free play time on the playground?

A: (At this point all three women broke into smiles at our incredulity. Waving their hands back and forth to underscore their words, they said): No, no, nothing like that. We believe in persuasion.

Q: Do other children ever participate in criticism?

A: Generally, no. Unless a third child saw what happened—then he'll be asked to tell.

Q: Let's say the incident was unobserved by any third party and the two kids involved give conflicting versions of what happened. Then how does the teacher act?

A: If the teacher finds a contradiction when both tell what happened, she will try to educate the children. She will note that everyone can make a mistake, including the teachers. The mistake that led to the fight is not important, she will say, but telling the truth is very important. At this point the children will probably tell the truth.

This sounded like fine theory, but it provoked some skepticism among those of us who had been teachers. What about teachers who do not have the patience to use such positive techniques? we asked. How do you deal with teachers who don't observe the school's policy? The reply: "We all—teachers and leadership—have the same goal: to cultivate revolutionary successors. So we all work together and help each other. We study our profession together. We have regular criticism and self-criticism sessions, and sometimes we help each other on specific problems."

If we had not already seen many teachers in action here and elsewhere on our trip, we might have been dissatisfied with this answer. But we were constantly struck by the teachers' apparent love for their work in all the early child care institutions we visited. These women, we learned (there were no men), were chosen for their jobs after having shown a particular interest in children, and "sensitivity and love for children" were the criteria most often cited for their recruitment.

Credentials were secondary. Since the Cultural Revolution, the amount of training teachers receive has ranged all the way from university graduation to short-term training classes and "learning through practice."

Three of us in the group who were especially interested in child rearing and education often asked to see child care centers and schools under normal operating conditions. Our guides accommodated these requests by arranging for us to stay behind after the formal tour to make a low-key visit to a kindergarten, say, without the rest of the group. Some of our most revealing insights occurred during our observation of everyday free playground activities.

One afternoon, for example, at the child care center serving workers of the Fan Ga Chong coal mine area near Tangshan, I spent nearly an hour outside among the four-and-a-half to six-year-olds and their teachers, or "nurses." Here was the one place where I saw what might be called a disruptive child—a little boy who, in the United States, would probably have been labeled hyperkinetic and put on Ritalin. While the other 50 or so children busied themselves with various games—rope jumping, drop the handkerchief, tricycle riding, playing with toys and each other—this boy ran constantly from place to place, trying to be in on everything at once and occasionally interfering with someone else's fun. The nurses, who themselves were taking part in the games, were obviously aware of the boy's actions, but they made no fuss over him. Instead, each time he ran by a nurse, she would reach out, place her hand on the back of his head, and gently guide him away from trouble or toward an activity he might like—usually with a few soothing words. Soon he was off again, and once or twice it was necessary to intervene when he began picking on another child. But always the adults acted cheerfully and patiently, and the boy never became a center of attention. His actions were the closest thing to aggressive or disruptive behavior among children that I saw on the entire trip.

After visiting several classrooms at the Pei Hai Kindergarten, a full-time kindergarten located in a park in Peking, I spent an even longer time on the playground watching free play. Once again I was struck by the way teachers enthusiastically joined in. The children, well over a hundred of them, had formed into a variety of play groups. Some played on slides, a merry-go-round, monkey bars, and swings. Some were organized into class-sized groups for games. Others were in smaller groups, jumping rope or kicking a ball around. There were kids in pairs and kids alone. One gleeful little boy, holding aloft a leafy twig, ran, danced, and twirled with it till he fell down from dizziness. And ranging over the whole playground, sweeping past and through everyone else's games, was a whooping pack of boys chasing a soccer ball, a laughing teacher in the lead.

In one group that especially caught my eye, seven or eight girls were jumping rope, taking turns at the ends of a pink plastic rope and lining up to jump one by one. No teacher was with them. They were very absorbed and used chants and songs to accompany each jumper. Several times while I watched, a minor controversy of some kind would erupt and everything would come to a halt. Maybe it concerned whose turn was next on the rope or how many times one had jumped before missing. Whatever it was, the whole group would come together and heatedly debate their points. With no single girl taking charge, they would quickly work out a settlement that seemed to satisfy everyone and then resume their jumping with all the gusto of before. These little girls were good jumpers, incidentally. So good that after a while they attracted an audience: six little boys found chairs, lined them up to form a small gallery, and proceeded to join in the jumping chants, applauding for each jumper. Great fun for all, highly organized, and by all indications spontaneous and undirected by adults.

In the United States the growing demand for facilities for the care of infants and preschool children has provoked a chorus of urgent questions: Doesn't a baby need a single individual to relate to and identify with as mother? How can a mother be sure that those to whom she entrusts her child will teach the same values she holds? Isn't it the mother's natural role to care for her own children? What is the effect of institutionalized child care on the family?

Obviously, the answers the Chinese have found to these questions are not directly applicable to this country. Yet the insights they provide can be instructive as we seek our own solutions.

There is a strong likelihood that the average child in China will undergo "multiple mothering" of some kind. Even if the mother does not choose to leave her infant in the nursing room where she works, chances are the child will wind up in the care of a neighbor or the grandmother. Offsetting this diversity of "mothers," however, is the near-uniform consensus of values and methods of child rearing I have described. This consistency seems to go a long way toward providing young children with the kind of security we in the United States might normally associate only with single mothering.

Another aspect of multiple or "shared" mothering, as Ruth Sidel, author of the excellent recent book *Women & Child Care in China*, points out, "is that infants can thrive physically and emotionally if the mother-surrogates are constant, warm, and giving. Babies in China are not subjected to serial mothering; we were repeatedly told that aunties (i.e., nurses) and teachers rarely leave their jobs. And they are warm and loving with the children. The children show none of the lethargy or other intellectual, emotional, or physical problems of institutionalized children. Quite the opposite!"

"Everything is planned," and the position of mothers in China is the consequence of a society-wide effort to provide for the economic liberation of women. In keeping with Mao Tse-tung's edict calling for "genuine equality between the sexes," a broad series of programs, including birth control information and prenatal care with maternity leave, in addition to the system of child care facilities, is underway to assume the full participation of women in "building socialism." The objects of unspeakable oppression in prerevolutionary society, Chinese women today have been thoroughly integrated into the labor force, both in factory and commune. And a growing number of them are entering professions—for example, 50 percent of the medical students are now women.

Despite the enormous progress, even the Chinese will concede that full parity with men is not yet a reality. Top government, military, and management posts continue to be mostly male preserves. However, women do wield considerable political and administrative power at the local level, where they often run the smallest governmental units, the neighborhood revolutionary committees.

But the key to liberation is still economic independence, which depends on the availability of work. Since 1971 a new source of work for women has appeared: the so-called housewives' factories. These have been organized locally by women who live in housing areas like the Kung Kiang Workers' Residential Area in Shanghai, and whose husbands work in the various nearby factories. As they describe it to us, the housewives were looking for ways in which they could contribute productively to the revolution without having to leave the residential area. So they set up their own light industries in workshops near their homes, and by working full- or part-time were able to produce needed commodities, such as flashlight bulbs or men's trousers, while earning extra money for themselves. The entire operation in each case was staffed and run by women.

Since nearly all working-age women in China today work and are no longer economically dependent on their husbands or families, one might well wonder about the effects of these conditions on the family.

By all available evidence the family is thriving in China, and the individual household continues to be the basic social unit. A featured item in every home we visited, as ubiquitous as a portrait of Chairman Mao, was a display of a great many photographs of family members, usually pressed under a piece of glass on top of a bureau or framed on the wall. Our host or hostess would invariably point this out with pride. Signs of active and full participation in family life were everywhere, and all generations were included. A man out with his children is a common sight, as is a child with a grandmother or grandfather.

Parents are obviously revered by children, and so are grandparents. In fact, the complete absence of a "generation gap" is a striking phenomenon to an American. Not only are grandparents well integrated into family life, but old people who have no family or who are disabled live in well-tended "respect for aged" homes and are given important functions that serve the neighborhood.

Far from undermining the family structure, we were repeatedly told, jobs for women and day care for children have made home life easier, having eliminated many former sources of friction and frustration. A major factor here is undoubtedly the mass commitment to working for the betterment of China. Personal gratification seems to derive from each individual's knowledge that he or she makes an important contribution, no matter how small, to the national effort and that the benefits of this contribution, and others like it, will be distributed to all.

26

American Schoolrooms:
Learning the Nightmare

Jules Henry

Cultural values are reflected in social institutions. In institutions of socialization like schools, culture is recreated for a new generation—an important theme in the previous selection about postrevolutionary China. There is a critical linkage between a society's economic system, the organization of institutions, and the cultural values that are taught young children. Consider this provocative view of the unconscious cultural learning that goes on in American elementary schools.

When studying other societies, anthropologists often conclude that there are important differences between what the natives say they are doing and what they actually are doing. We are somewhat less comfortable when such an observation is made about our own society. In ideal terms, we believe that our educational institutions encourage cooperation, creativity, and free expression, allowing individual students to fulfill their own potential. But in this selection, Jules Henry argues that the function of education is to bind the mind and spirit, to make children fit the culture as it already exists. An institution like the school, therefore, functions as a mechanism of social control. Some of this control comes from people in positions of authority, but much of it is located in peer pressure to conform to the culture of the group.

Teachers (like parents) are probably doing this unconsciously, even when they are trying to make learning fun. In the process of education, children learn to sing off key—along with the rest of the group—and also learn not to question certain things. The author believes that American children also learn to become destructively competitive and that this produces a deep-seated fear of failure in their personalities. Paradoxically, whereas learning these parts of our culture might ultimately drive some students to succeed, it teaches others how to fail.

American cultural values, including competition and individual achievement, fit our capitalist economy and social meritocracy. The structure of the institutions of socialization, including tests and grades, probably influenced you to read this.

As you read this selection, ask yourself the following questions:

☐ *This selection is more than thirty years old. How have American schoolrooms changed or stayed the same over that time period? Does the author's description fit your experience?*

☐ *What does the author mean when he says that students "learn to be absurd"?*

☐ *Identify several cultural values that are expressed in schools.*

☐ *What do you think education should be? Are there any positive functions of the "noise" in classrooms?*

The following terms discussed in this selection are included in the Glossary at the back of the book:
cultural values
sanctions
social control
socialization

School is an institution for drilling children in cultural orientations. Educators have attempted to free the school from drill, but have failed because they have always chosen the most obvious "enemy" to attack. Furthermore, with every enemy destroyed, new ones are installed among the old fortifications that are the enduring contradictory maze of the culture. Educators think that when they have made arithmetic or spelling into a game; made it unnecessary for children to "sit up straight"; defined the relation between teacher and children as democratic; and introduced plants, fish, and hamsters into schoolrooms, they have settled the problem of drill. They are mistaken.

The paradox of the human condition is expressed more in education than elsewhere in human culture, because learning to learn has been and continues to be *Homo sapiens'* most formidable evolutionary task. Although it is true that mammals, as compared to birds and fishes, have to learn so much that it is difficult to say by the time we get to chimpanzees which behavior is inborn and which is learned, the learning task has become so enormous for man that today, education, along with survival, constitutes a major preoccupation. In all the fighting over education we are simply saying that after a million years of struggling to become human, we are not yet satisfied that we have mastered the fundamental human task, learning.

Another learning problem inherent in the human condition is this: We must conserve culture while changing it, we must always be *more* sure of surviving than of adapting. When a new idea appears, our first concern *as animals* must be that it does not kill us; then, and only then, can we look at it from other points of view. In general, primitive people solved this problem simply by walling their children off from new possibilities by educational methods that, largely through fear, so narrowed the perceptual sphere that nontraditional ways of viewing the world became unthinkable.

The function of education has never been to free the mind and the spirit of man, but to bind them. To the end that the mind and spirit of his children should never escape, *Homo sapiens* has wanted acquiescence, not originality, from his offspring. It is natural that this should be so, for where every man is unique there is no

society, and where there is no society there can be no man. Contemporary American educators think they want creative children, yet it is an open question as to what they expect these children to create. If all through school the young were provoked to question the Ten Commandments, the sanctity of revealed religion, the foundations of patriotism, the profit motive, the two-party system, monogamy, the laws of incest, and so on, we would have more creativity than we could handle. In teaching our children to accept fundamentals of social relationships and religious beliefs without question we follow the ancient highways of the human race.

American classrooms, like educational institutions anywhere, express the values, preoccupations, and fears found in the culture as a whole. School has no choice; it must train the children to fit the culture as it is. School can give training in skills; it cannot teach creativity. Since the creativity that *is* encouraged—as in science and mathematics, for example—will always be that which satisfies the cultural drives at the time, all the American school can do is nurture that creativity when it appears.

Creative intellect is mysterious, devious, and irritating. An intellectually creative child may fail in social studies, for example, simply because he cannot understand the stupidities he is taught to believe as "fact." He may even end up agreeing with his teachers that he is "stupid" in social studies. He will not be encouraged to play among new social systems, values, and relationships, if for no other reason than that the social studies teachers will perceive such a child as a poor student. Furthermore, such a child will simply be unable to fathom the absurdities that seem transparent *truth* to the teacher. What idiot believes in the "law of supply and demand," for example? But the children who do, tend to *become* idiots; and learning to be an idiot is part of growing up! Or, as Camus put it, learning to be *absurd*. Thus the intellectually creative child who finds it impossible to learn to think the absurd the truth, who finds it difficult to accept absurdity as a way of life, usually comes to think himself stupid.

Schools have therefore never been places for the stimulation of young minds; they are the central conserving force of the culture, and if we observe them closely they will tell us much about the cultural pattern that binds us.

Much of what I am now going to say pivots on the inordinate capacity of a human being to learn more than one thing at a time. A child writing the word "August" on the board, for example, is not only learning the word "August," but also how to hold the chalk without making it squeak, how to write clearly, how to keep going even though the class is tittering at his slowness, how to appraise the glances of the children in order to know whether he is doing it right or wrong. If a classroom can be compared to a communications

---

The author of this article used the term *man* to refer to humanity in general. The term is not used by modern anthropologists because, to many people, it reflects an unconscious sexist bias in language and rhetoric. At the time that this article was written, however, the generalized *man* was a common convention in writing. In the interest of historical accuracy we have not changed the wording in this article, but students should be aware that nonsexist terms (humans, people, *Homo sapiens*, and so on) are preferred. —The Editors.

From *Columbia University Forum*, Spring 1963, pp. 24–30, by permission of Columbia University Press.

system—a flow of messages between teacher (transmitter) and pupils (receivers)—it is instructive to recall another characteristic of communications systems applicable to classrooms: their inherent tendency to generate *noise*. *Noise*, in communications theory, applies to all those random fluctuations of the system that cannot be controlled, the sounds that are not part of the message. The striking thing about the child is that along with his "messages about spelling" he learns all the noise in the system also. But—and mark this well—it is *not* primarily the message (the spelling) that constitutes the most important subject matter to be learned, but the noise! The most significant cultural learning—primarily the cultural drives—are communicated as *noise*. Let us see the system operate in some of the contemporary suburban classrooms my students and I studied over a period of six years.

> It is March 17 and the children are singing songs from Ireland and her neighbors. The teacher plays on the piano, while the children sing. While some children sing, a number of them hunt in the index, find a song belonging to one of Ireland's neighbors, and raise their hands in order that they may be called on to name the next song. The singing is of that pitchless quality always heard in elementary school classrooms. The teacher sometimes sings through a song first, in her off-key, weakishly husky voice.

The usual reason for this kind of song period is that the children are "broadened" while they learn something about music and singing. But what the children in fact learn about singing is to sing like everybody else. (This phenomenon—the standard, elementary school pitchlessness of the English-speaking world—was impressive enough for D. H. Lawrence to mention it in *Lady Chatterley's Lover*. The difficulty in achieving true pitch is so pervasive among us that missionaries carry it with them to distant jungles, teaching the natives to sing hymns off key. Hence on Sundays we would hear our Pilagá Indian friends, all of them excellent musicians in the Pilagá scale, carefully copy the missionaries by singing Anglican hymns, translated into Pilagá, off key exactly as sharp or as flat as the missionaries sang.) Thus one of the first things a child with a good ear learns in elementary school is to be musically stupid; he learns to doubt or to scorn his innate musical capacities.

But possibly more important than this is the use to which teacher and pupils put the lesson in ways not related at all to singing or to Ireland and her neighbors. To the teacher this was an opportunity to let the children somehow share the social aspects of the lesson with her. The consequence was distraction from singing as the children hunted in the index, and the net result was to activate the children's drives toward competition, achievement, and dominance. In this way

the song period was scarcely a lesson in singing, but rather one in extorting the maximal benefit for the Self from *any* situation.

The first lesson a child has to learn when he comes to school is that lessons are not what they seem. He must then forget this and act as if they were. This is the first step toward "school mental health"; it is also the first step in becoming absurd. The second lesson is to put the teachers' and students' criteria in place of his own. The child must learn that the proper way to sing is tunelessly and not the way he hears the music; that the proper way to paint is the way the teacher says, not the way he sees it; that the proper attitude is not pleasure, but competitive horror at the success of his classmates, and so on. And these lessons must be so internalized that he will fight his parents if they object. The early schooling process is not successful unless it has produced in the child an acquiescence in its criteria, unless the child *wants* to think the way school has taught him to think. What we see in kindergarten and the early years of school is the pathetic surrender of babies. How could it be otherwise?

Now nothing so saps self-confidence as alienation from the Self. It would follow that school, the chief agent in the process, must try to provide the children with "ego support," for culture tries to remedy the ills it creates. Hence the effort to give children recognition in our schools. Hence the conversion of the songfest into an exercise in Self-realization. That anything essential was nurtured in this way, is an open question, for the kind of individuality that was recognized as the children picked titles out of the index was mechanical, without a creative dimension, and under the strict control of the teacher. In short, the school metamorphoses the child, giving it the kind of Self the school can manage, and then proceeds to minister to the Self it has made.

We can see this at work in another example:

> The observer is just entering her fifth-grade classroom for the observation period. The teacher says, "Which one of you nice, polite boys would like to take (the observer's) coat and hang it up?" From the waving hands, it would seem that all would like to claim the honor. The teacher chooses one child, who takes the observer's coat. . . . The teacher conducted the arithmetic lessons mostly by asking, "Who would like to tell the answer to the next problem?" This question was followed by the usual large and agitated forest of hands, with apparently much competition to answer.

What strike us here are the precision with which the teacher was able to mobilize the potentialities in the boys for the proper social behavior, and the speed with which they responded. The large number of waving hands proves that most of the boys have already become absurd; but they have no choice. Suppose they sat there frozen?

A skilled teacher sets up many situations in such a way that *a negative attitude can be construed only as treason*. The function of questions like, "Which one of you nice, polite boys would like to take (the observer's) coat and hang it up?" is to bind the children into absurdity—to compel them to acknowledge that absurdity is existence, to acknowledge that it is better to exist absurd than not to exist at all. The reader will have observed that the question is not put, "Who *has* the answer to the next problem?" but, "Who *would like to tell*" it? What at one time in our culture was phrased as a challenge to skill in arithmetic, becomes here an invitation to group participation. The essential issue is that *nothing is but what it is made to be by the alchemy of the system.*

In a society where competition for the basic cultural goods is a pivot of action, people cannot be taught to love one another. It thus becomes necessary for the school to teach children how to hate, and without appearing to do so, for our culture cannot tolerate the idea that babes should hate each other. How does the school accomplish this ambiguity? Obviously through fostering competition itself, as we can see in an incident from a fifth-grade arithmetic lesson.

> Boris had trouble reducing 12/16 to the lowest terms, and could only get as far as 6/8. The teacher asked him quietly if that was as far as he could reduce it. She suggested he "think." Much heaving up and down and waving of hands by the other children, all frantic to correct him. Boris pretty unhappy, probably mentally paralyzed. The teacher, quiet, patient, ignores the others and concentrates with look and voice on Boris. After a minute or two, she turns to the class and says, "Well, who can tell Boris what the number is?" A forest of hands appears, and the teacher calls Peggy. Peggy says that four may be divided into the numerator and the denominator.

Boris's failure has made it possible for Peggy to succeed; his misery is the occasion for her rejoicing. This is the standard condition of the contemporary American elementary school. To a Zuñi, Hopi, or Dakota Indian, Peggy's performance would seem cruel beyond belief, for competition, the wringing of success from somebody's failure, is a form of torture foreign to those noncompetitive cultures. Yet Peggy's action seems natural to us; and so it is. How else would you run our world?

Looked at from Boris's point of view, the nightmare at the blackboard was, perhaps, a lesson in controlling himself so that he would not fly shrieking from the room under enormous public pressure. Such experiences force every man reared in our culture, over and over again, night in, night out, even at the pinnacle of success, to dream not of success, but of failure. In school the external nightmare is internalized for life.

Boris was not learning arithmetic only; he was learning the *essential nightmare also. To be successful in our culture one must learn to dream of failure.*

When we say that "culture teaches drives and values" we do not state the case quite precisely. We should say, rather, that culture (and especially the school) provides the occasions in which drives and values are *experienced in events* that strike us with *overwhelming and constant force*. To say that culture "teaches" puts the matter too mildly. Actually culture invades and infests the mind as an obsession. If it does not, it will be powerless to withstand the impact of critical differences, to fly in the face of contradiction, to so engulf the mind that the world is seen only as the culture decrees it shall be seen, to compel a person to be absurd. The central emotion in obsession is fear, and the central obsession in education is fear of failure. In school, one becomes absurd through being afraid; but paradoxically, *only by remaining absurd can one feel free from fear.*

Let us see how absurdity is reinforced: consider this spelling lesson in a fourth-grade class.

> The children are to play "spelling baseball," and they have lined up to be chosen for the two teams. There is much noise, but the teacher quiets it. She has selected a boy and a girl and sent them to the front of the room as team captains to choose their teams. As the boy and girl pick the children to form their teams, each child takes a seat in orderly succession around the room. Apparently they know the game well. Now Tom, who has not yet been chosen, tries to call attention to himself in order to be chosen. Dick shifts his position to be more in the direct line of vision of the choosers, so that he may not be overlooked. He seems quite anxious. Jane, Tom, Dick, and one girl whose name the observer does not know are the last to be chosen. The teacher even has to remind the choosers that Dick and Jane have not been chosen. . . .
>
> The teacher now gives out words for the children to spell, and they write them on the board. (Each word is a pitched ball, and each correctly spelled word is a base hit. The children move around the room from base to base as their teammates spell the words correctly.) The outs seem to increase in frequency as each side gets near the children chosen last. The children have great difficulty spelling "August." As they make mistakes, those in the seats say, "No!" The teacher says, "Man on third." As a child at the board stops and thinks, the teacher says, "There's a time limit; you can't take too long, honey." At last, after many children fail on "August" one child gets it right and returns, grinning with pleasure, to her seat. . . . The motivation level in this game seems terrific. All the children seem to watch the board, to know what's right and wrong, and seem quite keyed up. There is no lagging in moving from base to base. The child who is now writing "Thursday" stops to think after the first letter, and the children snicker. He stops after another letter. More snickers. He gets the word wrong. There are frequent signs of joy from the children when their side is right.

"Spelling baseball" is an effort to take the "weariness, the fever, and the fret" out of spelling by absurdly transforming it into a competitive game. Children are usually good competitors, though they may never become good spellers; and although they may never learn to *spell* success, they know what it *is*, how to go after it, and how it feels not to have it. A competitive game is indicated when children are failing, because the drive to succeed in the *game* may carry them to victory over the subject matter. But once a spelling lesson is cast in the form of a game of baseball a great variety of *noise* enters the system; because the sound of *baseball* (the baseball "messages") cannot but be *noise* in a system intended to communicate *spelling*. If we reflect that one could not settle a baseball game by converting it into a spelling lesson, we see that baseball is bizarrely irrelevant to spelling. If we reflect further that a child who is a poor speller might yet be a magnificent ballplayer, we are even further impressed that learning spelling through baseball is learning by absurd association.

In making spelling into a baseball game one drags into the classroom whatever associations a child may have to the impersonal sorting process of kid baseball, but there are differences between the baseball world and the "spelling baseball" world also. One's failure is paraded before the class minute upon minute, until, when the worst spellers are the only ones left, the conspicuousness of the failures has been enormously increased. Thus the *noise* from baseball is amplified by a *noise* factor specific to the classroom.

It should not be imagined that I "object" to all of this, for in the first place I am aware of the indispensable social functions of the spelling game, and in the second place, I can see that the rendering of failure conspicuous cannot but intensify the quality of the essential nightmare, and thus render an important service to the culture. Without nightmares human culture has never been possible. Without hatred competition cannot take place except in games.

The unremitting effort by the system to bring the cultural drives to a fierce pitch must ultimately turn the children against one another; and though they cannot punch one another in the nose or pull one another's hair in class, they can vent some of their hostility in carping criticism of one another's work. Carping criticism, painfully evident in almost any American classroom, is viciously destructive of the early tillage of those creative impulses we say we cherish.

Listen to a fifth-grade class: The children are taking turns reading stories they have made up. Charlie's is called *The Unknown Guest*.

"One dark, dreary night, on a hill a house stood. This house was forbidden territory for Bill and Joe, but they were going in anyway. The door creaked, squealed, slammed. A voice warned them to go home. They went upstairs. A stair cracked. They entered a room. A voice said they might as well stay and find out now; and their father came out. He laughed and they laughed, but they never forgot their adventure together."

Teacher: Are there any words that give you the mood of the story?

Lucy: He could have made the sentences a little better . . . .

Teacher: Let's come back to Lucy's comment. What about his sentences?

Gert: They were too short. (Charlie and Jeanne have a discussion about the position of the word "stood" in the first sentence.)

Teacher: Wait a minute; some people are forgetting their manners. . . .

Jeff: About the room: the boys went up the stairs and one "cracked," then they were in the room. Did they fall through the stairs, or what?

The teacher suggests Charlie make that a little clearer. . . .

Teacher: We still haven't decided about the short sentences. Perhaps they make the story more spooky and mysterious.

Gwynne: I wish he had read with more expression instead of all at one time.

Rachel: Not enough expression.

Teacher: Charlie, they want a little more expression from you. I guess we've given you enough suggestions for one time. (Charlie does not raise his head, which is bent over his desk as if studying a paper.) Charlie! I guess we've given you enough suggestions for one time, Charlie, haven't we?

If American children fail while one of their number succeeds, they carp. And why not? We must not let our own "inner Borises" befog our thinking. A competitive culture endures by tearing people down. Why blame the children for doing it?

The contemporary school is not all horrors; it has its gentler aspects as well. Nearing a conclusion, let us examine impulse release and affection as they appear in the suburban classrooms.

Impulse is the root of life, and its release in the right amount, time, and place is a primary concern of culture. Nowadays the problem of impulse release takes on a special character because of the epoch's commitment to "letting down the bars." This being the case, teachers have a task unique in the history of education: the fostering of impulse release rather than the installation of controls. Everywhere controls are breaking down, and firmness with impulse is no part of contemporary pedagogy of "the normal child." Rather, impulse release, phrased as "spontaneity," "life adjustment," "democracy," "permissiveness," and "mothering," has become a central doctrine of education. It persists despite tough-minded critics from the Eastern Seaboard who concentrate on curriculum. The teachers know better; the real, persisting, subject matter is *noise*.

How can the teacher release children's emotions without unchaining chaos? How can she permit so much *noise* and not lose the message? Were they alive, the teachers I had in P.S. 10 and P.S. 186 in New York City, who insisted on absolute silence, would say that chaos does prevail in many modern classrooms and that the message *is* lost. But lest old-fashioned readers argue that the social structure has fallen apart, I will point out what does *not* happen: The children do not fight or wrestle, run around the room, throw things, sing loudly, or whistle. The boys do not attack the girls or vice versa. Children do not run in and out of the room. They do not make the teacher's life miserable. All this occurs when the social structure *is* torn down, but in the average suburban classrooms we studied, it never quite happens. Why not? Here are some excerpts from an interview with a second-grade teacher I'll call Mrs. Olan:

> In the one-room schoolhouse in which I first taught, the children came from calm homes. There was no worry about war, and there was no TV or radio. Children of today know more about what is going on; they are better informed. So you can't hold a strict rein on them.
>
> Children need to enjoy school and like it. They also need their work to be done; it's not all play. You must get them to accept responsibility and to do work on their own.

To the question, "What would you say is your own particular way of keeping order in the classroom?" Mrs. Olan says:

> Well, I would say I try to get that at the beginning of the year by getting this bond of affection and relationship between the children and me. And we do that with stories; and I play games *with* them—don't just teach them how to play. It's what you get from living together comfortably. We have "share" times. . . . These are the things that contribute toward discipline. Another thing in discipline—it took me a long time to learn it, too: I thought I was the boss, but I learned that even with a child, if you speak to him as you would to a neighbor or a friend you get a better response than if you say, "Johnny, do this or that."

Mrs. Olan has a creed: Love is the path to discipline through permissiveness; and school is a continuation of family life, in which the values of sharing and democracy lead to comfortable living and ultimately to discipline. She continues:

> With primary children the teacher is a mother during the day; they have to be able to bring their problems to you. They get love and affection at home, and I see no reason not to give it in school.

To Mrs. Olan, mother of a 21-year-old son, second-grade children are pussy-cats. When asked, "Do you think the children tend to be quieter if the teacher is affectionate?" she says:

> If a teacher has a well-modulated voice and a pleasing disposition, her children are more relaxed and quiet. Children are like kittens: If kittens have a full stomach and lie in the sun they purr. If the atmosphere is such that the children are more comfortable, they are quiet. It is comfortable living that makes the quiet child. When you are shouting at them and they're shouting back at you, it isn't comfortable living.

It is clear to the observer that Mrs. Olan is no "boss," but lodges responsibility in the children. She clarifies the matter further:

> It means a great deal to them to give their own direction. When problems do come up in the room we talk them over and discuss what is the right thing to do when this or that happens. Usually you get pretty good answers. They are a lot harder on themselves than I would be; so if any punishment comes along like not going to an assembly you have group pressure.

As the interviewer was leaving, Mrs. Olan remarked, "My children don't rate as high (on achievement tests) as other children. I don't push, and that's because I believe in comfortable living." *Noise* has indeed become subject matter.

In such classrooms the contemporary training for impulse release and fun is clear. There the children are not in uniform, but in the jerkins and gossamer of *A Midsummer Night's Dream*; it is a sweet drilling without pain. Since impulse and release and fun are a major requirement of the classroom, and since they must be contained within the four walls, the instrument of containment can only be affection. The teacher must therefore become a parent, for it is a parent above all who deals with the impulses of the child.

It is hard for us to see, since we consider most people inherently replaceable, that there is anything remarkable in a parent-figure like a teacher showering the symbols of affection on a child for a year and then letting him walk out of her life. However, this is almost unheard of outside the stream of Western civilization; and even in the West it is not common. As a matter of fact, the existence of *children* willing to accept such demonstrations is in itself an interesting phenomenon, based probably on the obsolescence of the two-parent family. (Today our children *do not have enough parents*, because parents are unable to do all that has to be done *by* parents nowadays.) The fact that a teacher can be demonstrative without inflicting deep wounds on *herself* implies a character structure having strong brakes on involvement. Her expressions of tenderness, then, must imply "so far and no farther"; and over the years, children must come to recognize this. If this were not so, children would have to be dragged shrieking from grade to grade and teachers would flee teaching, for the mutual attachment would be so deep that its annual severing would be too much for either to bear. And so this noise, too, teaches two lessons important to today's culture. From regular replacement-in-affection children learn that the affection-giving figure, the teacher, is replaceable also, and so they are drilled in uninvolvement. Meanwhile, they learn that the symbols of affectivity can be used ambiguously, and that they are not binding—that they can be scattered upon the world without commitment.

Again, the reader should not imagine that I am "against" affectionate classrooms. They are a necessary adjunct to contemporary childhood and to the socialization of parenthood (the "three-parent family") at this stage of our culture. Meanwhile, the dialectic of culture suggests that there is some probability that when love like this enters by the door, learning leaves by the transom.

What, then, is the central issue? The central issue is *love of knowledge* for its own sake, not as the creature of drive, exploited largely for survival and for prestige.

Creative cultures have loved the "beautiful person"—meditative, intellectual, and exalted. As for the individual, the history of great civilizations reveals little except that creativity has had an obstinate way of emerging only in a few, and that it has never appeared in the mass of the people. Loving the beautiful person more, we may alter this.

The contemporary school is a place where children are drilled in very general cultural orientations, and where subject matter becomes to a very considerable extent the instrument for instilling them. Because school deals with masses of children, it can manage only by reducing children all to a common definition. Naturally that definition is determined by the cultural preoccupations and so school creates the *essential nightmare* that drives people away from something (in our case, failure) and toward something (success). Today our children, instead of loving knowledge, become embroiled in the nightmare.

27

"Edutaining" Children:
Consumer and Gender Socialization in Japanese Marketing[1]

Millie R. Creighton

Gerber baby food is an American cultural icon. Most of us probably had our share of it when we were growing up. For Americans the ability to quickly and easily open a jar of baby food fits well with the high value we place on home-making efficiency. But such values are not universal. In fact, this is no way to sell baby food in Japan. In that country, marketing Gerber required the company to take aim at a different cultural value. This value had to do with the proper role of mothers in their children's education.

Once again we address the fundamental question of how individuals are socialized into particular sex roles. In Selection 23 ("Society and Sex Roles"), Ernestine Friedl demonstrated the relationship between sex roles and control over the distribution of valued resources. And in the selections by Bruce Dollar and Jules Henry, we saw the role of pre-school and formal education in socializing children into societally defined roles.

This selection looks at how Japanese businesses combine entertainment and education to market products, bring consumers into their stores for a purpose that is culturally acceptable, and use values of cooperative participation to build long-term relations with customers and among customers. Moreover, it will become clear that the "edutainment" of youth plays its own role in socializing the next generation.

We are used to thinking of the family, schools, and religious groups as influencing the socialization of the next generation; we less often think of marketing in this way. Yet American children probably spend more time listening

to radio or television and reading advertisements in magazines than they do listening to their parents. As both the previous selection and this one suggest, the messages are often both subtle and effective.

As you read this selection, ask yourself the following questions:

☐ *What is meant by gender-appropriate behavior?*

☐ *Does education happen only in schools? Where else might children learn gender roles?*

☐ *How is the high value placed on education in Japan reflected in Japan's shopping environment?*

☐ *How does the importance of belonging affect Japanese consumer behavior?*

☐ *In what ways do the characters in Dr. Kids Town reinforce gender stereotypes? Is gender socialization a conscious process?*

☐ *How does American culture (particularly advertising) socialize children to behave in ways that fit traditional gender stereotypes?*

The following terms discussed in this selection are included in the Glossary at the back of the book:

consumer society   *socialization*
edutainment   *socially validated*
gender

From *Ethnology* 33(1):35–52, 1994. Reprinted by permission of Department of Anthropology, University of Pittsburgh and the author.

A common Japanese expression asserts, *"ko wa takara"* (children are treasures). Japan's earliest poetry anthology, The *Manyōshū*, compiled in A.D. 753, expresses the sentiment as, "a treasure which excels everything else, could there be anything equal to children" (Kojima 1986:123–24). In present day Japan, the perception of children as treasures often implies indulging them with unprecedented consumer offerings. A spokesperson for a company that designs child-oriented shopping theme parks told me in a 1991 interview that the children's market was the predicted preeminent arena of Japanese consumerism for the decade of the 1990s. What was perhaps most significant about this statement is that in 1990 Japan marked a new all-time record low birthrate for the eleventh year in a row (Shibaguchi 1991).[2]

Far from foretelling the doom of children's sales, Japan's declining birthrate has propelled goods and services directed at children to new extremes. Takayama Hideo, director of the Children's Research Institute, explains, "Fewer children are surrounded by more rich adults and that means that the money spent on each child increases" (quoted in Blustein 1991). Children themselves also have more money to spend. As the actual birthrate declined, Japan witnessed the birth of the "five pocket child," meaning that with so few children, each child now receives larger gifts of money, such as . . . "New Year's Money" from several indulging sources, and hence metaphorically needs one pocket each for money received from parents, grandparents, aunts and uncles, neighboring households, and others.

This article reports on the construction of shopping worlds for parents and children in Japan. . . . It presumes that . . . consumer goods, . . . promotional catalogues and even the physical space of store layouts constitute cultural objects. These establish a physical reality heavily imbued with symbolic meaning and . . . [creates] a setting . . . that compels people toward certain forms of action. Despite Japan's burgeoning economy and its characterization as a consumer society, there is very little research on how children are socialized for culture- and gender-appropriate shopping behavior.

. . . ["Edutainment" (Creighton 1992)] is the fusion of education and entertainment offerings, particularly popular or mass culture entertainments that take on educating functions or invoke a pretense of having such functions. What Graburn (1983) calls the "Pray, Pay, and Play" philosophy of Japanese tourism reveals that pleasure travel is often socially validated in the guise of pilgrimage. I suggest that in a similar vein, invoking education in Japan serves to legitimize many hobbies or leisure activities that might otherwise be construed as overly indulgent fun.

Of course, this is not a uniquely Japanese phenomenon. The genesis of consumer cultures elsewhere generated amusements frequently proffered in the guise of education. . . . (Heininger (1984:30) for example, educational toys promising self-improvement and self-education were an important part of the American children's market by the early nineteenth century. How-ever, in order to understand how edutainment operates within a cultural setting, it is essential to explore its relationship to that culture's ideologies of education.

A great deal has been written about early childhood education and socialization through schools in Japan. Schools and preschools are embedded in cultures. Tobin, Wu, and Davidson (1989:2) point out that they "reflect and affect social change." Stores also reflect the cultures in which they are found, and they can shape social trends. Stores can operate as what Beauchamp (1991) calls institutions of informal schooling. According to Beauchamp (1991:189), education is conveyed through formal, nonformal, and informal arenas "through which the values and behaviors of a society are preserved and passed on to new generations." Stores, fashion, popular culture, and entertainment are all part of informal education. The following discussion shows that the edutainment permeating the Japanese children's market reflects dominant educational attitudes, the basic ideological value exalting education in Japan, and the contrasting tensions that surround it.

GOODS AND SERVICES FOR CHILDREN AND PARENTS

The example of marketing baby food in Japan reveals that the values and behaviors discussed in studies of formal educational institutions permeate the informal education situated in children's marketing. Processed, canned baby food has never been a best seller in Japan, in part because of the Japanese emphasis on fresh foods but also due to the expectation that good mothers, whether employed or not, sacrifice time and effort to prepare elaborate meals even for young children (Allinson 1991). Gerber baby foods were introduced to Japan by a Japanese company, Meijiya. Meijiya did not promote Gerber as a convenience food or timesaver for mothers, but stressed the educational advantages. Gerber baby foods were packaged as "lessons." Each jar of baby food has a prominent red label giving the lesson number followed by a brief description. For example, Lesson 4 (suggested age category six to seven months) involves achieving the state at which taste preferences in food begin to develop. . . . Thus even a jar of baby food caters to parents' fervent desires to educate their children. The significance of this example is further reflected in Fujita's (1989) suggestion that mothers are blamed for any problem a child manifests. According to Fujita (1989:78), if preschool children cannot chew food properly, mothers are blamed for not providing the appropriate solid food during the weaning period. Hence the educational-style baby food package strikes a responsive chord for mothers who must bear such social rebuke.

The cultural ideology of motherhood in Japan emphasizes mother-child bonding as the basis for human relationships, defines the mother as the best caretaker and educator of her children, and thus calls for extensive maternal involvement with children (Fujita 1989:72–80). Japanese mothers, who are expected to spend as much time as possible with young children, receive little support for leaving children with sitters, at day care, or at preschool while shopping. As one preschool teacher told Fujita (1989:78), mothers "should come pick them up before going shopping. Besides, taking children shopping is itself educational."

Large stores strive to maximize this view by emphasizing the educational nature of special store activities in order to win mothers' allegiance. These stores frequently host in-store events such as safety promotionals, math tournaments, and geography contests. For one common type of event, which combines a treasure hunt with test-taking skills, special booths are set up throughout a floor. At the starting booth each child is given a small passportlike booklet of blank pages. At each booth the child must solve a test problem and can then stamp her or his booklet with that booth's special stamp. Clues to the location of the next booth are posted to help children continue the treasure hunt. Children who pass through each checkpoint, successfully receiving a stamp at each one, are awarded a small present at the end. In its construction, this treasure hunt edutainment mimics domestic travel pastimes. Children commonly take a small booklet along while traveling, collecting stamp imprints at each location they visit for souvenirs. Mothers often express the view that the stores are nice to offer these children's events for free, even to the extent of providing presents. For the store such edutainment is also quite strategically aimed. It pulses children through all areas of a selling floor, usually accompanied by their mothers who are therefore exposed to the store goods.

Many stores, such as the main Seibu store, have an in-store classroom where "seminars for housewives" are given on topics related to home management and childhood development. So mothers may participate, Seibu also offers baby-sitting services free of charge, in an adjoining area. In this way the pursuit of education legitimizes behavior not otherwise fully condoned: The free baby-sitting services are not provided for mothers to leave children while shopping in the store or eating out with friends in store restaurants, but specifically for these self-development studies geared toward women's "career development" as . . . ["professional housewives"].

Store facilities are designed to make shopping with young children easy. Some stores, such as Takashimaya, have "baby restaurants," with posted meal menus that allow mothers to choose from several full meal assortments, each of which offers a selection of different baby foods.[3] Every department store or large shopping complex provides a fully equipped baby care area, containing cribs, changing tables, weighing scales, a kitchenette, hot water for formula, vending machines with baby food and diapers, small partitioned rooms for breast-feeding privacy, and a child's restroom with toddler-size toilets. . . .

Most women's restrooms have long been equipped with small cribs for women to change their infants' diapers or child-size potties so women can help their toddlers use the toilets. Only recently, however, have store architects addressed the problems of women with small children who want to use the restroom facilities themselves, as if the social construction of femininity and motherhood precluded openly viewing mothers in this way. The first facilities providing "parking places" for babies within stalls, making it easier for mothers to use the facilities, began appearing in 1985 when discussions surrounding Japan's Equal Employment Opportunity Law prompted new conceptualizations of women. In 1985, Seibu built a new store in Tsukuba to correspond with the 1985 World Expo held there. One of the women's restrooms contained an innovative stall with a toddler-size toilet, a western-style adult toilet, and a bassinet connected to the wall at a height allowing anyone using the adult toilet to reach it. Many stores now contain a new device that fits into the small public toilet stall of a Japanese-style floor toilet. When a baby or toddler is placed on the protruding wall seat, bands automatically lock in place around the seated child. This new toilet device was named the "baby keep" . . . a take-off on the more common phrase "bottle keep" which refers to bottles of alcohol purchased by regular clientele to small drinking establishments and kept on the premises under the purchaser's name. . . . This contrast symbolically expresses a persisting dichotomy of gender spheres in which "bottle keeps" (maintenance of the public realm, careers with responsible work, and late night business socializing) are for men, while "baby keeps" (maintenance of the domestic realm including the education of children, support roles, and daytime consumerism) are for women.

Every department store will provide some or all of the following services free of charge: a store-employed midwife and/or nutrition specialist always available for advice, consultations with physicians at specified times, a lending library of infant- and childcare books and videos, lectures on natural childbirth, maternity concerts, psychological counseling, and classes in stress management for new mothers. The last two items were widespread by the late 1980s, reflecting increasing social concern with . . . ["child-rearing neurosis"], interpreted as a new problem in Japan which began to attract attention in the mid-1960s as the pressure to pass entrance examinations intensified and academic achievement became the primary focus in evaluating child and maternal performance. . . .

Customer responses to special service offerings such as the maternity concerts show that parents eagerly utilize store edutainment in attempts to maximize childhood development. Maternity concerts became popular in the 1970s and 1980s, along with a boom in music tapes promoted for the purpose of fetal listening, to enhance early development during the mother's pregnancy. The rising sales of such products paralleled the development of consumer industries geared toward such objectives. Yamazaki (1993:200) describes a prenatal class for birthing a brilliant baby, where mothers alternate periods of caressing their stomachs with drill periods during which they shout out responses to flash cards or answers to test questions in unison, so that their developing fetuses are audibly exposed to the educative influences. . . . Japanese mothers' commitment to their children's educational development begins at conception. . . .

Stores present their offerings as educational to appeal to mothers, but also struggle to make such activities pleasant, playful, and fun for children in the hope that children will learn to look forward to a trip to the store. Most stores have special play areas set aside on sales floors where children can play with toys or put together construction assemblages. Stores commonly provide a playground and amusement park, complete with rides, on their roofs. Several stores have brought playground-size jungle-gyms inside so children can play uninterrupted by rain. Sales areas devoted to women's goods also commonly have play tables located nearby to occupy young children while their mothers are browsing through the merchandise.

Japanese store shopping clubs, which begin in early infancy and proceed through adult life, reflect the critical importance placed on belonging to a group found in other aspects of Japanese life. The so-called consumer clubs (i.e., store clubs, diner's clubs, credit card clubs, airline mileage clubs) that exist in North America usually offer benefits such as discounts or free items. Store shopping clubs in Japan are frequently organized around the idea of participatory interaction. In consumerism, as in other spheres, the group one belongs to is observed, and to an extent internalized, for standards of appropriate purchases for one's status and age category.

Research on Japanese education . . . shows that the strong mother-child bond is transferred to childhood groups. Attempts are then made to transfer these to each succeeding group level that embraces a person. In this way membership in a group is maintained as an essential element of personal identity and psychological satisfaction, while rigid self-reliance and individualism remain a bit disconcerting. Store shopping clubs mimic these attributes of school groups. Age-appropriate clubs exist for each stage of the life cycle, group bonds are not severed but transferred to succeeding groups, and the clubs create the boundaries of a shopping category which becomes the basis for many personal consumer decisions.

Recruitment to such consumer clubs begins very early in life. In fact, babies do not have to wait to be born, for while still wrapped in the process of "fetusing" their parents typically enroll them. Seibu's shopping club for infants, Baby Circle, provided expectant parents with pamphlets giving advice on prenatal care and childbirth preparation. When baby was born, the Baby Circle sent baby a congratulatory gift of a photo album, a birthday card, and baby's first shopping catalogue. The catalogue, addressed and mailed directly to baby, not to parents, was appropriately entitled *Faasuto Guzza* (First Goods).

The Baby Circle also sent parents many complimentary aids, such as free books on childcare and medical guides. Mothers could submit questions regarding problems, which were answered. Periodically such questions and answers were compiled into another free booklet sent to the parents of Baby Circle members. Members' parents were eligible for free consulting services with gift specialists regarding appropriate return gifts for well-wishers who gave congratulatory birth presents. Given the importance of obligatory gift exchanges in Japanese social relationships, this was an important concern for new parents, while the stores hoped parents would buy the return gifts at their locations.

It is customary to send both New Year's and midsummer greeting cards in Japan. After I enrolled my own son in a Baby Circle, the store sent him, at the age of seven months, a lovely midsummer's . . . greeting card. As these cards often do, the store's card commiserated with him on the heat, but went a bit further. It expressed sympathies that he had not been feeling so well, was always cranky, and crying late at night because he was suffering from the heat. It also noted the frustrations babies like him had to endure when they could not explain to their parents that they needed an air conditioner. That this midsummer greeting card was really directed at parents, and was an attempt to prompt the purchase of an air conditioner was obvious. Japanese mothers I knew whose babies also belonged to the Baby Circle expressed amusement at this ploy rather than any irritation. Items such as this, clearly an advertising message to parents, tended to be mailed to baby, while free gifts, medical books, advice books, and other items which did not suggest any direct advantage for the store were mailed to mothers.

Baby Circles provide occasions and the space for new members to play together while members' mothers also meet to discuss the strains of child-rearing, or to exchange advice. As baby gets a bit older the bonds created by membership in this first club are transferred to a new focus. This is called the *Chibbiko* Circle, or *Chibbiko* Club. (*Chibbiko* is an endearing word for child, similar to the English "tyke.") Chibbiko clubs are directed at boys and girls from three to twelve years of age. Chances to meet and participate in organized activities together increase during the Chibbiko Club years. Beginning in the preteen to teen years, a greater emphasis on gender-specific clubs appears. Then boys' clubs fade away, while girls' clubs continue and lead into the . . . ["gathering of friends"] women's clubs, which include participation in special interest classes (plays, crafts, etc.) for club members.

This review of some of the goods and services aimed at children and mothers shows how retailing amusements are cloaked in appeals to education. Invoking education strikes a responsive chord both because of the high cultural value given to education as an ideal, and because of parents' pragmatic concerns with propelling children through the crucial school entrance exam system. A form of social education is also taking place. Children are learning how to be shoppers, in ways that are culturally appropriate and often gender specific. Both types of educational experiences are also apparent in the expanding phenomenon of shopping theme parks for children.

CHILDREN'S SHOPPING THEME PARKS

Beginning in the 1980s, then escalating rapidly from 1990, the upsurge in children's marketing resulted in the appearance of shopping theme parks for children, which many observers feel now rival the entertainment atmosphere of Tokyo Disneyland. . . . In addition to their amusement orientation, these specialty shopping parks echo the educational and cultural development themes, while again providing kids' clubs where members actually meet and interact. Conceived in the same decade that internationalization became a buzz word proclaiming the goal for Japanese society from the 1980s onwards, this theme is reflected in the depiction of foreign fantasy characters, as well as in the presentation of foreign goods.

One of the first children's shopping theme parks constructed in Tokyo was *Ichigo no ouchi* (Strawberry House), opened by the Sanrio toy company in 1984. This three-story strawberry-shaped building, flanked on either side by brightly colored mushroom and strawberry constructions, sits conspicuously among the densely packed concrete gray utilitarian buildings of Tokyo that surround it. The entire Strawberry House concept is one which knows no fear of thematic redundancy. The store's mezzanine level contains . . . Strawberry Parlor, a child's version of the coffee/tea shops ubiquitous in Japan's urban centers. The third floor contains a plaza known as Strawberry Room . . . , which is full of strawberry stuff. Room furnishings include strawberry-shaped tables, strawberry-shaped cupboards, strawberry-shaped light fixtures, and a strawberry-shaped mirror. Children can sit on the strawberry-shaped cushions that are placed along the light grass-green floor carpet. The employees of Strawberry House, young women dressed in indigo blue uniforms with cardigans, sing and tell stories to children, creating the atmosphere of a kindergarten or elementary school. When the Strawberry Parlor is not used as a refreshment shop for children, these female employees conduct special birthday or thank-you parties for mothers, children, and teachers there. . . .

Sanrio publishes a periodical called the Strawberry Newspaper. . . . Subscribers automatically become members of the Strawberry Mates. . . . Once a month the Strawberry Mates gather in the Strawberry Room for a Strawberry Conference. They meet, socialize, establish friendships, and interact with their *oneesan* (big sisters) (store employees), discussing their lives and the problems they face. Although designed primarily for middle- to upper-elementary school girls, the popularity of Strawberry House is great among junior-high and senior-high girls, and extends to kindergarten girls. People often come from distant parts of Japan on a "pilgrimage" to Strawberry House. The shop chief finds nothing surprising in this, proclaiming that for children and Sanrio fans, Strawberry House is a "sacred place" (Izumi 1989:27–51).

From 1990, shopping theme parks designed as play floors for children were opened one after another. Seibu transformed the entire seventh floor of its main store into kids farm [sic], which opened in September 1990. Tokyo Sesame Place, fashioned after the Sesame Place built a decade earlier in the U.S., opened in October 1990, along with Dr. Kids Town at the Kichijōji branch of Isetan Department Store. In December 1990, the supermarket chain Seiyu opened Kids' Park in Tokyo's Shibuya district, while Odakyū Department Store finalized plans for the autumn 1991 opening of a mother and child shopping theme park in the nearby Harajuku district. Not restricted to Japan's core urban centers, this trend can even be seen in a new shopping center opened in Okinawa in 1990, which is built around a huge central children's plaza containing a mountain and castle maze. The mountain/castle complex, which children can climb, crawl through, and play on, rises through all three stories of the mall.

When Seibu opened kids farm, it amalgamated all previous store sections dealing with child-related goods or services, and also amalgamated its former Baby Circle, Young Tyke's Circle, and other children's clubs into a new "escalator" club series called the kids farm club. Seibu added several highly sophisticated children's boutiques, such as Ralph Lauren, Christine Dior, and Tartine et Chocolat (a Paris designer line for children), all aimed at fashion conscious "campus-minded mamas" . . . (Shibaguchi 1991:92).

Kids farm combines new amusement services, such as employees dressed as clowns to entertain children or a mountain-climbing play area, with new learning opportunities. At a special area of kids farm, called "First Science Corner," specialist employees conduct science experiments with children. Kids farm also offers English conversation lessons specifically for children.

Kids farm also has a pretend coffee shop, a quaint looking refreshment shop constructed in wood with blue ruffled curtains. Its young female employees dressed in long skirts and ruffled aprons serve Aunt Stella's cookies free with any drink purchase. These are served on store flyers which teach about the "cute Amish children" . . . of the Pennsylvania Dutch country who, dressed "like miniature adults," play and study with their friends healthily and freely (from Seibu kids farm, "Children's Country: Aunt Stella's" placemat/flyer). The ambience of the refreshment shop was designed in accordance with Seibu's asserted purpose for kids farm to serve as a symbol of parent and child togetherness . . . (Nikkei Sangyō Shimbun 1990).

The highly innovative Dr. Kids Town occupies the fifth floor of an annex to the main Isetan Department Store building. A bridge shaped like a train connects the two. En route to Dr. Kids Town customers pass a hair and beauty salon for children only. Television monitors in the salon show videos of children's programs or popular cartoon characters like Chibbi Maruko-chan. The bright pink hippos in the salon are really trash cans. Sink backs are shaped like elephants, with the elephants' trunks serving as water jets to wet or shampoo hair. Childlike drawings (illustrations by adults which mimic the style of children's drawings) line the walls. This "children's only" salon was so successful that within months of opening three chairs were added.

As its name suggests, Dr. Kids Town has been designed as a miniature town for children, and is said to be a representation of a small American rural town. In this town there are forests with log homes (which are teddy bear shops), a zoo (with real-like and often full-size stuffed animals), police stations, a real fire engine (bought and remodeled at a cost of five million yen,

about U.S. $47,000), the town's local businesses such as an optical store . . . a central fountain with a sponge pool near a replica of the Statue of Liberty, and, along the town's paved brick streets, the houses of five foreign character children. The young female staff at Dr. Kids Town socialize with the children, contributing to an atmosphere reminiscent of a preschool or elementary school. On the weekends they dress up as the town mayor, fire chief, police officers, and nurses. Dr. Kids Town also has a real children's *juku* (tutoring school) called the "budding class" which accepts children from 32 months to six years old.

Visitors are allowed to play freely throughout town. Children can [ride] tricycles or skate[board] (using store merchandise) through the brick streets, or [play] in the sponge pool while adults rest on town benches. Children climb the fire engine [and] enter the log homes and the five houses of the foreign character playmates. Within these houses they can play with their foreign playmates' toys, or rest in their beds (like Goldilocks?). Mothers [commonly play] with toddlers on the streets outside of these houses. The scene is reminiscent of real residential areas in Tokyo where, due to space limitations, mothers play with young children on the streets in front of their apartment complexes. However, the atmosphere of Dr. Kids Town is much more pleasant and idyllic than the real streets of Tokyo. Nearly all the goods that people are interacting with are actually for sale, but purchasing merchandise usually involves removing it from its space in Dr. Kids Town and bringing it to a central register or one on the "outskirts of the town." Visitors to Dr. Kids Town are fully aware that this is, after all, a store. However, the physical separation of the selling/purchasing transaction from the thematic town locations minimizes the feeling that this is business, and maximizes the sense of involvement in a fantasy wonderland.

The designers of Dr. Kids Town not only created a theme park for children, but constructed an educational philosophy to go along with it. The educational philosophy of Dr. Kids Town can be found on placards located on the shop floor, and also in the user's guide to Dr. Kids Town for parents, called *For Your Future Growth: Dr. Kids*. A Dr. Kids spokesperson explained that the theme park has a social message. It is that all Japanese must start thinking about developing children as Japan's resources for the 21st century, that parents are really only concerned with their own child or children, hoping they get into good universities and so on. But, she continued, not all children will get into prestigious universities, and Japan as a society could not exist in the future if this were possible, since the society needs all kinds of people, with different abilities, doing different things.

In addition to criticizing Japan's so-called academic pedigree society . . . and the corresponding obsession with entrance examinations, Dr. Kids tackles social concerns related to education or child development such as school bullying, school refusal syndrome, or child-rearing neurosis. The Dr. Kids philosophy of education emphasizes creating a balanced being by optimally developing all areas of human endeavor. To represent this, the Dr. Kids team developed a representation of a child standing with head high, arms and legs spread wide, creating an impression almost like a five-pointed star, or revolving pinwheel. Various elements of human experience (motivation, appreciation, imagination, communicability, originality, etc.) flow toward the child from different directions. Each of the five body appendages represent one important aspect of human life. To the common food, clothing, and shelter have been added learning and playing to make the five theme concepts eating, wearing, dwelling, learning, and playing. The five theme concepts are represented on the child image as follows: Learning is written across the head, eating on the right arm, playing on the right leg, dwelling on the left leg, and wearing on the left arm. "Balance" is imprinted across the torso of the child.

The Dr. Kids Project also created five foreign playmates to correspond with each of these elementary aspects of human existence. These are the five character children whose houses are constructed in Dr. Kids Town. With the exception of Cathy, who is French, all are American. A Dr. Kids representative explained why the characters are foreign: "Japanese are so very fond of foreigners—well, when I say 'foreigners' I really mean that Japanese are so fond of Americans." For each simulated foreign child a complete identity has been established, from physical appearance, personality, and abilities, extending to details of other family members. Although the fantasy foreign playmates never appear, visitors to Dr. Kids Town are thoroughly introduced to them. There are drawings of the children, along with detailed information about their hobbies and habits. Cathy, for example, is the playmate who represents "wearing," a category also referred to as "Fashion Life." Cathy wants to be a fashion designer when she grows up. She also has good "gathering information" skills. Therefore, when the five children travel over the world in the UFO they discovered, Cathy's position is secretary.

Cathy, whom the guide describes as "poised," "graceful," and "altruistic," has very good social skills. Comments made by a company employee who first guided me through the complex included insights such as, "Cathy is good with people;" and, "Right away, one notices the warm pleasant feelings one has when entering Cathy's house." Cathy is good at arranging furniture, giving parties, and sending invitations and thank-you cards. Such goods designed for children can be picked up while playing at Cathy's

house. Another simulated child is nine-year-old Jim, who represents learning and excels academically. There is even the suggestion he might be a future Nobel Prize winner. Jim will be an astronaut when he grows up, and, of course, pilots the children's UFO. Tom, the representative child for dwelling, also does well academically, and it is suggested, will be an architect. In constructing Tom, the Dr. Kids Project expresses the concern that the creative genius of this type of child is too often sacrificed to Japan's examination-oriented education system. George, who represents playing, is not very good at academic subjects, but excels at athletics. George will be a professional athlete. The Dr. Kids philosophy wants parents to realize that just because children like George cannot pass the exams for prestigious universities, they still have abilities which should be developed, and special "gifts" that can enhance society. The representative child for eating is Diane. She has very creative skills when it comes to cooking (which is her job on the children's UFO), and someday she will be a baker. At Diane's house visitors can get creative cooking utensils designed for use by young children.

These images of foreign children created for the consumption of Japanese children function less to enhance an understanding of foreigners than to enhance issues of Japanese identity and reinforce Japanese gender socialization. The imaging of Cathy, as the only French child, perpetuates existing Japanese associations with French fashion, style, and cuisine. Cathy also images a contemporary concern surrounding *kikokushijo*, children who return to Japan after living abroad. By living outside her native country (in the U.S.) Cathy risks losing her native identity. Her French and ballet lessons represent her struggle to retain her Frenchness while abroad, just as Japanese children must struggle to retain their Japaneseness in order to be accepted back into Japanese society upon their return (Goodman 1990).

Although presented as foreign, the five character children at Dr. Kids Town reflect gender stereotypes consistent with long-held expectations in Japanese society. The children who excel in spatial, mathematical, and scientific abilities are both boys, who have very prestigious careers ahead of them as an astronaut and as an architect. Even though the child who does poorly in academic subjects is also male, his special abilities are those more likely to be admired in male children, namely athletics. The two girls epitomize domestic and consumer roles expected of women in Japan. Their abilities and future occupations center around cooking, creating fashionable outfits, arranging furnishings attractively, attending social events, handling gift-giving situations, and making other people feel good. In fact, even the children's parents are cast in gender-typed roles with Cathy's mother (who is three years younger than Cathy's father) as a flower arranger, while her father is a doctor.

When I raised the suggestion that these fantasy playmates evoked gender stereotypes, the project designers expressed surprise. One spokesperson said there was never any conscious attempt to present these as gender-specific roles, since according to the philosophical ideal all areas of every child's development should be enhanced, and that from a business perspective they would also be happy if all children (or their parents) bought the broadest range of goods. However, it seems likely that given the strength and persistence of these gender concepts in Japan, they permeate retailing constructions even when this is not an overt objective.

The theme park shopping centers for children presented here show how far retailers' inclination to provide "princess and lord service" to Japan's youngest consumer market extends. The theme parks themselves, the special learning corners found within them, the accredited classes offered, the special entertainments, and even the merchandise for sale, all promise to educate the young. Often children do learn about science, math, language, etc., while their parents learn ways to cope with Japan's educational challenge. However, perhaps more than anything else, the edutainment offerings of the theme parks are educating children about their future roles, sometimes indirectly through sex-typed characters, and socializing them into expected patterns of consumer activity.

EDUTAINMENT, EDUCATION, AND SOCIAL LEARNING

Japan ethnologists such as Bestor . . . and Robertson . . . have shown that appeals to tradition provide effective, "unassailably legitimate" symbols imbued with a cultural legitimacy . . . no one could or would dispute. . . . Invoking education similarly sparks a responsive chord among consumers and surrounds marketing with a cloak of legitimacy. The cultural legitimacy of education stems in part from the very high value placed on education found in Japan's Confucian heritage, but also from highly pragmatic concerns, given that educational achievement is viewed as the route to security and success in Japan. Claims of educational or developmental value are a common element in the marketing of children's goods and toys elsewhere. However, the pervasiveness of these in Japan is notable, extending to nearly all types of goods and services. The specific forms marketing suggestions of education take also reflect Japanese cultural expectations. For example, the packaging transformation of processed baby meals into "lessons" reflects the idea that children are not just raised, they are created . . . ;

development does not just happen, it results from the painstaking efforts of committed mothers dedicated to the holistic educational development of their children—expressed even in meals. . . . Cultural expectations of motherhood make it inappropriate to resort to processed baby food because it is easy, but not if it is educational. Early childhood goods are presented in Japan, as elsewhere, as developmental objects. However, as expressed in the sentiments of Seibu's "First Goods" catalogue, these are not, in western cognitive developmental terms, transitional objects helping a child separate from mother. They instead create a bridge between the highly emphasized initial bond, symbolized even in the prenatal period by mother's voice, and the child's union with the larger social world as an interconnected social being.

The shopping clubs pervasive in Japan's children's marketing also reflect the general importance placed on belongingness in Japanese society. These clubs do not necessarily provide the same extensive basis of identity that preschool and school groups offer, but significantly they mimic a pattern of group formation and bond transferral that is a familiar aspect of Japanese custom. Unlike most consumer clubs in North America, these children's shopping clubs do not just offer discounts, free promotional goods, or services, but are actual clubs where members regularly meet, interact, and play together. This participatory involvement helps socialize children into expectations of group behavior—something that appeals to mothers who often feel judged by how well their children adapt to group play and learning activities in school settings.

By providing science and technology corners, English lessons, treasure hunts suggested to build knowledge or test-taking skills, and actual in-store *juku* (cram schools or tutoring classes), stores cater to parental concerns with maneuvering their children through the examination-oriented education system. However, in the store offerings, as in the society at large, there is often a contradiction between the exalted value of education as an ideal and the compelling pressure to succeed in the academic pedigree route. This tension surrounding education in Japan is aptly reflected in the paradoxical educational philosophy of Dr. Kids Town.

The Dr. Kids Project presents itself as a daring new concept in educational development. It has received tremendous media coverage in Japan, partly because of its critical stance towards the educational system. However, this is not really a novel perspective in Japan. The rise of biking gangs in the 1980s, frequently composed of high school dropouts or youth who did not do well academically (frustrated Georges whose own abilities went unrecognized and undeveloped) was attributed by many social scientists to the society's overemphasis on entrance examinations and academic credentials (Sato 1991). According to Rohlen (1983:81), the condemnation of exam-oriented education has long been part of Japan's national obsession with it.

> Like all great obsessions, this one evokes much regret and denial. . . . Time and again one reads how examinations are ruining the schools, the young and Japanese society; how cramming produces warped personalities, crushes enthusiasm, and nips creativity in the bud. . . . Yet, ironically, the critics are themselves graduates of the best universities, and their readers are the middle-class parents who will go to extremes to improve their children's performance.

The emphasis on balance and holistic development found in the Dr. Kids philosophy is consistent with the attitudes espoused by early childhood educational institutions, rather than a revolutionary shift from them. Cummings's (1980:13) depiction of Japan's educational system reiterates its emphasis on the "whole child." According to Peak (1991:64), "The primary goal of preschools is neither academic nor focused on preparing children for first grade. Rather, it is to provide a foundation of good character and develop a wholesome personality." Although the suggestion of uninhibited playfulness projected by the theme parks seems distantly removed from an emphasis on strict discipline often found in Japanese education, it is nonetheless consistent with the frequently expressed opposing ideal of . . . free, unencumbered development (Katsube 1984).

The edutainments proffered by stores and shopping theme parks appeal because they are consistent with commonly espoused social attitudes about education and underlying expectations for behavior. Dr. Kids, for example, echoes the condemnation of the examination system that reverberates throughout Japanese society while, like other critics, it simultaneously perpetuates the system. The importance of pursuing academic credentials is symbolically affirmed in the Dr. Kids logo, a mischievous looking young scholar wearing a graduation cap and tassel, and most obviously in the chosen name for the project—these are, after all, "Dr. Kids."

In addition to reflecting the attitudes and tensions surrounding formal education, stores function as agents of socialization. . . . Social learning theory suggests that children in part learn to conform with role and behavior expectations through observation and imitation. . . . The social learning of expected consumer behavior occurs in many ways. Whether at the large theme parks or at play tables amidst adult goods, children play surrounded by shopping activity, able to observe and thus learn consumer behavior. Japanese consumer behavior is coded in the metaphor of a host/guest relationship. Even the Japanese word for customer, *okyakusan*, is the same word used for guests

to a household. Hosts are expected to indulge guests, catering unasked to their whims. The theme parks in particular express the extension of the host/guest idiom to Japan's youngest customers. At Dr. Kids Town the metaphor of store guest and the image of household guest merge, as store visitors become guests in the houses of their fantasy playmates. Guests are indulged, but they are also expected to behave appropriately. For consumers this usually suggests making at least some small purchase in repayment for receiving the host's hospitality.

By imitating adult offerings, store edutainment teaches children that there is more to consumerism than purchasing things. Since many Japanese households are saturated with material goods, a 1990s marketing slogan stresses . . . selling "things other than things" (Creighton 1992:53). Hair salons, travel campaigns, pretend coffee shops, and catering services designed for children represent a shift toward teaching children early on to be consumers of these soft menu items.

Children's shopping clubs socialize Japanese consumers for the *tomo no kai* (gathering of friends) shopping clubs that are a prevalent aspect of adult consumerism. The adult clubs, comprised almost exclusively of women, create loyal store customers while providing club activities women pursue together. Among women *tomo no kai* prompt consumer expenditures at particular stores and also function as a hub of women's informal networking.

The social learning of appropriate gender and consumer behaviors are closely entwined, as consumerism is a gendered female construction; retailing employees are overwhelmingly female as are 80 percent of customers. Edutainments and facilities for children can also be seen as services directed at mothers. The cultural ideal of motherhood, the limited hours of available day care, and the structure of Japan's permanent employment system where seniority derives from years of service and extensive overtime commitments all pose barriers to women who wish to have both a family and a career. In contrast, their consumer role is facilitated since shopping is constructed to be easy and pleasurable for women despite the demands of motherhood. Despite some progress in career options for women, there persists a widespread gender dichotomy in Japan that assigns men and women to different spheres of activity. Without consciously thinking about it, Japanese shoppers observe that even among foreign fantasy playmates boys aspire to prominent career roles. In contrast, girls pursue socially situated nurturing and support activities such as attractive cooking, fashionable redecorating, and successful gift-giving—all activities imbued with an implicit consumer orientation. Whereas shopping clubs for boys fade away in the teen years, girls are led completely through these escalator schools of shopping socialization, directly into the *tomo no kai* (friendship clubs) which are a focus of both consumer and social networking for adult women.

CONCLUSIONS

. . . The large Japanese retailing complexes described here fulfill a socialization function through edutainment in three ways. The first involves direct messages about education. Store promotions and special events reflect the strong ideological value exalting education in Japan, as well as the pragmatic concerns surrounding education as the means to a desired lifestyle. Educational philosophies espoused by stores even reflect the contradictions surrounding the contemporary educational system in Japan. Like other voices in the society, stores actively renounce the academic pedigree orientation of modern education, while nonetheless further reinforcing this tendency.

Like other behaviors, consumerism involves learned, patterned actions. A second way in which store edutainment functions as a socializing agent is through the inculcation of appropriate consumer behavior. While socializing children into culturally defined appropriate age and gender consumer behavior, store discourse, communicated through the cultural objects of catalogues, advertisements, and the physical space of store layouts, constructs a role for modern consumerism consistent with prevailing cultural values. Consumerism is presented not so much as a way of finding oneself but as a means of linking selves to others. Just as aspects of adult consumerism such as gift-giving purchases in Japan serve to affirm networks of relationships, children are drawn into a similar process of linking consumer behavior to frameworks of human interactions. Consumerism is thus projected as the operator connecting young children to greater participation in the social world.

The third way store edutainment functions as a socializing agent is by prompting people more generally toward socially accepted values and behaviors. Stores do this by perpetuating themes common in Japanese society, providing images which define various social roles, and by replicating gender expectations. The images of children presented by the stores, and even the fantasy constructions of foreign children, serve to mirror desired characteristics for Japanese children. As such, they fulfill functions outlined by Barnouw and Kirkland (1992:52), who contend that popular culture provides the public with "a social repertoire of characters, relationships and outcomes that is used in the ongoing attempt to make sense of the world."

NOTES

1. The material presented here is based on fieldwork conducted under a Nakasone research grant to study Japan's internationalization, and on a Social Sciences and Humanities Research Council of Canada (UBC/HSS) grant to study consumer behavior among Japanese youth. The project also utilized insights from earlier research conducted under a Fulbright-Hays, U.S. Department of Education grant. I am grateful to Merry White for comments, and to all those in Japan who helped with this research, in particular the representatives of Tsumura Pyxis International for their participation and assistance.
2. This trend persists. In 1991 the average number of children born to a woman in her lifetime dropped to 1.53 (Iwao 1993), and in 1992 this figure was 1.5, the lowest since such statistics were first recorded in 1899.
3. Given the reluctance to use processed baby foods discussed earlier, such baby restaurants can also be seen as attempts to promote the use of canned baby foods among Japanese mothers by fostering greater acceptance for these products.

REFERENCES

Allinson, A. 1991. Japanese Mothers and Obentōs: The Lunch-box as Ideological State Apparatus. *Anthropological Quarterly* 64(4):195–208.
Barnouw, E., and C. E. Kirkland. 1992. *Entertainment, Folklore, Cultural Performances, and Popular Entertainments*, ed. R. Bauman, Pp. 50–52. Oxford.
Beauchamp, E. R. 1991. Education and Identity in Modern Japan, 1868–Present. *Asian Thought and Society* 16(48):189–98.
Blustein, P. 1991. Catering to Children in Japan: Businesses Respond as Parents Lavish Money on Youngsters. *The Washington Post,* 11 February.
Creighton, M. R. 1992. The Depaato: Merchandising the West While Selling Japaneseness. In *Re-made in Japan*, ed. J. Tobin, Pp. 42–57. New Haven.
Cummings, W. K. 1980. *Education and Equality in Japan.* Princeton.
Fujita, M. 1989. "It's All Mother's Fault": Childcare and the Socialization of Working Mothers in Japan. *The Journal of Japanese Studies* 15(1):67–91.
Goodman, R. 1990. *Japan's 'International Youth': The Emergence of a New Class of School Children.* Oxford.
Graburn, N. 1983. *To Pray, Pay and Play: The Cultural Structure of Japanese Domestic Tourism.* Series B, no 26. Aix-en-Provence.
Heininger, M. L. S. 1984. *Children, Childhood and Change in America, 1820–1920.* A Century of Childhood, 1820–1920. Pp. 1–33. Rochester.
Iwao, S. 1993. *The Japanese Woman: Traditional Image and Changing Reality.* New York.
Izumi, A. 1989. *Okosama Gyōkai Monogatari.* Tokyo.
Katsube, M. 1984. *Nobi Nobi Kosodateron.* Tokyo.
Kojima, H. 1986. Becoming Nurturant in Japan: Past and Present. In *Origins of Nurturance: Developmental, Biological and Cultural Perspectives on Caregiving,* eds. A. Fogel and G. F. Melson, Pp. 123–39. Hillsdale, NJ.

Nikkei Sangyō Shimbun. 1990. *Hyakkaten, TDL ni Manabu: Kodomo yohin uriba o teemapaakugata ni.* 28 November.

Peak, L. 1991. *Learning to Go to School in Japan: The Transition from Home to Preschool Life.* Berkeley.

Robertson, J. 1987. A Dialectic of Native and Newcomer: The Kodaira Citizen's Festival in Suburban Tokyo. *Anthropological Quarterly* 60(3):124–36.

Rohlen, T. P. 1983. *Japan's High Schools.* Berkeley.

Satō, I. 1991. *Kamikaze Biker: Parody and Anomy in Affluent Japan.* Chicago.

Shibaguchi, I. 1991. 'Hime-Tono Saabisu' ni hashiru kodomo yohin uriba. *Nikkei Torendii.* 4:92–93.

Tobin, J., D. Wu, and D. Davidson. 1989. *Preschool in Three Cultures: Japan, China and the United States.* New Haven.

Yamazaki, K. 1993. *Kishōtenten: Yōjieisai Kyōiku. Sekai* 5:200–201.

28

When Brothers Share a Wife

Melvyn C. Goldstein

Marriage is a social institution that formalizes certain aspects of the relationship between males and females. It is an institution that evokes in us deep-seated emotions about questions of right and wrong, good and evil, and traditional versus modern. Within families, arguments may occur about what is appropriate premarital behavior, what is a proper marriage ceremony, and how long a marriage should last. Although these arguments may be traumatic for parents and their offspring, from a cross-cultural perspective, they generally involve minor deviations from the cultural norms. In contrast, anthropology textbooks describe an amazing variety of marriage systems that fulfill both biological and social functions. This selection will show just how different things could be.

Social institutions are geared to operate within and adapt to the larger social and ecological environment. This was the case in the earlier selections on gender roles and family planning; the organization of the family must also be adapted to the ecology. For example, the nuclear family is more adapted to a highly mobile society than is an extended family unit that includes grandparents and others. As society increasingly focuses on technical education, career specialization, and therefore geographic mobility for employment purposes, a system has evolved that emphasizes the nuclear family over the extended family.

In a similar way, fraternal polyandry in Tibet, as described in this selection, can meet the social, demographic, and ecological needs of its region.

As you read this selection, ask yourself the following questions:

☐ *What is meant by the term* fraternal polyandry?

☐ *Is this the only form of marriage allowed in Tibet?*

☐ *How do husbands and wives feel about the sexual aspects of sharing a spouse?*

☐ *Why would Tibetans choose fraternal polyandry?*

☐ *How is the function of fraternal polyandry like that of nineteenth-century primogeniture in England?*

The following terms discussed in this selection are included in the Glossary at the back of the book:

arable land
corvée
fraternal polyandry
monogamy
nuclear family
population pressure
primogeniture

Eager to reach home, Dorje drives his yaks hard over the 17,000-foot mountain pass, stopping only once to rest. He and his two older brothers, Pema and Sonam, are jointly marrying a woman from the next village in a few weeks, and he has to help with the preparations.

Dorje, Pema, and Sonam are Tibetans living in Limi, a 200-square-mile area in the northwest corner of Nepal, across the border from Tibet. The form of marriage they are about to enter—fraternal polyandry in anthropological parlance—is one of the world's rarest forms of marriage but is not uncommon in Tibetan society, where it has been practiced from time immemorial. For many Tibetan social strata, it traditionally represented the ideal form of marriage and family.

With permission from *Natural History*, vol. 96, no. 3. Copyright © 1987 the American Museum of Natural History.

The mechanics of fraternal polyandry are simple. Two, three, four, or more brothers jointly take a wife, who leaves her home to come and live with them. Traditionally, marriage was arranged by parents, with children, particularly females, having little or no say. This is changing somewhat nowadays, but it is still unusual for children to marry without their parents' consent. Marriage ceremonies vary by income and region and range from all the brothers sitting together as grooms to only the eldest one formally doing so. The age of the brothers plays an important role in determining this: very young brothers almost never participate in actual marriage ceremonies, although they typically join the marriage when they reach their midteens.

The eldest brother is normally dominant in terms of authority, that is, in managing the household, but all the brothers share the work and participate as sexual partners. Tibetan males and females do not find the sexual aspect of sharing a spouse the least bit unusual, repulsive, or scandalous, and the norm is for the wife to treat all the brothers the same.

Offspring are treated similarly. There is no attempt to link children biologically to particular brothers, and a brother shows no favoritism toward his child even if he knows he is the real father because, for example, his older brothers were away at the time the wife became pregnant. The children, in turn, consider all of the brothers as their fathers and treat them equally, even if they also know who is their real father. In some regions children use the term "father" for the eldest brother and "father's brother" for the others, while in other areas they call all the brothers by one term, modifying this by the use of "elder" and "younger."

Unlike our own society, where monogamy is the only form of marriage permitted, Tibetan society allows a variety of marriage types, including monogamy, fraternal polyandry, and polygyny. Fraternal polyandry and monogamy are the most common forms of marriage, while polygyny typically occurs in cases where the first wife is barren. The widespread practice of fraternal polyandry, therefore, is not the outcome of a law requiring brothers to marry jointly. There is choice, and in fact, divorce traditionally was relatively simple in Tibetan society. If a brother in a polyandrous marriage became dissatisfied and wanted to separate, he simply left the main house and set up his own household. In such cases, all the children stayed in the main household with the remaining brother(s), even if the departing brother was known to be the real father of one or more of the children.

The Tibetans' own explanation for choosing fraternal polyandry is materialistic. For example, when I asked Dorje why he decided to marry with his two brothers rather than take his own wife, he thought for a moment, then said it prevented the division of his family's farm (and animals) and thus facilitated all of them achieving a higher standard of living. And when I later asked Dorje's bride whether it wasn't difficult for her to cope with three brothers as husbands, she laughed and echoed that rationale of avoiding fragmentation of the family land, adding that she expected to be better off economically, since she would have three husbands working for her and her children.

Exotic as it may seem to Westerners, Tibetan fraternal polyandry is thus in many ways analogous to the way primogeniture functioned in nineteenth-century England. Primogeniture dictated that the eldest son inherited the family estate, while younger sons had to leave home and seek their own employment—for example, in the military or the clergy. Primogeniture maintained family estates intact over generations by permitting only one heir per generation. Fraternal polyandry also accomplishes this but does so by keeping all the brothers together with just one wife so that there is only one set of heirs per generation.

While Tibetans believe that in this way fraternal polyandry reduces the risk of family fission, monogamous marriages among brothers need not necessarily precipitate the division of the family estate: brothers could continue to live together, and the family land could continue to be worked jointly. When I asked Tibetans about this, however, they invariably responded that such joint families are unstable because each wife is primarily oriented to her own children and interested in their success and well-being over that of the children of other wives. For example, if the youngest brother's wife had three sons while the eldest brother's wife had only one daughter, the wife of the youngest brother might begin to demand more resources for her children since, as males, they represent the future of the family. Thus, the children from different wives in the same generation are competing sets of heirs, and this makes such families inherently unstable. Tibetans perceive that conflict will spread from the wives to their husbands and consider this likely to cause family fission. Consequently, it is almost never done.

Although Tibetans see an economic advantage to fraternal polyandry, they do not value the sharing of a wife as an end in itself. On the contrary, they articulate a number of problems inherent in the practice. For example, because authority is customarily exercised by the eldest brother, his younger male siblings have to subordinate themselves with little hope of changing their status within the family. When these younger brothers are aggressive and individualistic, tensions and difficulties often occur despite there being only one set of heirs.

In addition, tension and conflict may arise in polyandrous families because of sexual favoritism. The bride normally sleeps with the eldest brother, and

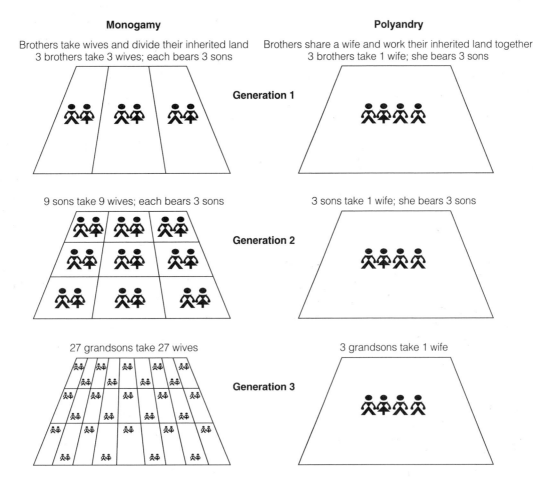

Monogamy

Brothers take wives and divide their inherited land
3 brothers take 3 wives; each bears 3 sons

Polyandry

Brothers share a wife and work their inherited land together
3 brothers take 1 wife; she bears 3 sons

Generation 1

9 sons take 9 wives; each bears 3 sons

3 sons take 1 wife; she bears 3 sons

Generation 2

27 grandsons take 27 wives

3 grandsons take 1 wife

Generation 3

the two have the responsibility to see to it that the other males have opportunities for sexual access. Since the Tibetan subsistence economy requires males to travel a lot, the temporary absence of one or more brothers facilitates this, but there are also other rotation practices. The cultural ideal unambiguously calls for the wife to show equal affection and sexuality to each of the brothers (and vice versa), but deviations from this ideal occur, especially when there is a sizable difference in age between partners in the marriage.

Dorje's family represents just such a potential situation. He is fifteen years old and his two older brothers are twenty-five and twenty-two years old. The new bride is twenty-three years old, eight years Dorje's senior. Sometimes such a bride finds the youngest husband immature and adolescent and does not treat him with equal affection; alternatively, she may find his youth attractive and lavish special attention on him. Apart from this consideration, when a younger male like Dorje grows up, he may consider his wife "ancient" and prefer the company of a woman his own age or younger. Consequently, although men and women do not find the idea of sharing a bride or a bridegroom repulsive, individual likes and dislikes can cause familial discord.

Two reasons have commonly been offered for the perpetuation of fraternal polyandry in Tibet: that Tibetans practice female infanticide and therefore have to marry polyandrously, owing to a shortage of females; and that Tibet, lying at extremely high altitudes, is so barren and bleak that Tibetans would starve without resort to this mechanism. A Jesuit who lived in Tibet in the eighteenth century articulated this second view: "One reason for this most odious custom is the sterility of the soil, and the small amount of land that can be cultivated owing to the lack of water. The crops may suffice if the brothers all live together, but if they form separate families they would be reduced to beggary."

Both explanations are wrong, however. Not only has there never been institutionalized female infanticide in Tibet, but Tibetan society gives females considerable rights, including inheriting the family estate in the absence of brothers. In such cases, the woman takes a bridegroom who comes to live in her family and adopts her family's name and identity. Moreover, there is no demographic evidence of a shortage of females. In Limi, for example, there were (in 1974) sixty females and fifty-three males in the fifteen- to thirty-five-year age category, and many adult females were unmarried.

The second reason is also incorrect. The climate in Tibet is extremely harsh, and ecological factors do play a major role perpetuating polyandry, but polyandry is not a means of preventing starvation. It is characteristic, not of the poorest segments of the society, but rather of the peasant landowning families.

In the old society, the landless poor could not realistically aspire to prosperity, but they did not fear starvation. There was a persistent labor shortage throughout Tibet, and very poor families with little or no land and few animals could subsist through agricultural labor, tenant farming, craft occupations such as carpentry, or by working as servants. Although the per person family income could increase somewhat if brothers married polyandrously and pooled their wages, in the absence of inheritable land, the advantage of fraternal polyandry was not generally sufficient to prevent them from setting up their own households. A more skilled or energetic younger brother could do as well or better alone, since he would completely control his income and would not have to share it with his siblings. Consequently, while there was and is some polyandry among the poor, it is much less frequent and more prone to result in divorce and family fission.

An alternative reason for the persistence of fraternal polyandry is that it reduces population growth (and thereby reduces the pressure on resources) by relegating some females to lifetime spinsterhood. Fraternal polyandrous marriages in Limi (in 1974) averaged 2.35 men per woman, and not surprisingly, 31 percent of the females of child-bearing age (twenty to forty-nine) were unmarried. These spinsters either continued to live at home, set up their own households, or worked as servants for other families. They could also become Buddhist nuns. Being unmarried is not synonymous with exclusion from the reproductive pool. Discreet extramarital relationships are tolerated, and actually half of the adult unmarried women in Limi had one or more children. They raised these children as single mothers, working for wages or weaving cloth and blankets for sale. As a group, however, the unmarried women had far fewer offspring than the married women, averaging only 0.7 children per woman, compared with 3.3 for married women, whether polyandrous, monogamous, or polygynous. While polyandry helps regulate population, this function of polyandry is not consciously perceived by Tibetans and is not the reason they consistently choose it.

If neither a shortage of females nor the fear of starvation perpetuates fraternal polyandry, what motivates brothers, particularly younger brothers, to opt for this system of marriage? From the perspective of the younger brother in a landholding family, the main incentive is the attainment or maintenance of the good life. With polyandry, he can expect a more secure and higher standard of living, with access not only to his family's land and animals, but also to its inherited collection of clothes, jewelry, rugs, saddles, and horses. In addition, he will experience less work pressure and much greater security because all responsibility does not fall on one "father." For Tibetan brothers, the question is whether to trade off the greater personal freedom inherent in monogamy for the real or potential economic security, affluence, and social prestige associated with life in a larger, labor-rich polyandrous family.

A brother thinking of separating from his polyandrous marriage and taking his own wife would face various disadvantages. Although in the majority of Tibetan regions all brothers theoretically have rights to their family's estate, in reality Tibetans are reluctant to divide their land into small fragments. Generally, a younger brother who insists on leaving the family will receive only a small plot of land, if that. Because of its power and wealth, the rest of the family usually can block any attempt of the younger brother to increase his share of land through litigation. Moreover, a younger brother may not even get a house and cannot expect to receive much above the minimum in terms of movable possessions, such as furniture, pots, and pans. Thus, a brother contemplating going it on his own must plan on achieving economic security and the good life not through inheritance but through his own work.

The obvious solution for younger brothers—creating new fields from virgin land—is generally not a feasible option. Most Tibetan populations live at high altitudes (above 12,000 feet), where arable land is extremely scarce. For example, in Dorje's village, agriculture ranges only from about 12,900 feet, the lowest point in the area, to 13,300 feet. Above that altitude, early frost and snow destroy the staple barley crop. Furthermore, because of the low rainfall caused by the Himalayan rain shadow, many areas in Tibet and northern Nepal that are within appropriate altitude range for agriculture have no reliable sources of irrigation. In the end, although there is plenty of unused land in such areas, most of it is either too high or too arid.

Even where unused land capable of being farmed exists, clearing the land and building the substantial terraces necessary for irrigation constitute a great undertaking. Each plot has to be completely dug out to a depth of two to two and a half feet so that the large rocks and boulders can be removed. At best, a man might be able to bring a few new fields under cultivation in the first years after separating from his brothers, but he could not expect to acquire substantial amounts of arable land this way.

In addition, because of the limited farmland, the Tibetan subsistence economy characteristically includes a strong emphasis on animal husbandry. Tibetan farmers regularly maintain cattle, yaks, goats, and sheep, grazing them in the areas too high for agriculture. These herds produce wool, milk, cheese, butter, meat, and skins. To obtain these resources, however, shepherds must accompany the animals on a daily basis. When first setting up a monogamous household, a younger brother like Dorje would find it difficult to both farm and manage animals.

In traditional Tibetan society, there was an even more critical factor that operated to perpetuate fraternal polyandry—a form of hereditary servitude somewhat analogous to serfdom in Europe. Peasants were tied to large estates held by aristocrats, monasteries, and the Lhasa government. They were allowed the use of some farmland to produce their own subsistence but were required to provide taxes in kind and corvée (free labor) to their lords. The corvée was a substantial hardship, since a peasant household was in many cases required to furnish the lord with one laborer daily for most of the year and more on specific occasions such as the harvest. This enforced labor, along with the lack of new land and the ecological pressure to pursue both agriculture and animal husbandry, made polyandrous families particularly beneficial. The polyandrous family allowed an internal division of adult labor, maximizing economic advantage. For example, while the wife worked the family fields, one brother could perform the lord's corvée, another could look after the animals, and a third could engage in trade.

Although social scientists often discount other people's explanations of why they do things, in the case of Tibetan fraternal polyandry, such explanations are very close to the truth. The custom, however, is very sensitive to changes in its political and economic milieu and, not surprisingly, is in decline in most Tibetan areas. Made less important by the elimination of the traditional serf-based economy, it is disparaged by the dominant non-Tibetan leaders of India, China, and Nepal. New opportunities for economic and social mobility in these countries, such as the tourist trade and government employment, are also eroding the rationale for polyandry, and so it may vanish within the next generation.

29

African Polygyny:
Family Values and Contemporary Changes

Philip L. Kilbride

Marriage is a cultural universal, although particular forms of marriage and family structure vary throughout the world. In the United States, polygamy, or plural marriage, is illegal. People have very strong feelings about what marriage is supposed to be like. The ideal of romantic love and lifelong monogamous marriage between people who are intimate companions—even best friends—is a dominant theme in American culture. Yet in all societies, including our own, there are significant differences between the sociocultural ideals and social realities. Divorce is so common in American society that many anthropologists and sociologists say that we actually practice serial monogamy; that is, we have more than one spouse but not at the same time. The nature of marriage is also being debated in our society in regard to gay and lesbian couples and adoption of children by gay couples.

In this selection, Philip Kilbride argues that marriage has much more to do with children and community than it does with sex. Divorce, he says, has negative effects on children's psychological and economic well-being. Deadbeat dads who fail to pay court-ordered child support are a major cause of the impoverishment of single-parent households and are a national disgrace. Teenage pregnancy is yet another problem to contend with.

From the child's point of view, is it better to have blended families linked through plural marriages? In contemporary Africa, this subject raises lively discussion—in part because it pits traditional culture against Christian morality and in part because marriage structure is a critical factor for understanding gender relations. Kilbride has examined polygyny in Africa and among Mormons and

has also studied a phenomenon called "man sharing" in the African American community. It is a controversial topic that has led him to some TV talk shows. But for an anthropologist to stir up controversy—that's nothing new.

As you read this selection, ask yourself the following questions:

☐ *Why do Americans think that polygamy is immoral?*

☐ *Is the author correct in saying that American men might be mildly for polygyny but American women are strongly against it? Why would this be so?*

☐ *Even in societies that allow polygyny, most people live in monogamous marriages. The author says that this is because polygyny is too expensive. What social functions does marriage serve that involve economic resources?*

☐ *Would the problem of deadbeat dads go away if polygyny were an option?*

☐ *Why do Africans see the American marriage system, with its high frequency of divorce, as inferior to traditional polygyny? Is this really from the child's perspective?*

The following terms discussed in this selection are included in the Glossary at the back of the book:

extended family	polygyny
polyandry	serial monogamy
polygamy	

RETHINKING POLYGAMY

In the Western world today, the term *marriage* is defined as a social institution that legally joins one man and one woman at the same time; that is, it is synonymous with monogamy. Nevertheless, anthropologists define marriage more broadly as to include cultural variation, such as number of mates, at the same time recognizing the universal function of marriage as a public contract that makes socially legitimate any offspring resulting from the marital union or unions. Anthropologists tell us that monogamy is the norm around the world (Fisher 1992). This assertion is correct in the pragmatic sense because even in cultures that permit polygyny, or marriage between one man and more than one woman at a time, the majority of individuals, in actuality, are married monogamously. Nevertheless, in the majority of the world's cultures, polygyny exists along with monogamy as a viable and, in many cases, ideal form of marriage. Ford and Beach (1951), for example, found that in 84 percent of the 185 cultures they studied, men were permitted to have more than one wife at a time. One common misconception in the West about polygyny is that its function is primarily one of sexual gratification. That this is not the case can be derived from the sociology of polygynous family life, which reveals that in all cultures in which polygyny is practiced, there are a number of commonalities. Ideally, for example, work is divided evenly among wives; the fair practice visiting rule requires the husband to visit each wife equally; wives usually have separate houses and sleeping quarters; and the first wife is given the most respected status of senior wife.

One of the best-known cases of polygyny comes from the Islamic religion. An important ordinance in Islam provides limits on the institution of polygyny: "And if you fear that you cannot act equitably toward orphans, then marry such women as seem good to you, 2, 3, or 4, of if you fear you will not do justice (between them) then marry only one or what your right hand possesses" (the Koran 4:3). Polygyny, in this case, cannot be understood apart from community obligations toward widows and children. The actual practice allows considerable variation, although as set forth as a religious ideology in the Koran, its basis is understood best in a humanitarian, communitarian context.

Polyandry, found in less than 1 percent of the world's cultures, always exists in combination with polygyny. Among the Irigwe of Nigeria (Sangree 1969), there are two basic types of marriage. The first type, the "primary marriage," is arranged by parents prior to the couple's adolescence. "Second marriage" is arranged later by the couple itself. When a woman leaves her primary husband and goes to a secondary husband or later on to still another secondary husband, she leaves behind everything except the clothes and jewelry she is wearing. She may be fetched back by her former husband, or she may decide to stay and take up residence with her new husband, who then provides her with a house and everything she needs for housekeeping. The traditional Irigwe marriage system has no divorce. A woman's prior marriages are not terminated by her switching residence to another spouse. At any point in time, she may return to any of her spouses and resume residence with him. Paternity is settled by consensus, and a husband competes with his wife's other husbands for the paternity of the child she bears.

Advocates for Euro-American polygamy have met with stiff resistance. For example, the great nineteenth-century explorer Captain Richard Francis Burton shocked and angered the Victorians by writing openly about sexual matters. He also angered his wife with his private opinions concerning polygamy. Nevertheless, he believed that polygamy would help keep families stable, lessen the need for prostitutes, and help the single wife with her many household chores. Although Victorians may not have understood Burton's opinion, it is probably fair to say that most Irigwe men and women would have agreed with him.

AFRICAN POLYGYNY AS A CULTURAL VALUE

In her research on family structure among the Yoruba of Nigeria, Sudarkasa (1982) describes the typical situation. Whether or not a husband is polygynous, he has his own room separate from that of his wife or wives who, in turn, have their own rooms and their own household belongings. Although separated physically at times, the polygynous family should be thought of as one family, not as separate families sharing a common husband. Sudarkasa points out that the latter view would rule out the very significant role that the senior wife plays in the polygynous family. The senior wife must be a confidant and a cowife to the other wives, and she sometimes serves as an intermediary between her cowives and their common husband. Wives of the same husband frequently cooperate in economic activities. Distinction is made between children of the same father and children of the same mother by the same father. Sudarkasa emphasizes that for certain purposes, a mother and her children constitute a "*subunit* within the family, but they do not constitute a separate *unit* within the family" (p. 142). After her many years of studying African social organization, it is her opinion that widespread in Africa is the preference for a system of cowives rather than one where women bear children outside of marriage or where women may choose to live as childless spinsters. In Africa, spinsterhood would be perceived as very much outside the normal range of human behavior.

The anthropological literature frequently reports that African cultures in fact value polygyny; however, some evidence suggests that this may be primarily a male's point of view. At a minimum, this requires us to consider a possible gender bias in this generalization. There is evidence that women, in fact, do traditionally value polygyny. There is also evidence that suggests that men value it even more. There is also strong evidence that modernizing or Westernizing women most likely value it not at all. We will consider some evidence in this direction, since the gender question has occurred over and over again when polygyny is considered in any particular cultural context. Sudarkasa writes that before being bombarded with Western propaganda against polygyny, African women valued the companionship of cowives. In fact, in one study of Nigerian women conducted within the last 15 years, a majority of the women interviewed stated that they would be "pleased" to have a second wife in the home (Ware 1979). The negative bias of some Western-educated African women toward polygyny cannot, Sudarkasa emphasizes, be taken as indicative of the traditional attitude toward it.

On many occasions, female students from Bryn Mawr College have been taken to Uganda and Kenya, where they lived with families in both urban and rural locations. When the subject of polygyny has been introduced into our "theoretical" discussions, these highly educated students who, by their academic training, are sympathetic toward and knowledgeable about cultural variation, uniformly expressed unfavorable comments concerning the practice or even the concept of polygyny in our initial discussions. A conversation that took place in a Nairobi pub one evening is a good illustration of the cultural gap between Western-educated male and female values and East African male values concerning polygyny.

Two female students had been living in the home of one of the married Kenyan men present in the pub with us. They had quickly become attached to his wife and children and sympathized with her when her husband was not present at dinnertime because, like many urban Kenyan men, he stopped regularly at a pub after work before going home. Nevertheless, they could see that he was a good father and provider for his family. Although not meeting their Western ideal of the "husbandly role," they liked him very much and could understand why he might be thought of favorably by his family, friends, and colleagues. They were therefore somewhat shocked and dismayed when he mentioned to the group that he was thinking about taking a second wife. With such a charming, intelligent, and attractive wife at home, the students especially could not understand why he should be contemplating this. He

explained that he was getting a lot of pressure from his mother to do so because she was all alone in the rural area and needed someone to help her farm. His mother also stated that there were many single women in her village who needed husbands, and she wanted grandchildren who would live near or with her rather than far away in the city. This man's wife opposed the idea because she was afraid that there would then not be enough money to pay for her own children's school fees. Besides, the second wife might want to come to the city to live also. He said that he told his wife that he would make sure that she stayed on the farm. One African man who pragmatically supported monogamy stated that there was no way to guarantee that the second wife wouldn't want to come to the city. He stated that he might consider polygyny himself if he could ensure that one would stay in the rural area, but he didn't think that was probable.

For the sake of argument (and because one might accept the practice of polygyny under the right circumstances), the professor asked whether a "feminist" perspective shouldn't look favorably on this man being compassionate to the needs of an older woman, his mother, should he decide to marry a second wife. To make more salient to the students the cultural influence on their negative attitudes toward polygyny, another dimension to our cross-cultural discussion of marriage was added. The group was asked their opinion of two men marrying each other and adopting children. While the two students, in conformity with their liberal ideology and anthropological training, felt that this would be perfectly reasonable, the reaction of the African males present was one of stunned silence followed by asking the professor to repeat what their ears could not have heard correctly. When he did so, these men, who had just been divided on the question of polygyny, laughed heartily and stated that this would be impossible because it was not natural. Their disbelief and laughter at what *to them* was such a culturally dissonant idea were still evident on the way home.

POLYGAMY AND GENDER

While there appears to be a female bias against the institution of polygamy among Western-educated women, including those in Africa, there is considerable evidence that traditional African women do value polygyny, at least under certain circumstances. At this time, it may be informative for us to consider some of the evidence for this contention. Those Africans who have written in praise of polygyny have invariably been men, but some African women have noted that polygyny is to be preferred over stigmatized concubinage. In general, little is known about the issue of "women's views of polygyny in the broad context of their perceptions of marriage and women's issues as a whole" (Ware 1979). A survey of over 6,000 Yoruba females, ranging in age from 15 to 59, from the city of Ibadan, Nigeria, found that about one wife in two lives in a polygynous marriage; the proportion for women over 40 rises to about two out of three. About 60 percent of the women in the survey reported that they would be "pleased" if their husbands took another wife. They would then have some companionship and someone with whom they could share housework, husband care, and child care. Only 23 percent expressed anger at the idea of sharing with another wife. More traditionally oriented women without education (67 percent) were more favorable toward polygyny than women with some formal education (54 percent).

Ware (1979) suggests that sharing economic and domestic responsibilities among women might well appeal to modern feminists. She goes on to point out that the sharing of a husband might be viewed as a detriment or an advantage, depending on the extent to which husbands as such are considered to be assets or liabilities. Some Ibadan wives see little value in having a husband except as a "recognized progenitor for their children" (1979:190). When these women, who live in a society where 99 percent of women marry by the age of 40, were asked whether there was a need for a husband apart from his role in begetting children, 47 percent answered that women do not need husbands. They felt that there were many disadvantages in marriage, and since women were equal to men, they often did better on their own. Those women who did consider other roles played by husbands (in addition to progenitor) mentioned companionship most frequently.

Around the time of the Ware study, a survey was undertaken in western Kenya by a Catholic nun and a Kenyan nurse. Lwanga (1976) reports the following concerning their discussions of polygyny with 27 Samia women living in a remote rural area of western Kenya. Many women felt that polygyny can be a happy and beneficial experience if the cowives cooperate with each other. They caution, however, that this is not likely to happen unless the husband allows the senior wife the chance to look for a second wife. Then she may choose a relative or the daughter of another family of which she approves. If he should require a third wife, these two wives would then be informed so that they could help to look for someone with whom they would wish to share their lives and work. Women felt that the most common reason a wife would advise her husband to take another wife was that he was a rich man with lots of cattle and land, too much for one wife to handle alone. Twenty-five out of the 27 women considered polygyny to be better than monogamy. Other studies have also suggested that traditional (usually rural, uneducated) women view polygyny more positively than their educated counterparts.

Susan Whyte (1980) provides information from Marachi, Kenya, on the practice known as *okhwenda eshiebo*, in which a wife could bring her sister's or brother's daughter or occasionally her mother's brother's daughter to be her cowife. She points out that this often happened at the instigation of the husband, but the Mariachi view of it is that "it is the woman who brings herself a cowife" (p. 137). Whyte states that polygyny has become more problematic in today's deteriorating economic climate. Many men still want the respect they can gain by having many wives and children, but women emphasize the difficulties of polygyny due to a shortage of land and labor and an increasing need for money for school fees, clothing, labor, and food. Whyte points out that while polygyny, in her opinion, has never been popular with women, it is even less so at present because the resources of individual men are becoming less adequate; thus, there is an increase in competition for the already scarce resources of the polygynous husband.

Studying another Kenyan society, Monique Mulder (1992) found that married women have strong views concerning polygyny that are generally positive. Seventy-six percent of the women in her survey viewed polygyny favorably. In general, cowife relations are not full of tension, nor do polygynously married women suffer reproductive costs. Neither women nor their parents expressed antipathy toward polygyny (Mulder 1989:179).

Whatever the value orientation is toward polygyny, the reality is that throughout Africa, most men turn out to be monogamous. A recent study among the Zulu of southern Africa by Moller and Welch (1990) helps explain this male point of view regarding polygyny. Among the Zulus, polygynists account for about 10 percent of rural married men. There continues to be a shift from overt polygyny to covert polygyny or monogamy owing to several factors. Among these are (1) a shortage of agriculturally productive land and other economic changes; (2) social pressures to accept the values of politically and socially dominant whites; and (3) the inflexible teachings and policy of Christian mission churches. From their research surveys, Moller and Welch (1990) found that a majority of monogamist and polygynist men reported both economic advantages and disadvantages to the practice of polygyny, although most men professed to favor monogamy. In the views of the majority who favored monogamy, the main disadvantage of polygyny, as they saw it, was an economic one. They found, for example, that the notion of the large polygynous family as a social security investment is now being replaced by the problems associated with educating children during an extended period of their life cycle. It must be pointed out, however, that these are views of men who are faced with the prospect of polygyny in a modern economy for which many of the advantages of the past are not available to them. One of the frequently mentioned circumstances resulting in polygyny is the practice of labor migration, in which many Africans travel away from their home areas in search of cash income. For these men, polygyny provides a solution to the problem of being required to spend lengthy periods away from their home families. Thus, one wife may visit the husband in town while the other one cares for the rural homestead. Polygynist wives may also share labor and keep each other company in the rural area when the husband is away (Moller and Welch 1990:208).

One serendipitous finding from this study was that polygynist men reported higher-quality work lives than did monogamous men. The former had higher job satisfaction, more voluntary retirement, better health, and higher degrees of social adjustment, including a better adjustment to aging and retirement. Very significantly, Moller and Welch discovered that in a mood index analysis, polygynous men overall felt less lonely and neglected than other men in the survey. It may be that part of this positive mood adjustment can be seen by reference to spiritual values in Zulu society as men age. The older cohorts of returned migrants are more likely to be traditionally oriented and therefore more likely to choose polygynous lifestyles, since it may be seen as pleasing to the ancestors. More research needs to be done in this area, however, before one can conclude that the practice of polygyny per se has a directly positive effect on the morale of these men.

There is not much evidence available to consider whether polygyny does cut down on male infidelity, but one recent study conducted in Nigeria by Orubuloye, Caldwell, and Caldwell (1990) suggests that it might. In this extensive survey done in the Akiki district of Nigeria, the researchers found that for monogamous males in the rural area, 56 percent of their most recent sexual experiences were outside their marriages; this figure rose to 67 percent in the urban area. Contributing to this practice is sexual abstinence during pregnancy and for two years postpartum, but also the belief common in polygynous societies that men need more than one woman. Sexual variety may be achieved by acquiring another wife. Polygynous men are more likely to turn to one of their other wives for gratification while another one is sexually abstaining. Only 38 percent of polygynous men in the rural area had their most recent sexual experience outside of marriage, and in the urban area 44 percent of polygynous men's most recent sexual partners were women other than their wives. These data suggest that, at least in this society, monogamous men are much more likely to have extramarital partners than are polygynous men. However, we see the opposite pattern for female respondents. Thirty-four percent of rural polygynous wives and 47 percent of urban polygynous wives reported that their most recent sexual encounter was an extramarital one. Only 14 percent of monogamous rural women and 36 percent of their urban counterparts reported that their most recent sexual partner was someone other than their spouse (Orubuloye, J. Caldwell, and P. Caldwell 1990:12). Thus, it appears that polygyny allows greater sexual equality, at least in terms of extramarital sexual relations, than does monogamy. Future research on marital relationships within monogamous and polygynous households should attempt a closer examination of de facto male and female balance of power and responsibilities within these two marital forms.

DELOCALIZED POLYGYNY

The fate of polygyny in Africa is very much caught up in the processes of moral and economic change. The churches vary considerably in terms of overt condemnation of polygyny, with the mainstream churches being predominantly opposed and many independent churches being favorable toward polygyny. Community sanctions traditionally at work in regulating polygyny have changed as well, and elders and other traditional moral leaders have lost the authority they had in the past when practices like polygyny were closely monitored. One finds, for example, that today in Kenya, many men who traditionally would not have been considered acceptable as polygynists in terms of their economic resources are practicing polygyny because community sanctions no longer operate with the same degree of salience as in the past. As traditions change and the modern economy and moral order impose themselves more and more into the everyday lives of people, polygyny increasingly takes on a negative ambiance. Much of the current female opposition to polygyny may in fact be related to the irresponsible practice of this custom by many men in modernizing circumstances throughout the African continent. A few examples drawn from the Kenya media will provide readers with a sense of the tone surrounding what can be thought of as a public discourse concerning doubts over the suitability of polygyny in contemporary times.

Kilbride and Kilbride (1990), in discussing the modernization of tradition in East Africa, present excerpts from newspapers and magazines published in Nairobi, Kenya. The gist of the polygyny debate as seen in mass media discourse will be presented here. Many Western-educated, urban Kenyan women no longer find polygyny acceptable. One prominent female Kenyan politician, in her address at a seminar on "Women and the Church," urged that the churches ban polygyny, which she described as "more dangerous than malaria" (*Daily Nation*, May 18, 1985). She was, however, compassionate with the plight of single women who, because of an imbalance in the sex ratio, found themselves chasing after other women's husbands or settling for second or third wives. As the following argument from a male Kenyan politician will illustrate, modern educated men tend to be more favorable to polygyny. In his view, foreign influences are responsible for present social ills. To counteract this moral decline, he suggests returning to their traditions, including polygyny, which he believes would "help reduce the number of unmarried women roaming the streets as prostitutes" (*Daily Nation*, July 9, 1985).

Unlike the Roman Catholic Church, which is officially opposed to the practice of polygyny, some Protestant churches are becoming more tolerant of it. A bishop of the Anglican Church in Kenya stated that while monogamy may be ideal "for the expression of love between husband and wife," the church should consider that in certain cultures polygyny is socially acceptable and that the belief that polygyny is contrary to Christianity was no longer tenable (*The Weekly Review*, August 1, 1987). The Catholic Archbishop of Nairobi, who himself was raised in a polygynous home, expressed the Catholic Church's opposition to it when he spoke to a gathering of young people about the sacrament of marriage. He admonished them to do "the will of God" rather than blindly following their customs. As he put it, "God wanted one Adam and one Eve, not one Adam and three Eves nor five Adams and one Eve" (*Daily Nation*, February 11, 1985). Sometimes differences of opinion regarding polygyny erupt within splinter groups of a particular religion. The Friends Church in Kakamega, Kenya, for example, faced a leadership crisis between its "old and monogamist founders" and its "young and polygamist followers" who formed a splinter group over the parent church's opposition to polygyny (*Sunday Nation*, January 6, 1985).

GROWING UP IN A POLYGYNOUS HOME

In general, our interviews revealed that East Africans have both positive and negative memories about growing up in polygynous homes. Although jealousy and conflict were present, especially between cowives concerning economic injustices, this was less likely to be the case when the polygynous home was a wealthy one. Importantly, in keeping with traditional values, whether talking about the past or the present, more positive impressions about life in a polygynous home as parents or as children were given if the family was rich. Two cases from Kenyan research will illustrate this variation.

The first case deals with the recollections of a Ugandan woman, here called Marjorie, who is 40 years old; she is a high school graduate whose father is a wealthy agricultural officer. He has four wives and 25 children. Her own mother was the senior wife. Before taking a second wife, her father provided her mother with her own home and land near to where two of her other children were attending boarding school. When Marjorie was in sixth grade, she went to live with her father and his second wife and her children so that she could attend school nearby their residence. Interestingly, she states that although her stepmother gave her a lot of chores to do, she didn't mind. She liked her stepmothers, whom she described as being good. On school holidays, she went back to her own mother, who was even stricter with her because it was her mother's job to teach Marjorie all her female duties. Marjorie states that although their family was large, everyone always had enough to eat and plenty of land to farm. The children treated each other well. "Myself and the stepsisters, we don't say, 'Who is your mother?' We are all like sisters and brothers" (Kilbride and Kilbride 1990:207). As behooves a good polygynous husband, her father showed no favoritism—at least as could be perceived by Marjorie. She stated that she never knew who her father loved best. The cowives also followed the traditional custom of giving respect and deference to the senior wife. Marjorie also reported that she liked her father very much.

Our next account is a less favorable recollection of growing up in a polygynous home by a man in his mid-20s, here called Robert. His father, like Majorie's, also has four wives. Unfortunately, this man's economic situation is much less favorable. He has 31 children, thus far, with his youngest being less than one year old. Also, Robert's mother is not in as favorable a position economically or in terms of respect in that she is his father's second wife. In Robert's early childhood, his father had only two wives, both of whom Robert called "mother." It was not until he was seven years old that he began to question his status. When he was eight years old, he recollects going to school for awhile with the sons of the first wife. It was not a pleasant memory in that his stepbrothers beat him, made him carry their books to and from school, and forced him to get money from his mother to give to them for their own lunches. He finally refused to go to that school, which was 10 kilometers away, so he was transferred to a school near his home. After fourth grade, he states that he was forced to go to another primary school near the home of the fourth wife. While living at her house, which is 15 miles from the home of his mother and the other two wives, who all share the same compound, Robert complains that he was forced to do many household chores, including cooking, cleaning, and tending livestock, at times going without food from breakfast until dinner. He also disliked the fact that when he had friends over to visit, his stepmother would say that he wasn't living in the home of his mother. "It made me feel that I was born somewhere else but was now under the control of another person" (Kilbride and Kilbride 1990:208).

As an adult, Robert understands that there are some advantages to polygyny, such as sharing the workload, protection from outsiders, helping to care for other family members when they or their children are sick, and preventing childlessness and thus gaining immortality through one's children. Nevertheless, the disadvantages he has experienced personally, which he sees as being mainly the result of a lack of sufficient economic resources on the part of his father, who married more wives and had more children than he could support, makes him unfavorable to polygyny and what he perceives to be its many problems of jealousy and conflict over insufficient resources for food, clothing, and education. He reports that during times of food shortage, each mother looked after only her own children rather than sharing with the others, while his father tended to "disappear" until the worst was over. In Robert's case, we can see the workings of modernized polygyny in that his father did not fit the traditional ideal of being wealthy enough to be a polygynist, at least on the scale that he practiced it. There are indications that two wives would have been better for all concerned.

MONOGAMY RECONSIDERED

A very definite pattern is visible in Kenya today: professional women rejecting marriage altogether because many of them feel that men on the whole are unsympathetic to their attempts to have careers, to seek education beyond the B.A., and to practice independent lifestyles frequently associated with modern, professional occupations. At the same time, many women feel that men involve themselves too frequently with other women (mistresses) while they expect their wives to remain at home caring for the children. There is also the problem of wife beating, which women have traditionally agreed is the "right" of the husband if they do not perform their duties or act properly. Although many professional women are opting against marriage, they have not given up their desire to have children. For this reason, such women frequently find themselves in a position of seeking out a man, married or single, to give them a child or to become a father to that child or to one that they already have.

Perlez (1991) reports the views of a Miss Makuku, who is a postgraduate student in French at Nairobi University and a former schoolteacher. She sees herself ten years from now as a single parent with a male companion, but not a husband. She points out that this is a choice made not only by herself but by many of her over-30 female friends with occupations ranging from television producers to professors. For example, many educated women are delaying marriage; more than half of the 16 female law graduates of Nairobi University in 1980 are still single. Miss Makuku admonishes that traditionally, African men looked after their women, but today the average man contributes to the rent if one is lucky while using the rest for mistresses and beer. According to Perlez, anecdotal evidence from Kenya abounds concerning professional women who have been previously married but have left their husbands because they cannot tolerate the restrictions imposed by these men. Eventually, these women seek a relationship of some kind with a man. Miss Makuku points out that it is difficult to raise a child without the financial help of a man. By the age of 35, however, most of her economically self-sufficient, single, female friends have decided to have children even though they are not married. Some choose to have a child by a younger man because he is less likely to "boss them around" than would an older man. A second choice would be to have a child by a married man, paradoxically choosing to do one of the very things that has turned them against marriage to begin with.

We see here that exclusive monogamy, in Kenya as in the United States, does not appear to be working very well. There seems to be a tendency for polygyny to be reinvented as more and more single women have relationships with married men. Perhaps these men will involve themselves in the role of father to their outside children. Here we have a situation, similar to that described for man sharing in the African American community, developing in the East African setting where, ironically, polygamy was, until recently, the ideal. Very much present in Kenya at this time is a consciousness of the importance of having fathers for children. For example, the July 18, 1993, issue of the *Sunday Nation,* a prominent Kenyan newspaper, published a cartoon that accompanied a story entitled "Choice: The New Trend." The cartoon shows a woman dressed in fashionable clothing and a young boy, presumably her son, leaning against their car with a man standing beside them looking at them. The woman says, "I have everything I want, a good job, a good house, and a good child. Why should I need a man?" The child, however, is shown to be thinking: "But a daddy, we don't have." The story itself reported that in nearly all their interviews, women stated that they would find it acceptable having children without marriage if they were financially secure. One woman who is a company executive replied that she had reached the age where she was ready for a child, but not a husband, since she wanted to advance in her career and found that men were usually intolerant of ambitious women. Many of the single women interviewed were involved with men who were already married. While encouraging his mistress to have his child, he may promise that he is going to divorce his wife, which ten years later she finally realizes will never happen. At this point, the woman may feel that it is too late for her, given her increasing age, to meet anyone else. The article does not offer any analysis of this situation in terms of whether or not, on balance, quasi-polygyny is more or less desirable than divorce, especially when children are involved.

The interview material with Kenyan men in Kilbride and Kilbride (1990) presents a similar picture of frustration and difficulties associated with the current situation. One man in his late 40s, for example, responded to the AIDS crisis by curtailing his outside girlfriends so that he had a long-standing relationship with a single woman from an ethnic group other than his own. He required secrecy from this woman so that his wife and family would not be offended. The child that resulted from this relationship, who is now a young girl, is presently being raised entirely by her mother, since my informant no longer gives her any support. In spite of this, he seemed to feel that everything would be fine for his daughter. Another informant who spoke openly about polygyny is a wealthy Kenyan who is Roman Catholic and states that although he does not himself favor polygyny, he is not opposed to others practicing it. He believes that it is, in fact, a fairly common practice. He himself has been "offered" a wife when he has gone into rural areas, although he has not involved himself because of his wife's opposition to polygyny. He nevertheless confesses that at present he has numerous girlfriends and would like to know whether his wife would prefer him to be polygynous with a small number of wives or monogamous with the large number of mistresses that he now has. Moreover, each of his mistresses is unaware of the other women in his life and are themselves in search of a permanent relationship. Some of his girlfriends do not even know that he is married.

PLURAL MARRIAGE AS A REINVENTED OPTION

Is it worth considering plural marriage as a morally viable option for American men and women, particularly in light of our national family crisis and increased calls for cultural pluralism? A myriad of legal considerations, including property ownership, inheritance, child disciplinary obligations, and health insurance, to name but a few, will require special study and legal adjustment. In the United States, the monogamous companionate marriage, though viewed as an ideal, is not in the majority. In fact, given our high divorce rate, it can be argued that the United States now has a high rate of informal, unrecognized polygyny, at least as we would

infer from Remi Clignet's comment that "Africans argue that remarriage subsequent to a divorce is merely another form of polygyny, one less desirable because it imposes on Westerners succession and discontinuity in married life" (1970:3). Blended families are known to be particularly stressful for children, given the ambiguous status of this rapidly emerging family structure. Once marriage is consistently considered from the perspective of children, perhaps more people will come to see that seemingly radical forms of now improper plurality are actually "smart" opportunities for children to have multiple parents and often access to a better life through foster parents or blended parents who are *added* to their biological family.

REFERENCES

Clignet, R. 1970. *Many Wives, Many Powers: Authority and Power in Polygynous Families.* Evanston, IL: Northwestern University Press.
Fisher, H. E. 1992. *Anatomy of Love: The Natural History of Monogamy, Adultery, and Divorce.* New York: W. W. Norton and Company.
Ford, C., and F. Beach. 1951. *Patterns of Sexual Behavior.* New York: Harper & Row.
Kilbride, P. L., and J. E. Kilbride. 1990. *Changing Family Life in East Africa: Women and Children at Risk.* University Park: Pennsylvania State University Press.
Lwanga, G. 1976. Report on the Health Education of Clan Health Workers. Nangina Hospital, Nangina, Kenya.
Moller, V., and G. J. Welch. 1990. Polygamy, Economic Security, and Well-being of Retired Zulu Migrant Workers. *Journal of Cross-Cultural Gerontology* 5:205–216.
Mulder, M. 1989. Polygyny and the Extent of Women's Contributions to Subsistence: A Reply to White. *American Anthropologist* 91:178–180.
———. 1992. Women's Strategies in Polygynous Marriage. *Human Nature* 3(1):45–70.
Orubuloye, I. O., J. Caldwell, and P. Caldwell. 1990. Experimental Research on Sexual Networking in the Ekti District of Nigeria. Health Transition Working Paper No. 3.
Perlez, J. 1991. Elite Kenyan Women Avoid a Rite: Marriage. *The New York Times*, March 3, p. 14.
Sangree, W. 1969. Going Home to Mother: Traditional Marriage Among the Irigwe of Benue-Plateau State, Nigeria. *Journal of the American Anthropological Association* 71(6): 946–1056.
Sudarkasa, N. 1982. African and Afro-American Family Structure. In *Anthropology for the Eighties*, J. Cole, ed. Pp. 132–161. New York: Free Press.
Ware, H. 1979. Polygyny, Women's Views in a Transitional Society, Nigeria 1975. *Journal of Marriage and the Family* 41(1):185–195.
Whyte, S. 1980. Wives and Co-wives in Marachi, Kenya. *Folk* 21–22; 134–136.

30

Law, Custom, and Crimes Against Women:

The Problem of Dowry Death in India

John van Willigen and V. C. Channa

Anthropologists find many societies with unusual customs, beliefs, and behaviors. Usually they discover, after careful study and reflection, that these perform some useful function within the society, as in the case of polygyny and polyandry discussed in the previous selections. But is this always the case? Must we assume that simply because a custom exists it is healthy for the members of society? We think not, and the Christians who were fed to lions and the Aztec slaves who were sacrificed to a bloodthirsty god would most likely agree.

Times change; hunters and gatherers plant crops, tribal people rush headlong into peasantry, and small-scale farmers become urban wage earners. Traditions that helped maintain a healthy society in one context may become dysfunctional in another. For better or worse, traditions and beliefs run deep and are almost impossible to unlearn. It is the nature of culture to resist change.

As you will read, the practice of dousing a bride with kerosene and creating a human torch certainly indicates that the payment of dowry is a traditional practice gone awry. That said, what can be done? Laws, even those that carry serious penalties, are light ammunition against the armor of strongly held cultural beliefs. Governments will solve such problems only through public policy based on in-depth cultural understanding.

As you read this selection, ask yourself the following questions:

- ☐ *What do you think the authors mean when they suggest that dowry death presents a problem for ethnologists because of ethnological theory's functional cast?*

- ☐ *Why does the institution of dowry make college education problematic for some young women?*

- ☐ *What are the present-day approaches to solving the dowry death problem?*

- ☐ *How can women's access to production roles and property, delocalization of social control, and economic transformation affect the problem of dowry death?*

- ☐ *Dowry-related violence in India is related to the economic value of women. What might be said about the relationship between the economic position and the social status of women in America?*

The following terms discussed in this selection are included in the Glossary at the back of the book:

caste	*ethnology*
cultural materialism	*peasants*
demography	*sex roles*
dowry	

A 25-year-old woman was allegedly burnt to death by her husband and mother-in-law at their East Delhi home yesterday. The housewife, Mrs. Sunita, stated before her death at the Jaya Prakash Narayana Hospital that members of her husband's family had been harassing her for bringing inadequate dowry.

The woman told the Shahdara subdivisional magistrate that during a quarrel over dowry at their Pratap Park house yesterday, her husband gripped her from behind while the mother-in-law poured kerosene over her clothes.

Her clothes were then set ablaze. The police have registered a case against the victim's husband, Suraj Prakash, and his mother.

—*Times of India,* February 19, 1988

This routinely reported news story describes what in India is termed a "bride-burning" or "dowry death." Such incidents are frequently reported in the newspapers of Delhi and other Indian cities. In addition, there are cases in which the evidence may be ambiguous, so that deaths of women by fire may be recorded as kitchen accidents, suicides, or murders. Dowry violence takes a characteristic form. Following marriage and the requisite giving of dowry, the family of the groom makes additional demands for the payment of more cash or the provision of more goods. These demands are expressed in unremitting harassment of the bride, who is living in the household of her husband's parents, culminating in the murder of the woman by members of her husband's family or by her suicide. The woman is typically burned to death with kerosene, a fuel used in pressurized cook stoves, hence the use of the term "bride-burning" in public discourse.

Dowry death statistics appear frequently in the press and parliamentary debates. Parliamentary sources report the following figures for married women 16 to 30 years of age in Delhi: 452 deaths by burning for 1985; 478 for 1986 and 300 for the first six months of 1987 (Bhatia 1988). There were 1,319 cases reported nationally in 1986 (*Times of India,* January 10, 1988). Police records do not match hospital records for third degree burn cases among younger married women; far more violence occurs than the crime reports indicate (Kumari 1988).

There is other violence against women related both directly and indirectly to the institution of dowry. For example, there are unmarried women who commit suicide so as to relieve their families of the burden of providing a dowry. A recent case that received national attention in the Indian press involved the triple suicide of three sisters in the industrial city of Kanpur. A photograph was widely published showing the three

Reproduced by permission of the Society for Applied Anthropology from *Human Organization*, vol. 50, no. 4, 1991, pp. 369–377.

young women hanging from ceiling fans by their scarves. Their father, who earned about 4,000 Rs. [rupees] per month, was not able to negotiate marriage for his oldest daughter. The grooms were requesting approximately 100,000 Rs. Also linked to the dowry problem is selective female abortion made possible by amniocentesis. This issue was brought to national attention with a startling statistic reported out of a seminar held in Delhi in 1985. Of 3,000 abortions carried out after sex determination through amniocentesis, only one involved a male fetus. As a result of these developments, the government of the state of Maharashtra banned sex determination tests except those carried out in government hospitals.

The phenomenon of dowry-death presents a difficult problem for the ethnologist. Ethnological theory, with its residual functionalist cast, still does not deal effectively with the social costs of institutions of what might be arguably referred to as custom gone bad, resulting in a culturally constituted violence syndrome.

This essay examines dowry and its violent aspects, and some of the public solutions developed to deal with it in India. Our work consists of a meta-analysis of some available literature. We critique the legal mechanisms established to regulate the cultural institution of dowry and the resultant social evils engendered by the institution, and argue that policies directed against these social evils need to be constructed in terms of an underlying cause rather than of the problem itself. We consider cause, an aspect of the problem infrequently discussed in public debate. As Saini asserts, "legal academicians have shown absolutely no interest in the causal roots of dowry as practiced in contemporary India" (1983:143).

THE INSTITUTION

Since ancient times, the marriage of Hindus has required the transfer of property from the family of the bride to the family of the groom. Dowry or *daan dehej* is thought by some to be sanctioned by such religious texts as the *Manusmriti*. Seen in this way, dowry is a religious obligation of the father of a woman and a matter of *dharma* (religious duty) whereby authority over a woman is transferred from her father to her husband. This transfer takes different forms in different communities in modern India (Tambiah 1973). In public discussion, the term "dowry" covers a wide range of traditional payments and expenses, some presented to the groom's family and others to be retained by the bride. Customs have changed through time. The financial burdens of gifts and the dowry payments per se are exacerbated by the many expenses associated with the marriage celebration itself, but dowry payment is especially problematic because of its open-ended nature. As Tambiah notes, "marriage payments in India usually comprise an elaborate series of payments back and forth between the marrying families" and "this series extends over a long period of time and persists after marriage" (1973:92). Contemporary cases such as the death of Mrs. Sunita, often revolve around such continued demands.

A daughter's marriage takes a long time to prepare and involves the development of an adaptive strategy on the part of her family. An important part of the strategy is the preparation for making dowry payments; family consumption may be curtailed so as to allow accumulation of money for dowry. Seeing to marriage arrangements may be an important aspect of retirement planning. The dowries that the family receives on behalf of their sons may be "rolled over" to deal with the daughter's requirements. Families attempt to cultivate in both their sons and daughters attributes that will make them more attractive in marriage negotiations. Many things besides dowry are considered in negotiations: "non-economic" factors have demonstrable effect on the expectations for dowry and the family's strategy concerning the dowry process.

Education is a variable to be considered in the negotiation process. Education of young women is somewhat problematic because suitable husbands for such women must also be college educated. The parents of such young men demand more dowry for their sons. A consideration in sending a young woman to college will therefore be her parents' capacity to dower her adequately so as to obtain an appropriate groom. In any case, education is secondary to a man's earning power and the reputation of a woman's family. Education is, however, important in the early stages of negotiation because of the need to coordinate the level of the education of the men and women. Education qualifications are also less ambiguously defined than other dimensions of family reputation. Physical attractiveness is a consideration, but it is thought somewhat unseemly to emphasize this aspect of the decision.

Advertisements in newspapers are used for establishing marriage proposals (Aluwalia 1969, Niehoff 1959, Weibe and Ramu 1971), but contacts are more typically established through kin and other networks. Some marriages may be best termed "self-arranged," and are usually called "love marriages." In these cases, young men and women may develop a relationship independent of their families and then ask that negotiations be carried out on their behalf by family representatives.

Analysis of matrimonial advertisements shows some of the attributes considered to be important. Listed in such advertisements are education, age, income and occupation, physical attributes, *gotra* (a kind of unilineal descent group) membership, family background, place of residence, personality features, consideration of dowry, time and type of marriage, and language.

Consideration of dowry and other expenditures are brought out early in the negotiations and can serve as a stumbling block. Dowry negotiations can go on for some time. The last stage is the actual "seeing of the groom" and the "seeing of the bride," both rather fleeting encounters whose position at the end of the process indicates their relative lack of importance.

Marriage is a process by which two families mutually evaluate each other. The outcome of the negotiations is an expression of the relative worth of the two persons, a man and a woman, and, by extension, the worth of their respective families. This estimation of worth is expressed in marriage expenditures, of which dowry is but a part. There are three possible types of expenditures: cash gifts, gifts of household goods, and expenditures on the wedding celebration itself. The cash gift component of the dowry goes to the groom's father and comes to be part of his common household fund. The household goods are for use by the groom's household, although they may be used to establish a separate household for the newlyweds. When separate accommodations are not set up, the groom's family may insist that the goods do not duplicate things they already have.

Dates for marriages are set through consideration of horoscopes; horoscopy is done by professional astrologers (*pandits*). This practice leads to a concentration of marriage dates and consequent high demand for marriage goods and services at certain times of the year. During marriage seasons, the cost of jewelry, furniture, clothes, musicians' services and other marriage related expenditures goes up, presumably because of the concentration of the demand caused by the astrologers.

The expenditures required of the woman's family for the wedding in general and the dowry in particular are frequently massive. Paul reports, for a middle-class Delhi neighborhood, that most dowries were over 50,000 Rs. (1986). Srinivas comments that dowries over 200,000 Rs. are not uncommon (1984).[1]

ETHNOLOGICAL THEORIES ABOUT DOWRY

Dowry had traditionally been discussed by ethnologists in the context of the functionalist paradigm, and much theorizing about dowry appears to be concerned with explaining the "contribution" that the institution makes to social adaptation. The early theoretician Westermarck interpreted dowry as a social marker of the legitimacy of spouse and offspring, and as a mechanism for defining women's social roles and property rights in the new household (Westermarck 1921:428).

Murdock suggests that dowry may confirm the contract of marriage (1949). Dowry is interpreted by Friedl as a means to adjust a woman to her affinal home as it rearranges social relationships including the social separation of the man from his parents (1967). Dowry payments are public expressions of the new relationship between the two families, and of the social status of the bride and groom.

Dowry is seen in the social science literature as a kind of antemortem or anticipated inheritance by which a widow is assured of support, and provision for her offspring (Friedl 1967; Goody 1973, 1976). It transfers money to where the women will be and where they will reproduce; as a result, resources are also placed where the children will benefit, given the practice of patrilineal inheritance of immovable, economically valuable property like farm land.

In India, dowry is also seen as an expression of the symbolic order of society. According to Dumont, dowry expresses the hierarchal relations of marriage in India and lower status of the bride (Dumont 1957). The amount of dowry given is an expression of prestige. The capacity to buy prestige through dowry increases the potential for social mobility (Goody 1973). Dowry is a kind of delayed consumption used to demonstrate or improve social rank (Epstein 1960).

There is a significant discontinuity between discussions of dowry in the ethnological theory and in public discourse. Certainly the dowry problem does appear in the writing of contemporary ethnologists, but it is simply lamented and left largely uninterpreted and unexplained.

THE EXTANT SOLUTIONS TO THE PROBLEM

The Dowry Prohibition Act of 1961, as amended in 1984 and 1986, is the primary legal means for regulating the dowry process and controlling its excesses. The laws against dowry are tough. Dowry demand offenses are "cognizable" (require no warrant) and non-bailable, and the burden of proof is on the accused. There are, in fact, convictions under the law.

The act defines dowry as "any property of valuable security given or agreed to be given either directly or indirectly—(a) by one party to a marriage to the other party to a marriage; or (b) by parents of either party to a marriage or by any other person, to either party to the marriage or to any other person" (Government of India 1986:1). The act makes it illegal to give or take dowry, "If any person after the commencement of this act, gives or takes or abets the giving or taking of dowry, he shall be punishable with imprisonment for a term which shall be not less than five years; and with fine which shall not be less than fifteen thousand rupees or the amount of the value of such

dowry which ever is more" (Government of India 1986:1). While this section unambiguously prohibits dowry, the third section allows wedding presents to be freely given. Thus the law does not apply to "presents which are given at the time of marriage to the bride (without demand having been made in that behalf)" (Government of India 1986:1). Identical provisions apply to the groom. Furthermore, all such presents must be listed on a document before the consummation of the marriage. The list is to contain a brief description and estimation of the value of the gifts, name of presenting person, and the relationship that person has with the bride and groom. This regulation also provides "that where such presents are made by or on the behalf of the bride or any other person related to the bride, such presents are of a customary nature and the value thereof is not excessive having regard to the financial status of the person by whom, or on whose behalf, such presents are given" (Government of India 1986:2). Amendments made in 1984 make it illegal for a person to demand dowry with the same penalty as under the earlier "giving and taking" provision. It was also declared illegal to advertise for dowry, such an offense being defined as not bailable, with the burden of proof on the accused person.

This legislation was coupled with some changes in the Indian Penal Code that legally established the concept of "dowry death." That is, "where the death of a woman is caused by any burns or bodily injury or occurs otherwise than under normal circumstances within seven years of her marriage and it is shown that soon before her death she was subjected to cruelty or harassment by her husband or any relative of her husband for, or in connection with, any demand for dowry, such death shall be called 'dowry death,' and such husband or relative shall be deemed to have caused her death" (Government of India 1987:4). The Indian Evidence Act of 1871 was changed so as to allow for the presumption of guilt under the circumstances outlined above. Changes in the code allowed for special investigation and reporting procedures of deaths by apparent suicide of women within seven years of marriage if requested by a relative. There were also newly defined special provisions for autopsies.

To this point, however, these legal mechanisms have proved ineffective. According to Sivaramayya, the "act has signally failed in its operation" (1984:66). Menon refers to the "near total failure" of the law (1988:12). A similar viewpoint is expressed by Srinivas, who wrote, "The Dowry Prohibition Act of 1961 has been unanimously declared to be an utterly ineffective law" (1984:29).

In addition to the legal attack on dowry abuses, numerous public groups engage in public education campaigns. In urban settings, the most noteworthy of these groups are specialized research units such as the

Special Cell for Women of the Tata Institute of Social Sciences (Bombay), and the Center for Social Research (New Delhi). Also involved in the effort are private voluntary organizations such as the Crimes Against Women Cell, Karmika, and Sukh Shanti.

These groups issue public education advertising on various feminist issues. The anti-dowry advertisement of the Federation of Indian Chambers of Commerce and Industry Ladies Organization exemplifies the thrust of these campaigns. In the following advertisement, which was frequently run in the winter of 1988 in newspapers such as the *Times of India*, a photograph of a doll dressed in traditional Indian bridal attire was shown in flames.

> Every time a young bride dies because of dowry demands, we are all responsible for her death. Because we allow it to happen. Each year in Delhi hospitals alone, over 300 brides die of third degree burns. And many more deaths go unreported. Most of the guilty get away. And we just shrug helplessly and say, "what can we do?" We can do a lot.
>
> Help create social condemnation of dowry. Refuse to take or give dowry. Protest when you meet people who condone the practice. Reach out and help the girl being harassed for it. Act now.
>
> Let's fight it together.
>
> As parents, bring up educated, self-reliant daughters. Make sure they marry only after 18. Oppose dowry; refuse to even discuss it. If your daughter is harassed after marriage stand by her.
>
> As young men and women, refuse marriage proposals where dowry is being considered. As friends and neighbors, ostracize families who give or take dowry. Reach out to help victims of dowry harassment.
>
> As legislators and jurists, frame stronger laws. Ensure speedy hearings, impose severe punishments. As associations, give help and advice. Take up the challenge of changing laws and attitudes of society. Let us all resolve to fight the evil. If we fight together we can win.
>
> SAY NO TO DOWRY.

Also engaged in anti-dowry work are peasant political action groups such as Bharatiya Kisan Union (BKU). BKU consists of farmers from western Uttar Pradesh whose political program is focused more generally on agricultural issues. The group sponsored a massive 25-day demonstration at Meerut, Uttar Pradesh, in 1988. The leadership used the demonstration to announce a social reform program, most of it dealing with marriage issues. According to news service reports, "The code of social reforms includes fixing the maximum number of persons in a marriage party at 11, no feasts relating to marriage, and no dowry except 10 grams of gold and 30 grams of silver" (*Times of India*, February 11, 1988). Buses plying rural roads in western Uttar Pradesh are reported to have been painted with the slogan "The bride is the dowry."

Private campaigns against dowry occur in the countryside as well as among the urban elites, although it is likely that the underlying motivations are quite different.

POLICY ANALYSIS

Our argument is based on the assumption that social problems are best dealt with by policies directed at the correction of causative factors, rather than at the amelioration of symptoms. While current legal remedies directly confront dowry violence, the linkage between cause and the problematic behavior is not made. Here we develop an argument consisting of three components: women's access to production roles and property; delocalization of social control; and economic transformation of society. The pattern of distribution of aspects of the institution of dowry and its attendant problems is important to this analysis. Although dowry practices and the related crimes against women are distributed throughout Indian society, the distribution is patterned in terms of geography, caste rank, socioeconomic rank, urban/rural residence, and employment status of the women. In some places and among some people there is demonstrably more violence, more intensity of dowry practices, and more commitment to dowry itself. Much of the distributional data are problematic in one way or another. The most frequent problem is that the studies are not based on national samples. Furthermore, the interpretation of results is often colored by reformist agendas. There is a tendency to deemphasize differences in frequency from one segment of the population to another so as to build support of dowry death as a general social reform issue. Nevertheless, while the data available for these distributions are of inconsistent quality, they are interpretable in terms of our problem.

Women's Access to Production Roles and Property

Dowry violence is most frequent in north India. Some say that it is an especially severe problem in the Hindi Belt (i.e., Uttar Pradesh, Haryana, Punjab, Delhi, Bihar) (Government of India 1974:75). It is a lesser, albeit increasing problem in the south. There is also a north/south difference in the marriage institution itself. To simplify somewhat, in the north hypergamy is sought after in marriage alliances, in which case brides seek grooms from higher rank descent groups within their caste group (Srinivas 1984). In the south, marriages are more typically isogamous.

The literature comparing north and south India indicates important contrasts at both the ecological and the institutional levels. Based on conceptions developed by Boserup (1970) in a cross-cultural comparative framework on the relationship between the farming system and occupational role of women, Miller (1981) composed a model for explaining the significant north-south differences in the juvenile sex ratio [the ratio of males to females ten years of age and below]. The farming systems of the north are based on "dry-field plow cultivation," whereas in the south the farming systems are dominated by "swidden and wet-rice cultivation" (Miller 1981:28). These two systems make different labor demands. In the wet rice or swidden systems of the south, women are very important sources of labor. In the north, women's involvement in agricultural production is limited. According to Miller, women in the north are excluded from property holding and receive instead a "dowry of movables." In the south, where women are included in the production activities, they may receive "rights to land" (Miller 1981:28). In the north, women are high-cost items of social overhead, while in the south, women contribute labor and are more highly valued. In the north there is a "high cost of raising several daughters" while in the south there is "little liability in raising several daughters." There is thus "discrimination against daughters" and an "intense preference for sons" in the north, and "appreciation for daughters" and "moderate preference for sons" in the south. Miller thus explains the unbalanced-toward-males juvenile sex ratios of the north and the balanced sex ratios of the south (Miller 1981:27–28). The lower economic value of women in the north is expressed in differential treatment of children by sex. Females get less food, less care, and less attention, and therefore they have a higher death rate. In general the Boserup and Miller economic argument is consistent with Engels's thesis about the relationship between the subordination of women and property (Engels 1884, Hirschon 1984:1).

Miller extended her analysis of juvenile sex ratios to include marriage costs (including dowry), female labor participation, and property owning, and found that property owning was associated with high marriage costs and low female labor force participation, both of which were associated with high juvenile sex ratios. That is, the death rate of females is higher when marriage costs are high and women are kept from remunerative employment. Both of these patterns are associated with the "propertied" segment of the population (Miller 1981:156–159). Her data are derived from the secondary analysis of ethnographic accounts. The literature concerning the distribution of dowry practices and dowry death is consistent with these results.

Miller's analysis shows a general pattern of treatment of females in India. Their access to support in various forms is related to their contribution to production (Miller 1981). This analysis does not explain

the problem of dowry violence, but it does demonstrate a fundamental pattern within which dowry violence can be interpreted.

The distribution of dowry varies by caste. In her study of dowry violence victims in Delhi, Kumari found that members of the lower ranking castes report less "dowry harassment" than do those in higher ranking castes (Kumari 1988:31). These results are consistent with Miller's argument since the pattern of exclusion of women from economic production roles varies by caste. Women of lower castes are less subject to restrictions concerning employment outside the realm of reproduction within the household. These women are often poor and uneducated, and are subject to other types of restrictions.

In the framework of caste, dowry practices of higher caste groups are emulated by lower caste groups. This process is known as "Sanskritization" and it may relate to the widely held view that dowry harassment is increasing in lower ranking castes. Sanskritization is the process by which lower ranked caste groups attempt to raise their rank through the emulation of higher rank castes. The emulation involves discarding certain behaviors (such as eating meat or paying bride price) and adopting alternatives (Srinivas 1969). Attitudinal research shows that people of the lower socio-economic strata have a greater commitment to dowry than do those of higher strata (Hooja 1969, Khanna and Verghese 1978, Paul 1986). Although the lower and middle classes are committed to dowry, the associated violence, including higher death rates, is more typically a middle class problem (Kumari 1988).

Employment status of women has an effect on dowry. In her survey of dowry problems in a south Delhi neighborhood, Paul (1986) found that the amount of dowry was less for employed middle class women than it was for the unemployed. This pattern is also suggested by Verghese (1980) and van der Veen (1972:40), but disputed by others (Murickan 1975). This link is also manifested among tribal people undergoing urbanization. Tribal people, ranked more toward the low end of the social hierarchy, typically make use of bride price (i.e., a payment to the bride's family) rather than dowry (Karve 1953). As these groups become more integrated into national life, they will shift to dowry practices to emulate high castes while their women participate less in gainful employment (Luthra 1983). Croll finds a similar relationship in her analysis of post-revolutionary China. She says, "it is the increased value attributed to women's labor which is largely responsible for the decline in the dowry" (1984:58).

Both Kumari (1988) and Srinivas (1984) developed arguments based on non-economic factors. Kumari in effect indicated that if dowry could be explained in economic terms, marriage would be simply a calculation of the value of a woman: if the value were high, bride price would be paid, and if the value were low, dowry transactions would occur. This formulation was presented as a refutation of Madan's dowry-as-compensation argument (Kumari 1988). We agree that reducing this practice to purely economic terms is an absurdity. The argument is not purely economic, but it is certainly consistent with a cultural materialist perspective (Harris 1979) in which symbolic values are shaped by an underlying material relationship that is the basis for the construction of cultural reality.

Delocalization of Social Control

Dowry violence is more frequent in cities (Saini 1983). Delhi has the reputation of having a high frequency of problems of dowry (Srinivas 1984:7). The urban-rural distribution pattern may be a manifestation of the effects of the delocalization of dowry. Dowry, when operative in the relationships among local caste groups in related villages, was to an extent self-regulating through caste *panchayats* (councils) and by the joint families themselves. These groups easily reach into peoples' lives. By contrast, the national level laws have inadequate reach and cannot achieve regulation. While in some areas caste groups continue to function to limit abuses, these groups are less effective in urban settings. Population movements and competition with state level social control mechanisms limit the effectiveness of self-regulation. A government commission study of women's status argues "that because of changed circumstances in which a son generally has a separate establishment and has a job somewhere away from home, the parents cannot expect much help from him, and so they consider his marriage as the major occasion on which their investment in his education can be recovered" (Government of India 1974:74). These views are consistent with the research results reported by Paul, who demonstrates that dowry amounts are higher among people who have migrated to Delhi and those who live in nuclear families, because the families in general and the women in particular are less subject to social constraints (Paul 1986). New brides do not seem to have adequate support networks in urban settings.

Economic Transformation of Society

The custom of dowry has been thrown into disarray by inflationary pressures. The consumer price index for urban non-manual workers has increased from its reference year of 1960 value of 100 to 532 for 1984–85 (Government of India 1987). The media of dowry exchange have changed dramatically because of the increasing availability of consumer goods. It has become increasingly difficult to prepare for giving dowry for a daughter or a sister. Sharma argues that, in part, dowry problems are caused by rapid change in the nature of consumer goods which made it no longer possible to accumulate gift goods over a long period as the latest styles in material goods could not be presented (1984: 70–71).

The current regime of individual dowry seeking and giving is constituted as a kind of rational behavior. That is, it is achieved through choice, is consistent with certain values, and serves to increase someone's utility. There are a number of things sought by the groom's family in these transactions. Wealth and family prestige are especially important. The family prestige "bought" with marriage expenditures, which is relevant to both the bride and groom's side in the transaction, is no doubt very much worth maximizing in the Indian context. From the perspective of the bride's family, dowry payments involve trading present consumption for future earning power for their daughter through acquiring a groom with better qualities and connections. In a two-tier, gender segregated, high unemployment, inflationary economy such as that of India, one can grasp the advantage of investing in husbands with high future earning potential. It is also possible to argue that in societies with symbolic mechanisms of stratification, it is expected that persons will attempt to make public displays of consumption in order to improve their overall performance and so to take advantage of the ambiguities of the status hierarchy system. The demand for both symbolic goods and future earnings is highly elastic. Family connections, education, and wealth seem especially important in India, and they all serve as hedges against inflation and poverty. With women having limited access to jobs and earning lower pay, it is rational to invest in a share of the groom's prospects. If you ask people why they give dowry when their daughters are being married they say, "because we love them." On the other hand, grooms' families will find the decision to forgo dowry very difficult.

SUMMARY

The distributional data indicate that the relationship between the way females are treated in marriage and their participation in economic production is consistent with Miller's development of the Boserup hypothesis. It is assumed that the pattern of maltreatment of females has been subject to various controls operating at the levels of family, caste, and community. Urbanization reduces the effectiveness of these mechanisms, thus increasing the intensity of the problem. This trend is exacerbated by the economic transformations within contemporary Indian society. It is our viewpoint that policies developed to reduce dowry-related violence will fail if they do not increase the economic value of women.

The criminalization of dowry may have been a politically useful symbol, but it has not curtailed the practice. As dowry is attacked, the state has not adequately dealt with the ante-mortem inheritance aspect of the custom. If dowry continues to provide a share of the family wealth to daughters before the death of the parents, then legally curtailing the practice is likely to damage the economic interests of women in the name of protecting them. One might argue that the primary legal remedy for the dowry problem actually makes it worse because it limits the transfer of assets to women. Perhaps this is why research on attitudes toward dowry indicates a continued positive commitment to the institution (Mathew 1987). India is a society in which most people (most particularly the elite) have given and received dowry; most people are even today giving and taking dowries. Declaring dowry a crime creates a condition in which the mass of society are technically criminals. The moral-legal basis of society suffers, and communal, parochial, and other fissiparous forces are encouraged.

To be effective, anti-dowry legislation must make sure that the social utility provided by dowry practices be displaced to practices that are less problematic, and that the apparent causes of the practice be attacked. To do so would mean that attempts to eradicate the social evils produced by the dowry institution need to be based on an examination of women's property rights so as to increase their economic access. Traditional Hindu customs associated with inheritance give sons the right from birth to claim the so-called ancestral properties. This principle is part of the Mitakshara tradition of Hindu law, which prevails throughout India except in Bengal, Kerala, Assam, and northern parts of Orissa. These properties are obtained from father, paternal grandfather, or paternal great-grandfather. According to Sivaramayya (1984:71), "The Hindu Succession Act (the law which controls inheritance) did not abrogate this right by birth which exists in favor of a son, paternal grandson and paternal great grandson. The availability of the right in favor of these male descendants only is a discrimination against daughters." The right is derived from ancient texts. According to Tambiah (1973:95), the Dharmasastras provide that it is "essentially males who inherit the patrimony while women are entitled to maintenance, marriage expenses and gifts." While the Hindu Succession Act abrogates much traditional law, it specifically accepts the principle of male birth right to the property of the joint family. That is, "When a male Hindu dies after the commencement of the Act, having at the time of death an interest in a Mitakshara coparcenary property, his

interest in the property shall devolve by survivorship upon the surviving members of the coparcenary and not in accordance with this Act" (Government of India 1985:3). The Hindu Succession Act in its most recent form provides for the intestate or testamentary inheritance of a female of a share of the family property. Yet the prior right of males at birth is not abrogated. Hindu males own a share of the family rights at birth; females can inherit it. Testamentary succession overrides the principle of intestate succession, and therefore the interests of females can be usurped simply by writing a will. The other procedures for a female to renounce an interest in family property are very simple. Moreover, according to Sivaramayya (1984:58), "no specific formality is required for the relinquishment of the interest beyond the expression of a clear intention to that effect." Instruments of relinquishment can be and are forged.

The antemortem inheritance function of dowry has been eroded or perhaps supplanted by transfer of goods to the groom's family for their consumption and the expression of the so-called prestige of the family. Indeed social science commentary on dowry in India suggests that this aspect of dowry is relatively unimportant in any case because only a small portion of the total marriage expenditure is under the bride's control. There is evidence that even the clothing and ornaments and other personal property of the bride are being usurped (Verghese 1980). Implementation of a gender-neutral inheritance law as advocated by the Government of India Committee on the Status of Women may serve to increase the economic value of women in general, while it serves as an alternative to the ante-mortem inheritance aspect of dowry. Since dowry constitutes a kind of ante-mortem inheritance, it is logical to change the inheritance laws in conjunction with the restrictions on dowry behavior. Sisters as well as brothers need to have a share in the family wealth from birth, and that right should be associated with legal procedures that increase the difficulty of alienation of property rights. There is no question that such a procedure would serve to erode the stability of the patrilineal family by diluting its economic base.

The Government of India has passed legislation such as the Hindu Succession Act (1956) and the Hindu Adoption and Maintenance Act (1956), both of which inter-alia provide for a woman's right of inheritance from her father. For example, under the Adoption and Maintenance Act, a woman has a claim of rights of maintenance from her husband's father in case she is widowed. Moreover, she has the right to claim inheritance from her deceased husband's estate. In spite of these changes, inheritance provisions are quite different for males and females. The Chief Justice of the Supreme Court of India, Honorable Mr. Justice Y. V. Chandrachud, wrote that in spite of changes, "some inequalities like the right of birth in favor of a son, paternal grandson and paternal great grandson still persist" (1984:vii). Provision of females with equal rights to inherit ancestral property from birth, or from a bequest, or at the death may reduce dowry problems. Furthermore, property that is allowed to remain in the name of the deceased for any length of time, as is frequently the case in India, should revert to the state. As it stands, property may remain in the name of a deceased ancestor, while his descendants divide it informally among themselves.

The establishment of a gender-neutral inheritance law represents a significant shift in public policy. We argue that there is a link between pro-male property laws and violence toward women. While we assert this position, we also need to recognize that the property laws give coherence and stability to an essential Indian institution, the joint family. The Mitakshara principle of male inheritance rights is both a reflection and a cause of family solidarity. Modifying this principle in an attempt to reduce violence toward women could have a deleterious effect on family coherence. In addition, the fundamental nature of these institutions makes it inconceivable that there would be substantial resistance to these changes. Yet if one considers this issue in historic terms, it is apparent that during the 20th century, legal change is in the direction of gender neutrality, a process that started with the Hindu Law of Inheritance (Amendment) Act (1929) and the Hindu Succession Act (1956), and continues through judicial decisions to the present (Diwan 1988:384). As Diwan notes in reference to the changes brought by the Hindu Succession Act of 1956, "the Mitakshara bias towards preference of males over females and of agnates over cognates has been considerably whittled down" (1988:358). Such change is not easy. The changes brought with the Hindu Succession Act in 1956 were achieved only after overcoming "stiff resistance from the traditionalists" (Government of India 1974:135). The same report states, "The hold of tradition, however, was so strong that even while introducing sweeping changes, the legislators compromised and retained in some respects the inferior position of women" (Government of India 1974:135). It must be remembered that the texts that are the foundations of contemporary law include legislation (such as the Hindu Succession Act itself), case law, and religious texts, so that the constitutional question is also a question for religious interpretation, despite the constitutional commitment to secularism.

We are advocating further steps toward gender neutrality of the inheritance laws so that women and men will receive an equal share under intestate succession, and have an equal chance to be testamentary heirs. The law should thus be gender-neutral while still permitting a range of decisions allowing property to stay in a male line if the holder of the property so chooses. The required social adjustment could be largely achieved through the decisions of a family, backed by the power of the state. Families could express their preferences, but the state would not serve to protect the economic interests of males. The process could involve the concept of birthright as well as succession at death. We do not choose to engage those arguments, but do point out that the rapid aging of the Indian population may suggest that a full abrogation of the Mitakshara principle of birthright would be the best social policy because doing so would give older people somewhat greater control over their property in an economy virtually devoid of public investment in social services for older people (Bose and Gangrade 1988, Sharma and Dak 1987).

There are precedents for such policy at the state level. In Andhra Pradesh, the Hindu Succession Act was amended to provide for a female's birthright interest in the Mitakshara property. In Kerala, the Mitakshara property concept was legally abrogated altogether. Other gender asymmetries in the laws of India need to be attacked. The overall goal of policy should be to increase the economic value of women.

Ethnological theory directs our attention to social recognition of marriage and property transfer as functionally important features of the institution. The state can provide a means of socially recognizing marriage through registration and licensure. The law expresses no explicit preference for traditional marriage ritual, and it is possible to have a civil marriage under the provisions of the Special Marriage Act (1954) through registration with a magistrate. Nevertheless, this system co-exists parallel with the traditional system of marriage, which is beyond the reach of state control. Other marriages may be registered under this act if the persons involved so choose, and if a ceremony has been carried out. These special marriages are an alternative to an unregistered marriage.

We conclude that a useful mechanism for state control of dowry problems is the establishment of universal marriage registration, which does not exist at the present time. Marriage registration is also called for by the first Round Table on Social Audit of Implementation of Dowry Legislation (Bhatia 1988), which may serve to provide some monitoring of dowry abuses and perhaps to manifest the state's interest in an effective marriage institution. It would be naive to assume that such a policy would be widely honored, but as it is, low-income persons do not get married because they do not have the resources for marriage under the traditional non-state controlled regime. There are numerous reform groups that organize mass marriage ceremonies of village people so as to help them escape the burden of marriage expenditures. The point is that compliance is a large problem even under current circumstances.

In conclusion, we feel that the causes of the dowry problems are a product of the low economic value of women, loss of effective social control of abuse through delocalization, and pressures caused by economic transformation. The traditional family, caste group, and community controls which have been reduced in effectiveness should be replaced by state functions. The foundation of state control is universal marriage registration and licensure. The impact of the economic value of women on the problem is indicated by the transition from bride price to dowry among tribal people. It is also associated with a reduction in the extent of gainful employment and lower dowry amounts demonstrated for employed women. A broad program to increase the economic value of women would be the most useful means of dealing with the problem of dowry. Further restrictions on dowry without providing for a radically different property right for females is probably not in the interests of Indian women, since dowry represents ante-mortem inheritance. This underlying paradox may explain the commitment to dowry revealed in attitudinal research with Indian women, even though it is also an important feminist issue. The alternatives include the abolishment of the legal basis for the joint family as a corporate unit as has been done in Kerala, or the legal redefinition of the joint family as economically duolineal, as has occurred in Andhra Pradesh.

NOTE

1. For purposes of comparison, a mid-career Indian academic might be paid 60,000 Rs. per year.

REFERENCES

Aluwalia, H. 1969. Matrimonial Advertisements in Panjab. *Indian Journal of Social Work* 30:55–65.

Bhatia, S. C. 1988. Social Audit of Dowry Legislation. Delhi: Legal Literacy Project.

Bose, A. B., and K. D. Gangrade. 1988. *The Aging in India, Problems and Potentialities*. New Delhi: Abhinav.

Boserup, Ester. 1970. *Women's Role in Economic Development*. New York: St. Martin's Press.

Chandrachud, Y. V. 1984. Foreword. In *Inequalities and the Law*. B. Sivaramayya, ed. Pp. iv–vi. Lucknow: Eastern Book Company.

Croll, Elisabeth. 1984. The Exchange of Women and Property: Marriage in Post-revolutionary China. In *Women and Property—Women as Property*. Renee Hirschon, ed. Pp. 44–61. London/New York: Croom Helm/St. Martin's Press.

Diwan, Paras. 1988. *Modern Hindu Law, Codified and Uncodified*. Allahabad: Allahabad Law Agency.

Dumont, Louis. 1957. *Hierarchy and Marriage Alliance in South Indian Kinship*. London: Royal Anthropological Institute.

Engels, Fredrich. 1884. *The Origin of Family, Private Property and the State*. New York: International.

Epstein, T. Scarlett. 1960. Peasant Marriage in South India. *Man in India* 40:192–232.

Friedl, Ernestine. 1967. *Vasilika, A Village in Modern Greece*. New York: Holt, Rinehart and Winston.

Goody, Jack. 1973. Bridewealth and Dowry in Africa and Eurasia. In *Bridewealth and Dowry*. Jack Goody and S. J. Tambiah, eds. Pp. 1–58. Cambridge: Cambridge University Press.

———. 1976. *Production and Reproduction, A Comparative Study of the Domestic Domain*. Cambridge: Cambridge University Press.

Government of India. 1974. *Towards Equality: Report of the Committee on the Status of Women*. New Delhi: Government of India, Ministry of Education and Social Welfare.

———. 1985. The Hindu Succession Act. New Delhi: Government of India.

———. 1986. The Dowry Prohibition Act, 1961 (Act No. 28 of 1961) and Connected Legislation (as on 15th January, 1986). New Delhi: Government of India.

———. 1987. *India 1986, A Reference Manual*. Delhi: Ministry of Information and Broadcasting.

Harris, Marvin. 1979. *Cultural Materialism: The Struggle for a Science of Culture*. New York: Random House.

Hirschon, Renee. 1984. Introduction: Property, Power and Gender Relations. In *Women and Property—Women as Property*. Renee Hirschon, ed. Pp. 1–22. London/New York: Croom Helm/St. Martin's Press.

Hooja, S. L. 1969. *Dowry System in India*. New Delhi: Asia Press.

Karve, Irawati. 1953. *Kinship Organization in India*. Bombay: Asia Publishing.

Khanna, G. and M. Verghese. 1978. *Indian Women Today*. New Delhi: Vikas Publishing House.

Kumari, Ranjana. 1988. Practice and Problems of Dowry: A Study of Dowry Victims in Delhi. In *Social Audit of Dowry Legislation*. S. C. Bhatia, ed. Pp. 27–37. Delhi: Legal Literacy Project.

Luthra, A. 1983. Dowry Among the Urban Poor, Perception and Practice. *Social Action* 33:207.

Mathew, Anna. 1987. Attitudes Toward Dowry. *Indian Journal of Social Work* 48:95–102.

Menon, N. R. Madhava. 1988. The Dowry Prohibition Act: Does the Law Provide the Solution or Itself Constitute the Problem? In *Social Audit of Dowry Legislation*. S. C. Bhatia, ed. Pp. 11–26. Delhi: Legal Literacy Project.

Miller, Barbara D. 1981. *The Endangered Sex, Neglect of Female Children in Rural North India*. Ithaca, NY: Cornell University Press.

Murdock, George P. 1949. *Social Structure*. New York: Macmillan.

Murickan, J. 1975. Women in Kerala: Changing Socio-economic Status and Self Image. In *Women in Contemporary India*. A. de Souza, ed. Pp. 73–95. Delhi: Manohar.

Niehoff, Arthur H. 1959. A Study of Matrimonial Advertisements in North India. *Eastern Anthropologist* 12:37–50.

Paul, Madan C. 1986. *Dowry and the Position of Women in India. A Study of Delhi Metropolis*. New Delhi: Inter India Publishers.

Saini, Debi. 1983. Dowry Prohibition Law, Social Change and Challenges in India. *Indian Journal of Social Work* 44(2):143–147.

Sharma, M. L. and T. Dak. 1987. *Aging in India, Challenge for the Society*. Delhi: Ajanta Publications.

Sharma, Ursula. 1984. Dowry in North India: Its Consequences for Women. In *Women and Property—Women as Property*. Renee Hirschon, ed. Pp. 62–74. London/New York: Croom Helm/St. Martin's Press.

Sivaramayya, B. 1984. *Inequalities and the Law*. Lucknow: Eastern Book Company.

Srinivas, M. N. 1969. *Social Change in Modern India*. Berkeley, CA: University of California Press.

———. 1984. *Some Reflections on Dowry*. Delhi: Oxford University Press.

Tambiah, S. J. 1973. Dowry and Bridewealth and the Property Rights of Women in South Asia. In *Bridewealth and Dowry*. Jack Goody and S. J. Tambiah, eds. Pp. 59–169. Cambridge: Cambridge University Press.

van der Veen, Klaus W. 1972. *I Give Thee My Daughter—A Study of Marriage and Hierarchy Among the Anavil Brahmins of South Gujarat*. Assen: Van Gorcum.

Verghese, Jamila. 1980. *Her Gold and Her Body*. New Delhi: Vikas Publishing House.

Weibe, P. O. and G. N. Ramu. 1971. A Content Analysis of Matrimonial Advertisements. *Man in India* 51:119–120.

Westermarck, Edward. 1921. *The History of Human Marriage*. London: MacMillan and Co.

31

The Kpelle Moot

James L. Gibbs, Jr.

Some scholars argue that law, like marriage, is a major institution found in all societies, although in widely divergent forms. Others argue that law exists only where some individual or group possesses the authority to impose punishments. Debates about what is and what isn't law aside, conflict exists in all societies. Further, all societies have culturally defined mechanisms by which people attempt to settle their differences.

Conflict-management procedures must be geared to meet the needs of particular social systems. In the urban centers of Western society, people live in faceless anonymity. Relations between people can be characterized as single interest. For example, generally a person's landlord is neither kin nor neighbor. The landlord–tenant relationship is not complicated by any other social bonds. A person who has a car accident is unlikely to have run into a friend or a relative. Our legal system, with its narrow focus on the grievance itself, fits our social system of one-dimensional relationships.

In small-scale social systems, people are often involved with one another on multiple levels. A landlord may also be a neighbor and a relative. In such settings, people are born, grow up, grow old, and die in the same community. Because their social relationships are long-term and highly valued, people in such communities need to resolve disputes in a way that maintains good relations.

Today in the United States, government agencies and grassroots organizations are establishing programs—Neighborhood Justice Centers or Dispute Resolution Centers—based on models of consensus and conciliation. According to the **Citizen's Dispute Resolution Handbook**, the potential of local-level conflict resolution was originally recognized in the work of an anthropologist who had described these processes in Africa.

As you read this selection, ask yourself the following questions:

☐ How are formal courtroom hearings different from moots?

☐ In what kinds of cases is the formal court effective and in what kinds is it ineffective?

☐ How is a mediator different from a judge?

☐ What is the function of the blessing at the beginning of the moot?

☐ In contrast to the official court, how does the procedure used during the moot facilitate harmony and reconciliation?

☐ Why does the author consider the moot therapeutic?

The following terms discussed in this selection are included in the Glossary at the back of the book:

clan
culture area
extended family
mediator
moot
multiplex relationship
palaver
patrilineal
single-interest relationship
social control

Reprinted from James L. Gibbs, "The Kpelle Moot," *Africa*, vol. 33, no. 1, 1963.

Africa as a major culture area has been characterized by many writers as being marked by a high development of law and legal procedures.[1] In the past few years research on African law has produced a series of highly competent monographs such as those on law among the Tiv, the Barotse, and the Nuer.[2] These and related shorter studies have focused primarily on formal processes for the settlement of disputes, such as those which take place in a courtroom, or those which are, in some other way, set apart from simpler measures of social control. However, many African societies have informal, quasi-legal, dispute-settlement procedures, supplemental to formal ones, which have not been as well studied, or—in most cases—adequately analysed.

In this paper I present a description and analysis of one such institution for the informal settlement of disputes, as it is found among the Kpelle of Liberia; it is the moot, the *bɛrɛi mu meni saa* or 'house palaver.' Hearings in the Kpelle moot contrast with those in a court in that they differ in tone and effectiveness. The genius of the moot lies in the fact that it is based on a covert application of the principles of psychoanalytic theory which underlie psychotherapy.

The Kpelle are a Mande-speaking, patrilineal group of some 175,000 rice cultivators who live in Central Liberia and the adjoining regions of Guinea. This paper is based on data gathered in a field study which I carried out in 1957 and 1958 among the Liberian Kpelle of Panta Chiefdom in north-east Central Province.

Strong corporate patrilineages are absent among the Kpelle. The most important kinship group is the virilocal polygynous family which sometimes becomes an extended family, almost always of the patrilineal variety. Several of these families form the core of a residential group, known as a village quarter, more technically, a clan-barrio.[3] This is headed by a quarter elder who is related to most of the household heads by real or putative patrilineal ties.

Kpelle political organization is centralized although there is no single king or paramount chief, but a series of chiefs of the same level of authority, each of whom is superordinate over district chiefs and town chiefs. Some political functions are also vested in the tribal fraternity, the Poro, which still functions vigorously. The form of political organization found in the area can thus best be termed the polycephalous associational state.

The structure of the Kpelle court system parallels that of the political organization. In Liberia the highest court of a tribal authority and the highest tribal court chartered by the Government is that of a paramount chief. A district chief's court is also an official court. Disputes may be settled in these official courts or in unofficial courts, such as those of town chiefs or quarter elders. In addition to this, grievances are settled informally in moots, and sometimes by associational groupings such as church councils or cooperative work groups.

In my field research I studied both the formal and informal methods of dispute settlement. The method used was to collect case material in as complete a form as possible. Accordingly, immediately after a hearing, my interpreter and I would prepare verbatim transcripts of each case that we heard. These transcripts were supplemented with accounts—obtained from respondents—of past cases or cases which I did not hear litigated. Transcripts from each type of hearing were analysed phrase by phrase in terms of a frame of reference derived from jurisprudence and ethno-law. The results of the analysis indicate two things: first, that courtroom hearings and moots are quite different in their procedures and tone, and secondly, why they show this contrast.

Kpelle courtroom hearings are basically coercive and arbitrary in tone. In another paper[4] I have shown that this is partly the result of the intrusion of the authoritarian values of the Poro into the courtroom. As a result, the court is limited in the manner in which it can handle some types of disputes. The court is particularly effective in settling cases such as assault, possession of illegal charms, or theft where the litigants are not linked in a relationship which must continue after the trial. However, most of the cases brought before a Kpelle court are cases involving disputed rights over women, including matrimonial matters which are usually cast in the form of suits for divorce. The court is particularly inept at settling these numerous matrimonial disputes because its harsh tone tends to drive spouses farther apart rather than to reconcile them. The moot, in contrast, is more effective in handling such cases. The following analysis indicates the reasons for this.[5]

The Kpelle *bɛrɛi mu meni saa*, or 'house palaver,' is an informal airing of a dispute which takes place before an assembled group which includes kinsmen of the litigants and neighbors from the quarter where the case is being heard. It is a completely *ad hoc* group, varying greatly in composition from case to case. The matter to be settled is usually a domestic problem: alleged mistreatment or neglect by a spouse, an attempt to collect money paid to a kinsman for a job which was not completed, or a quarrel among brothers over the inheritance of their father's wives.

In the procedural description which follows I shall use illustrative data from the Case of the Ousted Wife:

> Wama Nya, the complainant, had one wife, Yua. His older brother died and he inherited the widow, Yokpo, who moved into his house. The two women were classificatory sisters. After Yokpo moved in, there was strife in

the household. The husband accused her of staying out late at night, of harvesting rice without his knowledge, and of denying him food. He also accused Yokpo of having lovers and admitted having had a physical struggle with her, after which he took a basin of water and 'washed his hands of her.'

Yokpo countered by denying the allegations about having lovers, saying that she was accused falsely, although she had in the past confessed the name of one lover. She further complained that Wama Nya had assaulted her and, in the act, had committed the indignity of removing her headtie, and had expelled her from the house after the ritual hand-washing. Finally, she alleged that she had been thus cast out of the house at the instigation of the other wife who, she asserted, had great influence over their husband.

Kɔlɔ Waa, the Town Chief and quarter elder, and the brother of Yokpo, was the mediator of the moot, which decided that the husband was mainly at fault, although Yua and Yokpo's children were also in the wrong. Those at fault had to apologize to Yokpo and bring gifts of apology as well as local rum[6] for the disputants and participants in the moot.

The moot is most often held on a Sunday—a day of rest for Christians and non-Christians alike—at the home of the complainant, the person who calls the moot. The mediator will have been selected by the complainant. He is a kinsman who also holds an office such as town chief or quarter elder, and therefore has some skill in dispute settlement. It is said that he is chosen to preside by virtue of his kin tie, rather than because of his office.

The proceedings begin with the pronouncing of blessings by one of the oldest men of the group. In the Case of the Ousted Wife, Gbenai Zua, the elder who pronounced the blessings, took a rice-stirrer in his hand and, striding back and forth, said:

This man has called us to fix the matter between him and his wife. May ɤala (the supreme, creator deity) change his heart and let his household be in good condition. May ɤala bless the family and make them fruitful. May He bless them so they can have food this year. May He bless the children and the rest of the family so they may always be healthy. May He bless them to have good luck. When Wama Nya takes a gun and goes in the bush, may he kill big animals. May ɤala bless us to enjoy the meat. May He bless us to enjoy life and always have luck. May ɤala bless all those who come to discuss this matter.

The man who pronounces the blessings always carries a stick or a whisk (kpung) which he waves for effect as he paces up and down chanting his injunctions. Participation of spectators is demanded, for the blessings are chanted by the elder (kpung namu or 'kpung owner') as a series of imperatives, some of which he repeats. Each phrase is responded to by the spectators who answer in unison with a formal response, either e ka ti (so be it), or a low, drawn-out eeee. The kpung namu delivers his blessings faster and faster, building up a rhythmic interaction pattern with the other participants. The effect is to unite those attending in common action before the hearing begins. The blessing focuses attention on the concern with maintaining harmony and the well-being of the group as a whole.

Everyone attending the moot wears their next-to-best clothes or, if it is not Sunday, everyday clothes. Elders, litigants, and spectators sit in mixed fashion, pressed closely upon each other, often overflowing onto a veranda. This is in contrast to the vertical spatial separation between litigants and adjudicators in the courtroom. The mediator, even though he is a chief, does not wear his robes. He and the oldest men will be given chairs as they would on any other occasion.

The complainant speaks first and may be interrupted by the mediator or anyone else present. After he has been thoroughly quizzed, the accused will answer and will also be questioned by those present. The two parties will question each other directly and question others in the room also. Both the testimony and the questioning are lively and uninhibited. Where there are witnesses to some of the actions described by the parties, they may also speak and be questioned. Although the proceedings are spirited, they remain orderly. The mediator may fine anyone who speaks out of turn by requiring them to bring some rum for the group to drink.

The mediator and others present will point out the various faults committed by both the parties. After everyone has been heard, the mediator expresses the consensus of the group. For example, in the Case of the Ousted Wife, he said to Yua: 'The words you used towards your sister were not good, so come and beg her pardon.'

The person held to be mainly at fault will then formally apologize to the other person. This apology takes the form of the giving of token gifts to the wronged person by the guilty party. These may be an item of clothing, a few coins, clean hulled rice, or a combination of all three. It is also customary for the winning party in accepting the gifts of apology to give, in return, a smaller token such as a twenty-five cent piece[7] to show his 'white heart' or good will. The losing party is also lightly 'fined'; he must present rum or beer to the mediator and the others who heard the case. This is consumed by all in attendance. The old man then pronounces blessings again and offers thanks for the restoration of harmony within the group, and asks that all continue to act with good grace and unity.

An initial analysis of the procedural steps of the moot isolates the descriptive attributes of the moot and shows that they contrast with those of the courtroom hearing. While the airing of grievances is incomplete in courtroom hearings, it is more complete in the moot. This fuller airing of the issues results, in many marital cases, in a more harmonious solution. Several specific features of the house palaver facilitate this wider airing of grievances. First, the hearing takes place soon after a breach has occurred, before the grievances have hardened. There is no delay until the complainant has time to go to the paramount chief's or district chief's headquarters to institute suit. Secondly, the hearing takes place in the familiar surroundings of a home. The robes, writs, messengers, and other symbols of power which subtly intimidate and inhibit the parties in the courtroom, by reminding them of the physical force which underlies the procedures, are absent. Thirdly, in the courtroom the conduct of the hearing is firmly in the hands of the judge but in the moot the investigatory initiative rests much more with the parties themselves. Jurisprudence suggests that, in such a case, more of the grievances lodged between the parties are likely to be aired and adjusted. Finally, the range of relevance applied to matters which are brought out is extremely broad. Hardly anything mentioned is held to be irrelevant. This too leads to a more thorough ventilation of the issues.

There is a second surface difference between court and moot. In a courtroom hearing, the solution is, by and large, one which is imposed by the adjudicator. In the moot the solution is more consensual. It is, therefore, more likely to be accepted by both parties and hence more durable. Several features of the moot contribute to the consensual solution: first, there is no unilateral ascription of blame, but an attribution of fault to both parties. Secondly, the mediator, unlike the chief in the courtroom, is not backed by political authority and the physical force which underlies it. He cannot jail parties, nor can he levy a heavy fine. Thirdly, the sanctions which are imposed are not so burdensome as to cause hardship to the losing party or to give him or her grounds for a new grudge against the other party. The gifts for the winning party and the potables for the spectators are not as expensive as the fines and the court costs in a paramount chief's court. Lastly, the ritualized apology of the moot symbolizes very concretely the consensual nature of the solution.[8] The public offering and acceptance of the tokens of apology indicate that each party has no further grievances and that the settlement is satisfactory and mutually acceptable. The parties and spectators drink together to symbolize the restored solidarity of the group and the rehabilitation of the offending party.

This type of analysis describes the courtroom hearing and the moot, using a frame of reference derived from jurisprudence and ethno-law which is explicitly comparative and evaluative. Only by using this type of comparative approach can the researcher select features of the hearings which are not only unique to each of them, but theoretically significant in that their con-

tribution to the social-control functions of the proceedings can be hypothesized. At the same time, it enables the researcher to pin-point in procedures the cause for what he feels intuitively: that the two hearings contrast in tone, even though they are similar in some ways.

However, one can approach the transcripts of the trouble cases with a second analytical framework and emerge with a deeper understanding of the implications of the contrasting descriptive attributes of the court and the house palaver. Remember that the coercive tone of the courtroom hearing limits the court's effectiveness in dealing with matrimonial disputes, especially in effecting reconciliations. The moot, on the other hand, is particularly effective in bringing about reconciliations between spouses. This is because the moot is not only conciliatory, but *therapeutic*. Moot procedures are therapeutic in that, like psychotherapy, they re-educate the parties through a type of social learning brought about in a specially structured interpersonal setting.

Talcott Parsons[9] has written that therapy involves four elements: support, permissiveness, denial of reciprocity, and manipulation of rewards. Writers such as Frank,[10] Klapman,[11] and Opler[12] have pointed out that the same elements characterize not only individual psychotherapy, but group psychotherapy as well. All four elements are writ large in the Kpelle moot.

The patient in therapy will not continue treatment very long if he does not feel support from the therapist or from the group. In the moot the parties are encouraged in the expression of their complaints and feelings because they sense group support. The very presence of one's kinsmen and neighbors demonstrates their concern. It indicates to the parties that they have a real problem and that the others are willing to help them to help themselves in solving it. In a parallel vein, Frank, speaking of group psychotherapy, notes that: 'Even anger may be supportive if it implies to a patient that others take him seriously enough to get angry at him, especially if the object of the anger feels it to be directed toward his neurotic behavior rather than himself as a person.'[13] In the moot the feeling of support also grows out of the pronouncement of the blessings which stress the unity of the group and its harmonious goal, and it is also undoubtedly increased by the absence of the publicity and expressive symbols of political power which are found in the courtroom.

Permissiveness is the second element in therapy. It indicates to the patient that everyday restrictions on making anti-social statements or acting out anti-social impulses are lessened. Thus, in the Case of the Ousted Wife, Yua felt free enough to turn to her ousted co-wife (who had been married leviratically) and say:

You don't respect me. You don't rely on me any more. When your husband was living, and I was with my husband, we slept on the farm. Did I ever refuse to send you what you asked me for when you sent a message? Didn't I always send you some of the meat my husband killed? Did I refuse to send you anything you wanted? When your husband died and we became co-wives, did I disrespect you? Why do you always make me ashamed? The things you have done to me make me sad.

Permissiveness in the therapeutic setting (and in the moot) results in catharsis, in a high degree of stimulation of feelings in the participants and an equally high tendency to verbalize these feelings.[14] Frank notes that: 'Neurotic responses must be expressed in the therapeutic situation if they are to be changed by it.'[15] In the same way, if the solution to a dispute reached in a house palaver is to be stable, it is important that there should be nothing left to embitter and undermine the decision. In a familiar setting, with familiar people, the parties to the moot feel at ease and free to say *all* that is on their minds. Yokpo, judged to be the wronged party in the Case of the Ousted Wife, in accepting an apology, gave expression to this when she said:

I agree to everything that my people said, and I accept the things they have given me—I don't have *anything else* about them on my mind. (*My italics.*)

As we shall note below, this thorough airing of complaints also facilitates the gaining of insight into and the unlearning of idiosyncratic behaviour which is socially disruptive. Permissiveness is rooted in the lack of publicity and the lack of symbols of power. But it stems, too, from the immediacy of the hearing, the locus of investigatory initiative with the parties, and the wide range of relevance.

Permissiveness in therapy is impossible without the denial of reciprocity. This refers to the fact that the therapist will not respond in kind when the patient acts in a hostile manner or with inappropriate affection. It is a type of privileged indulgence which comes with being a patient. In the moot, the parties are treated in the same way and are allowed to hurl recriminations that, in the courtroom, might bring a few hours in jail as punishment for the equivalent of contempt of court. Even though inappropriate views are not responded to in kind, neither are they simply ignored. There is denial of *congruent* response, not denial of *any* response whatsoever. In the *bɛrɛi mu meni saa*, as in group psychotherapy, 'private ideation and conceptualization are brought out into the open and all their facets or many of their facets exposed. The individual gets a "reading" from different bearings on the compass, so to speak,[16] and perceptual patterns . . . are joggled out of their fixed positions. . . .'[17]

Thus, Yua's outburst against Yokpo quoted above was not responded to with matching hostility, but its inappropriateness was clearly pointed out to her by the group. Some of them called her aside in a huddle and said to her:

You are not right. If you don't like the woman, or she doesn't like you, don't be the first to say anything. Let her start and then say what you have to say. By speaking, if she heeds some of your words, the wives will scatter, and the blame will be on you. Then your husband will cry for your name that you have scattered his property.

In effect, Yua was being told that, in view of the previous testimony, her jealousy of her co-wife was not justified. In reality testing, she discovered that her view of the situation was not shared by the others and, hence was inappropriate. Noting how the others responded, she could see why her treatment of her co-wife had caused so much dissension. Her interpretation of her new co-wife's actions and resulting premises were not shared by the co-wife, nor by the others hearing a description of what had happened. Like psychotherapy, the moot is gently corrective of behavior rooted in such misunderstandings.

Similarly, Wama Nya, the husband, learned that others did not view as reasonable his accusing his wife of having a lover and urging her to go off and drink with the suspected paramour when he passed their house and wished them all a good evening. Reality testing for him taught him that the group did not view this type of mildly paranoid sarcasm as conducive to stable marital relationships.

The reaction of the moot to Yua's outburst indicates that permissiveness in this case was certainly not complete, but only relative, being much greater than in the courtroom. But without this moderated immunity the airing of grievances would be limited, and the chance for social relearning lessened. Permissiveness in the moot is incomplete because, even there, prudence is not thrown to the winds. Note that Yua was not told not to express her feelings at all, but to express them only after the co-wife had spoken so that, if the moot failed, she would not be in an untenable position. In court there would be objection to her blunt speaking out. In the moot the objection was, in effect, to her speaking *out of turn*. In other cases the moot sometimes fails, foundering on this very point, because the parties are *too* prudent, all waiting for the others to make the first move in admitting fault.

The manipulation of rewards is the last dimension of therapy treated by Parsons. In this final phase of therapy[18] the patient is coaxed to conformity by the granting of rewards. In the moot one of the most important rewards is the group approval which goes to the wronged person who accepts an apology and to the person who is magnanimous enough to make one.

In the Case of the Ousted Wife, Kɔlɔ Waa, the mediator, and the others attending decided that the husband and the co-wife, Yua, had wronged Yokpo. Kɔlɔ Waa said to the husband:

> From now on, we don't want to hear of your fighting. You should live in peace with these women. If your wife accepts the things which the people have brought you should pay four chickens and ten bottles of rum as your contribution.

The husband's brother and sister also brought gifts of apology, although the moot did not explicitly hold them at fault.

By giving these prestations, the wrong-doer is restored to good grace and is once again acting like an 'upright Kpelle' (although, if he wishes, he may refuse to accept the decision of the moot). He is eased into this position by being grouped with others to whom blame is also allocated, for, typically, he is not singled out and isolated in being labelled deviant. Thus, in the Case of the Ousted Wife, the children of Yokpo were held to be at fault in 'being mean' to their step-father, so that blame was not only shared by one 'side,' but ascribed to the other also.

Moreover, the prestations which the losing party is asked to hand over are not expensive. They are significant enough to touch the pocketbook a little; for the Kpelle say that if an apology does not cost something other than words, the wrong-doer is more likely to repeat the offending action. At the same time, as we noted above, the tokens are not so costly as to give the loser additional reason for anger directed at the other party which can undermine the decision.

All in all, the rewards for conformity to group expectations and for following out a new behaviour pattern are kept within the deviant's sight. These rewards are positive, in contrast to the negative sanctions of the courtroom. Besides the institutionalized apology, praise and acts of concern and affection replace fines and jail sentences. The mediator, speaking to Yokpo as the wronged party, said:

> You have found the best of the dispute. Your husband has wronged you. All the people have wronged you. You are the only one who can take care of them because you are the oldest. Accept the things they have given to you.

The moot in its procedural features and procedural sequences is, then, strongly analogous to psychotherapy. It is analogous to therapy in the structuring of the role of the mediator also. Parsons has indicated that, to do his job well, the therapist must be a member of two social systems: one containing himself and his patient; and the other, society at large.[19] He must not be seduced into thinking that he belongs only to the therapeutic dyad, but must gradually pull the deviant back into a relationship with the wider group. It is significant, then, that the mediator of a moot is a

kinsman who is also a chief of some sort. He thus represents both the group involved in the dispute and the wider community. His task is to utilize his position as kinsman as a lever to manipulate the parties into living up to the normative requirements of the wider society, which, as chief, he upholds. His major orientation must be to the wider collectivity, not to the particular goals of his kinsmen.

When successful, the moot stops the process of alienation which drives two spouses so far apart that they are immune to ordinary social-control measures such as a smile, a frown, or a pointed aside.[20] A moot is not always successful, however. Both parties must have a genuine willingness to cooperate and a real concern about their discord. Each party must be willing to list his grievances, to admit his guilt, and make an open apology. The moot, like psychotherapy, is impotent without well-motivated clients.

The therapeutic elements found in the Kpelle moot are undoubtedly found in informal procedures for settling disputes in other African societies also; some of these are reported in literature and others are not. One such procedure which seems strikingly parallel to the Kpelle *bɛrɛi mu meni saa* has been described by J. H. M. Beattie.[21] This is the court of neighbors or *rukurato rw'enzarwa* found in the Banyoro kingdom of Uganda. The group also meets as an *ad hoc* assembly of neighbors to hear disputes involving kinsmen or neighbors.[22]

The intention of the Nyoro moot is to 'reintegrate the delinquent into the community and, if possible, to achieve reconciliation without causing bitterness and resentment; in the words of an informant, the institution exists "to finish off people's quarrels and to abolish bad feeling."'[23] This therapeutic goal is manifested in the manner in which the dispute is resolved. After a decision is reached the penalty imposed is always the same. The party held to be in the wrong is asked to bring beer (four pots, modified downwards according to the circumstances) and meat, which is shared with the other party and all those attending the *rukurato*. The losing party is also expected to 'humble himself, not only to the man he has injured but to the whole assembly.'[24]

Beattie correctly points out that, because the council of neighbors has no power to enforce its decision, the shared feast is *not* to be viewed primarily as a penalty, for the wrong-doer acts as a host and also shares in the food and drink. 'And it is a praiseworthy thing; from a dishonourable status he is promoted to an honourable one . . .'[25] and reintegrated into the community.[26]

Although Beattie does not use a psychoanalytic frame of reference in approaching his material, it is clear that the communal feast involves the manipulation of rewards as the last step in a social-control measure which breaks the progressive alienation of the deviance cycle. The description of procedures in the *rukurato* indicates that it is highly informal in nature, convening in a room in a house with everyone 'sitting around.' However, Beattie does not provide enough detail to enable one to determine whether or not the beginning and intermediate steps in the Nyoro moot show the permissiveness, support, and denial of reciprocity which characterize the Kpelle moot. Given the structure and outcome of most Nyoro councils, one would surmise that a close examination of their proceedings[27] would reveal the implicit operation of therapeutic principles.

The fact that the Kpelle court is basically coercive and the moot therapeutic does not imply that one is dysfunctional while the other is eufunctional. Like Beattie, I conclude that the court and informal dispute-settlement procedures have separate but complementary functions. In marital disputes the moot is oriented to a couple as a dyadic social system and serves to reconcile them wherever possible. This is eufunctional from the point of view of the couple, to whom divorce would be dysfunctional. Kpelle courts customarily treat matrimonial matters by granting a divorce. While this may be dysfunctional from the point of view of the couple, because it ends their marriage, it may be eufunctional from the point of view of society. Some marriages, if forced to continue, would result in adultery or physical violence at best, and improper socialization of children at worst. It is clear that the Kpelle moot is to the Kpelle court as the domestic and family relations courts (or commercial and labour arbitration boards) are to ordinary courts in our own society. The essential point is that both formal and informal dispute-settlement procedures serve significant functions in Kpelle society and neither can be fully understood if studied alone.[28]

NOTES

1. The field work on which this paper is based was carried out in Liberia in 1957 and 1958 and was supported by a grant from the Ford Foundation, which is, of course, not responsible for any of the views presented here. The data were analyzed while the writer was the holder of a pre-doctoral National Science Foundation Fellowship. The writer wishes to acknowledge, with gratitude, the support of both foundations. This paper was read at the Annual Meeting of the American Anthropological Association in Philadelphia, Pennsylvania, in November 1961.

   The dissertation, in which this material first appeared, was directed by Philip H. Gulliver, to whom I am indebted for much stimulating and provocative discussion of many of the ideas here. Helpful comments and suggestions have also been made by Robert T. Holt and Robert S. Merrill.

   Portions of the material included here were presented in a seminar on African Law conducted in the Department of Anthropology at the University of Minnesota by E. Adamson Hoebel and the writer. Members of the seminar were generous in their criticisms and comments.

2. Paul J. Bohannan, *Justice and Judgment among the Tiv*, Oxford University Press, London, 1957; Max Gluckman, *The Judicial Process among the Barotse of Northern Rhodesia*, Manchester University Press, 1954; P. P. Howell, *A Handbook of Nuer Law*, Oxford University Press, London, 1954.

3. Cf. George P. Murdock, *Social Structure*, Macmillan, New York, 1949, p. 74.

4. James L. Gibbs, Jr., 'Poro Values and Courtroom Procedures in a Kpelle Chiefdom,' *Southwestern Journal of Anthropology* (in press). A detailed analysis of Kpelle courtroom procedures and of procedures in the moot together with transcripts appears in: James L. Gibbs, Jr., *Some Judicial Implications of Marital Instability among the Kpelle* (unpublished Ph.D. Dissertation, Harvard University, Cambridge, Mass., 1960).

5. What follows is based on a detailed case study of moots in Panta Chiefdom and their contrast with courtroom hearings before the paramount chief of that chiefdom. Moots, being private, are less susceptible to the surveillance of the anthropologist than courtroom hearings, thus I have fewer transcripts of moots than of court cases. The analysis presented here is valid for Panta Chiefdom and also valid, I feel, for most of the Liberian Kpelle area, particularly the north-east where people are, by and large, traditional.

6. This simple distilled rum, bottled in Monrovia and retailing for twenty-five cents a bottle in 1958, is known in the Liberian Hinterland as 'cane juice' and should not be confused with imported varieties.

7. American currency is the official currency of Liberia and is used throughout the country.

8. Cf. J. F. Holleman, 'An Anthropological Approach to Bantu Law (with special reference to Shona law)' in the *Journal of the Rhodes-Livingstone Institute*, vol. x, 1950, pp. 27–41. Holleman feels that the use of tokens for effecting apologies—or marriages—shows the proclivity for reducing events of importance to something tangible.

9. Talcott Parsons, *The Social System*, The Free Press, Glencoe, Ill., 1951, pp. 314–19.

10. Jerome D. Frank, 'Group Methods in Psychotherapy,' in *Mental Health and Mental Disorder: A Sociological Approach*, edited by Arnold Rose, W. W. Norton Co., New York, pp. 524–35.

11. J. W. Klapman, *Group Psychotherapy: Theory and Practice*, Grune & Stratton, New York, 1959.

12. Marvin K. Opler, 'Values in Group Psychotherapy,' *International Journal of Social Psychiatry*, vol. iv, 1959, pp. 296–98.

13. Frank, op. cit., p. 531.

14. Ibid.

15. Ibid.

16. Klapman, op. cit., p. 39.

17. Ibid., p. 15.

18. For expository purposes the four elements of therapy are described as if they always occur serially. They may,

and do, occur simultaneously also. Thus, all four of the factors may be implicit in a single short behavioural sequence. Parsons (op. cit.) holds that these four elements are common not only to psychotherapy but to all measures of social control.

19. Parsons, op. cit., p. 314. Cf. loc. cit., chap. 10.
20. Cf. Parsons, op. cit., chap. 7. Parsons notes that in any social-control action the aim is to avoid the process of alienation, that 'vicious-cycle' phenomenon whereby each step taken to curb the non-conforming activity of the deviant has the effect of driving him further into his pattern of deviance. Rather, the need is to 'reach' the deviant and bring him back to the point where he is susceptible to the usual everyday informal sanctions.
21. J. H. M. Beattie, 'Informal Judicial Activity in Bunyoro,' *Journal of African Administration*, vol. ix, 1957, pp. 188–95.
22. Disputes include matters such as a son seducing his father's wives, a grown son disobeying his father, or a husband or wife failing in his or her duties to a spouse. Disputes between unrelated persons involve matters like quarrelling, abuse, assault, false accusations, petty theft, adultery, and failure to settle debts. (Ibid., p. 190.)
23. Ibid., p. 194.
24. Beattie, op. cit., p. 194.
25. Ibid., p. 193.
26. Ibid., p. 195. Moreover, Beattie also recognizes the functional significance of the Nyoro moots, for he notes that: 'It would be a serious error to represent them simply as clumsy, "amateur" expedients for punishing wrong-doers or settling civil disputes at an informal, sub-official level.' (Ibid.)
27. The type of examination of case materials that is required demands that field workers should not simply record cases that meet the 'trouble case' criterion (cf. K. N. Llewellyn and E. A. Hoebel, *The Cheyenne Way*, Norman, Okla., University of Oklahoma Press, 1941; and E. A. Hoebel, *The Law of Primitive Man*, Cambridge, Mass., Harvard University Press, 1954), but that cases should be recorded in some transcript-like form.
28. The present study has attempted to add to our understanding of informal dispute-settlement procedures in one African society by using an eclectic but organized collection of concepts from jurisprudence, ethno-law, and psychology. It is based on the detailed and systematic analysis of a few selected cases, rather than a mass of quantitative data. In further research a greater variety of cases handled by Kpelle moots should be subjected to the same analysis to test its merit more fully.

32

Gauging the Winds of War

Bruce Bower

Of all the insidious and pernicious evils that humankind has brought upon its own head, certainly warfare must rank at the top. Throughout history, and apparently prehistory as well, man (and we do mean man, not woman) has sought to maim and murder his brothers for an endless variety of real and imagined insults, beliefs, and gains. Wars may have been more common in earlier times (and they certainly may have been as deadly, given the size of armies that marched into battle, leaving grotesque numbers on history's killing fields), but never before have men held in their hands the power to end humanity. It is no small irony that the policy of mutually assured destruction should go by the acronym MAD.

MAD may have kept the two superpowers from the oft-predicted Armageddon, or we may have reached the end of the cold war despite, rather than because of, MAD. No one will ever know. What is certain is that the end of the cold war has brought a renaissance of ethnic warfare, rape, and genocide, euphemistically referred to as ethnic cleansing. From Somalia to Bosnia to the Middle East, tensions between groups override individuals' desire for safety and well-being. Do these behaviors make sense for individuals, or are people swept up by cultural forces beyond their control? Do wars fulfill some biological, ecological, social, or cultural function?

Warfare is violent conflict between politically autonomous groups, be they nation-states, chiefdoms, tribes, or bands. If there is a root cause of war, examining the cross-cultural literature may very well help us understand why human groups are so often unable to simply get along.

What are the roots of warfare?

As you read this selection, ask yourself the following questions:

- ☐ *What are three themes that might distinguish different approaches to the causes of war?*

- ☐ *What are several theoretical approaches to the causes of war?*

- ☐ *How does warfare affect reproductive success for males among the Yanomamo and the Cheyenne?*

- ☐ *How might warfare be related to population size (or population density)?*

- ☐ *Did the rise of chiefdoms, agriculture, and a more sedentary lifestyle lead to an increase or decrease in warfare?*

The following terms discussed in this selection are included in the Glossary at the back of the book:

extended family
feud
polygyny
reproductive success
war

In a 1971 Motown hit single, Edwin Starr posed the musical question, "War—what is it good for?" His gruff response: "Absolutely nothin'."

Despite the grimly predictable tragedies of armed conflict, almost all ancient and modern societies studied by anthropologists have engaged in at least periodic bouts of warfare. The ubiquity of organized fighting between human groups—currently brought home by the war[s] in the Middle East [and Bosnia]—has fired up the scientific study of warfare over the last 30 years and has sparked some bruising academic skirmishes.

. . . Warfare researchers . . . do not praise fighting, but they assume that anything so common in human experience serves some purpose. They search for the "absoluty somethin' " that lights the fuse of violence in bands of foragers, tribes of hunter-gatherers, rudimentary political states and modern nations alike.

In the 1960s, as U.S. involvement in Vietnam deepened, anthropological theories of war's causes and consequences flourished, numbering at least 16 by 1973, observes Keith F. Otterbein of the State University of New York at Buffalo. However, he says, only about half of those theories still receive strong scientific support, and no persuasive new theories have emerged.

Current notions about the roots of war stem mainly from studies of nonindustrial societies lacking centralized political power and extensive military organizations. In Otterbein's view, all of these theoretical approaches focus on three themes:

- "Ultimate" causes of war that influence the goals people fight for, such as competition within a society for scarce resources or mates, and intense divisions between groups of related men.

- "Proximate" causes of war, such as a society's military preparedness and the goals of its leaders, often centering on the desire for land, natural resources, or control of trade routes.

- Consequences of war that influence further conflict, including population decline, improved access to resources, and increased prestige and power accorded to victorious warriors.

Although some anthropologists and sociobiologists contend that a genetic tendency toward physical violence greases the human war machine, theories of innate aggression attract few advocates today, Otterbein maintains. Nevertheless, disputes over the alleged biological roots of combat continue to erupt, ignited in many cases by the work of Napoleon A. Chagnon of the University of California, Santa Barbara, whose studies of warfare have become the most widely publicized research in this field.

Since 1964, Chagnon has conducted fieldwork among the 15,000 Yanomamo Indians who inhabit some 200 villages in the Amazonian jungle of Brazil and Venezuela. He has long stressed the ferocity and frequency of combat between Yanomamo villages. Some other anthropologists who have studied the jungle tribe argue that Chagnon emphasizes a misleading slice of Yanomamo life.

Chagnon's . . . report in the Feb. 26, 1988, *Science* concludes that revenge fuels protracted, bloody battles between groups of men from different Yanomamo villages. Competition for food, water, territory, or women creates the initial friction, he says. Minor bow-and-arrow confrontations ensue, escalating rapidly when a death results and the victim's male relatives exact revenge through raids on the offending village.

Blood vengeance apparently raises the social status and reproductive success of Yanomamo warriors, who represent nearly half of the men in the tribe, Chagnon maintains. On average, killers have more than twice as many wives and three times as many children as their peaceable counterparts.

Chagnon refrains from arguing that warfare generally proves biologically advantageous among the Yanomamo or in any other culture. He does contend, however, that reproductive success and fighting prowess probably go hand-in-hand in many human groups, and that this may help explain the great prestige attached to military conquest in both modern and ancient states.

Even if Chagnon's Yanomamo data hold up, responds anthropologist John H. Moore, successful warriors in similar tribal societies sometimes contribute few genes to subsequent generations. Moore, of the University of Oklahoma in Norman, cites the 19th-century Cheyenne Indians of the North American plains as a case in point. The Cheyenne, with a population of about 3,000 divided into bands of 150 to 400 individuals, engaged in fierce warfare with other Indian tribes as well as with U.S. military forces, achieving historical notoriety with their defeat of Custer at the battle of Little Big Horn. In addition to seven warrior bands led by numerous war chiefs, Cheyenne society included 44 peace chiefs, sometimes more than one to a band, who led polygynous extended families.

U.S. Census data collected in 1880 and 1892 reveal that men in the Cheyenne peace bands had a striking reproductive advantage over warriors, reports Moore in the June 1990 *Current Anthropology*. The war chiefs stressed celibacy and ritual suicide, while the peace chiefs had numerous wives and children, he notes.

Moore asserts that many societies without centralized political systems, including the Cheyenne, undergo periodic cultural reorganizations, and he says researchers have no evidence suggesting that recent Yanomamo behavior reflects all or most of human prehistory or even the Yanomamo of several generations ago.

Another critic of Chagnon's research, Marvin Harris of the University of Florida in Gainesville, theorizes that war occurs among hunter-gatherers and other "band-and-village" peoples when population growth creates increasingly intense competition for food, especially protein-rich game. He maintains that warfare, for all its brutality, effectively prunes these populations, preventing malnutrition and hunger among survivors—whether the combatants hail from Yanomamo villages or from horticultural groups in Papua New Guinea.

"Band-and-village societies must pay a heavy price for keeping population and food supply in balance, and warfare is part of that price," Harris writes in *Our Kind* (1989, Harper & Row, New York). Conflicts sometimes veer out of control, wiping out more lives than malnutrition would have claimed, but "no system is fail-safe," he notes.

Harris' theory may help explain widespread fighting among North America's Anasazi Indians around 700 years ago, says Jonathan Haas of the Field Museum of Natural History in Chicago. Although Anasazi culture extended back at least to A.D. 500, Haas points out that burnt houses, decapitated skeletons, and other archaeological evidence of warfare date only to the second half of the 13th century A.D. At that time, the ingredients for war coalesced, he says: A burgeoning population fostered the emergence of distinct cultural groups with an "us versus them" mentality, and periodic droughts reduced crop yields and drained food reserves.

When the Anasazi abandoned their population centers at the end of the 13th century and the droughts also eased, warfare again diminished, Haas observes.

"Tribal peoples cycle in and out of warfare because of environmental stress," he says. "Warfare has increased with the evolution of states because environmental stresses are more unrelenting now."

The nearly unrelenting warfare of most early states, which spread throughout the world from 3200 B.C. until around A.D. 1800, often reflects the "predatory accumulation" practiced by rulers sitting atop centralized political hierarchies, asserts Stephen P. Reyna of the University of New Hampshire in Durham. However, early or "archaic" states possessed nowhere near the political complexity or destructive means of modern "nation-states," he notes.

A violent conflict in the Chad Basin of north central Africa around 200 years ago illustrates the dynamics of warfare between archaic states, Reyna says. A leader of one state accused a neighboring leader of a crime against Islam—incest with his daughter—and the charge sparked a war. But the real problem stemmed from the rapid growth of both states due to a brutal type of arms race, Reyna holds. These leaders had engaged in constant warfare with weaker neighbors to accumulate wealth and larger armies. In a vicious cycle, each victory enabled them to accumulate even more means of destruction to wage more successful wars, he says. Eventually their "fields of empire" overlapped, and war between the two soon followed.

Reyna notes that the incest charge, though probably unfounded, served a strategic purpose: It led to the defection of several generals aligned with the accused ruler, undermining his army and helping to seal his eventual defeat.

Such hostilities grew out of a long history of warfare among human groups, says Robert L. Carneiro of the American Museum of Natural History in New York City. In his view, war played a critical role in the evolution of large political and social systems.

The origins of war probably stretch back through a couple of million years to Stone Age times, Carneiro contends. Stone Age battles—fought to avenge murders, wife-stealing, or other trespasses often observed among modern hunter-gatherers—served to push small bands of humans apart and keep them separate.

But around 10,000 years ago, the nature of warfare changed, he maintains. The spread of agriculture increased permanent settlements and human populations. Adjacent villages then began to fight over access to farmland. Instead of pushing the communities apart in traditional Stone Age fashion, these wars forged the emergence of the chiefdom, a forced coalition of several formerly independent villages under the control of a paramount chief. With chiefdoms came district chiefs, village chiefs, advisers, and other early representatives of social and political complexity.

Archaeological signs of war, such as the number of weapons found in graves and heavily fortified occupation sites, increase with the growth of chiefdoms, Carneiro observes. The push from chiefdoms to even larger state-societies did not occur swiftly or irreversibly throughout the world, he says, but early hotbeds of state growth appeared where limited areas of prime farmland prevented vanquished villagers from fleeing to greener pastures. Prime examples include Mesopotamia, the Nile valley, and the Peruvian coast.

War was the one instrument capable of surmounting autonomous villages and deserves careful study as a cause of social evolution," Carneiro says.

Perhaps the most wide-ranging warfare study to date was conducted during the 1980s by Carol R. Ember and Melvin Ember of Human Relations Area Files, a privately funded research organization in New Haven, Conn. The team analyzed anthropological descriptions of 186 nonindustrial societies, virtually all of which operated on a much smaller scale than modern nation-states. Descriptions ranged from 18th-century writings on Native American tribes to recent accounts of African hunter-gatherers.

Two independent coders read the voluminous literature and rated the presence and frequency of warfare, aggressive acts, natural disasters, and other social and psychological factors, focusing on a 25-year period in each society.

The Embers say their unpublished findings offer a tentative theory of war, at least among "simple" societies: The societies that engage in the most warfare express considerably more fear of food shortages caused by expected but unpredictable natural disasters, such as drought, flood, or infestation. The fear of others—indicated by child-rearing practices stressing mistrust of neighbors—further fuels the tendency to fight, the researchers say.

Their data provide no backing for other explanations of warfare. For example, the Embers found that societies already experiencing chronic food and protein shortages did not engage in excessive fighting. The study also failed to support the idea that a shortage of women stimulates warfare and regulates population.

Some researchers have suggested a penchant for warfare among sexually restrictive societies and among societies with high levels of interpersonal aggression, as reflected in elevated rates of murder and theft. The Embers' study showed no such links.

Parents in warlike societies do tend to encourage toughness and aggression among boys, but warfare apparently *causes* this practice rather than vice versa, the Embers argue. When these societies lose wars and come under the control of outside forces, harsh child-rearing methods diminish sharply, they found.

Three-quarters of the sample's "simple" societies fought wars every two years, Carol Ember notes, although "this doesn't mean war is inevitable."

The Embers hope to expand their analyses to modern nation-states. In the meantime, they suspect that the link between the risk of war and the fear of unpredictable disasters extends to a wide variety of situations.

Several researchers say contact with Westerners has whipped up local conflicts in Africa and elsewhere since the early days of European colonialism.

More than a century ago, for example, Tuareg tribes of northern Africa limited their attacks to small-scale raids on caravans passing through their territory, says Candelario Saenz of the State University of New York at Purchase. The Tuareg extorted camels and other goods from the caravans to support their pastoral way of life, Saenz says. But when France took control of Algeria in the late 1800s, it imposed numerous restrictions on trade in the region. Tuareg groups soon entered into a period of nearly constant warfare among themselves as they competed for the rapidly decreasing supply of goods passing along traditional trade routes, Saenz says.

Another instance of Western contact helping to foment violence occurred more recently in the ethnically mixed African nation of Mauritania, says Michael M. Horowitz of the State University of New York at Binghamton, who has conducted fieldwork there for the past four years.

The completion of a large dam on the Senegal River several years ago expanded farmable floodplains and drew the promise of considerable outside investment by Western agricultural companies, Horowitz says. But the local population, long dependent on farming this fertile river valley, already occupied much of the area.

"The Mauritanian government is now killing and torturing these people to get the land," Horowitz says. "In the process they've created 100,000 refugees and intensified violence between ethnic groups."

Whether stimulated by Western contact or not, most of the 120 wars documented since the end of World War II similarly pit large states against smaller nations or ethnic groups the states claim to represent, says Jason Clay of Cultural Survival, a public-interest organization in Cambridge, Mass.

In the aftermath of the international conflict sparked by the aggressions of the Axis powers, he notes, dictatorships and one-party states ironically solidified their power in many parts of the world, including Africa, the Soviet Union, and Eastern Europe. Diverse nations and groups of people with separate languages and cultural histories were yoked to the goals of unresponsive, unelected leaders of both the political right and left, Clay says.

Moreover, those leaders socked away whatever taxes, internal resources, foreign aid, and international loans they could extract for themselves, leaving the rest of the populace destitute, he maintains.

"The destruction of social and political life at the local level and the stripping away of resources by modern one-party states has led to longer, more widespread wars," Clay argues. "We'll have more violence at the regional level and the settling of old scores as states fall apart in the post–Cold War world."

Although Clay's dire prediction gathers support from the bloody Soviet crackdown on Lithuania's independence movement and the increasing tensions in other Soviet republics, anthropological research provides room for optimism, says R. Brian Ferguson of Rutgers University in Newark, N.J.

"War is not the natural human condition," Ferguson says. "Research shows that war varies over time due to factors such as trade, population growth, and outside contacts."

Often, leaders must paint the enemy as inhuman in order to motivate people to kill, he says—and even then, many soldiers come out of combat with severe psychological aftereffects.

We need to dispense with the idea that people love violence and are doomed to fight," Ferguson concludes.

33

Contemporary Warfare in the New Guinea Highlands

Aaron Podolefsky

Within political units—whether tribes or nations—there are well-established mechanisms for handling conflict nonviolently. Anthropologists have described a wide range of conflict resolution mechanisms within societies. Between politically autonomous groups, however, few mechanisms exist. Consequently, uncontained conflict may expand into armed aggression—warfare. In both primitive and modern forms, warfare always causes death, destruction, and human suffering. It is certainly one of the major problems confronting humankind.

New Guinea highlanders can tell you why they go to war—to avenge ghosts or to exact revenge for the killing of one of their own. As we have seen in previous selections, people do not seem to comprehend the complex interrelationship among the various parts of their own social system. Throughout the world, anthropologists find that people do not fathom the causes of their own social behavior. If they did, finding solutions would certainly be a far simpler matter.

The leaders of Papua New Guinea see intertribal fighting as a major social problem with severe economic consequences. Although fighting itself may be age-old, the reemergence of warfare in this area in the 1970s appears to have a new set of causes. In this selection, Aaron Podolefsky shows how the introduction of Western goods may have inadvertently resulted in changes in economic arrangements, marriage patterns, and, ultimately, warfare.

As you read this selection, ask yourself the following questions:

☐ *What is the theoretical orientation (research strategy) of this paper?*

☐ *When did tribal fighting reemerge as a national problem in New Guinea?*

☐ *How did intertribal marriage constrain the expansion of minor conflict into warfare?*

☐ *How has the rate of intertribal marriage changed? Why did it change?*

☐ *How are the introduction of Western goods, trade, marriage, and warfare interrelated?*

The following terms discussed in this selection are included in the Glossary at the back of the book:

affinal kin
aggression
agnates
blood relatives
cross-cutting ties
cultural materialism
hypothesis
lineage
multiplex relationships
pacification
tribe

From *Ethnology*, 1984. Reprinted by permission of *Ethnology*.

After decades of pacification and relative peace, intergroup warfare reemerged in the Papua New Guinea highlands during the late 1960s and early 1970s, only a few years before national independence in 1975. Death and destruction, martial law, and delay in highlands development schemes have been the outcome.

Most explanations of the resurgence either posit new causes (such as psychological insecurity surrounding political independence from Australian rule or disappointment at the slow speed of development) or attribute the increased fighting to relaxation of government controls which suppressed fighting since the pacification process began. None of the explanations thus far advanced has looked at changes in the structure or infrastructure of highlands societies themselves which could account for behavioral changes in the management of conflict.

This paper employs a cultural materialist strategy in which the efficacy of explanatory models are ranked: infrastructure, structure, and superstructure.[1] From a macrosociological perspective, infrastructural changes unintentionally induced during the colonial era resulted in changes in the structural relations between groups. These changes reduced existing (albeit weak) indigenous mechanisms constraining conflict. Traditionally, groups maintained differential access to resources such as stone used for axes and salt. Axe heads and salt were produced in local areas and traded for valuables available elsewhere. I argue that the introduction and distribution of items such as salt and steel axes reduced the necessity for trade, thereby altering the need for intertribal marriage as well as reducing extratribal contacts of a type which facilitated marriage between persons of different tribes. The reduction of intertribal marriage, over time, resulted in a decay of the web of affinal and nonagnatic kin ties which had provided linkages between otherwise autonomous tribal political units. Thus, the resurgence of tribal fighting is, in part, a result of the reduction of constraints which might otherwise have facilitated the containment of conflict rather than its expansion into warfare. This view sees warfare as one possible end result of a process of conflict management.

An advantage of this strategy is that it suggests a testable hypothesis which runs counter to conventional wisdom and informed opinion that the rate of intertribal marriage would increase after pacification. Some researchers believed that once tribal fighting ended men would be able to wander farther afield and develop relationships with single teenage girls over a wide area. Pacification, then, might reasonably be expected to result in an increase in intertribal marriage. An increase or lack of change in the rate of intergroup marriage since contact would invalidate the explanation. The hypothesis will be tested on data collected in the Gumine District, Simbu (formerly Chimbu) Province, Papua New Guinea.

BACKGROUND

Warfare in traditional highlands societies has been regarded as chronic, incessant, or endemic, and is said to have been accepted as a part of social living in most areas. Indeed, the pattern of warfare was one of the most continuous and violent on record.

However, hostilities were neither random nor did highlanders live in a perpetual state of conflict with all surrounding groups. Some neighboring groups maintained relations of permanent hostility and had little to do with one another. In contrast, most neighboring tribes intermarried and attended one another's ceremonies.

Pacification was an early goal of the colonial administration. By the end of the 1930s fighting was rare in the vicinity of Simbu province government stations. By 1940 Australian authority was accepted and attacks on strangers and tribal fighting had nearly ended, although the entire highlands was not pacified until the 1960s. This period also witnessed the introduction of Western goods such as salt and the steel axe.

Change came quickly to New Guinea. Sterling writes in 1943: "Headhunters and cannibals a generation ago, most of the natives of British New Guinea have now become so accustomed to the ways of the whites that they have been trained as workers and even to assist in administering the white man's law."

From the end of World War II through the 1970s, educational and business opportunities expanded, local government and village courts were introduced, and national self-government was attained in 1975. Highlanders came to expect that development would lead to material gains.[2]

Tribal warfare began to reemerge as a significant national problem in about 1970, five years before independence. By 1973 the government had become concerned that the situation might deteriorate to a point that they could no longer effectively administer parts of the highlands. In 1972, according to government report, 28 incidents involving 50 or more persons were reported in the Western Highlands District. A decade later, Bill Wormsley (1982) reports 60 fights per year in the Enga Province (the figures are of course not directly comparable). Although the level of fighting declined in Enga during 1980 due to the declaration of a state of emergency, it increased again in 1981 and 1982. Martial law has also been declared in the Simbu Province. Deaths lead to payback killing and to demands for compensation payments. Inflated demands for "excess" compensation further compound the problem.

232

Of the five major theories of warfare outlined by Koch in 1974 (biological evolution, psychological theories, cultural evolution, ecological adaptation, and social-structure analysis), scholars have used only psychological theories and social-structural analysis to explain the recent emergence of tribal warfare.

Some researchers favor explanations which combine the traditional cultural heritage of violence with issues in development. Others seem to argue that the problem lies in the Enga's perception that the government, especially the courts, has become weaker and that this had led to the breakdown in law and order. Rob Gordon notes, however, that the police force in Enga has increased from 72 in 1970 to 300 in 1981, and that the average sentence for riotous behavior has grown from 3 months in 1970 to 9.6 months in 1978–9 with no apparent deterrent effect. Kiaps (field officers), Gordon suggests, have in fact lost power for several reasons. Most interesting from the perspective of the present analysis involves the kiaps' loss of control over access to goods. He (1983:209) states that "The importance that the Enga attach to trade-goods should not be underestimated." An old Engan is quoted as saying "The first Kiaps gave beads, salt, steel axes—everyone wanted it so they all followed the Kiap and stopped fighting. We stopped fighting because we did not want to lose the source of these things." I would add that once they "followed the kiaps" for these goods, previous important trade relations no longer needed to be kept up. In a 1980 study, Gordon also acknowledges problems created by intergroup suspicion, generational conflict exacerbated by education, and decline in men's houses and clan meetings. Similarly, Paula Brown (1982a) believes that pacification was a temporary effect in which fighting was suppressed. The Simbu do not see the government as holding power.

Explanations also combine development problems with psychologically oriented theories. Contemporary violence is sometimes thought to be a protest rising out of psychological strain created by the drastic social change of an imposed economic and political system. In a 1973 paper Bill Standish describes the period leading up to independence as one of stress, tension, and insecurity. He argues that the fighting is an expression of primordial attachments in the face of political insecurity surrounding national independence from Australian colonial rule. Paula Brown (1982a, 1982b) suggests that during the colonial period expectations for the future included security, wealth, and the improvement of life. "Disappointment that these goals have not been realized is expressed in disorder." She suggests that what is needed is a political movement rather than the imposition of Western institutions and suppression of fighting.

The present paper cannot and does not formally refute any of these explanations. Indeed, some make a great deal of sense and fill in part of a very complex picture. However, it is difficult to evaluate the validity of these explanations since very little data are presented. For example, Standish (1973) presents no evidence to assess whether, in fact, the level of stress has changed over time (precontact, postcontact, or independence era), or whether stress is associated with fighting or even with differential levels of awareness about independence, the latter likely expressing itself geographically around centers of population and development.

ETHNOGRAPHIC BACKGROUND— THE MUL COMMUNITY

Mul lies approximately 3 miles east of the Gumine District Headquarters and 32 miles south of Kundiawa, the capital of the Simbu province. The Gumine patrol post was established in 1954. During the early 1960s a dirt road was constructed linking Gumine to the capital and within a few years the road was extended through Mul. Lying at an elevation of about 5,500 feet, Mul is the central portion of a larger tribal territory which extends steeply from the southern edge of the Marigl Gorge to elevations of 8 to 9,000 feet.

The area is densely populated. Land is either cultivated or fallow in grass or scrub regrowth. Individually owned trees are scattered and there are a yearly increasing number of coffee trees. With 295 persons per square mile on cultivatable land, this density is high compared with other highland groups (see Brown and Podolefsky 1976).

The people of Mul are Simbus. Social relations and cultural patterns follow in most important respects those extensively documented by Paula Brown in numerous publications. I will describe here only those dimensions of organization most directly relevant to the resurgence of tribal fighting.

Mul residents trace kinship through males, and their social groupings are patrilineal. Hierarchical segments link themselves as father/son, while parallel segments are seen as brothers. Individuals, however, are less concerned with this overall construct and tend to interact in terms of group composition and alignments. The likelihood of an individual conflict escalating into warfare is directly related to the structural distance between conflicting parties.

The largest political group to unite in warfare is the tribe, a group of several thousand individuals. Tribes are segmented into clans whose members see themselves as a unified group. Generally, individually owned plots of land tend to cluster and people can point out rough boundaries between adjacent clans. Plots of land belonging to members of a particular subclan tend to cluster within the clan area. The subclan section (or one-blood group) is the first to mobilize for warfare. The potential for expansion of such conflicts depends to a large degree on whether the relative position of the groups in the segmentary system lends itself to opposing alignments at the higher levels of segmentation and upon the past relations between the groups.

Unlike subclan sections in most highlands societies there is no restriction upon fighting between sections of the subclan. Within the subclan section, however, there are moral restrictions on internal fighting. If comembers become extremely angry they may attack with fists, clubs, or staffs, but not with axes, arrows, or spears. These restrictions are related to the notion that members of the subclan have "one-blood," and that this common blood should not be shed.

Segmentary principles operate in situations of cooperation as well as conflict. Members of a subclan section may enclose garden plots within a single fence and cooperate in the construction of men's houses. Brown (1970:99–103) similarly notes that in the central Simbu transactions between clans and tribes are competitive while those within the clan are reciprocal. Generally speaking, in terms of proximity of land holdings and residence, cooperation in gardening and house construction and the willingness to unite in common defense and ceremonial exchange, the solidarity of a social group is inversely related to the position in the segmentary hierarchy.

Cross-cutting these segmentary principles are a variety of interpersonal ties (e.g., affinal and other non-agnatic relations, exchange ties and personal friendships) which affect behavior in conflict situations. It is these ephemeral or transitory linkages which provide the avenues through which structurally autonomous tribal groups interact.

MARRIAGE AND WARFARE

Marriage and warfare are linked in the minds of New Guinea highlanders. Early writers report indigenous notions that highlanders marry their enemies. The Siane say, "They are our affinal relatives; with them we fight" (Salisbury 1962:25). Enga informants report, "We marry those whom we fight" (Meggitt 1958:278). In an extensive study of Enga warfare, Meggitt (1977: 42) supports these assertions by reporting quite strong correlations between rates of intergroup marriage and killing.

While there is little doubt that there is a strong association between marriage and warfare, it is not clear at all that they are causally related in any direct fashion, i.e., warfare causing marriage or marriage causing warfare. It is highly unlikely that warfare causes marriage. Researchers have noted the difficulty in arranging marriages between hostile groups. It is similarly unlikely that marriage causes warfare (although exceptions can certainly be pointed out). While disputes may arise between bride and groom or their families, the relations are generally highly valued and long term. The association between marriage and warfare can be reduced to two separate relationships. First, highlanders most frequently marry their neighbors. Second, highlanders most frequently go to war with their neighbors. This is because in the highlands, where travel is restricted and relations are multiplex, neighbors are the parties most likely to be involved in a dispute. Thus propinquity is causally related to both marriage and warfare; the positive correlation between marriage and warfare is spurious. Indeed, the essence of the argument made here is that if other variables could be "controlled" the association between warfare and marriage would in fact be negative.

The notion that there is no direct (as opposed to inverse) causal relationship between warfare and marriage is critical. Warfare results from precipitating disputes in the absence of sufficiently powerful third party mechanisms and other constraints which control the dispute. One dimension of constraint stems from marriage links.

In her paper "Enemies and Affines," Paula Brown (1964) carefully describes the relevant social relations among the central Simbu. During wedding ceremonies speeches proclaim that the groups of the bride and groom (consisting of subclansmen, some clansmen, kin, and affines) should remain on friendly terms and exchange visits and food. The marriage creates individual ties and obligations outside the clan which, while not institutionalized, are not wholly voluntary. At various stages in the life cycle payments are obligatory. Given the widely documented emphasis on transaction in highlands social relations, it is important to note that whenever a formal food presentation occurs between clans, the donors and recipients are related to one another through marriage. Extratribal relatives play an important role in conflict situations.

> The prevailing hostility between neighboring tribes gives extratribal relatives a special complex role. Men try not to injure their close kin and affines in any conflict between their agnatic group and the group of their relatives, but they may not attempt to prevent or stop hostilities. In any dealings between neighboring tribes, men with connections in both take a leading part; their political sphere of action encompasses both. When intermediaries and peacemakers are required these men are active (Brown 1964:348).

Thus, in Central Simbu, affines played some role in attempting to prevent warfare and were important in restoring peace. No amount of oral history data will tell us how many wars did not occur due to efforts made through these channels. Nor can such data tell us how many wars were shorter or less intense than they would have been had there been fewer cross-cutting ties. The importance of cross-cutting ties is recognized among the densely populated Enga.

> Even while or after two men or groups fight over an issue, others may intervene to urge negotiation and compromise. . . . Whether, however, noncombatants initiate some kind of conciliation or simply stand by and watch the fighting spread depends on a complex set of conditions . . . relevant factors . . . include, for instance, the importance traditionally ascribed to the object in contention (is it a pig or a sweet potato garden?), the number of antagonists, the kinship, affinal, or exchange connections among some or all of them, and between them and interested noncombatants (Meggitt:12).

Moreover, the frequency of intergroup marriage is related to the expansion or containment of a dispute. That is, the more intermarriage the greater the chance that disputes will be handled without violence or that the violence can be contained.

> Especially within the tribe, the supporters of each party include men with affines on the other side, most of whom are on good terms with their in-laws and have no wish to offend them. In such cases some men stay out of the fight while others, while participating, avoid meeting their affines in combat. This may serve to confine interclan conflict. Between tribes, similar serious disputes can more easily lead to fighting because fewer men have close ties which restrain them from supporting their fellow tribesmen (Brown 1964:352).

In sum, while there is an apparent correlation between marriage and warfare, marriage, in fact, establishes a social relationship which acts primarily as a constraint upon the expansion of a dispute. Second, as Meggitt suggests, it is not merely the marriage ties between the two groups, but also between them and their allies, i.e., the web of affinal relations. Third, the frequency of marriage, or density of the web, is related to efficacy of conflict management processes.

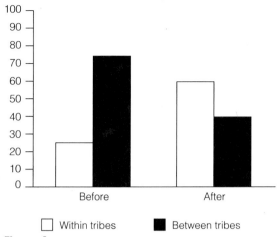

Figure 1
Percentage of Marriage Ties

CHANGING PATTERN OF INTERTRIBAL MARRIAGE

A null hypothesis that the proportion of intertribal marriages has gone up or remained the same can be rejected ($p < 0.001$) on the basis of the data shown in Table 1. Thus, we tend to believe, based upon these data, that there has in fact been an overall decline in intertribal marriage.

The data reveal a statistically significant change in the marriage pattern in the anticipated direction. Figure 1 describes the proportion of marriage ties within and between tribes, before and after Western influence. Comparing the intertribal (between) and intratribal (within) marriage rates in the precontact sample (labeled before), we see that intertribal marriage was nearly three times as frequent as intratribal marriage. Of the 114 marriage ties recorded in the precontact sample, 85 (75 percent) were between members of different tribes while only 29 (25 percent) were within the tribe. This allowed for a dense network of affinal ties between autonomous political groups. In the recent postcontact period (labeled after), in contrast, the number of intertribal marriages drops below the number of intratribal marriages. Of the 74 marriage ties in the postcontact sample, only 30 (40 percent) were between persons of different tribes while 44 (60 percent) were within the tribe. The intertribal marriage rate in the recent period is nearly half that of the precontact period.

The argument presented in this paper is that the dramatic reduction of intertribal marriage rates had significant implications for the structure of relations between politically autonomous tribal groups.

Table 1 MARRIAGE TIES BY TIME PERIOD

	Before Contact		After Contact	
	N	%	N	%
Between tribes	85	75%	30	40%
Within tribes	29	25%	44	60%
Total	114	100%	74	100%

chi squared = 21.86 1 df

$p < 0.001$ (one tail)

phi = .341

A Secondary Analysis

Sometimes it is possible to replicate one's findings by performing a secondary analysis on data collected by other researchers.

In 1964, Paula Brown published data on the marriage of some men in the Naregu tribe who live in the central Simbu near the capital of Kundiawa. Data for two clans are divided into previous generations (prior to 1930) and present generation. Brown's categories for marriage ties may be collapsed to match those used above.

What should we expect, a priori? Since Brown did not arrange the data to address this particular question, we expect some differences. Her temporal dichotomy is previous and present generation rather than before and after contact. Europeans did not reach this area until the mid-1930s and Brown's data are dichotomized at 1930. This means that precontact marriages are included in the present generation sample. Neither do Brown's data allow for a decade of transition. Based upon these differences in the data sets, we would expect the difference between the previous and present samples to be less extreme than the difference between the before and after sample in the Mul data (i.e., we expect a lower measure of association).

The data in Table 2 reveal a statistically significant change in the marriage pattern, although the association is lower (as we expected it would be) than in Mul. The between-tribe marriage rate (in the sample) dropped from 60 to 47 percent. This change was sufficient to draw Brown's attention. While the analysis fits our predictions, we cannot be certain that the change in marriage pattern observed by Paula Brown in central Simbu represents the same process occurring in Mul nearly twenty years later. Nevertheless, the analysis is intriguing. I think Brown was observing the initial stages of a process of change initiated by a reduction in the necessity for trade.[3]

Table 2 MARRIAGES OF SOME MEN IN THE NAREGU TRIBE

	Pre-1930 (Before)		Post-1930 (After)	
	N	%	N	%
Between tribes	154	60%	130	47%
Within tribes	102	40%	144	53%
Total	256	100%	274	100%

chi squared = 8.597 1 df

$p < 0.005$ (one tail)

phi = .1272

TRADE AND MARRIAGE

Given the conventional wisdom that pacification would lead to greater intertribal contact and, therefore, an increase in the rate of intertribal marriage, it remains to be explained why the proportion of intertribal marriages decreased. In other words, what forces or situations affected the marriage pattern?

Interviews with young men of marriageable age and some of the oldest men in the community elicited two different perspectives. (Unfortunately, it was not possible for me, being a male, to maintain serious conversation with women on this topic.) Young men typically explained that they do not find wives from other areas because they are "tired"; they just do not have any desire to travel the long distances to visit women of other areas when there are women close at hand. This emic explanation is not particularly satisfactory from an anthropological perspective.

While the older men could not explain why the distribution of marriages in their younger days differed from that of more recent years, they were able to describe the ways young men and women met prospective spouses from other tribes prior to the coming of Europeans scarcely twenty years earlier. The old men reported that when they were young trade was very important. Salt, stone axes, bird of paradise feathers, shells of different kinds, pandanus oil, carpul fur, and the like were traded between tribes during trading expeditions. Figure 2 maps the trade network as described by the older residents of Mul.

When they were young, the old men reported, they would dress in their finest decorations and travel to the places described in Figure 2. The women at these places, they said, would see them arrayed in all their finery and want to marry them. Of course, the situation may not have been quite this straightforward.

These reports drew my attention to the link between intertribal marriage and trade for scarce necessary and luxury resources. What would be the effect of the introduction of European goods upon trade? And, could this affect marriage patterns?

According to the old men, pigs from Mul were traded south to the lower elevation, less densely populated areas in return for bird of paradise feathers and carpul fur (see Figure 2). Some of the fur and feathers were traded for cowrie shells with people from Sina. Cowries, in turn, were traded to the Gomgales for kina shells. Carpul fur and pandanus oil were traded to the east for salt. Finally, some of the fur and feathers obtained from the south and the salt obtained from the east were traded to the northeast for stone axes and small shells, which had in turn been brought in from even further off.

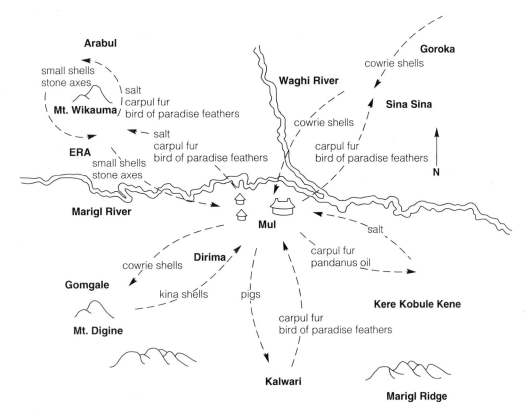

Figure 2
Traditional Exchange Network

Enter the ubiquitous steel axe; exit the stone axe. No one in Mul today would use a stone axe. Indeed, it was difficult to find someone who recalled how to attach stone to handle. The effect was that the primary reason for trade between the peoples of Mul and Era (i.e., the need for stone axes) was eliminated and the Muls' need for fur, feathers, and salt was reduced (what may have begun to increase was a need for cash). Similarly, salt increasingly became more readily available. Nowadays it can be purchased at the store on the government station or in small trade stores which stock, for example, three bags of salt, two packs of cigarettes, a bit of rice, and two or three tins of mackerel. The availability of salt locally eliminates the need to trade for it and further reduces the need for fur. Thus, two of the five trade routes shown on Figure 2 become totally unnecessary and the usefulness of trade items from a third is reduced.

The elimination of the need to trade for necessary scarce resources allowed some trade relations to atrophy. I use the term *atrophy* since the process was probably one of gradual disuse of trade networks rather than a catastrophic change. The remaining trade relations were reliant upon the need for luxury items such as shells and feathers. Scholars who have done long-term research in New Guinea have described the highlanders' declining interest in these decorative items.

With the introduction of Western goods and the reduction of trade, both the need and the opportunity for intermarriage declined. Intertribal marriage was functional in that it facilitated intergroup economic transactions. While there are a range of rights and obligations as well as affective ties which make marriage into neighboring groups preferable, more distant marriages have recognized importance. This same point was made by Roy Rappaport in his study of the Tsembaga Maring:

> While unions between men and women of a single local group are generally preferred, the Tsembaga recognize certain advantages in marriage to members of other local groups . . . unions with groups north of the Sambai River and south of the Bismarks strengthen trading relationships. Bird-of-paradise plumes and shell ornaments are still obtained from these groups and until the 1950s stone axes from the Jimi Valley were traded for salt manufactured in the Simbai Valley (1969:121).

An early paper on the Siani linked trade and marriage directly by focusing on the exchange of nonutilitarian valuables which occurred at marriage and at the rites of passage for children of the marriage (Salisbury 1956). Valuables were traded in from the coast about 70 miles to the northeast. Trading took the form of ceremonial gift exchange between affines. At the same time, Salisbury reports a statistically significant trend for Siane men to obtain wives from the south and west while their sisters marry into groups from the north and east (the direction from which valuables come).

Even more interesting for the present purpose is Salisbury's report on the effect of the introduction of European wealth goods. The European settlements nearest the Siane were in Goroka and Asaroka, 30 miles to the east and north. Groups nearest these (who were already closer than the Siane to coastal wealth) quickly became wealthy in shells, cloth, and other European goods. Salisbury reports that, as a result of this increased wealth, the movement of women in that direction became more pronounced. He also notes that "Neither the wealth difference nor the movement of women is recognized in Siane idealogy."

Thus, Salisbury clearly links marriage patterns to the need to obtain wealth not locally available, although no mention is made of utilitarian goods. While the initial response to "wealthy neighbors" is to increase "wife giving," it is easy to see that once wealth is more evenly (and locally) distributed this reason for marrying out will no longer be of major consequence.

Particularly in the many areas of the highlands where marriages were arranged by families with minimal, if any, consultation with the bride or groom, consideration of trade relations was likely to play a role in the selection of a spouse. Families had an interest in the establishment or maintenance of trade relations.

At the same time that the function of intertribal marriage for maintaining the economic system in terms of access to necessary resources was eliminated, the decline in trade itself reduced the opportunity to make marriage arrangements between non-adjacent groups. Generally speaking, opportunity for marriage is not random but may be structured by factors such as class, caste, religious affiliation, sorority membership, or political borders. Changes in this structure of opportunity may lead to observable changes in marriage patterns. In other words, a change in the visiting (or trading) pattern between autonomous political groups could affect the structure of opportunity. The importance of opportunity remains whether the individuals are free to choose their own mates or whether such choices are made for them.

In central Simbu elders choose a person's spouse for them and, although they can refuse, the bride and groom usually accept even though they may never have met. Brown (1969) reports that some groups do not intermarry because of the lack of opportunity to make arrangements.

Administrative policy and mission influence may have speeded the process. In some areas, such as South Fore or Manga, Australian patrol officers insisted (or at least strongly urged) that brides consent and that

women have a right to choose a spouse. Nowadays in central Simbu more marriages are being initiated by the couples themselves. Choice in a mate is likely to further increase the importance of the structure of opportunity.

In sum, the argument here is that the replacement, by Western goods, of resources secured through trade reduced the economic need (function) for intergroup marriage and the opportunity to arrange such marriages. The effects of these changes were not felt immediately because of the extant relations between groups. Over time fewer and fewer intertribal marriages were arranged to replace those of the passing generation. The net effect was a gradual decay of the web of affinal and non-agnatic ties which cut across tribal boundaries.

CONCLUSION

Gordon (1989) has insightfully pointed out that there is very little sense in talking about or planning development if people live in fear of renewed tribal fighting. Moreover, he notes that this is a testing time for anthropologists "who find that their explanatory models are somewhat inadequate." Indeed, few of the explanations begin from a particular theoretical position nor even a unified conceptual model; there is little discussion of the mechanisms by which suggested "causes" result in the behavior being explained; and, little evidence is presented to test the explanations.

In this paper, I have employed a particular theoretic strategy, namely, cultural materialism, in which the efficacy of explanatory models are ranked: infrastructure, structure, and superstructure.

Prior to contact with the outside world, stone axe heads and salt were produced in local areas where these resources were available. Redistribution was accomplished through trade. One of the functions of intertribal marriage was the facilitation of trade between autonomous political groups. With the early introduction of Western goods, particularly steel axes and salt, local production was discontinued and marriage was no longer necessary to maintain these trade relations. As trade was discontinued, so declined the opportunity to make marriage arrangements between non-adjacent groups. Of course, existing marriage ties facilitated continued contact between groups, but probably less frequently, and there was no pragmatic reason for young people to marry others from distant areas. Particularly in the case of women, where such a marriage necessitated a move far from her natal family, there were distinct disadvantages. Thus, as older people died and fewer marriages were arranged between groups, the web of affinal and non-agnatic kin ties decayed. Intertribal marriages provided a linkage through which groups could communicate, and a mechanism and reason for containing conflict. With the decline in intergroup marriage over time, the likelihood of a dispute expanding into full-scale warfare increased.

This explanation began with infrastructural conditions (production) and showed how they were causally related to structural changes (trade relations) which in turn caused further structural changes (the web of kin ties), finally leading to changes in conflict behaviors. I have tried to explain each of the stages in this temporal process, i.e., the relationship between trade and marriage and the relationship between marriage and warfare.

Scientific hypotheses and models can be tested by examining predictions which can be deduced from them. The model which I have outlined predicts the unlikely occurrence that, with pacification and the ability to wander further afield without the threat of life and limb, intertribal marriage actually declined rather than rose as was thought would be the case. The hypothesis was tested on genealogical data collected in this research site as well as on data published earlier from a different area of the Simbu province. This is but a single case study and there is no statistical reason to extend the findings to other areas of the highlands. However, the inability to falsify the hypothesis in this case lends support to the general efficacy of the explanation.

NOTES

1. Financial support from the National Science Foundation (Grant No. BNS76-218 37) is gratefully acknowledged.
2. For a more extensive discussion of this period with special reference to the resurgence of fighting, see Brown 1982a and 1982b.
3. Paula Brown reports (pers. comm.) that recently many Simbu women are marrying outside the Simbu to men they had met in the district or on visits. She notes that there are, now, advantages for older men having a daughter married to a prestigious outsider. Naregu men who migrate probably also marry outsiders.

Such marriages further the process described here since, although they are extra-tribal, they do not link neighboring potential enemy groups.

REFERENCES

Brown, P. 1964. Enemies and Affines. *Ethnology* 3:335–356.

——. 1969. Marriage in Chimbu. *In* R. M. Glasse and M. Meggitt (eds.), *Pigs, Pearlshells and Women*, pp. 77–95. Englewood Cliffs, NJ: Prentice-Hall.

——. 1970. Chimbu Transactions. *Man* 5:99–117.

——. 1982a. Conflict in the New Guinea Highlands. *Journal of Conflict Resolution* 26:525–546.

——. 1982b. Chimbu Disorder: Tribal Fighting in Newly Independent Papua New Guinea. *Pacific Viewpoint* 22:1–21.

Gordon, R. 1980. Rituals of Governance and the Breakdown of Law and Order in Papua New Guinea. Paper presented at the annual meeting of the American Anthropological Association. Washington, D.C.

——. 1983. The Decline of the Kiapdom and the Resurgence of "Tribal Fighting" in Enga. *Oceania* 53:205–223.

Howlett, D., et al. 1976. *Chimbu: Issues in Development.* Development Studies Centre Monograph No. 4 Canberra.

Koch, K. 1974. *The Anthropology of Warfare.* Addison-Wesley Module in Anthropology No. 52.

Meggitt, M. 1958. The Enga of the New Guinea Highlands. *Oceania* 28:253–330.

——. 1977. *Blood Is Their Argument: Warfare Among the Mae Enga Tribesmen of the New Guinea Highlands.* Palo Alto, CA: Mayfield.

Rappaport, R. 1969. Marriage Among the Maring. *In* R. M. Glasse and M. Meggitt (eds.), *Pigs, Pearlshells and Women*, pp. 117–137. Englewood Cliffs, NJ: Prentice-Hall.

Salisbury, R. F. 1956. Asymmetrical Marriage Systems. *American Anthropologist* 58:639–655.

——. 1962. *From Stone to Steel.* London: Cambridge University Press.

Standish, B. 1973. The Highlands. *New Guinea* 8:4–30.

Wormsley, W. 1982. *Tribal Fighting, Law and Order, and Socioeconomic Development in Enga, Papua New Guinea.* Paper presented at the meetings of the American Anthropological Association. Washington, D.C.

34

Ritual Regulation
of Environmental Relations
Among a New Guinea People

Roy A. Rappaport

Environmental regulation is a hot topic. Air and water pollution, the overuse of land, and overpopulation are among the many interrelated factors implicated in the degradation of the environment and the predicted global warming. Although government regulation has been an important strategy, businesses have recently argued that these regulations limit their efforts to profitably expand and thereby create new jobs. We have seen in several selections that environmental problems, such as deforestation, are not limited to the United States and other highly industrialized nations. We find, however, that some indigenous cultural institutions regulate behavior that would, if left unchecked, damage society in the long run.

Religious rituals are found in all societies, from the technologically most simple to the most sophisticated. Such rituals are, of course, explained in terms of the spiritual well-being of individuals or groups. Most people have also long recognized that rituals have important sociological and psychological functions. In this classic study of the Tsembaga people of the New Guinea highlands, Roy Rappaport goes further to suggest that ritual "helps to maintain an undegraded environment, limits fighting to frequencies which do not endanger the existence of the regional population, adjusts man-land ratios, facilitates trade, distributes local surpluses of pig throughout the regional population in the form of pork, and assures people of high quality protein when they are most in need of it."

If today's religious rituals protected the environment, maybe we wouldn't need government regulation.

As you read this selection, ask yourself the following questions:

☐ What was the traditionally dominant anthropological view of the functions of religious rituals? Was ritual thought to produce practical results?

☐ What, specifically, does Rappaport believe are the functions of ritual among the Tsembaga?

☐ Is there an ecological balance between the productivity of gardens and fallow periods, on the one hand, and the human and animal population on the other?

☐ When are pigs killed? What is the context? How and why is this related to stress?

☐ How does the ritual cycle affect the distribution of land and membership in groups?

☐ How does the ritual cycle affect intergroup conflict?

The following terms discussed in this selection are included in the Glossary at the back of the book:

affines	chief	feral
agnates	cognatic kin	patrilineal
big men	demography	population
biotic community	ecosystem	ritual
bridewealth	egalitarian	swidden cultivation
bush-fallow	etiology	taboo
carrying capacity	fecundity	trophic exchanges

From *Ethnology*, 6:17–30, 1967. Reprinted by permission of Department of Anthropology, University of Pittsburgh and the author.

Most functional studies of religious behavior in anthropology have as an analytic goal the elucidation of events,[1] processes, or relationships occurring within a social unit of some sort. The social unit is not always well defined, but in some cases it appears to be a church, that is, a group of people who entertain similar beliefs about the universe, or a congregation, a group of people who participate together in the performance of religious rituals. There have been exceptions. Thus Vayda, Leeds, and Smith (1961) and J. K. Moore (1957) have clearly perceived that the functions of religious ritual are not necessarily confined within the boundaries of a congregation or even a church. By and large, however, I believe that the following statement by Homans (1941:172) represents fairly the dominant line of anthropological thought concerning the functions of religious ritual:

> Ritual actions do not produce a practical result on the external world—that is one of the reasons why we call them ritual. But to make this statement is not to say that ritual has no function. Its function is not related to the world external to the society but to the internal constitution of the society. It gives the members of the society confidence, it dispels their anxieties, it disciplines their social organization.

No argument will be raised here against the sociological and psychological functions imputed by Homans, and many others before him, to ritual. They seem to me to be plausible. Nevertheless, in some cases at least, ritual does produce, in Homans' terms, "a practical result on the world" external not only to the social unit composed of those who participate together in ritual performances but also to the larger unit composed of those who entertain similar beliefs concerning the universe. The material presented here will show that the ritual cycles of the Tsembaga, and of other local territorial groups of Maring speakers living in the New Guinea interior, play an important part in regulating the relationships of these groups with both the nonhuman components of their immediate environments and the human components of their less immediate environments, that is, with other similar territorial groups. To be more specific, this regulation helps to maintain the biotic communities existing within their territories, redistributes land among people and people over land, and limits the frequency of fighting. In the absence of authoritative political statuses or offices, the ritual cycle likewise provides a means for mobilizing allies when warfare may be undertaken. It also provides a mechanism for redistributing local pig surpluses in the form of pork throughout a large regional population while helping to assure the local population of a supply of pork when its members are most in need of high quality protein.

Religious ritual may be defined, for the purposes of this paper, as the prescribed performance of conventionalized acts manifestly directed toward the involvement of nonempirical or supernatural agencies in the affairs of the actors. While this definition relies upon the formal characteristics of the performances and upon the motives for undertaking them, attention will be focused upon the empirical effects of ritual performances and sequences of ritual performances. The religious rituals to be discussed are regarded as neither more nor less than part of the behavioral repertoire employed by an aggregate of organisms in adjusting to its environment. The data upon which this paper is based were collected during fourteen months of field work among the Tsembaga, one of about twenty local groups of Maring speakers living in the Simbai and Jimi Valleys of the Bismarck Range in the Territory of New Guinea. The size of Maring local groups varies from a little over 100 to 900. The Tsembaga, who in 1963 numbered 204 persons, are located on the south wall of the Simbai Valley. The country in which they live differs from the true highlands in being lower, generally more rugged, and more heavily forested. Tsembaga territory rises, within a total surface area of 3.2 square miles, from an elevation of 2,200 feet at the Simbai river to 7,200 feet at the ridge crest. Gardens are cut in the secondary forests up to between 5,000 and 5,400 feet, above which the area remains in primary forest. Rainfall reaches 150 inches per year.

The Tsembaga have come into contact with the outside world only recently: The first government patrol to penetrate their territory arrived in 1954. They were considered uncontrolled by the Australian government until 1962, and they remain unmissionized to this day.

The 204 Tsembaga are distributed among five putatively patrilineal clans, which are, in turn, organized into more inclusive groupings on two hierarchical levels below that of the total local group.[2] Internal political structure is highly egalitarian. There are no hereditary or elected chiefs, nor are there even "big men" who can regularly coerce or command the support of their clansmen or co-residents in economic or forceful enterprises.

It is convenient to regard the Tsembaga as a population in the ecological sense, that is, as one of the components of a system of trophic exchanges taking place within a bounded area. Tsembaga territory and the biotic community existing upon it may be conveniently viewed as an ecosystem. While it would be permissible arbitrarily to designate the Tsembaga as a population and their territory with its biota as an ecosystem, there are also nonarbitrary reasons for doing so. An ecosystem is a system of material exchanges, and the Tsembaga maintain against other human groups exclusive access to the resources within their territorial borders. Conversely, it is from this territory alone that the Tsembaga ordinarily derive all of their foodstuffs and most of the other materials they require for survival. Less anthropocentrically, it may be justified to regard Tsembaga territory with its biota as an ecosystem in view of the rather localized nature of cyclical material exchanges in tropical rainforests.

As they are involved with the nonhuman biotic community within their territory in a set of trophic exchanges, so do they participate in other material relationships with other human groups external to their territory. Genetic materials are exchanged with other groups, and certain crucial items, such as stone axes, were in the past obtained from the outside. Furthermore, in the area occupied by the Maring speakers, more than one local group is usually involved in any process, either peaceful or warlike, through which people are redistributed over land and land redistributed among people.

The concept of the ecosystem, though it provides a convenient frame for the analysis of interspecific trophic exchanges taking place within limited geographical areas, does not comfortably accommodate intraspecific exchanges taking place over wider geographical areas. Some sort of geographical population model would be more useful for the analysis of the relationship of the local ecological population to the larger regional population of which it is a part, but we lack even a set of appropriate terms for such a model. Suffice it here to note that the relations of the Tsembaga to the total of other local human populations in their vicinity are similar to the relations of local aggregates of other animals to the totality of their species occupying broader and more or less continuous regions. This larger, more inclusive aggregate may resemble what geneticists mean by the term *population*, that is, an aggregate of interbreeding organisms persisting through an indefinite number of generations and either living or capable of living in isolation from similar aggregates of the same species. This is the unit which survives through long periods of time while its local ecological (*sensu stricto*) subunits, the units more or less independently involved in interspecific trophic exchanges such as the Tsembaga, are ephemeral.

Since it has been asserted that the ritual cycles of the Tsembaga regulate relationships within what may be regarded as a complex system, it is necessary, before proceeding to the ritual cycle itself, to describe briefly, and where possible in quantitative terms, some aspects of the place of the Tsembaga in this system.

The Tsembaga are bush-fallowing horticulturalists. Staples include a range of root crops, taro (*Colocasia*) and sweet potatoes being most important, yams and manioc less so. In addition, a great variety of greens are raised, some of which are rich in protein. Sugar cane and some tree crops, particularly *Pandanus conoideus*, are also important.

All gardens are mixed, many of them containing all of the major root crops and many greens. Two named garden types are, however, distinguished by the crops which predominate in them. "Taro-yam gardens" were found to produce, on the basis of daily harvest records kept on entire gardens for close to one year, about 5,300,000 calories[3] per acre during their harvesting lives of 18 to 24 months; 85 percent of their yield is harvested between 24 and 76 weeks after planting. "Sugar–sweet potato gardens" produce about 4,600,000 calories per acre during their harvesting lives, 91 percent being taken between 24 and 76 weeks after planting. I estimated that approximately 310,000 calories per acre is expended on cutting, fencing, planting, maintaining, harvesting, and walking to and from taro-yam gardens. Sugar–sweet potato gardens required an expenditure of approximately 290,000 calories per acre.[4] These energy ratios, approximately 17:1 on taro-yam gardens and 16:1 on sugar–sweet potato gardens, compare favorably with figures reported for swidden cultivation in other regions.[5]

Intake is high in comparison with the reported dietaries of other New Guinea populations. On the basis of daily consumption records kept for ten months on four households numbering in total sixteen persons, I estimated the average daily intake of adult males to be approximately 2,600 calories, and that of adult females to be around 2,200 calories. It may be mentioned here that the Tsembaga are small and short statured. Adult males average 101 pounds in weight and approximately 58.5 inches in height; the corresponding averages for adult females are 85 pounds and 54.5 inches.[6]

Although 99 percent by weight of the food consumed is vegetable, the protein intake is high by New Guinea standards. The daily protein consumption of adult males from vegetable sources was estimated to be between 43 and 55 grams, of adult females 36 to 48 grams. Even with an adjustment for vegetable sources, these values are slightly in excess of the recently published WHO/FAO daily requirements (Food and Agriculture Organization of the United Nations 1964). The same is true of the younger age categories, although soft and discolored hair, a symptom of protein deficiency, was noted in a few children. The WHO/FAO protein requirements do not include a large "margin for safety" or allowance for stress; and, although no clinical assessments were undertaken, it may be suggested that the Tsembaga achieve nitrogen balance at a low level. In other words, their protein intake is probably marginal.

Measurements of all gardens made during 1962 and of some gardens made during 1963 indicate that, to support the human population, between 0.15 and 0.19 acres are put into cultivation per capita per year. Fallows range from 8 to 45 years. The area in secondary forest comprises approximately 1,000 acres, only 30 to 50 of which are in cultivation at any time. Assuming calories to be the limiting factor, and assuming an unchanging population structure, the territory could support—with no reduction in lengths of fallow and without cutting into the virgin forest from which the Tsembaga extract many important items—between 290 and 397 people if the pig population remained minimal. The size of the pig herd, however, fluctuates widely. Taking Maring pig husbandry procedures into consideration, I have estimated the human carrying capacity of the Tsembaga territory at between 270 and 320 people.

Because the timing of the ritual cycle is bound up with the demography of the pig herd, the place of the pig in Tsembaga adaptation must be examined.

First, being omnivorous, pigs keep residential areas free of garbage and human feces. Second, limited numbers of pigs rooting in secondary growth may help to hasten the development of that growth. The Tsembaga usually permit pigs to enter their gardens one and a half to two years after planting, by which time second-growth trees are well established there. The Tsembaga practice selective weeding; from the time the garden is planted, herbaceous species are removed, but tree species are allowed to remain. By the time cropping is discontinued and the pigs are let in, some of the trees in the garden are already ten to fifteen feet tall. These well-established trees are relatively impervious to damage by the pigs, which, in rooting for seeds and remaining tubers, eliminate many seeds and seedlings that, if allowed to develop, would provide some competition for the established trees. Moreover, in some Maring-speaking areas swiddens are planted twice, although this is not the case with the Tsembaga. After the first crop is almost exhausted, pigs are penned in the garden, where their rooting eliminates weeds and softens the ground, making the task of planting for a second time easier. The pigs, in other words, are used as cultivating machines.

Small numbers of pigs are easy to keep. They run free during the day and return home at night to receive their ration of garbage and substandard tubers, particularly sweet potatoes. Supplying the latter requires little extra work, for the substandard tubers are taken from the ground in the course of harvesting the daily ration for humans. Daily consumption records kept over a period of some months show that the ration of tubers received by the pigs approximates in weight that consumed by adult humans, i.e., a little less than three pounds per day per pig.

If the pig herd grows large, however, the substandard tubers incidentally obtained in the course of harvesting for human needs become insufficient and it becomes necessary to harvest especially for pigs. In other words, people must work for the pigs and perhaps even supply them with food fit for human consumption. Thus, as Vayda, Leeds, and Smith (1961:71) have pointed out, there can be too many pigs for a given community.

This also holds true of the sanitary and cultivating services rendered by pigs. A small number of pigs is sufficient to keep residential areas clean, to suppress superfluous seedlings in abandoned gardens, and to soften the soil in gardens scheduled for second plantings. A larger herd, on the other hand, may be troublesome; the larger the number of pigs, the greater the possibility of their invasion of producing gardens, with concomitant damage not only to crops and young secondary growth but also to the relations between the pig owners and garden owners.

All male pigs are castrated at approximately three months of age, for boars, people say, are dangerous and do not grow as large as barrows. Pregnancies, therefore, are always the result of unions of domestic sows with feral males. Fecundity is thus only a fraction of its potential. During one twelve-month period only fourteen litters resulted out of a potential 99 or more pregnancies. Farrowing generally takes place in the forest, and mortality of the young is high. Only 32 of the offspring of the above-mentioned fourteen pregnancies were alive six months after birth. This number is barely sufficient to replace the number of adult animals which would have died or been killed during most years without pig festivals.

The Tsembaga almost never kill domestic pigs outside of ritual contexts. In ordinary times, when there is no pig festival in progress, these rituals are almost always associated with misfortunes or emergencies, notably warfare, illness, injury, or death. Rules state not only the contexts in which pigs are to be ritually slaughtered, but also who may partake of the flesh of the sacrificial animals. During warfare it is only the men participating in the fighting who eat the pork. In cases of illness or injury, it is only the victim and certain near relatives, particularly his co-resident agnates and spouses, who do so.

It is reasonable to assume that misfortune and emergency are likely to induce in the organisms experiencing them a complex of physiological changes known collectively as "stress." Physiological stress reactions occur not only in organisms which are infected with disease or traumatized, but also in those experiencing rage or fear (Houssay et al. 1955:1096), or even prolonged anxiety (National Research Council 1963:53). One important aspect of stress is the increased catabolization of protein (Houssay et al. 1955:451; National Research Council 1963:49), with a net loss of nitrogen from the tissues (Houssay et al. 1955:450). This is a serious matter for organisms with a marginal protein intake. Antibody production is low (Berg 1948:311), healing is slow (Large and Johnston 1948:352), and a variety of symptoms of a serious nature are likely to develop (Lund and Levenson 1948:349; Zintel 1964:1043). The status of a protein-depleted animal, however, may be significantly improved in a relatively short period of time by the intake of high quality protein, and high protein diets are therefore routinely prescribed for surgical patients and those suffering from infectious diseases (Burton 1959:231; Lund and Levenson 1948:350; Elman 1951:85ff; Zintel 1964:1043ff).

It is precisely when they are undergoing physiological stress that the Tsembaga kill and consume their pigs, and it should be noted that they limit the consumption to those likely to be experiencing stress most profoundly. The Tsembaga, of course, know nothing of physiological stress. Native theories of the etiology and treatment of disease and injury implicate various categories of spirits to whom sacrifices must be made. Nevertheless, the behavior which is appropriate in terms of native understandings is also appropriate to the actual situation confronting the actors.

We may now outline in the barest of terms the Tsembaga ritual cycle. Space does not permit a description of its ideological correlates. It must suffice to note that Tsembaga do not necessarily perceive all of the empirical effects which the anthropologist sees to flow from their ritual behavior. Such empirical consequences as they may perceive, moreover, are not central to their rationalizations of the performances. The Tsembaga say that they perform the rituals in order to rearrange their relationships with the supernatural world. We may only reiterate here that behavior undertaken in reference to their "cognized environment"— an environment which includes as very important elements the spirits of ancestors—seems appropriate in their "operational environment," the material environment specified by the anthropologist through operations of observation, including measurement.

Since the rituals are arranged in a cycle, description may commence at any point. The operation of the cycle becomes clearest if we begin with the rituals performed during warfare. Opponents in all cases occupy adjacent territories, in almost all cases on the same valley wall. After hostilities have broken out, each side performs certain rituals which place the opposing side in the formal category of "enemy." A number of taboos prevail while hostilities continue. These include prohibitions on sexual intercourse and on the ingestion of certain things—food prepared by women, food grown on the lower portion of the territory, marsupials, eels, and, while actually on the fighting ground, any liquid whatsoever.

One ritual practice associated with fighting which may have some physiological consequences deserves mention. Immediately before proceeding to the fighting ground, the warriors eat heavily salted pig fat. The ingestion of salt, coupled with the taboo on drinking,

has the effect of shortening the fighting day, particularly since the Maring prefer to fight only on bright sunny days. When everyone gets unbearably thirsty, according to informants, fighting is broken off.

There may formerly have been other effects if the native salt contained sodium (the production of salt was discontinued some years previous to the fieldwork, and no samples were obtained). The Maring diet seems to be deficient in sodium. The ingestion of large amounts of sodium just prior to fighting would have permitted the warriors to sweat normally without a lowering of blood volume and consequent weakness during the course of the fighting. The pork belly ingested with the salt would have provided them with a new burst of energy two hours or so after the commencement of the engagement. After fighting was finished for the day, lean pork was consumed, offsetting, at least to some extent, the nitrogen loss associated with the stressful fighting (personal communications from F. Dunn, W. MacFarlane, and J. Sabine, 1965).

Fighting could continue sporadically for weeks. Occasionally it terminated in the rout of one of the antagonistic groups, whose survivors would take refuge with kinsmen elsewhere. In such instances, the victors would lay waste their opponents' groves and gardens, slaughter their pigs, and burn their houses. They would not, however, immediately annex the territory of the vanquished. The Maring say that they never take over the territory of an enemy for, even if it has been abandoned, the spirits of their ancestors remain to guard it against interlopers. Most fights, however, terminated in truces between the antagonists.

With the termination of hostilities a group which has not been driven off its territory performs a ritual called "planting the *rumbim*." Every man puts his hand on the ritual plant, *rumbim* (*Cordyline fruticosa* (L.). A. Chev; *C. terminalis*, Kunth), as it is planted in the ground. The ancestors are addressed, in effect, as follows:

> We thank you for helping us in the fight and permitting us to remain on our territory. We place our souls in this *rumbim* as we plant it on our ground. We ask you to care for this *rumbim*. We will kill pigs for you now, but they are few. In the future, when we have many pigs, we shall again give you pork and uproot the *rumbim* and stage a *kaiko* (pig festival). But until there are sufficient pigs to repay you the *rumbim* will remain in the ground.

This ritual is accompanied by the wholesale slaughter of pigs. Only juveniles remain alive. All adult and adolescent animals are killed, cooked, and dedicated to the ancestors. Some are consumed by the local group, but most are distributed to allies who assisted in the fight.

Some of the taboos which the group suffered during the time of fighting are abrogated by this ritual. Sexual intercourse is now permitted, liquids may be taken at any time, and food from any part of the territory may be eaten. But the group is still in debt to its allies and ancestors. People say it is still the time of the *bamp ku,* or "fighting stones," which are actual objects used in the rituals associated with warfare. Although the fighting ceases when *rumbim* is planted, the concomitant obligations, debts to allies and ancestors, remain outstanding; and the fighting stones may not be put away until these obligations are fulfilled. The time of the fighting stones is a time of debt and danger which lasts until the *rumbim* is uprooted and a pig festival (*kaiko*) is staged.

Certain taboos persist during the time of the fighting stones. Marsupials, regarded as the pigs of the ancestors of the high ground, may not be trapped until the debt to their masters has been repaid. Eels, the "pigs of the ancestors of the low ground," may neither be caught nor consumed. Prohibitions on all intercourse with the enemy come into force. One may not touch, talk to, or even look at a member of the enemy group, nor set foot on enemy ground. Even more important, a group may not attack another group while its ritual plant remains in the ground, for it has not yet fully rewarded its ancestors and allies for their assistance in the last fight. Until the debts to them have been paid, further assistance from them will not be forthcoming. A kind of "truce of god" thus prevails until the *rumbim* is uprooted and a *kaiko* completed.

To uproot the *rumbim* requires sufficient pigs. How many pigs are sufficient, and how long does it take to acquire them? The Tsembaga say that, if a place is "good," this can take as little as five years; but if a place is "bad," it may require ten years or longer. A bad place is one in which misfortunes are frequent and where, therefore, ritual demands for the killing of pigs arise frequently. A good place is one where such demands are infrequent. In a good place, the increase of the pig herd exceeds the ongoing ritual demands, and the herd grows rapidly. Sooner or later the substandard tubers incidentally obtained while harvesting become insufficient to feed the herd, and additional acreage must be put into production specifically for the pigs.

The work involved in caring for a large pig herd can be extremely burdensome. The Tsembaga herd just prior to the pig festival of 1962–63, when it numbered 169 animals, was receiving 54 percent of all of the sweet potatoes and 82 percent of all of the manioc harvested. These comprised 35.9 percent by weight of all root crops harvested. This figure is consistent with the difference between the amount of land under cultivation just previous to the pig festival, when the herd was at maximum size, and that immediately afterwards, when the pig herd was at minimum size. The former was 36.1 percent in excess of the latter.

I have estimated on the basis of acreage yield and energy expenditure figures, that about 45,000 calories per year are expended in caring for one pig 120 to 150 pounds in size. It is upon women that most of the burden of pig keeping falls. If, from a woman's daily intake of about 2,200 calories, 950 calories are allowed for basal metabolism, a woman has only 1,250 calories a day available for all her activities, which include gardening for her family, child care, and cooking, as well as tending pigs. It is clear that no woman can feed many pigs; only a few had as many as four in their care at the commencement of the festival; and it is not surprising that agitation to uproot the *rumbim* and stage the *kaiko* starts with the wives of the owners of large numbers of pigs.

A large herd is not only burdensome as far as energy expenditure is concerned; it becomes increasingly a nuisance as it expands. The more numerous pigs become, the more frequently are gardens invaded by them. Such events result in serious disturbances of local tranquillity. The garden owner often shoots, or attempts to shoot, the offending pig; and the pig owner commonly retorts by shooting, or attempting to shoot, either the garden owner, his wife, or one of his pigs. As more and more such events occur, the settlement, nucleated when the herd was small, disperses as people try to put as much distance as possible between their pigs and other people's gardens and between their gardens and other people's pigs. Occasionally this reaches its logical conclusion, and people begin to leave the territory, taking up residence with kinsmen in other local populations.

The number of pigs sufficient to become intolerable to the Tsembaga was below the capacity of the territory to carry pigs. I have estimated that, if the size and structure of the human population remained constant at the 1962–1963 level, a pig population of 140 to 240 animals averaging 100 to 150 pounds in size could be maintained perpetually by the Tsembaga without necessarily inducing environmental degradation. Since the size of the herd fluctuates, even higher cyclical maxima could be achieved. The level of toleration, however, is likely always to be below the carrying capacity, since the destructive capacity of the pigs is dependent upon the population density of both people and pigs, rather than upon population size. The denser the human population, the fewer pigs will be required to disrupt social life. If the carrying capacity is exceeded, it is likely to be exceeded by people and not by pigs.

The *kaiko* or pig festival, which commences with the planting of stakes at the boundary and the uprooting of the *rumbim,* is thus triggered by either the additional work attendant upon feeding pigs or the destructive capacity of the pigs themselves. It may be said, then, that there are sufficient pigs to stage the *kaiko* when the relationship of pigs to people changes from one of mutualism to one of parasitism or competition.

A short time prior to the uprooting of the *rumbim*, stakes are planted at the boundary. If the enemy has continued to occupy its territory, the stakes are planted at the boundary which existed before the fight. If, on the other hand, the enemy has abandoned its territory, the victors may plant their stakes at a new boundary which encompasses areas previously occupied by the enemy. The Maring say, to be sure, that they never take land belonging to an enemy, but this land is regarded as vacant, since no *rumbim* was planted on it after the last fight. We may state here a rule of land redistribution in terms of the ritual cycle: *If one of a pair of antagonistic groups is able to uproot its rumbim before its opponents can plant their rumbim, it may occupy the latter's territory.*

Not only have the vanquished abandoned their territory; it is assumed that it has also been abandoned by their ancestors as well. The surviving members of the erstwhile enemy group have by this time resided with other groups for a number of years, and most if not all of them have already had occasion to sacrifice pigs to their ancestors at their new residences. In so doing they have invited these spirits to settle at the new locations of the living, where they will in the future receive sacrifices. Ancestors of vanquished groups thus relinquish their guardianship over the territory, making it available to victorious groups. Meanwhile, the *de facto* membership of the living in the groups with which they have taken refuge is converted eventually into *de jure* membership. Sooner or later the groups with which they have taken up residence will have occasion to plant *rumbim*, and the refugees, as co-residents, will participate, thus ritually validating their connection to the new territory and the new group. A rule of population redistribution may thus be stated in terms of ritual cycles: *A man becomes a member of a territorial group by participating with it in the planting of rumbim.*

The uprooting of the *rumbim* follows shortly after the planting of stakes at the boundary. On this particular occasion the Tsembaga killed 32 pigs out of their herd of 169. Much of the pork was distributed to allies and affines outside of the local group.

The taboo on trapping marsupials was also terminated at this time. Information is lacking concerning the population dynamics of the local marsupials, but it may well be that the taboo which had prevailed since the last fight—that against taking them in traps—had conserved a fauna which might otherwise have become extinct.

The *kaiko* continues for about a year, during which period friendly groups are entertained from time to time. The guests receive presents of vegetable foods, and the hosts and male guests dance together throughout the night.

These events may be regarded as analogous to aspects of the social behavior of many nonhuman animals. First of all, they include massed epigamic, or courtship, displays (Wynne-Edwards 1962:17). Young women are presented with samples of the eligible males of local groups with which they may not otherwise have had the opportunity to become familiar. The context, moreover, permits the young women to discriminate amongst this sample in terms of both endurance (signaled by how vigorously and how long a man dances) and wealth (signaled by the richness of a man's shell and feather finery).

More importantly, the massed dancing at these events may be regarded as epideictic display, communicating to the participants information concerning the size or density of the group (Wynne-Edwards 1962:16). In many species such displays take place as a prelude to actions which adjust group size or density, and such is the case among the Maring. The massed dancing of the visitors at a *kaiko* entertainment communicates to the hosts, while the *rumbim* truce is still in force, information concerning the amount of support they may expect from the visitors in the bellicose enterprises that they are likely to embark upon soon after the termination of the pig festival.

Among the Maring there are no chiefs or other political authorities capable of commanding the support of a body of followers, and the decision to assist another group in warfare rests with each individual male. Allies are not recruited by appealing for help to other local groups as such. Rather, each member of the groups primarily involved in the hostilities appeals to his cognatic and affinal kinsmen in other local groups. These men, in turn, urge other of their co-residents and kinsmen to "help them fight." The channels through which invitations to dance are extended are precisely those through which appeals for military support are issued. The invitations go not from group to group, but from kinsman to kinsman, the recipients of invitations urging their co-residents to "help them dance."

Invitations to dance do more than exercise the channels through which allies are recruited; they provide a means for judging their effectiveness. Dancing and fighting are regarded as in some sense equivalent. This equivalence is expressed in the similarity of some pre-fight and pre-dance rituals, and the Maring say that those who come to dance come to fight. The size of a visiting dancing contingent is consequently taken as a measure of the size of the contingent of warriors whose assistance may be expected in the next round of warfare.

In the morning the dancing ground turns into a trading ground. The items most frequently exchanged include axes, bird plumes, shell ornaments, an occasional baby pig, and, in former times, native salt. The *kaiko* thus facilitates trade by providing a market-like setting in which large numbers of traders can assemble. It likewise facilitates the movement of two critical items, salt and axes, by creating a demand for the bird plumes which may be exchanged for them.

The *kaiko* concludes with major pig sacrifices. On this particular occasion the Tsembaga butchered 105 adult and adolescent pigs, leaving only 60 juveniles and neonates alive. The survival of an additional fifteen adolescents and adults was only temporary, for they were scheduled as imminent victims. The pork yielded by the Tsembaga slaughter was estimated to weigh between 7,000 and 8,500 pounds, of which between 4,500 and 6,000 pounds were distributed to members of other local groups in 163 separate presentations. An estimated 2,000 to 3,000 people in seventeen local groups were the beneficiaries of the redistribution. The presentations, it should be mentioned, were not confined to pork. Sixteen Tsembaga men presented bridewealth or child-wealth, consisting largely of axes and shells, to their affines at this time.

The *kaiko* terminates on the day of the pig slaughter with the public presentation of salted pig belly to allies of the last fight. Presentations are made through the window in a high ceremonial fence built specially for the occasion at one end of the dance ground. The name of each honored man is announced to the assembled multitude as he charges to the window to receive his hero's portion. The fence is then ritually torn down, and the fighting stones are put away. The pig festival and the ritual cycle have been completed, demonstrating, it may be suggested, the ecological and economic competence of the local population. The local population would now be free, if it were not for the presence of the government, to attack its enemy again, secure in the knowledge that the assistance of allies and ancestors would be forthcoming because they have received pork and the obligations to them have been fulfilled.

Usually fighting did break out again very soon after the completion of the ritual cycle. If peace still prevailed when the ceremonial fence had rotted completely—a process said to take about three years, a little longer than the length of time required to raise a pig to maximum size—*rumbim* was planted as if there had been a fight, and all adult and adolescent pigs were killed. When the pig herd was large enough so that the *rumbim* could be uprooted, peace could be made with former enemies if they were also able to dig out their *rumbim*. To put this in formal terms: *If a pair of antagonistic groups proceeds through two ritual cycles without resumption of hostilities, their enmity may be terminated.*

The relations of the Tsembaga with their environment have been analyzed as a complex system composed of two subsystems. What may be called the "local subsystem" has been derived from the relations of the Tsembaga with the nonhuman components of their immediate or territorial environment. It corresponds to the ecosystem in which the Tsembaga participate. A second subsystem, one which corresponds to the larger regional population of which the Tsembaga are one of the constituent units and which may be designated as the "regional subsystem," has been derived from the relations of the Tsembaga with neighboring local populations similar to themselves.

It has been argued that rituals, arranged in repetitive sequences, regulate relations both within each of the subsystems and within the larger complex system as a whole. The timing of the ritual cycle is largely dependent upon changes in the states of the components of the local subsystem. But the *kaiko*, which is the culmination of the ritual cycle, does more than reverse changes which have taken place within the local subsystem. Its occurrence also affects relations among the components of the regional subsystem. During its performance, obligations to other local populations are fulfilled, support for future military enterprises is rallied, and land from which enemies have earlier been driven is occupied. Its completion, furthermore, permits the local population to initiate warfare again. Conversely, warfare is terminated by rituals which preclude the reinitiation of warfare until the state of the local subsystem is again such that a *kaiko* may be staged and completed. Ritual among the Tsembaga and other Maring, in short, operates as both transducer, "translating" changes in the state of one subsystem into information which can effect changes in a second subsystem, and homeostat, maintaining a number of variables which in sum comprise the total system within ranges of viability. To repeat an earlier assertion, the operation of ritual among the Tsembaga and other Maring helps to maintain an undegraded environment, limits fighting to frequencies which do not endanger the existence of the regional population, adjusts man-land ratios, facilitates trade, distributes local surpluses of pig throughout the regional population in the form of pork, and assures people of high quality protein when they are most in need of it.

Religious rituals and the supernatural orders toward which they are directed cannot be assumed *a priori* to be mere epiphenomena. Ritual may, and doubtless frequently does, do nothing more than validate and intensify the relationships which integrate the social unit or symbolize the relationships which bind the social unit to its environment. But the interpretation of such presumably *sapiens*-specific phenomena as religious ritual within a framework which will also accommodate the behavior of other species shows, I think, that religious ritual may do much more than symbolize, validate, and intensify relationships. Indeed, it would not be improper to refer to the Tsembaga and the other entities with which they share their territory as a "ritually regulated ecosystem" and to the Tsembaga and their human neighbors as a "ritually regulated population."

NOTES

1. The field work upon which this paper is based was supported by a grant from the National Science Foundation, under which Professor A. P. Vayda was principal investigator. Personal support was received by the author from the National Institutes of Health. Earlier versions of this paper were presented at the 1964 annual meeting of the American Anthropological Association in Detroit, and before a Columbia University seminar on Ecological Systems and Cultural Evolution. I have received valuable suggestions from Alexander Alland, Jacques Barrau, William Clarke, Paul Collins, C. Glen King, Marvin Harris, Margaret Mead, M. J. Meggitt, Ann Rappaport, John Street, Marjorie Whiting, Cherry Vayda, A. P. Vayda and many others, but I take full responsibility for the analysis presented herewith.

2. The social organization of the Tsembaga will be described in detail elsewhere.

3. Because the length of time in the field precluded the possibility of maintaining honest records on single gardens from planting through abandonment, figures were based in the case of both "taro-yam" and "sugar–sweet potato" gardens on three separate gardens planted in successive years. Conversions from the gross weight to the caloric value of yields were made by reference to the literature. The sources used are listed in Rappaport (1966: Appendix VIII).

4. Rough time and motion studies of each of the tasks involved in making, maintaining, harvesting, and walking to and from gardens were undertaken. Conversion to energy expenditure values was accomplished by reference to energy expenditure tables prepared by Hipsley and Kirk (1965:43) on the basis of gas exchange measurements made during the performance of garden tasks by the Chimbu people of the New Guinea highlands.

5. Marvin Harris, in an unpublished paper, estimates the ratio of energy return to energy input ratio on Dyak (Borneo) rice swiddens at 10:1. His estimates of energy ratios on Tepotzlan (Meso-America) swiddens range from 13:1 on poor land to 29:1 for the best land.

6. Heights may be inaccurate. Many men wear their hair in large coiffures hardened with pandanus grease, and it was necessary in some instances to estimate the location of the top of the skull.

REFERENCES

Berg, C. 1948. Protein Deficiency and Its Relation to Nutritional Anemia. Hypoproteinemia, Nutritional Edema, and Resistance to Infection. In *Protein and Amino Acids in Nutrition.* ed. M. Sahyun. Pp. 290–317. New York.

Burton, B. T., ed. 1959. *The Heinz Handbook of Nutrition.* New York.

Elman, R. 1951. *Surgical Care.* New York.

Food and Agriculture Organization of the United Nations. 1964. Protein: At the Heart of the World Food Problem. *World Food Problems* 5. Rome.

Hipsley, E., and N. Kirk. 1965. Studies of the Dietary Intake and Energy Expenditure of New Guineans. South Pacific Commission. Technical Paper 147. Noumea.

Homans, G. C. 1941. Anxiety and Ritual: The Theories of Malinowski and Radcliffe-Brown. *American Anthropologist* 43: 164–172.

Houssay, B. A. et al. 1955. *Human Physiology.* 2nd ed. New York.

Large, A., and C. G. Johnston. 1948. Proteins as Related to Burns. In *Proteins and Amino Acids in Nutrition.* ed. M. Sahyun. Pp. 386–396. New York.

Lund, C. G., and S. M. Levenson. 1948. Protein Nutrition in Surgical Patients. In *Proteins and Amino Acids in Nutrition.* ed. M. Sahyun. Pp. 349–363. New York.

Moore, O. K. 1957. Divination—a New Perspective. *American Anthropologist* 59:69–74.

National Research Council. 1963. Evaluation of Protein Quality. National Academy of Sciences—National Research Council Publication 1100. Washington.

Rappaport, R. A. 1966. Ritual in the Ecology of a New Guinea People. Unpublished doctoral dissertation, Columbia University.

Vayda, A. P., A. Leeds, and D. B. Smith. 1961. The Place of Pigs in Melanesian Subsistence. *Proceedings of the 1961 Annual Spring Meeting of the American Ethnological Society.* ed. V. E. Garfield. Pp. 69–77. Seattle.

Wynne-Edwards, V. C. 1962. *Animal Dispersion in Relation to Social Behaviour.* Edinburgh and London.

Zintel, Harold A. 1964. Nutrition in the Care of the Surgical Patient. In *Modern Nutrition in Health and Disease*, 3rd ed., ed. M. G. Wohl and R. S. Goodhart. Pp. 1043–1064. Philadelphia.

35

Hallucinogenic Plants and Their Use in Traditional Societies

Wade Davis

In Western society, drugs are used for either medicinal purposes or pleasure. Our culture sometimes defines those who use drugs for nonmedicinal purposes as deviant, and we have begun to view the use of drugs as a pathological condition unique in the annals of human history. The illegal use of drugs is considered a major social problem. In Selection 3, an ethnography of "Crack Street," we saw the human dimension of that problem.

The use of drugs is widespread in traditional cultures around the world. However, in traditional societies hallucinogenic plants are used for religious purposes and in ritual settings. Throughout history, people have sought ways to see beyond the normal reality of everyday life. They have endured the risk of poison in experimenting with ways to prepare mind-altering substances. These substances may be smoked, chewed, eaten, sniffed, drunk, rubbed onto the skin or into cuts, or even taken as intoxicating enemas. They have taken these risks, not for pleasure or kicks, but for curing illnesses through magic, divining truth, peering into the future, and making contact with the spirit world. This is serious and important for the people involved.

Another difference highlighted by the comparative study of drug use is the important effect of culture and context on the drug experience. Used in different settings, under different sets of expectations, the same drug may cause very different reactions, from nausea on the one hand to a religious experience on the other. Today we may find it odd that Native Americans (Amerindians) smoked tobacco to cause

giddiness (one of the universal symptoms of ecstasy) and to open the pathways through which shamans disassociated themselves from the normal state of awareness.

In light of America's drug problem, getting a broader historical and comparative vision of the role of drugs in society makes sense.

As you read this selection, ask yourself the following questions:

- ☐ *Were hallucinogenic plants discovered by chance?*

- ☐ *What is the relationship between medicinal drugs, psychotropic drugs, and poisons?*

- ☐ *What factors influence what an individual sees under the influence of hallucinogens?*

- ☐ *How do ritual and the role of the shamanistic leader create a different context for the use of hallucinogenic drugs in traditional and modern societies?*

- ☐ *Do drug users in our society have their own secular rituals?*

The following terms discussed in this selection are included in the Glossary at the back of the book:

Amerindian	*psychoactive drugs*
decoction	*rite of passage*
hallucinogen	*ritual*
indigenous	*sorcery*

The passionate desire which leads man to flee from the monotony of everyday life has made him instinctively discover strange substances. He has done so, even where nature has been most niggardly in producing them and where the products seem very far from possessing the properties which would enable him to satisfy this desire.

Thus early in this century did Lewis Lewin, perhaps the preeminent pioneer in the study of psychoactive drugs, describe the primal search that led to man's discovery of hallucinogens. Strictly speaking, a hallucinogen is any chemical substance that distorts the senses and produces hallucinations—perceptions or experiences that depart dramatically from ordinary reality. Today we know these substances variously as psychotomimetics (psychosis mimickers), psychotaraxics (mind disturbers) and psychedelics (mind manifesters); dry terms which quite inadequately describe the remarkable effects they have on the human mind. These effects are varied but they frequently include a dreamlike state marked by dramatic alterations "in the sphere of experience, in the perception of reality, changes even of space and time and in consciousness of self. They invariably induce a series of visual hallucinations, often in kaleidoscopic movement, and usually in indescribably brilliant and rich colours, frequently accompanied by auditory and other hallucinations"—tactile, olfactory, and temporal. Indeed the effects are so unearthly, so unreal that most hallucinogenic plants early acquired a sacred place in indigenous cultures. In rare cases, they were worshipped as gods incarnate.

The pharmacological activity of the hallucinogens is due to a relatively small number of types of chemical compounds. While modern chemistry has been able in most cases successfully to duplicate these substances, or even manipulate their chemical structures to create novel synthetic forms, virtually all hallucinogens have their origins in plants. (One immediate exception that comes to mind is the New World toad, *Bufo marinus*, but the evidence that this animal was used for its psychoactive properties is far from complete.)

Within the plant kingdom the hallucinogens occur only among the evolutionarily advanced flowering plants and in one division—the fungi—of the more primitive spore bearers. Most hallucinogens are alkaloids, a family of perhaps 5,000 complex organic molecules that also account for the biological activity of most toxic and medicinal plants. These active compounds may be found in the various concentrations in different parts of the plant—roots, leaves, seeds, bark and/or flowers—and they may be absorbed by the human body in a number of ways, as is evident in the wide variety of folk preparations. Hallucinogens may be smoked or snuffed, swallowed fresh or dried, drunk in decoctions and infusions, absorbed directly through the skin, placed in wounds or administered as enemas.

To date about 120 hallucinogenic plants have been identified worldwide. On first glance, given that estimates of the total number of plant species range as high as 800,000, this appears to be a relatively small number. However, it grows in significance when compared to the total number of species used as food. Perhaps 3,000 species of plants have been regularly consumed by some people at some period of history, but today only 150 remain important enough to enter world commerce. Of these a mere 12–15, mostly domesticated cereals, keep us alive.

In exploring his ambient vegetation for hallucinogenic plants, man has shown extraordinary ingenuity, and in experimenting with them all the signs of pharmacological genius. He has also quite evidently taken great personal risks. Peyote (*Lophophora williamsii*), for example, has as many as 30 active constituents, mostly alkaloids, and is exceedingly bitter, not unlike most deadly poisonous plants. Yet the Huichol, Tarahumara and numerous other peoples of Mexico and the American Southwest discovered that sundried and eaten whole the cactus produces spectacular psychoactive effects.

With similar tenacity, the Mazatec of Oaxaca discovered amongst a mushroom flora that contained many deadly species as many as 10 that were hallucinogenic. These they believed had ridden to earth upon thunderbolts, and were reverently gathered at the time of the new moon. Elsewhere in Oaxaca, the seeds of the morning glory (*Rivea corymbosa*) were crushed and prepared as a decoction known at one time as ololiuqui—the sacred preparation of the Aztec, and one that we now realize contained alkaloids closely related to LSD, a potent synthetic hallucinogen. In Peru, the bitter mescaline-rich cactus *Trichocereus pachanoi* became the basis of the San Pedro curative cults of the northern Andes. Here the preferred form of administration is the decoction, a tea served up at the long nocturnal ceremonies during which time the patients' problems were diagnosed. At dawn they would be sent on the long pilgrimages high into the mountains to bathe in the healing waters of a number of sacred lakes.

Lowland South America has provided several exceedingly important and chemically fascinating hallucinogenic preparations, notably the intoxicating yopo (*Anadenanthera peregrina*) and ebene (*Virola calophylla, V. calophylloidea, V. theiodora*) snuffs of the upper Orinoco of Venezuela and adjacent Brazil and the

From *Cultural Survival* 9(4):2–5, 1985. Reprinted by permission of *Cultural Survival*.

ayahuasca-caapi-yagé complex (*Banisteriopsis caapi*) found commonly among the rainforest peoples of the Northwest Amazon. Yopo is prepared from the seeds of a tall forest tree which are roasted gently and then ground into a fine powder, which is then mixed with some alkaline substance, often the ashes of certain leaves. Ebene is prepared from the blood red resin of certain trees in the nutmeg family. Preparations vary but frequently the bark is stripped from the tree and slowly heated to allow the resin to collect in a small earthenware pot where it is boiled down into a thick paste, which in turn is sundried and powdered along with the leaves of other plants. Ayahuasca comes from the rasped bark of a forest liana which is carefully heated in water, again with a number of admixture plants, until a thick decoction is obtained. All three products are violently hallucinogenic and it is of some significance that they all contain a number of subsidiary plants that, in ways not yet fully understood, intensify or lengthen the psychoactive effects of the principal ingredients. This is an important feature of many folk preparations and it is due in part to the fact that different chemical compounds in relatively small concentrations may effectively potentiate each other, producing powerful synergistic effects—a biochemical version of the whole being greater than the sum of its parts. The awareness of these properties is evidence of the impressive chemical and botanical knowledge of the traditional peoples.

In the Old World may be found some of the most novel means of administering hallucinogens. In southern Africa, the Bushmen of Dobe, Botswana, absorb the active constituents of the plant kwashi (*Pancratium trianthum*) by incising the scalp and rubbing the juice of an onion-like bulb into the open wound. The fly agaric (*Amanita muscaria*), a psychoactive mushroom used in Siberia, may be toasted on a fire or made into a decoction with reindeer milk and wild blueberries. In this rare instance the active principals pass through the body unaltered, and the psychoactive urine of the intoxicated individual may be consumed by the others. Certain European hallucinogens—notably the solanaceous belladonna (*Atropa belladonna*), henbane (*Hyoscyamus niger*), mandrake (*Mandragora officinarum*) and datura (*Datura metel*)—are topically active; that is the active principals are absorbed through the skin. We now know, for example, that much of the behavior associated with the medieval witches is as readily attributable to these drugs as to any spiritual communion with the diabolic. The witches commonly rubbed their bodies with hallucinogenic ointments. A particularly efficient means of self-administering the drug for women is through the moist tissue of the vagina; the witches broomstick or staff was considered the most effective applicator. Our own popular image of the haggard woman on a broomstick comes from the me-

dieval belief that the witches rode their staffs each midnight to the sabbat, the orgiastic assembly of demons and sorcerers. In fact, it now appears that their journey was not through space but across the hallucinatory landscape of their minds.

There is in the worldwide distribution of the hallucinogenic plants a pronounced and significant discrepancy that has only inadequately been accounted for but which serves to illustrate a critical feature of their role in traditional societies. Of the 120 or more such plants found to date, over 100 are native to the Americas; the Old World has contributed a mere 15–20 species. How might this be explained? To be sure it is in part an artifact of the emphasis of academic research. A good many of these plants have entered the literature due to the efforts of Professor R. E. Schultes and his colleagues at the Harvard Botanical Museum and elsewhere, and their interest has predominantly been in the New World. Yet were the hallucinogenic plants a dominant feature of traditional cultures in Africa and Eurasia, surely they would have shown up in the extensive ethnographic literature and in the journals of traders and missionaries. With few notable exceptions, they don't. Nor is this discrepancy due to floristic peculiarities. The rainforests of West Africa and Southeast Asia, in particular, are exceedingly rich and diverse. Moreover, the peoples of these regions have most successfully explored them for pharmacologically active compounds for use both as medicines and poisons. In fact, as much as any other material trait the manipulation of toxic plants remains a consistent theme throughout sub-Saharan African cultures. The Amerindians, for their part, were certainly no strangers to plant toxins which they commonly exploited as fish, arrow and dart poisons. Yet it is a singular fact that while the peoples of Africa consistently used these toxic preparations on each other, the Amerindian almost never did. And while the Amerindian successfully explored his forest for hallucinogens, the African did not. This suggests the critical fact that the use of any pharmacologically active plant—remembering that the difference between hallucinogen, medicine and poison is often a matter of dosage—is firmly rooted in culture. If the peoples of Africa did not explore their environment for psychoactive drugs, surely it is because they felt no need to. In many Amerindian societies the use of plant hallucinogens lies at the very heart of traditional life.

To begin to understand the role that these powerful plants play in these societies, however, it is essential to place the drugs themselves in proper context. For one, the pharmacologically active components do not produce uniform effects. On the contrary, any psychoactive drug has within it a completely ambivalent potential for good or evil, order or chaos. Pharmacologically it induces a certain condition, but that condition is mere raw material to be worked by particular cultural or psychological forces and expectations. This is what our own medical experts call the "set and setting" of any drug experience. *Set* in these terms is the individual's expectation of what the drug will do to him; *setting* is the environment —both physical and social—in which the drug is taken. This may be illustrated by an example from our own country. In the northwest rainforests of Oregon are a native species of hallucinogenic mushrooms. Those who go out into the forest deliberately intending to ingest these mushrooms generally experience a pleasant intoxication. Those who inadvertently consume them while foraging for edible mushrooms invariably end up in the poison unit of the nearest hospital. The mushroom itself has not changed.

Similarly the hallucinogenic plants consumed by the Amerindian induce a powerful but neutral stimulation of the imagination; they create a template, as it were, upon which cultural beliefs and forces may be amplified a thousand times. What the individual sees in the visions is dependent not on the drug but on other factors—the mood and setting of the group, the physical and mental states of the participants, his own expectations based on a rich repository of tribal lore and, above all in Indian societies, the authority, knowledge and experience of the leader of the ceremony. The role of this figure—be it man or woman, shaman, curandero, paye, maestro or brujo—is pivotal. It is he who places the protective cloak of ritual about the participants. It is he who tackles the bombardment of visual and auditory stimuli and gives them order. It is he who must interpret a complex body of belief, reading the power in leaves and the meaning in stones, who

must skillfully balance the forces of the universe and guide the play of the winds. The ceremonial use of hallucinogenic plants by the Amerindian is (most often) a collective journey into the unconscious. It is not necessarily, and in fact rarely is, a pleasant or an easy journey. It is wondrous and it may be terrifying. But above all it is purposeful.

The Amerindian enters the realm of the hallucinogenic visions not out of boredom, or to relieve an individual's restless anxiety, but rather to fulfill some collective need of the group. In the Amazon, for example, hallucinogens are taken to divine the future, track the paths of enemies, ensure the fidelity of women, diagnose and treat diseases. The Huichol in Mexico eat their peyote at the completion of long arduous pilgrimages in order that they may experience in life the journey of the soul of the dead to the underworld. The Amahuaca Indians of Peru drink yage that the nature of the forest animals and plants may be revealed to their apprentices. In eastern North America during puberty rites, the Algonquin confined adolescents to a longhouse for two weeks and fed them a beverage based in part on datura. During the extended intoxication and subsequent amnesia—a pharmacological feature of this drug—the young boys forgot what it was to be a child so that they might learn what it meant to be a man. But whatever the ostensible purpose of the hallucinogenic journey, the Amerindian imbibes his plants in a highly structured manner that places a ritualistic framework of order around their use. Moreover the experience is explicitly sought for positive ends. It is not a means of escaping from an uncertain existence; rather it is perceived as a means of contribution to the welfare of all one's people.

36

The Doctor's White Coat:

The Image of the Physician in Modern America

Dan Blumhagen

Symbolic communication is an important characteristic of our species. What people wear provides others with a symbolic statement of who they are—that is, of their status and role. This selection by an anthropologist-physician presents a historical and symbolic analysis of the costume worn by medical doctors.

Symbols are central to both sacred and secular rituals because they have meaning; they are things that stand for something else. In the analysis of cultural symbols, anthropologists can uncover layers of meaning, so that a single symbolic behavior can communicate a rich and complex set of ideas.

Most of the time, people are unaware of the symbols being communicated in their ritual behavior. However, anthropologists believe that symbolic analysis can lead us to deeper understandings of the belief systems of other people. Like all aspects of culture, symbol systems change through time. As such, the anthropologist can use history to show how a particular object or behavior came to be associated with particular meanings.

In this selection, the author traces the social history of medicine in the United States by examining the white coat as a symbol. Such symbols are also employed in our pre-sentation of self to others, and, as we see in this selection, in silently communicating messages about social relationships.

As you read this selection, ask yourself the following questions:

☐ *Why is the physician's coat white? Can you think of some impractical aspects of this cultural convention?*

☐ *Is the white coat simply a marker of an occupation, or are other cultural beliefs communicated through it?*

☐ *What taboos do we allow and expect a physician to violate?*

☐ *Does this symbolic analysis fit with your own experiences with physician–patient interactions?*

The following terms discussed in this selection are included in the Glossary at the back of the book:

cultural values
status
symbol
taboo

Reproduced, with permission, from: Dan Blumhagen, "The Doctor's White Coat: The Image of the Physician in Modern America." *Annals of Internal Medicine*, 91: 111–116, 1979.

All societies have healers who care for the sick.[1] The healer's interaction with a patient is often surrounded by a symbolic system that expresses the implicit cultural concepts of what "healing" means.[2] As changes occur in the social meanings attributed to healing, the symbols used to express those concepts also change. This paper will use the symbol-analysis approach, widely used in cultural anthropology, to examine the historical origins and the function of the symbol systems that surround American physicians and their patients. An understanding of how these were adopted first by the profession and then by the greater society will elucidate what it means to be a healer in American culture. This knowledge can be usefully applied to problematic patient consultations, as well as to understanding some of the conflicts that have arisen between the medical profession and society at large.

THE NATURE OF SYMBOL ANALYSIS

Most physicians are aware of the importance of symbol analysis in individual psychotherapy.[3] What is less widely appreciated is the application of a similar approach to understanding entire cultures. Anthropologists have found that symbols are often used as a way to express and reaffirm the fundamental belief systems that a society holds.[4] This is often done in ritualized events. Perhaps cultural symbols can be most usefully viewed as a form of communication, analogous to words in a natural language.[5] Like words, they can be used in social settings to define the shared interpretation of "what's really going on here," to direct each actor's behavior, and to express the dominance relationships that exist between the various individuals who are interacting. Since most symbol analyses have dealt with small-scale preliterate societies, there is no well-defined formula for doing such a study in a complex, literate society such as modern America. My approach here will be to look at doctor-patient interactions to determine what symbols may be used, then to examine historical data documenting how these came into use and the original meanings they bore. Finally, the use of these symbols in the medical setting will be compared with similar symbols used in other American rituals to develop the full spectrum of meaning that they communicate.

SYMBOLS OF THE PHYSICIAN

What, then, are the symbols surrounding physicians, and what do they mean? Table 1 shows how physicians are depicted in advertisements for medical journals and in newspaper comic strips. These sources were chosen because they represent stereotypes of the

doctor as presented to the profession and to the public. They represent "all physicians in general" and do not merely reflect the idiosyncracies of a particular physician.

Table 1 shows that although there are some differences in the way physicians are depicted in medical and popular media, there appear to be four principal objects used to depict the doctor: the white coat, stethoscope, head mirror, and black bag. In this survey, there was only one physician depicted in a patient-care setting who did not have at least one of these items. The most frequent component of the image seems to be the white coat. Of 43 doctors pictured in patient-care settings (Table 1), 36 were wearing white. In the symbolism of white coats, the social concept of "what it means to be a physician" is summarized, intensified, and extended. Its importance as the symbol of physicians is seen in that when the advertising media—a reflection of the current social stereotype—wish to depict a person with the authority of a physician, he is usually shown wearing a white coat. Although professionals are reluctant to articulate the meanings they attribute to white coats, on occasion, under stress, such interpretations may be given.

> The relationship between a physician and his patient is serious and purposeful, not social, casual or random. In this relation the patient unburdens himself or herself of a set of concerns regarding health matters and transfers them to the accepting physician. For a very long time it has been customary for individuals in society to dress rather formally when conducting serious business, and less formally when they are at leisure. The physician's dress should convey to even his most anxious patient a sense of seriousness of purpose that helps to provide reassurance and confidence that his or her complaints will be dealt with competently. True, the white coat is only a symbol of this attitude, but it also has the additional practical virtue of being identifiable, easily laundered, and more easily changed than street clothes if accidentally soiled. . . . Casual or slovenly dress is likely to convey, rightly or wrongly, casual or inattentive professional handling of their problem. Such a patient may respond in an inhibited manner, fail to volunteer infor-

Table 1 DEPICTION OF PHYSICIANS IN MEDICAL AND LAY MEDIA

	Medical Journals	Newspaper Comics
Number	45	11
White coats	29	7
Stethoscopes	13	5
Head mirror	6	5
Black bag	0	5
No special identifiers	14	0

mation, refuse to carry out a recommended diagnostic or management program, fail to keep appointments, and be uncomfortable enough to seek help elsewhere. The rapport, so anxiously sought for with your patient, may be irretrievably lost.[6]

To fully understand how the white coat has achieved this position, we must look at the historical origins of white coats as the symbol of physicians. I have been able to identify three major origins for the white coat as it has been used until fairly recently: the operating room, the scientific, specifically microbiological, laboratory, and the hospital. Each adds a layer of meaning.

THE WHITE COAT IN THE OPERATING ROOM

Operating-room garb appears to have originated with the concept of aseptic surgery, which began in this country about 1889.[7] Photographs from that year in the Massachusetts General Hospital Archives show the surgeons and nurses (but not the anesthesiologist or observers in the balcony) wearing short-sleeved white coats over their street clothes. Masks and gloves had not yet come into use. The purpose of the coats in this setting appears to be twofold: to protect the patient from being contaminated by the physician, and to protect the physician from contamination by the patient during the procedure being performed. We will find that the white coat repeatedly serves to protect both the patient and the physician.

Another implication that surgery has for the public image of the physician is its incredible power to send a person into a deathlike state, open the previously inviolable body cavities, correct whatever was "wrong" and resurrect the patient, healed.

> I have said that the modern surgeon has become a popular hero. . . . One has only to glance through the month's illustrated magazines, or turn a few pages of the latest novel to find him in the act of revealing his demonical subtlety or demonstrating his incredible skill. The tall spare frame is capable on emergency of strength and endurance that would make Sandow stand aghast.[8]

White coats had not yet become symbolic of this heroism, but the newly developing film industry ground out a remarkable number of amplifications of this theme.[9] One such film, "Society Doctor," is described as being "played in spotless white. . . . and with an appropriate sense of glamor and nobility. . . . [The hero] persuades his best friend to operate on him, directing the work himself with the aid of mirrors."[10] In these quotations we see that the social image of the physician had become one of immense power and authority. These attributes were associated with the white clothing he wore.

Even though the operating room provided one of the earliest examples of doctors wearing white, and provides some of the basic cultural meaning, it does not appear to be the main source. Stahel's otherwise valuable article[11] confuses this point. With the goal of better aseptic technique, the white coats of 1889 rapidly became full-length gowns, and were referred to as such.[12] Aseptic surgery required that these gowns only be used in the operating room to avoid the risk of cross contamination. The back opening, a necessity for sterile technique, also made it impractical for other patient-care settings.[11] Additionally, the term "gown" in our culture usually refers to women's clothing, and thus is not suitable as a symbol for those who were "active, scientific men, virile, ambitious . . . upon whose shoulders the actual work of the institution will fall."[12]

White coats diverged from operating-room gowns. The step that took the garb of the scientific laboratory into a clinical setting appears to be the main source of our current white coats. The term "lab coat," the primary term used for the white coat, refers to this origin.

THE WHITE COAT IN THE LABORATORY

The representation of the physician as a scientist has a long history that culminated during the first decades of this century. In the middle of the 19th century, science had nearly destroyed the reputability of medicine by demonstrating that its cures were worthless, but it was unable to substitute more effective remedies. Medicine became simply one of a wide variety of healing cults and quackery.[13] Despite this inauspicious start, both the profession and public turned to science as the means by which healing would come. After all, the laboratories, whose inventions had transformed night into day, could transmit messages instantaneously, and had revolutionized transportation, were certainly the most important hope for the conquest of disease. Physicians were urged to present themselves as scientists. Cathell, whose book *The Physician Himself* went through many editions between 1882 and 1922, advised: "Show aesthetic cultivation in your office arrangement, and make it look fresh, neat, clean *and scientific*" [emphasis added].[14] Above all, one must avoid "forcing on everybody the conclusion that you are, after all, but an ordinary person."[14] By 1922, Cathell had become more emphatic in describing "*the office, the sanctuary—of an earnest, working scientific medical man . . .* " [emphasis in original] as the place where one will make "judicious and intelligent use of your scientific instruments of precision . . . to assist you in curing nervous and terrified people by increasing their confidence in your armamentarium and in your professional ability."[15] The authority of science is seen as validating the practice of medicine.

Demonstrations of the efficacy of modern science, such as the construction of the Panama Canal (1905), led to its public acceptance as the foundation of modern healing. An intense feeling of hope about the future of scientific medicine was expressed in cartoons. Other healing cults, particularly homeopathy and eclecticism, which had threatened the existence of scientific medicine only a few years earlier, withered away. Their schools closed or converted to biomedicine.

The medical profession rapidly consolidated its position as part of the scientific enterprise. Within a decade of the publication of the *Flexner Report* in 1910, medical education was restructured around laboratory science. The *content* of medicine changed. Textbooks were rewritten: Of all the books popular enough to go through multiple editions before the "progressive era," almost none were still being printed when it ended. (This was ascertained by a review of the books in the open stacks of the Countway Library. The most notable exceptions, of course, are *Gray's Anatomy* and Osler's *Textbook of Medicine* (1892), both of which are still being printed in revised editions. There were no technical or theoretical advances that would outdate the former, and the latter was written by one of the men who led medical education during this change.) Towards the end of this radical transformation of the profession of medicine, and as a reflection of it, physicians became stereotyped as scientists wearing white coats. The message of power and protection emerge: While wearing a white coat the physician is able to handle safely the deadly scourges that plague mankind and is able to render them innocuous. One result of this perception of power was that physician-scientists were granted tremendous authority. No mere individual desires or beliefs were allowed to stand in the way of the public's health as determined by medical laboratories.[16]

THE WHITE COAT IN THE HOSPITAL

The shift in locus of sick care from the home to the hospital was the third historical trend. The basis for this lay in the development of aseptic surgery and modern diagnostic and therapeutic techniques, which necessitated the use of personnel and resources that could not readily be taken to the patient's home. With the impact of the change in medical care, the image of the hospital changed from that of being a place where social outcasts died to being the only place where the sick could be healed. The image changed from death to life. This was reflected in the change of the clothing of the healing staff. The black habits of the religious nursing orders, for example, became the white uniforms of the modern nursing profession.[17] Hornsby, then director of Michael Reese Hospital in Chicago, tells us in *The Modern Hospital* (12, pp. 543–5) that all people connected with the healing process (including patients and visitors) were to be dressed in white, whereas the *nonmedical* employees were to be given colored uniforms. White became associated with the *institutions* of healing, and it was within their halls that the use of white coats as the symbol of medicine was most pronounced. Physicians in private practice have never completely adopted their use.

This transition is most clearly indicated in the photographs of house staff that often accompany a hospital's annual report. These pictures show that during the period 1905–15 apprentice physicians exchanged their street clothes for white coats and pants. Hornsby indicates that this was not merely for the convenience of the hospital laundry; indeed, "Intern's white uniforms are difficult to launder, and should be done by hand."[12] In other words, there were compelling reasons for dressing interns in white that outweighed the economic disadvantages.

THE MEANING OF WHITENESS

Given the historical backdrop of the meaning of the white coat, what is added by the cultural conception of the meaning of whiteness? Originally, laboratory coats were tan and appear to have changed to white as they became associated with medicine. Why was not another, perhaps more functional, color adopted? Why were both the profession and the public so profoundly disturbed when Nobel Laureate Alexis Carrel wore *black gowns* in his laboratories and operating rooms at the fledgling Rockefeller Institute of Medicine?[18]

The significance of white as a symbol of life has already been mentioned. Since there are few celebrations of life in our society, this meaning is derived from its opposite color, black, which is clearly the color of death and mourning. The association with purity has also received comment. But this purity contains two strands of meaning: First is the concept of innocence. No shadow of malice, of intentional harm, can mar the white coat—the patient is safe in the hands of this powerful figure. Second is the purity of unaroused sexuality, particularly as this meaning is evoked in another ritual that uses the white bridal gown.

Closely allied to the concept of purity is the concept of superhuman power. The saying "cleanliness is next to godliness" originated long before the germ theory of disease! Whiteness as an attribute of superhuman power, at once irresistibly attractive and infinitely dangerous, is clearly expressed in Melville's *Moby Dick*[19] and, as has been shown, was explicitly applied to physicians. In religious symbols, Christ and the saints who have exercised their power over death and all other human frailties are robed in white (*Bible*, Revelations 7:9–17). But these are not merely powerful, they are supremely good.

A final meaning comes from the term *candor*, itself derived from the Latin *candidus* (white). This impartial truth-telling is often portrayed in statues of "justice," who is usually depicted wearing white.

If symbols affect behavior, the use of the white coat should affect how patients and physicians act. There appear to be two behavioral changes that have been mediated by the white coat: the physician's access to his patient's body, and the shift in the locus of the sick role from the home to an institution.

BODY AND SEXUAL TABOOS IN AMERICAN CULTURE

In many societies, the most powerful symbol systems are found in situations where strong social values appear to be challenged.[20] One of the strongest beliefs in our society is the inviolability of a person's physical body.[21, 22] There is even a legal term for the violation of a person's rights over his own body: battery. Merely touching another individual without that person's permission is to be at jeopardy of civil and criminal action.[23] The extent to which the physical examination is a serious breach of social custom has been clearly stated by Lief and Fox.[24]

> The amounts and occasions of bodily contact are carefully regulated in all societies, and very much so in ours. The kind of access to the body of the patient that a physician in our society has is a uniquely privileged one. Even in the course of a so-called routine physical examination, the physician is permitted to handle the patient's body in ways otherwise permitted to special intimates, and in the case of procedures such as rectal and vaginal examination in ways normally not even permitted to a sexual partner.

The physical body is not merely a threat to the person whose body is revealed, it is also considered to be dangerous to the one exposed to it. This is the basis of much of the American film rating system. Given these taboos, the perfunctory way that physicians are given permission to do the most intimate examination is remarkable.

> The individual must stand before his doctor man to man, unclothed physically, mentally, and morally, revealing to him as he does to no other mortal, not even to his father confessor, the secrets of his most inmost soul; submitting his person to the most thorough scrutiny of the physician and to varied tests, physical, clinical, instrumental and what not, and without hesitation committing to his keeping the keys of the family skeleton closet.[25]

Physical examinations of apparently healthy people are a relatively recent phenomenon. Referring to the late 19th century, Duffy writes: "Physical diagnosis remained handicapped by the reluctance of patients, particularly females, to bare their skins to the probing, palpation or percussion of the physicians."[26] Rectal and pelvic examinations do not appear to have been frequently used. As late as 1927, Richard Cabot, a prominent *medical* educator, claimed that "it is not and should not be a part of the routine physical examination to examine the rectum."[27] Buttressed, however, by the successes of medicine in improving public health, a campaign was waged from 1922 to 1929 that promoted periodic physical examinations as a means of *improving the individual's* health.[28] These included pelvic and rectal examinations.

For this crusade to be successful, the cultural dangers of the physical contact had to be muted. A mechanism was needed that would reinterpret an ordinarily taboo activity into a socially acceptable, even desirable, one.[29] A set of symbols was needed to protect both the doctor and patient in this dangerous setting. The white coat, with its meanings of bilateral protections, purity, goodness, and unaroused sexuality, was ideally suited for the task. In the less-threatening situation where a male physician examined a man, the white coat was all that was needed: The patient was nude.[30] When the physician was a woman, however, a reciprocal symbolic dress was required, leading to the development of the examination gown. In one of the early descriptions of such a garment, the symbolic themes come out. Fisk[30] claims that this gown "gives the examinee a sense of protection and lessens the embarrassment." The disparate treatment of men and women can not be maintained, and soon men, too, were offered the protection of examination gowns.

The second behavioral change was a shift in the concept of where it was appropriate to act sick.[31] Previously, of course, illness had been a personal drama played in the bedroom, the most secluded, intimate, and protective area of the home. The physician could enter at the invitation of the family and be made privy to the physical and behavioral secrets contained therein without violating any social norms. Only those unfortunate persons who lacked a protective home sought care in an institution. It was only the "fallen women who enter hospitals,"[32] that is, only those people without anything worth concealing or without anyone to shield them. Symbols were required that would protect patients from the unwarranted intrusions that could occur in an institution and that would legitimize private behavior in a public place. The physician's white coat and the patient's examination gown met these needs perfectly.

These shared meanings direct patient and physician behavior in the following way: The physician is an active scientist, the patient is passive material; the physician prescribes, the patient complies; the physician is self-concealing, the patient is self-revealing. Clearly, as long as this social definition of the healing encounter exists, the physician will dominate the setting.

DEVELOPMENTS FROM 1930 TO 1960

The above set of symbols appears to have been fully functional by the early 1930s and remained largely intact until recently. There were minor changes, such as the adoption of blue or green garb in operating rooms when high-intensity lighting made the glare from white drapes unbearable, but these pastel shades did not conflict with the underlying value system as black or red, for example, would have.

Other practitioners found that some of the meanings communicated by the white coat were so overpowering that it interfered with their practice. Pediatricians and psychiatrists have discovered that this mark of authority has a tendency to overwhelm their patients, and they therefore tend to wear pastel coats or normal street clothes. As has been noted, many physicians, particularly those in private practice, did not adopt the white coat. Nonetheless, these trends did not affect the public image of what a physician should be. If anything, the beliefs were intensified, as is evidenced by the meteoric rise in the funding of medical research after World War II, which resulted in the National Institutes of Health and much of the rest of the academic medical enterprise.[33]

CURRENT TRENDS

During the past decade, however, much of this has changed. Physician-scientists who were once seen as validating medical practice no longer necessarily protect and heal patients, but may endanger them. A good example of this attitude is seen in the widespread laetrile movement, which is perceived as a direct assault on the biomedical establishment. Other social symbols of authority are also being rejected. Hospitals are often accused of prolonging agony rather than renewing life. Body taboos do not seem to be as strong as they once were.

These social changes strike at the heart of the meanings communicated by white coats. No new consensus has developed that will define the nature of healing and give direction for patient behavior. This has had an effect on the use of both white coats and examination gowns.

The quote from Kriss[6] earlier in this paper that expounded the significance of white coats is the result of widespread student challenges of authority of this symbol. Debate over whether medical students should wear one still continues.[34] Voices from some of the countercultural movements recognize the implications of this symbolism and reject it. Some feminists, for example, "advise women to discard the drape by throwing it on the floor when the doctor enters. If he replaces it, throw it on the floor again."[35] This type of symbolic action tends to make physicians uncomfortable, for the rejection of symbols of established roles means that there is little guidance as to how they or their patients should act.

Cousins[36] comments on this redefinition of roles in the healing encounter when he claims that "the most important thing happening in American medicine today is not the discovery of magical new drugs but the new relationship that is emerging between physicians and patients."[36] The old model of the scientist-healer is rejected for a more humanistic relationship. He continues: "Traditionally the doctor is the authoritarian figure . . . the new relationship is more in the nature of a partnership." Note that the "traditional authoritarian figure" is, as has been documented here, a tradition that has only existed since the turn of the century. There were reasons for adopting that role at the time, there may be similar reasons for abandoning it now.

The dynamic relationship that exists between physicians and American culture is only beginning to be explored. As we learn more about the social meaning and function of healing, we will better understand some of the conflicts that we feel between society and the profession. This in turn may enable us to devise better institutional and individual means of meeting these needs. But even before that global understanding is reached, there may be benefits that accrue on a smaller scale. In all patient-physician encounters, careful consideration of the symbolic and other nonverbal communication may be important. In particularly unsettled interactions, painstaking, explicit discussion and negotiation on the exact role that the patient and the physician will take may be required for healing to occur.

NOTES

1. Landy, D. (ed.). 1977. *Culture, Disease and Healing: Studies in Medical Anthropology*, New York: Macmillan, 1.
2. Kleinman, A. M. 1975. The symbolic context of Chinese medicine: A comparative approach to the study of traditional medical and psychiatric forms of care in Chinese cultures. *Am J Chin Med*. 3:103–24.
3. Freud, S. 1900. *The Interpretation of Dreams*. New York: Macmillan.
4. Dolgin, J. L., Kemnitzer, D. S., Schneider, D. M. 1977. *Symbolic Anthropology: A Reader in the Study of Symbols and Meaning*. New York: Columbia University Press, 3–47.

5. Leach, E. 1976. *Culture and Communication: The Logic by Which Symbols Are Connected*. Cambridge: Cambridge University Press, 10.

6. Kriss, J. P. 1975. On white coats and other matters. *N. Engl J Med*. 292:1024–5.

7. Potter, R. A., ed. 1976. *Surgery in the United States*. The American College of Surgeons and the American Surgical Association, 17.

8. Whitby, C. J. 1912. *The Doctor and His Work*. London: Swift and Co., 23.

9. Spears, J. 1955. The doctor on the screen. *Films in Review*. 19 November 6:436–44.

10. *New York Times Film Review: 1913–1968: Volume 2, 1932–1938*. 1970. New York: New York Times, 1143.

11. Stahel, H. R. 1970. Der weisse Mantel in der Medizin. *Zürcher Medizingeschichtliche Abhandlungen*, 78:1–22.

12. Hornsby, J. A., Schmidt, R. E. 1913. *The Modern Hospital*. Philadelphia: W. B. Saunders, 543.

13. Shryock, R. H. 1947. *The Development of Modern Medicine*. New York: Alfred A. Knopf, Inc., 248–72.

14. Cathell, D. W. 1882. *The Physician Himself and What He Should Add to the Strictly Scientific*. Baltimore: Clishay and Barley, 10.

15. Cathell, D. W. 1922. *Book on the Physician Himself from Graduation to Old Age*. Emerson Hotel, Baltimore: Published by the author, 10.

16. Rosen, G. 1958. *A History of Public Health*. New York: MD Publications, 464–78.

17. Dietz, L. D. 1967. Lehozky, A. R. *History and Modern Nursing*. Philadelphia: F. A. Davis, 168–73.

18. Conner, G. W. 1964. *A History of the Rockefeller Institution*. New York: Rockefeller Foundation, 154.

19. Melville, H. 1930. *Moby Dick, or The White Whale*. New York: The Modern Library, 272–83.

20. Berger, P. L., Luckmann, T. 1966. *The Social Construction of Reality*. Garden City, New York: Doubleday and Co., 96.

21. Miner, H. 1975. Body ritual among the Nacirema. *In* J. P. Spradley and M. A. Rynkiewich (eds.), *The Nacirema*. Boston: Little, Brown and Co.

22. Glaser, B. G., Strauss, A. L. 1965. *Awareness of Dying*. Chicago: Aldine Publishing Co., 162.

23. Black, H. C. 1957. *Black's Law Dictionary*. St. Paul, Minnesota: West Publishing Co., 193.

24. Lief, H. I., Fox, R. C. 1963. Training for detached concern in medical students. *In* H. I. Lief, V. F. Lief, N. R. Lief, (eds.), *The Psychological Basis of Medical Practice*. New York: Harper and Row, 32.

25. Finney, J. M. T. 1923. *The Physician*. New York: Charles Scribner and Sons.

26. Duffy, J. 1976. *The Healers*. New York: McGraw-Hill, 232.

27. Cabot, R. C. 1927. *Physical Diagnosis*. New York: William Wood and Co., 435.

28. Rosen, G. 1975. *Preventive Medicine in the United States, 1900–1975*. New York: Science History Press, 59.

29. Emerson, J. P. 1970. Behavior in private places: sustaining definitions of reality in gynecological examinations. *In* H. P. Dreitzel, (ed.), *Recent Sociology: No. 2, Patterns of Communicative Behavior*. New York: Macmillan Publishing Co.

30. Fisk, E. L., Crawford, J. R. 1928. *How to Make the Periodic Physical Examination*. New York: Macmillan Publishing Co., 41.

31. Friedson, E. 1970. *Profession of Medicine*. New York: Harper and Row, 220.

32. Trousseau, A. 1882. *Clinical Medicine Letters*. Philadelphia: Blinkerston, 43.

33. Bordley, J. III, Harvey, A. M. 1976. *Two Centuries of American Medicine: 1776–1976*. Philadelphia: W. B. Saunders, 419.

34. McKinnon, J. A. 1977. Life in a short white coat. *New Physician*. November 26:24–30.

35. Dreifus, C. (ed.), *Seizing Our Bodies*. New York: Random House, 226.

36. Cousins, N. "A Better Rx for Patients." Los Angeles Times Syndicate; 2 April 1978. Syndicated editorial column.

37

PROFILE OF AN ANTHROPOLOGIST

Anthropology and the World of Physicians

Thomas M. Johnson

Anthropologists frequently study traditional medical practitioners to understand this aspect of culture and to improve people's health in a Third World context. Medical anthropologists also work closer to home. Some analyze the culture of biomedicine as practiced in American hospitals, and some actually work within the system by trying to improve medical education for effective cross-cultural clinical care.

As a clinical faculty member in a medical school, Thomas Johnson not only helps train physicians but also is involved in patient care. In this selection, he describes his work in the hospital of the University of Alabama at Huntsville. As a true participant-observer, he offers many insights about the culture of biomedicine. Take, for instance, his comments about the meaning of time for clinicians. We are reminded not only of the cultural construction of time but also of the differences in the pace of life in traditional and modern societies. Notice also how medical students have to be socialized (enculturated) into the culture of medicine.

As you read this selection, ask yourself the following questions:

- ☐ *What are Thomas Johnson's goals in practicing his "specialized form of applied medical anthropology"?*

- ☐ *How did he gain acceptance in the world of clinicians?*

- ☐ *What is the difference between "explaining" and "understanding" in the clinical setting?*

- ☐ *What are some of the unspoken assumptions in the culture of biomedicine that can have a negative impact on clinical care?*

The following terms discussed in this selection are included in the Glossary at the back of the book:

biomedicine
epistemology
ethos
medical anthropology
socialization
world view

Reprinted by permission of the American Anthropological Association from *Anthropology Newsletter*, November and December 1991. Not for further reproduction.

Biomedicine has always fascinated me: the complex social organization of hospitals; the elaborate rituals and specialized language of practitioners; the poignancy of human emotions made exquisitely palpable in time of sickness; the powerful, even brutal molding of young people into physicians by the process of medical education. I have worked in medical settings for the past 25 years—from exploring every nook and cranny of a hospital as a maintenance worker/undergraduate sociology major, to discovering the existence of a specialty called medical anthropology that encouraged me to conduct ethnographic studies of hospital wards, indigent clinics and migrant farm worker health care as a graduate student. I learned about the power of medical education by immersing myself in the process—from cadaver dissection to bedside rounds—during dissertation research.

I concluded that the 1960s activist dreams I had about improving health care in this country could best be achieved by attempting to change the medical education process. Knowing that the most powerful professional socialization in medicine takes place in clinical settings rather than in the lecture hall, I became one of only a few nonphysician medical anthropologists whose primary teaching role has been in hospital wards and outpatient clinics. Ultimately, also I recognized that, for me at least, the immediacy of patient care was so rewarding that I completed another graduate degree in clinical psychology. With dual training and clinical credentials I consider almost everything I do—from leading a staff support group for nurses in a burn unit to being a psychotherapist—as a specialized type of applied medical anthropology.

With this background, I have spent most of the last fifteen years in clinical and teaching activities on the faculties of three medical schools and residency programs, although during that time I also taught for seven years in a graduate medical anthropology program. Currently, I am on the faculty of a family medicine residency program, in which I act as a consultant to residents and physician faculty in the care of their patients. I also give seminars and supervise residents in a required month-long clinical rotation in medical behavioral science.

Over the years, interacting with medical students and residents while interviewing a severely burned patient or a parent whose baby was stillborn an hour earlier not only has permitted me to influence medical practice, but has also allowed me to view with ever greater acuity the cultural contrasts between medicine and anthropology—differences in world views and epistemologies that must be understood to work successfully in medicine. My experiences suggest that any medical anthropologists desiring to work in biomedicine will have to struggle with these implicit, unspoken assumptions that characterize the culture of biomedicine. My purpose here is to present some of these distinctive features of biomedicine, particularly as they contrast with those of academic anthropology.

Most anthropologists recognize that culture can be defined in Kroeberian terms (as "acts, artifacts, beliefs, etc."), but it is also clear that culture is a phenomenon involving basic assumptions about the world. These assumptions, sometimes thought of as "core values," not only guide people in their activities, but also underlie group identity and serve boundary maintenance functions (defines who is "us" and who is "not us"). Because identity and boundary maintenance functions are a major feature of professionalization in complex cultures, many medical anthropologists may anticipate that being accepted by practitioners in a biomedical setting will be difficult. I have not experienced this to be true. In fact, I have found that physicians unconsciously divide the world moiety-like into two groups: practitioners and the public. Because *therapeutic activism* is a core value among practitioners, anyone willing to be even peripherally involved in the process of patient care will find acceptance. Anyone not involved in the therapeutic process is automatically relegated to the lay moiety.

Thus, although it is true that physicians may anticipate criticisms from a social scientist in their midst, once a medical anthropologist has demonstrated even a modicum of therapeutic activism, which initially involves passing what I call "ethnographic tests" (such as helping to remove an encrusted incisional drain without overt expressions of disgust, or enduring caustic and insensitive remarks about patients without becoming defensive), ready acceptance will follow. Such inevitable ethnographic tests are not unlike those in traditional cross-cultural fieldwork settings where anthropologists are expected to accept offers of certain indigenous foods or to witness rituals like clitoridectomy or infanticide without overt judgmentalism. As in any cross-cultural setting, it is axiomatic that learning "medicalese"—both informally through informants and by taking a course in medical terminology—is essential for effective participation.

My participation in biomedical settings has led me to see inevitable epistemological differences between anthropology and biomedicine. For example, among my biomedical colleagues there is an unspoken assumption that medical science is rational and objective. This ethos of *positivism* provides for a sense of certainty and control in the face of sickness. The touchstone of this view is "hard data": an emphasis on quantification, which predisposes physicians to value phenomena that can be reduced to numerical equivalents, such as blood pressure, serum amylase levels, and the like, but to be much more uncomfortable with phenomena such as anxiety or depression (unless, of course, these can be "measured" using psychological testing).

Thus, the very modes of acquiring knowledge in medical anthropology and biomedicine stand in sharp contrast. In biomedicine, diagnosis based on the core value of *affective neutrality*, is the *sine qua non* of inquiry. The term "diagnosis" literally means "to tell apart": not only to differentiate one disease from another, but also to separate those who are well or "in control" from those who are sick, which may effectively distance practitioners from patients. Of course, diagnosis is also a process that improves the confidence and reduces the anxiety of practitioners. Diagnosis emphasizes *explaining*, while knowledge acquisition in academic medical anthropology increasingly emphasizes *understanding*—bemoaning the decontextualization and disembodying of sickness and demanding that empathic attention be paid to the individual experiences and social contexts of people who are ill. Whenever I am asked to render a diagnosis, I debate with myself to clarify if the process will permit me to better understand and help the patient, or if it will distance me because I am feeling uncomfortable.

In actual treatment activities, this key difference in the way physicians and medical anthropologists are predisposed to gather and value data creates an inevitable tension within me. Although the anthropological predilection to immerse oneself in the life-world of patients is compelling, unless one is actively involved in the therapeutic process it is difficult to appreciate how *too much* understanding actually can be paralyzing. When agonizing clinical decisions have to be made, I have experienced how too much empathy can lead to overwhelming feelings of vulnerability and uncertainty. Nonetheless, I see how dangerous it can be to objectify patients so that, in my own clinical work, I constantly challenge myself to walk a tightrope between explaining and understanding—between distancing and empathy—recognizing always the liabilities of each.

While treatment decisions ostensibly are attempts to "control" the diseases to be treated, I have noticed an unconscious tendency for physicians to want to control patients themselves (the term "patient management" is common in biomedicine, and betrays this posture—I insist on the term "disease management," but recognize that this still involves a cooperative effort between physician and patient). When hospitalized and seriously ill, illusions of control of patients and their diseases are easier; in primary care outpatient settings, however, patient behavior is frustratingly difficult to predict, making attention to the psychosocial dimensions of patient care—the grist for a medical anthropologist's mill—essential.

I have discovered that work in biomedicine demands constant attention to other unspoken assumptions about the world, such as the *concept of time*, which is viewed differently in medical and academic anthropology settings. In the latter, time is one's own, and scholarship that results from working in relative isolation is expected and valued. Time is something that one can "control," as when a long-distance runner consciously sets an individual pace. In biomedicine, time is both a scarce commodity and a compelling force, in relation to which practitioners see themselves as out of control. In clinical settings one responds almost exclusively to demands from others, there is never enough time to meet all the demands, and it is impossible to predict when demands will be made. Although it seems trivial on the surface, one of the most frustrating aspects of working as an anthropologist in the biomedical world is seldom being able to enjoy conversations over meals, which invariably are eaten hurriedly for fear that one's beeper will go off at any moment.

Availability is another important core value in biomedical culture. Carrying a beeper is a symbolic statement that one is "always available": this is a powerful anxiety-allaying mechanism, reassuring all that help is always close when the inevitable emergencies occur. Although there are seldom emergencies demanding my involvement, I have found it imperative (albeit sometimes annoying) to adopt the "beeper mentality" that exists in biomedicine. Interestingly, my academic anthropology colleagues regularly questioned the presence of my beeper with derogatory suggestions that I was "playing doctor." The importance of availability in clinical settings is also symbolized in daily ritual activities in clinical settings: "making rounds" on patients starting at 7:00 AM, being "on call" at night, or working on holidays become rites of intensification that solidify group identity. I have found that I must be available to participate in such activities, even at onerous times, to remain an effective part of the group.

In individual physicians, the behavioral and attitudinal manifestations of therapeutic activism, positivism, affective neutrality, time pressure and expectations of availability are often expressed and/or perceived by outsiders as arrogance. Successful medical anthropologists must not be put off by such a posture in physician colleagues, but recognize it as a psychological defense against the uncertainties that attend patient care—something I truly believe most of my academic colleagues have never experienced (here, I recognize my own apparent arrogance!).

In truth, unspoken assumptions within biomedicine can and sometimes do have negative effects on clinical reasoning and decision making. Unless physicians can step back and examine these assumptions within biomedicine, there is very real likelihood that medical practice will become a compulsion to change patients, rather than an opportunity to help them. There is a danger that these unconscious assumptions of biomedicine will be a source of clinical distortion. Thus, in every patient care consultation, my goal is to get medical students and residents to understand themselves, and not simply help them explain their patients' problems. My work is an attempt to help physicians become more genuine and flexible in their care of patients by better understanding the unconscious motivations and assumptions underlying their clinical activities.

38

Ritual in the Operating Room

Pearl Katz

Whether we recognize them or not, we are surrounded by rituals, only some of which are religious. Rituals provide a precise set of routine behaviors for performing certain tasks. Often they mark the beginning of some event (meals, sports) or stages in an ongoing process. Rituals often mark critical junctures in the life cycle, such as birth, adulthood, marriage, and death. They may define a time or a place that is in some sense nonordinary and, as such, allows nonordinary behavior. Rituals produce cultural meaning by using symbols and symbolic behavior. We saw earlier how the Nacirema use ritual to express unconscious cultural ideas about the body and its tendency to degenerate.

The medical profession generally deals with the body rather than the soul. It cloaks itself with the most up-to-date scientific technologies. Most people would never associate medicine with something as "archaic" as ritual. Therefore, the following study of operating room procedure as ritual is particularly fascinating. Surprisingly, we find that ritual is an integral part of the efficient functioning of the operating room. This leads us to wonder what other fields might be profitably analyzed from a ritual perspective, and, moreover, in what situations might we consciously introduce ritual to reduce risk and improve performance.

As you read this selection, ask yourself the following questions:

☐ *What is the meaning of the term* ritual *as it is used in this selection?*

☐ *What are the similarities between the sacred and the profane, on the one hand, and the clean and the dirty, on the other?*

☐ *How do ritualized movements within the operating room maintain the separation of sterile and nonsterile people and objects?*

☐ *What are the three stages of operations, and what rituals are performed during each?*

☐ *As you come to understand the definition and function of rituals as described in this selection, can you identify other arenas—at home, at work, or at school—in which the ritualization of behavior functions in a fashion similar to that described here?*

The following terms discussed in this selection are included in the Glossary at the back of the book:

pollution
ritual
symbol

From *Ethnology*, 1981. Reprinted by permission of *Ethnology*.

Ritual has been defined as standardized ceremonies in which expressive, symbolic, mystical, sacred, and nonrational behavior predominates over practical, technical, secular, rational, and scientific behavior, although anthropologists have acknowledged that rational, technical acts may occur as part of ritual behavior.

The analysis of ritual has assumed various forms. One is to investigate the meanings, types, and structures of the symbols used in rituals. Another is to examine the thought processes that occur in ritual, or how the actors believe in the effectiveness of the rituals, how the thoughts expressed in ritual reflect their social structure, and how thought processes in ritual compare with those in science. Another form of analysis of ritual focuses upon the structure and function of ritual in society. Van Gennup's pioneering work describes the ways in which rituals deal with movements of people through passages in time, place, and statuses, and distinctive phases. Gluckman shows how ritual may exaggerate the distinctions between different events enacted by the same people, and explained some means by which rituals masked conflicts by emphasizing solidarity. Douglas describes the ways in which rituals resolve anomaly by avoiding the dangers of pollution.

According to these studies of ritual, behavior in an operating room in a modern hospital would not be defined as ritual because it involves predominately technical, rational, and scientific activity. By relegating behavior in an operating room to a nonritual realm, the meanings of the symbols, movements, and thought processes they reveal are not likely to be subject to the same kinds of analyses as they would if they were termed ritual behavior. Even in Horton's provocative essay, in which he compares traditional and modern thought, traditional thought is conceived as magical, religious, and expressed in ritual; modern thought as secular, technical, and expressed in scientific activity. Although Horton emphasizes the similarities as well as the differences of these two kinds of thinking, he deliberately defines the two thinking styles as embedded in two separate and different contexts.

Recently, some anthropologists have acknowledged that secular ceremonies may be examined as rituals because they share the symbolic and communicative functions of rituals. In the same spirit this paper examines both ritual and science in one technical context, the hospital operating room. It describes behavior and thinking in the operating room in order to understand the functions of ritual in a scientific context. Specifically, it examines the functions and efficacy of sterility procedures.

Despite the elaborate rituals, and despite the rigorous application of advanced scientific knowledge in the operating room, infections do occur as a result of surgery. In the vast majority of cases the specific cause of these infections remains unknown. In the United States each year there are approximately two million postoperative infections, causing 79,000 deaths among surgical patients. This paper argues that the elaborate rituals and technical procedures of the modern hospital operating room, manifestly designed to prevent infection, better serve latent functions. Ritual actually contributes to the efficiency of a technical, goal-oriented, scientific activity, such as surgery, by permitting autonomy of action to the participants and enabling them to function in circumstances of ambiguity.

THE OPERATING ROOM

In most modern hospitals the surgical area is isolated from the rest of the hospital, and the operating room is further isolated from other parts of the surgical area. The surgical area may include dressing rooms, lounges, storage rooms, offices, and laboratories as well as operating rooms. Entrance to the surgical area is restricted to those people who are properly costumed and who are familiar with the rituals within. These include surgeons, anesthesiologists, pathologists, radiologists, operating room and recovery room nurses, student doctors, nurses, and ward orderlies who work in that area.[1] The major exception to these occupational roles is that of the surgical patient who, although costumed, is unfamiliar with the rituals. All of the people in the surgery area wear costumes which identify both their general role in the hospital, as well as denoting the specific areas within the surgical area which they are permitted to enter.

The restrictive entrance procedures and costume requirements contribute to the maintenance of cleanliness and prevention of contamination. Identification and separation of cleanliness and dirt are the most important concepts in the operating room. They govern the organization of the activities in surgery, the spatial organization of rooms and objects, the costumes worn, as well as most of the rituals.

The surgical area of University Hospital[2] has four parts: the periphery, outer, middle, and inner areas. Physical barriers separate these four areas. They function to prevent contamination from dirtier areas to cleaner ones. From outside to inside, these areas are differentiated according to increasing degrees of cleanliness. The periphery, the least clean area, includes the offices of the anesthesiologists, a small pathology laboratory for quick analyses of specimens, dressing rooms for men and women, and lounges for nurses and doctors. To enter the periphery area a person must wear a white jacket for identification as a member of the medical staff.

The outside area is separated from the periphery by a sliding door. Within the outer area, a nurse at the main desk can prevent the door from opening if an unauthorized person tries to enter. Entrance to the outer area is restricted to patients and to those medical personnel who wear blue or green costumes. The largest and most populated part of the outer area consists of an open corridor in which the daily operating schedule is posted and a blackboard indicating the current use of operating rooms. Patients awaiting surgery lie in narrow beds lined in a single row along one wall of the open corridor. A nurse, in charge of coordinating the timing and activities in each operating room, sits at an exposed desk in the outer area. She is in continual intercom communication with each operating room. The outer area also contains a large recovery room which houses patients immediately after their surgery is completed.

The middle area consists of three separate areas called "aseptic cores." Each aseptic core contains five doors. One of them links the outer area to the aseptic core. Each of the other four doors leads to an operating room. Each aseptic core contains a long sink, three sterilizing machines (autoclaves), and many carts and shelves containing surgical equipment, sheets, and towels. In order to enter an aseptic core, a person must wear a mask which covers the mouth and nose, coverings for shoes and for hair, and a blue or green outfit.

The innermost area contains the operating rooms and small laundry rooms. In each aseptic core there are four operating rooms and two laundry rooms. Each operating room contains three doors. One door adjoins the outer area and is used exclusively for the patient to enter and leave the operating room. A door with a small glass window connects the aseptic core to the operating room. This is used by the operating room staff. The third door leads to the laundry room which serves as a depository for contaminated clothing and instruments.

PREOPERATIVE RITUALS

One of the more important operating room rituals, scrubbing, takes place in the aseptic core before each operation begins. It is a procedure by which selected personnel wash their hands and lower arms according to rigidly prescribed timing and movements. The purpose of scrubbing is to remove as many bacteria as possible from the fingers, nails, hands, and arms to the elbows. The people who scrub are those who actually carry out, or directly assist in, the surgery; not everyone in the operating room scrubs. The surgeon, assistant surgeon(s), and the scrub nurse, participate in the scrubbing ritual. Medical students and other surgical

assistants consider it an honor if they are asked to scrub with a surgeon.

Before a person begins scrubbing he checks the clock in order to time the seven-minute procedures. He turns on the water by pushing a button with his hip, and reaches for a package which contains a nail file, a brush and sponge which is saturated with an antiseptic solution. For two minutes he cleans under each of his nails with the nail file. For two-and-a-half minutes, he scrubs his fingers, hands and arms to his elbows, intermittently wetting the sponge and brush with running water. Using a circular motion he scrubs all of the surfaces of his fingers on one hand, his hand, and, finally, an arm to the elbow. After rinsing that arm thoroughly under running water, he repeats the procedure for two-and-a-half minutes on his second hand. After having scrubbed for seven minutes, he discards the sponge, brush, file, and paper and turns off the tap water by pressing a button on the sink with his hip.

After scrubbing, the surgeon and his assistant(s) enter the operating room by pushing the door with their hips. They hold their lower arms and hands in an upright position, away from the rest of their bodies. They are forbidden to allow their scrubbed hands and arms to come into contact with any object or person. The scrub nurse hands them a sterile towel to dry their hands. They dry each finger separately, and throw the towel into a container on the floor. The scrub nurse holds the outside, sterile part of a green gown for the surgeon and his assistant(s) to wear. They insert their hands through the sleeves, without allowing their hands to touch the outside of the gown. At this point, their hands, although scrubbed and clean, are not sterile. But the outside of the gown is sterile. After their arms pass through the sleeves, the scrub nurse holds their sterile gloves in place with the open side facing their hands. The surgeon, followed by his assistant, thrusts one hand at a time into each glove. They accomplish this in one quick movement, in which a hand is brought down from its upward position, thrust forward inside the glove and snapped in place over the sleeve. When only one glove is on, the surgeon is not permitted to adjust it with the other hand. However, when the second glove is on, he can adjust his glove and the sleeve of his gown and any other part of the front of the gown.

At this stage, the gown is not completely fastened. In order to fasten his gown, the surgeon unties a tie of his gown at waist level. Although this tie had been sterile, he hands it to the circulating nurse, who has not scrubbed. The circulating nurse brings the tie to the back of his gown. The back is a nonsterile area of the gown. The surgeon helps her reach the back by making a 360° turn, while she holds the tie. The circulating nurse secures this and two more ties to the back of the gown.

PRINCIPLES OF STERILITY AND CONTAMINATION

The rituals of scrubbing, gowning, and gloving suggest some basic principles underlying most of the rituals in the operating room.

1. In the operating room, objects, or parts of objects and people, are classified either as sterile or nonsterile (S = sterile; NS = nonsterile);
    (a) Nonsterile objects are further classified as clean, dirty, or contaminated.
    (b) No part of the circulating nurse or the anesthesiologist is sterile.
    (c) Parts of the surgeon and the scrub nurse are sterile.

2. To remain sterile, sterile objects may only come into contact with other objects that are sterile (c = contact; > = remains, becomes, or is transformed into; therefore S c S > S).

3. To remain sterile, sterile objects may not come into contact with anything that is not sterile (~ = not; therefore, S ~ c NS > S).

4. Nonsterile objects may come into contact with other nonsterile objects, and both remain nonsterile (NS c NS > NS).

5. Sterile objects may be transformed into nonsterile by contact with objects which are nonsterile. This process is called contamination (S c NS > NS).

6. Contaminated objects can only be restored to sterility by either placing them in an autoclave for a specified period of time, or, in the case of a person's clothes, by discarding the contaminated clothes and replacing them with sterile clothes. If gloves become contaminated, rescrubbing for three minutes is required before replacing the gloves and the gown.

Before the operation begins, most sterile objects are either symbolized by the color green, or are in contact with an object colored green. Sterile instruments, for example, are placed upon a green towel which lies on a nonsterile tray. Although the green towel has been sterilized, it becomes contaminated at the bottom through contact with the nonsterile tray (S c NS > NS). The towel remains sterile at the top, however, and the sterile instruments laying on the top remain sterile (S c S > S).

The surgeon, his assistant(s), and the scrub nurse wear sterile gloves and a green or blue gown which is sterile in the front from the waist to the armpits. However, the gown is not sterile in the back nor above the armpits and below the waist in the front. That is why the surgeon unties the tie at the sterile side of his gown

with his sterile gloves, and the circulating (nonsterile) nurse holds the tie without touching the surgeon's (sterile) gloves, and brings the tie toward the (nonsterile) back of the surgeon's gown. The sterile tie becomes contaminated when the circulating nurse's hand touches it. It remains contaminated because it is tied in the back of the surgeon's gown.

The potentials for manipulating the overhead light in the center of the operating room illustrate some principles of sterility and contamination. Before the operation begins, the scrub nurse places a sterile handle on the huge, movable, overhead light. This permits the light to be adjusted by the surgeon, his assistant(s), and the scrub nurse through contact with the sterile handle (S c S > S). The circulating nurse and anesthesiologist, however, are also able to manipulate the light by touching the nonsterile frame of the light (NS c NS > NS).

In order for a person to move to the other side of the person next to him, as the scrubbed members of the operating team stand next to the patient's table, a ritual must be enacted. The person making the move turns 360° in the direction of his move, allowing his back to face the back of his neighbor. This movement prevents his sterile front from coming into contact with his neighbor's nonsterile back (S ~ c NS > S). Instead, his nonsterile back only comes into contact with his neighbor's nonsterile back (NS c NS > NS).

Before the operation begins each member of the operating team is busily engaged in activities that are essentially similar for each operation. The surgeon and his assistant(s) gown and glove and check last-minute details about the forthcoming operation. The anesthesiologist checks his tools, his gas supply, and his respirator. He also prepares the instruments for monitoring the patient's vital functions, and prepares the patient for receiving anaesthesia. In the outer area, a nurse checks to insure that the patient is properly identified and his operative site is verified. She independently checks the preoperative instructions written by the surgeon with the administrative order written when the surgery was booked, and asks the surgeon to identify the proposed operation and the precise site of the operation. Finally, she asks the patient to identify his name and the site of the operation.

Within the operating room, the words "clean," "dirty," "sterile," and "contaminated" assume different meanings according to different stages of the operation. Before the operation begins, the operating room is considered to be clean. Dirty objects have been removed or cleaned. Instruments and clothes which have been contaminated by the previous operation have been removed. Floors, walls, permanent fixtures, and furniture have been cleaned with antiseptic solution. The air in the operating room is continually cleaned during, and between, operations by a filter system.

Fields of sterility and cleanliness within the operating room are mapped out. Everyone in the operating room, with the exception of the patient, is knowledgeable about these fields. Some of the fields, such as that surrounding the patient, are invisible. Other fields are distinguished by the use of sterile paper sheets colored green. The sheets provide only a minimal material barrier against airborne bacteria yet serve as a symbolic shield separating fields of sterility and nonsterility. They are also used to isolate the operative area of the body from the rest of the patient's body. The sheets cover the entire body of the patient leaving a small opening for the operative area, or separate the head end of the patient from the rest of his body. The head end is considered nonsterile and is accessible to the anesthesiologist and his equipment, which are also nonsterile.

After the patient is rendered unconscious by the anesthesiologist, the scrub nurse applies an orange-brown antiseptic solution (Providine) onto the patient's skin. She pours the Providine liberally onto the skin, and distributes it with circular movements radiating outward from the center of the operative site. This action is repeated at least once, using a sterile sponge on a long holder which is discarded and replaced with each action. The sterile sponges become contaminated through contact with the patient's nonsterile skin (S c NS > NS). This action, which transforms the sterile sponge into a contaminated sponge, also transforms the dirty body area of the patient into a clean area. When this act is completed, sterile green paper towels are placed on the patient's body, exposing only his aseptic, painted, operative site.

Before the operation begins both nurses lay out and count all the sterile instruments and sponges that are likely to be used. The circulating nurse obtains articles from their nonsterile storage place. When the outside of sealed packages is nonsterile and contains sterile objects inside, the circulating nurse holds the outside of the package. She either thrusts the objects onto a green sterile towel, or asks the scrub nurse to grasp the sterile object by reaching down into the package and lifting the object upwards, with a straight, quick movement. These procedures are followed for each sterile needle, thread, or vial that is wrapped in a nonsterile wrapping in order to prevent contamination of sterile parts by the nonsterile parts of the same package. The two nurses also simultaneously count items that are laid out for use during surgery. The circulating nurse records the amounts of each item that is counted. Each item must be accounted for before the operation is completed, and the last count must concur with the total of the previous counts.

Different operations are classified according to the degree of sterility and contamination likely to be present. At University Hospital there are four categories of operations classified according to decreasing sterility: (1) clean; (2) clean contaminated; (3) contaminated; and (4) dirty. Eye operations, for example, are clean. Most gall bladder operations are clean contaminated. Duodenal operations are contaminated. Colonic operations are dirty. Intestinal operations are considered dirtier than many other operations because the contents of the intestines are highly contaminated with bacteria, requiring additional measurements for vigilance against contamination during the operation. Ritual during most operations is concerned with avoidance of contamination of the patient from the outside. Rituals in operations which are classified as contaminated or dirty are concerned, in addition, with contamination of the patient and the medical staff from inside the patient.

After the completion of dirty operations, the medical staff is required to discard all their outside garments before leaving the operating room. Since the unscrubbed members of the operating team wear only one set of clothing, before the operation they don an additional white, clean, nonsterile gown over their green or blue costume. After the operation is completed they discard the gown.

THE OPERATION

Although extensive variation exists among types of operations, as well as variations among the medical conditions of patients, there is, nevertheless, considerable similarity in the structure of all operations. Operations contain three distinct stages. Specific rituals are performed during these stages. Stage One consists of the incision, or opening. Stage Two consists of the excision and repair. Stage Three consists of the closure.[3]

The operation begins after the anaesthetized patient is draped, all sterilized instruments are counted and placed in orderly rows upon trays, and the nurses and doctors, wearing their appropriate costumes, are standing in their specified places. The anesthesiologist stands behind the green curtain at the head of the patient, outside of the sterile field. The surgeon stands next to the operative site, on one side of the patient. His assistant usually stands on the opposite side of the patient from that of the surgeon. The scrub nurse stands next to the surgeon, with the pole of an instrument tray between them. The instrument tray is suspended over the patient's body. The circulating nurse stands outside of the sterile field, near the outer part of the operating room.

Silence and tension prevail as the first stage of the operation begins. With a sterile scalpel, the surgeon makes the first incision through the layers of the patient's skin, then discards the scalpel in a sterile basin. He has transformed both the scalpel and the basin from sterile to nonsterile. The transformation takes place because the sterile scalpel touches the patient's nonsterile skin. (The patient's skin, although cleaned with an antiseptic, is not sterile.) The scalpel, which has become nonsterile (S c NS > NS), touches the sterile basin and contaminates the basin (NS c S > NS). The surgeon uses another sterile scalpel to cut through the remaining layers of fat, fascia, muscle, and, in an abdominal operation, the peritoneum. The same scalpel may be used for all the layers underlying the skin because, unlike the contaminated skin, these layers are considered to be sterile.

As the surgeon cuts, he or his assistant cauterizes or ties the severed blood vessels. The patient's blood is considered sterile once the operation has begun. Before the operation, however, the patient's blood is considered to be nonsterile. This was illustrated graphically at University Hospital before a particular emergency operation in which a patient was bleeding externally from an internal hemorrhage. The nurses complained about "the man who is dirtying our clean room!" However, once the operation on this man began, his blood was considered sterile. Sterile instruments which touched his blood during the operation remained sterile (S c S > S) until contaminated by touching something nonsterile.

The rituals enacted during the first stage of the operation involve the transformation of objects defined as sterile and nonsterile, at the same time that the appropriate instruments are made accessible and are being used to make the incisions. The beginning of the first stage, in which the first incision is made, introduces new definitions of sterile and nonsterile. For example, the patient's blood and internal organs, which had been considered nonsterile before the operation, are considered sterile once the operation begins. (The surgeon's blood, however, remains nonsterile.) The patient's skin, although cleansed with antiseptic before the operation, becomes nonsterile once the operation begins and the incision is made. The rituals also enforce the segregation of the sterile and nonsterile objects while the initial incisions are being made. The surgeon typically utters terse commands, usually stating the specific names of the instrument he needs. The scrub nurse immediately places the requested instrument securely in the palm of the surgeon's hand. If the instrument remains clean, the surgeon returns it to the scrub nurse and the scrub nurse places it upon the sterile tray. If it becomes contaminated, as occurs to the skin scalpel after the first incision, the surgeon places it into a container which could only be handled by the circulating nurse.

As the technical tasks become routinized during the first stage of the operation, joking begins. Most of the joking at this stage revolves around the operative procedures which are to be carried out during the next stage: "I can't wait to get my hands on your gallblad-der, Mr. Smith." "Okay, sports fans, we're going to have some action." The first stage of the operation ends when the first incision has been completed and the organs are exposed. The joking abruptly ends just as the second stage of the operation is about to begin.

The second stage of the operation consists either of repair, implantation or the isolation and excision of the organ, and the anastomosis. (An anastomosis is the connection of two parts of the body which are not normally connected.) This stage contains the greatest amount of tension of the entire operation, and adherence to ritual is strictly enforced. It begins with the identification and isolation of structures surrounding the organ to be excised. The surgeon identifies vessels, nerves, ducts, and connective tissues, carefully pulling them aside, and preserving, clamping, severing, or tying them. The surgeon utters abrupt, abbreviated commands for instruments to be passed by the scrub nurse, structures to be cut by the assistant(s), basins and materials to be readied by the circulating nurse, and the operating table to be adjusted by the anesthesiologist. These people respond to the surgeon's commands quickly, quietly, and efficiently. A delayed, or an incorrect, response may be met with noticeable disapproval from the others.

During the second stage of the operation many of the classifications of sterility differ from those of the first stage. In a cholecystectomy (gallbladder removal), for example, the gallbladder is considered to be nonsterile before the operation begins. Yet during the first and second stages the gallbladder is considered to be sterile, before it is severed. Once it is severed, however, although it is considered to be clean, it transforms to nonsterile. It is placed in a sterile container, but the container becomes contaminated by its contact with the nonsterile gallbladder (S c NS > NS). Because it is nonsterile after it has been removed, it can only be handled by a nonsterile person such as the circulating nurse. But, since the gallbladder is clean and must be examined, it must not be further contaminated from sources outside of the patient. To prevent further contamination, the circulating nurse wears a sterile glove over her nonsterile hand to examine the gallbladder and its contents. The gallbladder is not sterile, but it is not grossly contaminated. It is clean, but nonsterile. It is avoided by the sterile members of the team, yet only touched by the nonsterile members if they wear sterile gloves. The ritual surrounding its removal and examination is complex, and the removed organ is avoided by most members of the operating team because its classification is ambiguous.

Once the gallbladder has been removed, x-rays of its ducts (which remain inside the patient) are taken to determine if gallstones remain. A masked, gowned and lead-shielded radiologist enters the operating room with a large x-ray machine that is draped with green sterile sheets. The surgeon injects a radio-opaque dye into the ducts, and everyone, except the radiologist, leaves the room to avoid the invisible x-rays. When the x-rays have been taken, the radiologist and the machine exit, the staff enter, and the operation proceeds.

Although unexpected events may occur at any stage of the operation, they are more likely to occur at the second stage because this stage contains the greatest trauma to the patient's body. If a sudden hemorrhage or a cardiac arrest occurs, the rituals segregating sterile from nonsterile may be held in abeyance, and new rituals designed to control the unanticipated event take over. If, for example, hemorrhaging occurs, all efforts are dedicated to locating and stopping the source of the hemorrhage and replacing the blood that is lost. Even though immediate replacement of blood is required, rituals are enacted which delay the replacement, yet ensure accurate matching. The anesthesiologist and the circulating nurse independently check, recheck, record and announce the blood type, the number and date of the blood bank supply and the operating room request. They glue stickers onto the patient's record and onto the blood bank record. This complex ritual involves repetition, separation and matching records before the blood is transfused into the hemorrhaging patient.

If a patient's heart ceases beating, a prescribed ritual is enacted by a cardiac-arrest team, whose members enter the operating room with a mobile cart, and enact prescribed procedures to resuscitate the patient. Considerations of preserving the separation of sterility and nonsterility (including most of the rituals previously described) are ignored while this emergency ritual is enacted.

Tension remains high throughout the second stage of the operation. There is virtually no joking or small talk. As the remaining internal structures are repaired and restored in place, some of the tension is lifted, and the routinization of rituals continues. The second stage of the operation ends when all the adjustments to the internal organs are finished and only the suturing of the protective layers for the third stage remains.

The third stage of the operation begins with the final counting of the materials used in surgery. Both nurses engage in this ritual of counting. They simultaneously orally count all the remaining materials, including tools, needles, and sponges. The circulating nurse checks the oral count with her written tally of materials recorded at the beginning of the operation. When the circulating nurse has accounted for each item, she informs the surgeon that he may begin the closing.

The rituals enacted during this stage of the operation are similar to those enacted during the first stage. The surgeon, or his assistant(s), requests specific nee-

dles and sutures from the nurses. They sew the patient closed, layer by layer, beginning with the inside layer. Although careful suturing is an essential part of the operation, this stage is enacted in a comparatively casual manner. There is considerably less tension than there was during the second stage, and greater toleration for deviations from the rituals. Questions about the procedures are acknowledged and answered. Minor mistakes may be overlooked. If the surgeon touched his nonsterile mask with his sterile glove during this part of the operation, he would be less likely to reglove and regown than he would if the same incident had occurred during the second stage.

The silence of the second stage is replaced in the third stage by considerable talking, including jokes and small talk. Most of the joking revolves around events which occurred during the second stage and references are made to actual or potential danger during this stage. "I thought he'd never stop bleeding." "You almost choperated [sic] his spleen by mistake." "Well, I hope he has good term life insurance." Much of the small talk revolves around future activities of the medical staff. The subject of small talk rarely relates to the patient. It may involve the next operation, lunch plans, or sports results.

When the closure has been completed, the surgeon signals to the anesthesiologist to waken the patient. The staff members finish recording information, transport the patient to the recovery room, and prepare for the next case. The operation is finished.

DISCONTINUITY AND OPERATING ROOM RITUALS

The observed rituals help to establish the operating room as a separate place, discontinuous from its surroundings. They also help to establish and define categories of appropriate and inappropriate behavior. This includes indicating behavior categories and their limits.

The rituals in the operating room and the meanings of many of the words used there are exclusive to that setting. The observed rituals express beliefs and values which are exclusive to the operating room. The use of the words "clean," "dirty," "contaminated" in the operating room do not correspond to their use elsewhere. This indicates the existence of discontinuity between the operating room and the outside. Discontinuity between the operating room and the outside is also reflected in the restricted entrances, the specific costumes required for entrance, the special language used, the classification and segregation of objects into sterile and nonsterile, and the dispassionate emotional reactions to parts of the human body. A person can be prohibited from entering the operating room if he were not properly dressed, if he transgressed the rules for segregating sterile from nonsterile, and he did not behave in a dispassionate manner upon viewing or touching parts of the body.

The boundaries which separate the operating room from the outside contribute to a particular mental set for the participants, which enables them to participate in a dispassionate manner in activities they would ordinarily view with strong emotion. For example, in the operating room, they look dispassionately upon, and touch internal organs and their secretions, blood, pus, and feces. Outside of the operating room context, these same objects provoke emotions of embarrassment, fear, fascination and disgust in the same persons. Discontinuity was illustrated during a movie shown to the surgeons outside of the surgical area of the hospital. The film illustrated different techniques for draining and lancing pus-filled abscesses. The reactions observed for the surgeons watching this movie were unlike any reactions observed for the same surgeons while they drained abscesses in the operating room. They uttered comments and noises indicating their disgust. They looked away from the screen. Outside of the context of the operating room, with its rituals and its isolation, the same events are experienced differently. In the operating room a purulent lesion is mentally linked to the rituals that are enacted during the act of lancing. The image of the lesion is embedded in the entire operating room context, including the ritual prescriptions for managing that lesion and for organizing the behavior of others in the room. In contrast, outside of the operating room, the image of the lesion is embedded in images of everyday life. In that context, the reaction to the lesion is one of disgust. Outside of the operating room there are no rituals to diffuse their concentration. Moreover, sitting in a darkened room, watching a movie, the viewers are forced to focus on the picture of the lesion. The only opportunity they have to diffuse their focus is to look away, or to make noises indicating their disgust. The operating room, with its focus upon precise rituals, permits diffusion of emotions and encourages discontinuity from everyday life.

The different stages of an operation express discontinuity of mental sets. For example, blood, internal organs, feces, and skin are classified differently during different stages of the operation, and some are different outside of the operating room. For each of the parts of the body—the patient's washed skin, gallbladder, colon, feces, blood, and the surgeon's blood—the greatest transformation of dirty and clean categories occurs before the first stage of the operation (incision) and between the second and third stage (the excision and closure). For example, the patient's blood is considered to be dirty outside of the operating room, yet is considered to be clean during the first and second

stages of the operation. But during the third stage, blood is again classified as dirty. Similarly, the patient's skin, after having been thoroughly cleaned with antiseptic, is considered extremely clean outside of the operating room. However, once the operation begins, the patient's skin is classified as "dirty." It remains dirty for the first and second stages of the operation. Once closure takes place, during the third stage, the patient's skin is transformed again to "clean."

Rituals exaggerate the discontinuity in the operating room and they proclaim definite categories. An instrument is either sterile or nonsterile; it is never almost sterile or mostly sterile. A person is either scrubbed, gowned, and gloved, and, therefore, sterile, or he is not scrubbed, gowned, or gloved, and, therefore, not sterile. An operation is either in Stage One, Two, or Three, or it has not yet begun, or it has ended.

Rituals in the operating room are prescribed for four different kinds of situations: (1) passing through the three stages of surgery, (2) managing unanticipated events, such as cardiac arrest or sudden hemorrhaging, (3) matching information, such as blood types, operative sites or instrument counts, and (4) separating sterile from nonsterile objects. In each of these situations there exists a potential confusion about the appropriate classification of events. There is danger that objects and events can be confused or indistinct or there is danger of contact of forbidden categories: blood may not be properly matched; the wrong operative site may be selected; an instrument may remain in the patient's body; objects or events may not match or fit; or sterile objects may touch nonsterile ones. For those situations in which behavior categories are not clear, rituals clarify. In a recent textbook for operating room nurses, more than one hundred prescriptions for precise behavior are spelled out in which confusion existed about definitions of categories. At University Hospital, the head operating room nurse claimed that the rituals performed in the operating room "were introduced in response to actual mistakes, problems, conflicts that we had, when how to behave was not clearly spelled out." Rituals in the operating room not only indicate the categories which are potentially confusing, they also indicate the boundaries, or limits, for these categories. Through the use of rituals it is clear to all the participants when Stage One ends and Stage Two begins. It is clear to them which part of the surgeon's body is sterile (between the armpits and waist in front) and which part is not sterile (the remainder). Rituals, then, make salient, and even exaggerate, the boundaries of categories.

Rituals in the operating room have much in common with rituals in other contexts, sacred or secular. Rituals are enacted during periods of transition. In the operating room they are enacted during transitions of events or classifications of objects. Danger is perceived during these periods of transitions. Indeed, Van Gennep emphasizes the dangers which lie in transitional states because the classification of neither state is clear. When states are not clearly defined, ritual controls the danger. Similarly Douglas (1966) claims that pollution behavior takes place when categories are confused, or when accepted categories are not adhered to, as in anomaly.

Beyond the operating room, rituals also indicate categories and limits or boundaries for these categories. These include rituals which define passages—of time, seasons, stages of life, or passages through different lands—as well as rituals of pollution. Rituals proclaim that something is in one category and not in another. One is an adult, not a child. It is the rainy season, not the dry season. We are in the new land, not the old land. I belong to this kinship group now, not that group. Even the middle, liminal stage of ritual, which Turner describes as a kind of limbo, has limits. Although the middle state is neither incorporated into the first stage, nor reintegrated into the last stage, its boundaries are clearly recognized and known to all the participants.

In all societies rituals take place when categories are not clearly defined and when limits of categories are not known. Gluckman suggests, for example, that primitive societies have more rituals than modern societies because different roles are enacted with the same people in primitive societies. This may be understood as exaggerating the boundaries or limits of each of their roles, precisely because they are unclear. Indeed, ritual is found in modern secular society in those situations in which boundaries are unclear, not only during changes of status, such as marriages and deaths, but also in situations such as entering or leaving a house, installing a political officer, and beginning a team sport.

The operating room observations suggest that through its elaborate, stylized behavioral prescriptions and obsession with detail, ritual exaggerates the boundaries between categories. Rituals create boundaries because boundaries have been transgressed or are unclear. When boundaries are not precisely defined, confusion may result about which category is operative at a particular time or place. The actors do not know to which situation to respond. Knowing the limits or boundaries gives shape and definition to the categories. Ritual by defining categories and prescribing specific behavior within these categories, creates boundaries. Moreover, when the boundaries are known, autonomy to function can increase.

AUTONOMY AND RITUAL

At first glance, it seems improbable that ritual, with its emphasis upon specific detailed prescriptions for behavior, may provide autonomy for its participants. To be sure, it is known that ritual exaggerates and often provides license for behavior which may be prohibited in everyday life. Studies by Katz suggest that autonomy increases when the limits of the system are known and implemented. On this basis one will expect that rituals, by indicating and clarifying boundaries of behavior categories—such as sterile/nonsterile or child/adult—increase the autonomy of the participants. Conversely, when the rituals have not been fully carried out—when a person is not clearly within the prescribed limits—there will be very little autonomy.

For example, when the surgeon enters the operating room after he has scrubbed, but before he has gowned and gloved, he is helpless. He has virtually no autonomy. His scrubbed, clean hands are not clearly classified as sterile, nor as contaminated (although strictly speaking, they are nonsterile). He has to exercise extreme caution lest his hands touch anything. If he touches a sterile object, that object becomes contaminated. If he touches a contaminated object, his hands become further contaminated, and he is required to rescrub. He is so helpless that he can do almost nothing. His hands are raised in a helpless position. He depends upon a nurse to give him a towel and to provide him with a gown and gloves. He is not able to put the gown on himself, nor to tie his gown once it is on. Even when he is gowned, he has no autonomy to touch anything. He cannot pull the sleeve of the gown from his hands. The nurse has to put his gloves on his hands for him. His classification of sterility is confusing because, being half sterile and half nonsterile, he does not clearly fit in either category. His autonomy is severely restricted. The autonomy of others interacting with him is also reduced. Only after he has completely scrubbed, gowned, and gloved, and become unequivocally sterile, does he attain his autonomy. He can move about within the sterile field and touch all sterile objects.

In the operating room, boundaries of categories are likely to become confused if a person is present who does not know the appropriate rituals. When this occurs, autonomy decreases, both for the uninitiated person, and for others who interact with him. On one occasion during surgery in University Hospital, the circulating nurse requested a scrubbed medical student to remove a sterile needle from the nonsterile wrapping which she held in her hand. Although the student knew that the wrapping was nonsterile and the needle was sterile, and he was familiar with many rituals, he did not know the precise ritual required for removing the needle. The ritual required him to grasp the needle between his forefinger and thumb, quickly thrust his fingers upwards, and place the needle upon the sterile tray. The circulating nurse was required to pull downward on the wrapping, discard the wrapping in a contaminated bag, and record the addition of that needle. Neither person had autonomy to deviate from this behavior.

The student succeeded in contaminating his glove and the needle by touching both with the nonsterile wrapping. A great deal of autonomy was lost through his failure to follow the prescribed ritual. The student had to reglove and regown. The circulating nurse had to aid him in regloving and regowning. The needle had to be discarded. Since the needle had contaminated the sterile green towel on the tray, the towel had to be replaced, the sterile contents of the tray removed from the contaminated towel and replaced on the sterile towel. In addition, the circulating nurse had mistakenly recorded the addition of that needle, and, near the end of the operation, it appeared that a needle was missing. All the people present searched for the needle, both inside and outside the patient. This activity delayed the completion of the operation until the circulating nurse realized the source of the mismatching. In this case, the autonomy of most of the staff was restricted because one person did not follow the ritual properly.

The surgical patient who is awake can reduce the autonomy of the operating team. The conscious patient has autonomy to express his fears and concerns about the operation. Most members of the medical staff in the operating room regard the waking patient as a hindrance to the smooth performance of preoperative rituals. The waking patient may restrict discussions which are necessary for planning the strategy of the operation. Rendering the patient unconscious deprives the patient of all autonomy, while increasing the autonomy of the staff. The staff gains the autonomy to ignore the patient's psyche, to consider only the parts of his body relevant to the operative procedure, to joke about the patient and his expressions of fear, and to discuss subjects that have nothing to do with the operation. Although the patient loses autonomy, the staff gains autonomy.

It is well known to most laymen that irreverent behavior in the form of jokes and small talk occurs in the operating room. Jokes and small talk in the operating room represent autonomous behavior *par excellence*. They are autonomous because they are not a prescribed part of the operative procedure. They often express values which are antithetical to the serious and dangerous nature of the operation itself. Jokes differ from small talk in that jokes explicitly focus on events of surgery (whether real or imagined), whereas small talk revolves around events unrelated to surgery. Both jokes and small talk trivialize the solemnity, significance, discipline and danger that typically accompany surgery. Although the precise content of jokes and small talk in the operating room is unpredictable, their

timing is. They are not expressed while transitions take place—when stages are crossed, transformations from sterile to nonsterile occur, or when mismatching or emergencies occur. During transitions danger is often perceived to be present. All attention becomes focused on the rituals which are enacted to restore the boundaries. Jokes and small talk are expressed during those periods in which categories—of stages, sterility, or matching—are clearly defined. They occur when ritual succeeds in restoring and bounding these categories, and activities are routinized. Once the boundaries have been restored by ritual, autonomy flourishes. When rituals are enacted routinely, the boundaries are defined and autonomy increased.

Jokes and small talk do not occur during periods of transition, when danger is present, although they express concern about these periods. Jokes are not expressed during the times that autonomy is most severely restricted, such as during the transitions. Autonomous behavior of joking and small talk occurs after the transitions pass, after the tension subsides, after the rituals have been enacted in their carefully prescribed manner.

Most of the jokes focus on events which occur during transitional or dangerous periods. Jokes about organs to be severed do not occur during the dangerous period while the organ is being severed. Jokes about the incision do not occur while the incision is being made. Jokes about the incision only occur before or after the incision is made. When jokes touched on dangerous or transitional situations, they did so only after rituals had clearly indicated that the situation was over. Only then did the surgical staff make irreverent jokes about the most dangerous and vulnerable aspects of the operation. They made jokes in the crudest terms about internal organs, external appearances, sexual organs, the personality of the patient, or other members of the operating team. But they did not joke about the rituals themselves. The operating room staff treated the rituals with reverence and less questioning than other surgical activities.

Many anthropologists have tried to understand the simultaneous presence of both controlling and autonomous aspects of ritual. Van Gennup and later Firth emphasized the controlling and regulating function of ritual. Munn describes how ritual myths function as social control mechanisms by regulating states and bodily feelings. Turner describes the presence of elaborate autonomous improvisation within highly structured ritual. Leach suggests that stylization in secular ritual may be either "escetic, representing the intensification of formal restraint, or ecstatic, signifying the elimination of restraint." Gluckman describes license in rituals as reversals that express behavior outlawed in everyday life. Gluckman also recognizes that license is only permitted in ritual when the limits are known and agreed upon by the participants: "The acceptance of the established order as right and good, and even sacred, seems to allow unbridled license, very rituals of rebellion, for the order itself keeps this rebellion within bounds."

The rituals in the operating room, as well as those described by Gluckman, Leach, and Turner, suggest that the boundaries of behavior are not open to questioning. They are firm. However, within those boundaries there is a great deal of autonomy. In the operating room, the rituals themselves, as signposts indicating boundaries, are not open to question, nor to ridicule. However, within the boundaries considerable autonomy exists. There is autonomy to joke about everything, except the rituals. There is autonomy to question details about the rituals (e.g., how long to scrub), but virtually no autonomy to question the ritual itself (e.g., whether scrubbing was necessary).

CONCLUSION

In modern operating rooms rituals, as stylized, arbitrary, repetitive and exaggerated forms of behavior, occur as integral parts of surgical procedures. Most of the rituals in the operating room symbolize separation of areas containing micro-organisms from areas free of micro-organisms, or separation of realms of cleanliness (sterility, asepsis) from realms of pollution (nonsterility, sepsis, contamination).

Most rituals considered by anthropologists, especially those in sacred settings, express and communicate values, and are linked to institutions of everyday life. Such rituals are amenable to serious questioning of their major premises. It is different, however, with rituals in the hospital operating room. That setting is discontinuous with everyday life, and rituals there have no continuity with values or categories of thought outside of the medical setting. Inspection and introspection of their premises are thereby discouraged or overlooked, but nonetheless neglected. It is through the examination of rituals in extraordinary settings, whether in traditional or modern contexts, that we can become aware of some of the functions of rituals that, heretofore, have largely gone unrecognized in the anthropological literature. The study of the hospital operating room suggests that ritual defines categories and clarifies boundaries between important states by exaggerating the differences between them, doing so precisely where the boundaries normally are not clear and well-defined. It is then that rituals are enacted in order to avoid the confusion that may result when it is uncertain which categories are operative at a particular time.

By imposing exaggerated definitions upon categories, rituals also serve to increase the autonomy of the participants by providing them with an unambiguous understanding of precisely which categories are operative at a certain time. Without the boundaries provided by rituals, participants do not know to which situation to respond. When boundaries are known, autonomy is increased. Extreme license in ritual is an expression of this. In the operating room irreverent joking, as an example, is only possible after the ritual has succeeded in establishing a boundary between indistinct states. Autonomy is limited, and reverence and awe prevail during transitional states of ritual, when boundaries are not yet firm. When indistinct categories are ritually separated and given sharp definition, ambiguity of behavior is lowered and autonomy enhanced.

NOTES

1. Occasionally others, such as salesmen or filmmakers, are allowed in parts of the surgical area. I was allowed free access to all surgical areas at all times, which included scrubbing and standing next to the surgeons and patient during surgery.
2. University Hospital is a pseudonym for a hospital in North America affiliated with a medical school.
3. The stages are heuristic. I have not encountered surgeons nor surgery texts which describe three distinct stages.

39

Women, Minorities, and Indigenous Peoples:
Universalism and Cultural Relativity

Carole Nagengast

Cultural relativity is among the first concepts introduced to new students in cultural anthropology, as you will no doubt recall. It was developed by anthropologists and remains a core concept because it is critical that people respect cultural difference. It remains as true today as when this concept was developed that cultural practices and traditions should be understood within their own historical context.

But what happens when such traditions violate what many consider fundamental human rights? Does cultural relativity excuse forcing girls to undergo hideous genital surgery? Does it justify genocide, torture, bride burning, or religious persecution? Are there no universal principles of human rights? Do we not wish to rid the globe of human rights abuses? This is a difficult paradox.

This selection "problematizes" a concept that may have seemed straightforward as you began your study of cultural anthropology. The more you have learned, the less simple the answers seem to be.

As you read this selection, ask yourself the following questions:

☐ *What is cultural relativity, and why is this perspective important?*

☐ *Are there basic human rights that should be guaranteed to all people?*

☐ *Are human rights culturally relative?*

☐ *How do civil and political rights differ from social, economic, and cultural rights?*

☐ *How are individual rights similar to or different from group rights?*

The following terms discussed in this selection are included in the Glossary at the back of the book:

clitoridectomy
cultural relativity
essentialize
ethnocide
infanticide
infibulation
primordial
universalism

Reprinted by permission from the *Journal of Anthropological Research*, 53:349–369, 1997.

I am always a little surprised at the number of students who, when I query them during the first week of my Human Rights and Anthropology class, agree with popular media assertions that poverty is inevitable; who believe that ethnic hatreds are primordial and thus beyond human action; who are initially willing, if it is "the custom," to accede to forced veiling, bride burning, clitoridectomy, infibulation,[1] and the imprisonment of women accused of adultery, even if men are not subject to the same treatment. They acquiesce in the name of the same "respect for cultural difference" that the spokespersons for various governments demand when defending their human rights records. That this view has a certain facile seductiveness is the primary motive for this paper. The more repressive aspects of the politics of identity seem sometimes to be taking us backward as a profession, even while appearing on the surface to be moving us beyond the essentializing and totalizing images of the past.

The questions I wish to pose are: Does the Universal Declaration of Human Rights and other human rights standards of the United Nations objectify and essentialize Others by undermining cultural integration? In other words, are all human rights universal, or are some of them culturally determined? Specifically, should women and girls always have the same human rights as men and boys? Should Kurds, Moslems, Yanomami, Tibetans, and Ogoni, as individuals and as collectivities within multination states, have the same rights as majorities? Do they have the right to peacefully speak their languages, practice their religions, occupy and exploit their traditional lands, and have equal access to the benefits enjoyed by majorities?

Even though it has become rather unfashionable, I shall make a plea for a kind of universalism, mediated and partial, but still universalism. However, in spite of my universalistic tendencies, I am not prepared to discard cultural relativity altogether (nor am I supporting the claims of repressive states).

The very reasons cultural relativity developed as one of the central themes of American anthropology have far from disappeared, and it can indeed be used to defend basic rights. By the same token, some of the ways in which the concept of culture is today used also grievously penalize those "minorities"[2] to whom respect may be intended.

HUMAN RIGHTS STANDARDS

The Universal Declaration of Human Rights came into being in 1948 at a historical moment when fascism had been defeated and when belief in the future was unassailable. Fifty years later, Western dominance has faltered, and most Communist regimes have left the world stage. Even as economy and society have become more globalized in some respects, the world system has also fragmented, e.g., the creation of the European Union and the splintering of nation-states in Europe. Paradoxically, overall, globalization is matched by a process of profound localization as various societies adopt the symbols and practices of modernity differently. The desire to identify and understand the universal dilemmas of humankind and the search for equally universal solutions has given way in many quarters to postmodern cynicism and disjuncture, on the one hand, and celebration of difference and relativity, on the other. The great projects of social transformation have been replaced with quests for roots and explorations of identity, while the assertion of local and regional identities and calls for autonomy and self-determination have been accompanied by a renaissance of "culture"; newly emergent states and separatist movements alike purport or aspire to ethnic, racial, religious, or cultural purity (Friedman 1994:70–71). As modernity has waned worldwide, so has faith in the future and in the unquestioned belief in the existence of universals, including the universality of human rights.

Human rights standards and procedures as they have developed between 1948 and the present are intended to be neutral—that is, they apply to all humans by virtue of common humanity and are not supposed to take account of sex, gender, sexual preference, skin color, ethnicity, nationality, religion, or politics. However, women, minorities, and indigenous peoples have long recognized that, even though variable but large numbers of political foes of any given state may suffer torture, disappearance, political imprisonment, or assassination at the hands of the state, they are more often and more severely subject to specific abuses based on their gender or ethnic identity (Amnesty International 1992; Peters and Wolper 1995; Burger 1988; Stavenhagen 1990).

For example, the legal apparatuses of many states worldwide condone or implicitly tolerate physical, sexual, and psychological violence towards women in the so called private spaces of family and household. Others actually mandate second-class legal status for women. In both Chile and Argentina, for example, adultery is a crime for women but not for men. In Indonesia, Malaysia, Iraq, and China, among others, laws justify and vindicate differential status for women in access to education, employment, and other public sectors, including in some cases health care and less than equal protection before the law (Peters and Wolper 1995; Cook 1994). The latest instance concerns the Taleban[3] movement in Afghanistan. Beginning in October 1996, the Taleban has banned women from schools at all levels in the areas under its control, as well from employment and public service, and has mandated that women conceal their bodies from head to toe. Justification is religious in nature, and penalties to those who challenge these edicts or appear in public unaccompanied by a male kinsperson include beatings and arrest. Human rights organizations have documented numerous cases of women attacked by clerics or other men for the stray strand of hair or briefly exposed ankle. These assaults occur with impunity (Amnesty International 1996). The majority of Arab spokespersons, even the government of Iran, have officially condemned the Taleban's treatment of women, calling it "uncompassionate, and thus un-Islamic" (King-Irani 1996:12).

As for minorities, in Turkey it was long illegal to identify oneself as a Kurd, speak the Kurdish language in public, or assert the existence of Kurds as a separate linguistic and cultural group with a distinct history. Kurds were officially referred to as "mountain Turks" and their language falsely described as a "dialect" of Turkish. While this changed in the 1990s, Kurds are still subject to unofficial but no less intimidating persecution complicated by the decade-long war in southeastern Turkey between Kurdish separatists and government forces.[4] In Pakistan, certain Christian sects are singled out and deprived of the right to congregate and worship according to their rights on the grounds that they would be a scandal to Moslems and would interfere with the stability of the state. In parts of India in which they are a minority, Moslems as both a cultural and religious group are subject to restrictions of their freedom on grounds similar to those endured by Christians in Pakistan. The Chinese state persecutes, imprisons, and executes Tibetans who attempt to claim their national patrimony. Ogoni tribal and group rights to speak out against the environmental policies of transnational corporations were violated when Nobel Peace prize nominee Ken Saro-Wiwa and eight associates were executed in November 1995 by the Nigerian government. Dissidents continue to be imprisoned and tortured. The annual reports of Amnesty International are filled with accounts of people deprived of political and civil rights on the basis of their language, religion, or ethnic status (see, for example, Amnesty International 1995a, 1995b, 1996).

In addition to the deprivation of their civil and political rights, women, indigenous peoples, and minorities are differentially subject to endemic and largely structural economic, social, and cultural violences that are *not* committed by the state, though they may be implicitly tolerated by it or are the result of state policies (see, for example, Bodley 1988b; Peters and Wolper 1995; Cultural Survival 1993; George 1984; Kohler 1996). The Indian state, for example, overtly defends the right to deny education to the poorest sectors of society, which are of course the historical "untouchable castes," on the grounds that education will simply cause them to be discontent with the economic structure of society (M. Weiner 1996). The Venezuelan and Brazilian states

allow gold miners to operate with impunity on the ancestral land of Yanomami and other indigenous groups, causing harm to them as well as being the perhaps unwitting agents of introduced disease (Sponsel 1994). Everywhere, indigenous peoples are evicted from their lands, both legally and illegally, in the name of regional or local development (Cultural Survival 1993) and are prevented from enjoying their chosen ways of life. Everywhere, women suffer differential access to food, health care, and other material necessities.

The right to development must, according to commonly understood United Nations principles, "be consistent with the existing body of international human rights law" and "derive from the inherent dignity and worth of the human person" (Steiner and Alston 1996a:1111). Nonetheless, governments require that indigenous peoples assimilate and give up their land in the name of development and the greater good. For example, the Bangladesh state has encouraged Bengali settlers to occupy what it defined as "underpopulated land" long inhabited by foraging Chittagong Hills peoples (Pitsch n.d.). The rationale is that land shortages contribute to the impoverishment of the majority Bengalis and that the lands of the Chittagong Hills peoples are needed to alleviate that poverty. Similar circumstances pertain in Highland New Guinea (Grossman 1988), South American rain forests (Kroeger and Barbira-Freedman 1988), and many other parts of the globe (Bodley 1988a, 1990). Critics of these projects reject governmental assertions that denunciations infringe on state sovereignty and are motivated by culturally inappropriate Western ideas about property and freedom (Bodley 1988b, 1990). They contend that governments have an obligation to protect indigenous lands and thus avoid ethnocide (Maybury-Lewis 1996).

As for the rights of women, the Convention on Ending Discrimination against Women (CEDAW), part of the international human rights debate over the last decade, has been given additional impulse by the World Conference of Human Rights in Vienna in 1993 and the 1995 Bejing Conference. Increasingly, governments that perpetuate or permit discrimination or the actual abuse of women have been criticized. In counterattack, they often invoke religious purity, tradition, and "culture," accusing commentators of cultural imperialism and attacks on their honor (Afkhami 1996; Charlesworth, Chinkin, and Wright 1996; Moughaizel 1996). Among rhetorical claims, for example, is the declaration that extending equal rights to women leads to "inappropriate" sexual freedom, the breakdown of "traditional" religion, and the decline of the "traditional" family (Mayer 1995:104–31). Thus, human rights are said to be culturally relative, and Northern or Western liberal views which stress freedom and individual rights are inappropriate to Eastern or Southern circumstances which emphasize communitarian values and community solidarity. One scholar notes that "more reservations with the potential to modify or exclude most, if not all, of the terms of the treaty have been entered to CEDAW than to any other international convention" (Mayer 1995:104).

Thus, the concept of cultural relativity, developed by anthropologists to induce respect for difference, is deployed to excuse, rationalize, or explain the differential treatment before the law of women, minorities, and indigenous groups and to justify what many call human rights abuses. Accusations of cultural imperialism—regardless of the source—chill the anthropological soul and raise difficult questions for us in terms of our research questions and our advocacy (or lack thereof).

TERMS OF DEBATE

In addition to universalism versus cultural relativity, I've implicitly invoked several other dichotomies that need exploration. Individual versus group rights, civil and political versus cultural and economic rights, and the public versus the private sphere are all dichotomies that speak to the dispute over what does and should constitute universal human rights and what ought to be relegated to "cultural choice." Critical commentaries in both the popular and academic press over the last years are often couched in terms of these dichotomies. First, cultural imperialism intersects the public/private split and also invokes individual versus group rights (King-Irani 1996). Denunciations from this quarter charge human and women's rights activists and Northern-based nongovernmental organizations with insensitivity, liberal individualism, Eurocentrism, and the inability to imagine or appreciate the central role traditional communitarian practices have in culture (Lewis 1996; Gunning 1991–1992; Davies 1996; Hicks 1993; Peters and Wolper 1995). That is, they claim that activists misunderstand, undervalue, or disparage cultural and traditional practices that reinforce community solidarity at the expense of individual liberty (Lewis 1996).

Those who invoke the public/private split (which pertains primarily to women) take a different stance. They say that marital battering, marital rape, dowry violence, wife burning, and genital surgeries (all included in the 1993 Declaration against All Forms of Violence against Women, adopted by the Vienna Conference) are regrettable but are essentially private acts committed against private individuals. While they may be criminal and excoriated in some states, they cannot be characterized as human rights abuses within the framework of international law, especially since some of them are voluntary practices of which women themselves are the primary agents (Hayter 1996). Moreover, gender violence affects relatively small numbers of women in the developing world compared to the numbers who suffer poverty, malnutrition, and environmental degradation as a result of colonialism and the neoimperialism of the capitalist world. The right to development in which peoples have the right to choose the kind, direction, and rate of development, in the view of some, takes precedence over the liberal emphasis on the rights of individuals (Hyndman 1992).[5] Minorities and indigenous peoples will benefit from sustainable development, and change in traditional practices that negatively affect them or women, if it comes at all, should be initiated by those most affected by it. Further, such change should only be introduced from the states in which those practices are most detrimental (Dawit and Mekuria 1993). Even those who take this stance, however, condemn the practice of genital surgeries (Toubia 1993).

CULTURES, NATIONS, AND STATES

Other articles . . . discuss the origins of contemporary ideas of universal human rights, especially the codification of the concept in the Universal Declaration of Human Rights in 1948, and the inclusion of the provisions of the UDHR in international written and customary law through various treaties and covenants ratified by the states of the world. . . . Major nongovernmental human rights organizations, including Amnesty International,[6] base their work on the UDHR, the Torture Convention, the Genocide Convention, and other such documents and agreements. The rights listed in the UDHR and elsewhere are intended to protect people from the excesses of the state and to insure equal and fair treatment for all those living within the boundaries of that state. Thus they appeal to a universal notion of humanness.[7] As important, however, by appealing to a wider and broader transnational authority, they transcend the boundaries, constitutions, penal codes, and the very hegemonic nature of stateness by challenging the grounds on which a putative nation-state is constructed in the first place (Nagengast 1994; Clay 1996; Abrams 1988). The continued salience of "the" nation-state as the arbiter of social events is called into question (Appadurai 1996).

These points are worth elaborating. First, human rights treaties, covenants, and customary law are not intended to protect people from individual acts of violence, reprehensible though they may be, but from the illegal violence of the state or from the state that selectively enforces its own laws. International enforcement mechanisms, feeble though they may be, also hold states responsible for ensuring that the basic principles of human rights are upheld within their borders. In other words, the state which is the main violator of human rights is also supposed to be the main enforcer of human rights standards. So, for example, the Mexican state is called upon to bring murderous landowners, who target emerging local political leaders, to justice. Quite often those same landowners are apparently acting at the behest of state officials who have an interest in preventing oppositional politics (Amnesty International 1995a:210–12). The Indian state should bring those accused of killing young women over dowry disputes to trial for murder, yet to do so may mean that the functionaries of the state come up against the locally powerful men whose efforts helped to put them in office in the first place (Stone and James 1997). Still, the endorsement of the UDHR by the United Nations and the variable but still widespread ratification of other treaties and covenants suggest that the theory of universality has worldwide acceptance.

Indeed, Falk (1992), Afkhami (1996), Dwyer (1991), and An-Na'im (1992), among others, make a compelling argument for the cross-cultural foundation of rights, suggesting that the idea can be found in ancient Chinese, Hindi, and Islamic civilizations. All argue that even if human rights as presently codified are the product of Western thought, that does not make them, *ipso facto*, inapplicable to other places in the world. To say that it does begs the question of what the power politics of those other places are. Certain universal moral principles may well be essential for and inherent in all social life (Milne 1986), an argument that has been often made (see, for example, Nickel 1987; Winston 1989; Donnelly 1993; Howard 1992; Cranston 1967; Steiner and Alston 1996c). Indeed, in many countries with diverse "cultures," there are nongovernmental organizations focused on human rights, suggesting that human rights do not simply depend on Western moral imperatives (see, for example, Human Rights Internet 1992). Likewise, tens of thousands of survivors of human rights abuses around the world also probably favor certain universal standards.

It is not the concept of human rights that is in question, it is the content. In every modern state, murder, torture, and slavery are condemned. In notable contrast to official reactions to charges of gender violence or the infringement of minority or indigenous rights, the many states accused of perpetrating torture, disappearance, or extrajudicial executions (or of allowing them to happen) generally plead ignorance or claim to be pursuing the culprits. International prohibitions against such practices can be reasonably said to be universal. Indeed, some of the most egregious human rights violators in the world have constitutions and penal codes guaranteeing protection against the abuses of especially civil and political rights. Many of the rights contained in international documents, compliance with which is reviewed by the United Nations Human Rights Committee and by nongovernmental organizations, thus have not been subject to a great deal of debate with respect to cultural relativity.

The question then is whose human rights should the state protect and which rights should they ensure? The liberal states of the West and the North have long given preference to the subset of civil and political rights, and the developing states of the South and the once socialist states have emphasized social, economic, and cultural rights (Nickel 1987). Civil and political rights, largely enshrined in the International Covenant on Civil and Political Rights (ICCPR), are often said to apply primarily to individuals and to pertain to public life. While most Western legal scholars agree that these are immediately realizable and that states have the obligation to extend them to all without delay (Weissbrodt 1988), some Asians and Africans disagree. For example, Bilhari Kausikan, a spokesperson for the Singapore government, asserted that "good government may well require . . . detention without trial to deal with military rebels or religious or other extremists; curbs on press freedoms to avoid fanning racial tensions or exacerbating social divisions; and draconian laws to break the power of entrenched interests in order to, for instance, establish land reforms" (Kausikan 1996:226).

Economic, social, and cultural rights and rights to development, on the other hand, though realizable by individuals (e.g., the right to a job or adequate nutrition), still often also pertain to groups and largely, though not entirely, to private life (Donnelly 1993). These rights, it is argued by those made especially nervous by socialism, are fundamentally different from, even secondary to, civil and political rights (see, for example, Vierdag 1978; Bossuyt 1975). The grounds most often cited for their secondary status have to do with the sheer cost of implementing them (Cranston 1967) and what critics call the relative or subjective nature of economic, social, and cultural rights compared to the absoluteness of civil and political rights (Bossuyt 1975). However, it is easy to find legal scholars on the opposite side. Van Hoof (1996) notes that it is impossible to refute views ascribing an absolute character to some kinds of rights when they are based on a vague concept of "Natural Law" rather than on a set of evolving norms. In fact, he claims to know "of no convincing argument to support the contention that, for instance, the right to life is absolute because it emanates from human dignity while the right to food does not have the same absolute character" (Van Hoof 1996:281).

A second question arises, namely, should the rights of individuals be privileged or should the concept of human rights also be invoked to protect substate *groups* of people against the power of the state, and is this necessarily a dichotomy? Anthropologists argue that one is not automatically an individual, but that this identity only emerges in a complex constitutive web of social relations (Watson 1997; Morgan 1996; Collier, Mauer, and Navaz 1995). Rights constitute identity, in other words, and are useful in political struggle. "[F]or the historically disempowered, the conferring of rights is symbolic of all the denied aspects of their humanity. Rights imply a respect that places one in the referential range of self and others, that elevates one's status from human body to social being. . . . The attainment of rights signifies the respectful behavior, the collective responsibility, properly owed by a society to one of its own" (Williams 1991:148).

A conundrum arises, however, when individual rights are pitted against group rights. Here is where people who support the rights of groups to live lives in keeping with their cultural mores on ancestral lands flounder. Part of the quandary has to do with some conceptual slippage. In other words, when one moves away from theoretical treatises of anthropology and cultural studies into the realm of other social sciences, law, and journalism, one discerns a tendency to use "culture," "nation," and "state" more or less synonymously. This is especially noticeable among those who defend and justify what others call "human rights violations" by invoking cultural imperialism.

First, most anthropologists nowadays avoid use of the term "a" culture. Second, most agree that "culture" is not a homogeneous web of meanings that a bounded group creates and reproduces and that can be damaged by change but, rather, that "culture" is an evolving process, an always changing, always fragmented product of negotiation and struggle that flows from multiple axes of inequality (Appadurai 1996; Comaroff and Comaroff 1991). Thus, culture is a set of contested signs and practices that are historically and socially situated; shifting power relations within and between societies imply that signs and practices are evanescent rather than inert and static. Further, people who share them may or may not view them in the same way, give them the same meanings, or hold them in precisely the same reverence (Abu-Lughod 1991; Comaroff and Comaroff 1992).

A nation is similar to a state in popular and some anthropological usages (Kottak 1996:40–41), appearing in its hyphenated form as a nation-state. However, many theorists agree that it is more useful to style a people as a nation if they claim to share the same language, the same version of history, and the same set of beliefs about the nature of the world, and if they can lay claim to specific territory (Clay 1996; Maybury-Lewis 1996; Comaroff and Comaroff 1992). If they can defend that claim, they may even aspire to statehood or, as in the case of the Serbs, to expand the boundaries of their state.

In contrast, a state is a political organization, a set of institutions that govern the people who live upon a bounded and internationally recognized territory (Nietschmann 1987). A nation is *not* the same thing as a state. A state can and usually does encompass a number of "nations." The project of a state that wishes to define itself as a "nation-state" is to efface differences among "cultures," "peoples," and "nations" who live within the bounds of the state, so that it can create the illusion of a single homogeneous nation that coincides with the physical boundaries it manages to defend (Abrams 1988). Thus "the state" strives to make the statistical majority the norm. In the most benign scenario, deviation from that norm is stigmatized or is punishable by assimilation or disenfranchisement; in a more sinister scenario, deviation can lead to imprisonment, torture, or death. This latter possibility was made abundantly clear when Saro-Wiwa and friends were hung for insisting that Ogoni have the right to make decisions about their economic circumstances apart from the decisions the Nigerian state makes on their behalf. This is also no doubt what the above-quoted Kausikan, the spokesman for Singapore, had in mind. The state seeks to eliminate, assimilate, normalize, or domesticate dissidents, not only as individuals, but as groups, whether Ogoni in Nigeria, Tibetans in China, Kurds in Turkey, Native Americans in the U.S. or Canada, Christians in Pakistan, or Moslems in Kashmir.

Cultures, nations, and states intersect and overlap, and those who inhabit them must negotiate different roles at different moments. *All* of them are internally differentiated, cut by class inequalities (perhaps caste) and always by gender differences. There are dominant and subordinate sectors, there are factions, there are power blocs, there is contestation. There is no thing that we can call *a* culture, or even a pure nation that will be damaged if *any* aspect of it is criticized. The ostensible object of claims of cultural relativity is liberal democracy or "the West," but the more realistic, though more obscured, object may be the elite of a state, nation, or "culture." Indeed, India's defense of its right to fund education for elites, while denying it to poor children, notwithstanding the very real problem of resources, is a way of maintaining the status quo and inhibiting the emergence of opposition to that status quo.

The anthropological question of how any state legislates "difference" such that it means "lesser" is at issue. The assertion that a state may construct minority status and then punish it, or that it will *permit* differential treatment of state residents based on cultural differences, is to fall prey to a relativity that equates certain cultural practices with state routines of power and control and that regulates others to the category of punishable dissidents. The same argument, and this is crucial, also applies to smaller-than-state groups and their rights and prerogatives. For example, we need to ask about the rights of women in traditional patriarchal societies, and we need to discuss the implications of "traditions" that assign second-class status, rights, and prerogatives to some segments based on gender or outsider position. Just as the ideological underpinnings of state rules are subject to analysis and discussion, so too are the analogous practices of nations, tribes, minorities, and indigenous groups.

DICHOTOMIES AND WOMEN'S RIGHTS

Arati Rao (1995) has identified four components to any discussion about culture and women's rights that can be extended to minority rights:

1. What is the status of the person or group who asserts that human rights are relative; who claims that men and women or minorities and majorities have different rights as a matter of cultural principle or tradition? The Committee for Human Rights of the American Anthropology Association suggests that anthropologists should be concerned whenever "difference" in any of its linguistic, cultural, gender, or biological manifestations is the basis on which people are deprived of human rights (Commission for Human Rights 1993; Turner, this issue).

2. In whose name is the assertion that human rights are relative advanced?

3. In whose interest are these cultural principles? Who benefits from them?

4. To what degree do women and girls, minorities, or indigenous peoples have a say in the formulation and perpetuation of cultural rules and customs that demean them or accord them fewer advantages than men and boys or majorities?

The answer to the first two questions about the status of those who assert that different people have different rights, when different means lesser, and in whose name they advance that argument has to do at least in part with the forum in which this claim is deployed. The resort to "cultural" explanations of women's status and rights is usually specifically intended to influence internal politics and economics. For example, the violation of women's rights is often cloaked by legislation that purports to protect women; this is one of the justifications that the Taleban has invoked. Saudis offer similar arguments about protection to prevent women from driving and otherwise participating in public life and in justifying their differential treatment before the law. Similarly, laws that claim to protect indigenous peoples persist in many parts of the world. Contributors to a forthcoming volume on indigenous rights speak directly to the economics and politics of such paternalistic measures, demonstrating that, in reality, indigenous peoples are

but rarely afforded benefits from them (Morris and Hitchcock n.d.). Cultural explanations for the secondary status of minorities and women are also communicated to international audiences of political leaders and diplomats in response to the criticisms of nongovernmental organizations and other states. Such charges are difficult to demonstrate, however, and envoys are also forced by their own governments to consider their trade policies and "realpolitik" before or instead of human rights.

Historically, no larger group has suffered greater violations of its human rights in the name of culture and tradition than women. And, in answer to the third question above, they have little or no voice in politics or economic decisions, and they are often legally or practically defenseless against domestic violence. They are the object of varying degrees of genital surgeries, some of them health and life threatening; they eat only after men and boys have finished; and they suffer a great variety of other penalties in the name of culture and tradition (Sargent and Brettell 1996; Anderson and Collins 1992). What is more, the concept of culture in the modern state circumscribes women's lives in deeply symbolic as well as in immediately real and concrete ways. Through their clothing, body embellishments, and demeanor, women and girls are visible and vulnerable embodiments of practices that designate them as the repositories and guardians of cultural meanings that ironically also imply second-class status. Men treat women like "angels of culture" who must be protected both from themselves and from the outside world. Thus the primary identification of women with the family and home as reproducers and caretakers, in what has long been cogently argued to be a problematic separation of public and private spheres of life (Lamphere 1997; A. Weiner 1976; Rosaldo and Lamphere 1974; Rogers 1975; Leacock 1978), further contributes to women's secondary status in the very realm in which their lives are debated and decided—in that so-called public sphere to which they are denied full access.

That Southern Hemisphere and Fourth World women should continue to take the lead and set the pace in solving what they define as women's rights in their own groups, in their own countries, is not at issue. Nor is the contention that there are those in the North who have popularized images of the barbarian African or Asian "Other" because they are insensitive or for other objectionable reasons.[8] And it is incontrovertible that Northern states and spokespersons, men and women, have been guilty of imperialism, including cultural imperialism. But *all* states, Northern and Southern alike, sometimes have agendas at international human rights congresses and at the United Nations which have little or nothing to do with women's rights (Rao 1995). We should be deeply suspicious of cries for cultural integration that come from bureaucratic cadres whose very existence depends on governmental approval or from patriarchal elites who stand to benefit from the continued oppression of women. As Barrington Moore (1966:523) has noted:

> [T]he dominant groups are the ones with the most to hide about the way society works. Very often therefore truthful analyses . . . seem like exposures rather than objective statements. . . . For all students of human society, sympathy with the victims of historical processes and skepticism about the victors' claims provide essential safeguards against being taken in by the dominant mythology.[9]

Poverty and inequality along the dimensions of class, caste, and ethnicity in addition to gender plague states and societies of the South but are endemic in the North as well. However, that should not mean that group rights to development, with their implications for the alleviation of poverty (or not) and often their intensification of inequalities as part of the fallout of global capitalism, should always be given pride of place over the integrity of the person. What *do* we do when group rights to cultural principles and traditions mean that women's rights to be free of violence and to realize their human and bodily integrity are violated? Group rights that do not allow a person to opt out of the group seem hollow indeed.

Dr. Mahnaz Afkhami, Iranian professor of English and presently director of the "Sisterhood is Global Institute," a women's human rights organization, notes that Western people who are trying to be sensitive and culturally aware "can go too far, as we see among those women who say that female circumcision [genital surgeries] is just another cultural practice. This cultural relativism is an example of arrogance. It is as if Western feminists are saying 'okay, a whole set of norms apply to us and our culture, and a whole other set of norms apply to these other cultures'" (Afkhami 1996:17).

Thus, both people of good will and those that criticize the universality of women's human rights for less innocuous reasons make a conceptual leap from private, women's space to just that reified culture concept critiqued above (Sullivan 1995). It is impossible to talk about cultural self-determination without locating culture in a changing historical, social, and political matrix. And it is impossible to talk about conceptual schemes which define that which occurs in the family and the household as private, traditional, and inviolate, for these terms are often code for power and dominance (Freeman 1995). The dichotomies of the individual versus the collective, the public versus the private, universalism versus particular obscure the pitched battle that is occurring on all fronts over shifting relations of power and dominance, over the very meaning of "culture."

So among the questions that must be asked before any practice is assigned the status of inviolate cultural principle is this: Does it undermine human integrity? Milne (1986:139), for example, suggests that "the right to life, to justice in the form of fair treatment, to aid, to freedom in the negative sense of freedom from arbitrary interference, to honorable treatment, to civility and, in the case of children, to care" constitute the aspects of humanity that define human integrity. To these, many theorists add bodily integrity (Allen 1996; Martin 1987; Scarry 1985). Few people anywhere, regardless of their views on other issues, regard international prohibitions on torture as cultural imperialism, even if prisoners in their own society had long been (and in some cases still are) subject to invasions of their bodies, to dismemberment, disfigurements, and excruciating pain. These, no less than gender violence and other abuses of women's rights, as well as practices that diminish the humanity of minorities, violate human integrity or "humanity."

Activists and anthropologists alike often contend that it is not "culture" that lies at the root of the problems faced by women worldwide but lack of education about the concept of equality and lack of access to, and experience with, political and economic power (King-Irani 1996). Some women voluntarily seek breast implants and forego education; others may believe that they should have permission from husbands, father, brothers, or sons before seeking medical care; some may believe that they should be beaten or even that they "asked" to be raped. Some women undergo genital excisions voluntarily, but most are performed on children who are not in a position to choose otherwise. Further, significant numbers of women and girls never have any opportunity to exercise alternatives to *any* of these because they will suffer the dire consequences of having made the wrong choice. However, in large part as an outcome of the 1995 Bejing Conference, women's groups all over the world have initiated educational projects whose aim is to discover which human rights concepts, symbols, and images are most relevant in their own societies and how they can best combat abuses (Afkhami 1996).

It is appropriate for women to ask whose interests are served by the imprisonment, torture, and ill-treatment, by the disappearance of political opponents of a regime, as do nongovernmental human rights organizations. But it is also appropriate for them to ask who benefits from traditions, routines, customs, and habits that control their autonomy, their production and reproduction, and their sexuality. Whose interests are served by the differential abortion of female fetuses (Sen 1996) and infanticide (Miller 1997); who benefits when police and military rape with impunity, either because women are defined as legitimate spoils of war (Enloe 1983) or because genocidal rape is a deliberate tactic to undermine "the enemy" (Allen 1996)? What are the long- and short-term implications for themselves and their society if they are allocated a smaller share of food resources, medical care, educational opportunities, and political offices than men (Lockwood 1997)? And finally, whose interests are served when they suffer disproportionately from the contradictions of the global process of capitalist development (Sen 1996)?

When minorities and indigenous peoples ask a similar set of questions, it becomes apparent that some members of some groups suffer pain, sometimes death, and often deprivation and indignity, in the name of a depoliticized tradition and culture. At a minimum, anthropologists need to avoid essentializing any aspect of tradition or culture. To the degree that we do not, we risk helping to create and intensify the penalties of difference. This does not mean that we subsume others to a Western, Northern, or Eurocentric world view or that we promote assimilation and disrespect difference.

COMPLICATIONS

But we might ask whether those who depart from tradition, either as individuals or collectively, enhance their lives or further endanger their well-being. The answer is ambiguous and variable. The case of the Togo woman, Fauziya Kasindja,[10] is instructive. Kasindja fled Togo in 1994 at age seventeen to avoid the imposition of a marriage she did not want and to avoid customary genital surgery. Her parents had managed to protect her and her four sisters from this practice, but when her father died, her mother was forced to leave the home in which she had lived for many years, and Kasindja came under the tutelage of her father's brother and his wife. (Her sisters were already married.) Kasindja's uncle and aunt took a more "traditional" view of culture than did her own parents—perhaps because the uncle as the political leader of the community had a stake in so doing. Kasindja had to leave school—"we don't think girls should be too civilized," said the aunt (Dugger 1996:B8). Arrangements were soon made for the customary surgery, which was to precede Kasindja's marriage to a man of forty-five who already had three wives.[11] Fauziya Kasindja gained international prominence when she was imprisoned in the United States for two years pending the outcome of deportation hearings for entering illegally in order to escape her fate. In May 1996, through the efforts of many women's organizations, she was declared a political refugee and granted asylum because of her well-founded fear of persecution—forced genital surgery—should she be compelled to return to Togo. She is now attending school in the Washington, D.C., area.

On a follow-up to this story, the *New York Times* ran an article on 11 September 1996 about the effects of all this on Kasindja's mother, who, as a widow without brothers or a living father and unable to support herself in a country in which there are few or no opportunities for women without male protection, had no choice but to return to the village where her brother-in-law is headman. While Kasindja's mother was accepted back, it was only after she debased herself before her brother-in-law and other male elders, apologized for her rebellion in allowing her daughter to escape, and performed other acts of obeisance.

I was struck by the fact that Kasindja's mother was not allowed to speak for herself, but had to have a male cousin as spokesperson, and that her uncle was more willing than her sister-in-law to discuss eliminating the surgeries in the future. Indeed, many women in Togo and elsewhere in West and North Africa and Western Asia, including the midwives whose source of livelihood would be imperiled without them, support genital surgeries as a source of women's solidarity. Further, not to have the operation or to allow your daughters to escape it would imply moral turpitude, making it difficult or impossible to obtain a spouse, a disastrous fate in a place with few or no roles for single women (Gruenbaum 1997). We must constantly remind ourselves that there can never be a "culture" that is not mediated by multiple axes of inequality which must be mapped against the larger economic and social conditions of a state. Genital surgeries are outlawed in Togo, one of the poorest of African states, but the law is not enforced, probably because uncircumcised women would, in the short run, be left without economic or social alternatives, as the case of Kasindja's mother demonstrates.

When anyone speaks of "culture" as an explanation for or source of defense of human rights abuse, whether that person is a man or a woman, a member of a feminist group or of the established power bloc, a religious practitioner, or a government spokesperson, it would behoove us to inquire about the overall political, social, and economic, as well as the cultural, context in which human rights violations occur. Fauziya Kasindja as an individual is a survivor of human rights abuses, but her mother and other rural women in Togo still suffer the indignities that accompany gender oppression there. Without dramatic overall and far-reaching changes in the economic and social fabric of life, demands that bodily integrity be respected may be disregarded even by those who might privately agree with a person's right to refuse. The same can be said for extending educational rights to the children of the poor in India. Yet, through Kasindja's flight and the global media attention to her community, a new imaginary has penetrated the quotidian imagination of Togoland and may one day be the basis for change.

There is one final issue—an implicit tendency to regard all the human rights enumerated in various declarations, treaties, and covenants as epistemologically equal. Yet, certainly, the need for protection against torture and summary execution should not be compared to the need for rest and leisure. First is survival, physical and emotional. Individual people cannot be sacrificed in order to insure another's survival, even the survival of another group. That's what leads to massive disappearances, as well as to both genocide and ethnocide. After pure survival comes bodily integrity and the right to protection from physical injury and disease; then human dignity and fundamental freedoms. Essential to the priorities is the notion of individual and collective freedoms—with the stipulation that an individual's rights are protected only to the extent that they do not jeopardize the survival, health, dignity, or equally basic freedoms for others, individually or collectively.

CONCLUSION

My argument is that the concept of human rights applies to everyone, universally, though the actual content of the concept is somewhat more ambiguous and subject to historical, economic, and political considerations. Further, human rights are in my view both individual and collective. But if individuals are not free to choose whether they are in or out of the group, are not free to choose to support or oppose the dictates of the collectivity, then the notion of collective rights is vacuous. It is against the state that collective rights must be exacted, not against individuals. Finally, we should not insist on radical cultural relativity; nor should we suppose that there are universal standards awaiting discovery. Better that we promote dialogue such that universal values capable of insuring the integrity of all humans emerge. Better that we use our anthropological skills and insights to examine the dialectic among the material conditions, power dynamics, and ideas that maintain certain groups of people in secondary or tertiary positions rather than insist on either a kneejerk relativity or a similarly unmediated universality.

NOTES

1. Following Isabelle R. Gunning (1991–1992), I shall use the term "genital surgery" rather than "genital mutilations" to refer to these practices because surgery is less sensational. As many as eighty million women worldwide are subject to these surgeries which are often health and life threatening (Lightfoot-Klein 1989; see also Slack 1988). They entail cutting away a woman's or more likely a child's external genitalia, including the cli-

toris. In its most drastic and most widespread form, the labia minora and majora are also removed, and the wound is sutured such that only a very tiny opening remains for the purpose of urination and menstruation.

2. The category of minority, a technical one in international usage, is defined as "a group numerically inferior to the rest of the population of a state, in a non-dominant position, whose members . . . possess ethnic, religious, or linguistic characteristics differing from those of the rest of the population, and show, if only implicitly, a sense of solidarity, directed towards preserving their culture, traditions, religions, or language" (F. Capotorti, quoted in Stavenhagen 1990:59). Women, though not a numerical minority, are effective minorities in many societies by virtue of their subordinate status. The peoples described as "minorities" often find the label paternalistic, with its connotations of "minor," but the term and definition remain in general usage in both the United Nations and in social science literature. With apologies to those so offended, I'll retain it here as a shorthand for "categorical difference."

3. While "Taliban" is the form of the word used in U.S. newspapers, it is spelled "Taleban" in the magazine *Al-Raida*, the journal of the Institute for Women's Studies in the Arab World, published in Beirut. This would appear to be the preferred spelling.

4. In 1995, Yasar Kemal, Turkey's best-known novelist, who is a Kurd, was charged with "advocating separatism" because of an article he wrote for *Der Spiegel*, the German newsmagazine, in January 1995. The article describes the oppressive conditions of fellow Kurds in southeastern Turkey. Amnesty International and Helsinki Watch, among other human rights organizations, have documented widespread summary executions, torture, and disappearances of Kurds in the southeast while they were in the custody of the security forces. Entire villages have been burned, and general conditions for all Kurds are harsh (Amnesty International 1995a:291–94). Mr. Kemal does not advocate separatism or other illegal action in the article, but he faces a possible total of sixteen years in prison if he is convicted on all charges (Steiner and Alston 1996b:6–7).

5. Hyndman discusses this issue in the context of Aboriginal peoples in Australia.

6. The author has been an activist with Amnesty International for many years, serving on the Board of Directors of Amnesty International USA for six years and as Chair of the Board for two years (1991–1992). The views expressed are those of the author, not Amnesty International. Amnesty International has a restricted mandate and does not take up issues of collective rights or social, economic, and cultural rights.

7. See Turner, this issue, for a discussion of what it means to be human.

8. A book, *Warrior Marks*, by Alice Walker (1993) about genital surgeries has been widely read as disrespectful, as exoticizing and representing African women as dramatically dissimilar to North American women.

9. Moore (1966:522) also notes that "there is a strong tendency to assume that mild-mannered statements in favor of the status quo are 'objective' and that anything

else is a form of 'rhetoric.' . . . This type of bias . . . confuses objectivity with triviality and meaninglessness."

10. Some sources transcribe Kasindja's name as Kasinga. The *New York Times* attributes this to an error by U.S. Immigration, which has been perpetuated (Dugger 1996:B7).

11. The man later claimed he was only twenty-eight but did admit to three wives.

REFERENCES

Abrams, P., 1988, Notes on the Difficulty of Studying the State. Journal of Historical Sociology 1(1):58–89.

Abu-Lughod, L., 1991, Writing against Culture. Pp. 137–62 in Recapturing Anthropology (ed. by R. Fox). Santa Fe, N. M.: School of American Research Press.

Afkhami, M., 1996, Building on Indigenous Conceptions of Women's Human Rights. Al-Raida 13(74/75):13–18.

Allen, B., 1996, Rape Warfare: The Hidden Genocide in Bosnia-Herzegovina and Croatia. Minneapolis: University of Minnesota Press.

Amnesty International (AI), 1992, Human Rights Violations against Indigenous Peoples of the Americas. London and New York: Amnesty International Publishers.

Amnesty International (AI), 1995a, Annual Report. London and New York: Amnesty International Publishers.

Amnesty International (AI), 1995b, Human Rights are Women's Rights. London and New York: Amnesty International Publishers.

Amnesty International (AI), 1996, Annual Report. London and New York: Amnesty International Publishers.

Anderson, M. L., and P. H. Collins, 1992, Race, Class and Gender: An Anthology. Belmont, Calif.: Wadsworth Publishing Company.

An-Na'am, A. A., ed., 1992, Human Rights in Cross-Cultural Perspectives: A Quest for Consensus. Philadelphia: University of Pennsylvania Press.

Appadurai, A., 1996, Modernity At Large: Cultural Dimensions of Globalization. Minneapolis: University of Minnesota Press.

Bodley, J., ed., 1988a, Tribal Peoples and Development Issues: A Global Overview. Mountain View, Calif.: Mayfield Publishing Company.

Bodley, J., 1988b, The World Bank Tribal Policy: Criticisms and Recommendations. Pp. 406–13 in Tribal Peoples and Development Issues: A Global Overview (ed. by J. Bodley). Mountain View, Calif.: Mayfield Publishing Company.

Bodley, J., 1990, Victims of Progress. Mountain View, Calif.: Mayfield Publishing Company.

Bossuyt, M., 1975, La Distinction entre les Droits Civils et Politiques et les Droits Economiques, Sociaux et Culturels. Human Rights Journal 8:783.

Burger, J., 1988, Indigenous Peoples: New Rights for Old Wrongs. Pp. 99–110 in Human Rights (ed. by P. Davies). London and New York: Routledge.

Charlesworth, H., C. Chinkin, and S. Wright, 1996, Feminist Approaches to International Law. Pp. 900–910 in International Human Rights in Context (ed. by H. J. Steiner and P. Alston). Oxford: Clarendon Press.

Clay, J., 1996, What's a Nation? Latest Thinking. Pp. 188–90 in Talking about People: Readings in Contemporary Anthropology (ed. by W. Haviland and R. Gordon). Mountain View, Calif.: Mayfield Publishing Company.

Collier, J., B. Mauer, and L. S. Navaz, 1995, Legal Constructions of Modern Personhood. Identities 2(1–2):1–28.

Comaroff, J., and J. Comaroff, 1991, Of Revelation and Revolution: Christianity, Colonialism and Consciousness in South Africa. Chicago: University of Chicago Press.

Comaroff, J., and J. Comaroff, 1992, Ethnography and the Historical Imagination. Boulder, Colo.: Westview Press.

Commission for Human Rights of the American Anthropological Association, 1993, Report of the American Anthropological Association Commision for Human Rights. Anthropology Newsletter 34:1, 5.

Cook, R. J., ed., 1994, Human Rights of Women. Philadelphia: University of Pennsylvania Press.

Cranston, M., 1967, Human Rights: Real and Supposed. Pp. 43–51 in Political Theory and the Rights of Man (ed. by D. D. Raphael). Bloomington: Indiana University Press.

Cultural Survival, 1993, State of the Peoples: A Global Human Rights Report on Societies in Danger (M. S. Miller, project director). Boston: Beacon Press.

Davies, M., 1996, A Statement on Genital Mutilation. Pp. 251–52 in International Human Rights in Context (ed. by H. J. Steiner and P. Alston). Oxford: Clarendon Press.

Dawit, S., and S. Mekuria, 1993, The West Just Doesn't Get It. New York Times, 7 December, p. A27.

Donnelly, J., 1993, International Human Rights. Boulder, Colo.: Westview Press.

Dugger, C. W., 1996, A Refugee's Body Is Intact but Her Family Is Torn. New York Times, 11 September, pp. A1, B6–8.

Dwyer, K, 1991, Arab Voices: The Human Rights Debate in the Middle East. Berkeley: University of California Press.

Enloe, C., 1983, Does Khaki Become You? The Militarization of Women's Lives. Boston: South End Press.

Falk, R, 1992, Cultural Foundations for the International Protection of Human Rights. Pp. 44–64 in Human Rights in Cross-Cultural Perspectives: A Quest for Consensus (ed. by A. A. An-Na'im). Philadelphia: University of Pennsylvania Press.

Freeman, M . A., 1995, The Human Rights of Women in the Family: Issues and Recommendations for Implementation of the Women's Convention. Pp. 135–48 in Women's Rights, Human Rights: International Feminist Perspectives (ed. by J. Peters and A. Wolper). London: Routledge.

Friedman, J., 1994, Cultural Identity and Global Processes. London and Thousand Oaks, Calif.: Sage.

George, S., 1984, Ill Fares the Land: Essays on Food, Hunger, and Power. Washington, D.C.: Institute for Policy Studies.

Grossman, L. S., 1988, Cattle and Rural Economic Differentiation in the Highlands of Papua, New Guinea. Pp. 237–48 in Tribal Peoples and Development Issues: A Global Overview (ed. by J. Bodley). Mountain View, Calif.: Mayfield Publishing Company.

Gruenbaum, E., 1997, The Movement against Clitoridectomy and Infibulation in Sudan: Public Health Policies and the Women's Movement. Pp. 441–52 in Gender in Cross-Cultural Perspective (ed. by C. B. Brettell and C. Sargent). Upper Saddle River, N.J.: Prentice Hall.

Gunning, I. R., 1991–1992, Arrogant Perception, World Travelling and Multi-Cultural Feminism. Columbia Human Rights Law Review 23:189–248.

Hayter, K., 1996, Female Circumcision—Is There a Legal Solution? Pp. 250–51 in International Human Rights in Context (ed. by H. J. Steiner and P. Alston). Oxford: Clarendon Press.

Hicks, E. K., 1993, Infibulation: Female Mutilation in Islamic Northeastern Africa. London: Transaction Publishers.

Howard, R, 1992, Dignity, Comrnunity, and Human Rights. Pp. 81–102 in Human Rights in Cross-Cultural Perspectives: A Quest for Consensus (ed. by A. A. An-Na'im). Philadelphia: University of Pennsylvania Press.

Human Rights Internet, 1992, Masterlist of Human Rights Organizations and Serial Publications. Ottawa: Human Rights Internet Reporter.

Hyndman, P., 1992, Cultural Legitimacy in Law and Policy in Australia Pp. 295–338 in Human Rights in Cross-Cultural Perspectives: A Quest for Consensus (ed. by A. A. An-Na'im). Philadelphia: University of Pennsylvania Press.

Kausikan, B., 1996, Asia's Different Standard. Pp. 226–33 in International Human Rights in Context (ed. by H. J. Steiner and P. Alston). Oxford: Clarendon Press.

King-lrani, L., 1996, Women's Rights are Human Rights. Al-Raida 13(74/75):11–12.

Kohler, G., 1996, Global Apartheid. Pp. 262–69 in Talking about People: Readings in Contemporary Anthropology (ed. by W. Haviland and R. Gordon). Mountain View, Calif.: Mayfield Publishing Co.

Kottak, C. P., 1996, Mirror for Humanity. New York: McGraw-Hill.

Kroeger, A., and F. Barbira-Freedman, 1988, Cultural Change and Health: The Case of South American Rain Forest Indians. Pp. 221–36 in Tribal Peoples and Development Issues: A Global Overview (ed. by J. Bodley). Mountain View, Calif.: Mayfield Publishing Company.

Lamphere, L., 1997, The Domestic Sphere of Women and the Public World of Men: The Strengths and Weaknesses of an Anthropological Dichotomy. Pp. 82–92 in Gender in Cross-Cultural Perspective (ed. by C. B. Brettell and C. Sargent). Upper Saddle River, N.J.: Prentice Hall.

Leacock, E., 1978, Women's Status in Egalitarian Society: Implications for Social Evolution. Current Anthropology 19(2):247–75.

Lewis, H., 1996, Between "Irua" and "Female Genital Mutilation." Pp. 252–53 in International Human Rights in Context (ed. by H. J. Steiner and P. Alston). Oxford: Clarendon Press.

Lightfoot-Klein, H., 1989, Prisoners of Ritual: An Odyssey into Female Genital Circumcision in Africa. New York and London: Harrington Park Press.

Lockwood, V., 1997, The Impact of Development on Women: The Interplay of Material Conditions and Gender Ideology. Pp. 504–17 in Gender in Cross-Cultural Perspective (ed. by C. B. Brettell and C. Sargent). Upper Saddle River, N.J.: Prentice Hall.

Martin, E., 1987, The Woman in the Body: A Cultural Analysis of Reproduction. Boston: Beacon Press.

Maybury-Lewis, D., 1996, A Special Sort of Pleading: Anthropology at the Service of Ethnic Groups. Pp. 15–23 in Talking about People: Readings in Contemporary Anthropology (ed. by W. Haviland and R. Gordon). Mountain View, Calif.: Mayfield Publishing Co.

Mayer, A. E., 1995, Rhetorical Strategies and Official Policies on Women's Rights: The Merits and Drawbacks of the New World Hypocrisy. Pp. 104–31 in Faith and Freedom: Women's Human Rights in the Muslim World (ed. by M. Afkhami). Syracuse, N.Y.: Syracuse University Press.

Miller, B., 1997, Female Infanticide and Child Neglect in Rural North India. Pp. 453–65 in Gender in Cross-Cultural Perspective (ed. by C. B. Brettell and C. Sargent). Upper Saddle River, N.J.: Prentice Hall.

Milne, A. J. M., 1986, Human Rights and Human Diversity. London: Macmillan Press. Moore, B., 1966, Social Origins of Dictatorship and Democracy: Lord and Peasant in the Making of Democracy. Boston: Beacon Press.

Morgan, L., 1996, When Does Life Begin? A Cross-Cultural Perspective on the Personhood of Fetuses and Young Children. Pp. 24–34 in Talking about People: Readings in Contemporary Anthropology (ed. by W. Haviland and R. Gordon). Mountain View, Calif.: Mayfield Pubiishing Company.

Morris, C. P., and R. Hitchcock, eds., n.d., International Human Rights, Indigenous Peoples, and the Environment. Tucson: University of Arizona Press. In press.

Moughaizel, L., 1996, Laure Moughaizel Evaluates Lebanese Laws. An interview conducted by Ghena Ismail. Al-Raida 13(74/75):23–25.

Nagengast, C., 1994, Violence, Terror, and the Crisis of the State. Annual Review of Anthropology 23:109–36.

Nickel, J.W., 1987, Making Sense of Human Rights: Philosophical Reflections on the Universal Declaration of Human Rights. Berkeley: University of California Press.

Nietschmann, B., 1987, Militarization and Indigenous People: The Third World War. Cultural Survival Quarterly 11(3):1–16.

Peters, J., and A. Wolper, eds., 1995, Women's Rights, Human Rights: International Feminist Perspectives. New York: Routledge.

Pitsch, A. R, n d., Human Rights and Development: Chittagong Hill Tracts of Bangladesh, 1980–1995. In International Human Rights, Indigenous Peoples, and the Environment (ed. by C. P. Morris and R. Hitchcock). Tucson: University of Arizona Press. In press.

Rao, A., 1995, The Politics of Gender and Culture in International Human Rights Discourse. Pp. 167–75 in Women's Rights, Human Rights: International Feminist Perspectives (ed. by J. Peters and A. Wolper). New York: Routledge.

Rogers, S., 1975, Female Forms of Power and the Myth of Male Domination: A Model of Female/Male Interaction. American Ethnologist 2:727–56.

Rosaldo, M . Z., and L. Lamphere, 1974, Women, Culture and Society. Stanford, Calif.: Stanford University Press.

Sargent, C., and C. B. Bretell, eds., 1996, Gender and Health: An International Perspective. Upper Saddle River, N.J.: Prentice-Hall.

Scarry, E., 1985, The Body in Pain: The Making and Unmaking of the World. Oxford and New York: Oxford University Press.

Sen, A., 1996, More Than 100 Million Women Are Missing. Pp. 896–99 in International Human Rights in Context (ed. by H. J. Steiner and P. Alston). Oxford: Clarendon Press.

Slack, A. T., 1988, Female Circumcision: A Critical Appraisal. Human Rights Quarterly 10:437–86.

Sponsel, L., 1994, The Yanomami Holocaust Continues. Pp. 37–46 in Who Pays the Price? The Sociocultural Context of Environmental Crisis (ed. by B. Johnson). Covelo, Calif.: Island Press.

Stavenhagen, R, 1990, The Ethnic Question: Conflicts, Development and Human Rights. New York: United Nations University Press.

Steiner, H. J., and P. Alston, 1996a, Development and Human Rights. Pp. 1110–12 in International Human Rights in Context (ed. by H. J. Steiner and P. Alston). Oxford: Clarendon Press.

Steiner, H. J., and P. Alston,1996b, Global Snapshots. Pp. 3–21 in International Human Rights in Context (ed. by H. J. Steiner and P. Alston). Oxford: Clarendon Press.

Steiner, H. J., and P. Alston, eds., 1996c, International Human Rights in Context. Oxford: Clarendon Press.

Stone, L., and C. James, 1997, Dowry, Bride-Burning, and Female Power in India. Pp. 270–79 in Gender in Cross-Cultural Perspective (ed. by C. B. Brettell and C. Sargent). Upper Saddle River, N.J.: Prentice Hall.

Sullivan, D., 1995, The Public/Private Distinction in International Human Rights Law. Pp. 126–34 in Women's Rights, Human Rights: International Feminist Perspectives (ed. by J. Peters and A. Wolper). New York: Routledge.

Toubia, N., 1993, Female Genital Mutilation: A Call for Global Action. New York: Women Ink.

Van Hoof, G. J. H., 1996, The Legal Nature of Economic, Social, and Cultural Rights: A Rebuttal of Some Traditional Views. Pp. 279–83 in International Human Rights in Context (ed. by H. J. Steiner and P. Alston). Oxford: Clarendon Press.

Vierdag, E., 1978, The Legality of the Rights Granted by the International Covenant on Economic, Social and Cultural Rights. Ninth Netherlands Yearbook International 69.

Walker, A., 1993, Warrior Marks: Female Genital Mutilation and the Sexual Blinding of Women. New York: Harcourt Brace.

Watson, R., 1997, The Named and the Nameless: Gender and Person in Chinese Society. Pp. 137—49 in Gender in Cross-Cultural Perspective (ed. by C. B. Brettell and C. Sargent). Upper Saddle River, N.J.: Prentice Hall.

Weiner, A. B., 1976, Women of Value, Men of Renown: New Perspectives in Trobriand Exchange. Austin: University of Texas Press.

Weiner, M., 1996, The Child and the State in India: Child Labor and Education Policy in Comparative Perspective. Pp. 287–89 in International Human Rights in Context (ed. by H. J. Steiner and P. Alston). Oxford: Clarendon Press.

Weissbrodt, D., 1988, Human Rights: An Historical Perspective. Pp. 1–20 in Human Rights (ed. by P. Davies). London and New York: Routledge.

Williams, P., 1991, The Alchemy of Race and Rights. Cambridge, Mass.: Harvard University Press.

Winston, M. E., 1989, The Philosophy of Human Rights. Belmont, Calif.: Wadsworth Publishing Company.

40

Advertising and Global Culture

Noreene Janus

Cultures have always undergone change, whether slow and evolutionary or rapid and revolutionary. Sometimes these changes make people's lives better and sometimes they make them worse. Some social change is spontaneous and unplanned; at other times change is the result of conscious efforts. Planned change can produce socially disastrous results or significant social benefits.

In this selection, Noreene Janus describes changes that are occurring on a global scale. The change agents—those creating the change—are transnational corporations and transnational advertising agencies. Through their efforts, Western goods and Western values are being introduced throughout the Third World, causing significant cultural transformations.

This selection raises the question of conflicting inalienable rights among the members of our global village. Some people believe that transnational advertisers have the inalienable right to sell their products on a free market without worrying about the burden of long-term social consequences. Most Third World people feel they have the right to access the world's consumer goods. But in doing so, are they aware of the long-term consequences that buying into the Western consumer model may have on the continuation of their cultural heritage? Some people think that Third World leaders should be warned of these consequences and have the opportunity to reject the consumer model by restricting advertising. The big question is whether Third World peoples are the beneficiaries or the victims of this global process of change.

As you read this selection, ask yourself the following questions:

☐ Are these global cultural changes spontaneous or planned? Who is responsible?

☐ What is the underlying value, the core, of transnational culture?

☐ What do you think is meant by "consumer democracy"?

☐ Do transnational advertisers seem to have their own culture, or set of values, about the legitimacy of their work?

☐ Do you think transnational advertisers have an inalienable right to advertise, or should restrictions be imposed on them?

The following terms discussed in this selection are included in the Glossary at the back of the book:

economy
social stratification
transnational culture
values

From *Cultural Survival* 7(2): 28–31, 1983. Reprinted with permission of *Cultural Survival*.

No one can travel to Africa, Asia, or Latin America and not be struck by the Western elements of urban life. The symbols of transnational culture—automobiles, advertising, supermarkets, shopping centers, hotels, fast food chains, credit cards, and Hollywood movies—give the feeling of being at home. Behind these tangible symbols are a corresponding set of values and attitudes about time, consumption, work relations, etc. Some believe global culture has resulted from gradual spontaneous processes that depended solely on technological innovations—increased international trade, global mass communications, jet travel. Recent studies show that the processes are anything but spontaneous; that they are the result of tremendous investments of time, energy and money by transnational corporations.

This "transnational culture" is a direct outcome of the internationalization of production and accumulation promoted through standardized development models and cultural forms.

The common theme of transnational culture is consumption. Advertising expresses this ideology of consumption in its most synthetic and visual form.

Advertisers rely on few themes: happiness, youth, success, status, luxury, fashion, and beauty. In advertising, social contradictions and class differences are masked and workplace conflicts are not shown. Advertising campaigns suggest that solutions to human problems are to be found in individual consumption, presented as an ideal outlet for mass energies . . . a socially acceptable form of action and participation which can be used to defuse potential political unrest. "Consumer democracy" is held out to the poor around the world as a substitute for political democracy. After all, as the advertising executive who transformed the U.S. Pepsi ad campaign "Join the Pepsi Generation" for use in Brazil as "Join the Pepsi Revolution" explains, most people have no other means to express their need for social change other than by changing brands and increasing their consumption.

Transnational advertising is one of the major reasons both for the spread of transnational culture and the breakdown of traditional cultures. Depicting the racy foreign lifestyles of a blond jetsetter in French or English, it associates Western products with modernity. That which is modern is good; that which is traditional is implicitly bad, impeding the march of progress. Transnational culture strives to eliminate local cultural variations. Barnett and Muller (1974:178) discuss the social impact of this process:

> What are the long range social effects of advertising on people who earn less than $200 a year? (Peasants, domestic workers, and laborers) learn of the outside world through the images and slogans of advertising. One

message that comes through clearly is that happiness, achievement, and being white have something to do with one another. In mestizo countries (sic) such as Mexico and Venezuela where most of the population still bear strong traces of their Indian origin, billboards depicting the good life for sale invariably feature blond, blue-eyed American-looking men and women. One effect of such "white is beautiful" advertising is to reinforce feelings of inferiority which are the essence of a politically immobilizing colonial mentality . . . The subtle message of the global advertiser in poor countries is "Neither you nor what you create are worth very much; *we will sell you a civilization*" (emphasis added).

But global culture is the incidental outcome of transnational marketing logic more than it is the result of a conscious strategy to subvert local cultures. It is marketing logic, for example, that created the "global advertising campaign," one single advertising message used in all countries where the product is made or distributed. This global campaign is both more efficient and less expensive for a firm. Thus, before the intensification of violence in rural Guatemala, for example, farmers gathered around the only television set in their village to watch an advertisement for Revlon perfume showing a blonde woman strolling down Fifth Avenue in New York—the same advertisement shown in the U.S. and other countries.

Transnational firms and global advertising agencies are clearly aware of the role of advertising in the creation of a new consumer culture in Third World countries. A top Israeli advertising executive says,

> Television antennas are gradually taking the place of the tom-tom drums across the vast stretches of Africa. Catchy jingles are replacing tribal calls in the Andes of Latin America. Spic-and-span supermarkets stand on the grounds where colorful wares of an Oriental Bazaar were once spread throughout Asia. Across vast continents hundreds of millions of people are awakening to the beat of modern times. Is the international advertiser fully aware of the magnitude of this slow but gigantic process? Is he alert to the development of these potential markets? Does he know how to use and apply the powerful tools of modern advertising to break into these vast areas of emerging consumers despite the barriers of illiteracy, tribal customs, religious prejudices and primitive beliefs? How great is the potential, and how promising are the prospects of the pioneer industrialist, marketer or advertiser who will venture into this vast Terra Incognita? [Tal, 1974].

Increasingly advertising campaigns are aimed at the vast numbers of poor in Third World countries. As one U.S. advertising executive observes about the Mexican consumer market, even poor families, when living together and pooling their incomes, can add up to a household income of more than $10,000 per year. He explains how they can become an important marketing target:

> The girls will need extra for cosmetics and clothes, but Jaime needs date money and, of course, something is going into the bank to send Carlito to the university. Once all day-to-day expenses have been covered there will come the big decisions that change lifestyles from month to month.
>
> First will probably be a TV set. Nobody can visit Latin America and not be shocked at the number of antennas on top of shacks. And once the TV set goes to work the Fernandez family is like a kid in a candy store. They are the audience that add up to five and one-half hours of viewing a day. They are pounded by some 450 commercials a week. They see all the beautiful people and all the beautiful things. And what they see, they want [Criswell, 27 October 1975].

Since an important characteristic of transnational culture is the speed and breadth with which it is transmitted, communications and information systems play an important role, permitting a message to be distributed globally through television series, news, magazines, comics, and films. The use of television to spread transnational culture is especially effective with illiterates. Grey Advertising International undertook a worldwide study of television to determine its usefulness as an advertising channel and reported that:

> Television is undisputedly the key communications development of our era. It has demonstrated its power to make the world a global village; to educate and inform; to shape the values, attitudes, and lifestyles of generations growing up with it. In countries where it operates as an unfettered commercial medium it has proven for many products the most potent of all consumer marketing weapons as well as a major influence in establishing corporate images and affecting public opinion on behalf of business [Grey Advertising International, 1977].

What do we know about the impact of transnational culture on Third World cultures? Personal observations are plentiful. Anyone who has heard children singing along with television commercials and introducing these themes into their daily games begins to see the impact. There are more extensive analyses as well. Pierre Thizier Seya studied the impact of transnational advertising on cultures in the Ivory Coast. He notes that transnational firms such as Colgate and Nestle have helped to replace traditional products—often cheaper and more effective—with industrialized toothpastes and infant formulas.

> By consuming Coca-Cola, Nestle products, Marlboro, Maggi, Colgate or Revlon, Ivorians are not only fulfilling unnecessary needs but also progressively relinquishing their authentic world outlook in favor of the transnational way of life [Seya, 1982:17].

Advertising of skin-lightening products persuades the African women to be ashamed of their own color and try to be white.

> In trying to be as white as possible, that is to say, in becoming ashamed of their traditional being, the Ivorians are at the same time relinquishing one of the most powerful weapons at their disposal for safeguarding their dignity as human beings: their racial identity. And advertising is not neutral in such a state of affairs [Seya, 1982:18].

He also mentions that advertising is helping to change the Ivorian attitude toward aging, making women fear looking older and undermining the traditional respect for elders.

The consumption of soft drinks and hard liquor points to another social change. Traditionally drinks are consumed only in social settings, as evidenced by the large pot where they are stored. Yet, the advertising of Coca-Cola and Heinekens portrays drinking as an individual act rather than a collective one.

A study carried out in Venezuela explores the relationship between television content and children's attitudes. Santoro (1975) analyzed a week of television programming and interviewed 900 sixth grade children. The children were asked to invent a story by drawing the characters in a television screen and then to describe what they had drawn. The imaginary scenes were primarily stories about violence, crime, physical force, and competition, and the large majority of them depicted destructive actions motivated by greed. The "good" characters were primarily from the U.S., white, rich, of varied professions and English surnames. The "bad" characters were mostly from other countries including China and Germany, of black color, poor, workers or office personnel, and with English or Spanish surnames. Santoro concluded that these stereotypes held by children were largely the same ones to be found in typical Venezuelan television and advertising contents.

In another study carried out in Mexico by the National Consumer's Institute in 1981, more than 900 sixth grade children were quizzed on the contents of their textbooks and the contents of commercial television. They knew more about television personalities than about national heroes and recognized more trademarks for snacks, soft drinks, chewing gum and so on than national symbols such as the flag, a map of the country, the major party's symbol, etc. They knew much more about soap operas and action series than they did about episodes of Mexican history. The researchers concluded that advertising and the television medium are far more effective teachers than the public school system. If children are learning about consumption, soap operas and transnational symbols, their parents must be also.

In another research project, seven-year-old Mexican children from different economic backgrounds were interviewed to determine the role of the mass media—primarily television—as sources of information, the relationship established between children and television, and the degree to which the children have internalized transnational consumption patterns (Janus, 1982).

Children were shown pictures of the same man in three different settings—family, nature, and luxury possessions and asked to choose which of these three was the happiest. The question was meant to show the degree to which the children accept the fundamental assumption of advertising: consumption brings happiness. While slightly more than half of the children chose the family scene, poorer children were significantly more likely to associate the luxury possessions with happiness than the rich children.

In the same study, children were shown a series of industrial products along with the traditional products they had replaced: Tang and fresh orange juice, Wonder bread and traditional rolls, Nescafe and coffee beans. The question was designed to determine the degree to which these children actually thought of the industrialized product as the principal form of the food. Again, poor children more often answered that Nescafe *is* coffee, and Tang *is* orange juice.

Perhaps the most interesting result of the study concerns the ability of children to analyze consumption in terms of class. They were shown different categories of consumer products such as cigarettes and television sets, and asked which a rich person could buy and which a poor person could buy. Virtually every child showed an acute awareness of the different access to these products by class. They knew very well that a rich person could buy any or all of the products whereas the poor could buy only the cigarettes, the Coca-Cola, the snackfoods, and the lipstick.

These results, while very tentative, suggest that the impact of transnational culture is greater among the poor—the very people who cannot afford to buy the lifestyle it represents. The poor are more likely to associate consumption with happiness and feel that industrialized products are better than the locally made ones. But at the same time they are painfully aware that only the rich have access to the lifestyle portrayed.

This leads us to the most important questions. What political impact does the spread of transnational culture have on the poor for whom luxury lifestyles are not possible? How do they deal with the daily contradictions that this awareness implies? How much will they accept and how much will they reject? How can they maintain their own identities in the face of transnational culture?

REFERENCES

Barnett, R. and R. Muller, 1974. *Global Reach*. New York: Simon and Schuster.

Criswell, R. 1975. "Keeping up with the Fernandez." *Advertising Age*. October 27.

Grey Advertising International. 1977. "Survey of International Television." *Grey Matter*.

Instituto Nacional del Consumidor (INCO). 1981. *La Television y Los Niños: Conocimiento de la "Realidad Televisiva" vs. Conocimiento de la "Realidad Nacional."* Mexico City: INCO.

Janus, N. 1982. "Spiderman Drinks Tang: Television and Transnational Culture in Mexican Children." Mexico: Instituto Latinoamericano de Estudios Transnacionales (ILET).

Santoro, E. 1975. *La Television Venezolana y La Formacion de Estereotipos en el Niño*. Caracas: Universidad Central de Venezuela.

Seya, P. T. 1982. "Advertising as an Ideological Apparatus of Transnational Capitalism in the Ivory Coast." Mimeographed copy.

41

The Price of Progress

John H. Bodley

Anthropologists are not against progress: We do not want everyone to return to the "good old days" of our Paleolithic ancestors. On the other hand, the discoveries of cultural anthropologists have made us painfully aware of the human costs of unplanned social and economic change. Anthropologists do not want our society to plunge blindly into the future, unaware and unconcerned about how our present decisions will affect other people or future generations. Cultures are always changing, and the direction of that change is toward a single world system. As seen in the previous selection on advertising, cultures change because a society's economy is pulled into the world economy. "Progress" is a label placed on cultural and economic change, but whether something represents "progress" or not depends on one's perspective.

In this selection, John Bodley reviews some of the unexpected consequences of economic development in terms of health, ecological change, quality of life, and relative deprivation. We have seen this same theme in several previous selections—the invention of agriculture, for example. The benefits of economic development are not equally distributed within a developing society. In this selection, we see the relative costs and benefits of economic progress for some of the most marginalized people of the world—the tribal peoples who have been the traditional focus of cultural anthropology research. We believe that the problems detailed here should make our society think about the way cultural change can make people's lives worse; these are issues of social justice.

Anthropologists have been active in seeking solutions to many serious problems. At the same time, most anthro-pologists believe that tribal peoples have a right to lead their traditional lifestyles and not to be forced into change. In this regard, an organization called Cultural Survival has been active in the international political arena in protecting the land and rights of native peoples.

As you read this selection, ask yourself the following questions:

☐ What is meant by quality of life? Why might it increase or decrease for a population?

☐ What are the three ways in which economic development can change the distribution of disease?

☐ Why do people's diets change? Do people choose diets and behaviors that are harmful to them?

☐ What is meant by relative deprivation? Can you think of other examples of this process?

☐ Are tribal peoples more vulnerable to the negative impact of social and economic change than larger industrial societies?

The following terms discussed in this selection are included in the Glossary at the back of the book:

dental anthropology	relative deprivation
ecosystem	self-sufficient
ethnocentrism	swidden
nomadic band	tribe
population pressure	urbanization

In aiming at progress . . . you must let no one suffer by too drastic a measure, nor pay too high a price in upheaval and devastation, for your innovation.

—Maunier, 1949:725

Until recently, government planners have always considered economic development and progress beneficial goals that all societies should want to strive toward. The social advantages of progress—as defined in terms of increased incomes, higher standards of living, greater security, and better health—are thought to be positive, *universal* goods, to be obtained at any price. Although one may argue that tribal peoples must sacrifice their traditional cultures to obtain these benefits, government planners generally feel that this is a small price to pay for such obvious advantages.

In earlier chapters, evidence was presented to demonstrate that autonomous tribal peoples have not *chosen* progress to enjoy its advantages, but that governments have *pushed* progress upon them to obtain tribal resources, not primarily to share with the tribal peoples the benefits of progress. It has also been shown that the price of forcing progress on unwilling recipients has involved the deaths of millions of tribal people, as well as their loss of land, political sovereignty, and the right to follow their own life style. This chapter does not attempt to further summarize that aspect of the cost of progress, but instead analyzes the specific effects of the participation of tribal peoples in the world-market economy. In direct opposition to the usual interpretation, it is argued here that the benefits of progress are often both illusory and detrimental to tribal peoples when they have not been allowed to control their own resources and define their relationship to the market economy.

PROGRESS AND THE QUALITY OF LIFE

One of the primary difficulties in assessing the benefits of progress and economic development for any culture is that of establishing a meaningful measure of both benefit and detriment. It is widely recognized that *standard of living*, which is the most frequently used measure of progress, is an intrinsically ethnocentric concept relying heavily upon indicators that lack universal cultural relevance. Such factors as GNP, per capita income, capital formation, employment rates, literacy, formal education, consumption of manufactured goods, number of doctors and hospital beds per thousand persons, and the amount of money spent on government welfare and health programs may be irrelevant measures of actual *quality* of life for autonomous or even semiautonomous tribal cultures. In its 1954 report, the Trust Territory government indicated that since the Micronesian population was still largely satisfying its own needs within a cashless subsistence economy, "Money income is not a significant measure of living standards, production, or well-being in this area" (TTR, 1953:44). Unfortunately, within a short time the government began to rely on an enumeration of certain imported goods as indicators of a higher standard of living in the islands, even though many tradition-oriented islanders felt that these new goods symbolized a lowering of the quality of life.

A more useful measure of the benefits of progress might be based on a formula for evaluating cultures devised by Goldschmidt (1952:135). According to these less ethnocentric criteria, the important question to ask is: Does progress or economic development increase or decrease a given culture's ability to satisfy the physical and psychological needs of its population, or its stability? This question is a far more direct measure of quality of life than are the standard economic correlates of development, and it is universally relevant. Specific indication of this *standard* of living could be found for any society in the nutritional status and general physical and mental health of its population, the incidence of crime and delinquency, the demographic structure, family stability, and the society's relationship to its natural resource base. A society with high rates of malnutrition and crime, and one degrading its natural environment to the extent of threatening its continued existence, might be described as at a lower standard of living than is another society where these problems did not exist.

Careful examination of the data, which compare, on these specific points, the former condition of self-sufficient tribal peoples with their condition following their incorporation into the world-market economy, leads to the conclusion that their standard of living is *lowered*, not raised, by economic progress—and often to a dramatic degree. This is perhaps the most outstanding and inescapable fact to emerge from the years of research that anthropologists have devoted to the study of culture change and modernization. Despite the best intentions of those who have promoted change and improvement, all too often the results have been poverty, longer working hours, and much greater physical exertion, poor health, social disorder, discontent, discrimination, overpopulation, and environmental deterioration—combined with the destruction of the traditional culture.

DISEASES OF DEVELOPMENT

Perhaps it would be useful for public health specialists to start talking about a new category of diseases. . . . Such diseases could be called the "diseases of development" and would consist of those pathological conditions which are based on the usually unanticipated consequences of the implementation of development schemes [Hughes & Hunter, 1972:93].

Economic development increases the disease rate of affected peoples in at least three ways. First, to the extent that development is successful, it makes developed populations suddenly become vulnerable to all of the diseases suffered almost exclusively by "advanced" peoples. Among these are diabetes, obesity, hypertension, and a variety of circulatory problems. Second, development disturbs traditional environmental balances and may dramatically increase certain bacterial and parasite diseases. Finally, when development goals prove unattainable, an assortment of poverty diseases may appear in association with the crowded conditions of urban slums and the general breakdown in traditional socioeconomic systems.

Outstanding examples of the first situation can be seen in the Pacific, where some of the most successfully developed native peoples are found. In Micronesia, where development has progressed more rapidly than perhaps anywhere else, between 1958 and 1972 the population doubled, but the number of patients treated for heart disease in the local hospitals nearly tripled, mental disorder increased eightfold, and by 1972 hypertension and nutritional deficiencies began to make significant appearances for the first time (TTR, 1959, 1973, statistical tables).

Although some critics argue that the Micronesian figures simply represent better health monitoring due to economic progress, rigorously controlled data from Polynesia show a similar trend. The progressive acquisition of modern degenerative diseases was documented by an eight-member team of New Zealand medical specialists, anthropologists, and nutritionists, whose research was funded by the Medical Research Council of New Zealand and the World Health Organization. These researchers investigated the health status of a genetically related population at various points along a continuum of increasing cash income, modernizing diet, and urbanization. The extremes on this acculturation continuum were represented by the relatively traditional Pukapukans of the Cook Islands and the essentially Europeanized New Zealand Maori, while the busily developing Rarotongans, also of the Cook Islands, occupied the intermediate position. In 1971, after eight years of work, the team's preliminary findings were summarized by Dr. Ian Prior, cardiologist and leader of the research, as follows:

> We are beginning to observe that the more an islander takes on the ways of the West, the more prone he is to succumb to our degenerative diseases. In fact, it does not seem too much to say our evidence now shows that the farther the Pacific natives move from the quiet, care-free life of their ancestors, the closer they come to gout,

diabetes, atherosclerosis, obesity, and hypertension [Prior, 1971:2].

In Pukapuka, where progress was limited by the island's small size and its isolated location some 480 kilometers from the nearest port, the annual per capita income was only about thirty-six dollars and the economy remained essentially at a subsistence level. Resources were limited and the area was visited by trading ships only three or four times a year; thus, there was little opportunity for intensive economic development. Predictably, the population of Pukapuka was characterized by relatively low levels of imported sugar and salt intake, and a presumably related low level of heart disease, high blood pressure, and diabetes. In Rarotonga, where economic success was introducing town life, imported food, and motorcycles, sugar and salt intakes nearly tripled, high blood pressure increased approximately ninefold, diabetes two- to threefold, and heart disease doubled for men and more than quadrupled for women, while the number of grossly obese women increased more than tenfold. Among the New Zealand Maori, sugar intake was nearly eight times that of the Pukapukans, gout in men was nearly double its rate on Pukapuka, and diabetes in men was more than fivefold higher, while heart disease in women had increased more than sixfold. The Maori were, in fact, dying of "European" diseases at a greater rate than was the average New Zealand European.

Government development policies designed to bring about changes in local hydrology, vegetation, and settlement patterns and to increase population mobility, and even programs aimed at reducing certain diseases, have frequently led to dramatic increases in disease rates because of the unforeseen effects of disturbing the preexisting order. Hughes and Hunter (1972) published an excellent survey of cases in which development led directly to increased disease rates in Africa. They concluded that hasty development intervention in relatively balanced local cultures and environments resulted in "a drastic deterioration in the social and economic conditions of life."

Traditional populations in general have presumably learned to live with the endemic pathogens of their environments, and in some cases they have evolved genetic adaptations to specific diseases, such as the sickle-cell trait, which provided an immunity to malaria. Unfortunately, however, outside intervention has entirely changed this picture. In the late 1960s, sleeping sickness suddenly increased in many areas of Africa and even spread to areas where it did not formerly occur, due to the building of new roads and migratory labor, both of which caused increased population movement. Large-scale relocation schemes, such as the Zande Scheme, had disastrous results when natives were moved from their traditional disease-free refuges into infected areas. Dams and irrigation developments inadvertently created ideal conditions for the rapid proliferation of snails carrying schistosomiasis (a liver fluke disease), and major epidemics suddenly occurred in areas where this disease had never before been a problem. DDT spraying programs have been temporarily successful in controlling malaria, but there is often a rebound effect that increases the problem when spraying is discontinued, and the malarial mosquitoes are continually evolving resistant strains.

Urbanization is one of the prime measures of development, but it is a mixed blessing for most former tribal peoples. Urban health standards are abysmally poor and generally worse than in rural areas for the detribalized individuals who have crowded into the towns and cities throughout Africa, Asia, and Latin America seeking wage employment out of new economic necessity. Infectious diseases related to crowding and poor sanitation are rampant in urban centers, while greatly increased stress and poor nutrition aggravate a variety of other health problems. Malnutrition and other diet-related conditions are, in fact, one of the characteristic hazards of progress faced by tribal peoples and are discussed in the following sections.

The Hazards of Dietary Change

The traditional diets of tribal peoples are admirably adapted to their nutritional needs and available food resources. Even though these diets may seem bizarre, absurd, and unpalatable to outsiders, they are unlikely to be improved by drastic modifications. Given the delicate balances and complexities involved in any subsistence system, change always involves risks, but for tribal people the effects of dietary change have been catastrophic.

Under normal conditions, food habits are remarkably resistant to change, and indeed people are unlikely to abandon their traditional diets voluntarily in favor of dependence on difficult-to-obtain exotic imports. In some cases it is true that imported foods may be identified with powerful outsiders and are therefore sought as symbols of greater prestige. This may lead to such absurdities as Amazonian Indians choosing to consume imported canned tunafish when abundant high-quality fish is available in their own rivers. Another example of this situation occurs in tribes where mothers prefer to feed their infants expensive and nutritionally inadequate canned milk from unsanitary, but *high status*, baby bottles. The high status of these items is often promoted by clever traders and clever advertising campaigns.

Aside from these apparently voluntary changes, it appears that more often dietary changes are forced upon unwilling tribal peoples by circumstances beyond their control. In some areas, new food crops have been introduced by government decree, or as a consequence of forced relocation or other policies designed to end hunting, pastoralism, or shifting cultivation. Food habits have also been modified by massive disruption of the natural environment by outsiders—as when sheepherders transformed the Australian Aborigine's foraging territory or when European invaders destroyed the bison herds that were the primary element in the Plains Indians' subsistence patterns. Perhaps the most frequent cause of diet change occurs when formerly self-sufficient peoples find that wage labor, cash cropping, and other economic development activities that feed tribal resources into the world-market economy must inevitably divert time and energy away from the production of subsistence foods. Many developing peoples suddenly discover that, like it or not, they are unable to secure traditional foods and must spend their newly acquired cash on costly, and often nutritionally inferior, manufactured foods.

Overall, the available data seem to indicate that the dietary changes that are linked to involvement in the world-market economy have tended to *lower* rather than raise the nutritional levels of the affected tribal peoples. Specifically, the vitamin, mineral, and protein components of their diets are often drastically reduced and replaced by enormous increases in starch and carbohydrates, often in the form of white flour and refined sugar.

Any deterioration in the quality of a given population's diet is almost certain to be reflected in an increase in deficiency diseases and a general decline in health status. Indeed, as tribal peoples have shifted to a diet based on imported manufactured or processed foods, there has been a dramatic rise in malnutrition, a massive increase in dental problems, and a variety of other nutrition-related disorders. Nutritional physiology is so complex that even well-meaning dietary changes have had tragic consequences. In many areas of Southeast Asia, government-sponsored protein supplementation programs supplying milk to protein-deficient populations caused unexpected health problems and increased mortality. Officials failed to anticipate that in cultures where adults do not normally drink milk, the enzymes needed to digest it are no longer produced and milk *intolerance* results (Davis & Bolin, 1972). In Brazil, a similar milk distribution program caused an epidemic of permanent blindness by aggravating a preexisting vitamin A deficiency (Bunce, 1972).

Teeth and Progress

There is nothing new in the observation that savages, or peoples living under primitive conditions, have, in general excellent teeth. . . . Nor is it news that most civilized populations possess wretched teeth which begin to decay almost before they have erupted completely, and that dental caries is likely to be accompanied by periodontal disease with further reaching complications [Hooton, 1945:xviii].

Anthropologists have long recognized that undisturbed tribal peoples are often in excellent physical condition. And it has often been noted specifically that dental caries and the other dental abnormalities that plague industrialized societies are absent or rare among tribal peoples who have retained their traditional diets. The fact that tribal food habits may contribute to the development of sound teeth, whereas modernized diets may do just the opposite, was illustrated as long ago as 1894 in an article in the *Journal of the Royal Anthropological Institute* that described the results of a comparison between the teeth of ten Sioux Indians and a comparable group of Londoners (Smith, 1894:109–116). The Indians were examined when they came to London as members of Buffalo Bill's Wild West Show and were found to be completely free of caries and in possession of all their teeth, even though half of the group were over thirty-nine years of age. Londoners' teeth were conspicuous for both their caries and their steady reduction in number with advancing age. The difference was attributed primarily to the wear and polishing caused by the traditional Indian diet of coarse food and the fact that they chewed their food longer, encouraged by the absence of tableware.

One of the most remarkable studies of the dental conditions of tribal peoples and the impact of dietary change was conducted in the 1930s by Weston Price (1945), an American dentist who was interested in determining what caused normal, healthy teeth. Between 1931 and 1936, Price systematically explored tribal areas throughout the world to locate and examine the most isolated peoples who were still living on traditional foods. His fieldwork covered Alaska, the Canadian Yukon, Hudson Bay, Vancouver Island, Florida, the Andes, the Amazon, Samoa, Tahiti, New Zealand, Australia, New Caledonia, Fiji, the Torres Strait, East Africa, and the Nile. The study demonstrated both the superior quality of aboriginal dentition and the devastation that occurs as modern diets are adopted. In nearly every area where traditional foods were still being eaten, Price found perfect teeth with normal dental arches and virtually no decay, whereas caries and abnormalities increased steadily as new diets were adopted. In many cases the change was sudden and striking. Among Eskimo groups subsisting entirely on traditional food he found caries totally absent, whereas in groups eating a considerable quantity of store-bought food approximately 20 percent of their teeth were decayed. The figure rose to more than 30 percent with Eskimo groups subsisting almost exclusively on purchased or government-supplied food,

and reached an incredible 48 percent among the Vancouver Island Indians. Unfortunately for many of these people, modern dental treatment did not accompany the new food, and their suffering was appalling. The loss of teeth was, of course, bad enough in itself, and it certainly undermined the population's resistance to many new diseases, including tuberculosis. But new foods were also accompanied by crowded, misplaced teeth, gum diseases, distortion of the face, and pinching of the nasal cavity. Abnormalities in the dental arch appeared in the new generation following the change in diet, while caries appeared almost immediately even in adults.

Price reported that in many areas the affected peoples were conscious of their own physical deterioration. At a mission school in Africa, the principal asked him to explain to the native schoolchildren why they were not physically as strong as children who had had no contact with schools. On an island in the Torres Strait the natives knew exactly what was causing their problems and resisted—almost to the point of bloodshed—government efforts to establish a store that would make imported food available. The government prevailed, however, and Price was able to establish a relationship between the length of time the government store had been established and the increasing incidences of caries among a population that showed an almost 100 percent immunity to them before the store had been opened.

In New Zealand, the Maori, who in their aboriginal state are often considered to have been among the healthiest, most perfectly developed of peoples, were found to have "advanced" the furthest. According to Price:

> Their modernization was demonstrated not only by the high incidence of dental caries but also by the fact 90 percent of the adults and 100 percent of the children had abnormalities of the dental arches [Price, 1945:206].

Malnutrition

Malnutrition, particularly in the form of protein deficiency, has become a critical problem for tribal peoples who must adopt new economic patterns. Population pressures, cash cropping, and government programs all have tended to encourage the replacement of traditional crops and other food sources that were rich in protein with substitutes high in calories but low in protein. In Africa, for example, protein-rich staples such as millet and sorghum are being replaced systematically by high-yielding manioc and plantains, which have insignificant amounts of protein. The problem is increased for cash croppers and wage laborers whose earnings are too low and unpredictable to allow purchase of adequate amounts of protein. In some rural areas, agricultural laborers have been forced systematically to deprive nonproductive members (principally children) of their households of their minimal nutritional requirements to satisfy the need of the productive members. This process has been documented in northeastern Brazil following the introduction of large-scale sisal plantations (Gross & Underwood, 1971). In urban centers the difficulties of obtaining nutritionally adequate diets are even more serious for tribal immigrants, because costs are higher and poor quality foods are more tempting.

One of the most tragic, and largely overlooked, aspects of chronic malnutrition is that it can lead to abnormally undersized brain development and apparently irreversible brain damage; it has been associated with various forms of mental impairment or retardation. Malnutrition has been linked clinically with mental retardation in both Africa and Latin America (see, for example, Mönckeberg, 1968), and this appears to be a worldwide phenomenon with serious implications (Montagu, 1972).

Optimistic supporters of progress will surely say that all of these new health problems are being overstressed and that the introduction of hospitals, clinics, and the other modern health institutions will overcome or at least compensate for all of these difficulties. However, it appears that uncontrolled population growth and economic impoverishment probably will keep most of these benefits out of reach for many tribal peoples, and the intervention of modern medicine has at least partly contributed to the problem in the first place.

The generalization that civilization frequently has a broad negative impact on tribal health has found broad empirical support (see especially Kroeger & Barbira-Freedman [1982] on Amazonia; Reinhard [1976] on the Arctic; and Wirsing [1985] globally), but these conclusions have not gone unchallenged. Some critics argue that tribal health was often poor before modernization, and they point specifically to tribals' low life expectancy and high infant mortality rates. Demographic statistics on tribal populations are often problematic because precise data are scarce, but they do show a less favorable profile than that enjoyed by many industrial societies. However, it should be remembered that our present life expectancy is a recent phenomenon that has been very costly in terms of medical research and technological advances. Furthermore, the benefits of our health system are not enjoyed equally by all members of our society. High infant mortality could be viewed as a relatively inexpensive and egalitarian tribal public health program that offered the reasonable expectation of a healthy and productive life for those surviving to age fifteen.

Some critics also suggest that certain tribal populations, such as the New Guinea highlanders, were "stunted" by nutritional deficiencies created by tribal culture and are "improved" by "acculturation" and cash cropping (Dennett & Connell, 1988). Although this argument does suggest that the health question requires careful evaluation, it does not invalidate the empirical generalizations already established. Nutritional deficiencies undoubtedly occurred in densely populated zones in the central New Guinea highlands. However, the specific case cited above may not be widely representative of other tribal groups even in New Guinea, and it does not address the facts of outside intrusion or the inequities inherent in the contemporary development process.

ECOCIDE

> "How is it," asked a herdsman . . . "how is it that these hills can no longer give pasture to my cattle? In my father's day they were green and cattle thrived there; today there is no grass and my cattle starve." As one looked one saw that what had once been a green hill had become a raw red rock [Jones, 1934].

Progress not only brings new threats to the health of tribal peoples, but it also imposes new strains on the ecosystems upon which they must depend for their ultimate survival. The introduction of new technology, increased consumption, lowered mortality, and the eradication of all traditional controls have combined to replace what for most tribal peoples was a relatively stable balance between population and natural resources, with a new system that is imbalanced. Economic development is forcing *ecocide* on peoples who were once careful stewards of their resources. There is already a trend toward widespread environmental deterioration in tribal areas, involving resource depletion, erosion, plant and animal extinction, and a disturbing series of other previously unforeseen changes.

After the initial depopulation suffered by most tribal peoples during their engulfment by frontiers of national expansion, most tribal populations began to experience rapid growth. Authorities generally attribute this growth to the introduction of modern medicine and new health measures and the termination of intertribal warfare, which lowered mortality rates, as well as to new technology, which increased food production. Certainly all of these factors played a part, but merely lowering mortality rates would not have produced the rapid population growth that most tribal areas have experienced if traditional birth-spacing mechanisms had not been eliminated at the same time. Regardless of which factors were most important, it is clear that all of the natural and cultural checks on population growth have suddenly been pushed aside by culture change, while tribal lands have been steadily reduced and consumption levels have risen. In many tribal areas, environmental deterioration due to overuse of resources has set in, and in other areas such deterioration is imminent as resources continue to dwindle relative to the expanding population and increased use. Of course, population expansion by tribal peoples may have positive political consequences, because where tribals can retain or regain their status as local majorities they may be in a more favorable position to defend their resources against intruders.

Swidden systems and pastoralism, both highly successful economic systems under traditional conditions, have proven particularly vulnerable to increased population pressures and outside efforts to raise productivity beyond its natural limits. Research in Amazonia demonstrates that population pressures and related resource depletion can be created indirectly by official policies that restrict swidden peoples to smaller territories. Resource depletion itself can then become a powerful means of forcing tribal people into participating in the world-market economy—thus leading to further resource depletion. For example, Bodley and Benson (1979) showed how the Shipibo Indians in Peru were forced to further deplete their forest resources by cash cropping in the forest area to replace the resources that had been destroyed earlier by the intensive cash cropping necessitated by the narrow confines of their reserve. In this case, a certain species of palm trees that had provided critical housing materials were destroyed by forest clearing and had to be replaced by costly purchased materials. Research by Gross (1979) and others showed similar processes at work among four tribal groups in central Brazil and demonstrated that the degree of market involvement increases directly with increases in resource depletion.

The settling of nomadic herders and the removal of prior controls on herd size have often led to serious overgrazing and erosion problems where these had not previously occurred. There are indications that the desertification problem in the Sahel region of Africa was aggravated by programs designed to settle nomads. The first sign of imbalance in a swidden system appears when the planting cycles are shortened to the point that garden plots are reused before sufficient forest regrowth can occur. If reclearing and planting continue in the same area, the natural pattern of forest succession may be disturbed irreversibly and the soil can be impaired permanently. An extensive tract of tropical rainforest in the lower Amazon of Brazil was reduced to a semiarid desert in just fifty years through such a process (Ackermann, 1964). The soils in the Azande area are also now seriously threatened with laterization and other problems as a result of the government-promoted cotton development scheme (McNeil, 1972).

The dangers of overdevelopment and the vulnerability of local resource systems have long been recognized by both anthropologists and tribal peoples themselves, but the pressures for change have been overwhelming. In 1948 the Maya villagers of Chan Kom complained to Redfield (1962) about the shortening of their swidden cycles, which they correctly attributed to increasing population pressures. Redfield told them, however, that they had no choice but to go "forward with technology" (Redfield, 1962:178). In Assam, swidden cycles were shortened from an average of twelve years to only two or three within just twenty years, and anthropologists warned that the limits of swiddening would soon be reached (Burling, 1963:311–312). In the Pacific, anthropologists warned of population pressures on limited resources as early as the 1930s (Keesing, 1941:64–65). These warnings seemed fully justified, considering the fact that the crowded Tikopians were prompted by population pressures on their tiny island to suggest that infanticide be legalized. The warnings have been dramatically reinforced since then by the doubling of Micronesia's population in just the fourteen years between 1958 and 1972, from 70,600 to 114,645, while consumption levels have soared. By 1985 Micronesia's population had reached 162,321.

The environmental hazards of economic development and rapid population growth have become generally recognized only since worldwide concerns over environmental issues began in the early 1970s. Unfortunately, there is as yet little indication that the leaders of the now developing nations are sufficiently concerned with environmental limitations. On the contrary governments are forcing tribal peoples into a self-reinforcing spiral of population growth and intensified resource exploitation, which may be stopped only by environmental disaster or the total impoverishment of the tribals.

The reality of ecocide certainly focuses attention on the fundamental contrasts between tribal and industrial systems in their use of natural resources. In many respects the entire "victims of progress" issue hinges on natural resources, who controls them, and how they are managed. Tribal peoples are victimized because they control resources that outsiders demand. The resources exist because tribals managed them conservatively. However, as with the issue of the health consequences of detribalization, some anthropologists minimize the adaptive achievements of tribal groups and seem unwilling to concede that ecocide might be a consequence of cultural change. Critics attack an exaggerated "noble savage" image of tribals living in perfect harmony with nature and having no visible impact on their surroundings. They then show that tribals do in fact modify the environment, and they conclude that there is no significant difference between how tribals and industrial societies treat their environments. For example, Charles Wagley declared that Brazilian Indians such as the Tapirape are not "natural men." They have human vices just as we do. . . . They do not live "in tune" with nature any more than I do; in fact, they can often be as destructive of their environment, within their limitations, as some civilized men. The Tapirape are not innocent or childlike in any way [Wagley, 1977:302].

Anthropologist Terry Rambo demonstrated that the Semang of the Malaysian rain forests have measurable impact on their environment. In his monograph *Primitive Polluters*, Rambo (1985) reported that the Semang live in smoke-filled houses. They sneeze and spread germs, breathe, and thus emit carbon dioxide. They clear small gardens, contributing "particulate matter" to the air and disturbing the local climate because cleared areas proved measurably warmer and drier than the shady forest. Rambo concluded that his research "demonstrated the essential functional similarity of the environmental interactions of primitive and civilized societies" (1985:78) in contrast to a "noble savage" view (Bodley, 1983) which, according to Rambo (1985:2), mistakenly "claims that traditional peoples almost always live in essential harmony with their environment."

This is surely a false issue. To stress, as I do, that tribals tend to manage their resources for sustained yield within relatively self-sufficient subsistence economies is not to make them either innocent children or natural men. Nor is it to deny that tribals "disrupt" their environment and may never be in absolute "balance" with nature.

The ecocide issue is perhaps most dramatically illustrated by two sets of satellite photos taken over the Brazilian rain forests of Rôndonia (Allard & McIntyre, 1988:780–781). Photos taken in 1973, when Rôndonia was still a tribal domain, show virtually unbroken rain forest. The 1987 satellite photos, taken after just fifteen years of highway construction and "development" by outsiders, show more than 20 percent of the forest destroyed. The surviving Indians were being concentrated by FUNAI (Brazil's national Indian foundation) into what would soon become mere islands of forest in a ravaged landscape. It is irrelevant to quibble about whether tribals are noble, childlike, or innocent, or about the precise meaning of balance with nature, carrying capacity, or adaptation, to recognize that for the past 200 years rapid environmental deterioration on an unprecedented global scale has followed the wresting of control of vast areas of the world from tribal groups by resource-hungry industrial societies.

DEPRIVATION AND DISCRIMINATION

Contact with European culture has given them a knowledge of great wealth, opportunity and privilege, but only very limited avenues by which to acquire these things [Crocombe, 1968].

Unwittingly, tribal peoples have had the burden of perpetual relative deprivation thrust upon them by acceptance—either by themselves or by the governments administering them—of the standards of socioeconomic progress set for them by industrial civilizations. By comparison with the material wealth of industrial societies, tribal societies become, by definition, impoverished. They are then forced to transform their cultures and work to achieve what many economists now acknowledge to be unattainable goals. Even though in many cases the modest GNP goals set by development planners for the developing nations during the "development decade" of the 1960s were often met, the results were hardly noticeable for most of the tribal people involved. Population growth, environmental limitations, inequitable distribution of wealth, and the continued rapid growth of the industrialized nations have all meant that both the absolute and the relative gap between the rich and poor in the world is steadily widening. The prospect that tribal peoples will actually be able to attain the levels of resource consumption to which they are being encouraged to aspire is remote indeed except for those few groups who have retained effective control over strategic mineral resources.

Tribal peoples feel deprivation not only when the economic goals they have been encouraged to seek fail to materialize, but also when they discover that they are powerless, second-class citizens who are discriminated against and exploited by the dominant society. At the same time, they are denied the satisfactions of their traditional cultures, because these have been sacrificed in the process of modernization. Under the impact of major economic change family life is disrupted, traditional social controls are often lost, and many indicators of social anomie such as alcoholism, crime, delinquency, suicide, emotional disorders, and despair may increase. The inevitable frustration resulting from this continual deprivation finds expression in the cargo cults, revitalization movements, and a variety of other political and religious movements that have been widespread among tribal peoples following their disruption by industrial civilization.

REFERENCES

Ackermann, F. L. 1964. *Geologia e Fisiografia da Região Bragantina, Estado do Pará*. Manaus, Brazil: Conselho Nacional de Pesquisas, Instituto Nacional de Pesquisas da Amazônia.

Allard, William Albert, and Loren McIntyre. 1988. Rôndonia's settlers invade Brazil's imperiled rain forest. *National Geographic* 174(6):772–799.

Bodley, John H. 1983. The World Bank tribal policy: Criticisms and recommendations. *Congressional Record*, serial no. 98-37, pp. 515–521. (Reprinted in Bodley, 1988.)

Bodley, John H., and Foley C. Benson. 1979. Cultural ecology of Amazonian palms. *Reports of Investigations*, no. 56. Pullman: Laboratory of Anthropology, Washington State University.

Bunce, George E. 1972. Aggravation of vitamin A deficiency following distribution of non-fortified skim milk: An example of nutrient interaction. In *The Careless Technology: Ecology and International Development*, ed. M. T. Farvar and John P. Milton, pp. 53–60. Garden City, N.Y.: Natural History Press.

Burling, Robbins. 1963. *Rengsanggri: Family and Kinship in a Garo Village*. Philadelphia: University of Pennsylvania Press.

Crocombe, Ron. 1968. Bougainville!: Copper, R. R. A. and secessionism. *New Guinea* 3(3):39–49.

Davis, A. E., and T. D. Bolin. 1972. Lactose intolerance in Southeast Asia. In *The Careless Technology: Ecology and International Development*, ed. M. T. Farvar and John P. Milton, pp. 61–68. Garden City, N.Y.: Natural History Press.

Dennett, Glenn, and John Connell. 1988. Acculturation and health in the highlands of Papua New Guinea. *Current Anthropology* 29(2):273–299.

Goldschmidt, Walter R. 1952. The interrelations between cultural factors and acquisition of new technical skills. In *The Progress of Underdeveloped Areas*, ed. Bert F. Hoselitz, pp. 135–151. Chicago: University of Chicago Press.

Gross, Daniel R., and Barbara A. Underwood. 1971. Technological change and caloric costs: Sisal agriculture. *American Anthropologist* 73(3):725–740.

Gross, Daniel R., et al. 1979. Ecology and acculturation among native peoples of Central Brazil. *Science* 206(4422):1043–1050.

Hooton, Earnest A. 1945. Introduction. In *Nutrition and Physical Degeneration: A Comparison of Primitive and Modern Diets and Their Effects* by Weston A. Price. Redlands, Calif.: The author.

Hughes, Charles C., and John M. Hunter. 1972. The role of technological development in promoting disease in Africa. In *The Careless Technology: Ecology and International Development*, ed. M. T. Farvar and John P. Milton, pp. 69–101. Garden City, N.Y.: Natural History Press.

Jones, J. D. Rheinallt. 1934. Economic condition of the urban native. In *Western Civilization and the Natives of South Africa*, ed. I. Schapera, pp. 159–192. London: George Routledge and Sons.

Keesing, Felix M. 1941. *The South Seas in the Modern World*. Institute of Pacific Relations International Research Series. New York: John Day.

Kroeger, Axel, and Françoise Barbira-Freedman. 1982. *Culture Change and Health: The Case of South American Rainforest Indians*. Frankfurt am Main: Verlag Peter Lang. (Reprinted in Bodley, 1988:221–236).

Maunier, René. 1949. *The Sociology of Colonies*. Vol. 2. London: Routledge and Kegan Paul.

McNeil, Mary. 1972. Lateritic soils in distinct tropical environments: Southern Sudan and Brazil. In *The Careless Technology: Ecology and International Development*, ed. M. T. Farvar and John P. Milton, pp. 591–608. Garden City, N.Y.: Natural History Press.

Mönckeberg, F. 1968. Mental retardation from malnutrition. *Journal of the American Medical Association* 206:30–31.

Montagu, Ashley. 1972. Sociogenic brain damage. *American Anthropologist* 74(5):1045–1061.

Price, Weston Andrew. 1945. *Nutrition and Physical Degeneration: A Comparison of Primitive and Modern Diets and Their Effects*. Redlands, Calif.: The author.

Prior, Ian A. M. 1971. The price of civilization. *Nutrition Today* 6(4):2–11.

Rambo, A. Terry. 1985. *Primitive Polluters: Semang Impact on the Malaysian Tropical Rain Forest Ecosystem*. Anthropological Papers no. 76, Museum of Anthropology, University of Michigan.

Redfield, Robert. 1962. *A Village That Chose Progress: Chan Kom Revisited*. Chicago: University of Chicago Press, Phoenix Books.

Reinhard, K. R. 1976. Resource exploitation and the health of western arctic man. In *Circumpolar Health: Proceedings of the Third International Symposium, Yellowknife, Northwest Territories*, ed. Roy J. Shephard and S. Itoh, pp. 617–627. Toronto: University of Toronto Press. (Reprinted in Bodley, 1988.)

Smith, Wilberforce. 1894. The teeth of ten Sioux Indians. *Journal of the Royal Anthropological Institute* 24:109–116.

TTR: *See under* United States.

United States, Department of State. 1955. *Seventh Annual Report to the United Nations on the Administration of the Trust Territory of the Pacific Islands* (July 1, 1953, to June 30, 1954).

———. 1959. *Eleventh Annual Report to the United Nations on the Administration of the Trust Territory of the Pacific Islands* (July 1, 1957, to June 30, 1958).

———. 1973. *Twenty-Fifth Annual Report to the United Nations on the Administration of the Trust Territory of the Pacific Islands* (July 1, 1971, to June 30, 1972).

Wagley, C. 1977. *Welcome of Tears: The Tapirape Indians of Central Brazil*. New York: Oxford University Press.

Wirsing, R. 1985. The health of traditional societies and the effects of acculturation. *Current Anthropology* 26: 303–322.

Glossary

acculturation The process of extensive borrowing of aspects of another culture, usually as a result of external pressure, and often resulting in the decline of traditional culture.

adaptation The process by which an organism or a culture is modified, usually through selection, enhancing the ability of individuals to survive and reproduce in a particular environment.

adispose tissue Fat. A physiological mechanism of energy storage; some adipose tissue, especially when deposited on the central body, is associated with chronic diseases.

adjudication A process of handling disputes in which the ultimate decision is made by a third party appointed by the legal system.

affinal kin A kin relationship created by marriage.

affines Individuals related to one another because of marriage between their families; related through marriage rather than birth.

Afrocentric An explanation based on African origins.

age grade A social category of people who fall within a particular, culturally distinguished age range; age grades often undergo life cycle rituals as a group.

aggression A forceful action, sometimes involving physical violence, intended for social domination.

agnates Individuals sharing a patrilineal kinship tie; people related through the male line.

agnatic Related through the male kinship line.

agrarian Relating to agriculture.

agricultural development Changes in agricultural production intended to improve the system by producing more harvest per unit of land.

AIDS Acquired Immune Deficiency Syndrome, a fatal disease caused by the human immunodeficiency virus (HIV) and usually transmitted through semen or blood.

Amerindian Native American populations.

anthropology The systematic study of humans, including their biology and culture, both past and present.

applied research Study directed at gaining valid knowledge to help in the solution of human problems.

arable land Land suitable for cultivation.

arbitration The hearing and determination of a dispute by a person chosen by the parties or appointed by the legal system with the consent of the parties.

archaeology The field of anthropology concerned with cultural history; includes the systematic retrieval, identification, and study of the physical and cultural remains deposited in the earth.

argot A specialized, sometimes secret, vocabulary peculiar to a particular group.

artifact An object manufactured and used by human beings for a culturally defined goal.

AZT An antiviral drug used to slow down the replication of HIV, the human immunodeficiency virus that causes AIDS; AZT is very expensive.

basic research Study directed toward gaining scientific knowledge primarily for its own sake.

big men Political leaders in tribal-level societies whose status has been achieved and whose authority is limited.

biogenetic Genetic.

biological anthropology Subfield of anthropology that studies the biological nature of humans and includes primatology, paleoanthropology, population genetics, anthropometry, and human biology.

biomedicine Modern medicine as practiced in the United States and Europe; emphasizes the biological causation and remedy for illness.

biophysical diversity Outward biological appearance resulting from interaction of genes and environment; phenotype.

biotic community Plants and animals sharing a niche within an ecosystem.

blood relatives A folk term referring to consanguineal kin, that is, kin related through birth.

bridewealth The presentation of goods or money by the groom's family to the bride's family at the time of marriage; an economic exchange that legitimates the marriage and offspring as members of the father's patrilineage.

bush-fallow A technique used by horticulturalists that allows a garden plot to return to the wild state after a period of cultivation.

cadastral A government survey and record-keeping system for recording land ownership and property boundaries.

canton A small territorial division of a country.

capitalism An economic system characteristic of modern state societies where land, labor and, capital all become commodities exchanged on the market and in which socioeconomic inequality is a constant feature.

carrying capacity The maximum population size that can be maintained in a given area without causing environmental degradation of the ecology.

caste A ranked group, sometimes linked to a particular occupation, with membership determined at birth and with marriage restricted to others within the group.

ceremony Public events involving special symbols that signify important cultural values or beliefs.

chief The political leader of a society that is more complex than a tribal society and is characterized by social ranking, a redistributive economy, and a centralized political authority.

chiefdom A society more complex than a tribal society, characterized by social ranking, a redistributive economy, and a centralized political authority.

civilization The culture of state-level societies characterized by the following elements: (1) agriculture; (2) urban living; (3) a high degree of occupational specialization and differentiation; (4) social stratification; and (5) literacy.

clan A kinship group whose members assume, but need not demonstrate, descent from a common ancestor.

clitoridectomy The surgical removal of the clitoris.

clustering In epidemiology, the concentration of cases by place of residence and time of diagnosis.

cognates Words that belong to different languages but have similar sounds and meanings.

cognatic kin Kinship traced simultaneously through the male and female lines in a nonunilineal pattern of descent.

collective behavior Patterns of social action.

comparative framework An analytical approach in anthropology using the comparison of cultures across time and place.

consumer society A characteristic of modern capitalist societies in which the purchase of non-essential material goods and services is an important marker of social status and identity.

contingent truths Truth based upon the best scientific evidence available at the time and subject to revision as knowledge expands.

conversational analysis A technique in sociolinguistics that focuses on the social and symbolic attributes of verbal interactions.

corporate culture The cultural characteristics of a workplace.

corporate kin groups Social groups, like lineages, that share political responsibilities and access to land; characteristic of tribal societies.

correlate A variable that stands in a consistent observed relationship with another variable.

correlation A statistical relationship between two variables.

corvée A system of required labor; characteristic of ancient states.

creole A type of language that results from the widespread adoption of a pidgin language as the primary language of a group.

Cro-Magnon A term broadly referring to the first anatomically modern humans, from roughly 40,000 to 10,000 B.C.; named after a site in southwestern France.

cross-cultural research The exploration of cultural variation by using ethnographic data from many societies.

cross-cutting ties Affinal or trading relationships that serve to counteract the political isolation of social groups in tribal societies.

cross-sectional Research done across different geographic locales.

cultural anthropology A field of anthropology emphasizing the study of the cultural diversity of contemporary societies, including their economies, sociopolitical systems, and belief systems.

cultural dissonance A situation arising from the incompatibility of two or more interacting cultural systems.

cultural evolution The process of invention, diffusion, and elaboration of the behavior that is learned and taught in groups and is transmitted from generation to generation; often used to refer to the development of social complexity.

cultural ideals A valued characteristic or belief of a society.

cultural materialism The idea, often associated with Marvin Harris, that cultural behaviors are best explained in relation to material constraints (including food-producing technology) to which humans are subjected.

cultural pluralism The simultaneous existence of two or more cultural systems within a single society; multiculturalism.

cultural relativism/cultural relativity The principle that all cultural systems are inherently equal in value and, therefore, that each cultural item must be understood on its own terms.

cultural reproduction The process by which cultural behaviors and beliefs are regenerated across generations or spread among people of the same generation; cultural construction creates reality.

cultural values Ideas, beliefs, values, and attitudes learned as a member of a social group.

culture Learned patterns of thought and behavior characteristic of a particular social group.

culture area A largely outmoded idea that the world can be divided into a limited number of geographical regions, each defined by a certain set of cultural features that result from common ecological adaptation or history and are shared by all groups in the region.

culture brokers Individuals, often anthropologists, who function as mediators or translators between members of two cultures.

culture shock The experience of stress and confusion resulting from moving one culture to another; the removal or distortion of familiar cues and the substitution of strange cues.

decoction The extraction of flavor by boiling.

demography The statistical study of human populations, including size, growth, migration, density, distribution, and vital statistics.

dental anthropology A specialization within biological anthropology; the study of the morphology of teeth across time and populations.

dependency   A theory of international economic relations in which an economically powerful nation creates ties with other nations in ways that reduce the possibility of economic independence of the poorer nations.

dependent variable   The resultant phenomenon that is explained by its relationship with an independent variable.

dialect   A regional or class-based version of a spoken language, although the difference between dialect and language can be influenced by historical and political considerations.

diffusion   A process of cultural change by which traits of one society are borrowed by another; the spread of cultural traits.

diseases of civilization   Chronic diseases, such as cardiovascular disease and obesity, that characterize the epidemiological profile of modern capitalist societies and are the result of infrequent exercise and high fat diets.

domestication of plants and animals   The invention of farming.

dowry   Presentation of goods or money by the bride's family, to the bride, the groom, or the groom's family.

Ebonics   The rule-based and pattern dialect of English spoken by many working-class urban African Americans; black English vernacular.

economy   The production, distribution, and consumption of resources, labor, and wealth within a society.

ecosystem   A community of plants and animals, including humans, within a physical environment and the relationship of organisms to one another.

edutainment   A marketing technique in consumer-oriented societies where consumerism and education are simultaneously valued.

egalitarian   A society organized around the principle of social equality; characteristic social formation of food foraging groups.

egalitarian society   A society that emphasizes the social equality of members and makes achieved statuses accessible to all adults.

epidemic   Higher-than-expected disease prevalence affecting individuals within a population at the same time.

epidemiology   A science that studies the incidence, distribution, and control of disease in a poulation.

epistemology   The study of the nature of knowledge and its limits.

ergonomics   Human engineering; an applied science concerned with the anthropometric characteristics of people in the design of technology for improved human-machine interaction and safety.

essentialize   The assumption that all individuals of the same social category (e.g., class, caste, race, gender) have the same beliefs, values, experiences, and other characteristics.

ethnic groups   A group of people within a larger society with a distinct cultural or historical identity; ethnicity is a common mechanism of social separation in complex, heterogeneous societies.

ethnocentrism   The assumption that one's own group's lifestyle, values, and patterns of adaptation are superior to all others.

ethnocide   The attempt to exterminate an entire ethnic group (similar to genocide).

ethnographic methods   The research techniques of cultural anthropology based on long-term participant observations, yielding a description of another culture.

ethnography   The intensive and systematic description of a particular society; ethnographic information is usually collected through the method of long-term participant-observation fieldwork.

ethnology   The study and explanation of cultural similarities and differences.

ethnomedicine   The medical theories, diagnosis systems, and therapeutic practices of a culture or ethnic group.

ethos   The world view of a particular society, including its distinctive character, sentiments, and values.

etiology   The theory of causation of a disease or illness.

evolutionary medicine   An anthropological approach to disease, symptoms, and medical care based upon our evolutionary heritage.

exchange   A social system for the distribution of goods; reciprocity is widespread system of exchange between social equals while markets act as a mode of exchange between strangers.

exogamous   Relating to a custom that forbids members of a specific group from selecting a spouse from within that group.

extended family   A domestic unit created by the linking together of two or more nuclear families.

fallow   The period during which a unit of agricultural land is not cultivated so that nutrients can be restored to the soil.

family of origin   Nuclear family into which an individual is born and in which he or she is reared.

fecundity   A demographic characteristic of a society referring to its overall capacity for reproduction.

feral   Living in, or pertaining to, the wild; without the benefit of society or culture.

feud   A pattern of reciprocal hostility between families or kin groups, usually involving retribution for past wrongs or deaths; such as blood feud.

fieldwork   The hallmark of research in cultural anthropology, it usually involves long-term residence with the people being studied.

fission   The splitting of a descent group—a residential unit based on shared kinship—into two or more new descent groups or domestic units.

folk taxonomy   A culture's system of classification or grouping of objects, which can reveal the cognitive categories of that group.

food foragers   People living in a society with an economic pattern harvesting of wild food resources, usually by gathering plants or hunting animals; hunting and gathering.

food scarcity   The lack of sufficient food to meet the energy requirements of a population; may be the result of failed food production or a socially unequal distribution system.

foraging   Hunting and gathering; the original human economic system relying on the collection of natural plant and animal food sources.

fraternal polyandry   An uncommon form of plural marriage in which a woman is married to two or more brothers at one time.

gender   The social classification of masculine or feminine.

gender dimorphism   Physical and physiological differences between males and females; sexual dimorphism.

genealogy   The systematic study of the consanguineal and affinal kin of a particular person, including his or her ancestors; a common method used in anthropological field studies.

ghetto   A subsection of a city in which members of a minority group live because of social, legal, or economic pressure.

hallucinogen   A substance that induces visions or auditory hallucinations in normal individuals.

hierarchy   The categorization of a group of people according to status, whether it be ascribed at birth or achieved. A hierarchy refers to group organized in this way.

HIV   The human immunodeficiency virus that causes AIDS.

holistic   Refers to viewing the whole society as an integrated and interdependent system; an important characteristic of the anthropological approach to understanding humans.

horticulture   A plant cultivation system based upon relatively low energy input, like gardening by using only the hoe or digging stick; often involves use of the slash-and-burn technique.

human universal   A trait or behavior found in all human cultures.

hunter-gatherers   Peoples who subsist on the collection of naturally occurring plants and animals; food foragers.

hypothesis   A tentative assumption or proposition about the relationship(s) between specific events or phenomena, tentatively set forth as a "target" to be tested.

ideal body images   Culturally defined standards for attractive body shapes.

indigenous   The original or native population of a particular region or environment.

infanticide   Killing a baby soon after birth.

infibulation   Sewing together the lips of the vagina.

informant   A member of a society who has established a working relationship with an anthropological fieldworker and who provides information about the culture; the subject of intensive interviewing.

institutions   Formal organizations within a society.

intensive interviewing   The ethnographic method of repeated interviews with a single informant.

intercultural communication   The exchange of meanings and messages between people from different societies characterized by different underlying ideas, beliefs, and world views; may or may not be complicated by the speaking of different languages.

kinship   A network of culturally recognized relationships among individuals, either through affinal or consanguineal ties.

Koran   The sacred text of Islam.

kula   Traditional long-distance trading network for valuable objects among Trobriand islanders first described by B. Malinowski.

lactose intolerance   The inability of adults to digest milk because they no longer produce the enyzme lactase; a biological characteristic of a large proportion of the world's population.

land concentration   The degree to which land ownership is concentrated among a small number of people in a society.

land tenure   A system of land ownership and inheritance.

language   A rule-based and patterned system of communication.

levirate   The practice by which a man is expected to marry the wife or wives of a deceased brother; commonly found in patrilineal descent systems.

lexicon   The vocabulary set characteristic of a group; argot.

life history   A methodological technique of cultural anthropologists in which a key informant's biography is compiled using multiple interviews.

lineage   Refers to a kin group tracing common descent through one sex from a known ancestor.

linguistic anthropology   A subfield of anthropology entailing the study of language forms across space and time and their relation to culture and social behavior.

linguistic relativity   A principle of anthropological linguistics referring to the fact that all languages are equally adequate as systems of communication.

linguistics   The study of language, consisting of: (1) historical linguistics, which is concerned with the evolution of languages and language groups through time; (2) descriptive linguistics, which focuses on recording and analysis of the structures of languages; (3) sociolinguistics, the way in which speech patterns reflect social phenomena; and (4) ethnosemantics, the study of the connection between reality, thought, and language.

literacy   The ability to read; not possible for people who speak unwritten languages.

longitudinal   A research strategy that examines changes in a particular group over time.

mana   A supernatural force inhabiting objects or people.

mediator   The role of a disinterested third party in dispute settlement.

medical anthropology   The study of health and medical systems in a cross-cultural perspective; includes the study of biocultural adaptations to disease, ethnomedical systems, and cultural factors in health-seeking behavior.

meritocracy   A system in which advancement is purportedly based upon ability or achievement of the individual.

metalinguistics   Elements of communication beyond verbal speech; includes the use of gesture, personal space, silence, and nonlinguistic sounds.

moiety system   A social system in which the entire group is divided into two kinship units, which are usually based on unilineal descent and exogamous.

monogamy   marriage between one man and one woman at a given time.

moot   A public hearing or community assembly to decide local problems and administer justice.

multiplex relationships   Complex social relations characterized by multiple patterns of interaction, for example by kinship, business, political party, ethnicity, and religion.

national character studies   Descriptions of the cultural belief and "typical" personality of people from another culture, an approach used by the culture and personality school of anthropology.

negotiation   The use of direct argument and compromise by the parties to a dispute to voluntarily arrive at a mutually satisfactory agreement.

Neolithic   A stage in cultural evolution marked by the appearance of ground stone tools and, more importantly, the domestication of plants and animals, starting some 10,000 years ago.

nomadic band   A food-foraging group that moves among a variety of campsites; a society without sedentary villages.

nonreactive measure of behavior   Various methods for collecting social science data that are unobtrusive and unsubjected to bias introduced by the population under study.

norms   Standards of behavior characteristic of a society or social group to which members are expected to conform.

nuclear family   A basic social grouping consisting of a husband and wife and their children, typical of societies with monogamous marriage with the family living at a distance from the parents of the husband and wife.

obesity   A medically defined condition of excessive fat storage.

origin myth   A story found in most cultures that explains the creation and population of the world.

orthography   The way in which words in a particular language are written phonetically to include sounds (phonemes) not represented in our alphabet; anthropological linguists usually use the International Phonetic Alphabet (IPA).

ovulation   The part of the menstrual cycle in which the egg (ovum) is released and fertilization can occur.

pacification   In tribal areas like New Guinea, the establishment by outside authorities of peace from blood-feud warfare.

palaver   A discussion for purposes of dispute settlement, typically informal and following customary law.

Paleolithic   Old stone age; the archaeological period that includes the beginning of culture to the end of the Pleistocene glaciation.

paleontology   The study of the fossils of ancient, usually extinct, animals and plants.

paleopathology   The study of disease patterns in extinct populations, primarily through the examination of skeletal remains.

paramount chief   In a ranked society of ascribed statuses, the position at the top of the hierarchy.

participant observation   The primary research method of cultural anthropology, involving long-term observations conducted in natural settings.

patriarchy   A form of social organization in which power and authority are vested in the males and in which descent is usually in the male line.

patrilineal   Descent traced exclusively through the male line for purposes of group membership or inheritance.

patrilocal   A postmarital residence rule by which a newlywed couple takes up permanent residence with or near the groom's father's family.

peasants   Rural, agricultural populations of state-level societies who maintain parts of their traditional culture while they are tied into the wider economic system of the whole society through economic links of rent, taxes, and markets.

physical anthropology   Another term for biological anthropology; includes the study of paleoanthropology, population genetics, human adaptation, and primatology.

Pleistocene   The geological period approximately from 600,000 years ago to 12,000 years ago, characterized by recurrent glaciations.

pollution   The act of defilement, uncleanness.

polyandry   A relatively rare form of plural marriage in which one woman is married to two or more men.

polygamy   A general term for plural marriage, either polygyny or polyandry.

polygyny   A common form of plural marriage in which one man is married to two or more women; in societies that permit polygyny, the majority of marital unions are monogamous. Extended families may be formed through polygyny.

population   In genetics and biological anthropology, a discrete demographic unit often characterized by inmarriage.

population density   The ratio of the number of people per area of land; closely related to carrying capacity.

population pressure   The situation of population growth in a limited geographical area causing a decline in food production and resources and sometimes triggering technological change.

potlatch   A feast given by a Northwest Coast Native American chief often involving competitive gift-giving, first described by Franz Boas.

prehistoric   The time before written records.

primogeniture   A rule of inheritance in which the homestead is passed down to the firstborn (male) child.

primordial   Belonging to or characteristic of the earliest stage of development; first in sequence of time.

privilege   A special advantage, immunity, permission, right, or benefit granted to or enjoyed by an individual, class, caste, or race. Such advantage may be held consciously or unconsciously and exercised to the exclusion or detriment of others.

probability sampling   A data collection sampling technique based on the known proportions of various social groups.

proletariat   The working class in a state-level society, usually residing in urban areas.

psychoactive drugs   Chemicals that affect the mind or behavior and that may cause, among other things, hallucinations.

purdah   The Hindu or Muslim system of sex segregation, which is practiced by keeping women in seclusion.

qualitative methods   Research strategies that emphasize description, in-depth interviewing, and participant observation.

quantitative methods Research methods that translate behaviors or attitudes into reliable and valid numeric measures suitable for statistical analysis for hypothesis testing.

race A folk category of the English language that refers to discrete groups of human beings who are uniformly separated from one another on the basis of arbitrarily selected phenotypic traits.

random sample A data sample selected by a method in which all individuals in a population have equal chance of being selected.

reciprocal gift A mechanism of establishing or reinforcing social ties between equals involving a "present," which is repaid at a later date.

reciprocity The principle of mutual obligations to give, to receive and to repay.

reforestation To renew forest cover by seeding or planting.

relative deprivation A concept wherein individuals perceive that they are less well off only in relation to another group or to their own expectations.

religion Attitudes, beliefs, and practices related to supernatural powers.

reproductive success A variable used in Darwinian analyses referring to an individual's overall achievement in reproduction of their own genes (through direct offspring or kin).

rite of passage Religious rituals that mark important changes in individual status or social position at different points in the life cycle, such as birth, marriage, or death.

ritual A set of acts, usually involving religion or magic, following a sequence established by tradition.

sample A subpopulation that is studied in order to make generalizations.

sanctions Generally negative responses by a social group as a consequence of an individual's behavior; used to maintain social control.

segmentary system A hierarchy of more and more inclusive lineages; functions primarily in contexts of conflict between groups.

self-sufficient Refers to a characteristic of most pre-state societies; the ability to maintain a viable economy and social system with minimal outside contact.

serial monogamy The marriage of one woman and one man at a time but in a sequence, usually made possible through divorce.

sex roles Learned social activities and expectations made on the basis of gender.

sexual dimorphism A condition of having the two sexes dissimilar in appearance.

shaman A part-time religious practitioner typical of tribal societies who goes into trance to directly communicate with the spirit world for the benefit of the community.

sickle-cell anemia An often fatal genetic disease caused by a chemical mutation that changes one of the amino acids in normal hemoglobin; the mutant sickle-cell gene occurs with unusually high frequency in parts of Africa where malaria is present.

SIDA The Spanish, French, Italian, and Haitian Creole acronym for AIDS.

SIDS Sudden Infant Death syndrome—the sudden and unexpected death of an infant, also known as crib death.

single-interest relationship A relationship based solely on one connection, such as landlord-tenant.

slang A small set of new and usually short-lived words in the vocabulary of a dialect of a language.

slash-and-burn techniques Shifting form of cultivation (horticulture) with recurrent, alternate clearing and burning of vegetation and planting in the burnt fields; swidden.

social class In state-level societies, a stratum in a social hierarchy based on differential group access to means of production and control over distribution; often endogamous.

social cohesion The process by which a social group binds itself together, producing greater cooperation and conformity.

social control Practices that induce members of a society to conform to the expected behavior patterns of their culture; includes informal mechanisms, like gossip, legal systems, and punishment.

socialization The development, through the influence of parents and others, of patterns of thought and behavior in children that conform to beliefs and values of a particular culture.

social mobility The upward or downward movement of individuals or groups in a society characterized by social stratification.

social networks An informal pattern of organization based on the complex web of social relations linking individuals; includes factors like kinship, friendship, economics, and political ties.

social organization A culturally inherited system that orders social relations within social groups.

social stratification An arrangement of statuses or groups within a society into a pattern of socially superior and inferior ranks; based on differential access to strategic resources.

socially validated Approved or recognized by the culture of a particular social group.

society A socially bounded, spacially contiguous group of people who interact in basic economic and political institutions and share a particular culture; societies retain relative stability across generations.

sociocultural Refers to the complex combination of social and cultural factors.

sociolinguistics A subfield of anthropological linguistics emphasizing the study of the social correlates to variations in speech patterns.

solidarity Unity based on community interest, objectives, and culture.

sorcery The use of supernatural knowledge or power for purposes of evil, for example causing sickness; used to further the sorcerer's individual social goals.

species The largest naturally occurring population that is capable of interbreeding and producing fully fertile offspring.

spurious Not an actual or causal relationship, as in the correlation between the number of storks and birth rate.

states A complex society characterized by urban centers, agricultural production, labor specialization, standing armies, permanent boundaries, taxation, centralized authority, public works, and laws designed to maintain the status quo.

status   Position in a social system that is characterized by certain rights, obligations, expected behaviors (roles), and certain social symbols.

stigma   Socially constructed shame or discredit.

stratified societies   A society in which groups experience structured inequality of access not only to power and prestige but also to economically important resources.

structure   In anthropology, generally referring to social institutions and patterns of organization.

subculture   The culture of a subgroup of a society that has its own distinctive ideas, beliefs, values, and world view.

superstructure   In the theory of cultural materialism, refers to a society's ideology.

swidden cultivation   A tropical gardening system, also known as slash-and-burn horticulture where forest is cleared, burned, cultivated, and then left for bush fallow.

symbol   A sign that consistently but arbitrarily represents an object or meaning; the basis of communication within a culture.

taboo   A supernaturally forbidden act as defined by a culture, violation of which can have severe negative consequences.

TFR (total fertility rate)   The average number of children born to a woman during her lifetime.

time-allocation study   A quantitative method that identifies what people do and how much time they spend doing various activities; useful for cross-cultural comparison.

totem   A symbolic plant or animal associated with a social group (clan) used for identification and religious expression.

transnational culture   A pattern of cultural beliefs and behaviors characteristic of elites throughout the world and often spread through mass media.

tribe   A relatively small, usually horticultural, society organized on principles of kinship, characterized by little social stratification and no centralized political authority, and whose members share a culture and language.

trophic exchanges   Relationships between organisms having to do with food; eating or being eaten.

universalism   The understanding that certain beliefs, values, rights, or conditions are or should be universal.

urbanization   The worldwide process of the growth of cities at the expense of rural populations.

urban villages   Small (usually segregated) communities of minorities or rural migrants located in cities.

usufruct rights   The legal right of using land (or resources on land) that is not one's private property.

validity   The quality of a measurement tool or variable actually measuring what is intended.

values   The ideals of a culture that are concerned with appropriate goals and behavior.

virilocal residence   Patrilocal postmarital residence.

walkabout   A custom of Australian Aborigines involving a long circular journey to sacred places and a return to home.

war   Violence between political entities, such as nations, using soldiers; to be distinguished from the smaller scale feud.

Western culture   A generic term referring to the common beliefs, values, and traditions of Europeans and their descendants.

world view   The particular way in which a society constructs ideas of space, time, social relationship, and the meaning of life.

zeitgeist   The general intellectual, moral, and cultural climate of an era.

Index